An Insider's Guide to Academic Writing

NORTHERN ILLINOIS UNIVERSITY | ENGLISH 103/203

Susan Miller-Cochran | Roy Stamper | Stacey Cochran

with selected chapters from:

From Critical Thinking to Argument, Fifth Edition, by Sylvan Barnet, Hugo Bedau, and John O'Hara

Team Writing, First Edition, by Joanna Wolfe

macmillan learning
curriculum solutions

Additional chapters taken from:
From Critical Thinking to Argument, Fifth Edition
By Sylvan Barnet, Hugo Bedau, and John O'Hara
Copyright © 2017 by Bedford/St. Martin's

Team Writing
By Joanna Wolfe
Copyright © 2010 by Bedford/St. Martin's

Copyright © 2018 by Bedford/St. Martin's

Cover photo by Michael Day

2   1   0   9   8   7
f   e   d   c   b   a

Macmillan Learning Curriculum Solutions
14903 Pilot Drive
Plymouth, MI 48170
www.macmillanlearning.com

978-1-319-14883-6

Acknowledgments (listed alphabetically)

Microsoft product screenshots used with permission from Microsoft.

Acknowledgments and copyrights are continued at the back of the book on pages 669–670, which constitute an extension of the copyright page. Art acknowledgments and copyrights appear on the same page as the art selections they cover.

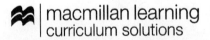

macmillan learning
curriculum solutions

bedford/st. martin's • hayden-mcneil
w.h. freeman • worth publishers

Table of Contents

Learning Outcomes for English 103, 203, and 204

(adapted from the Council of Writing Program Administrators' Outcomes Statement)

Introduction

This statement describes common knowledge, skills, and attitudes we seek in our first-year composition program in both online and traditional writing classrooms; that is, we seek to outline the programmatic expectations for English 103/203/204. The following statement articulates what composition teachers have learned from practice, research, and theory. This document defines "outcomes" or types of results and should be used in conjunction with appropriate rubrics to measure levels of achievement.

Learning to write is a complex process, both individual and social, that takes place over time with continued practice and informed guidance. Therefore, it is important that teachers, administrators, and concerned public do not imagine that these outcomes can be taught or reduced in simple ways. Helping students demonstrate these outcomes requires expert understanding of how students learn to write. For this reason, we expect the primary audience for this document to be well-prepared college writing teachers and college writing program administrators. Among such readers, terms such as "rhetorical" and "genre" convey a rich meaning that is not easily simplified. While we have also aimed at writing a document that the general public can understand, in limited cases we have aimed first at communicating effectively with expert writing teachers and writing program administrators.

These statements describe only what we expect to find at the end of first-year composition at NIU. As writers move beyond first-year composition, their writing abilities should be challenged not only to diversify along disciplinary and professional lines but also to move into new levels where outcomes expand, multiply, and diverge. For this reason, this statement encourages Writing Across the Curriculum (WAC) to build on these outcomes.

NIU's Outcomes for English 103, 203, and 204

Rhetorical Knowledge

Students should be able to:

- Establish a clear purpose for writing
- Identify and respond to the needs of different audiences
- Respond effectively to different kinds of rhetorical situations
- Use conventions of format and structure appropriate to the rhetorical situation
- Adopt voice, tone, and level of formality appropriate to the rhetorical situation
- Reflect on their own progress with regards to the above

Introduction written by First-Year Composition Committee, Northern Illinois University.

Critical Thinking, Reading, and Writing

Students should be able to:

- Use writing and reading for inquiry, critical thinking, and communicating

- Recognize and write in a variety of genres, such as narration, argument, analysis, synthesis, and research

- Invent, articulate, and understand their own ideas as they relate to those of others

- Question or analyze the rhetorical appeals of written, graphic, or multi-media discourse

- Recognize the relationships among language, knowledge, and power

Processes

Students should be able to:

- Understand that polished texts require multiple drafts for creation, development, and revision

- Develop strategies for generating, revising, editing, and proofreading texts

- Practice writing as a recursive process; that is, an ongoing process that allows writers to later invent and rethink as they revise their work

- Develop strategies for conducting efficient research

- Employ the collaborative and social aspects of writing processes—i.e., learn to balance the advantages of relying on others with the responsibility of doing their part

- Use appropriate technologies for each stage of the writing process

- Assemble a portfolio as a demonstration of the writing process

Knowledge of Conventions

Students should be able to:

- Apply appropriate genre conventions to their writing, including
  - Structure (sentence, paragraph, and essay levels)
  - Format
  - Documentation (where appropriate)
- Control such features as syntax, usage, punctuation, and spelling

Collaboration

The ability to learn and accomplish tasks in groups is a critical competency for success in and out of the classroom. Individuals who are skilled in this competency behave in ways that contribute to both accomplishing group goals as well as maintaining positive relationships among group members. Individuals who are proficient collaborators will:

- facilitate others' contributions by recognizing how group members' strengths and weaknesses can be best combined to accomplish group goals;
- participate in the organization and planning of the group;
- communicate clearly and respectfully while also actively listening to others' ideas and input;
- reliably keep agreements and make substantial contributions to the group's goals;
- help leverage contrasting viewpoints to help find innovative ways to accomplish group goals;
- demonstrate genuine concern for other group members and contribute to positive group morale.

The rubric that follows can be used by individuals within a group to provide ratings of other team members and/or to provide self-ratings, or by an outside observer to rate the behaviors of individuals within a group. The rubric is written so as to be applicable to many different types of group goals which could include: producing a tangible product such as a paper, presentation, or design; executing a task such as finding and sharing information; or solving a problem. The rubric can be particularly helpful if used in a formative fashion in that it can help students to understand and internalize what it means to be a proficient collaborator.

Collaboration Rubric

Criteria	Excelling 4	Accomplishing 3	Progressing 2	Developing 1
Facilitates team members' contributions	Instrumental in group planning and organization; proactively helps to develop roles and responsibilities that capitalize on team members' knowledge, skills and abilities to maximize team effectiveness.	Participates fully in planning and organization, identifying how team members' knowledge, skills, and abilities can contribute to achieving group goals.	Participates minimally in group planning and organization, aware only of how personal knowledge, skills, and abilities can contribute to goals.	Does not participate in group planning and organization.
Fosters a positive team climate	Clearly values other team members, exhibits concern for others' well-being, and contributes to a high level of morale among team members.	Treats team members with respect, develops positive working relationships with other members, and maintains a positive attitude.	Is respectful of other team members but exhibits little camaraderie toward other group members.	Shows little regard for the feelings of other team members and devotes little attention to maintaining positive working relationships.
Manages contrasting viewpoints	Leverages contrasting viewpoints to find innovative solutions that are embraced by the group.	Addresses contrasting viewpoints to find acceptable compromise solutions.	Identifies, but does not address, contrasting viewpoints among team members.	Ignores or actively suppresses contrasting viewpoints among team members.
Communicates clearly and listens actively	Communicates articulately and demonstrates active listening by building on and integrating others' perspectives / viewpoints.	Communicates clearly and appropriately; exhibits respect for others' viewpoints.	Communicates appropriately and listens to others' viewpoints.	Communicates unclearly or inappropriately and disregards others' input.
Contributes to the team	Assumes significant responsibility and completes tasks that make exceptional contributions to the group's goals.	Accepts responsibilities and completes tasks that make meaningful contributions to the group's goals.	Fulfills responsibilities and assigned tasks but makes minimal contributions to the group's goals.	Relies on others to do the groups' work and doesn't contribute to the group's goals.

Common Reading Experience

The Common Reading Experience (CRE) provides an opportunity for NIU students, faculty, and staff to have a campus-wide discussion about a book that raises important issues about our communities and our cultures.

NIU's CRE for 2017–2019 is Jennine Capó Crucet's *Make Your Home Among Strangers*, a 2015 novel that follows Lizet, daughter of Cuban immigrants, through her challenging journey as she navigates the all-encompassing process of becoming a first-generation college student.

NIU has invited each CRE author to campus to promote engagement and reflection, helping students connect academically and socially to what can be an intimidating large university campus.

How can you get involved? Enter an essay and/or speech contest, attend the author's talk and discussion workshops, and help celebrate the book at the Open Mic session!

Projects

Showcase

The Showcase of Student Writing is a spring event that provides a public forum for students to display the best research projects from ENGL 203 and ENGL 204 and to share their findings with friends, family, and members of the NIU community. A celebration of community-based writing, the Showcase is the perfect catalyst for engaged learning, as students demonstrate their research, critical thinking, and communication

skills through visual media and discussion with participants and judges. By engaging in critical discussion with audience members, students learn more about their topics and how to better craft their arguments.

The Electronic Portfolio (ePortfolio) in English 103, 203, and 204

In your English 103, 203, or 204 class, you will be asked to create an electronic portfolio showcasing your best writing and reflecting upon your writing process and progress. ePortfolios are widely recognized as a High Impact Practice (HIP) that promotes active and lifelong learning and helps you integrate vital writing skills into your academic and professional work at NIU and in your post-graduate career.

Your electronic portfolio on Blackboard provides an opportunity for you to develop your identity as a future professional in your field and engage with readers. It can be used in other classes and programs, potentially evolving into your final graduation and/or job search portfolio.

Why Portfolios?

Your portfolio allows your teacher to assess writing process through multiple drafts rather than through tests or timed essays. The process of creating your portfolio also invites YOU to assess YOUR OWN learning experience through your overall reflection. You can use your portfolio as a focal point for conversations with other students, your teacher, teachers of your other classes, and your advisors.

How Does This Work in Practice?

Collect: Your electronic portfolio will display the work you produce in FYComp classes at NIU and, potentially, many other classes as well. Starting early in the semester, remember to save electronic copies of everything you write for your FYComp class. Be sure to save your documents in multiple places or to back up your files using your NIU-provided network space, Google Docs, or an external drive, especially documents that will not be submitted to Blackboard.

Select: Later in the semester, talk with your instructor and your classmates during peer review, office hours, or conferences about which pieces of writing, and which passages in pieces of writing, best demonstrate your strengths as a writer and your ability to do specific writing tasks, such as introducing topics or citing sources. As you begin to select pieces and passages, you should also reflect on them, assembling a story of your growth as a writer throughout the semester.

Reflect: Research has shown that if you reflect on your own composing processes, you will not only improve your writing, but you will also be able to transfer the procedural (how-to-do-it) knowledge you gain in FYComp classes to other writing tasks in other contexts. Thus, you will be asked to reflect frequently at different stages of your writing process during the semester. If you reflect on all your assignments, including early ones, the overall reflection for your electronic portfolio will not come as a surprise; instead, it will be a natural outgrowth of the class's dual focus: (1) composing and revising the primary assignments and (2) telling the story of your writing process and your growth as a writer.

Connect: FYComp classes are designed to prepare you for the writing, reading, critical thinking, and problem solving work you will perform in other classes and in your life and work. The electronic portfolio is a space in which you can identify patterns in your writing, learning, and expression that extend outward from your FYComp class into other contexts and situations. You should frequently ask yourself how the tasks you complete in your FYComp class connect to tasks, challenges, and assignments in your other classes, your life, and your eventual career. Take note of and reflect on these connections. Your teacher may also encourage you to link to examples of your writing from outside your current FYComp class, particularly when those examples demonstrate how well you are meeting general education goals.

Project: Just as we ask you to find connections that extend outward from your FYComp classes, we also ask you to reflect back on who you were as a writer before your current FYComp class (in elementary and secondary education, for example), and to look forward to who you will become as a writer after your current FYComp class. This process extends your reflective practice to embrace both history and the future. Think about how teachers commented on your writing in high school, as well as how you see yourself growing and changing as a writer, not only at NIU, but in your future life and career. You need not create your job search portfolio yet, but remember that most employers prefer candidates with online portfolios. Use this opportunity to begin practicing how to express your professional identity online.

Resources

ESL Center

The ESL Center in the Department of English at NIU welcomes English language learners at all levels of ability and from all across campus. Our experienced tutorial staff work one-on-one with clients on reading, writing, conversation, pronunciation, grammar, and American culture. We also provide support and practice for a number of different tests and assessments. Whether you are writing a paper for a class or getting ready to defend your dissertation, we are here to support your English language needs.

Clients can meet our tutors and sign up for our services by stopping by the ESL Center in Reavis Hall 306B or by calling or e-mailing us: 815-753-6637 or niu.esl.center@gmail.com.

NIU University Writing Center

The NIU University Writing Center assists all current and former NIU students with both academic and non-academic writing projects. Our writing coaches work with you one-on-one to brainstorm, draft, revise, and perfect your work. At every stage, we encourage, advise, and offer constructive critique: our goal is not only to help you improve your current writing project, but also to help you become a stronger, more confident writer overall.

Call us at 815-753-6636 to schedule an appointment. For a full description of our hours, policies, and locations, visit us at http://uwc.niu.edu/uwc.

Awards

Mae Thomas Award for Excellence in First-Year Composition

This award honors the memory of Mae Thomas, a faculty member in the Department of English and an administrator in NIU's CHANCE program.

The Mae Thomas Award recognizes the best essays written in ENGL 102 or ENGL 103P. All essays written in ENGL 102 or ENGL 103P are welcome for submission.

Maude Uhland Award

The Maude Uhland Award honors the memory of a faculty member who taught composition at NIU from 1922 until her retirement in 1958.

The Maude Uhland Award recognizes the best essays written in a First-Year Composition course. All essays written in any First-Year Composition course are welcome for submission.

Jan Kiergaard Award

This award honors the memory of Jan Kiergaard, a faculty member in the Department of English and director of the ESL Center for many years.

The Jan Kiergaard Award recognizes the best essays written in any of the following courses: ENGL 103 ESL, ENGL 203 ESL, ENGL 451, ENGL 452, or ENGL 453. All essays from these courses are welcome for submission.

English Major and Minor

If you enjoy ENGL 103/203 and find the classes useful, please consider taking additional English classes and/or signing up for the major or minor in English.

English majors and minors develop writing, analytical, critical thinking, and creative skills that are useful in a variety of careers. Most importantly, they learn to communicate effectively as writers and speakers. An English major or minor is especially useful when combined with credentials in physical sciences, human sciences, technology, engineering, math, business, education, health, and visual or performing arts.

Employers know that students with a solid background in English read more closely and accurately, think more critically, speak more articulately, write more persuasively, and solve problems creatively. These skills are in high demand with small and large companies, including high-tech firms, such as Apple, Amazon, and Google. English majors and minors get jobs in a wide range of fields, including teaching, technical writing, copywriting, editing, web developing, grant writing, and communications management.

The English Department at Northern Illinois University offers three tracks for majors:	We also offer four English minors and one concentration:	The English Department's student clubs and organizations include:
• **Literary Studies** • **Teacher Licensure in English Language Arts** • **Writing Studies** (technical and/or creative writing)	• Linguistics • Professional Communication • Women's Studies in English • Traditional Literature Minor • Medieval Studies	• Sigma Tau Delta, international honor society • *Towers*, creative writers' and artists' magazine • Professional Writing Student Association • Linguistics Society • Film Club • Creative Writers Club • Comic Book Club

For additional information about these options, please contact askenglish@niu.edu or come visit us in Reavis 214. Ask about our scholarships, professional internships, 3 + 3 program toward a law degree, and opportunities to study abroad in Oxford, England.

From Critical Thinking to Argument and Research

Part One

Andrea Tsurumi

Part One

From Critical Thinking to Argument and Research

Chapter 1 Critical Thinking

What is the hardest task in the world? To think.

—Ralph Waldo Emerson

In all affairs it's a healthy thing now and then to hang a question mark on the things you have long taken for granted.

—Bertrand Russell

Although Emerson said the hardest task in the world is simply "to think," he was using the word *think* in the sense of *critical thinking*. By itself, *thinking* can mean almost any sort of cognitive activity, from idle daydreaming ("I'd like to go camping") to simple reasoning ("but if I go this week, I won't be able to study for my chemistry exam"). Thinking by itself may include forms of deliberation and decision-making that occur so automatically they hardly register in our consciousness ("What if I do go camping? I won't be likely to pass the exam. Then what? I better stay home and study").

When we add the adjective *critical* to the noun *thinking*, we begin to examine this thinking process consciously. When we do this, we see that even our simplest decisions involve a fairly elaborate series of calculations. Just in choosing to study and not to go camping, for instance, we weighed the relative importance of each activity (both are important in different ways); considered our goals, obligations, and commitments (to ourselves, our parents, peers, and professors); posed questions and predicted outcomes (using experience and observation as evidence); and resolved to take the most prudent course of action.

Many people associate being critical with fault-finding and nit-picking. The word *critic* might conjure an image of a sneering art or food critic eager to gripe about everything that's wrong with a particular work of art or menu item. People's low estimation of the stereotypical critic comes to light humorously in Samuel Beckett's play

Waiting for Godot, when the two vagabond heroes, Vladimir and Estragon, engage in a name-calling contest to see who can hurl the worst insult at the other. Estragon wins hands-down when he fires the ultimate invective:

V: Moron!

E: Vermin!

V: Abortion!

E: Morpion!

V: Sewer-rat!

E: Curate!

V: Cretin!

E: (*with finality*) Crritic!

V: Oh! (*He wilts, vanquished, and turns away.*)

However, being a good *critical* thinker isn't the same as being a "critic" in the derogatory sense. Quite the reverse: Because critical thinkers approach difficult questions and seek intelligent answers, they must be open-minded and self-aware, and they must interrogate *their own* thinking as rigorously as they interrogate others'. They must be alert to *their own* limitations and biases, the quality of evidence and forms of logic *they themselves* tentatively offer. In college, we may not aspire to become critics, but we all should aspire to become better critical thinkers.

Becoming more aware of our thought processes is a first step in practicing critical thinking. The word *critical* comes from the Greek word *krinein*, meaning "to separate, to choose"; above all, it implies *conscious* inquiry. It suggests that by breaking apart, or examining, our reasoning we can understand better the basis of our judgments and decisions—ultimately, so that we can make better ones.

Thinking through an Issue: Gay Marriage Licenses

By way of illustration, let's examine a case from Kentucky that was reported widely in the news in 2015. After the U.S. Supreme Court's landmark decision making gay marriage legal in all fifty states, a Rowan County clerk, Kim Davis, refused to begin issuing marriage licenses to same-sex couples. Citing religious freedom as her reason, Davis contended that the First Amendment of the Constitution protects her from being forced to act against her religious convictions and conscience. As a follower of Apostolic Christianity, she believes gay marriage is not marriage at all. To act against her belief, she said, "I would be asked to violate a central teaching of Scripture and of Jesus Himself regarding marriage.... It is not a light issue for me. It's a Heaven or Hell decision."

Let's think critically about this—and let's do it in a way that's fair to all parties and not just a snap judgment. Critical thinking means questioning not only the beliefs and assumptions of others, but also *one's own* beliefs and assumptions. We'll discuss this point at some length later, but for now we'll say only that when writing an argument you ought to be *thinking*—identifying important problems, exploring relevant issues, and evaluating available evidence—not merely collecting information to support a pre-established conclusion.

In 2015, Kim Davis was an elected county official. She couldn't be fired from her job for not performing her duties because she had been placed in that position by the vote of her constituency. And as her lawyers pointed out, "You don't lose your conscience rights, or your religious freedom rights, or your constitutional rights just because you accept public employment." However, once the Supreme Court established the legality of same-sex marriage, Davis's right to exercise her religious freedom impinged upon others' abilities to exercise their equal right to marriage (now guaranteed to them by the federal government). And so there was a problem: Whose rights have precedence?

Ty Wright/Getty Images

We may begin to identify important problems and explore relevant issues by using a process called *clustering*. (We illustrate clustering again on p. 14.) Clustering is a method of brainstorming, a way of getting ideas on paper to see what develops, what conflicts and issues exist, and what tentative conclusions you can draw as you begin developing an argument. To start clustering, take a sheet of paper, and in the center jot down the most basic issue you can think of related to the problem at hand. In our example, we wrote a sentence that we think gets at the heart of the matter. It's important to note that we conducted this demonstration in "real time"—just a few minutes—so if our thoughts seem incomplete or off-the-cuff, that's fine. The point of clustering is to get ideas on paper. Don't be afraid to write down whatever you think, because you can always go back, cross out, rethink. This process of working through an issue can be messy. In a sense, it involves conducting an argument with yourself.

At the top of our page we wrote, "The law overrides individual religious freedom." (Alternatively, we could have written from the perspective of Davis and her supporters, saying "Individual religious freedom supersedes the law," and seen where that might have taken us.) Once we have a central idea, we let our minds work and allow one thought to lead to another. We've added numbers to our thoughts so you can follow the progression of our thinking.

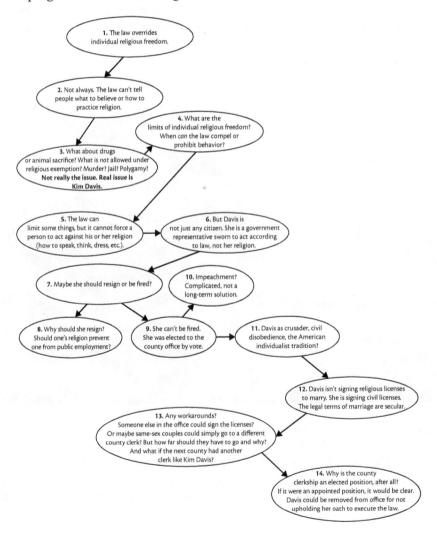

Notice that from our first idea about the law being more important than individual religious freedom, we immediately challenged our initial thinking. The law, in fact, protects religious freedom (2), and in some cases allows individuals to "break the law" if their religious rituals require it. We learned this when we wrote down a number of illegal activities sometimes associated with religion, and quickly looked up whether or not there was a legal precedent protecting these activities. We found the Supreme Court has allowed for the use of illegal drugs in some ceremonies (*Gonzalez v. O Centro Espirita*), and for the ritual sacrifice of animals in another (*Church of Lakumi Bablu Aye v. Hialeah*). Still, religions cannot do *anything they want* in the name of religious freedom. Religions cannot levy taxes, or incarcerate or kill people, for example. We then realized that what religions do as part of their ceremonies is not really the issue at all. The questions we are asking have to do with Kim Davis, her individual religious freedom, and what the law might force her to do (4).

Individuals cannot simply break the law and claim religious exemption. But the government cannot force people to act against their religious beliefs (5). Then (6) it occurred to us that Davis isn't just any citizen but a government employee whose job is to issue marriage licenses under the law. She may be free to believe what she wants and exercise her rights accordingly, but she cannot use her authority legally as a government official to deny people the rights they've been afforded by law.

We then posed several questions to ourselves in trying to determine the right way to think. We considered whether Davis should resign or be fired (7), which we then realized isn't possible (8, 9), and we wondered how else a person may be removed from office (10). We considered her as a figure of civil disobedience, defying the law in defense of religious liberties (11), trying to see the situation from her perspective. But we returned again to the idea that she isn't just a regular citizen but an agent of the law whose oath compels her to uphold the law (6). She shouldn't be able to use her authority to deprive others of exercising their rights. We also considered that the government doesn't take particular interest in the religious basis of marriage (12), so why should Davis be permitted to impose her religious beliefs on a lawful act of marriage?

By the time we got to (13), we thought, "Isn't there some workaround? Can't *deputy clerks* continue to sign the licenses as long as the state accepts them?" This way, Davis wouldn't have to violate the deeply held beliefs that she is free to hold, and yet those seeking to exercise their rights to marriage would still be satisfied. We also thought in (13) that maybe same-sex couples could just get their licenses from a different place, one where Davis doesn't work.

At this point, it may be useful to mention another facet of critical thinking and argument that we'll also explore in more detail later: considering the implications of the decisions to which our thinking leads. What happens when our judgments on matters are settled and we draw a reasonable conclusion? If we were to settle on a compromise in the Davis case, it might work for the moment, but what would happen if other clerks in the state held the same beliefs as Davis (13)? In (13), we also considered the implications if same-sex couples were simply asked to go to a different office. How far should a same-sex couple have to go to find someone willing to issue the license if all clerks can decide based on their religious convictions what kinds of marriage they will authorize? Additionally, and maybe even more important, why should same-sex couples be hindered in any way in acquiring their license or be treated as a different class of citizens?

Again, if you think with pencil and paper in hand and let your mind make associations by clustering, you'll find (perhaps to your surprise) that you have plenty of interesting ideas and that some can lead to satisfying conclusions. Doubtless you'll also have some ideas that represent gut reactions or poorly thought-out conclusions, but that's okay. When clustering, allow your thoughts to take shape without restriction; you can look them over again and organize them later. Originally, we wrote in our cluster (7) that Davis could be fired for not performing her job according to its requirements. We then realized that this wouldn't involve a simple process. Because she's an elected official, there would have to be a state legislative action to impeach her (9). This made us think, "The state of Kentucky could impeach Davis" (10). But then we also considered the consequences and decided this would not be a long-term solution. What if the next election cycle brought someone else who shares Davis's beliefs into the same position? In fact, what if citizens in Kentucky continued to elect county clerks in Rowan County—or any county—who refused to issue marriage licenses based on religious convictions? Would the state have to impeach clerks over and over again? We then thought, "Why is the county clerkship an elected position" (14)? Could it become an appointed position instead, such that governors could emplace county clerks, whose primary job is to administer legislative policy? Perhaps this is the argument we'll want to make. (Of course, it might open up new questions and issues that we would have to explore: What else does the clerk do? Is the autonomy of an elected position necessary? Do all states elect county clerks? And so on.)

At the time of this writing, Kim Davis had continued to refuse signing marriage licenses for same-sex couples. When ordered by a judge to do so or face contempt of court, she held firm to her position and spent six days in jail as a result. Her supporters cheered her act of civil disobedience (defined as breaking a law based on moral or religious conscience) and even compared her to Rosa Parks, Martin Luther King Jr., and other civil rights leaders who fought against unjust laws on the basis of religious principles. Davis returned to her position as Rowan County clerk and authorized her deputy clerks to issue marriage licenses to same-sex couples, but without her signature. Time will tell how the case plays out.

A Rule for Writers

One good way to start writing an essay is to generate ideas by clustering—and at this point not to worry that some ideas may be off-the-cuff or even nonsense. Just get ideas down on paper. You can evaluate them later.

Discussion Questions: Topics for Critical Thinking and Writing

1. As noted, some of Kim Davis's supporters have compared her to celebrated figures from American history like Rosa Parks who practiced civil disobedience by breaking laws they believed were immoral, unfair, or unjust. What are the similarities and differences in the case of Rosa Parks, who violated the law in Montgomery, Alabama, in 1955 by refusing to move to the "black" section of a public bus, and that of Kim Davis, who has refused to abide by laws established by the U.S. Supreme Court regarding gay marriage? How do the similarities and differences justify or not justify Davis's actions?

2. On a Facebook page dedicated to Davis's case, one commenter wrote, "Davis is a hero for all of us Christians who feel this country is abandoning our God." Think critically about this statement by writing about the assumptions it reveals.

3. In denying Davis's appeal to a federal court to not be forced to authorize same-sex marriage licenses, Judge David Bunning wrote that individuals "cannot choose what orders they follow" and that religious conscience "is not a viable defense" for not adhering to the law. At the same time, the free exercise clause of the First Amendment of the U.S. Constitution says that Congress shall make no law prohibiting the free exercise of religion. What do you think about Kim Davis's exercise of religion? Is it fair that in order to keep her job after the Court's decision about the legality of gay marriage, she has to regularly violate one of her religion's central beliefs about marriage? Explain your response.

On Flying Spaghetti Monsters: Analyzing and Evaluating from Multiple Perspectives

Let's think critically about another issue related to religious freedom, equality, and the law—one that we hope brings some humor to the activity but also inspires careful thinking and debate.

In 2005, in response to pressure from some religious groups, the Kansas Board of Education gave preliminary approval for teaching alternatives to evolution in public school science classes. New policies would require science teachers to present "intelligent design"—the idea that the universe was created by an intentional, conscious force such as God—as an equally plausible explanation for natural selection and human development.

In a quixotic challenge to the legislation, twenty-four-year-old physics graduate Bobby Henderson wrote an open letter that quickly became popular on the Internet and then was published in the *New York Times*. Henderson appealed for recognition of another theory that he said was equally valid: that an all-powerful deity called the Flying Spaghetti Monster created the world. While clearly writing satirically on behalf of science, Henderson nevertheless kept a straight face and argued that if creationism were to be taught as a theory in science classes, then "Pastafarianism" must also be taught as another legitimate possibility. "I think we can all look forward to the time," he wrote, "when these three theories are given equal time in our science classes.... One third time for Intelligent Design; one third time for Flying Spaghetti Monsterism (Pastafarianism); and one third time for logical conjecture based on overwhelming observable evidence."

Brian Cahn/Newscom/ZUMA Press/Washington/District of Columbia/U.S.

Since that time, the Church of the Flying Spaghetti Monster has become a creative venue where secularists and atheists construct elaborate mythologies, religious texts, and rituals, most of which involve cartoonish pirates and various noodle-and-sauce images. ("R'amen," they say at the end of their prayers.) However, although tongue-in-cheek, many followers have also used the organization seriously as a means to champion the First Amendment's establishment clause, which prohibits government institutions from *establishing*, or preferring, any one religion over another. Pastafarians have challenged policies and laws in various states that appear to discriminate among religions or to provide exceptions or exemptions based on religion. In Tennessee, Virginia, and Wisconsin, church members have successfully petitioned for permission to display statues or signs of the Flying Spaghetti Monster in places where other religious icons are permitted, such as on state government properties. One petition in Oklahoma argued that because the state allows a marble and granite Ten Commandments monument on the state courthouse lawn, then a statue of the Flying Spaghetti Monster must also be permitted; this effort ultimately forced the state to remove the Ten Commandments monument in 2015. In the past three years, individuals in California, Georgia, Florida, Texas, California, and Utah have asserted their right to wear religious head coverings in their driver's license photos—a religious exemption afforded to Muslims in those states—and have had their pictures taken with colanders on their heads.

Let's stop for a moment. Take stock of your initial reactions to the Church of the Flying Spaghetti Monster. Some responses might be quite uncritical, quite unthinking: "That's outrageous!" or "What a funny idea!" Others might be the type of snap judgment we discussed earlier: "These people are making fun of real religions!" or "They're just causing trouble." Think about it: If your hometown approved placing a Christmas tree on the town square during the holiday season, and the Church of the Flying Spaghetti Monster argued that it too should be allowed to set up its holiday symbol as a matter of religious equality—perhaps a statue—should it be afforded equal space? Why, or why not?

Be careful here, and exercise critical thinking. Can one simply say, "No, that belief is ridiculous," in response to a religious claim? What if members of a different religious group were asking for equal space? Should a menorah (a Jewish holiday symbol) be allowed? A mural celebrating Kwanzaa? A Native American symbol? Can some religious expressions be included in public spaces and not others? If so, why? If not, why not?

In thinking critically about a topic, we must try to see it from all sides before reaching a conclusion. We conduct an argument with ourselves, advancing and then questioning different opinions:

- What can be said *for* the proposition?
- What can be said *against* it?

Critical thinking requires us to support our position and also see the other side. The heart of critical thinking is a *willingness to face objections to one's own beliefs*, to adopt a skeptical attitude not only toward views opposed to our own but also toward our own common sense—that is, toward views that seem to us as obviously right. If we assume we have a monopoly on the truth and dismiss those who disagree with us as misguided fools, or if we say that our opponents are acting out of self-interest (or a desire to harass the community) and we don't analyze their views, we're being critical but we aren't engaging in critical thinking.

When thinking critically, it's important to ask key questions about any position, decision, or action we take and any regulation, policy, or law we support. We must ask:

- Is it fair?
- What is its purpose?
- Is it likely to accomplish its purpose?
- What will its effects be? Might it unintentionally cause some harm?
- If it might cause harm, to whom? What kind of harm? Can we weigh the potential harm against the potential good?
- Who gains something and who loses something as a result?
- Are there any compromises that might satisfy different parties?

What do you think? If you were on your hometown's city council, how would you answer the above questions in relation to a petition from the Church of the Flying Spaghetti Monster to permit a Spaghetti Monster display alongside the traditional Christmas tree on the town square? How would you vote, and why? What other questions and issues might arise from your engagement with this issue? (**Hint**: Try clustering. Place the central question in the middle of a sheet of a paper, and brainstorm the issues that flower from it.)

Call-Out: Obstacles to Critical Thinking

Because critical thinking requires engaging seriously with potentially difficult topics, topics about which you may already have strong opinions, and topics that elicit powerful emotional responses, it's important to recognize the ways in which your thinking may be compromised or clouded. Write down or discuss how each of the following attitudes might impede or otherwise negatively affect your critical thinking in real life. How might each one be detrimental in making conclusions?

1. The topic is too controversial and will never be resolved.
2. The topic hits "too close to home" (i.e., "I've had direct experience with this").
3. The topic disgusts me.
4. The topic angers me.
5. Everyone I know thinks roughly the same thing I do about this topic.
6. Others may judge me if I verbalize what I think.
7. My opinion on this topic is X because it benefits me, my family, or my kind the most.
8. My parents raised me to think X about this topic.
9. One of my favorite celebrities believes X about this topic, so I do too.
10. I know what I think, but my solutions are probably unrealistic. It's impossible to change the system.

Think of some more obstacles to critical thinking, and provide examples of how they might lead to unsound conclusions or poor solutions.

A Rule for Writers

Early in the process of jotting down your ideas on a topic, stop to ask yourself, "What might someone reasonably offer as an *objection* to my view?"

In short, as we will say several times (because the point is key), *argument is an instrument of learning* as well as of persuasion. In order to formulate a reasoned position and make a vote, you'll have to gather some information, find out what experts say, and examine the points on which they agree and disagree. You'll likely want to gather opinions from religious leaders, community members, and legal experts (after all, you wouldn't want the town to be sued for discrimination). You'll want to think beyond a knee-jerk value judgment like, "No, a Spaghetti Monster statue would be ugly."

Seeing the issue from multiple perspectives will require familiarizing yourself with current debates—perhaps about religious equality, free speech, or the separation of church and state—and considering the responsibility of public institutions to accommodate different viewpoints and various constituencies. Remember, the Church of the Flying Spaghetti Monster didn't gain so much traction by being easy to dismiss. Thus, you must do the following:

Survey, considering as many perspectives as possible.

Analyze, identifying and then separating out the parts of the problem, trying to see how its pieces fit together.

Evaluate, judging the merit of various ideas and claims and the weight of the evidence in their favor or against them.

If you survey, analyze, and evaluate comprehensively, you'll have better and more informed ideas; you'll generate a wide variety of ideas, each triggered by your own responses and the ideas your research brings to light. As you form an opinion and prepare to vote, you'll be constructing an argument to yourself at first, but also one you may have to present to the community, so you should be as thorough as possible and sensitive to the ideas and rights of many different people.

Critical Thinking at Work: From Jottings to a Short Essay

We have already seen an example of clustering on page 6, which illustrates the prewriting process of thinking through an issue and generating ideas by imagining responses—counterthoughts—to our initial thoughts. Here's another example, this time showing an actual student's thoughts about an issue related to the Church of the Flying Spaghetti Monster. The student, Alexa Cabrera, was assigned to write approximately 500 words about a specific legal challenge made by a member of the Church of the Flying Spaghetti Monster. She selected the case of Stephen Cavanaugh, a prisoner who made a complaint against the Nebraska State Penitentiary after being denied the right to practice Pastafarianism while incarcerated there. Because the Department of Corrections denied him those privileges, Cavanaugh filed suit citing civil rights violations and asked for his rights to be accommodated. Notice that in the essay—the product of several revised drafts—the student introduced points she had *not* thought of while clustering. The cluster, in short, was a *first* step, not a road map of the final essay.

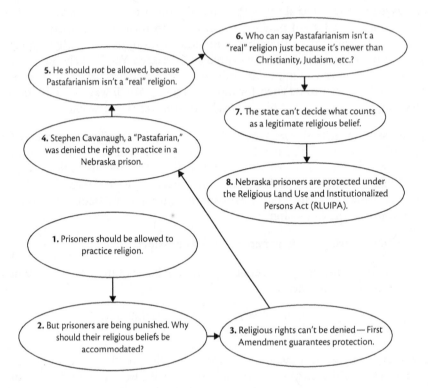

A Student's Essay, Developed from a Cluster and a List

Stirred and Strained: Pastafarians Should Be Allowed to Practice in Prison

Stephen Cavanaugh is a member of the Church of the Flying Spaghetti Monster, a mostly Web-based religious group that has earned notoriety for its members' demands that they be treated under the First Amendment like any other religion. The group strives to show that if Christians can place Nativity scenes on public grounds, or if Muslims can wear head coverings in state driver's license photographs, then by god (or pasta, as the case may be), they can too. Cavanaugh is in the Nebraska State Penitentiary, where inmates are permitted under the Religious Land Use and Institutionalized Persons Act (RLUIPA) to exercise religious freedoms guaranteed by the First Amendment. He wants the same rights and privileges given to incarcerated Christians, Muslims, Jews, and Buddhists—namely, to be able to wear religious clothing, to eat specially prepared meals, and to be given resources, space, and time to conduct worship with his fellow "believers." For Cavanaugh, this means being able to dress up as a pirate, eat pasta on selected holidays, order satirical holy books, and lead a weekly "prayer" group. Many people consider these requests absurd, but Cavanaugh should be permitted under the First Amendment and the RLUIPA to practice his faith.

Some arguments against Cavanaugh are easier to dismiss than others. One of these simply casts aside the spiritual needs and concerns of prisoners: They are being punished, after all, so why should they receive any religious accommodations? This position is both immoral and unconstitutional. Religion is an important sustaining force for prisoners who might otherwise struggle to find meaning and purpose in life, and it is protected by the First Amendment *because* it helps prisoners find purpose and become rehabilitated—the fundamental goal of correctional facilities (even for those serving life without parole). Another argument sees religion as important as long as it conforms to Judeo-Christian belief structures, which has for a long time been the only spiritual path available in American prisons. But today, in our diverse society, the RLUIPA *requires* prisons to provide religious accommodations for all faiths equally unless an undue administrative, financial, or security burden can be proven. Obviously, many religious observances cannot be accommodated. Prisons cannot permit inmates to carry crosses and staves, construct temples and sweat lodges, or make required religious pilgrimages. However, as long as some religious accommodations can be and are made—such as Catholics being offered fish on Fridays, or Jewish and Muslim prisoners receiving kosher and halal meals—all religious groups must be similarly accommodated.

The more challenging question about the Church of the Flying Spaghetti Monster is whether it is a religion at all, whether it deserves equal treatment among more established religions. When Cavanaugh was first denied his request, the prison claimed that FSM was not a religion but a "parody" of religion. The Nebraska State Penitentiary suggested it could not grant privileges to anyone who presents his whimsical desires as part of a religious philosophy. In dealing with a humorous and politically motivated "religion" without a strong tradition and whose founder may write a new gospel at any time, should the prison have to keep up with the possibility of constantly changing prisoner demands? Can anyone just make up a religion and then expect to be accommodated?

For better or worse, the answer is yes—as long as the accommodations represent valid forms of observance, are reasonable, and do not pose a substantial burden to the institution. Many religions have councils that at times alter the tenets of their faith. The state does not have the authority to determine what is or is not a "real" religion or religious practice. It does have an obligation under the RLUIPA to accommodate not just some but all forms of faith for incarcerated persons. As long as individuals sincerely hold certain beliefs, and as long as the accommodations requested meet the standards of reasonability and equity, state prisons, like all other government agencies and institutions, cannot discriminate. Some might argue that Cavanaugh's faith is not sincere—that he does not *really* believe that the Earth was literally created by a ball of pasta with meatball-shaped eyes. But this is not the point. The government cannot apply a religious test to measure the degree of one's sincerity or faith. Like others in the Flying Spaghetti Monster movement—secularists, atheists, and professed believers—Cavanaugh should not be treated as an exploiter of religious freedom. In fact, in a pluralistic society with laws to ensure religious freedom and equality, his challenge helps protect all faiths.

The Essay Analyzed

The title, in its words *stirred* and *strained*, engages readers' attention by playing with words related to pasta, prison, and the frustration likely to be encountered by an individual who is denied religious freedom. The subtitle states the thesis. This introductory material—a paper begins with its title, not with its first paragraph—makes readers curious and lets them know where the essay will take them.

Paragraph 1 sets the stage. The first sentence clarifies what the Church is and uses a nifty turn of phrase, "by god (or by pasta)," to encourage engagement and make the author's voice, like the FSM, playful but dead serious. The second, third, and fourth sentences provide the basis for Cavanaugh's claims. The last sentence presents a clear thesis.

Paragraph 2 draws on the student's preliminary map. It sets forth objections to making religious accommodations for prisoners and disputes them, providing a citation of the law that guarantees religious freedom in prison, a definition of its limits, and a few examples of these limits. The last sentence sustains the thesis by arguing that accommodations must be equal among religions. However, it also anticipates that readers are likely to agree on this point but still not consider the FSM as a religion.

Paragraph 3 addresses the potential counterargument set up by paragraph 2 and highlights the most common criticism of the FSM: that it isn't *really* a religion at all. The writer raises the problematic question that if prisons must accommodate Cavanaugh, then where would the protest end? What new accommodations might he ask for in the future? Paragraph 3 in effect suggests the *implications* of granting Cavanaugh his request, inviting the reader to imagine a potentially slippery argumentative slope.

Paragraph 4 halts readers' imaginings, reminding them that the writer is still in the realm of talking about *reasonable* and *fair* treatment among inmates, not an "anything goes" proposition. It reminds readers that the state cannot determine a "real" or "unreal" religion, just as it cannot judge the depth, rigor, or literalness of an inmate's belief (Christian, Pastafarian, or otherwise). The fact is that our society has laws to ensure religious freedom and equality for all citizens. In this way, the writer makes a shrewd rhetorical move, presenting Cavanaugh's complaint not just as antagonistic but also as something essential to protecting prisoners of all faiths. Such an appeal to democratic insistence on fairness is normally effective, although in this instance a reader may wonder if the writer has demonstrated convincingly that fairness requires prisons to accommodate Pastafarians. Are you convinced that it would be *unfair* to deny Cavanaugh and other Pastafarian inmates their demands? Why, or why not?

Generating Ideas: Writing as a Way of Thinking

We have already seen, in the clusters that students have generated, concise examples of how the act of writing helps thinkers to think better. "To learn to write," Robert Frost said, "is to learn to have ideas." But how does one "learn to have ideas"? Often we discover ideas while talking with others. A friend says *X* about some issue, and we—who have never really thought much about the matter—say,

- "Well, yes, I see what you're saying, but come to think of it, I'm not of your opinion. I see it differently—*not as X but as Y.*"

Or maybe we say,

- "*Yes, X, sure, and also a bit of Y, too.*"

Mere chance—a friend's comment—has led us to an idea that we didn't know we had. This sort of discovery may seem like the one we make when reaching under the couch to retrieve the dog's ball and finding a ten-dollar bill instead: "How it got there, I'll never know, but I'm sure glad I found it."

In fact, learning to have ideas is not largely a matter of chance. Or if chance *is* involved, well, as Louis Pasteur put it, "Chance favors the prepared mind." This means that lurking in the mind are bits of information or hints or hunches that in the unexpected circumstance—when talking, when listening to a lecture or a classroom discussion, or especially when reading—are triggered and lead to useful thoughts. This is a sort of seat-of-the-pants knowledge that, when brought to the surface in the right circumstances, produces good results.

Consider the famous example of Archimedes, the ancient Greek mathematician who discovered a method to determine the volume of an irregularly shaped object. The problem: A king gave a goldsmith a specific weight of gold with which to make a crown in the shape of laurel leaves. When the job was finished, the king weighed the crown and found that it matched the weight of the gold he had provided, but he nevertheless suspected that the goldsmith might have substituted some silver for some of the gold. How could the king find out (without melting or otherwise damaging the crown) if the crown was pure gold? For Archimedes, meditating on this problem produced no ideas, but when he entered a bathtub he noticed that the water level rose as he immersed his body. He suddenly realized that he could thus determine the volume of the crown—by measuring the amount of displaced water. Since silver is less dense than gold, it takes a greater volume of silver to equal a given weight of gold. That is, a given weight of gold will displace less water than the same weight of silver. Archimedes then immersed the given weight of gold, measured the water it displaced, and found that indeed the crown displaced more water than the gold did. In his excitement at confirming his idea, Archimedes is said to have leaped out of the tub and run naked through the street, shouting "Eureka!" (Greek for "I have found [it]!").

Why do we tell this story? Partly because we like it, but chiefly because the word *eureka* comes from the same Greek word that has given our language the word **heuristic** (pronounced hyoo-RIS-tik), which refers to a method or process of discovering ideas—in short, of thinking. In this method, one thought triggers another. (**Note**: In computer science, *heuristic* has a more specialized meaning.) Of course, one of the best ways of generating ideas is to hear what's going on around you—and that is talk, both in and out of the classroom, as well as in the world of books. You'll find, as we said early in this discussion, that your response may be, "Well, yes, I see what you're saying, but come to think of it, I don't see it quite that way. I see it differently—not as *X* but as *Y*." As we've said, argument is an instrument of learning as well as of persuasion. For instance:

> *Yes*, solar power is a way of conserving energy, *but* do we need to despoil the Mojave Desert and endanger desert life with—literally—fifty thousand solar mirrors so that folks in Los Angeles can heat their pools? Doesn't it make sense to reduce our use of energy, rather than develop sources of renewable energy that violate the environment? Some sites should be off-limits.

Maybe your response to the proposal (now at least fifteen years old) that wind turbines be placed in the waters off Cape Cod, Massachusetts, would go like this:

Given our need for wind power, *how can a reasonable person object* to the proposal that we put 130 wind turbines in the waters off Cape Cod, Massachusetts? *Yes,* the view will be changed, *but* in fact the turbines are quite attractive. No one thinks that windmills in Holland spoil the landscape. So the view will be changed, but not spoiled; *and furthermore,* the verdict is still out on whether or not wind turbines pose a significant risk to birds or aquatic life.

When you're asked to write about something you've read in this book, if your first response is that you have no ideas, remember the responses that we have mentioned—"No, I don't see it that way" or "Yes, but" or "Yes, and moreover"—and see if one of them helps you respond to the work—helps you, in short, to develop ideas.

Confronting Unfamiliar Issues

Generating ideas can be a challenge when you, as a student, are asked to read about and respond to an unfamiliar issue. Sometimes, students wonder why they have to engage in particular topics and generate ideas about them. "I want to be a speech pathologist," you might say, "so why do I need to read essays and formulate ideas about capital punishment?"

One answer is that a college curriculum should spur students to think about pressing issues facing our society, so learning about capital punishment is important to all students. But this isn't the only answer. One could never study "all" the important social problems we face (anyway, many of them change very rapidly). Instead, colleges seek to equip students with tools, methods, and habits of mind that enable them to confront arguments about *any* potential issue or problem (including those within the field of speech pathology!). The primary goal of a college education (and of this book) is to help students develop an *intellectual apparatus*—a toolkit that can be applied to any subject matter, any issue.

The techniques presented in this book offer a practical framework for approaching issues, thinking about them carefully, asking good questions, identifying problems, and offering reasonable solutions—not necessarily because we want you to form opinions about the issues we have selected (though we hope you do), but because we want you to practice critical thinking, reading, and writing in ways that transfer to other aspects of your education as well as to your personal, professional, and civic life.

The playwright Edward Albee once said, "Good writers define reality; bad ones merely restate it." Rather than thinking that you must "agree or disagree" with the authors whose works you'll read in this book, imagine that you'll be practicing how to discover your unique point of view by finding pathways into debates, negotiating different positions, and generating new ideas. So when you confront an unfamiliar issue in this book (or elsewhere), consider the strategies discussed below as practical methods for generating new ideas. That is what critical thinking (and writing) is all about.

Topics

One way of generating ideas, practiced by the ancient Greeks and Romans and still regarded as among the best ways, is to consider what the ancients called **topics**—from the Greek *topos*, meaning "place," as in our word *topography* (a description or representation of a place). For the ancients, certain topics, when formulated as questions, were places where they went to find ideas. Among the classical topics were *definition, comparison, relationship,* and *testimony.* By prompting oneself with questions about these topics, one moves toward answers.

If you're at a loss for ideas when confronted with an issue (and an assignment to write about it), you might discover ideas by turning to the relevant classical topics and jotting down your responses. (In classical terminology, this means engaging in the process of invention, from the Latin *invenire*, "to come upon, to find.") Seeing your ideas on paper—even in the briefest form—will help bring other ideas to mind and will also help you evaluate them. For instance, after jotting down ideas as they come and your responses to them, you might do the following:

1. First, organize them into two lists, pro and con.

2. Next, delete ideas that, upon consideration, seem wrong or irrelevant.

3. Finally, develop the ideas that strike you as pretty good.

You probably won't know where you stand until you've gone through such a process. It would be nice to be able to make a quick decision, immediately justify it with three excellent reasons, and then give three further reasons showing why the opposing view is inadequate. In fact, however, people almost never can reach a reasoned decision without a good deal of preliminary thinking.

Consider the following brief essay about the Food and Drug Administration's approval, in 2015, of a genetically engineered salmon. Although GMO (genetically modified organisms) foods and medicines are common in the United States, this salmon will soon be the first genetically modified animal approved for food consumption in the United States. After you read the essay, refer to Thinking Critically: Generating Topics (pp. 22–23), which asks you to begin jotting down ideas on a sheet of paper along the lines of the classical topics. As an example of how to respond to the questions, we've included columns related to the Kim Davis and Stephen Cavanaugh cases. As you attempt to formulate ideas related to the essay about genetically engineered salmon, answer the questions related to the classical topics. There's no need to limit yourself to one answer per item as we did.

Nina Fedoroff

Nina Fedoroff (b. 1942) is the Evan Pugh professor emerita at Penn State University. She served as science and technology adviser to the U.S. secretary of state from 2007 to 2010. The following essay originally appeared in the *New York Times* in December 2015.

The Genetically Engineered Salmon Is a Boon for Consumers and Sustainability

This is great news for consumers and the environment. Wild salmon populations have long been in deep trouble because of overfishing, and open-water cage farming of salmon pollutes coastal waters, propagates fish diseases, and sacrifices a lot of wild-caught fish to be consumed as salmon feed.

The fish is virtually identical to wild salmon, but it is a more sustainable food source, growing faster to maturity.

But just imagine, you'll soon be able to eat salmon guilt-free. AquaBounty has spent more than 20 years developing and testing this faster-growing salmon that will require less feed to bring it to a marketable size. It can be farmed economically in closed, on-land facilities that recirculate water and don't dump waste into the sea. Since the fish live in clean, managed water, they don't get diseases that are spread among caged fish in the sea. And the growing facilities could be closer to markets, cutting shipping costs.

All of these elements take pressure off wild salmon and make salmon farming more sustainable.

Much of the concern about AquaBounty's salmon centers around several bits of added DNA, taken from another fish, that let the salmon grow continuously, not just seasonally. That does not make them "unnatural" or dangerous, it just makes them grow to market size on less feed.

5

We've been tinkering with our plants and animals to serve our food needs for somewhere between 10 and 20 thousand years. We created corn, for example. The seed-bearing structure of the original "wild" version, called teosinte, looked very different from the modern-day ear, packed with hundreds of soft, starch-and-protein-filled kernels. And it's people who developed the tomatoes we eat today. Mother Nature's are tiny: A pioneering breeder described them in an 1893 grower's guide as "small, hollow, tough, watery" fruits.

But there's money (and fame) in being anti-G.M.O. The organic food marketers want to sell their food, which is over-priced because organic farming is inefficient—not because the food's better—so they tell scare stories about the dangers of G.M.O.s.

There is also no reason to fear that these genetically engineered salmon will escape and destroy wild populations. Only sterile females will be grown for food. And since the fish will be grown in contained facilities on land, escapees can't survive either.

AquaBounty's salmon is salmon, plain and simple. I, for one, can't wait to taste it.

Thinking Critically: Generating Topics

Provide the relevant information for the topic of genetically engineered salmon.

Topics	Questions	Davis
Definition Categories Descriptions Definitions Explanations	*What is it?*	"The Kim Davis case involves one woman's dissent against the Supreme Court decision of 2015 legalizing gay marriage. The law says *X*, but Davis draws upon *Y*."
Comparison Similarities Differences Analogies Applications	*What is it like or unlike?*	"Other cases in which individuals defied the law because of conscience include *X*, *Y*, and *Z*. The Davis case is similar/different because…"
Relationship Antecedents Precedents Consequences Outcomes	*What caused it, and what will it cause?*	"The issue of gay marriage had been a state's rights issue but was unevenly applied across states. When the Court legalized it at the federal level, it required all public officials including judges and clerks to abide by the law, yet the result is…"
Testimony Statistics Maxims Laws Quotations	*What is known or said about it, especially by experts?*	"Supreme Court Justice Kennedy asserted in his opinion that the Constitution guarantees *X*, though Justice Scalia in his dissent said…"

Cavanaugh	Genetically Engineered Salmon
"The RLUIPA requires state prisons to provide religious accommodations under the First Amendment, which says *X*. Cavanaugh asserted his 'right' to…"	
"This case is like other challenges made by the FSM Church; however, since he is a prisoner asking for *XYZ*, Cavanaugh's case is different because…"	
"Prisoners deserve to exercise their religious freedom, but for most of U.S. history Christianity was the only available option, which violated the establishment clause…"	
"In American prisons, there are *over X* number of recognized religious groups, including Satanists and Wiccans. If they can have their rights, then…"	

Here's an inner dialogue that you might engage in as you think critically about the question of genetically engineered salmon:

> The purpose of genetically engineered salmon is to protect against the ecological effects of overfishing—that seems to be a good thing.
>
> Another purpose is to protect consumers by ensuring that the price of salmon, one of the most commonly eaten fish, will not become so high that few people could afford it.
>
> But other issues are apparent. Should we turn to altering the genes of animals to protect the environment or consumer prices? Are there other solutions, like eating less salmon or regulating overfishing?
>
> Who gains and who loses, and what do they stand to gain or lose, by this FDA approval of genetically modified salmon?
>
> The author says no one should worry about "several bits of DNA added"; but come to think of it, is this modification unethical or dangerous in any way? Is it okay to create a new type of animal by altering genes?
>
> The author attacks anti-GMO activists, saying they're just after money (and fame—why fame?). Isn't money (and fame?) also the goal of AquaBounty and other GMO food producers?

Notice how part of the job is *analytic*, recognizing the elements or complexities of the whole, and part is *evaluative*, judging the adequacy of all the ideas, one by one. Both tasks require critical thinking in the form of analyzing and evaluating, and those processes themselves require a disciplined *imagination*.

So far we have jotted down a few thoughts and then immediately given some second thoughts contrary to the first. Be aware that your own counterthoughts might not come to mind right away. For instance, they might not occur until you reread your notes or try to explain the issue to a friend, or until you begin drafting an essay aimed at supporting or undermining the new FDA rules. Most likely, in fact, some good ideas won't occur until a second or third or fourth draft.

Here are some further thoughts on the genetically modified salmon. We list them more or less as they occurred to us and as we typed them into a computer—not sorted neatly into two groups, pro and con, or evaluated as you should do in further critical thinking of your own. Of course, a later step would be to organize the material into a useful pattern. As you read, try writing your responses in the margin.

According to one article, the FDA is not requiring companies to label the salmon as genetically engineered. Should this information at least be made available to consumers? Maybe their religious, ethical, or personal preferences would be not to eat modified fish species. If the fish were properly labeled and people knew of any risks associated with eating it, they could avoid it if they wished.

Are there any animal rights issues at stake here? Is it okay to breed "only sterile females"? Critics say that scientists shouldn't create new kinds of animals. Is this even what AquaBounty is doing?

The author says we shouldn't worry about these fish breeding with other salmon, but is she understating the risks? I hadn't thought of the possibility, but clearly someone has. Is there an actual risk of threatening the natural species? If there was really zero risk, why are they bothering to breed only *sterile* females?

Maybe the FDA shouldn't have approved genetically modified salmon for food. If we start with the salmon, where will it end? What other foods are being reviewed for similar kinds of farming? Is this really the same as the development of corn and other vegetables, as the author suggests—or is animal life something different?

Doubtless there is much that we haven't asked or thought about, but we hope you'll agree that the issue deserves careful thought, given that the availability of genetically modified food animals has serious implications for the environment and the future of food production.

If you worked for the FDA and were part of this decision, you would *have* to think about these questions and issues. As a thought experiment, imagine you had to contribute to the decision about approving these fish. Try to put your tentative views into writing.

Note that you would want to get answers to questions such as the following:

- What sort of evidence exists about the safety of genetically engineered salmon? Who has studied it?

- What do biologists and bioethicists say about the genetically engineered salmon?

- What kind of people and organizations oppose the approval of this genetically engineered salmon, and what are their primary critiques?

Some of these questions require you to do **research** on the topic. Some raise issues of fact, and relevant evidence probably is available. In order to reach a conclusion in which you have confidence, you'll have to do some research to find out what the facts—the objective data—are. Merely explaining your position without giving the evidence will not be convincing.

Even without doing any research, however, you might want to look over the pros and cons, perhaps adding some new thoughts or modifying or even rejecting (for reasons that you can specify) some of those already given. If you do think further about this issue (and we hope that you will), notice an interesting point about *your own* thinking: It probably isn't *linear* (moving in a straight line from *A* to *B* to *C*) but *recursive*, moving from *A* to *C* and back to *B* or starting over at *C* and then back to *A* and *B*. By zigging and zagging almost despite yourself, you'll reach a conclusion that may finally seem correct. In retrospect, it might seem obvious; *now* you can chart a nice line from *A* to *B* to *C*—but that probably wasn't at all evident at the start.

✓ A Checklist for Critical Thinking

Attitudes

☐   Does my thinking show imaginative open-mindedness and intellectual curiosity?

☐   Am I willing to examine my assumptions?

☐   Am I willing to entertain new ideas—both those that I encounter while reading and those that come to mind while writing?

☐   Am I willing to exert myself—for instance, to do research—to acquire information and to evaluate evidence?

Skills

☐   Can I summarize an argument accurately?

☐   Can I evaluate assumptions, evidence, and inferences?

☐   Can I present my ideas effectively—for instance, by organizing and by writing in a manner appropriate to my imagined audience?

A Short Essay Calling for Critical Thinking

When reading an essay, we expect the writer to have thought carefully about the topic. We don't want to read every false start, every fuzzy thought, every ill-organized paragraph that the writer knocked off. Yes, writers make false starts, put down fuzzy thoughts, write ill-organized paragraphs; but then they revise and revise yet again, ultimately producing a readable essay that seems effortlessly written. Still—and this is our main point—writers of argumentative essays need to show readers that they have made some effort; they need to show *how* they got to their final (for the moment) views. It isn't enough for the writer to say, "I believe *X*"; rather, he or she must in effect say, "I believe X—and I hope you'll believe it also—because Y and Z, though attractive, just don't stand up to inquiry as well as X does. Y is superficially plausible, but…, and Z, which is an attractive alternative to Y, nevertheless fails because…."

Notice in the following short essay—on employers using biometric devices to monitor employees' performance—that the author, Lynn Stuart Parramore, positions herself against these workplace technologies in a compelling way. As you read, think critically about how she presents her position, how she encourages readers to sympathize with her views. Ask questions about what she includes and excludes, whether she presents other perspectives amply or fairly, and what additional positions might be valid on these recent developments in the rapidly growing field of biometrics in business.

Lynn Stuart Parramore

Lynn Stuart Parramore is a contributing editor of *AlterNet*, a frequent contributor to *Al-Jazeera America*, *Reuters*, and the *Huffington Post*, and a member of the editorial board of *Lapham's Quarterly*. Reprinted here is an essay published by *Al-Jazeera America* on September 18, 2015.

Fitbits for Bosses

Imagine you've just arrived at your job with the Anywhere Bank call center. You switch on your computer and adjust the height of your chair. Then, you slide on the headset, positioning the mic in front of your lips. All that's left to do is to activate your behavior-monitoring device—the gadget hanging from your neck that tracks your tone of voice, your heart rate, and your physical movements throughout the day, sending real-time reports to your supervisor.

A scene from a dystopian movie? Nope. It's already happening in America. Welcome to the brave new world of workplace biosurveillance.

It's obvious that wearable tracking technology has gone mainstream: Just look at the explosion of smart watches and activity monitors that allow people to count steps and check their calorie intake. But this technology has simultaneously been creeping into workplaces: The military uses sensors that scan for injuries, monitor heart rate, and check hydration. More and more, professional athletes are strapping on devices that track every conceivable dimension of performance. Smart ice skates that measure a skater's jump. Clothes that measure an athlete's breathing and collect muscle data. At this year's tryouts in Indianapolis, some NFL hopefuls wore the "Adidas miCoach," a device that sends data on speed and acceleration straight to trainers' iPads. Over the objection of many athletes, coaches and team owners are keen to track off-the-field activity, too, such as sleep patterns and diet. With million-dollar players at stake, big money seems poised to trump privacy.

Now employers from industries that don't even require much physical labor are getting in on the game.

Finance is adopting sophisticated analytics to ensure business performance from   5
high-dollar employees. Cambridge neuroscientist and former Goldman Sachs trader
John Coates works with companies to figure out how monitoring biological signals
can lead to trading success; his research focuses on measuring hormones that
increase confidence and other desirable states as well as those that produce negative, stressful states. In a report for Bloomberg, Coates explained that he is working
with "three or four hedge funds" to apply an "early-warning system" that would
alert supervisors when traders are getting into the hormonal danger zone. He calls
this process "human optimization."

People who do the most basic, underpaid work in our society are increasingly subject to physical monitoring, too—and it extends far beyond the ubiquitous urine test.
Bank of America has started using smart badges that monitor the voice and behavior patterns of call-center workers, partnering with the creepily named Humanyze,
a company specializing in "people analytics." Humanyze is the brainchild of the MIT
Media Lab, the fancy research institute at the Massachusetts Institute of Technology
dedicated to the "betterment of humanity," which, incidentally, receives a quarter of
its funding from taxpayers. Humanyze concocted a computer dashboard complete
with graphs and pie charts that can display the location of employees (Were you
hanging out in the lounge today?) and their "social context" (Do you spend a lot of
time alone?).

Humanyze founder Ben Waber points out that companies already spend enormous
resources collecting analytics on their customers. Why not their employees?

A growing number of workers are being monitored by GPS, often installed on their
smartphones. In the U.S. the Supreme Court ruled that law enforcement officials
need a warrant to use GPS devices to track a suspect. But employers don't worry
over such formalities in keeping tabs on employees, especially those who are
mobile, such as truck drivers. A *Washington Post* report on GPS surveillance noted a
2012 study by the research firm Aberdeen Group, which showed that 62 percent of
"field employees"—those who regularly perform duties away from the office—are
tracked this way. In May, a California woman filed a lawsuit against her former
employer, Intermex Wire Transfer, for forcing her to install a tracking app on her
phone, which she was required to keep on 24/7. She described feeling like a prisoner
wearing an ankle bracelet. After removing the app, the woman was fired.

Sensitive to Big Brother accusations, the biosurveillance industry is trying to keep
testing and tool evaluations under the radar. Proponents of the technology point
to its potential to improve health conditions in the workplace and enhance public
safety. Wouldn't it be better, they argue, if nuclear power plant operators, airline
pilots, and oil rig operatives had their physical state closely monitored on the job?

Young Americans nurtured in a digital world where their behavior is relentlessly   10
collected and monitored by advertisers may shrug at an employer's demands for
a biosurveillance badge. In a world of insecure employment, what choice do they
have, anyway? Despite the revelations of alarming National Security Agency spying

and increased government and corporate surveillance since 9/11, the young haven't had much experience yet with what's at stake for them personally. What could possibly go wrong?

A lot: Surveillance has a way of dehumanizing workers. It prevents us from experimenting and exercising our creativity on the job because it tends to uphold the status quo and hold back change. Surveillance makes everyone seem suspicious, creating perceptions and expectations of dishonesty. It makes us feel manipulated. Some researchers have found that increased monitoring actually decreases productivity.

Philosopher and social theorist Michel Foucault observed that the relationship between the watcher and the watched is mostly about power. The power of the observer is enhanced, while the person observed feels more powerless. When an employer or manager interprets our personal data, she gets to make categorical judgments about us and determine how to predict our behavior.

What if she uses the information to discriminate? Coerce? Selectively apply the rules? The data she uses to make her judgments may not even be telling the truth: Researchers have warned that big data can produce big errors. People looking at numbers tend to use them to confirm their own biases, cherry-picking the information that supports their beliefs and ditching the rest. And since algorithms are constructed by human beings, they are not immune to human biases, either. A consumer might be labeled "unlikely to pay a credit card bill" because of an ethnic name, thus promulgating a harmful stereotype.

As Americans, we like to tell ourselves that we value freedom and undue interference from authority. But when we are subjected to surveillance, we feel disempowered and disrespected. We may be more inclined to accept the government getting involved because of fears about terrorism—but when it comes to surveillance on the job, our tendency to object may be chilled by weakened worker protections and increased employment insecurity.

Instead of producing an efficient and productive workplace, biosurveillance may instead deliver troops of distracted, apathetic employees who feel loss of control and decreased job satisfaction. Instead of feeling like part of a team, surveilled workers may develop an us-versus-them mentality and look for opportunities to thwart the monitoring schemes of Big Boss. 15

Perhaps what we really need is biosurveillance from the bottom up—members of Congress and CEOs could don devices that could, say, detect when they are lying or how their hormones are behaving. Colorful PowerPoints could display the results of data collection on public billboards for the masses to pore over. In the name of safety and efficiency, maybe we ought to ensure that those whose behavior can do society the most harm do not escape the panopticon.

Overall View of the Essay

Before we comment in detail on Parramore's essay, we need to say that in terms of the length of some of its paragraphs, it isn't necessarily a model for you to imitate. Material in print or online news sources is typically presented in very short paragraphs (notice Parramore's one-sentence-long paragraph 4). This is partly because people read it while eating breakfast or commuting to work, and in the case of print newspapers partly because the columns are narrow (a paragraph of only two or three sentences may still be an inch or two deep).

The title, "Fitbits for Bosses," is provocative, captures readers' attention, and leaves them with a sense of where Parramore's argument is heading.

Paragraph 1 compels readers by asking them to imagine an ordinary day at work, presenting the routine activities of getting work under way—turning on the computer, adjusting the chair—before throwing in the "behavior-monitoring device" almost as an afterthought, as if to shock us with the possibility that such devices could become routine.

Paragraph 2 presses the idea of invasion of privacy, almost aggressively, by using words like *dystopian* and a reference to a science fiction novel ("brave new world") whose title has become a shorthand for technological intrusions into individuals' lives.

Paragraph 3 presents as "obvious" the fact that self-monitoring technology has gone mainstream. (One of the authors of this book just purchased a new mobile device that came preinstalled with an application that records the number of steps and miles the user walks in a day. Going deeper into the menu, it includes functions for recording everything from nutrient intake to sexual activity.) The writer is clearly drawing on readers' familiarity with these technologies. Then she presents the portent of these devices "creeping" into the workplace, first by showing how such technologies have already been used in military applications and in businesses like professional sports. "So what?" we might think, but Parramore is about to tell us.

Paragraph 4 is a single-sentence paragraph, turning the essay's focus from two specialized fields to the everyday jobs that millions of people hold. Notice how the language ("getting in on the game") reveals Parramore's position that this trend signals something new and troubling.

Paragraph 5 turns to the finance industry to show how some industries are beginning to monitor not just employee health but hormonal flows that have been correlated to emotional and psychological states. The dystopian theme is extended here as these technologies are presented as reaching into new realms where independent action and decision-making occur. Phrases like "human optimization" and references to an "early warning system" that would "alert supervisors" hint at potential limitations on human independence and deeper control of employees by managers.

Paragraph 6 focuses on Bank of America's partnership with Humanyze and shows more ways in which biosurveillance technologies could be used to monitor employees. Parramore is enhancing her argument through careful language use. In fact, her position is arguably coming most strongly through tone. What language cues indicate her position on these technologies? What specific words and phrases does she use ironically or sardonically?

Paragraph 7 quotes Humanyze's founder, Ben Waber, who rationally states that companies spend enormous amounts of money tracking consumers, so why not track employees too? But Parramore presents this statement as anything but appealing; instead, it comes across as a kind of dangerous rationality.

Paragraph 8 starts out by noting that the government doesn't permit law enforcement to do what employers regularly do in various industries. It cites a study showing how widespread the use of these devices is, and a case in which a woman lost her job by refusing to be monitored.

Paragraph 9 provides the defense offered by the industries that create these technologies, pointing out that some highly sensitive jobs such as power plant operator and airline pilot require the closest scrutiny of individuals' physical conditions.

Paragraph 10 mentions "Young Americans," raised in a digital world, who may just "shrug" at the latest developments in surveillance technology without realizing the implications to them personally. "What could go wrong?" Parramore asks.

Paragraph 11 answers that question, first with the word *dehumanizing*, then by claiming that surveillance dampens creativity and change, encourages suspicion, presumes dishonesty, and hurts productivity.

Paragraph 12 brings into the mix a philosopher, Michel Foucault—one of the twentieth century's most recognized theorists of power. Foucault leads Parramore to wonder about what kinds of power may be exercised by using the information gained from surveillance technology.

Paragraph 13 considers hypothetical scenarios in which a manager might be able to discriminate or coerce an employee by using collected data. Parramore seems to be asking how employees are protected from such strict oversight.

Paragraph 14 reminds readers that measurements are just measurements, prone to error and to biases that could lead to unfair or discriminatory uses of data.

Paragraph 15 presents a summary of the potentially harmful outcomes of widespread implementation of biometric surveillance of employees, pointing especially to decreased job satisfaction and an "us-versus-them" mentality among employees and employers.

Paragraph 16 drives home the author's point by offering a reversal of the expected order of surveillance arrangements. What if, Parramore suggests, the public demanded surveillance of those in power, especially since those in important managerial positions are presumably the ones whose behaviors and actions might impact the most people? The essay finishes with a suggestion that it is those in power who most need to be watched "in the name of safety and efficiency"—ostensibly the terms used to justify the practice as applied to workers.

Discussion Questions: Topics for Critical Thinking and Writing

1. Do you think biometric measurement by employers is ever justified, or do the privacy and security of one's own body always trump the concerns of employers? Why, or why not?

2. If your teachers or parents could monitor the time you spent, and how you felt, while doing homework and studying, what benefits and drawbacks might result? What types of personal monitoring are already in place (or possible) in schools and homes, and are these different from biometric surveillance?

3. Do you think Lynn Parramore fairly portrays the founder of Humanyze and others who see potential in the possibilities for biometric monitoring? Why, or why not? In what other ways might biometric measurements help employees and employers?

4. List some examples of Parramore's use of language, word choice, and phrasing that would influence readers to be suspicious of biometric monitoring. How does this language make the essay more or less effective or convincing?

5. In what way does Parramore's recommendation in the final paragraph support or contradict her argument about individuals' basic rights to privacy?

Examining Assumptions

In Chapter 3, we will discuss **assumptions** in some detail, but here we introduce the topic by emphasizing the importance of *identifying* and *examining* assumptions—those you'll encounter in the writings of others and those you'll rely on in your own essays.

With this in mind, let's again consider some of the assumptions suggested in this chapter's earlier readings. The student who wrote about Stephen Cavanaugh's case pointed out that Nebraska prison officials simply did not see the Church of the Flying Spaghetti Monster as a real religion. Their assumption was that some religions can be more or less "real" than others or can make more sense than others. Assumptions may be *explicit* or *implicit*, stated or unstated. In this case, the prison officials were forthright about their assumptions in their stated claim about the Church, perhaps believing their point was obvious to anyone who thought seriously about the idea of a Flying Spaghetti Monster. It didn't occur to them to consider that even major and mainstream religions honor stories, claims, and rituals that seem absurd to others.

An implicit assumption is one that is not stated but, rather, is taken for granted. It works like an underlying belief that structures an argument. In Lynn Stuart Parramore's essay on workplace biometric devices, the unstated assumption is that these sorts of technology in the workplace represent a kind of evil "big brother" intent on subduing and exploiting employees with newer and newer forms of invasion of privacy. Parramore's assumption, while not stated directly, is evident in her choice of language, as we've pointed out above. Another way to discern her assumption is by looking at the scenarios and selections of examples she chooses. For example, in imagining a company that would seek to know how much time an employee spends in the lounge area or alone, Parramore sees only obsessive monitoring of employees for the purposes of regulating their time. But what if these technologies could enable a company to discover that productivity or worker satisfaction increases in proportion to the amount of time employees spend collaborating in the lounge? Maybe workplace conditions would improve instead of deteriorating (a bigger lounge, more comfortable chairs), and maybe more efforts would be made for team-building and improving interpersonal employee relations.

✓ A Checklist for Examining Assumptions

- ☐ What assumptions does the writer's argument presuppose?

- ☐ Are these assumptions explicit or implicit?

- ☐ Are these assumptions important to the author's argument, or are they only incidental?

- ☐ Does the author give any evidence of being aware of the hidden assumptions in her or his argument?

- ☐ Would a critic be likely to share these assumptions, or are they exactly what a critic would challenge?

- ☐ What sort of evidence would be relevant to supporting or rejecting these assumptions?

- ☐ Am I willing to grant the author's assumptions? Would most readers grant them?

- ☐ If not, why not?

Consider now two of the assumptions involved in the Kim Davis case. Thanks to the clustering exercise (p. 6), these and other assumptions are already on display. Perhaps the most important and fundamental assumption Davis and her supporters made is this:

> Where private religious beliefs conflict with duly enacted laws, the former
> should prevail.

This assumption is widely held in our society; it is by no means unique to Davis and her supporters. Opponents, however, probably assumed a very different but equally fundamental proposition:

> Private religious practices and beliefs must yield to the demands of laws
> guaranteeing citizens equal rights.

Obviously, these two assumptions are opposed to each other, and neither side can prevail so long as the key assumption of the other side is ignored.

Assumptions can be powerful sources of ideas and opinions, and understanding our own and others' assumptions is a major part of critical thinking. Assumptions about race, class, disability, sex, and gender are among the most powerful sources of social inequality. The following essay arguing that women should be permitted to serve in combat roles in the military was published in 2012, well before the Department of Defense lifted the ban on women in combat roles in the armed forces in 2013. More recently, Defense Secretary Ashton Carter further lifted exclusions pertaining to women by granting them access to serve in all capacities in combat, including in elite special forces units. Following that development, General Lori J. Robinson made history as the first female combatant commander when she was appointed leader of the North American Aerospace Defense Command and U.S. Northern Command in Colorado in May 2016. Still, we reprint McGregor's essay because it compels readers to consider some of their assumptions about women (and men). Topics for discussion appear after the essay.

Jena McGregor

Jena McGregor, a graduate of the University of Georgia, is a freelance writer and a daily columnist for the *Washington Post*. This article was published on May 25, 2012.

Military Women in Combat: Why Making It Official Matters

It's been a big couple of weeks for women in the military.

Last week, female soldiers began formally moving into jobs in previously all-male battalions, a program that will later go Army-wide. The move is a result of rule changes following a February report that opened some 14,000 new positions to women in critical jobs much closer to the front lines. However, some 250,000 combat jobs still remain officially closed to them.

The same week, Rep. Loretta Sanchez (D, Calif.) and Sen. Kirsten Gillibrand (D, N.Y.) introduced legislation in both houses of Congress that would encourage the "repeal of the Ground Combat Exclusion policy" for women in the armed forces. Then this Wednesday, two female U.S. Army reservists filed a lawsuit that seeks to overturn the remaining restrictions on women in combat, saying they limit "their current and future earnings, their potential for promotion and advancement, and their future retirement benefits." (A Pentagon spokesperson told Bloomberg News that Defense Secretary Leon Panetta "is strongly committed to examining the expansion of roles for women in the U.S. military, as evidenced by the recent step of opening up thousands of more assignments to women.")

One of the arguments behind both the lawsuit and the new legislation is that the remaining restrictions hurt women's opportunities for advancement. Advocates for women in the military say that even if women like Gen. Ann Dunwoody have reached four-star general status, she and women like her without official frontline combat experience apparently haven't been considered for the military's very highest posts. "If women remain restricted to combat service and combat service support specialties, we will not see a woman as Commandant of the Marine Corps, or CENTCOM commander, or Chairman of the Joint Chiefs of Staff," writes Greg Jacob, policy director for the Service Women's Action Network. "Thus women in the military are being held back simply because they are women. Such an idea is not only completely at odds with military ethics, but is distinctly un-American."

Women have been temporarily "attached" to battalions for the last decade; still, allowing women to formally serve in combat operations could help to break down the so-called brass ceiling.

5

Another way to break down the ceiling would be to consider talented women for top military leadership positions, whether or not they've officially held certain combat posts. Presidents have chosen less-senior officers for Joint Chiefs roles, which are technically staff jobs, wrote Laura Conley and Lawrence Korb, a former assistant defense secretary in the Reagan administration and a senior fellow at the Center for American Progress, in the *Armed Forces Journal* last year. They argue that putting a woman on the Joint Chiefs would help the military grapple with rising sexual harassment issues, bring nontraditional expertise (which women have developed because of some of their role exclusions) at a time when that's increasingly critical, and send the signal that the military is not only open to women, but puts no barriers in their way.

Yes, putting women in combat roles beyond those that have been recently formalized would require many adjustments, both logistical and psychological, for the military and for its male troops. There are plenty of women who may not be interested in these jobs, or who do not meet the physical demands required of them. And gradual change may be prudent. The recent openings are a start; Army Chief of Staff Ray Odierno's acknowledgment last week that if women are allowed into infantry, they will at some point probably go through Ranger School, is encouraging.

But at a time when experience like the infantry is reportedly crucial for getting top posts, it's easy to see how official and sizable policy changes are needed in order to create a system that lets talented women advance to the military's highest echelons. In any field where there are real or perceived limitations for women's advancement, it's that much harder to attract the best and brightest. Indeed, the Military Leadership Diversity Commission recommended last March that the services end combat exclusion policies for women, along with other "barriers and inconsistencies, to create a level playing field for all qualified service members." As the commission chairman, Retired Air Force Gen. Lester L. Lyles, told the American Forces Press Service at the time, "we know that [the exclusion] hinders women from promotion."

For the military to achieve the diverse workforce it seeks, interested and capable women should either not face exclusions, or the culture of the armed forces needs to change so that women without that particular experience can still reach the very top. Both changes may be difficult, but the latter is extraordinarily so. Ending the restrictions is the shortest route to giving the military the best pool of talent possible and the most diverse viewpoints for leading it.

Discussion Questions: Topics for Critical Thinking and Writing

1. How would you characterize Jena McGregor's tone (her manner)? Is it thoughtful? Pushy? Identify passages that support your view.

2. Explain the term *brass ceiling* (para. 5).

3. One argument *against* sending women onto an actual battlefield, as infantry or as members of a tank crew, is that if they're captured they might be gang-raped. In your view, how significant is this argument? Explain your response.

4. Here is a second argument against sending women into direct combat: Speaking generally, women do not have the upper-body strength that men have, and a female soldier (again, speaking generally, not about a particular individual) would thus be less able to pull a wounded companion out of a burning tank or off a battlefield. To put the matter differently: Male soldiers might feel that they couldn't count on their female comrades in a time of need. What is your reply?

5. In her final paragraph, McGregor suggests that if the armed forces were to change their policy and not require battlefield experience for the very highest jobs, the military would achieve diversity at the top and women would have an opportunity for top pay. What are your thoughts? For instance, is the idea that the top officers should have experienced hand-to-hand combat out of date, romantic, hopelessly macho, or irrelevant to modern warfare? Explain.

6. What do you make of the following question? Since women are now permitted to serve in all military combat positions, should all women, like all men, have to register for Selective Service and be subject to the military draft, if one were needed? Construct an argument to defend your position on this question.

Inside Work: Four Exercises in Critical Thinking

As you draft essays for one or more of the assignments, consider typing your notes in a Google document or in Microsoft OneNote, or using another collaborative application or service (perhaps offered free by your school), so that you can easily share your thoughts and writing on the topic. As always, submit and complete assignments in the way that your instructor directs. However, remember that services such as Google and OneNote can be good places to maintain copies of your notes and essays for later consultation.

1. Think further about the issues of privacy and surveillance raised by Lynn Parramore's essay. Consider several different kinds of work, types of employers, and the various types of employee monitoring that do or may occur. Jot down pros and cons, and then write a balanced dialogue between two imagined speakers who hold opposing views on the issue. You'll doubtless have to revise your dialogue several times, and in revising your drafts you'll likely come up with further ideas. Present *both* sides as strongly as possible. (You may want to give the two speakers distinct characters; for instance, one may be an employer seeking to introduce a new technology, and the other may be an employee intent on protecting his privacy and freedom. Alternatively, one could be an employee looking forward to a new "healthy workplace" initiative using biometrics, and the other could be a colleague suspicious of the new program.)

2. Choose one of the following topics, and write down all the pro and con arguments you can think of in, say, ten minutes. Then, at least an hour or two later, return to your notes and see whether you can add to them. Finally, as in Exercise 1, write a balanced dialogue, presenting each idea as strongly as possible. (If none of these topics interests you, ask your instructor about the possibility of choosing a topic of your own.) Suggested topics:

    a. Colleges with large athletic programs should pay student athletes a salary or stipend.

    b. Bicyclists and motorcyclists should be required by law to wear helmets.

    c. High school teachers should have the right to carry concealed firearms in schools.

    d.   Smoking should be prohibited on all college campuses, including in all buildings *and* outdoors.

    e.   College students should have the right to request alternative assignments from their professors if class material is offensive or traumatic.

    f.   Students should have the right to drop out of school at any age.

    g.   Sororities and fraternities should be coeducational (allowing both males and females).

    h.   The government should tax sugary foods and drinks in order to reduce obesity.

3.   In April 2012, Williams College in Williamstown, Massachusetts, hosted a lecture and film screening of work by Jiz Lee, described in campus advertisements as a "genderqueer porn star." After inviting the adult entertainer to campus, the college came under fire by some students and members of the public (especially after the story was reported by national media). Opponents questioned the appropriateness and academic value of the event, which was brought to campus by the Mike Dively Committee, an endowment established to help "develop understanding of human sexuality and sexual orientation and their impact on culture." Proponents argued that (1) pornography is a subject that deserves critical analysis and commentary; (2) the Dively series is intended to create conversations about sexuality and sexual orientation in society and culture; and (3) treating any potential subject in an academic setting under the circumstances of the program is appropriate. What are your views? Should adult film stars ever be invited to college campuses? Should pornography constitute a subject of analysis on campus? Why, or why not?

    Imagine you're a student member of the campus programming board, and the Gender and Sexuality Program comes to your committee seeking funds to invite a female former adult film star to campus to lecture on "The Reality of Pornography." Faculty and student sponsors have assured your committee that the visit by the actress in question is part of an effort to educate students and the public about the adult film industry and its impact on popular culture. Images and short film clips may be shown. Pose as many questions as you can about the potential benefits and risks of approving this invitation. How would you vote, and why? (If you can find a peer who has an opposing view, construct a debate on the issue.)

4. In 1985, the U.S. Congress passed the National Minimum Drinking Age Act, mandating that all states implement and enforce raising the minimum drinking age from eighteen to twenty-one years. Through this legislation, the United States became one of a handful of developed countries to have such a high drinking age. In 2009, John McCardell, president of Middlebury College in Vermont, wrote a declaration signed by 135 college presidents supporting returning the drinking age to eighteen. McCardell's organization, Choose Responsibly, says that people age eighteen to twenty should be treated as the adults they are—for example, in terms of voting, serving on juries and in the military, or buying legal weapons. The organization encourages educational programs and awareness efforts that would introduce alcohol-related issues to young college students and demystify and discourage problem drinking. Such a move is opposed by Mothers Against Drunk Drivers (MADD), whose members argue that raising the drinking age to twenty-one has curbed traffic accidents and fatalities caused by drunk driving. Opponents to lowering the drinking age also claim that it would introduce alcohol to even younger people, as many eighteen-year-olds would inevitably interact in social situations with underage peers. Argue for the age you think might be the best legal minimum—eighteen, or twenty-one, or something in between?—trying to anticipate and address the counterarguments that will be made against your position.

Chapter 2

Critical Reading: Getting Started

Some books are to be tasted, others to be swallowed, and some few to be chewed and digested.

—Francis Bacon

Active Reading

In the passage that we quote above, Bacon makes two good points. One is that books are of varying worth; the second is that a taste of some books may be enough.

But even a book (or an essay) that you will chew and digest is one that you first may want to taste. How can you get a taste—that is, how can you get some sense of a piece of writing—*before* you sit down to read it carefully?

Previewing

Even before reading a work, you may have some ideas about it, perhaps because you already know something about the author. You know, for example, that a work by Martin Luther King Jr. will probably deal with civil rights. You know, too, that it will be serious and eloquent. In contrast, if you pick up an essay by Stephen King, you'll probably expect it to be about fear, the craft of writing, or his experiences as a horror novelist. It may be about something else, but it's probable the essay will follow your expectations. For one thing, you know that King writes for a broad audience, so his essay won't be terribly difficult to understand.

In short, a reader who has knowledge of the author probably has some idea of what the subject will be and what the writing will be like, so the reader approaches it in a certain light. But even if you don't know the author, you can often discern important information about him or her by looking at biographical information provided in the text or by doing a quick Internet search. You can use this information to predict not only the essay's subject and style but also the author's approach to the topic, which helps when trying to diagnose assumptions and biases, among other things.

Chapter 2, "Critical Reading: Getting Started," from *From Critical Thinking to Argument: A Portable Guide,* by Sylvan Barnet, Hugo Bedau, and John O'Hara, pp. 45–87 (Chapter 2). Copyright © 2017 by Bedford/St. Martin's.

The **place of publication** may also reveal something about the essay in terms of its subject, style, and approach. For instance, the *National Review* is a conservative journal. If you notice that an essay on affirmative action was published in the *National Review*, you're probably safe in tentatively assuming that the essay will not endorse affirmative action. In contrast, *Ms.* magazine is a liberal publication, and an essay on affirmative action published there will probably be an endorsement. You often can learn a good deal about a journal or magazine simply by flipping through it and noticing the kinds of articles and advertisements in it.

The **title** of an essay, too, may give an idea of what to expect. Of course, a title may announce only the subject and not the author's thesis or point of view ("On Gun Control"; "Should Drugs Be Legal?"), but fairly often it will indicate the thesis too (as in "Give Children the Vote" or "We Need Campaign Finance Reform Now"). By knowing more or less what to expect, you can probably take in some of the major points even on a quick reading.

When engaging with an essay, you can also consider the role of **context**—the situational conditions in which it was written. Context can refer to the time period, geographical location, cultural climate, political environment, or any other setting for a piece of writing. Recognizing the context of any piece of writing can reveal a lot about how an author treats a subject. For example, an essay written before September 11, 2001, about how to contain global terrorism might have a less urgent approach and advocate more lenient measures than one written today. An article about transgender identity or police brutality might convey different assumptions about those topics depending on whether it was written before or after Bruce Jenner publicly became Caitlyn Jenner, for instance, or before or after the events of Ferguson, Missouri, brought the issue of race and police violence into the public's consciousness in new ways.

Anything you read exists in at least two broad contexts: the context of its *production* (where and when it was written or published) and the context of its *consumption* (where and when it is encountered and read). One thing all good critical thinkers do when considering the validity of claims and arguments is to take *both* types of context into account. This means asking questions not only about the approach, assumptions, and beliefs that were in place when an essay was written, but also about how current events and understandings generate new issues and challenges within the subject of the essay. The state of affairs in the time and place in which that argument is made *and received* shapes the questions you might ask, the evidence you might consider, and the responses you might produce.

Notice that you can apply these previewing techniques before reading a single word of the essay. And once you have a good sense of the what, who, where, and when of an essay, you should keep them in mind while reading.

Your first reading might involve another previewing technique, **skimming**. Sometimes, you can find the **thesis** (the main point or major claim) of an essay by looking at the first paragraph. Other times, especially if the paragraphs are short, you can locate the thesis within the first several paragraphs. Depending on what you discover while skimming, you can speed up or slow down your reading as needed while you locate the thesis and get a sense of how the argument for it is structured. If the essay has sections, pay attention to *headings* and *subheadings*. Look for key expressions that indicate an author's conclusive statements, such as "Finally, then, it is time that we…" or "Given this evidence, it is clear that…." These kinds of sentences frequently appear at the beginnings or endings of paragraphs and sections. Final paragraphs are particularly important because they often summarize the argument and restate the thesis.

By previewing and skimming effectively, you can quickly ascertain quite a bit of information about an article or essay. You can detect the author's claims and methods, see the evidence he or she uses (experience, statistics, quotations, etc.), ascertain the tone and difficulty level, and determine whether the piece of writing offers useful ideas for you. This strategy works well if you're researching a topic and need to review many essays—you can read efficiently to find those that are most important or relevant to you, or those that offer different perspectives. Of course, if you do find an essay to be compelling during previewing, you can begin "chewing and digesting," as Francis Bacon put it—reading more closely and carefully (or else putting it aside for later when you can give it more time).

Call-Out: Critical Reading Tip

Instead of imagining previewing and close reading as two separate stages to be completed consecutively, think of previewing as an activity that might at any time develop into close reading.

A Short Essay for Previewing Practice

Before skimming the following essay, apply the previewing techniques discussed above, and complete the Thinking Critically: Previewing activity on pages 48–49.

Sanjay Gupta

Dr. Sanjay Gupta (b. 1969) is a neurosurgeon and multiple Emmy award–winning television personality. As a leading public health expert, he has appeared widely on television, including the *Oprah Winfrey Show*, the *Late Show with David Letterman*, the *Jon Stewart Show*, and *60 Minutes*. He is most well known as CNN's chief medical correspondent. In 2011, *Forbes* magazine named him one of the ten most influential celebrities in America. The essay reprinted below originally appeared on CNN.com in August 2013.

Why I Changed My Mind on Weed

Over the last year, I have been working on a new documentary called "Weed." The title "Weed" may sound cavalier, but the content is not.

I traveled around the world to interview medical leaders, experts, growers and patients. I spoke candidly to them, asking tough questions. What I found was stunning.

Long before I began this project, I had steadily reviewed the scientific literature on medical marijuana from the United States and thought it was fairly unimpressive. Reading these papers five years ago, it was hard to make a case for medicinal marijuana. I even wrote about this in a *Time* magazine article, back in 2009, titled "Why I Would Vote No on Pot."

Well, I am here to apologize.

I apologize because I didn't look hard enough, until now. I didn't look far enough. I didn't review papers from smaller labs in other countries doing some remarkable research, and I was too dismissive of the loud chorus of legitimate patients whose symptoms improved on cannabis.

5

Instead, I lumped them with the high-visibility malingerers, just looking to get high. I mistakenly believed the Drug Enforcement Agency listed marijuana as a Schedule 1 substance because of sound scientific proof. Surely, they must have quality reasoning as to why marijuana is in the category of the most dangerous drugs that have "no accepted medicinal use and a high potential for abuse."

They didn't have the science to support that claim, and I now know that when it comes to marijuana neither of those things are true. It doesn't have a high potential for abuse, and there are very legitimate medical applications. In fact, sometimes marijuana is the only thing that works. Take the case of Charlotte Figi, whom I met in Colorado. She started having seizures soon after birth. By age 3, she was having 300 a week, despite being on 7 different medications. Medical marijuana has calmed her brain, limiting her seizures to 2 or 3 per month.

I have seen more patients like Charlotte first hand, spent time with them and come to the realization that it is irresponsible not to provide the best care we can as a medical community, care that could involve marijuana.

We have been terribly and systematically misled for nearly 70 years in the United States, and I apologize for my own role in that.

I hope this article and upcoming documentary will help set the record straight.

10

On August 14, 1970, the Assistant Secretary of Health, Dr. Roger O. Egeberg, wrote a letter recommending the plant, marijuana, be classified as a Schedule 1 substance, and it has remained that way for nearly 45 years. My research started with a careful reading of that decades-old letter. What I found was unsettling. Egeberg had carefully chosen his words:

"Since there is still a considerable void in our knowledge of the plant and effects of the active drug contained in it, our recommendation is that marijuana be retained within Schedule 1 at least until the completion of certain studies now under way to resolve the issue."

Not because of sound science, but because of its absence, marijuana was classified as a Schedule 1 substance. Again, the year was 1970. Egeberg mentions studies that are under way, but many were never completed. As my investigation continued, however, I realized Egeberg did in fact have important research already available to him, some of it from more than 25 years earlier.

High Risk of Abuse

In 1944, New York mayor Fiorello LaGuardia commissioned research to be performed by the New York Academy of Science. Among their conclusions: they found marijuana did not lead to significant addiction in the medical sense of the word. They also did not find any evidence marijuana led to morphine, heroin or cocaine addiction.

We now know that while estimates vary, marijuana leads to dependence in around 9 to 10% of its adult users. By comparison, cocaine, a Schedule 2 substance "with less abuse potential than Schedule 1 drugs," hooks 20% of those who use it. Around 25% of heroin users become addicted.   15

The worst is tobacco, where the number is closer to 30% of smokers, many of whom go on to die because of their addiction.

There is clear evidence that in some people marijuana use can lead to withdrawal symptoms, including insomnia, anxiety and nausea. Even considering this, it is hard to make a case that it has a high potential for abuse. The physical symptoms of marijuana addiction are nothing like those of the other drugs I've mentioned. I have seen the withdrawal from alcohol, and it can be life threatening.

I do want to mention a concern that I think about as a father. Young, developing brains are likely more susceptible to harm from marijuana than adult brains. Some recent studies suggest that regular use in teenage years leads to a permanent decrease in IQ. Other research hints at a possible heightened risk of developing psychosis.

Much in the same way I wouldn't let my own children drink alcohol, I wouldn't permit marijuana until they are adults. If they are adamant about trying marijuana, I will urge them to wait until they're in their mid-20s, when their brains are fully developed.

Medical Benefit

While investigating, I realized something else quite important. Medical marijuana is not new, and the medical community has been writing about it for a long time.   20

There were in fact hundreds of journal articles, mostly documenting the benefits. Most of those papers, however, were written between the years 1840 and 1930. The papers described the use of medical marijuana to treat "neuralgia, convulsive disorders, emaciation," among other things.

A search through the U.S. National Library of Medicine this past year pulled up nearly 20,000 more recent papers. But the majority were research into the harm of marijuana, such as "Bad trip due to anticholinergic effect of cannabis," or "Cannabis induced pancreatitis" and "Marijuana use and risk of lung cancer."

In my quick running of the numbers, I calculated about 6% of the current U.S. marijuana studies investigate the benefits of medical marijuana. The rest are designed to investigate harm. That imbalance paints a highly distorted picture.

The Challenges of Marijuana Research

To do studies on marijuana in the United States today, you need two important things.

First of all, you need marijuana. And marijuana is illegal. You see the problem. Scientists can get research marijuana from a special farm in Mississippi, which is astonishingly located in the middle of the Ole Miss campus, but it is challenging. When I visited this year, there was no marijuana being grown.

The second thing you need is approval, and the scientists I interviewed kept reminding me how tedious that can be. While a cancer study may first be evaluated by the National Cancer Institute, or a pain study may go through the National Institute for Neurological Disorders, there is one more approval required for marijuana: NIDA, the National Institute on Drug Abuse. It is an organization that has a core mission of studying drug abuse, as opposed to benefit.

Stuck in the middle are the legitimate patients who depend on marijuana as a medicine, oftentimes as their only good option.

Keep in mind that up until 1943, marijuana was part of the United States drug pharmacopeia. One of the conditions for which it was prescribed was neuropathic pain. It is a miserable pain that's tough to treat. My own patients have described it as "lancinating, burning and a barrage of pins and needles." While marijuana has long been documented to be effective for this awful pain, the most common medications prescribed today come from the poppy plant, including morphine, oxycodone and dilaudid.

Here is the problem. Most of these medications don't work very well for this kind of pain, and tolerance is a real problem.

Most frightening to me is that someone dies in the United States every 19 minutes from a prescription drug overdose, mostly accidental. Every 19 minutes. It is a horrifying statistic. As much as I searched, I could not find a documented case of death from marijuana overdose.

25

It is perhaps no surprise then that 76% of physicians recently surveyed said they would approve the use of marijuana to help ease a woman's pain from breast cancer.

30

When marijuana became a Schedule 1 substance, there was a request to fill a "void in our knowledge." In the United States, that has been challenging because of the infrastructure surrounding the study of an illegal substance, with a drug abuse organization at the heart of the approval process. And yet, despite the hurdles, we have made considerable progress that continues today.

Looking forward, I am especially intrigued by studies like those in Spain and Israel looking at the anti-cancer effects of marijuana and its components. I'm intrigued by the neuro-protective study by Lev Meschoulam in Israel, and research in Israel and the United States on whether the drug might help alleviate symptoms of PTSD. I promise to do my part to help, genuinely and honestly, fill the remaining void in our knowledge.

Citizens in 20 states and the District of Columbia have now voted to approve marijuana for medical applications, and more states will be making that choice soon. As for Dr. Roger Egeberg, who wrote that letter in 1970, he passed away 16 years ago.

I wonder what he would think if he were alive today.

Inside Work: The "First and Last" Rule

As noted previously, authors often place main points of emphasis at the beginnings and endings of *essays*. They also place important material at the beginnings and endings of *paragraphs* and *sentences*.

When writing, you can emphasize main points by using the first and last rule. Don't bury your most important material in the middle of sentences, paragraphs, or entire papers. Make it stand out.

Consider the following observations. Select two that you find to be most important.

1. Gupta is one of the most respected voices in public health.

2. Gupta argues for the legalization of medical marijuana.

3. Gupta's article was written for CNN News in 2011.

4. Gupta rejects his previous position on medical marijuana and apologizes for his oversight.

5. The article was important because it represented a shift in approach by a leading doctor.

Thinking Critically: Previewing

Provide the missing information for Sanjay Gupta and his essay "Why I Changed My Mind on Weed."

Previewing Strategies	Types of Questions	Answers
Author	Who is he? What expertise does he have? What credibility does he have? How difficult is the writing likely to be?	
Title	What does the title reveal about the essay's content? Does it give any clues about how the argument will take shape?	
Place of Publication	How does the place of publication help you understand the argument? What type of audiences will it be likely to target?	
Context	By placing the article in the context of its time—given trends in the conversations about or popular understandings of the subject—what can you expect about the author's position?	
Skimming	As you skim over the first several paragraphs, where do you first realize the purpose of the essay? What is Gupta's argument? What major forms of evidence does he offer?	

Now arrange these statements in a short paragraph, using the first and last rule to emphasize the two that you selected as most important. Compare your paragraph to your classmates' paragraphs. How do they compare?

Reading with a Careful Eye: Underlining, Highlighting, Annotating

Once you have a general idea of the work—not only an idea of its topic and thesis but also a sense of the way in which the thesis is argued—you can go back and start reading it carefully.

As you read, underline or highlight key passages, and make annotations in the margins. Because you're reading actively, or interacting with the text, you won't simply let your eye rove across the page.

- Highlight what seem to be the chief points, so that later when reviewing the essay you can easily locate the main passages.

- But don't overdo a good thing. If you find yourself highlighting most of a page, you're probably not thinking carefully enough about what the key points are.

- Similarly, your marginal annotations should be brief and selective. They will probably consist of hints or clues, comments like "doesn't follow," "good," "compare with Jones," "check this," and "really?"

- In short, in a paragraph you might highlight a key definition, and in the margin you might write "good," or "in contrast," or "?" if you think the definition is unclear or incorrect.

- With many electronic formats, you can use tools to highlight or annotate. Also consider copying and pasting passages that you would normally highlight in a Google document. Include a link to the piece, and create an RSS feed to the journal's Web site. Having your notes in an electronic format makes it easy to access and use them later.

In all these ways, you interact with the text and lay the groundwork for eventually writing your own essay on what you have read.

What you annotate will depend largely on your purpose. If you're reading an essay in order to see how the writer organizes an argument, you'll annotate one sort of thing. If you're reading in order to challenge the thesis, you'll annotate other things. Here is a passage from an essay entitled "On Racist Speech," with a student's rather skeptical, even aggressive, annotations. But notice that the student apparently made at least one of the annotations—"Definition of 'fighting words'"—chiefly in order to remind herself to locate where the definition of an important term appears in the essay. The essay is by Charles R. Lawrence III, a professor of law at Georgetown University. It originally appeared in the *Chronicle of Higher Education* (October 25, 1989), a publication read chiefly by college and university faculty members and administrators.

University officials who have formulated <u>policies</u> to respond to incidents of racial harassment have been characterized in the press as "thought police," <u>but such policies</u> generally do nothing more than impose (sanctions) against intentional face-to-face insults. When <u>racist speech</u> takes the form of <u>face-to-face insults</u>, catcalls, or other assaultive speech aimed at an individual or small group of persons, it falls directly within the "<u>fighting words</u>" exception to First Amendment protection. The Supreme Court has held that <u>words "which 'by their very utterance inflict</u> injury or tend to incite an immediate breach of the peace'"</u> are not protected by the First Amendment.

[Marginal annotations: "?"; "Examples of such a policy?"; "Example?"; "Definition of 'fighting words'"; "What about sexist speech?"]

If the purpose of the First Amendment is to foster the greatest amount of speech, racial insults disserve that purpose. Assaultive racist speech functions as a preemptive strike. The <u>invective is experienced as a blow, not as a proffered idea,</u> and once the blow is struck, it is unlikely that a dialogue will follow. Racial insults are particularly undeserving of First Amendment protection because the perpetrator's <u>intention is not to discover truth</u> or initiate dialogue but to injure the victim. <u>In most situations,</u> members of minority groups realize that they are likely to lose if they respond to epithets by fighting and are forced to remain silent and submissive.

[Marginal annotations: "Why must speech always seek 'to discover truth'?"; "Really? Probably depends on the individual."; "How does he know?"]

"This; Therefore, That"

To arrive at a coherent thought or series of thoughts that will lead to a reasonable conclusion, a writer has to go through a good deal of preliminary effort. When we discussed heuristics in Chapter 1 (p. 18), we talked about patterns of thought that stimulate initial ideas. The path to sound conclusions involves similar thought patterns that carry forward the arguments presented in the essay:

- While these arguments are convincing, they fail to consider...
- While these arguments are convincing, they must also consider...
- These arguments, rather than being convincing, instead prove...
- While these authors agree, in my opinion...
- Although it is often true that...
- Consider also...
- What sort of audience would agree with such an argument?
- What sort of audience would be opposed?
- What are the differences in values between these two kinds of audiences?

All of these patterns can serve as heuristics or prompts—that is, they can stimulate the creation of ideas.

Moreover, for the writer to convince the reader that the conclusion is sound, the reasoning behind the conclusion must be set forth in detail, with a good deal of "This; therefore, that"; "If this, then that"; and "Others might object at this point that...." The arguments in this book require more comment than President Calvin Coolidge supposedly provided when his wife, who hadn't been able to attend church one Sunday, asked him what the preacher talked about in his sermon. "Sin," Coolidge said. His wife persisted: "What did the preacher say about it?" Coolidge's response: "He was against it."

But, again, when we say that most of the arguments in this book are presented at length and require careful reading, we don't mean that they are obscure; we mean, rather, that you have to approach the sentences thoughtfully, one by one. In this vein, recall an episode from Lewis Carroll's *Through the Looking-Glass*:

> "Can you do Addition?" the White Queen asked. "What's one and one and one and one and one and one and one and one and one and one?"

> "I don't know," said Alice. "I lost count."

> "She can't do Addition," the Red Queen said.

Alice with the Red Queen and the White Queen

It's easy enough to add one and one and one and so on, and of course Alice can do addition—but not at the pace that the White Queen sets. Fortunately, you can set your own pace in reading the cumulative thinking set forth in the essays we reprint in this book. Skimming won't work, but slow reading—and thinking about what you're reading—will.

When you first pick up an essay, you may indeed want to skim it, for some of the reasons mentioned on pages 42–43, but sooner or later you have to settle down to read it and think about it. The effort will be worthwhile. Consider what John Locke, a seventeenth-century English philosopher, said:

> *Reading* furnishes the mind with materials of knowledge; it is *thinking* [that] makes what we read ours. We are of the ruminating kind, and it is not enough to cram ourselves with a great load of collections; unless we chew them over again they will not give us strength and nourishment.

Often students read an essay just once, supposing that to reread would be repetitious. But much can be gleaned from a second reading, as new details will likely emerge and new ideas will be generated. Roland Barthes, a twentieth-century philosopher, warned against accepting a first reading as final. Far from being repetitive, "[r]e-reading," he wrote, "*saves* the text from repetition, multiplies it in its variety and plurality." What may actually be repetitious is reading something only once and, thinking you have it pinned down, repeating it (in your writing) and thereby sticking to your first and only impression.

Defining Terms and Concepts

Suppose you're reading an argument about whether a certain set of images is pornography or art. For the present purpose, let's use a famous example from 1992, when American photographer Sally Mann published *Immediate Family*, a controversial book featuring numerous images of her three children (then ages 12, 10, and 7) in various states of nakedness during their childhood on a rural Kentucky farm. Mann is considered a great photographer and artist ("America's Best Photographer," according to *Time* magazine in 2001), and *Immediate Family* is very well regarded in the art community ("one of the great photograph books of our time," according to the *New Republic*). But some critics couldn't separate the images of Mann's own naked children from the label "child pornography."

When reading, attend carefully to how terms and concepts are used for the purposes of advancing an argument. In this case, you might begin by asking, "What is *pornography*? What is *art*?" If writers and readers cannot agree on basic definitions of the terms and concepts that structure the debate, then argument is futile. And if an author doesn't share *your* definition of a term or concept, then you might challenge the premise of his or her argument. If someone were to define pornography to include *any* images of nude children, that definition would include photographs taken for any reason—medical, sociological, anthropological, scientific—and would include even the innocent photographs taken by proud parents of their children swimming, bathing, and so on. It would also apply to some of the world's great art. Most people do not seriously think the mere image of the naked body, adult or child, is pornography.

Pornography is often defined according to its intended effect on the viewer ("genital commotion," Father Harold Gardiner, S.J., called it in *Catholic Viewpoint on Censorship*). In this definition, if images are eroticized (i.e., made erotic through style or symbolism), if they invite a sexual gaze, they are pornographic. This seems to be the definition that novelist Mary Gordon applied in a 1996 critique of Sally Mann:

> Unless we believe it is ethically permissible for adults to have sex with children, we must question the ethics of an art which allows the adult who has the most power over these children—a parent, in this case a mother—to place them in a situation where they become the imagined sexual partner of adults.... It is inevitable that Sally Mann's photographs arouse the sexual imaginations of strangers.

But is it enough to say something is pornographic if it "arouses the sexual imagination"? No, you might contend, because there is no way to predict what will arouse people's sexual imaginations. Many kinds of images might arouse the sexual imaginations of different people. You might say in rebutting Gordon, "These are just pictures of children. Sure, they're naked in some of them, but children have been symbols of purity and innocence in art since the dawn of civilization. If some people see these images as sexual, that's their problem, not Mann's."

A Rule for Writers

Be alert to how terms and concepts are defined both in your source material and in your own writing. Are your terms broadly, narrowly, or technically construed?

Writers often attempt to provide a provisional definition of important terms and concepts in their arguments. They may write, for example, "For the purposes of this argument, let's define terrorism as X" (a broad definition) or "According to federal law, the term 'international terrorism' means A, B, and C" (a technical definition). If you do this and a reader wants to challenge your ideas, he must argue on your terms or else offer a different definition.

So that we are consistent with our own recommendations, allow us to define the difference between a "term" and a "concept." A rule of thumb is that a *term* is more concrete and fixed than a *concept*. You may be able to find an authoritative source (like a federal law or an official policy) to help define a *term*. A *concept* is more open-ended and may have a generally agreed-upon definition, but rarely a strict or unchanging one. Concepts can be abstract but can also function powerfully in argumentation; love, justice, morality, psyche, health, freedom, bravery, obscenity, masculinity—these are all concepts. You may look up such words in the dictionary for general definitions, but the source won't say much about how to apply the concepts.

Since you cannot assume that everyone has a shared understanding of concepts you may be using, it's prudent for the purposes of effective writing to define them. You may find a useful definition of a concept given by an authoritative person, such as an expert in a field, as in "Stephen Hawking defines time as...." You might cite a respected authority, as in "Mahatma Gandhi defines love as...." Alternatively, you can combine several views and insert your own provisional definition. See "Thinking Critically: Defining Terms and Concepts" for an exercise.

Thinking Critically: Defining Terms and Concepts

Examine each claim, and note the terms and concepts used. Provide a terminological (strict, codified by an authoritative source) or a conceptual (loose, self-generated) definition for each. what sources did you use? Compare your answers to those of your peers to see if they are similar or different.

Statement	Definition	Type of Defintion
Video games are **addictive**.		
Poor people will suffer most from the new law.		
The **epidemic of obesity** needs to be solved.		
We must send troops to protect **the national interest**.		
The Internet has ushered in a new age of **progress**.		

Summarizing and Paraphrasing

After a first reading, perhaps the best approach to a fairly difficult essay is to reread it and simultaneously take notes on a sheet of paper, summarizing each paragraph in a sentence or two. Writing a summary will help you to:

* understand the contents and

* see the strengths and weaknesses of the piece.

Don't confuse a summary with a paraphrase. A paraphrase is a word-by-word or phrase-by-phrase rewording of a text, a sort of translation of the author's language into your own. A paraphrase is therefore as long as the original or even longer; a summary is much shorter. An entire essay, even a whole book, may be summarized in a page, in a paragraph, even in a sentence. Obviously, the summary will leave out most details, but it will accurately state the essential thesis or claim of the original.

Why would anyone summarize, and why would anyone paraphrase? Because, as we've already said, these two activities—in different ways—offer a way to introduce other authors' ideas into your arguments in a way that readers can follow. You may do this for a number of reasons. Summaries and paraphrases can accomplish the following:

* **validate** the basis of your argument by providing an instance in which someone else wrote about the same topic

* **clarify** in short order the complex ideas contained in another author's work

* **support** your argument by showing readers where someone else "got it right" (corroborating your ideas) or "got it wrong" (countering your ideas, but giving you a chance to refute that position in favor of your own)

* **lend authority** to your voice by showing readers that you have considered the topic carefully by consulting other sources

* **help you build new ideas** from existing ideas on the topic, enabling you to insert your voice into an ongoing debate made evident by the summary or paraphrase

When you summarize, you're standing back, saying briefly what the whole adds up to; you're seeing the forest, as the saying goes, not the individual trees. **When you paraphrase**, you're inching through the forest, scrutinizing each tree—finding a synonym for almost every word in the original in an effort to ensure you know exactly what the original is saying. (*Caution*: Do not incorporate a summary or a paraphrase into your own essay without acknowledging the source and stating that you are summarizing or paraphrasing.)

Let's examine the distinction between summary and paraphrase in connection with the first two paragraphs of Paul Goodman's essay "A Proposal to Abolish Grading," excerpted from Goodman's book *Compulsory Miseducation and the Community of Scholars* (1966).

> Let half a dozen of the prestigious universities—Chicago, Stanford, the Ivy
> League—abolish grading, and use testing only and entirely for pedagogic
> purposes as teachers see fit.
>
> Anyone who knows the frantic temper of the present schools will under-
> stand the transvaluation of values that would be effected by this modest
> innovation. For most of the students, the competitive grade has come to be
> the essence. The naive teacher points to the beauty of the subject and the
> ingenuity of the research; the shrewd student asks if he is responsible for that
> on the final exam.

A summary of these two paragraphs might read like this:

> If some top universities used tests only to help students to learn and not for
> grades, students would stop worrying about whether they got an A, B or C and
> might begin to share the teacher's interest in the beauty of the subject.

Notice that the summary doesn't convey Goodman's style or voice (e.g., the wry tone
in his pointed contrast between "the naive teacher" and "the shrewd student"). That
is not the purpose of summary.

Now for a paraphrase. Suppose you're not sure what Goodman is getting at, maybe
because you're uncertain about the meanings of some words (e.g., *pedagogic* and *trans-
valuation*), or else you just want to make sure you understand the point. In such a
case, you may want to move slowly through the sentences, restating them in your own
words. You might turn Goodman's "pedagogic purposes" into "goals in teaching,"
"attempts to help students to learn," or something else. Here is a paraphrase—not a
summary, but a rewording—of Goodman's paragraphs:

> Suppose some of the top universities—such as Chicago, Stanford, Harvard, Yale,
> and others in the Ivy League—stopped using grades and instead used tests only
> in order to help students to learn.
>
> Everyone who is aware of the rat race in schools today will understand the
> enormous shift in values about learning that would come about by this small
> change. At present, idealistic instructors talk about how beautiful their subjects
> are, but smart students know that grades are what count. They only want to
> know if it will be on the exam.

In short, you may decide to paraphrase an important text if you want the reader to see
the passage itself but you know that the full passage will be puzzling. In this situation,
you offer help, *paraphrasing* before making your own point about the author's claim.

A second good reason to offer a paraphrase is if there is substantial disagreement
about what the text says. The Second Amendment to the U.S. Constitution is a good
example of this sort of text:

A well regulated Militia being necessary to the security of a free State, the right of the people to keep and bear Arms shall not be infringed.

Exactly what, one might ask, is a "Militia"? What does it mean for a militia to be "well regulated"? And does "the people" mean each individual or the citizenry as a unified group? After all, elsewhere in the document, where the Constitution speaks of individuals, it speaks of a "man" or a "person," not "the people." To speak of "the people" is to use a term (some argue) that sounds like a reference to a unified group—perhaps the citizens of each of the thirteen states—rather than a reference to individuals.

However, if Congress did mean a unified group rather than individuals, why didn't it say, "Congress shall not prohibit the states from organizing militias"? In fact, thousands of pages have been written about this sentence, and if you're going to talk about it, you certainly have to let readers know exactly how you interpret each word. In short, you almost surely will paraphrase the sentence, going word by word, giving readers your own sense of what each word or phrase means. Here is one possible paraphrase:

Gun control supporters marching in 2013 at the Washington Monument in Washington, D.C.

Because an independent society needs the protection of an armed force if it is to remain free, the government may not limit the right of the individuals (who may someday form the militia needed to keep the society free) to possess weapons.

In this interpretation, the Constitution grants individuals the right to possess weapons, and that is that.

Other students of the Constitution, however, offer very different paraphrases, usually along these lines:

Because each state that is now part of the United States may need to protect its freedom (from the new national government), the national government may not infringe on the right of each state to form its own disciplined militia.

This paraphrase says that the federal government may not prevent each state from having a militia; it says nothing about every individual person having a right to possess weapons.

The first paraphrase might be offered by the National Rifle Association or any other group that interprets the Constitution as guaranteeing individuals the right to own guns. The second paraphrase might be offered by groups that seek to limit the owner-ship of guns.

Why paraphrase? Here are two reasons why you might paraphrase a passage:

- To help yourself to understand it. In his case, the paraphrase does not appear in your essay.

- To help your reader to understand a passage that is especially important but that is not immediately clear. In this case, you paraphrase to let the reader know exactly what the passage means. This paraphrase does appear in your essay.

Paraphrase, Patchwriting, and Plagiarism

We have indicated that only rarely will you have reason to introduce a paraphrase into your essays. But in your preliminary work, when taking notes, you might sometimes do one or more of the following: copy word for word, paraphrase (usually to establish an author's idea clearly in your mind), summarize, and / or produce a medley of bor-rowed words and original words. The latter strategy is known as *patchwriting*, and it can be dangerous: If you submit such a medley in your final essay, you risk the charge of plagiarism *even if you have rearranged the phrases and clauses, and even if you have cited your source.*

Here's an example. First, we give the source: a paragraph from Jena McGregor's essay on whether women serving in the armed forces should be allowed to participate directly in combat. (The entire essay is printed on pp. 34–36.)

> Last week, female soldiers began formally moving into jobs in previously all-male battalions, a program that will later go Armywide. The move is a result of rule changes following a February report that opened some 14,000 new positions to women in critical jobs much closer to the front lines. However, some 250,000 combat jobs still remain officially closed to them.

Here is a student's patchwriting version:

> Women in the army recently began to formally move into jobs in battalions that previously were all-male. This program later will go throughout the Army. According to author Jena McGregor, the move comes from changes in the rules following a February report that opened about 14,000 new jobs to women in critical jobs that are much closer to the front lines. About 250,000 jobs, how-ever—as McGregor points out—continue to be officially closed to women.

As you can see, the student writer has followed the source almost phrase by phrase—certainly, sentence by sentence—making small verbal changes, such as substituting *Women in the army recently* for McGregor's *Last week, female soldiers* and substitut-ing *the move comes from changes in the rules* for McGregor's *The move is a result of rule changes....*

What the student should have done is either (1) *quote the passage exactly*, setting it off to indicate that it's a quotation and indicating the source, or (2) *summarize it briefly* and credit the source—maybe in a sentence such as this:

> Jena McGregor points out that although a recent change in army rules has resulted in new jobs being opened for women in the military, some 250,000 jobs "continue to be officially closed."

As opposed to the above example of a sentence that frankly summarizes a source, patchwriting is *not* the student's writing but, rather, the source material thinly disguised. In a given paragraph of patchwriting, usually some of the words are copied from the source, and all or most of the rest consists of synonyms substituted for the source's words, with minor rearrangement of phrases and clauses. That is, the sequence of ideas and their arrangement, as well as most of the language, are entirely or almost entirely derived from the source, even if some of the words are different.

The fact that you may cite a source is not enough to protect you from the charge of plagiarism. Citing a source tells the reader that some fact or idea—or some groups of words enclosed within quotation marks or set off by indentation—comes from the named source; it does *not* tell the reader that almost everything in the paragraph is, in effect, someone else's writing with a few words changed, a few words added, and a few phrases moved.

The best way to avoid introducing patchwriting into your final essay is to make certain that when taking notes you indicate, *in the notes themselves*, what sorts of notes they are. For example:

- When quoting word for word, put the passage within quotation marks, and cite the page number(s) of the source.

- When paraphrasing—perhaps to ensure that you understand the writer's idea, or because your readers won't understand the source's highly technical language unless you put it into simpler language—use some sign, perhaps (*par*), to remind yourself later that this passage is a paraphrase and thus is not really *your* writing.

- When summarizing, use a different key, such as (*sum*), and cite the page(s) of the source.

Make certain that your notes indicate the degree of indebtedness to your source, and again, do *not* think that if you name a source in a paraphrase you're not plagiarizing. The reader assumes that the name indicates the source of a fact or an idea—not that the paragraph is a rewriting of the original with an occasional phrase of your own inserted here and there.

If you have taken notes properly, with indications of the sort we've mentioned, when writing your paper you can say things like the following:

X's first reason is simple. He says, "…" (here you quote *X*'s words, putting them within quotation marks).

X's point can be summarized thus… (here you cite the page).

X, writing for lawyers, uses some technical language, but we can paraphrase her conclusion in this way: … (here you give the citation).

In short:

- Avoid patchwriting; it is *not* acceptable.
- Enclose direct quotations within quotation marks, or, if the quotations are long, set them off as a block quotation. (Consult your specific style guide for instructions on how to set off block quotations.)
- If you offer a paraphrase, tell readers that you are paraphrasing and explain *why* you are doing so rather than quoting directly or summarizing.

Strategies for Summarizing

As with paraphrases, summaries can be useful for helping you to establish your understanding of an essay or article. Summarizing each paragraph or each group of closely related paragraphs will enable you to follow the threads of the argument and will ultimately provide a useful map of the essay. Then, when rereading the essay, you may want to underline passages that you now realize are the author's key ideas—for instance, definitions, generalizations, summaries. You may also want to jot notes in the margins, questioning the logic, expressing your uncertainty, or calling attention to other writers who see the matter differently.

✓   A Checklist for a Paraphrase

- ☐   Do I have a good reason for offering a paraphrase rather than a summary?

- ☐   Is the paraphrase entirely in my own words—a word-by-word "translation"— rather than a patchwork of the source's words and my own, with some of my own rearrangement of phrases and clauses?

- ☐   Do I not only cite the source but also explicitly say that the entire passage is a paraphrase?

Summaries are also useful for your readers, for the reasons noted on page 55. How long should your summaries be? They can be as short as a single sentence or as long as an entire paragraph. Here's a one-sentence summary of Martin Luther King Jr.'s famous essay "Letter from Birmingham Jail." King wrote this essay after his arrest for marching against racial segregation and injustice in Birmingham, Alabama.

> In his letter, King argues that the time is ripe for nonviolent protest throughout the segregated South, dismissing claims by local clergymen who opposed him, and arguing that unjust laws need to be challenged by black people who have been patient and silent for too long.

King's essay, however, is quite long. Obviously, our one-sentence summary cannot convey substantial portions of King's eloquent arguments, sacrificing almost all the nuance of his rationale, but it serves as an efficient summation and allows the writer to move on to his own analysis promptly.

A longer summary might try to capture more nuance, especially if, for the purposes of your essay, you need to capture more. How much you summarize depends largely on the *purpose* of your summary (see again our list of reasons to summarize on p. 55). Here is a longer summary of King's letter:

> In his letter, King argues that the time is ripe for nonviolent protest in the segregated South despite the criticism he and his fellow civil rights activists received from various authorities, especially the eight local clergymen who wrote a public statement against him. King addresses their criticism point by point, first claiming his essential right to be in Birmingham with his famous statement, "injustice anywhere is a threat to justice everywhere," and then saying that those who see the timing of his group's nonviolent direct action as inconvenient must recognize at least two things: one, that his "legitimate and unavoidable impatience" resulted from undelivered promises by authorities in the past; and two, that African Americans had long been told over and over again to wait for change with no change forthcoming. "This 'wait' has almost always meant 'never,'" King writes. For those who criticized his leadership, which encouraged people to break laws prohibiting their march, King says that breaking *unjust* laws may actually be construed as a *just* act. For those who called him an extremist, he revels in the definition ("was not Jesus an extremist in love?" he asks) and reminds them of the more extremist groups who call for violence in the face of blatant discrimination and brutality (and who will surely rise, King suggests, if no redress is forthcoming for the peaceful southern protestors he leads). Finally, King rails against "silence," saying that to hold one's tongue in the face of segregation is tantamount to supporting it—a blow to "white moderates" who believe in change but do nothing to help bring it about.

A Rule for Writers

Your essay is *likely to include brief summaries* of points of view with which you agree or disagree, but it will *rarely include a paraphrase* unless the original is obscure and you feel compelled to present a passage at length in words that are clearer than those of the original. If you do paraphrase, explicitly identify the material as a paraphrase. Never submit patchwriting.

This summary, obviously much longer than the first, raises numerous points from King's argument and preserves through quotation some of King's original tone and substance. It sacrifices much, of course, but seeks to provide a thorough account of a long and complex document containing many primary and secondary claims.

If your instructor asks for a summary of an essay, most often he or she won't want you to include your own thoughts about the content. Of course, you'll be using your own words, but try to "put yourself in the original author's shoes" and provide a summary that reflects the approach taken by the source. It should *not* contain ideas that the original piece doesn't express. If you use exact words and phrases drawn from the source, enclose them in quotation marks.

Summaries may be written for exercises in reading comprehension, but the point of summarizing when writing an essay is to assist your own argument. A faithful summary—one without your own ideas interjected—can be effective when using a source as an example or showing another writer's concordance with your argument. Consider the following paragraph written by a student who was arguing that if a person today purchases goods manufactured in sweatshops or under other inadequate labor conditions, then he or she is just as responsible for the abuses of labor as the companies who operate them. Notice how the student provides a summary (underlined) along the way and how it assists her argument.

> Americans today are so disconnected from the source and origins of the products they buy that it is entirely possible for them one day to march against global warming and the next to collect a dividend in their 401k from companies that are the worst offenders. It is possible to weep over a news report on child labor in China and then post an emotional plea for justice on Facebook using a mobile device made by Chinese child laborers. In 1849, Henry David Thoreau wrote in "Resistance to Civil Government" how ironic it was to see his fellow citizens in Boston opposed to slavery in the South, yet who read the daily news and commodity prices and "fall asleep over them both," not recognizing their own investments in, or patronage of, the very thing that offends their consciences. To Thoreau, such "gross inconsistency" makes even well-intentioned people "agents of injustice." Similarly, today we do not see the connections between our consumer habits and the various kinds of oppression that underlie our purchases—forms of oppression we would never support directly and outright.

The embedded short summary addresses only one point of Thoreau's original essay, but it shows how summaries may serve in an integrative way—as analogy, example, or illustration—to support an argument even without adding the writer's own commentary or analysis.

Critical Summary

When writing a longer summary that you intend to integrate into your argument, you may interject your own ideas; the appropriate term for this is **critical summary**. It signifies that you're offering more than a thorough and accurate account of an original source, because you're adding your evaluation of it as well. Think of this as weaving together your neutral summary with your own argument so that the summary meshes seamlessly with your overall writing goal. Along the way, during the summary, you may appraise the original author's ideas, commenting on them as you go—even while being faithful to the original.

How can you faithfully account for an author's argument while commenting on its merits or shortcomings? One way is to offer examples from the original. In addition, you might assess the quality of those examples or present others that the author didn't consider. Remember, being critical doesn't necessarily mean refuting the author. Your summary can refute, support, or be more balanced, simply recognizing where the original author succeeds and fails.

A Strategy for Writing a Critical Summary

Follow these five steps when writing a critical summary:

1. **Introduce** the summary. You don't have to provide all these elements, but consider offering the *author's name* and *expertise*, the *title* of the source, the *place* of publication, the *year* of publication, or any other relevant information. You may also start to explain the author's main point that you are summarizing:

    Pioneering feminist Betty Friedan, in her landmark book *The Feminine Mystique* (1963), argued that...

    In an essay on the state of higher education today, University of Illinois English professor Cary Nelson complains about...

2. **Explain** the major point the source makes. Here you have a chance to tell your readers what the original author is saying, so be faithful to the original but also highlight the point you're summarizing:

    Pioneering feminist Betty Friedan, in her landmark book *The Feminine Mystique* (1963), argued that women of the early 1960s were falling victim to a media-created image of ideal femininity that pressured them to prioritize homemaking, beauty, and maternity above almost all other concerns.

Here you can control the readers' understanding through simple adjectives such as *pioneering* and *landmark*. (Compare how "*stalwart* feminist Betty Friedan, in her *provocative* book" might dispose the reader to interpret your material differently.)

> In a *blunt critique* of the state of higher education today, University of Illinois professor Cary Nelson complains that universities are underpaying and overworking part-time, adjunct teachers.

3. **Exemplify** by offering one or more representative examples or evidence on which the original author draws. Feel free to quote if needed, though it is not required in a summary.

> Friedan examines post–World War II trends that included <u>the lowering of the marriage age</u>, <u>the rise of the mass media</u>, and what she calls <u>"the problem that has no name"</u>—that of feminine un-fulfillment, or what we might today call "depression."

4. **Problematize** by placing your assessment, analysis, or question into the summary.

> While the word *depression* never comes up in Friedan's work, <u>one could assume</u> that terms like *malaise*, *suffering*, and *housewives' fatigue* <u>signal an emerging understanding of the relationship between stereotypical media representations of social identity and mental health</u>.

If you're working toward a balanced critique or rebuttal, here is a good place to insert your ideas or those of someone with a slightly different view.

> Nelson is right to say that schools should model themselves on the ideals being taught in classrooms, <u>but having a flexible workforce is perfectly logical for a large organization</u> (something probably also taught in many business classes).

5. **Extend** by tying the summary to your argument, helping transition out of the critical summary and back into your own analysis.

> Friedan's work should raise questions about how women are portrayed in the media today, and about what mental health consequences are attributable to the ubiquitous and consistent messages given to women about their bodies, occupations, and social roles.

> The biggest problem with using too many contingent faculty is with preserving the quality of undergraduate education and the basic principles of academic freedom. Paying contingent faculty more money while increasing the number of tenure-track positions is not just a question of principles but a hallmark of the investment a university makes in its students.

It is possible to use this method—**Introduce**, **Explain**, **Exemplify**, **Problematize**, and **Extend**—in many ways, but essentially it is a way of providing a critical summary, any element of which can be enhanced or built upon as needed.

A Rule for Writers

Remember that when writing a summary you are putting yourself into the author's shoes.

Having insisted earlier that you should read the essays in this book slowly because the writers build one reason on another, we will now seem to contradict ourselves by presenting an essay that you can almost skim. Susan Jacoby's piece originally appeared in the *New York Times*, a thoroughly respectable newspaper but not one that requires readers to linger over every sentence. Still, compared with most news accounts, Jacoby's essay requires close reading. Notice that it zigs and zags, not because Jacoby is careless but because in building a strong case to support her point of view, she must consider some widely held views that she does *not* accept; she must set these forth and then give her reasons for rejecting them.

Susan Jacoby

Susan Jacoby (b. 1946), a journalist since the age of seventeen, is well known for her feminist writings. "A First Amendment Junkie" (our title) appeared in the Hers column in the *New York Times* in 1978.

A First Amendment Junkie

It is no news that many women are defecting from the ranks of civil libertarians on the issue of obscenity. The conviction of Larry Flynt, publisher of *Hustler* magazine—before his metamorphosis into a born-again Christian—was greeted with unabashed feminist approval. Harry Reems, the unknown actor who was convicted by a Memphis jury for conspiring to distribute the movie *Deep Throat*, has carried on his legal battles with almost no support from women who ordinarily regard themselves as supporters of the First Amendment. Feminist writers and scholars have even discussed the possibility of making common cause against pornography with adversaries of the women's movement—including opponents of the Equal Rights Amendment and "right-to-life" forces.

All of this is deeply disturbing to a woman writer who believes, as I always have and still do, in an absolute interpretation of the First Amendment. Nothing in Larry Flynt's garbage convinces me that the late Justice Hugo L. Black was wrong in his opinion that "the Federal Government is without any power whatsoever under the Constitution to put any type of burden on free speech and expression of ideas of any kind (as distinguished from conduct)." Many women I like and respect tell me I am wrong; I cannot remember having become involved in so many heated discussions of a public issue since the end of the Vietnam War. A feminist writer described my views as those of a "First Amendment junkie."

Many feminist arguments for controls on pornography carry the implicit conviction that porn books, magazines, and movies pose a greater threat to women than similarly repulsive exercises of free speech pose to other offended groups. This conviction has, of course, been shared by everyone—regardless of race, creed, or sex—who has ever argued in favor of abridging the First Amendment. It is the argument used by some Jews who have withdrawn their support from the American Civil Liberties Union because it has defended the right of American Nazis to march through a community inhabited by survivors of Hitler's concentration camps.

If feminists want to argue that the protection of the Constitution should not be extended to *any* particularly odious or threatening form of speech, they have a reasonable argument (although I don't agree with it). But it is ridiculous to suggest that the porn shops on 42nd Street are more disgusting to women than a march of neo-Nazis is to survivors of the extermination camps.

The arguments over pornography also blur the vital distinction between expression of ideas and conduct. When I say I believe unreservedly in the First Amendment, someone always comes back at me with the issue of "kiddie porn." But kiddie porn is not a First Amendment issue. It is an issue of the abuse of power—the power adults have over children—and not of obscenity. Parents and promoters have no more right to use their children to make porn movies than they do to send them to work in coal mines. The responsible adults should be prosecuted, just as adults who use children for back-breaking farm labor should be prosecuted.

5

Susan Brownmiller, in *Against Our Will: Men, Women, and Rape,* has described pornography as "the undiluted essence of antifemale propaganda." I think this is a fair description of some types of pornography, especially of the brutish subspecies that equates sex with death and portrays women primarily as objects of violence.

The equation of sex and violence, personified by some glossy rock record album covers as well as by *Hustler,* has fed the illusion that censorship of pornography can be conducted on a more rational basis than other types of censorship. Are all pictures of naked women obscene? Clearly not, says a friend. A Renoir nude is art, she says, and *Hustler* is trash. "Any reasonable person" knows that.

But what about something between art and trash—something, say, along the lines of *Playboy* or *Penthouse* magazines? I asked five women for their reactions to one picture in *Penthouse* and got responses that ranged from "lovely" and "sensuous" to "revolting" and "demeaning." Feminists, like everyone else, seldom have rational reasons for their preferences in erotica. Like members of juries, they tend to disagree when confronted with something that falls short of 100 percent vulgarity.

In any case, feminists will not be the arbiters of good taste if it becomes easier to harass, prosecute, and convict people on obscenity charges. Most of the people who want to censor girlie magazines are equally opposed to open discussion of issues that are of vital concern to women: rape, abortion, menstruation, contraception, lesbianism—in fact, the entire range of sexual experience from a woman's viewpoint.

Feminist writers and editors and filmmakers have limited financial resources: 10
Confronted by a determined prosecutor, Hugh Hefner[1] will fare better than Susan
Brownmiller. Would the Memphis jurors who convicted Harry Reems for his role
in *Deep Throat* be inclined to take a more positive view of paintings of the female
genitalia done by sensitive feminist artists? *Ms.* magazine has printed color repro-
ductions of some of those art works; *Ms.* is already banned from a number of high
school libraries because someone considers it threatening and/ or obscene.

Feminists who want to censor what they regard as harmful pornography have essentially the same motivation as other would-be censors: They want to use the power of
the state to accomplish what they have been unable to achieve in the marketplace
of ideas and images. The impulse to censor places no faith in the possibilities of
democratic persuasion.

It isn't easy to persuade certain men that they have better uses for $1.95 each month
than to spend it on a copy of *Hustler*. Well, then, give the men no choice in the
matter.

I believe there is also a connection between the impulse toward censorship on the
part of people who used to consider themselves civil libertarians and a more general
desire to shift responsibility from individuals to institutions. When I saw the movie
Looking for Mr. Goodbar, I was stunned by its series of visual images equating sex
and violence, coupled with what seems to me the mindless message (a distortion
of the fine Judith Rossner novel) that casual sex equals death. When I came out of
the movie, I was even more shocked to see parents standing in line with children
between the ages of ten and fourteen.

I simply don't know why a parent would take a child to see such a movie, any more
than I understand why people feel they can't turn off a television set their child is
watching. Whenever I say that, my friends tell me I don't know how it is because I
don't have children. True, but I do have parents. When I was a child, they did turn off
the TV. They didn't expect the Federal Communications Commission to do their job
for them.

I am a First Amendment junkie. You can't OD on the First Amendment, because free   15
speech is its own best antidote.

---

1 **Hugh Hefner** Founder and longtime publisher of *Playboy* magazine.

Summarizing Jacoby

Suppose we want to make a *rough summary*, more or less paragraph by paragraph, of Jacoby's essay. Our summary might look like this:

Paragraph 1. Although feminists usually support the First Amendment, when it comes to pornography many feminists take pretty much the position of those who oppose the Equal Rights Amendment and abortion and other causes of the women's movement.

Paragraph 2. Larry Flynt produces garbage, but I think his conviction represents an unconstitutional limitation of freedom of speech.

Paragraphs 3, 4. Feminists who want to control (censor) pornography argue that it poses a greater threat to women than similar repulsive speech poses to other groups. If feminists want to say that all offensive speech should be restricted, they can make a case, but it is absurd to say that pornography is a "greater threat" to women "than a march of neo-Nazis is to survivors of the extermination camps."

Paragraph 5. Trust in the First Amendment is not refuted by kiddie porn; kiddie porn is not a First Amendment issue but an issue of child abuse.

Paragraphs 6, 7, 8. Some feminists think censorship of pornography can be more "rational" than other kinds of censorship, but a picture of a nude woman strikes some women as base and others as "lovely." There is no unanimity.

Paragraphs 9, 10. If feminists censor girlie magazines, they will find that they are unwittingly helping opponents of the women's movement to censor discussions of rape, abortion, and so on. Some of the art in the feminist magazine *Ms.* would doubtless be censored.

Paragraphs 11, 12. Like other would-be censors, feminists want to use the power of the state to achieve what they have not achieved in "the marketplace of ideas." They display a lack of faith in "democratic persuasion."

Paragraphs 13, 14. This attempt at censorship reveals a "desire to shift responsibility from individuals to institutions." The responsibility—for instance, to keep young people from equating sex with violence—is properly the parents'.

Paragraph 15. We can't have too much of the First Amendment.

Jacoby's **thesis** (i.e., major claim or chief proposition)—that any form of censorship of pornography is wrong—is clear enough, even as early as the end of paragraph 1, but it gains force from the **reasons** she offers throughout the essay. If we want to reduce our summary further, we might say that she supports her thesis by arguing several subsidiary points. Here we'll merely assert them briefly, but Jacoby **argues** them—that is, she gives reasons:

- Pornography can scarcely be thought of as more offensive than Nazism.

- Women disagree about which pictures are pornographic.

- Feminists who want to censor pornography will find that they help antifeminists to censor discussions of issues advocated by the women's movement.

- Feminists who favor censorship are in effect turning to the government to achieve what they haven't achieved in the free marketplace.

- One sees this abdication of responsibility in the fact that parents allow their children to watch unsuitable movies and television programs.

If we want to present a *brief summary* in the form of one coherent paragraph—perhaps as part of an essay arguing for or against—we might write something like the one shown in the paragraph below. (Of course, we would **introduce** it with a lead-in along these lines: "Susan Jacoby, writing in the *New York Times*, offers a forceful argument against censorship of pornography. Jacoby's view, briefly, is....")

> When it comes to censorship of pornography, some feminists take a position shared by opponents of the feminist movement. They argue that pornography poses a greater threat to women than other forms of offensive speech offer to other groups, but this interpretation is simply a mistake. Pointing to kiddie porn is also a mistake, for kiddie porn is an issue involving not the First Amendment but child abuse. Feminists who support censorship of pornography will inadvertently aid those who wish to censor discussions of abortion and rape or censor art that is published in magazines such as *Ms.* The solution is not for individuals to turn to institutions (i.e., for the government to limit the First Amendment) but for individuals to accept the responsibility for teaching young people not to equate sex with violence.

In contrast, a *critical summary* of Jacoby—an evaluative summary in which we introduce our own ideas and examples—might look like this:

> Susan Jacoby, writing for the *New York Times* in 1978, offers a forceful argument against censorship of pornography, but one that does not have foresight of the Internet age and the new availability of extreme and exploitative forms of pornography. While she dismisses claims by feminists that pornography should be censored because it constitutes violence against women, what would Jacoby think of such things as "revenge porn" and "voyeuristic porn" today, or the array of elaborate sadistic fantasies readily available to anyone with access to a search engine? Jacoby says that censoring pornography is a step toward censoring art, and she proudly wears the tag "First Amendment junkie," ostensibly to protect what she finds artistic (such as images of female genitalia in *Ms.* Magazine). However, her argument does not help us account for these new forms of exploitation and violence disguised as art or "free speech." Perhaps she would see revenge porn and voyeur porn in the same the way she sees kiddie porn—not so much as an issue of free speech but as an issue of other crimes. Perhaps she would hold her position that we can avoid pornography by just

> "turning off the TV," but the new Internet pornography is intrusive, entering our lives and the lives of our children whether we like it or not. Education is part of the solution, Jacoby would agree, but we could also consider....

The example above not only summarizes and applies the other techniques presented in this chapter (e.g., accounting for context and questioning definitions of terms and concepts) but also weaves them together with a central argument that offers a new response and a practicable solution.

Discussion Questions: Topics for Critical Thinking and Writing

1. What does Susan Jacoby mean by saying she is a "First Amendment junkie" (para. 15)?

2. The essay is primarily an argument against the desire of some feminists to censor the sort of pornography that appealed to some heterosexual adult males in 1978. How does the context of the article's publication reflect events and perspectives of that period? How are conditions different now, and how do these new contexts offer ways to support or challenge Jacoby's argument?

3. Evaluate the final paragraph as a conclusion. (Effective final paragraphs are not all of one sort. Some round off the essay by echoing one or more points from the opening; others suggest that the reader, having now seen the problem, should think further about it or act on it. No matter what form it takes, a good final paragraph should make the reader feel that the essay has come to a satisfactory conclusion, not a sudden breaking-off of the argument.)

4. This essay originally appeared in the *New York Times*. If you're unfamiliar with this newspaper, consult an issue or two in your school library. Next, in a paragraph, try to characterize the paper's readers—that is, Jacoby's audience.

5. Jacoby claims in paragraph 2 that she "believes...in an absolute interpretation of the First Amendment." What does such an interpretation involve? Would it permit shouting "Fire!" in a crowded theater even when there is no fire? Posting racist insults on the Internet? Spreading untruths about someone's past? (*Does* the First Amendment, as actually interpreted by the Supreme Court today, permit any or all of these claims? Consult your reference librarian for help in answering this question.)

6. Jacoby implies that permitting prosecution of persons on obscenity charges will lead eventually to censorship of "open discussion" of important issues such as "rape, abortion, menstruation, contraception, lesbianism" (para. 9). Do you find her fears convincing? Does she give evidence to support her claim? Explain your responses.

✓ A Checklist for Getting Started

- ☐ Have I adequately previewed the work?
- ☐ Can I state the thesis?
- ☐ If I have written a summary, is it accurate?
- ☐ Does my summary mention all the chief points?
- ☐ If there are inconsistencies, are they in the summary or the original selection?
- ☐ Will my summary be clear and helpful?
- ☐ Have I considered the audience for whom the author is writing?

Essays for Analysis

Zachary Shemtob and David Lat

Zachary Shemtob teaches criminal justice at Central Connecticut State University; David Lat is a former federal prosecutor. Their essay originally appeared in the *New York Times* in 2011.

Executions Should Be Televised

Earlier this month, Georgia conducted its third execution this year. This would have passed relatively unnoticed if not for a controversy surrounding its videotaping. Lawyers for the condemned inmate, Andrew Grant DeYoung, had persuaded a judge to allow the recording of his last moments as part of an effort to obtain evidence on whether lethal injection caused unnecessary suffering.

Though he argued for videotaping, one of Mr. DeYoung's defense lawyers, Brian Kammer, spoke out against releasing the footage to the public. "It's a horrible thing that Andrew DeYoung had to go through," Mr. Kammer said, "and it's not for the public to see that."

We respectfully disagree. Executions in the United States ought to be made public.

Right now, executions are generally open only to the press and a few select witnesses. For the rest of us, the vague contours are provided in the morning paper. Yet a functioning democracy demands maximum accountability and transparency. As long as executions remain behind closed doors, those are impossible. The people should have the right to see what is being done in their name and with their tax dollars.

This is particularly relevant given the current debate on whether specific methods of   5
lethal injection constitute cruel and unusual punishment and therefore violate the
Constitution.

There is a dramatic difference between reading or hearing of such an event and
observing it through image and sound. (This is obvious to those who saw the footage of Saddam Hussein's hanging in 2006 or the death of Neda Agha-Soltan during
the protests in Iran in 2009.) We are not calling for opening executions completely to
the public—conducting them before a live crowd—but rather for broadcasting them
live or recording them for future release, on the Web or TV.

When another Georgia inmate, Roy Blankenship, was executed in June, the prisoner
jerked his head, grimaced, gasped, and lurched, according to a medical expert's
affidavit. The *Atlanta Journal-Constitution* reported that Mr. DeYoung, executed in
the same manner, "showed no violent signs in death." Voters should not have to rely
on media accounts to understand what takes place when a man is put to death.

Cameras record legislative sessions and presidential debates, and courtrooms are
allowing greater television access. When he was an Illinois state senator, President
Obama successfully pressed for the videotaping of homicide interrogations and
confessions. The most serious penalty of all surely demands equal if not greater
scrutiny.

Opponents of our proposal offer many objections. State lawyers argued that making
Mr. DeYoung's execution public raised safety concerns. While rioting and pickpock-
eting occasionally marred executions in the public square in the eighteenth and
nineteenth centuries, modern security and technology obviate this concern. Little
would change in the death chamber; the faces of witnesses and executioners could
be edited out, for privacy reasons, before a video was released.

Of greater concern is the possibility that broadcasting executions could have a   10
numbing effect. Douglas A. Berman, a law professor, fears that people might come
to equate human executions with putting pets to sleep. Yet this seems overstated.
While public indifference might result over time, the initial broadcasts would
undoubtedly get attention and stir debate.

Still others say that broadcasting an execution would offer an unbalanced picture—
making the condemned seem helpless and sympathetic, while keeping the victims
of the crime out of the picture. But this is beside the point: the defendant is being
executed precisely because a jury found that his crimes were so heinous that he
deserved to die.

Ultimately the main opposition to our idea seems to flow from an unthinking
disgust—a sense that public executions are archaic, noxious, even barbarous. Albert
Camus related in his essay "Reflections on the Guillotine" that viewing executions
turned him against capital punishment. The legal scholar John D. Bessler suggests
that public executions might have the same effect on the public today; Sister Helen
Prejean, the death penalty abolitionist, has urged just such a strategy.

That is not our view. We leave open the possibility that making executions public could strengthen support for them; undecided viewers might find them less disturbing than anticipated.

Like many of our fellow citizens, we are deeply conflicted about the death penalty and how it has been administered. Our focus is on accountability and openness. As Justice John Paul Stevens wrote in *Baze v. Rees*, a 2008 case involving a challenge to lethal injection, capital punishment is too often "the product of habit and inattention rather than an acceptable deliberative process that weighs the costs and risks of administering that penalty against its identifiable benefits."

A democracy demands a citizenry as informed as possible about the costs and benefits of society's ultimate punishment.   15

Discussion Questions: Topics for Critical Thinking and Writing

1. In paragraphs 9–13, the authors discuss objections to their position. Are you satisfied with their responses to the objections, or do you think they do not satisfactorily dispose of one or more of the objections? Explain.

2. In paragraph 4, the authors say that "[t]he people should have the right to see what is being done in their name and with their tax dollars." But in terms of *rights*, should the person being executed have a right to die in privacy? Articulate a position that weighs the public's right to see what is being done with its tax dollars against death row prisoners' rights to privacy.

3. In the concluding paragraph, the authors imply that their proposal, if enacted, will help to inform citizens "about the costs and benefits of society's ultimate punishment." Do you agree? Why, or why not? What reasons do the authors offer to support their proposal?

4. In your view, what is the strongest argument the authors give on behalf of their proposal? What is the weakest? Explain why you made these choices.

Gwen Wilde—Student Essay

This essay was written for a composition course at Tufts University.

Why the Pledge of Allegiance Should Be Revised

All Americans are familiar with the Pledge of Allegiance, even if they cannot always recite it perfectly, but probably relatively few know that the *original* Pledge did *not* include the words "under God." The original Pledge of Allegiance, published in the September 8, 1892, issue of the *Youth's Companion*, ran thus:

> I pledge allegiance to my flag, and to the Republic for which it stands: one Nation indivisible, with Liberty and justice for all. (Djupe 329)

In 1923, at the first National Flag Conference in Washington, D.C., it was argued that immigrants might be confused by the words "my Flag," and it was proposed that the words be changed to "the Flag of the United States." The following year it was changed again, to "the Flag of the United States of America," and this wording became the official—or, rather, unofficial—wording, unofficial because no wording had ever been nationally adopted (Djupe 329).

In 1942, the United States Congress included the Pledge in the United States Flag Code (4 USC 4, 2006), thus for the first time officially sanctioning the Pledge. In 1954, President Dwight D. Eisenhower approved adding the words "under God." Thus, since 1954 the Pledge reads:

> I pledge allegiance to the flag of the United States of America, and to the Republic for which it stands: one nation under God, indivisible, with Liberty and Justice for all. (Djupe 329)

In my view, the addition of the words "under God" is inappropriate, and they are needlessly divisive—an odd addition indeed to a nation that is said to be "indivisible."

Very simply put, the Pledge in its latest form requires all Americans to say something that some Americans do not believe. I say "requires" because although the courts have ruled that students may not be compelled to recite the Pledge, in effect peer pressure does compel all but the bravest to join in the recitation. When President Eisenhower authorized the change, he said, "In this way we are reaffirming the transcendence of religious faith in America's heritage and future; in this way we shall constantly strengthen those spiritual weapons which forever will be our country's most powerful resource in peace and war" (Sterner).

Exactly what did Eisenhower mean when he spoke of "the transcendence of religious faith in America's heritage" and when he spoke of "spiritual weapons"? I am not sure what "the transcendence of religious faith in America's heritage" means. Of course, many Americans have been and are deeply religious—no one doubts it—but the phrase certainly goes far beyond saying that many Americans have been devout. In any case, many Americans have *not* been devout, and many Americans have *not* believed in "spiritual weapons," but they have nevertheless been patriotic Americans. Some of them have fought and died to keep America free.

In short, the words "under God" cannot be uttered in good faith by many Americans. True, something like 70 or even 80% of Americans say they are affiliated with some form of Christianity, and approximately another 3% say they are Jewish. I don't have the figures for persons of other faiths, but in any case we can surely all agree that although a majority of Americans say they have a religious affiliation, nevertheless several million Americans do *not* believe in God.

5

If one remains silent while others are reciting the Pledge, or even if one remains silent only while others are speaking the words "under God," one is open to the charge that one is unpatriotic, is "unwilling to recite the Pledge of Allegiance." In the Pledge, patriotism is connected with religious belief, and it is this connection that makes it divisive and (to be blunt) un-American. Admittedly, the belief is not very specific: one is not required to say that one believes in the divinity of Jesus, or in the power of Jehovah, but the fact remains, one is required to express belief in a divine power, and if one doesn't express this belief one is—according to the Pledge—somehow not fully an American, maybe even un-American.

Please notice that I am not arguing that the Pledge is unconstitutional. I understand that the First Amendment to the Constitution says that "Congress shall make no law respecting an establishment of religion, or prohibiting the free exercise thereof." I am not arguing that the words "under God" in the Pledge add up to the "establishment of religion," but they certainly do assert a religious doctrine. Like the words "In God we trust," found on all American money, the words "under God" express an idea that many Americans do not hold, and there is no reason why these Americans—loyal people who may be called upon to defend the country with their lives—should be required to say that America is a nation "under God."

It has been argued, even by members of the Supreme Court, that the words "under God" are not to be taken terribly seriously, not to be taken to say what they seem to say. For instance, Chief Justice Rehnquist wrote:

> To give the parent of such a child a sort of "heckler's veto" over a patriotic ceremony willingly participated in by other students, simply because the Pledge of Allegiance contains the descriptive phrase "under God," is an unwarranted extension of the establishment clause, an extension which would have the unfortunate effect of prohibiting a commendable patriotic observance. (qtd. in Stephens et al. 104)

Chief Justice Rehnquist here calls "under God" a "descriptive phrase," but descriptive of *what*? If a phrase is a "descriptive phrase," it describes something, real or imagined. For many Americans, this phrase does *not* describe a reality. These Americans may perhaps be mistaken—if so, they may learn of their error at Judgment Day—but the fact is, millions of intelligent Americans do not believe in God.

Notice, too, that Chief Justice Rehnquist goes on to say that reciting the Pledge is "a commendable patriotic observance." Exactly. That is my point. It is a *patriotic* observance, and it should not be connected with religion. When we announce that we respect the flag—that we are loyal Americans—we should not also have to announce that we hold a particular religious belief, in this case a belief in monotheism, a belief that there is a God and that God rules.

10

One other argument defending the words "under God" is often heard: The words "In God We Trust" appear on our money. It is claimed that these words on American money are analogous to the words "under God" in the Pledge. But the situation really is very different. When we hand some coins over, or some paper money, we are concentrating on the business transaction, and we are not making any affirmation about God or our country. But when we recite the Pledge—even if we remain silent at the point when we are supposed to say "under God"—we are very conscious that we are supposed to make this affirmation, an affirmation that many Americans cannot in good faith make, even though they certainly can unthinkingly hand over (or accept) money with the words "In God We Trust."

Because I believe that *reciting* the Pledge is to be taken seriously, with a full awareness of the words that is quite different from when we hand over some money, I cannot understand the recent comment of Supreme Court Justice Souter, who in a case said that the phrase "under God" is "so tepid, so diluted, so far from compulsory prayer, that it should, in effect, be beneath the constitutional radar" (qtd. in "Guide"). I don't follow his reasoning that the phrase should be "beneath the constitutional radar," but in any case I am willing to put aside the issue of constitutionality. I am willing to grant that this phrase does not in any significant sense signify the "establishment of religion" (prohibited by the First Amendment) in the United States. I insist, nevertheless, that the phrase is neither "tepid" nor "diluted." It means what it says—it *must* and *should* mean what it says, to everyone who utters it—and, since millions of loyal Americans cannot say it, it should not be included in a statement in which Americans affirm their loyalty to our great country.

Spencer Platt/Getty Images

In short, the Pledge, which ought to unite all of us, is divisive; it includes a phrase that many patriotic Americans cannot bring themselves to utter. Yes, they can remain silent when others recite these two words, but, again, why should they have to remain silent? The Pledge of Allegiance should be something that *everyone* can say, say out loud, and say with pride. We hear much talk of returning to the ideas of the Founding Fathers. The Founding Fathers did not create the Pledge of Allegiance, but we do know that they never mentioned God in the Constitution. Indeed, the only reference to

15

religion, in the so-called establishment clause of the First Amendment, says, again, that "Congress shall make no law respecting an establishment of religion, or prohibiting the free exercise thereof." Those who wish to exercise religion are indeed free to do so, but the place to do so is not in a pledge that is required of all schoolchildren and of all new citizens.

Works Cited

Djupe, Paul A. "Pledge of Allegiance." *Encyclopedia of American Religion and Politics.* Edited by Paul A. Djupe and Laura R. Olson, Facts on File, 2003.

"Guide to Covering 'Under God' Pledge Decision." *ReligionLink*, 17 Sept. 2005, religion-link.com/database/guide-to-covering-under-god/.

Stephens, Otis H., et al., editors. *American Constitutional Law.* 6th ed., vol. 1, Cengage Learning, 2014.

Sterner, Doug. "The Pledge of Allegiance." *Home of Heroes*, homeofheroes.com/hallofheroes/1st_floor/flag/1bfc_pledge_print.html. Accessed 13 Apr. 2016.

Discussion Questions: Topics for Critical Thinking and Writing

1. Summarize the essay in a paragraph.

2. What terms and concepts are defined in this essay? Explain how one term or concept is defined.

3. Does the writer, Gwen Wilde, give enough weight to the fact that no one is compelled to recite the Pledge? Explain your answer.

4. What arguments does Wilde offer in support of her position?

5. Does Wilde show an adequate awareness of counterarguments? Identify one place where she raises and refutes a counterargument.

6. What is Wilde's strongest argument? Are any of her arguments notably weak? If so, how could they be strengthened?

7. What assumptions—tacit or explicit—does Wilde make? Do you agree or disagree with them? Explain your response.

8. What do you take the words "under God" to mean? Do they mean "under God's special protection"? Or "acting in accordance with God's rules"? Or "accountable to God"? Or something else? Explain.

9. Chief Justice Rehnquist wrote that the words "under God" are a "descriptive phrase." What do you think he meant by this?

10. What is the purpose of the Pledge of Allegiance? Does the phrase "under God" promote or defeat that purpose? Explain your answer.

11. What do you think about substituting "with religious freedom" for "under God"? Set forth your response, supported by reasons, in about 250 words.

12. Wilde makes a distinction between the reference to God on U.S. money and the reference to God in the Pledge. Do you agree with her that the two cases are not analogous? Explain.

13. What readers might *not* agree with Wilde's arguments? What values do they hold? How might you try to persuade an audience who disagrees with Wilde to consider her proposal?

14. Putting aside your own views on the issue, what grade would you give this essay as a work of argumentative writing? Support your evaluation with reasons.

Chapter 3 Critical Reading: Getting Deeper into Arguments

He that wrestles with us strengthens our nerves, and sharpens our skill. Our antagonist is our helper.

—Edmund Burke

Persuasion, Argument, Dispute

When we think seriously about an argument, not only do we encounter ideas that may be unfamiliar but also we are forced to examine our own cherished opinions—and perhaps for the first time really see the strengths and weaknesses of what we believe. As John Stuart Mill put it, "He who knows only his own side of the case knows little."

It is useful to distinguish between **persuasion** and **argument**. Persuasion has the broader meaning. To **persuade** is to convince someone else to accept or adopt your position, which can be accomplished in a number of ways, including

- by giving reasons (i.e., by argument, by logic),
- by appealing to the emotions, or
- by using torture.

Argument, we mean to say, represents only one form of persuasion, one that relies on the cognitive or intellectual capacity for reason. Rhetoricians often use the Greek word *logos*, which means "word" or "reason," to denote this aspect of persuasive writing. An appeal to reason may by conducted by using such things as

- physical evidence,
- the testimony of experts,
- common sense, and
- probability.

We can put it this way: The goal of *argument* is to convince by demonstrating the truth (or probable truth) of an assertion, whereas the goal of *persuasion* is simply to convince by one means or another. *Logos*, the root word of *logic*, means appealing to the intellect to make rational claims and reasoned judgments.

The appeal to the emotions is known as **pathos**. Strictly speaking, *pathos* is Greek for "feeling." It covers all sorts of emotional appeals—for instance, appeals that elicit pity or sympathy (derived from the Greek for "feeling with"), or one's sense of duty or patriotism.

Notice that an argument doesn't require two speakers or writers with opposing positions. In practice, of course, they may, but it is not a requirement that arguments advance claims in opposition to another position. **Dispute** is a special kind of argument in which two or more people express views that are at odds. But the Declaration of Independence is also an argument, setting forth the colonists' reasons for declaring their independence. An essay showing indecisiveness to be Hamlet's tragic flaw would present an argument. Even when writing only for oneself, trying to clarify one's thinking by setting forth reasons and justifications for an idea, the result is an argument.

Most of this book is about argument in the sense of presenting reasonable support of claims, but reason is not the whole story. If an argument is to be effective, it must be presented persuasively. For instance, the writer's **tone** (presentation of self, topic, and audience) must be appropriate if the discourse is to persuade the reader. The careful presentation of the self is not something disreputable, nor is it something that publicity agents or advertising agencies invented. Aristotle (384–322 B.C.E.) emphasized the importance of impressing on the audience that the speaker is a person of good sense and high moral character. (He called this aspect of persuasion **ethos**, the Greek word for "character," a basis of persuasion different from *logos*, which involves persuasion by appealing to reason, and *pathos*, which persuades by appealing to emotion.)

Writers convey their *ethos*, their good character or trustworthiness, by doing the following:

* using language appropriate to the setting, avoiding vulgar language, slang, and colloquialism;

* showing an awareness of the issue's complexity (e.g., by offering other points of view in goodwill and by recognizing that contrary points of view may have some merit); and

* showing attention to detail (e.g., by citing relevant statistics).

In short, writers who are concerned with *ethos*—and all writers should be—employ devices that persuade readers that the writers are reliable, fair-minded, intelligent persons in whom their readers can have confidence.

We talk at length about tone, along with other matters such as the organization of an argument, in Chapter 5, Writing an Analysis of an Argument, but here we deal with some of the chief devices used in reasoning, and we glance at emotional appeals.

Thinking Critically: Establishing Trustworthiness and Credibility

For each method listed, provide your own example of a sentence that helps to establish trustworthiness and credibility. (Pick a topic that interests you. If you need ideas, look at the topics addressed by the authors presented in this chapter.) Be sure to use a tone and language that are appropriate and respectful of your audience.

Method	Examples	Your Turn
Acknowledge weaknesses, exceptions, and complexities.	"Although the unemployment rate continues to decline, further investigation into underemployment and the loss of jobless benefits is necessary in order to truly understand the unemployment crisis in the United States."	
Use personal experience when appropriate.	"As a student who works and attends school full-time, I can speak firsthand about the importance of increased availability of financial aid."	
Mention the qualifications of any sources as a way to boost your own credibility.	"Acording to Deborah Tannen, author and noted professor of linguistics at Georgetown University,..."	

We should note at once, however, that an argument presupposes a fixed **topic**. Suppose we're arguing about Thomas Jefferson's assertion, in the Declaration of Independence, that "all men are created equal." Jones subscribes to this statement, but Smith says it's nonsense and argues that some people are obviously brighter than others, or healthier, or better coordinated, and so on. Jones and Smith, if they intend to argue the point, will do well to examine what Jefferson actually wrote:

> We hold these truths to be self-evident, that all men are created equal: that they are endowed by their Creator with certain unalienable rights; and that among these are life, liberty, and the pursuit of happiness.

There is room for debate over what Jefferson really meant and whether he is right, but clearly he was talking about *equality of rights*. If Smith and Jones wish to argue about Jefferson's view of equality—that is, if they wish to offer their reasons for accepting, rejecting, or modifying it—they must first agree on what Jefferson said or probably meant to say. Jones and Smith may still hold different views; they may continue to disagree on whether Jefferson was right and proceed to offer arguments and counter-arguments to settle the point. But only if they can agree on *what* they disagree about will their dispute get somewhere.

Reason versus Rationalization

Reason may not be the only way of finding the truth, but it is a way on which we often rely. "The subway ran yesterday at 6:00 A.M. and the day before at 6:00 A.M. and the day before that, so I infer from this evidence that it will also run today at 6:00 A.M." (a form of reasoning known as **induction**). "Bus drivers require would-be passengers to present the exact change; I don't have the exact change; therefore, I infer I cannot ride on the bus" (**deduction**). (The terms *deduction* and *induction* are discussed in more detail on pp. 90 and 94.)

We also know that if we set our minds to a problem, we can often find reasons (not always necessarily sound ones) for almost anything we want to justify. Here's an entertaining example from Benjamin Franklin's *Autobiography:*

> I believe I have omitted mentioning that in my first voyage from Boston, being becalmed off Block Island, our people set about catching cod and hauled up a great many. Hitherto I had stuck to my resolution of not eating animal food, and on this occasion, I considered with my master Tryon the taking of every fish as a kind of unprovoked murder, since none of them had or ever could do us any injury that might justify the slaughter. All this seemed very reasonable. But I had formerly been a great lover of fish, and when this came hot out of the frying pan, it smelt admirably well. I balanced some time between principle and inclination, till I recollected that when the fish were opened I saw smaller fish taken out of their stomachs. Then thought I, if you eat one another, I don't see why we mayn't eat you. So I dined upon cod very heartily and continued to eat with other people, returning only now and then occasionally to a vegetable diet. So convenient a thing it is to be a *reasonable creature,* since it enables one to find or make a reason for everything one has a mind to do.

Franklin is being playful; he is *not* engaging in critical thinking. He tells us that he loved fish and that this fish "smelt admirably well," so we're prepared for him to find a reason (here one as weak as "Fish eat fish, therefore people may eat fish") to abandon his vegetarianism. (But think: Fish also eat their own young. May we therefore eat ours?)

Still, Franklin touches on a truth: If necessary, we can find reasons to justify whatever we want. That is, instead of reasoning, we may *rationalize* (devise a self-serving but dishonest reason), like the fox in Aesop's fables who, finding the grapes he desired were out of reach, consoled himself with the thought that they were probably sour.

Perhaps we can never be certain that we aren't rationalizing, except when being playful like Franklin. But we can seek to think critically about our own beliefs, scrutinizing our assumptions, looking for counterevidence, and wondering if it's reasonably possible to draw different conclusions.

Some Procedures in Argument

Definition

Definition, we mentioned in Chapter 1, is one of the classical topics, a "place" to which one goes with questions; in answering the questions, one finds ideas. When we define, we're answering the question "What is it?" In answering this question as precisely as we can, we will find, clarify, and develop ideas.

We have already glanced at an argument over the proposition that "all men are created equal," and we saw that the words needed clarification. *Equal* meant, in the context, not physically or mentally equal but something like "equal in rights," equal politically and legally. (And, of course, *men* meant "white men and women.") Words don't always mean exactly what they seem to mean: There's no lead in a lead pencil, and a standard 2-by-4 is currently $1\frac{5}{8}$ inches in thickness and $3\frac{3}{8}$ inches in width.

Definition by Synonym

Let's return for a moment to *pornography,* a word that is not easy to define. One way to define a word is to offer a **synonym**. Thus, pornography can be defined, at least roughly, as "obscenity" (something indecent). But definition by synonym is usually only a start because then we have to define the synonym; besides, very few words have exact synonyms. (In fact, *pornography* and *obscenity* are not exact synonyms.)

Definition by Example

A second way to define a word is to point to an example (this is often called **ostensive definition**, from the Latin *ostendere,* "to show"). This method can be very helpful, ensuring that both writer and reader are talking about the same thing, but it also has limitations. A few decades ago, many people pointed to James Joyce's *Ulysses* and D. H. Lawrence's *Lady Chatterley's Lover* as examples of obscene novels, but today these books are regarded as literary masterpieces. It's possible that they can be obscene and also be literary masterpieces. (Joyce's wife is reported to have said of her husband, "He may have been a great writer, but...he had a very dirty mind.")

"It all depends on how you define 'chop.'"

Tom Cheney, The New Yorker Collection/The Cartoon Bank

One of the difficulties of using an example, however, is that the example is richer and more complex than the term it's being used to define, and this richness and complexity get in the way of achieving a clear definition. Thus, if one cites *Lady Chatterley's Lover* as an example of pornography, a reader may erroneously think that pornography has something to do with British novels (because Lawrence was British) or with heterosexual relationships outside of marriage. Yet neither of these ideas relates to the concept of pornography.

We are not trying here to formulate a satisfactory definition of *pornography.* Our object is to make the following points clear:

- An argument will be most fruitful if the participants first agree on what they are talking about.
- One way to secure such agreement is to define the topic ostensively.
- Choosing the right example, one that has all the central or typical characteristics, can make a topic not only clear but also vivid.

Definition by Stipulation

Arguments frequently involve matters of definition. In a discussion of gun control, for instance, you probably will hear one side speak of *assault weapons* and the other side speak instead of *so-called assault weapons.* In arguing, you can hope to get agreement—at least on what the topic of argument is—by offering a **stipulative definition** (from a Latin verb meaning "to bargain"). For instance, you and a representative of the other side can agree on a definition of *assault weapon* based on the meaning of the term in the ban approved by Congress in 1994, which expired in 2004, and which President Obama in 2013 asked Congress to renew. Although the renewal of the ban was unsuccessful, the definition was this: a semiautomatic firearm (the spent cartridge case is automatically extracted, and a new round is automatically reloaded into the chamber but isn't fired until the trigger is pulled again) with a detachable magazine *and at least two of the following five characteristics*:

- collapsible or folding stock
- pistol grip (thus allowing the weapon to be fired from the hip)
- bayonet mount
- grenade launcher
- flash suppressor (to keep the shooter from being blinded by muzzle flashes)

Again, this was the agreed-upon definition for the purposes of the legislation. Congress put *fully* automatic weapons into an entirely different category, and the legislatures of California and of New York each agreed on a stipulation different from that of Congress: In these two states, an assault weapon is defined as a semiautomatic firearm with a detachable magazine and with any *one* (not two) of the five bulleted items. The point is that for an argument to proceed rationally, and especially in the legal context, the key terms need to be precisely defined and agreed upon by all parties.

Let's now look at stipulative definitions in other contexts. Who is a *Native American*? In discussing this issue, you might stipulate that *Native American* means any person with any Native American blood; or you might say, "For the purpose of the present discussion, I mean that a *Native American* is any person who has at least one grandparent of pure Native American blood." A stipulative definition is appropriate in the following cases:

- when no fixed or standard definition is available, and
- when an arbitrary specification is necessary to fix the meaning of a key term in the argument.

Not everyone may accept your stipulative definition, and there will likely be defensible alternatives. In any case, when you stipulate a definition, your audience knows what *you* mean by the term.

It would *not* be reasonable to stipulate that by *Native American* you mean anyone with a deep interest in North American aborigines. That's too idiosyncratic to be useful. Similarly, an essay on Jews in America will have to rely on a definition of the key idea. Perhaps the writer will stipulate the definition used in Israel: A Jew is a person who has a Jewish mother or, if not born of a Jewish mother, a person who has formally adopted the Jewish faith. Perhaps the writer will stipulate another meaning: Jews are people who consider themselves to be Jews. Some sort of reasonable definition must be offered.

To stipulate, however, that *Jews* means "persons who believe that the area formerly called Palestine rightfully belongs to the Jews" would hopelessly confuse matters. Remember the old riddle: If you call a dog's tail a leg, how many legs does a dog have? The answer is four. Calling a tail a leg doesn't make it a leg.

In an essay titled "When 'Identity Politics' Is Rational," the author, Stanley Fish, begins by stipulating a definition. His first paragraph begins thus:

> If there's anything everyone is against in these election times, it's "identity politics," a phrase that covers a multitude of sins. Let me start with a definition. (It may not be yours, but it will at least allow the discussion to be framed.) You're practicing identity politics when you vote for or against someone because of his or her skin color, ethnicity, religion, gender, sexual orientation, or any other marker that leads you to say yes or no independently of a candidates' ideas or policies.

Fish argues in later paragraphs that sometimes identity politics makes very good sense, that it is *not* irrational, is *not* logically indefensible; but here we simply want to make two points—one about how a definition helps the writer, and one about how it helps the reader:

- A definition is a good way to get started when drafting an essay, a useful stimulus (idea prompt, pattern, template, heuristic) that will help *you* to think about the issue, a device that will stimulate your further thinking.

- A definition lets readers be certain that they understand what the author means by a crucial word.

Readers may disagree with Fish, but at least they know what he means when he speaks of identity politics.

A stipulation may be helpful and legitimate. Here's the opening paragraph of a 1975 essay by Richard B. Brandt titled "The Morality and Rationality of Suicide." Notice that the author does two things:

- He first stipulates a definition.
- Then, aware that the definition may strike some readers as too broad and therefore unreasonable or odd, he offers a reason on behalf of his definition.

> "Suicide" is conveniently defined, for our purposes, as doing something which results in one's death, either from the intention of ending one's life or the intention to bring about some other state of affairs (such as relief from pain) which one thinks it certain or highly probable can be achieved only by means of death or will produce death. It may seem odd to classify an act of heroic self-sacrifice on the part of a soldier as suicide. It is simpler, however, not to try to define "suicide" so that an act of suicide is always irrational or immoral in some way; if we adopt a neutral definition like the above we can still proceed to ask when an act of suicide in that sense is rational, morally justifiable, and so on, so that all evaluations anyone might wish to make can still be made. (61)

Sometimes, a definition that at first seems extremely odd can be made acceptable by offering strong reasons in its support. Sometimes, in fact, an odd definition marks a great intellectual step forward. For instance, in 1990 the U.S. Supreme Court recognized that *speech* includes symbolic nonverbal expression such as protesting against a war by wearing armbands or by flying the American flag upside down. Such actions, because they express ideas or emotions, are now protected by the First Amendment. Few people today would disagree that *speech* should include symbolic gestures.

A definition that seems notably eccentric to many readers and thus far has not gained much support is from Peter Singer's *Practical Ethics*, in which the author suggests that a nonhuman being can be a *person*. He admits that "it sounds odd to call an animal a person" but says that it seems so only because of our habit of sharply separating ourselves from other species. For Singer, *persons* are "rational and self-conscious beings, aware of themselves as distinct entities with a past and a future." Thus, although a newborn infant is a human being, it isn't a person; however, an adult chimpanzee isn't a human being but probably is a person. You don't have to agree with Singer to know exactly what he means and where he stands. Moreover, if you read his essay, you may even find that his reasons are plausible and that by means of his unusual definition he has broadened your thinking.

The Importance of Definitions

Trying to decide on the best way to define a key idea or a central concept is often difficult as well as controversial. *Death,* for example, has been redefined in recent years. Traditionally, a person was considered dead when there was no longer any heartbeat. But with advancing medical technology, the medical profession has persuaded legislatures to redefine death as cessation of cerebral and cortical functions—so-called brain death.

Some scholars have hoped to bring clarity into the abortion debate by redefining *life.* Traditionally, human life has been seen as beginning at birth or perhaps at viability (the capacity of a fetus to live independently of the uterine environment). However, others have proposed a *brain birth* definition in the hope of resolving the abortion controversy. Some thinkers want abortion to be prohibited by law at the point where "integrated brain functioning begins to emerge," allegedly about seventy days after conception. Whatever the merits of such a redefinition may be, the debate is convincing evidence of just how important the definition of certain terms can be.

Last Words about Definition

Since Plato's time in the fourth century B.C.E, it has often been argued that the best way to give a definition is to state the *essence* of the thing being defined. Thus, the classic example defines *man* as "a rational animal." (Today, to avoid sexist implications, instead of *man* we would say *human being* or *person.*) That is, the property of *rational animality* is considered to be the essence of every human creature, so it must be mentioned in the definition of *man.* This statement guarantees that the definition is neither too broad nor too narrow. But philosophers have long criticized this alleged ideal type of definition on several grounds, one of which is that no one can propose such definitions without assuming that the thing being defined has an essence in the first place—an assumption that is not necessary. Thus, we may want to define *causality,* or *explanation,* or even *definition* itself, but it's doubtful whether it is sound to assume that any of these concepts has an essence.

A much better way to provide a definition is to offer a set of **sufficient and necessary conditions**. Suppose we want to define the word *circle* and are conscious of the need to keep circles distinct from other geometric figures such as rectangles and spheres. We might express our definition by citing sufficient and necessary conditions as follows: "Anything is a circle *if and only if* it is a closed plane figure and all points on the circumference are equidistant from the center." Using the connective "if and only if" (called the *biconditional*) between the definition and the term being defined helps to make the definition neither too exclusive (too narrow) nor too inclusive (too broad). Of course, for most ordinary purposes we don't require such a formally precise definition. Nevertheless, perhaps the best criterion to keep in mind when assessing a proposed definition is whether it can be stated in the "if and only if" form, and whether, if so stated, it is true; that is, if it truly specifies *all and only* the things covered by the word being defined. The Thinking Critically exercise that follows provides examples.

We aren't saying that the four sentences in the table below are incontestable. In fact, they are definitely arguable. We offer them merely to show ways of defining, and the act of defining is one way of helping to get your own thoughts going. Notice, too, that the fourth example, a "statement of necessary and sufficient conditions" (indicated by *if and only if*), is a bit stiff for ordinary writing. An informal prompt along this line might begin, "Essentially, something can be called *pornography* if it presents...."

Thinking Critically: Giving Definitions

In the spaces provided, define one of the "new terms" provided according to the definition type stipulated.

Definition Type	Example	New Term	Your Definition
Synonym	"*Pornography*, simply stated, is obscenity."	Police brutality Helicopter parenting Alternative music Organic foods	
Example	"*Pornography* can be seen, for example, in D. H. Lawrence's *Lady Chatterley's Lover*, in the scene where…"	Police brutality Helicopter parenting Alternative music Organic foods	
Stipulation	"For the purposes of this essay, *pornography* means any type of media that…"	Police brutality Helicopter parenting Alternative music Organic foods	
Statement of necessary and sufficient conditions	"Something can be called *pornography* if and only if it presents sexually stimulating material without offering anything of redeeming social value."	Police brutality Helicopter parenting Alternative music Organic foods	

Assumptions

In Chapter 1, we discussed the **assumptions** made by the authors of two essays on religious freedoms. But we have more to say about assumptions. We've already said that in the form of discourse known as argument, certain statements are offered as reasons for other statements. But even the longest and most complex chain of reasoning or proof is fastened to assumptions—one or more *unexamined beliefs.* (Even if writer and reader share such a belief, it is no less an assumption.) Benjamin Franklin argued against paying salaries to the holders of executive offices in the federal government on the grounds that men are moved by ambition (love of power) and by avarice (love of money) and that powerful positions conferring wealth incite men to do their worst. These assumptions he stated, although he felt no need to argue them at length because he assumed that his readers shared them.

An assumption may be unstated. A writer, painstakingly arguing specific points, may choose to keep one or more of the argument's assumptions tacit. Or the writer may be completely unaware of an underlying assumption. For example, Franklin didn't even bother to state another assumption. He must have assumed that persons of wealth who accept an unpaying job (after all, only persons of wealth could afford to hold unpaid government jobs) will have at heart the interests of all classes of people, not only the interests of their own class. Probably Franklin didn't state this assumption because he thought it was perfectly obvious, but if you think critically about it, you may find reasons to doubt it. Surely one reason we pay our legislators is to ensure that the legislature does not consist only of people whose incomes may give them an inadequate view of the needs of others.

As another example, here are two assumptions in the argument for permitting abortion:

1. Ours is a pluralistic society, in which we believe that the religious beliefs of one group should not be imposed on others.

2. Personal privacy is a right, and a woman's body is hers, not to be violated by laws that forbid her from doing certain things to her body.

But these (and other) arguments *assume* that a fetus is not—or not yet—a person and therefore is not entitled to the same protection against assaults that we are. Virtually all of us assume that it is usually wrong to kill a human being. Granted, there may be instances in which we believe it's acceptable to take a human life, such as self-defense against a would-be murderer. But even here we find a shared assumption that persons are ordinarily entitled not to be killed.

The argument about abortion, then, usually depends on opposed assumptions. For one group, the fetus is a human being and a potential person—and this potentiality is decisive. For the other group, it is not. Persons arguing one side or the other of the abortion issue ought to be aware that opponents may not share their assumptions.

Premises and Syllogisms

Premises are stated assumptions that are used as reasons in an argument. (The word comes from a Latin word meaning "to send before" or "to set in front.") A premise thus is a statement set down—assumed—before the argument begins. The joining of two premises—two statements taken to be true—to produce a conclusion, a third statement, is a **syllogism** (from the Greek for "a reckoning together"). The classic example is this:

Major premise:	All human beings are mortal.
Minor premise:	Socrates is a human being.
Conclusion:	Socrates is mortal.

Deduction

The mental process of moving from one statement ("All human beings are mortal") through another ("Socrates is a human being") to yet a further statement ("Socrates is mortal") is **deduction**, from the Latin for "lead down from." In this sense, deductive reasoning doesn't give us any new knowledge, although it's easy to construct examples that have so many premises, or premises that are so complex, that the conclusion really does come as news to most who examine the argument. Thus, the great fictional detective Sherlock Holmes was credited by his admiring colleague, Dr. Watson, with having unusual powers of deduction. Watson meant in part that Holmes could see the logical consequences of apparently disconnected reasons, the number and complexity of which left others at a loss. What is common in all cases of deduction is that the reasons or premises offered are supposed to contain within themselves, so to speak, the conclusion extracted from them.

Robert Mankoff, The New Yorker Collection/The Cartoon Bank

Often a syllogism is abbreviated. Martin Luther King Jr., defending a protest march, wrote in "Letter from Birmingham Jail":

> You assert that our actions, even though peaceful, must be condemned because they precipitate violence.

Fully expressed, the argument that King attributes to his critics would be stated thus:

> Society must condemn actions (even if peaceful) that precipitate violence.
>
> This action (though peaceful) will precipitate violence.
>
> Therefore, society must condemn this action.

An incomplete or abbreviated syllogism in which one of the premises is left unstated, of the sort found in King's original quotation, is an **enthymeme** (from the Greek for "in the mind").

Here is another, more whimsical example of an enthymeme, in which both a premise and the conclusion are left implicit. Henry David Thoreau remarked that "circumstantial evidence can be very strong, as when you find a trout in the milk." The joke, perhaps intelligible only to people born before 1930 or so, depends on the fact that milk used to be sold "in bulk"—that is, ladled out of a big can directly to the customer by the farmer or grocer. This practice was prohibited in the 1930s because for centuries the sellers, seeking to increase their profit, were diluting the milk with water. Thoreau's enthymeme can be fully expressed thus:

> Trout live only in water.
>
> This milk has a trout in it.
>
> Therefore, this milk has water in it.

These enthymemes have three important properties: Their premises are *true*, the form of their argument is *valid*, and they leave *implicit* either the conclusion or one of the premises.

Sound Arguments

The purpose of a syllogism is to present reasons that establish its conclusion. This is done by making sure that the argument satisfies both of two independent criteria:

- First, all of the premises must be *true*.
- Second, the syllogism must be *valid*.

Once these criteria are satisfied, the conclusion of the syllogism is guaranteed. Any such argument is said to establish or to prove its conclusion—to use another term, it is said to be **sound**. Here's an example of a sound argument, a syllogism that proves its conclusion:

> Extracting oil from the Arctic Wildlife Refuge would adversely affect the local ecology.
>
> Adversely affecting the local ecology is undesirable, unless there is no better alternative fuel source.
>
> Therefore, extracting oil from the Arctic Wildlife Refuge is undesirable, unless there is no better alternative fuel source.

Each premise is **true**, and the syllogism is **valid**, so it establishes its conclusion.

But how do we tell in any given case that an argument is sound? We perform two different tests, one for the truth of each of the premises and another for the validity of the argument.

The basic test for the **truth** of a premise is to determine whether what it asserts corresponds with reality; if it does, then it is true, and if it doesn't, then it is false. Everything depends on the premise's content—what it asserts—and the evidence for it. (In the preceding syllogism, it's possible to test the truth of the premises by checking the views of experts and interested parties, such as policymakers, environmental groups, and experts on energy.)

The test for **validity** is quite different. We define a valid argument as one in which the conclusion follows from the premises, so that if all the premises are true, then the conclusion *must* be true, too. The general test for validity, then, is this: If one grants the premises, one must also grant the conclusion. In other words, if one grants the premises but denies the conclusion, is one caught in a self-contradiction? If so, the argument is valid; if not, the argument is invalid.

The preceding syllogism passes this test. If you grant the information given in the premises but deny the conclusion, you contradict yourself. Even if the information were in error, the conclusion in this syllogism would still follow from the premises—the hallmark of a valid argument! The conclusion follows because the validity of an argument is a purely formal matter concerning the *relation* between premises and conclusion based on what they mean.

It's possible to see this relationship more clearly by examining an argument that is valid but that, because one or both of the premises are false, does *not* establish its conclusion. Here's an example of such a syllogism:

> The whale is a large fish.
>
> All large fish have scales.
>
> Therefore, whales have scales.

We know that the premises and the conclusion are false: Whales are mammals, not fish, and not all large fish have scales (sharks have no scales, for instance). But in determining the argument's validity, the truth of the premises and the conclusion is beside the point. Just a little reflection assures us that *if* both premises were true, then the conclusion would have to be true as well. That is, anyone who grants the premises of this syllogism yet denies the conclusion contradicts herself. So the validity of an argument does not in any way depend on the truth of the premises or the conclusion.

A sound argument, as we said, is one that passes both the test of true premises and the test of valid inference. To put it another way, a sound argument does the following:

- It passes the test of content (the premises are true, as a matter of fact).
- It passes the test of form (its premises and conclusion, by virtue of their very meanings, are so related that it is impossible for the premises to be true and the conclusion false).

Accordingly, an unsound argument, one that fails to prove its conclusion, suffers from one or both of two defects:

- Not all the premises are true.
- The argument is invalid.

Usually, we have in mind one or both defects when objecting to someone's argument as "illogical." In evaluating a deductive argument, therefore, you must always ask: Is it vulnerable to criticism on the grounds that one (or more) of its premises is false? Or is the inference itself vulnerable because even if all the premises are true, the conclusion still wouldn't follow?

A deductive argument proves its conclusion if and only if *two conditions* are satisfied: (1) All the premises are true, and (2) it would be inconsistent to assert the premises and deny the conclusions.

A Word about False Premises

Suppose that one or more of a syllogism's premises are false but the syllogism itself is valid. What does that indicate about the truth of the conclusion? Consider this example:

> All Americans prefer vanilla ice cream to other flavors.
>
> Jimmy Fallon is an American.
>
> Therefore, Jimmy Fallon prefers vanilla ice cream to other flavors.

The first (or major) premise in this syllogism is false. Yet the argument passes our formal test for validity; if one grants both premises, then one must accept the conclusion. So we can say that the conclusion *follows from* its premises, even though the premises *do not prove* the conclusion. This is not as paradoxical as it may sound. For all we know, the argument's conclusion may in fact be true; Jimmy Fallon may indeed prefer vanilla ice cream, and the odds are that he does because consumption statistics show that a majority of Americans prefer vanilla. Nevertheless, if the conclusion in this syllogism is true, it's not because this argument proved it.

A Word about Invaid Syllogisms

Usually, one can detect a false premise in an argument, especially when the suspect premise appears in someone else's argument. A trickier business is the invalid syllogism. Consider this argument:

> All terrorists seek publicity for their violent acts.
>
> John Doe seeks publicity for his violent acts.
>
> Therefore, John Doe is a terrorist.

In this syllogism, let's grant that the first (major) premise is true. Let's also grant that the conclusion may well be true. Finally, the person mentioned in the second (minor) premise could indeed be a terrorist. But it's also possible that the conclusion is false; terrorists aren't the only ones who seek publicity for their violent acts—consider, for example, the violence committed against doctors, clinic workers, and patients at clinics where abortions are performed. In short, the truth of the two premises is no guarantee that the conclusion is also true. It's possible to assert both premises and deny the conclusion without being self-contradictory.

How do we tell, in general and in particular cases, whether a syllogism is valid? Chemists use litmus paper to determine instantly whether the liquid in a test tube is an acid or a base. Unfortunately, logic has no litmus test to tell us instantly whether an argument is valid or invalid. Logicians beginning with Aristotle have developed techniques to test any given argument, no matter how complex or subtle, to determine its validity. But the results of their labors cannot be expressed in a paragraph or even a few pages; this is why entire semester-long courses are devoted to teaching formal deductive logic. All we can do here is repeat two basic points.

First, the validity of deductive arguments is a matter of their *form* or *structure*. Even syllogisms like the one on the Arctic Wildlife Refuge on page 111 come in a large variety of forms (256 forms, to be precise), and only some of these forms are valid. Second, all valid deductive arguments (and only such arguments) pass this test: If one accepts all the premises, then one must accept the conclusion as well. Hence, if it's possible to accept the premises but reject the conclusion (without self-contradiction, of course), then the argument is invalid.

Let's exit from further discussion of this important but difficult subject on a lighter note. Many illogical arguments masquerade as logical. Consider this example: If it takes a horse and carriage four hours to go from Pinsk to Chelm, does it follow that a carriage with two horses will get there in two hours?

Induction

Whereas deduction takes beliefs and assumptions and extracts their hidden consequences, **induction** uses information about observed cases to reach a conclusion about unobserved cases. (The word comes from the Latin *in ducere*, "to lead into" or "to lead up to.") If we observe that the bite of a certain snake is poisonous, we may conclude on the basis of this evidence that the bite of another snake of the same general type is also poisonous. Our inference might be even broader: If we observe that snake after snake of a certain type has a poisonous bite and that these snakes are all rattlesnakes, then we're tempted to **generalize** that all rattlesnakes are poisonous.

By far the most common way to test the adequacy of a generalization is to consider one or more **counterexamples**. If the counterexamples are genuine and reliable, then the generalization must be false. For example, an essay by Ronald Takaki on the "myth" of Asian racial superiority is full of examples that contradict the alleged superiority of Asians; they are counterexamples to that thesis, and they help to expose it as a "myth." What is true of Takaki's reasoning is true generally in argumentative writing: We constantly test our generalizations by considering them against actual or possible counterexamples, or by doing research on the issue.

Unlike deduction, induction yields conclusions that go beyond the information contained in the premises used in their support. It's not surprising that the conclusions of inductive reasoning are not always true, even when all the premises are true. On page 82, we gave as an example our observation that on previous days a subway has run at 6:00 A.M. and that therefore we conclude that it runs at 6:00 A.M. every day. Suppose, following this reasoning, we arrive at the subway platform just before 6:00 A.M. on a given day and wait for an hour without seeing a single train. What inference should we draw to explain this? Possibly today is Sunday, and the subway doesn't run before 7:00 A.M. Or possibly there was a breakdown earlier this morning. Whatever the explanation might be, we relied on a sample that wasn't large enough (a larger sample might have included some early morning breakdowns) or representative enough (a more representative sample would have included the later starts on Sundays and holidays).

A Word about Samples

When we reason inductively, much depends on the size and the quality of the sample (we say "sample" because a writer probably cannot examine every instance). If, for example, we're offering an argument concerning the politics of members of sororities and fraternities, we probably cannot interview *every* member. Rather, we select a sample. But is the sample a fair one? Is it representative of the larger group? We may interview five members of Alpha Tau Omega and find that all five are Republicans, yet we cannot legitimately conclude that all members of ATO are Republicans. The problem doesn't always involve failing to interview an adequately large sample group. For example, a poll of ten thousand college students tells us very little about "college students" if all ten thousand are white males at the University of Texas. Because such a sample leaves out women and minority males, it isn't sufficiently *representative* of "college students" as a group. Further, though not all students at the University of Texas are from Texas or even from the Southwest, it's quite likely that the student body is not fully representative (e.g., in race and in income) of American college students. If this conjecture is correct, even a truly representative sample of University of Texas students wouldn't enable us to draw firm conclusions about American college students.

In short: An argument that uses samples ought to tell the reader how the samples were chosen. If it doesn't provide this information, the reader should treat the argument with suspicion.

Evidence: Experimentation, Examples, Authoritative Testimony, Statistics

Different disciplines use different kinds of evidence:

- In literary studies, the texts are usually the chief evidence.

- In the social sciences, field research (interviews, surveys) usually provides evidence.

- In the sciences, reports of experiments are the usual evidence; if an assertion cannot be tested—if one cannot show it to be false—it is a *belief,* an *opinion,* not a scientific hypothesis.

Experimentation

Induction is obviously useful in arguing. If, for example, one is arguing that handguns should be controlled, one will point to specific cases in which handguns caused accidents or were used to commit crimes. In arguing that abortion has a traumatic effect on women, one will point to women who testify to that effect. Each instance constitutes **evidence** for the relevant generalization.

In a courtroom, evidence bearing on the guilt of the accused is introduced by the prosecution, and evidence to the contrary is introduced by the defense. Not all evidence is admissible (e.g., hearsay is not, even if it's true), and the law of evidence is a highly developed subject in jurisprudence. In the forum of daily life, the sources of evidence are less disciplined. Daily experience, a particularly memorable observation, an unusual event—any or all of these may serve as evidence for (or against) some belief, theory, hypothesis, or explanation. Science involves the systematic study of what experience can yield, and one of the most distinctive features of the evidence that scientists can marshal on behalf of their claims is that it is the result of **experimentation.** Experiments are deliberately contrived situations, often complex in their technology, that are designed to yield particular observations. What the ordinary person does with unaided eye and ear, the scientist does, much more carefully and thoroughly, with the help of laboratory instruments.

The variety, extent, and reliability of the evidence obtained in daily life are quite different from those obtained in the laboratory. It's no surprise that society attaches much more weight to the "findings" of scientists than to the corroborative (much less the contrary) experiences of ordinary people. No one today would seriously argue that the sun really does go around the earth just because it looks that way; nor would we argue that because viruses are invisible to the naked eye they cannot cause symptoms such as swellings and fevers, which are plainly evident.

Examples

One form of evidence is the **example.** Suppose we argue that a candidate is untrustworthy and shouldn't be elected to public office. We point to episodes in his career—his misuse of funds in 2008 and the false charges he made against an opponent in 2016—as examples of his untrustworthiness. Or if we're arguing that President Truman ordered the atom bomb dropped to save American (and, for that matter, Japanese) lives that otherwise would have been lost in a hard-fought invasion of Japan, we point to the stubbornness of the Japanese defenders in battles on the islands of Saipan, Iwo Jima, and Okinawa, where Japanese soldiers fought to the death rather than surrender.

These examples, we say, indicate that the Japanese defenders of the main islands would have fought to their deaths without surrendering, even though they knew defeat was certain. Or if we argue that the war was nearly won when Truman dropped the bomb, we can cite secret peace feelers as examples of the Japanese willingness to end the war.

An *example* is a *sample*. These two words come from the same Old French word, *essample,* from the Latin *exemplum,* which means "something taken out"—that is, a selection from the group. A Yiddish proverb shrewdly says, "'For example' is no proof," but the evidence of well-chosen examples can go a long way toward helping a writer to convince an audience.

In arguments, three sorts of examples are especially common:

- real events
- invented instances (artificial or hypothetical cases)
- analogies

We will treat each of these briefly.

Real Events   In referring to Truman's decision to drop the atom bomb, we've already touched on examples drawn from real events—the battles at Saipan and elsewhere. And we've also seen Ben Franklin pointing to an allegedly real happening, a fish that had consumed a smaller fish. The advantage of an example drawn from real life, whether a great historical event or a local incident, is that its reality gives it weight. It cannot simply be brushed off.

Yet an example drawn from reality may not be as clear-cut as we would like. Suppose, for instance, that someone cites the Japanese army's behavior on Saipan and on Iwo Jima as evidence that the Japanese later would have fought to the death in an American invasion of Japan and would therefore have inflicted terrible losses on themselves and on the Americans. This example is open to the response that in June and July 1945 certain Japanese diplomats sent out secret peace feelers, so that in August 1945, when Truman authorized dropping the bomb, the situation was very different.

Similarly, in support of the argument that nations will no longer resort to using atomic weapons, some people have offered as evidence the fact that since World War I the great powers have not used poison gas. But the argument needs more support than this fact provides. Poison gas wasn't decisive or even highly effective in World War I. Moreover, the invention of gas masks made its use obsolete.

In short, any *real* event is so entangled in historical circumstances that it might not be adequate or relevant evidence in the case being argued. In using a real event as an example (a perfectly valid strategy), the writer must demonstrate that the event can be taken out of its historical context for use in the new context of argument. Thus, in an argument against using atomic weapons in warfare, the many deaths and horrible injuries inflicted on the Japanese at Hiroshima and Nagasaki can be cited as effects of nuclear weapons that would invariably occur and did not depend on any special circumstances of their use in Japan in 1945.

Invented Instances   **Artificial** or **hypothetical cases—invented instances**—have the great advantage of being protected from objections of the sort we have just given. Recall Thoreau's trout in the milk; that was a colorful hypothetical case that illustrated his point well. An invented instance ("Let's assume that a burglar promises not to shoot a householder if the householder swears not to identify him. Is the householder bound by the oath?") is something like a drawing of a flower in a botany textbook or a diagram of the folds of a mountain in a geology textbook. It is admittedly false, but by virtue of its simplifications it sets forth the relevant details very clearly. Thus, in a discussion of rights, the philosopher Charles Frankel says:

> Strictly speaking, when we assert a right for X, we assert that Y has a duty. Strictly speaking, that Y has such a duty presupposes that Y has the capacity to perform this duty. It would be nonsense to say, for example, that a non-swimmer has a moral duty to swim to the help of a drowning man.

This invented example is admirably clear, and it is immune to charges that might muddy the issue if Frankel, instead of referring to a wholly abstract person, Y, talked about some real person, Jones, who did not rescue a drowning man. For then Frankel would get bogged down over arguing about whether Jones *really* couldn't swim well enough to help, and so on.

Yet invented examples have drawbacks. First and foremost, they cannot serve as evidence. A purely hypothetical example can illustrate a point or provoke reconsideration of a generalization, but it cannot substitute for actual events as evidence supporting an inductive inference. Sometimes, such examples are so fanciful that they fail to convince the reader. Thus, the philosopher Judith Jarvis Thomson, in the course of an argument entitled "A Defense of Abortion," asks the reader to imagine waking up one day and finding that against her will a celebrated violinist whose body is not adequately functioning has been hooked up into her body for life support. Does she have the right to unplug the violinist? As you read the essays we present in this textbook, you'll have to decide for yourself whether the invented cases proposed by various authors are helpful or whether they are so remote that they hinder thought. Readers will have to decide, too, about when they can use invented cases to advance their own arguments.

But we add one point: Even a highly fanciful invented case can have the valuable effect of forcing us to see where we stand. A person may say that she is, in all circumstances, against vivisection—the practice of performing operations on live animals for the purpose of research. But what would she say if she thought that an experiment on one mouse would save the life of someone she loves? Conversely, if she approves of vivisection, would she also approve of sacrificing the last giant panda to save the life of a senile stranger, a person who in any case probably wouldn't live longer than another year? Artificial cases of this sort can help us to see that we didn't really mean to say such-and-such when we said so-and-so.

Analogies   The third sort of example, **analogy**, is a kind of comparison. An analogy asserts that things that are alike in some ways are alike in yet another way as well. Here's an example:

> Before the Roman Empire declined as a world power, it exhibited a decline in morals and in physical stamina; our society today shows a decline in both morals (consider the high divorce rate and the crime rate) and physical culture (consider obesity in children). America, like Rome, will decline as a world power.

Strictly speaking, an analogy is an extended comparison in which different things are shown to be similar in several ways. Thus, if one wants to argue that a head of state should have extraordinary power during wartime, one can argue that the state at such a time is like a ship in a storm: The crew is needed to lend its help, but the decisions are best left to the captain. (Notice that an analogy compares things that are relatively *un*like. Comparing the plight of one ship to another or of one government to another isn't an analogy; it's an inductive inference from one case of the same sort to another such case.)

Let's consider another analogy. We have already glanced at Judith Thomson's hypothetical case in which the reader wakes up to find herself hooked up to a violinist in need of life support. Thomson uses this situation as an anal-

"Do you mind if I use yet another sports analogy?"

Gahan Wilson, The New Yorker Collection/The Cartoon Bank

ogy in an argument about abortion. The reader stands for the mother; the violinist, for the unwanted fetus. You may want to think about whether this analogy is close enough to pregnancy to help illuminate your own thinking about abortion.

The problem with argument by analogy is this: Two admittedly different things are agreed to be similar in several ways, and the arguer goes on to assert or imply that they are also similar in another way—the point being argued. (That's why Thomson argues that if something is true of the reader-hooked-up-to-a-violinist, it is also true of the pregnant-mother-hooked-up-to-a-fetus.) But the two things that are said to be analogous and that are indeed similar in characteristics *A*, *B*, and *C* are also differ-ent—let's say in characteristics *D* and *E*. As Bishop Butler is said to have remarked in the early eighteenth century, "Everything is what it is, and not another thing."

Analogies can be convincing, especially because they can make complex issues seem simple. "Don't change horses in midstream" isn't a statement about riding horses across a river but, rather, about choosing new leaders in critical times. Still, in the end, analogies don't necessarily prove anything. What may be true about riding horses across a stream may not be true about choosing new leaders in troubled times. Riding horses across a stream and choosing new leaders are fundamentally different things, and however much they may be said to resemble each other, they remain different. What is true for one need not be true for the other.

Analogies can be helpful in developing our thoughts and in helping listeners or readers to understand a point we're trying to make. It is sometimes argued, for instance—on the analogy of the doctor–patient, the lawyer–client, or the priest–penitent relationship—that newspaper and television reporters should not be required to reveal their confidential sources. That is worth thinking about: Do the similarities run deep enough, or are there fundamental differences? Consider another example: Some writers who support abortion argue that the fetus is not a person any more than the acorn is an oak. That is also worth thinking about. But one should also think about this response: A fetus is not a person, just as an acorn is not an oak; but an acorn is a potential oak, and a fetus is a potential person, a potential adult human being. Children, even newborn infants, have rights, and one way to explain this claim is to call attention to their potentiality to become mature adults. Thus, some people argue that the fetus, by analogy, has the rights of an infant, for the fetus, like the infant, is a potential adult.

Three analogies for consideration: First, let's examine a brief comparison made by Jill Knight, a member of the British Parliament, speaking about abortion:

> Babies are not like bad teeth, to be jerked out because they cause suffering.

Her point is effectively put; it remains for the reader to decide whether fetuses are *babies* and if a fetus is not a baby, *why* it can or cannot be treated like a bad tooth.

Now a second bit of analogical reasoning, again about abortion: Thomas Sowell, an economist at the Hoover Institute, grants that women have a legal right to abortion, but he objects to a requirement that the government pay for abortions:

> Because the courts have ruled that women have a legal right to an abortion, some people have jumped to the conclusion that the government has to pay for it. You have a constitutional right to privacy, but the government has no obligation to pay for your window shades. (*Pink and Brown People*, 1981, p. 57)

We leave it to you to decide whether the analogy is compelling—that is, if the points of resemblance are sufficiently significant to allow you to conclude that what's true of people wanting window shades should be true of people wanting abortions.

And one more: A common argument on behalf of legalizing gay marriage drew an analogy between gay marriage and interracial marriage, a practice that was banned in sixteen states until 1967, when the Supreme Court declared miscegenation statutes unconstitutional. The gist of the analogy was this: Racism and discrimination against gay and lesbian people are the same. If marriage is a fundamental right—as the Supreme Court held in its 1967 decision striking down bans on miscegenation—then it is a fundamental right for gay and lesbian people as well as heterosexual people.

Authoritative Testimony

Another form of evidence is **testimony**, the citation or quotation of authorities. In daily life, we rely heavily on authorities of all sorts: We get a doctor's opinion about our health, we read a book because an intelligent friend recommends it, we see a movie because a critic gave it a good review, and we pay at least a little attention to the weather forecaster.

In setting forth an argument, one often tries to show that one's view is supported by notable figures—perhaps Jefferson, Lincoln, Martin Luther King Jr., or scientists who won the Nobel Prize. You may recall that in Chapter 2, in talking about medical marijuana legalization, we presented an essay by Sanjay Gupta. To make certain that you were impressed by his ideas, we described him as CNN's chief medical correspondent and a leading public health expert. In our Chapter 2 discussion of Sally Mann, we qualified our description of her controversial photographs by noting that *Time* magazine called her "America's Best Photographer" and the *New Republic* called her book "one of the great photograph books of our time." But heed some words of caution:

- Be sure that the authority, however notable, is *an authority on the topic in question.* (A well-known biologist might be an authority on vitamins but not on the justice of war.)

- Be sure that the authority is *unbiased.* (A chemist employed by the tobacco industry isn't likely to admit that smoking may be harmful, and a producer of violent video games isn't likely to admit that playing those games stimulates violence.)

- Beware of *nameless* authorities: "a thousand doctors," "leading educators," "researchers at a major medical school." (If possible, offer at least one specific name.)

- Be careful when using authorities who indeed were great authorities in their day but *who now may be out of date.* (Examples would include Adam Smith on economics, Julius Caesar on the art of war, Louis Pasteur on medicine.)

- Cite authorities *whose opinions your readers will value*. (William F. Buckley Jr.'s conservative/libertarian opinions mean a good deal to readers of the magazine that he founded, the *National Review*, but probably not to most liberal thinkers. Gloria Steinem's liberal/feminist opinions carry weight with readers of the magazines that she cofounded, *New York* and *Ms.* magazine, but probably not with most conservative thinkers.) When writing for the general reader—your usual audience—cite authorities whom the general reader is likely to accept.

One other point: *You* may be an authority. You probably aren't nationally known, but on some topics you might have the authority of personal experience. You may have been injured on a motorcycle while riding without wearing a helmet, or you may have escaped injury because you wore a helmet. You may have dropped out of school and then returned. You may have tutored a student whose native language isn't English, you may be such a student who has received tutoring, or you may have attended a school with a bilingual education program. In short, your personal testimony on topics relating to these issues may be invaluable, and a reader will probably consider it seriously.

Statistics

The last sort of evidence we discuss here is quantitative, or statistical. The maxim "More is better" captures a basic idea of quantitative evidence: Because we know that 90 percent is greater than 75 percent, we're usually ready to grant that any claim supported by experience in 90 percent of cases is more likely to be true than an alternative claim supported by experience in only 75 percent of cases. The greater the difference, the greater our confidence. Consider an example. Honors at graduation from college are often computed on the basis of a student's cumulative grade-point average (GPA). The undisputed assumption is that the nearer a student's GPA is to a perfect record (4.0), the better scholar he or she is and therefore the more deserving of highest honors. Consequently, a student with a GPA of 3.9 at the end of her senior year is a stronger candidate for graduating summa cum laude than another student with a GPA of 3.6. When faculty members on the honors committee argue over the relative academic merits of graduating seniors, we know that these quantitative, statistical differences in student GPAs will be the basic (if not the only) kind of evidence under discussion.

Graphs, Tables, Numbers   Statistical information can be presented in many forms, but it tends to fall into two main types: the graphic and the numerical. Graphs, tables, and pie charts are familiar ways of presenting quantitative data in an eye-catching manner. (See pp. 149–50.) To prepare the graphics, however, one first has to decide how best to organize and interpret the numbers, and for some purposes it may be more appropriate to directly present the numbers themselves.

But is it better to present the numbers in percentages or in fractions? Should a report say that the federal budget (1) underwent a twofold increase over the decade; (2) increased by 100 percent; (3) doubled; or (4) at the beginning of the decade was one-half what it was at the end? These are equivalent ways of saying the same thing. Making a choice among them, therefore, will likely rest on whether one's aim is to dramatize the increase (a 100 percent increase looks larger than a doubling) or to play down its size.

Thinking about Statistical Evidence   Statistics often get a bad name because it's so easy to misuse them (unintentionally or not) and so difficult to be sure that they were gathered correctly in the first place. (One old saying goes, "There are lies, damned lies, and statistics.") Every branch of social science and natural science needs statistical information, and countless decisions in public and private life are based on quantitative data in statistical form. It's important, therefore, to be sensitive to the sources and reliability of the statistics and to develop a healthy skepticism when you confront statistics whose parentage is not fully explained.

Consider statistics that pop up in conversations about wealth distribution in the United States. In 2014, the Census Bureau calculated that the median household income in the United States was $53,657, meaning that half of households earned less than this amount and half earned above it. However, the average— technically, the mean—household income in the same year was $72,641, about $19,000 (or 39 percent) higher. Which number more accurately represents the typical household income? Both are "correct," but both are calculated with different measures, median and mean. If a politician wanted to argue that the United States has a strong middle class, he might use the average (mean) income as evidence, a number calculated by dividing the total income of all households by the total number of households. If another politician wished to make a rebuttal, she could point out that the average income paints a rosy picture because the wealthiest households skew the average higher. The median income (representing the number above and below which two halves of all households fall) should be the measure we use, the rebutting politician could argue, because it helps reduce the effect of the limitless ceiling of higher incomes and the finite floor of lower incomes at zero.

Consider the following statistics: Suppose in a given city in 2014, 1 percent of the victims in fatal automobile accidents were bicyclists. In the same city in 2015, the percentage of bicyclists killed in automobile accidents was 2 percent. Was the increase 1 percent (not an alarming figure), or was it 100 percent (a staggering figure)? The answer is both, depending on whether we're comparing (1) bicycle deaths in automobile accidents *with all deaths in automobile accidents* (that's an increase of 1 percent), or (2) bicycle deaths in automobile accidents *only with other bicycle deaths in automobile accidents* (an increase of 100 percent). An honest statement would say that bicycle deaths due to automobile accidents doubled in 2015, increasing from 1 to 2 percent. But here's another point: Although every such death is lamentable, if there was one such death in 2014 and two in 2015, the increase from one death to two (an increase of 100 percent!) hardly suggests a growing problem that needs attention. No one would be surprised to learn that in the next year there were no deaths at all, or only one or two.

If it's sometimes difficult to interpret statistics, it's often at least equally difficult to establish accurate statistics. Consider this example:

> Advertisements are the most prevalent and toxic of the mental pollutants. From the moment your radio alarm sounds in the morning to the wee hours of late-night TV, microjolts of commercial pollution flood into your brain at the rate of about three thousand marketing messages per day. (Kalle Lasn, *Culture Jam* [1999], 18–19)

Lasn's book includes endnotes as documentation, so, being curious about the statistics, we turn to the appropriate page and find this information concerning the source of his data:

> "three thousand marketing messages per day." Mark Landler, Walecia Konrad, Zachary Schiller, and Lois Therrien, "What Happened to Advertising?" *Business Week,* September 23, 1991, page 66. Leslie Savan in *The Sponsored Life* (Temple University Press, 1994), page 1, estimated that "16,000 ads flicker across an individual's consciousness daily." I did an informal survey in March 1995 and found the number to be closer to 1,500 (this included all marketing messages, corporate images, logos, ads, brand names, on TV, radio, billboards, buildings, signs, clothing, appliances, in cyberspace, etc., over a typical twenty-four hour period in my life). (219)

Well, this endnote is odd. In the earlier passage, the author asserted that about "three thousand marketing messages per day" flood into a person's brain. In the documentation, he cites a source for that statistic from *Business Week*—though we haven't the faintest idea how the authors of the *Business Week* article came up with that figure. Oddly, he goes on to offer a very different figure (16,000 ads) and then, to our confusion, offers yet a third figure, 1,500, based on his own "informal survey."

Probably the one thing we can safely say about all three figures is that none of them means very much. Even if the compilers of the statistics explained exactly how they counted—let's say that among countless other criteria they assumed that the average person reads one magazine per day and that the average magazine contains 124 advertisements—it would be hard to take them seriously. After all, in leafing through a magazine, some people may read many ads and some may read none. Some people may read some ads carefully—but perhaps just to enjoy their absurdity. Our point: Although the author in his text said, without implying any uncertainty, that "about three thousand marketing messages per day" reach an individual, it's evident (by checking the endnote) that even he is confused about the figure he gives.

Unreliable Statistics   We'd like to make a final point about the unreliability of some statistical information—data that looks impressive but that is, in fact, insubstantial. For instance, Marilyn Jager Adams studied the number of hours that families read to their children in the five or so years before the children start attending school. In her book *Beginning to Read: Thinking and Learning about Print* (1994), she pointed out that in all those preschool years, poor families read to their children only 25 hours, whereas in the same period middle-income families read 1,000 to 1,700 hours. The figures were much quoted in newspapers and by children's advocacy groups. Adams could not, of course, interview every family in these two groups; she had to rely on samples. What were her samples? For poor families, she selected 24 children in 20 families, all in Southern California. Ask yourself: Can families from only one geographic area provide an adequate sample for a topic such as this? Moreover, let's think about Adams's sample of middle-class families. How many families constituted that sample? Exactly one—her own. We leave it to you to judge the validity of her findings.

✓ A Checklist for Evaluating Statistical Evidence

Regard statistical evidence (like all other evidence) cautiously, and don't accept it until you have thought about these questions:

☐ Was it compiled by a disinterested (impartial) source? The source's name doesn't always reveal its particular angle (e.g., People for the American Way), but sometimes it lets you know what to expect (e.g., National Rifle Association, American Civil Liberties Union).

☐ Is it based on an adequate sample?

☐ Is the statistical evidence recent enough to be relevant?

☐ How many of the factors likely to be relevant were identified and measured?

☐ Are the figures open to a different and equally plausible interpretation?

☐ If a percentage is cited, is it the average (or *mean*), or is it the median?

We are not suggesting that everyone who uses statistics is trying to deceive or is unconsciously being deceived by them. We suggest only that statistics are open to widely different interpretations and that often those columns of numbers, which appear to be so precise with their decimal points, may actually be imprecise and possibly worthless if they're based on insufficient or biased samples.

Inside Work: Quiz

What is wrong with the following statistical proof that children do not have time for school?

One-third of the time they are sleeping (about 122 days).

One-eighth of the time they are eating (three hours a day, totaling 45 days).

One-fourth of the time they are on summer and other vacations (91 days).

Two-sevenths of the year is weekends (104 days).

Total: 362 days—so how can a kid have time for school?

Nonrational Appeals

Satire, Irony, Sarcasm, Humor

In talking about definition, deduction, and evidence, we've been talking about means of rational persuasion. However, as mentioned earlier, there are also other means of persuasion. Force is an example. If X kicks Y, threatens to destroy Y's means of livelihood, or threatens Y's life, X may persuade Y to cooperate. But writers, of course, cannot use such kinds of force on their readers. Instead, one form of irrational but sometimes highly effective persuasion is satire—that is, witty ridicule. A cartoonist may persuade viewers that a politician's views are unsound by caricaturing (thus ridiculing) her appearance or by presenting a grotesquely distorted (funny, but unfair) picture of the issue she supports.

Satiric artists often use caricature; satiric writers, also seeking to persuade by means of ridicule, often use verbal irony. This sort of irony contrasts what is said and what is meant. For instance, words of praise may actually imply blame (when Shakespeare's Cassius says, "Brutus is an honorable man," he wants his hearers to think that Brutus is dishonorable), and words of modesty may actually imply superiority ("Of course, I'm too dumb to understand this problem"). Such language, when heavy-handed, is sarcasm ("You're a great guy," said to someone who won't lend the speaker ten dollars). If it's witty and clever, we call it irony rather than sarcasm.

Although ridicule isn't a form of argument (because it isn't a form of reasoning), passages of ridicule, especially verbal irony, sometimes appear in argument essays. These passages, like reasons or like appeals to the emotions, are efforts to persuade the reader to accept the writer's point of view. The key to using humor in an argument is, on the one hand, to avoid wisecracking like a smart aleck, and on the other hand, to avoid mere clownishness. Later in this chapter (p. 111), we print an essay by George F. Will that is (or seeks to be) humorous in places. You be the judge.

Emotional Appeals

It is sometimes said that good argumentative writing appeals only to reason, never to emotion, and that any emotional appeal is illegitimate and irrelevant. "Tears are not arguments," the Brazilian writer Machado de Assis said. Logic textbooks may even stigmatize with Latin labels the various sorts of emotional appeal—for instance, *argumentum ad populam* (appeal to the prejudices of the mob, as in "Come on, we all know that schools don't teach anything anymore") and *argumentum ad misericordiam* (appeal to pity, as in "No one ought to blame this poor kid for stabbing a classmate because his mother was often institutionalized for alcoholism and his father beat him").

True, appeals to emotion may distract from the facts of the case; they may blind the audience by, in effect, throwing dust in its eyes or by provoking tears.

Learning from Shakespeare

A classic example is in Shakespeare's *Julius Caesar,* when Marc Antony addresses the Roman populace after Brutus, Cassius, and others have assassinated Caesar. The real issue is whether Caesar was becoming tyrannical (as the assassins claim) and would have curtailed the freedom of the Roman people. Antony turns from the evidence and stirs the mob against the assassins by appealing to its emotions. In the ancient Roman biographical writing that Shakespeare drew on, Sir Thomas North's translation of Plutarch's *Lives of the Noble Grecians and Romans,* Plutarch says this about Antony:

> perceiving that his words moved the common people to compassion,...[he] framed his eloquence to make their hearts yearn [i.e., grieve] the more, and, taking Caesar's gown all bloody in his hand, he laid it open to the sight of them all, showing what a number of cuts and holes it had upon it. Therewithal the people fell presently into such a rage and mutiny that there was no more order kept.

Here are a few extracts from Antony's speeches in Shakespeare's play. Antony begins by asserting that he will speak only briefly:

> Friends, Romans, countrymen, lend me your ears;
> I come to bury Caesar, not to praise him.

After briefly offering insubstantial evidence that Caesar gave no signs of behaving tyrannically (e.g., "When that the poor have cried, Caesar hath wept"), Antony begins to play directly on his hearers' emotions. Descending from the platform so that he may be in closer contact with his audience (like a modern politician, he wants to work the crowd), he calls attention to Caesar's bloody toga:

> If you have tears, prepare to shed them now.
> You all do know this mantle; I remember
> The first time ever Caesar put it on:
> 'Twas on a summer's evening, in his tent,
> That day he overcame the Nervii.
> Look, in this place ran Cassius' dagger through;
> See what a rent the envious Casca made;
> Through this, the well-belovèd Brutus stabbed....

In these few lines, Antony accomplishes the following:

- He prepares the audience by suggesting to them how they should respond ("If you have tears, prepare to shed them now").

- He flatters them by implying that they, like Antony, were intimates of Caesar (he credits them with being familiar with Caesar's garment).

- He then evokes a personal memory of a specific time ("a summer's evening")— not just any specific time, but a very important one, the day that Caesar won a battle against the Nervii (a particularly fierce tribe in what is now France).

In fact, Antony was not at the battle, and he did not join Caesar until three years later.

Antony doesn't mind being free with the facts; his point here is not to set the record straight but to stir the mob against the assassins. He goes on, daringly but successfully, to identify one particular slit in the garment with Cassius's dagger, another with Casca's, and a third with Brutus's. Antony cannot know which dagger made which slit, but his rhetorical trick works.

Notice, too, that Antony arranges the three assassins in climactic order, since Brutus (Antony claims) was especially beloved by Caesar:

> Judge, O you gods, how dearly Caesar loved him!
> This was the most unkindest cut of all;
> For when the noble Caesar saw him stab,
> Ingratitude, more strong than traitor's arms,
> Quite vanquished him. Then burst his mighty heart....

Nice. According to Antony, the noble-minded Caesar—Antony's words have erased all thought of the tyrannical Caesar—died not from wounds inflicted by daggers but from the heartbreaking perception of Brutus's ingratitude. Doubtless there wasn't a dry eye in the house. Let's all hope that if we are ever put on trial, we'll have a lawyer as skilled in evoking sympathy as Antony.

Are Emotional Appeals Fallacious?

Antony's oration was obviously successful in the play and apparently was successful in real life, but it is the sort of speech that prompts logicians to write disapprovingly of attempts to stir feeling in an audience. (As mentioned earlier, the evocation of emotion in an audience is *pathos*, from the Greek word for "emotion" or "suffering.") There is nothing inherently wrong in stimulating an audience's emotions when attempting to establish a claim, but when an emotional appeal confuses the issue being argued or shifts attention away from the facts, we can reasonably speak of the fallacy of emotional appeal.

No fallacy is involved, however, when an emotional appeal heightens the facts, bringing them home to the audience rather than masking them. In talking about legislation that would govern police actions, for example, it's legitimate to show a photograph of the battered, bloodied face of an alleged victim of police brutality. True, such a photograph cannot tell the whole truth; it cannot tell if the subject threatened the officer with a gun or repeatedly resisted an order to surrender. But it can demonstrate that the victim was severely beaten and (like a comparable description in words) evoke emotions that may properly affect the audience's decision about the permissible use of police evidence. Similarly, an animal rights activist who argues that calves are cruelly confined might reasonably talk about the inhumanely small size of their pens, in which they cannot turn around or even lie down. Others may argue that calves don't care about turning around or have no right to turn around, but the evocative verbal description of their pens, which makes an emotional appeal, cannot be called fallacious or irrelevant.

In appealing to emotions, then, important strategies are as follows:

- Do not falsify (especially by oversimplifying) the issue.
- Do not distract attention from the facts of the case.
- Do think ethically about how emotional appeals may affect the audience.

You should focus on the facts and offer reasons (essentially, statements linked with "because"), but you may also legitimately bring the facts home to your readers by seeking to provoke appropriate emotions. Your words will be fallacious only if you stimulate emotions that aren't connected with the facts of the case.

Does All Writing Contain Arguments?

Our answer to the question above is no—however, *most* writing probably *does* contain an argument of sorts. The writer wants to persuade the reader to see things the way the writer sees them—at least until the end of the essay. After all, even a recipe for a cherry pie in a food magazine—a piece of writing that's primarily expository (how to do it) rather than argumentative (how a reasonable person ought to think about this topic)—probably starts out with a hint of an argument, such as "*Because* [a sign that a *reason* will be offered] this pie can be made quickly and with ingredients (canned cherries) that are always available, give it a try. It will surely become one of your favorites." Clearly, such a statement cannot stand as a formal argument—a discussion that addresses counterarguments, relies chiefly on logic and little if any emotional appeal, and draws a conclusion that seems irrefutable.

Still, the statement is an argument on behalf of making a pie with canned cherries. In this case, we can identify a claim (the pie will become a favorite) and two *reasons* in support of the claim:

- It can be made quickly.
- The chief ingredient—because it is canned—can always be at hand.

There are two underlying *assumptions*:

- Readers don't have a great deal of time to waste in the kitchen.
- Canned cherries are just as tasty as fresh cherries—and even if they aren't, no one who eats the pie will know the difference.

When we read a lead-in to a recipe, then, we won't find a formal argument, but we'll probably see a few words that seek to persuade us to keep reading. And most writing does contain such material—sentences that engage our interest and give us a reason to keep reading. If the recipe is difficult and time consuming, the lead-in may say:

Although this recipe for a cherry pie, using fresh cherries that you will have to pit, is a bit more time consuming than the usual recipes that call for canned cherries, once you have tasted it you will never go back to canned cherries.

Again, although the logic is scarcely compelling, the persuasive element is evident. The assumption is that readers have a discriminating palate; once they've tasted a pie made with fresh cherries, they'll never again enjoy the canned stuff. The writer isn't making a formal argument with abundant evidence and detailed refutation of counterarguments, but we know where he stands and how he wishes us to respond.

In short, almost all writers are trying to persuade readers to see things *their* way.

✓ A Checklist for Analyzing an Argument

What is the writer's claim or thesis? Ask yourself:

☐   What claim is asserted?

☐   What evidence is imagined?

☐   What assumptions are being made—and are they acceptable?

☐   Are important terms satisfactorily defined?

What support (evidence) is offered on behalf of the claim? Ask yourself:

☐   Are the examples relevant and convincing?

☐   Are the statistics (if any) relevant, accurate, and complete? Do they allow only the interpretation that is offered in the argument?

☐   If authorities are cited, are they indeed authorities on this topic, and can they be considered impartial?

☐   Is the logic—deductive and inductive—valid?

☐   If there is an appeal to emotion (e.g., if satire is used to ridicule the opposing view), is this appeal acceptable?

Does the writer seem to be fair? Ask yourself:

☐   Are counterarguments adequately considered?

☐   Is there any evidence of dishonesty or of a discreditable attempt to manipulate the reader?

☐   How does the writer establish the image of himself or herself that readers sense in the essay? What is the writer's tone, and is it appropriate?

An Example: An Argument and a Look at the Writer's Strategies

This essay concerns President George W. Bush's proposal to allow drilling in part of the Arctic National Wildlife Refuge (ANWR, pronounced "An-war"). The ANWR section where drilling is proposed is called the 1002 area, as defined by Section 1002 of the Alaska National Interest Lands Conservation Act of 1980. In March 2003, the Senate rejected the Bush proposal, but the issue remains alive.

We follow George F. Will's essay with some comments about the ways in which he constructs his argument.

George F. Will

George F. Will (b. 1941), a syndicated columnist whose writing appears in 460 newspapers, was born in Champaign, Illinois, and educated at Trinity College (in Hartford), Oxford University, and Princeton University. Will has served as the Washington, D.C., editor of the *National Review* and now writes a regular column for *Newsweek*. His essays have been collected in several books.

This essay was originally published in 2002, so it is in some respects dated—for instance, in its reference to the price of gasoline—but it still serves as an excellent model of certain ways to argue.

Being Green at Ben and Jerry's

Some Environmental Policies Are Feel-Good Indulgences for an Era of Energy Abundance

If you have an average-size dinner table, four feet by six feet, put a dime on the edge of it. Think of the surface of the table as the Arctic National Wildlife Refuge in Alaska. The dime is larger than the piece of the coastal plain that would have been opened to drilling for oil and natural gas. The House of Representatives voted for drilling, but the Senate voted against access to what Sen. John Kerry, Massachusetts Democrat and presidential aspirant, calls "a few drops of oil." ANWR could produce, for twenty-five years, at least as much oil as America currently imports from Saudi Arabia.

Six weeks of desultory Senate debate about the energy bill reached an almost comic culmination in...yet another agriculture subsidy. The subsidy is a requirement that will triple the amount of ethanol, which is made from corn, that must be put in gasoline, ostensibly to clean America's air, actually to buy farmers' votes.

Over the last three decades, energy use has risen about 30 percent. But so has population, which means per capita energy use is unchanged. And per capita GDP has risen substantially, so we are using 40 percent less energy per dollar output. Which is one reason there is no energy crisis, at least none as most Americans understand such things—a shortage of, and therefore high prices of, gasoline for cars, heating oil for furnaces and electricity for air conditioners.

In the absence of a crisis to concentrate the attention of the inattentive American majority, an intense faction—full-time environmentalists—goes to work. Spencer Abraham, the secretary of Energy, says "the previous administration…simply drew up a list of fuels it *didn't* like—nuclear energy, coal, hydropower, and oil—which together account for 73 percent of America's energy supply." Well, there are always windmills.

Sometimes lofty environmentalism is a cover for crude politics. The United States has the world's largest proven reserves of coal. But Mike Oliver, a retired physicist and engineer, and John Hospers, professor emeritus of philosophy at USC, note that in 1996 President Clinton put 68 billion tons of America's cleanest-burning coal, located in Utah, off-limits for mining, ostensibly for environmental reasons. If every existing U.S. electric power plant burned coal, the 68 billion tons could fuel them for forty-five years at the current rate of consumption. Now power companies must import clean-burning coal, some from mines owned by Indonesia's Lippo Group, the heavy contributor to Clinton, whose decision about Utah's coal vastly increased the value of Lippo's coal.

5

The United States has just 2.14 percent of the world's proven reserves of oil, so some people say it is pointless to drill in places like ANWR because "energy independence" is a chimera.[1] Indeed it is. But domestic supplies can provide important insurance against uncertain foreign supplies. And domestic supplies can mean exporting hundreds of billions of dollars less to oil-producing nations, such as Iraq.

Besides, when considering proven reserves, note the adjective. In 1930 the United States had proven reserves of 13 billion barrels. We then fought the Second World War and fueled the most fabulous economic expansion in human history, including the electricity-driven "New Economy." (Manufacturing and running computers consume 15 percent of U.S. electricity. Internet use alone accounts for half of the growth in demand for electricity.) So by 1990 proven reserves were…17 billion barrels, not counting any in Alaska or Hawaii.

In 1975 proven reserves in the Persian Gulf were 74 billion barrels. In 1993 they were 663 billion, a ninefold increase. At the current rate of consumption, today's proven reserves would last 150 years. New discoveries will be made, some by vastly improved techniques of deep-water drilling. But environmental policies will define opportunities. The government estimates that beneath the U.S. outer continental shelf, which the government owns, there are at least 46 billion barrels of oil. But only 2 percent of the shelf has been leased for energy development.

---

1 **chimera** Something that is hoped or wished for but is impossible to actually achieve. [Editors' note.]

Opponents of increased energy production usually argue for decreased consumption. But they flinch from conservation measures. A new $1 gasoline tax would dampen demand for gasoline, but it would stimulate demands for the heads of the tax increasers. After all, Americans get irritable when impersonal market forces add 25 cents to the cost of a gallon. Tougher fuel-efficiency requirements for vehicles would save a lot of energy. But who would save the legislators who passed those requirements? Beware the wrath of Americans who like to drive, and autoworkers who like to make cars that are large, heavy, and safer than the gasoline-sippers that environmentalists prefer.

Some environmentalism is a feel-good indulgence for an era of energy abundance, which means an era of avoided choices. Or ignored choices—ignored because if acknowledged, they would not make the choosers feel good. Karl Zinsmeister, editor in chief of the *American Enterprise* magazine, imagines an oh-so-green environmentalist enjoying the most politically correct product on the planet—Ben & Jerry's ice cream. Made in a factory that depends on electricity-guzzling refrigeration, a gallon of ice cream requires four gallons of milk. While making that much milk, a cow produces eight gallons of manure, and flatulence with another eight gallons of methane, a potent "greenhouse" gas. And the cow consumes lots of water plus three pounds of grain and hay, which is produced with tractor fuel, chemical fertilizers, herbicides and insecticides, and is transported with truck or train fuel:

10

"So every time he digs into his Cherry Garcia, the conscientious environmentalist should visualize (in addition to world peace) a pile of grain, water, farm chemicals, and energy inputs much bigger than his ice cream bowl on one side of the table, and, on the other side of the table, a mound of manure eight times the size of his bowl, plus a balloon of methane that would barely fit under the dining room table."

Cherry Garcia. It's a choice. *Bon appétit*.

George F. Will's Strategies

Now let's look at Will's essay to see what techniques he uses to engage readers' interest and perhaps enable him to convince them—or at least make them think—that he is on to something. If you think some or all of his strategies are effective, consider adapting them for use in your own essays.

The title, "Being Green at Ben and Jerry's," does not at all prepare readers for an argument about drilling in the National Arctic Wildlife Refuge. But if you have read any of Will's other columns in *Newsweek*, you probably know that he is conservative and can guess that in this essay he'll poke some fun at the green folk—the environmentalists. Will can get away with using a title that isn't focused because he has a body of loyal readers who will read his pieces no matter what the topic is, but the rest of us have to give our readers some idea of our topic. In short, let your readers know early, perhaps in the title, where you'll be taking them.

The subtitle, "Some Environmental Policies Are Feel-Good Indulgences for an Era of Energy Abundance," perhaps added by the magazine's editor, suggests that the piece will concern energy. Moreover, the words "feel-good indulgences" signal to readers that Will believes the environmentalists are indulging themselves.

Paragraph 1 offers a striking comparison. Will wants his readers to believe that the area proposed for drilling is tiny, so he says that if they imagine the entire Arctic National Wildlife Refuge as a dinner table, the area proposed for drilling is the size of a dime. We think you'll agree that this opening seizes a reader's attention. Although some opponents to drilling in the ANWR have contested Will's analogy (saying the area would be much larger, perhaps comparable to the size of a dinner plate, or even a dinner plate broken in pieces, with roads and pipelines crossing between the fragments), the image is still highly effective. A dime is so small! And worth so little!

Another point about paragraph 1: Will's casual voice sounds like one you might hear in your own living room: "If you have an average-size dinner table," "The dime is larger," "at least as much oil." Your own essays need not adopt a highly formal style. Readers should think of you as serious but not solemn.

Will goes on to say that Senator John Kerry, an opponent of drilling and therefore on the side that Will opposes, dismisses the oil in the refuge as "a few drops." Will replies that it "could produce, for twenty-five years, at least as much oil as America currently imports from Saudi Arabia." Kerry's "a few drops" isn't literal, of course; he means that the oil is a drop in the bucket. But when one looks into the issue, one finds that estimates by responsible sources vary considerably—from 3.2 billion barrels to 11.5 billion barrels.

Paragraph 2 dismisses the Senate's debate ("almost comic...actually to buy farmers' votes").

Paragraph 3 offers statistics to make the point that "there is no energy crisis." Here, as in paragraph 1 (where he showed his awareness of Kerry's view), Will indicates that he's familiar with views other than his own. In arguing a case, it's important for a writer to let readers know that indeed there are other views—which the writer then shows are less substantial than the writer's own. Will is correct in saying that "per capita energy use is unchanged," but opponents might say, "Yes, per capita consumption hasn't increased; but given the population increase, the annual amount has vastly increased, which means that resources are being depleted and that pollution is increasing."

Paragraph 4 asserts again that there is no energy crisis, pokes fun at "full-time environmentalists" (perhaps even implying that such people ought to get respectable jobs), and ends with a bit of whimsy: These folks probably think we should go back to using windmills.

Paragraph 5, in support of the assertion that "Sometimes lofty environmentalism is a cover for crude politics," cites an authority (often an effective technique). Since readers aren't likely to recognize the name, Will also identifies him ("professor emeritus of philosophy at USC") and then offers further statistics. The paragraph begins by talking about "crude politics" and ends with this assertion: "Now power companies must import clean-burning coal, some from mines owned by Indonesia's Lippo Group, the heavy contributor to Clinton." In short, Will makes several strategic moves to suggest that at least some environmentalists' views are rooted in money and politics.

Paragraph 6 offers another statistic ("The United States has just 2.14 percent of the world's proven reserves of oil") and turns it against those who argue that therefore it's pointless to drill in Alaska. In effect, Will is replying to people like Senator Kerry who say that the Arctic refuge provides only "a few drops of oil." The point, Will suggests, is not that it's impossible for the nation to achieve independence; rather, the point is that "domestic supplies can provide important insurance against uncertain foreign supplies."

Paragraph 7 begins smoothly with a transition, "Besides," and then offers additional statistics concerning the large amount of oil that the United States has held in proven reserves. For instance, by the end of World War II these reserves were enough to fuel "the most fabulous economic expansion in human history."

Paragraph 8 offers additional statistics, first about "proven reserves in the Persian Gulf" and then about an estimate—but only an estimate—of oil "beneath the U.S. outer continental shelf." We are not certain of Will's point here, but in any case the statistics suggest that he has done some homework.

Paragraph 9 summarizes the chief position (as Will sees it) of those on the other side of this issue: They "usually argue for decreased consumption," but they're afraid to argue for the sort of gasoline tax that might indeed decrease consumption because they know that many Americans want to drive large, heavy cars. Further, the larger, heavier cars that the environmentalists object to are in fact "safer than the gasoline-sippers that environmentalists prefer."

Paragraph 10 uses the term "feel-good indulgence," which also appears in the essay's subtitle; and now in the paragraph's third sentence we hear again of Ben and Jerry, whose names we haven't seen since reading the essay's title, "Being Green at Ben and Jerry's." Perhaps we've been wondering all this time why the title mentions Ben and Jerry. Surely most readers know that Ben and Jerry are associated with ice cream and therefore with cows and meadows, and probably many readers know that Ben and Jerry support environmentalism and other liberal causes. Drawing on an article by Karl Zinsmeister, editor of the *American Enterprise*, Will writes an extremely amusing paragraph in which he points out that the process of making ice cream "depends on electricity-guzzling refrigeration" and that the cows are essentially supported by fuel that transports fertilizers, herbicides, and insecticides. Further, in the course of producing the four gallons of milk required for one gallon of ice cream, the cows themselves—those darlings of the environmentalists—contribute "eight gallons of manure, and flatulence with another eight gallons of methane, a potent 'greenhouse' gas." As we'll soon see in Will's next paragraph, the present paragraph is largely a lead-in for the quotation he gives in the next paragraph. He knows it isn't enough to give a quotation; a writer has to make use of it—by leading in to it, by commenting on it after inserting it, or both.

Paragraph 11 is entirely devoted to quoting Zinsmeister, who imagines an environmentalist digging into a dish of one of Ben and Jerry's most popular flavors, Cherry Garcia. We're invited to see the bowl of ice cream on one side of the table—here Will effectively evokes the table of paragraph 1—and a pile of manure on the other side, "plus a balloon of methane that would barely fit under the dining room table." This statement is vulgar, no doubt, but it's funny too. Will knows that humor as well as logic (and statistics and other evidence) can be among the key tools a writer uses in getting an audience to consider or accept an argument.

Paragraph 12 consists of three short sentences, adding up to less than a single line of type: "Cherry Garcia. It's a choice. *Bon appétit*." None of the sentences mentions oil or the Arctic Refuge or statistics; therefore, this ending might seem irrelevant to the topic, but Will is very effectively saying, "Sure, you have a choice about drilling in the Arctic Refuge; any sensible person will choose the ice cream (drilling) rather than the manure and the gas (not drilling)."

Discussion Questions: Topics for Critical Thinking and Writing

1. What, if anything, makes George Will's essay interesting to you? What, if anything, makes it highly persuasive? How might it be made more persuasive?

2. In paragraph 10, Will clowns about the gas that cows emit, but apparently this gas, which contributes to global warming, is no laughing matter. The government of New Zealand, in an effort to reduce livestock emissions of methane and nitrous oxide, proposed a tax that would subsidize future research on the emissions. The tax would cost the average farmer $300 a year. Imagine that you're a New Zealand farmer. Write a letter to your representative, arguing for or against the tax.

3. Senator Barbara Boxer, campaigning against the proposal to drill in ANWR, spoke of the refuge as "God's gift to us" (*New York Times*, March 20, 2002). How strong an argument is this? Some opponents of the proposal have said that drilling in ANWR is as unthinkable as drilling in Yosemite or the Grand Canyon. Again, how strong is this argument? Can you imagine circumstances in which you would support drilling in these places? Why, or why not? Do we have a moral duty to preserve certain unspoiled areas? Explain your response.

4. The Inupiat (Eskimo) who live in and near ANWR by a large majority favor drilling, seeing it as a source of jobs and a source of funding for schools, hospitals, and police. But the Ketchikan Indians, who speak of themselves as the "Caribou People," see drilling as a threat to the herds on which they depend for food and hides. How is it possible to balance the conflicting needs of these two groups?

5. Opponents of drilling in ANWR argue that over its lifetime of fifty years, the area would produce less than 1 percent of the fuel we need during the period and that therefore we shouldn't risk disturbing the area. Further, they argue that drilling in ANWR is an attempt at a quick fix to U.S. energy needs, whereas what the nation really needs are sustainable solutions, such as the development of renewable energy sources (e.g., wind and sun) and fuel-efficient automobiles. How convincing do you find these arguments? Explain your response.

6. Proponents of drilling include a large majority—something like 75 percent—of the people of Alaska, including its governor and its two senators. How much attention do their voices deserve?

7. Analyze the essay in terms of its use of *ethos*, *pathos*, and *logos*.

8. What sort of audience do you think Will is addressing? What values do his readers probably share? What makes you think so?

Chapter 4

Visual Rhetoric: Thinking about Images as Arguments

A picture is worth a thousand words.

—Proverb

"What is the use of a book," thought Alice, *"without pictures or conversations?"*

—Lewis Carroll

Uses of Visual Images

Most visual materials that accompany written arguments serve one of several functions. One of the most common is to appeal to the reader's emotions (e.g., a photograph of a sad-eyed calf in a narrow pen can assist an argument against eating meat by inspiring sympathy for the animal). Pictures can also serve as visual evidence, offering proof that something occurred or appeared in a certain way at a certain moment. Pictures can help clarify numerical data (e.g., a graph showing five decades of law school enrollment by males and females). They can also add humor or satire to an essay. In this chapter, we concentrate on thinking critically about visual images. This means reading images in the same way we read print (or electronic) texts: by looking closely at them and discerning not only *what* they show but also *how* and *why* they convey a particular message, or argument.

When we discussed the **appeal to emotion** in Chapter 3 (pp. 106–108), we quoted from Marc Antony's speech to the Roman populace in Shakespeare's play *Julius Caesar.* You'll recall that Antony stirred the mob by displaying Caesar's blood-stained mantle. He wasn't holding up a picture, but in a similar way he supplemented his words with visual material:

> Look, in this place ran Cassius' dagger through;
> See what a rent the envious Casca made;
> Through this, the well-belovèd Brutus stabbed....

Chapter 4, "Visual Rhetoric: Thinking about Images as Arguments," from *From Critical Thinking to Argument: A Portable Guide*, by Sylvan Barnet, Hugo Bedau, and John O'Hara, pp. 135–172 (Chapter 4). Copyright © 2017 by Bedford/St. Martin's.

In courtrooms today, trial lawyers and prosecutors accomplish the same thing when doing the following:

- exhibiting photos of a bloody corpse, or

- holding up a murder weapon for jurors to see, or

- introducing victims as witnesses who sob while describing their ordeal.

Lawyers know that such visuals help make good arguments. Whether presented sincerely or gratuitously, visuals can have a significantly persuasive effect. Such appeals to emotion work on feelings, not logic. Think about the suit and tie that lawyers advise their male clients to wear: The attire helps make an argument to the jury about the defendant's character or credibility, even if he is actually lacking these qualities. Images, too, may be rationally connected to an argument (e.g., a gruesome image of a diseased lung in an anti-smoking ad makes a reasonable claim), but their immediate impact is more on the viewer's heart than the mind.

Like any kind of evidence, images make statements and support arguments. When Congress debated over whether to allow drilling in the Arctic National Wildlife Refuge (ANWR), both opponents and supporters made use of images:

- *Opponents* of drilling showed beautiful pictures of polar bears frolicking, wildflowers in bloom, and caribou on the move.

- *Proponents* of drilling showed bleak pictures of what they called "barren land" and "a frozen wasteland."

Both sides knew very well that images are powerfully persuasive, and they didn't hesitate to use them as supplements to words.

We invite you to think about the appropriateness of using such images in arguments. Was either side manipulating the "reality" of the ANWR? Or do images such as those described provide reasonable support for the ideas under consideration? Should argument be entirely a matter of reason, of logic (*logos*), without appeals to the emotions (*pathos*)? A statement that "the Arctic National Wildlife Refuge is a home for abundant wildlife, notably polar bears, caribou, and wildflowers" may not mean much until it is reinforced with breathtakingly beautiful images. Similarly, a statement that "most of the ANWR land is barren" may not mean much until it is corroborated by images of the vast bleakness. Each side selected a particular kind of image for a specific purpose—to support its position on drilling in the ANWR. Neither side was being dishonest, but both were appealing to emotions.

Types of Emotional Appeals

We began the preceding chapter by distinguishing between *argument*, which relies on reason (*logos*), and *persuasion*, which is a broad term that can include appeals to the emotions (*pathos*)—for example, an **appeal to pity**, such as an image of a sad-eyed calf. You might say, "Well, eating meat implies confining and killing animals," and regard the image as both reasonable and emotionally powerful. Or you might say,

"Although it's emotionally powerful, this appeal to pity doesn't describe the condition of every meat animal. Some are treated humanely, slaughtered humanely, and eaten ethically." You might write a counterargument and include an image of free-range cattle on a farm (although in doing this, you too would be appealing to emotions).

The point is that images can be persuasive even if they don't make good arguments, in the same way threats of violence can be persuasive but do not make good arguments. The gangster Al Capone famously said, "You can get a lot more done with a kind word and a gun than with a kind word alone." Threats of violence appeal exclusively to the emotions—specifically, fear.

Advertisers commonly use the **appeal to fear** as a persuasive technique. While it is not a threat of violence, the appeal to fear is a threat of sorts. Showing a burglary, a car crash, embarrassing age spots, or a cockroach infestation can successfully convince consumers to buy a product—a home security system, a new car insurance policy, an age-defying skin cream, or a pesticide. Such images generate fear and anxiety at the same time that they offer the solution for it.

Appeal to self-interest is another persuasive tactic that writers can use. Consider these remarks, which use the word *interest* in the sense of "self-interest":

> Would you persuade, speak of Interest, not Reason.
> —BENJAMIN FRANKLIN

> There are two levers for moving men—interest and fear.
> —NAPOLEON BONAPARTE

Appeals to self-interest may be quite persuasive because they speak directly to what benefits you the most, not necessarily what benefits others in the community, society, or world. Such appeals are also common in advertising. "You can save bundles by shopping at Maxi-Mart," a commercial might claim, without making reference to sweatshop labor conditions, the negative impact of global commerce, or other troublesome aspects of what you see only as a great savings for yourself. You may be familiar with other types of emotional appeals in advertising that speak to the senses more than to the rational mind. Again, these kinds of appeals don't necessarily make good arguments for the products in question, but each can be highly persuasive—sometimes affecting us subconsciously. (The same applies to appeals in written arguments. This is why thinking critically about both words and images is so important.)

Here is a list of some additional kinds of appeals to emotion:

- Sexual appeals (Example: showing a bikini-clad model standing near a product)

- Bandwagon appeals (Example: showing crowds of people rushing to a sale)

- Humor appeals (Example: showing a cartoon animal drinking *X* brand of beverage)

- Celebrity appeals (Example: showing a famous person driving X brand of car)

- Testimonial appeals (Example: showing a doctor giving X brand of vitamins to her kids)

- Identity appeals (Example: showing a "good family" going to X restaurant)

- Prejudice appeals (Example: showing a "loser" drinking X brand of beer)

- Lifestyle appeals (Example: showing a jar of X brand of mustard on a silver platter)

- Stereotype appeals (Example: showing a Latino person enjoying X brand of salsa)

- Patriotic appeals (Example: showing X brand of mattress alongside an American flag)

Inside Work: Exercise

Watch the commercials that air during a television show, or examine the print advertisements in a popular magazine. Identify as many examples as possible of the types of appeals mentioned on the preceding pages. Is there a rational basis for any of the appeals you see? Are any appeals irrational even if they are effective? Why, or why not?

Seeing versus Looking: Reading Advertisements

Advertising is one of the most common forms of visual persuasion we encounter in everyday life. The influence of advertising in our culture is pervasive and subtle. Part of its power comes from our habit of internalizing the intended messages of words and images without thinking deeply about them. Once we begin decoding the ways in which advertisements are constructed—once we view them critically—we can understand how (or if) they work as arguments. We may then make better decisions about whether to buy particular products and what factors convinced us or failed to convince us.

To read an advertisement—or any image—critically, it helps to consider some basic rules from the field of semiotics, the study of signs and symbols. Fundamental to semiotic analysis is the idea that visual signs have shared meanings in a culture. If you approach a sink and see a red faucet and a blue faucet, you can be pretty sure which one will produce hot water and which one will produce cold. In a similar way, we almost subconsciously recognize the meanings of images in advertisements. Thus, one of the first strategies we can use in reading advertisements critically is deconstructing them, taking them apart to see what makes them work. It's helpful to remember that advertisements are enormously expensive to produce and disseminate, so nothing is left to chance. Teams of people typically scrutinize every part of an advertisement to ensure it communicates the intended message—although this doesn't imply that viewers must accept those messages. In fact, taking advertisements apart is the first step in being critical about them.

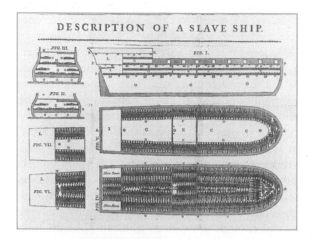

Images played an important role in the antislavery movement in the nineteenth century. On the top left is a diagram showing how human cargo was packed into a slave ship; it was distributed with Thomas Clarkson's *Essay on the Slavery and Commerce of the Human Species* (1804). On the top right is Frederick W. Mercer's photograph (April 2, 1863) of Gordon, a "badly lacerated" runaway slave. Images such as the slave ship and the runaway slave worked against slave owners' claims that slavery was a humane institution—claims that also were supported by illustrations, such as the woodcut at the bottom, titled *Attention Paid to a Poor Sick Negro*, from Josiah Priest's *In Defense of Slavery* (1843).

Taking apart an advertisement means examining each visual element. Consider the following advertisement for Nike shoes featuring basketball star LeBron James. Already, you should see the celebrity appeal—an implicit claim that Nike shoes help make James a star player. The ad creates an association between the shoes and the sports champion. James's uniform number, 23, assists in this association by referencing another basketball legend (and Nike spokesperson), Michael Jordan. James is, in a way, presented as the progeny of Michael Jordan, as a new incarnation of a sports "god." WE ARE ALL WITNESSES, the text reads, drawing on language commonly used in religious settings to describe the second coming of Christ. James's arms are outstretched, Christ-like, and seem to be illuminated by divine light from above. The uniform also references James's famous return to the Cleveland Cavaliers, his hometown team, after leaving the team abruptly to play four seasons with the Miami Heat. His "return" to Cleveland—his own second coming—the son of a sports god—and with the resonance of forgiveness, redemption, and salvation for Cleveland sports fans: All these associations work together to elevate James, Jordan, and Nike to exalted status. Of course, our description here is tongue-in-cheek. We're not gullible enough to believe this literally, and the ad's producers don't expect us to be; but they do hope that such an impression will be powerful enough to make us think of Nike the next time we shop for athletic shoes. If sports gods wear Nike, why shouldn't we?

This kind of analysis is possible when we recognize a difference between *seeing* and *looking*. Seeing is a physiological process involving light, the eye, and the brain. Looking, however, is a social process involving the mind. It suggests apprehending an image in terms of symbolic, metaphorical, and other social and cultural meanings. To do this, we must think beyond the *literal* meaning of an image or image element and consider its *figurative* meanings. If you look up *apple* in the dictionary, you'll find its literal, denotative meaning—a round fruit with thin red or green skin and a crisp flesh. But an apple also communicates figurative, connotative meanings. Connotative meanings are the cultural or emotional associations that an image suggests.

ABC/Photofest

The long-running ABC television series *Desperate Housewives*, which dramatized the furtive sex lives and exploits of suburban women, featured apples prominently in its advertisements.

Image Courtesy of The Advertising Archives

Image Courtesy of The Advertising Archives

How does the DKNY advertisement use the symbolic, connotative meanings of the apple? In what ways does the advertisement for Bulova watches attempt to make an argument about the product?

The connotative meaning of an apple in Western culture dates back to the biblical story of the Garden of Eden, where Eve, tempted by a serpent, eats the fruit from the forbidden tree of knowledge and brings about the end of paradise on earth. Throughout Western culture, apples have come to represent knowledge and the pursuit of knowledge. Think of the ubiquitous Apple logo gracing so many mobile phones, tablets, and laptops: With its prominent bite, it symbolizes the way technology opens up new worlds of knowing. Sometimes, apples represent forbidden knowledge, temptation, or seduction—and biting into one suggests giving in to desires for new understandings and experiences. The story of Snow White offers just one example of an apple used as a symbol of temptation.

Let's look at two additional advertisements (pictured on p. 127), each of which relies almost entirely on images rather than words. The first, an ad for a TV comedy that made its debut in 2009, boldly displays the show's title and highlights the network name by setting it apart, but the most interesting words are in much smaller print:

Funny. On so many levels.

These words flatter the ad's readers, thus making them susceptible to the implicit message: "Look at this program." Why do we say the words are flattering? For three reasons:

- The small type size implies that the reader isn't someone whose attention can be caught only by headlines.

- The pun on "levels" (physical levels, and levels of humor) is a witty way of saying that the show offers not only the low comedy of physical actions but also the high comedy of witty talk—talk that, for instance, may involve puns.

- The two terse, incomplete sentences assume that the sophisticated reader doesn't need to have things explained at length.

The picture itself is attractive, showing what seems to be a wide variety of people (though not any faces or body types that in real life might cause viewers any uneasiness) posed in the style of a family portrait. Indeed, these wholesome figures, standing in affectionate poses, are all dressed in white (no real-life ketchup stains here) and are neatly framed—except for the patriarch, at the extreme right—by a pair of seated youngsters whose legs dangle down from the levels. The modern family, we're told, is large and varied (this one includes a gay son and his partner, and their adopted Vietnamese baby), smart and warm. Best of all, it is "Funny. On so many levels."

The second ad features just a single line of text: "No In-App Purchases." These words are set below the image of a shopping cart with a plus sign, which has come to be an almost universally recognized symbol for an electronic shopping cart. Both the text and the icon are textured and look a little rough at the edges, suggesting that they are made out of the very item they are advertising. After all, Play-Doh has been around since the 1930s; though the way children play has changed dramatically since then (most kids born now will grow up knowing what an "in-app purchase" is), by fashioning the electronic icon and text out of a nearly century-old product, the ad implies that just because a toy—or anything else—is new and high-tech, that does not make it inherently better than old-fashioned things. After all, the product being advertised has been around for nearly a century; how long will an app on a smartphone or tablet last until it is replaced with a newer version?

Discussion Questions: Topics for Critical Thinking and Writing

1. Imagine that you work for a business—for instance, a vacation resort, a clothing manufacturer, or an automaker—that advertises in a publication such as *Time* or *Newsweek*. Design an advertisement for the business: Describe the picture and write the text, and then, in an essay of 500 words, identify your target audience (college students? young couples about to buy their first home? retired persons?) and explain your purpose in choosing certain types of appeals (e.g., to reason, to the emotions, to the audience's sense of humor).

2. It is often said that colleges, like businesses, are selling a product. Examine a brochure or catalog that is sent to prospective college applicants, or locate your own college's view book, and analyze the kinds of appeals that some of the images make.

✓   A Checklist for Analyzing Images (Especially Advertisements)

☐ What is the overall effect of the design? Colorful and busy (suggesting activity)? Quiet and understated (e.g., chiefly white and grays, with lots of empty space)? Old-fashioned or cutting edge?

☐ What single aspect of the image immediately captures your attention? Its size? Its position on the page? The beauty of the image? The grotesqueness of the image? Its humor?

☐ Who is the audience for the image? Affluent young men? Housewives? Retired persons?

☐ What is the argument?

☐ Does the text make a rational appeal (*logos*)? ("Tests at a leading university prove that…"; "If you believe *X*, you should vote 'No' on this referendum" appeal to our sense of reason.)

☐ Does the image appeal to the emotions or to dearly held values (*pathos*)? (Images of starving children or maltreated animals appeal to our sense of pity; images of military valor may appeal to our patriotism; images of luxury may appeal to our envy; images of sexually attractive people may appeal to our desire to be like them; images of violence or of extraordinary ugliness—as in ads showing a human fetus being destroyed—may seek to shock us.)

☐ Does the image make an ethical appeal—that is, does it appeal to our character as a good human being (*ethos*)? (Ads by charitable organizations often appeal to our sense of decency, fairness, and pity; but ads that appeal to our sense of prudence—such as ads for insurance companies or investment houses—also make an ethical appeal.)

☐ What is the relation of print to image? Does the image do most of the work, or does it serve to attract us and lead us on to read the text?

Other Aspects of Visual Appeals

As we saw with the uses of images relating to the Arctic National Wildlife Refuge, photographs can serve as evidence but have a peculiar relationship to the truth. We must never forget that images are constructed, selected, and used for specific purposes. When advertisers use images, they're trying to convince consumers to purchase a product or service. But when images serve as documentary evidence, we often assume they're showing the "truth" of the matter at hand. Our skepticism may be lower when we see an image in the newspaper or a magazine, assuming it captures a particular event or moment in time *as it really happened*. But historical images, images of events, news photographs, and other forms of visual evidence are not free from the potential for conscious or unconscious bias. Consider how liberal and conservative media sources portray the nation's president in images: One source may show him proud and smiling in bright light with the American flag behind him, while another might show him scowling in a darkened image suggestive of evil intent. Both are "real" images, but the framing, tinting, setting, and background can inspire significantly different responses in viewers.

As we saw with the image of LeBron James, certain postures, facial expressions, and settings can contribute to a photograph's interpretation. Martin Luther King Jr.'s great speech of August 28, 1963, "I Have a Dream," still reads very well on the page, but part of its immense appeal derives from its setting: King spoke to some 200,000 people in Washington, D.C., as he stood on the steps of the Lincoln Memorial. That setting, rich with associations of slavery and freedom, strongly assists King's argument. In fact, images of King delivering his speech are nearly inseparable from the very argument he was making. The visual aspects—the setting (the Lincoln Memorial with the Washington Monument and the Capitol in the distance) and King's gestures—are part of the speech's persuasive rhetoric.

Martin Luther King Jr. delivering his "I Have a Dream" speech on August 28, 1963, from the steps of the Lincoln Memorial.

Derrick Alridge, a historian, examined dozens of accounts of Martin Luther King Jr. in history books, and he found that images of King present him overwhelmingly as a messianic figure—standing before crowds, leading them, addressing them in postures reminiscent of a prophet. While King is an admirable figure, Alridge asserts, history books err by presenting him as more than human. Doing so ignores his personal struggles and failures and makes a myth out of the real man. This myth suggests he was the epicenter of the civil rights movement, an effort that was actually conducted in different ways via different strategies on the part of many other figures whom King eclipsed. We may even get the idea that the entire civil rights movement began and ended with King alone. When he's presented as a holy prophet, it becomes easier to focus on his abstract messages about love, equality, and justice, and not on the specific policies and politics he advocated—his avowed socialist stances, for instance. While photographs of King seek to help us remember, they may actually portray him in a way that causes us to forget other things—for example, the fact that his approval rating among whites at the time of his death was lower than 30 percent, and among blacks lower than 50 percent.

Martin Luther King Jr. on "Chicken Bone Beach" in Atlantic City.

John Mosley/Courtesy Charles L. Blockson Afro American Collection

Levels of Images

One helpful way of discerning the meanings of images by *looking* at them (see p. 124) is to utilize *seeing* first as a way to define what is plainly or literally present in them. You can begin by *seeing*—identifying the elements that are indisputably "there" in an image (the denotative level). Then you move on to *looking*—interpreting the meanings suggested by the elements that are present (the connotative level).

Semioticians distinguish between images' surface levels and deeper levels. The surface level is the syntagmatic level, and the deeper level is the paradigmatic level. The words *syntagmatic* and *paradigmatic* are related to the words *syntax* and *paradigm*.

Arguably, when we *see*, we pay attention only to the syntagmatic level. We notice the various elements included in an image. We *see* denotatively—that is, we observe just the explicit elements of the image. We aren't concerned with the meaning of the image's elements, but just with the fact that they're present.

When we *look*, we move to the paradigmatic level. That is, we speculate on the elements' deeper meanings—what they suggest figuratively, symbolically, or metaphorically in our cultural system. We may also consider the relationship of different elements to one another. When we do this, we look connotatively.

Syntagmatic analysis	Paradigmatic analysis
Seeing	Looking
Denotation	Connotation
Literal	Figurative
What is present	What it means
Understanding / Textual	Interpreting / Subtextual / Contextual

Inside Work: Exercise

Examine the images on this page. As you examine each one, do the following:

1. *See* the image. Perform a syntagmatic analysis thoroughly describing the image elements you observe. Write down as many elements as possible that you see.

2. *Look* at the image. Perform a paradigmatic analysis in which you take the elements you have observed and relate what they suggest by considering their figurative meanings, their meanings in relation to one another, and their meanings in the context of the images' production and consumption.

Margaret Bourke-White/Time & Life Pictures/Getty Images

Residents of Louisville, Kentucky, waiting in a bread line in 1937. A massive flood from January to February that year left nearly four hundred people dead and roughly one million people homeless across five states.

Adam Bettcher/Getty Images

Protestors rallying outside the office of Dr. Walter Palmer, a dentist from Bloomington, Minnesota. In July 2015, Palmer was accused of poaching a 13-year-old lion named Cecil that was living at Hwange National Park in Zimbabwe. Palmer reportedly paid $50,000 for the hunt and lured Cecil out of the sanctuary to shoot him.

The point here is that photographs promise a clear window into a past reality but are not unassailable guarantors of truth. In the digital age, it's remarkably easy to alter photographs, and we have become more suspicious of photographs as direct evidence of reality. Yet we still tend to trust certain sources more than others. To counteract this tendency, we can be more critical about images by asking three overarching questions about the contexts in which they are created, disseminated, and received. Within each question, other questions arise.

1. *Who produced the image?*   Who was the photographer? Under what circumstances was the picture taken? How is the subject of the image framed? What other visual information is included in the frame? What is emphasized and de-emphasized? What do you think is the image's intended effect?

2. *Who distributed the image?*   How widely has the image been distributed? Where has it been published (magazine, newspaper, blog, social media page)? What is the intended audience of the publication where the image appears? What purpose does the image serve? How does the image support the accompanying text? What alternative images exist?

3. *Who consumed the image?*   What type of audience is the likeliest viewer of the image? Are they likely to see it as negative or positive? Does the image inspire an emotional response? If so, what kind? What elements in the photograph are likely to generate certain kinds of responses?

A Rule for Writers

If you think that pictures will help you to make the point you are arguing, include them with captions explaining their sources and relevance.

Accommodating, Resisting, and Negotiating the Meaning of Images

Most images are produced, selected, and published in order to have a specific effect on readers and viewers. This dominant meaning of an image supposes that the audience will react in a predictable way, usually based on the widespread cultural codes that operate within a society. Images of elegant women in designer dresses, rugged men driving pickup trucks, stodgy teachers, cutthroat CEOs, hipster computer programmers, and so on speak to generally accepted notions of what certain types of people are like. An image of a suburban couple in an automobile advertisement washing their new car subconsciously confirms and perpetuates a certain ideal of middle-class suburban life (a heterosexual couple, a well-trimmed lawn, a neatly painted house and picket fence—and a brand-new midsize sedan). An image of a teary-eyed young woman accepting a diamond ring from a handsome man will likely touch the viewer in a particular way, in part because of our society's cultural codes about the rituals of romantic love and marriage, gender roles, and the diamond ring as a sign of love and commitment.

These examples demonstrate that images can be constructed according to dominant connotations of gender, class, and racial, sexual, and political identity. When analyzing an image, ask yourself what cultural codes it endorses, what ideals it establishes as natural, what social norms or modes of everyday life it idealizes or assumes.

As image consumers, we often *accommodate* (i.e., passively accept) the cultural codes promoted in the media. For example, in the hypothetical advertisement featuring a wedding proposal, you might accept the producer's communicated ideals that men should propose to women, that women are emotional beings, and that diamond rings are the appropriate objects to represent love and commitment. When you **accommodate** cultural codes without understanding them critically, you allow the media that perpetuate these codes to interpret the world for you. That is, you accept their interpretations without questioning the social and cultural values implicit in their assumptions, many of which may actually run counter to your own or others' social and cultural values.

If you *resist* the cultural codes of an image, you actively criticize its message and meaning. Suppose you (1) question how the ad presents gender roles and marriage, (2) claim that it idealizes heterosexual marriage, and (3) point out that it confirms and extends traditional gender roles in which men are active and bold and women are passive and emotional. Moreover, you (4) argue that the diamond ring represents a misguided commodification of love because diamonds are kept deliberately scarce by large companies and, as such, are overvalued and overpriced; meanwhile, the ad prompts young couples to spend precious money at a time when their joint assets might be better saved, and because many diamonds come from third-world countries under essentially slave labor conditions, the diamond is more a symbol of oppression than of love. If your analysis follows such paths, you **resist** the dominant message of the image in question. Sometimes, this is called an *oppositional reading*.

Negotiation, or a *negotiated reading*, the most useful mode of reading and viewing, involves a middle path—a process of revision that seeks to recognize and change the conditions that give rise to certain negative aspects of cultural codes. Negotiation implies a practical intervention into common viewing processes that help construct and maintain social conditions and relations. This intervention can be important when inequalities or stereotypes are perpetuated by cultural codes. A negotiated reading enables you to emphasize the ways in which individuals, social groups, and others relate to images and their dominant meanings, and how different personal and cultural perspectives can challenge those meanings. Without intervention there can be no revision, no positive social or cultural change. You **negotiate** cultural codes when:

- you understand the underlying messages of images and accept the general cultural implications of these codes, *but*

- you acknowledge that in some circumstances the general codes do not apply.

Using this scheme will help you analyze diverse kinds of images as well as develop more nuanced arguments about the messages those images convey.

Inside Work: Exercise

Examine the image on p. 133, which is an advertisement for Lego building blocks. Provide brief examples of how a viewer could accommodate, resist, or negotiate the images in the ad.

Are Some Images Not Fit to Be Shown?

Images of suffering—either human or animal—can be immensely persuasive. In the nineteenth century, for instance, the antislavery movement made extremely effective use of images in its campaign. We reproduce two antislavery images earlier in this chapter, as well as a counterimage that sought to assure viewers that slavery is a beneficent system (p. 123). But are there some images not fit to print?

Until recently, many newspapers did not print pictures of lynched African Americans, hanged and burned and maimed. The reasons for not printing such images probably differed between South and North: Southern papers may have considered the images to be discreditable to whites, while northern papers may have deemed the images too revolting. Even today, when it's commonplace for newspapers and television news to show pictures of dead victims of war, famine, or traffic accidents, one rarely sees bodies that are horribly maimed. (For traffic accidents, the body is usually covered, and we see only the smashed car.) The U.S. government has refused to release photographs showing the bodies of American soldiers killed in the war in Iraq, and it has been most reluctant to show pictures of dead Iraqi soldiers and civilians. Only after many Iraqis refused to believe that former Iraqi president Saddam Hussein's two sons had been killed did the U.S. government reluctantly release pictures showing the two men's blood-spattered faces—and some American newspapers and television programs refused to use the images.

There have been notable exceptions to this practice, such as Huynh Cong (Nick) Ut's 1972 photograph of children fleeing a napalm attack in Vietnam, which was widely reproduced in the United States and won the photographer a Pulitzer Prize in 1973. It's impossible to measure the influence of this particular photograph, but many people believe that it played a substantial role in increasing public pressure to end the Vietnam War. Another widely reproduced picture of horrifying violence is Eddie Adams's 1968 picture of a South Vietnamese chief of police firing a pistol into the head of a Viet Cong prisoner.

The issue remains: Are some images unacceptable? For instance, although capital punishment—by methods including lethal injection, hanging, shooting, and electrocution—is legal in parts of the United States, every state in the Union prohibits the publication of pictures showing a criminal being executed.[1]

Huynh Cong (Nick) Ut, *The Terror of War: Children on Route 1 near Trang Bang*, 1972

The most famous recent example of an image widely thought to be unprintable showed the murder of Daniel Pearl, a reporter for the *Wall Street Journal*. Pearl was captured and murdered in June 2002 by Islamic terrorists in Pakistan. His killers videotaped Pearl reading a statement denouncing American policy and then being decapitated. The video also shows a man's arm holding Pearl's head. The video ends with the killers making demands (such as the release of Muslim prisoners being held by the United States in Guantánamo Bay, Cuba) and asserting, "if our demands are not met, this scene will be repeated again and again."

Eddie Adams, *Execution of Viet Cong Prisoner, Saigon*, 1968

The chief arguments against newspapers reproducing material from this video were as follows:

- The video and still images from it are unbearably gruesome.
- Showing the video would traumatize the Pearl family.
- The video is enemy propaganda.

---

1 For more on this topic, see Wendy Lesser, *Pictures at an Execution* (1993).

Those who favored broadcasting the video on television and printing still images from it in newspapers offered these arguments:

- The photos would show the world what sort of enemy the United States is fighting.

- Newspapers have published pictures of other terrifying sights (notably, people leaping out of windows of the World Trade Center's Twin Towers on 9/11 and the space shuttle *Challenger* exploding in 1986).

- No one was worried about protecting the families of 9/11 or *Challenger* victims from seeing those traumatic images.

But is the comparison of the Daniel Pearl video to the photos of the Twin Towers and the *Challenger* valid? You may respond that individuals in the Twin Towers pictures aren't specifically identifiable and that the *Challenger* images, although horrifying, aren't as visually revolting as the picture of a severed head held up for view.

The *Boston Phoenix,* a weekly newspaper, published some images from the Pearl video and also put a link to the video (with a warning that the footage is "extremely graphic") on its Web site. The weekly's editor justified publication on the three grounds we list above. Pearl's wife, Mariane Pearl, was quoted in various newspapers as condemning the "heartless decision to air this despicable video." And a spokeswoman for the Pearl family, when asked for comment, referred reporters to a statement issued earlier, which said that broadcasters who show the video

Alexander Gardner, *Home of a Rebel Sharpshooter,* 1863. This photo illustrates the devastation wrought by the Battle of Gettysburg through focusing on a single dead soldier splayed out in a "sharpshooter's den."

Library of Congress, Prints & Photographs Division, Reproduction number LC-DIG-cwpb-04337 (digital file from original neg.) LC-B8171-7942 (b&w film neg.)

fall without shame into the terrorists' plan…. Danny believed that journalism was a tool to report the truth and foster understanding—not perpetuate propaganda and sensationalize tragedy. We had hoped that no part of this tape would ever see the light of day…. We urge all networks and news outlets to exercise responsibility and not aid the terrorists in spreading their message of hate and murder.[2]

---

2 Quoted in the *Hartford Courant,* June 5, 2002, and reproduced on the Internet by the Freedom of Information Center, under the heading "Boston Paper Creates Controversy."

Although some journalists expressed regret that Pearl's family was distressed, they insisted that journalists have a right to reproduce such material and that the images can serve the valuable purpose of shocking viewers into awareness.

Politics and Pictures

Consider, too, the controversy that erupted in 1991, during the Persian Gulf War, when the U.S. government decided that news media would not be allowed to photograph coffins returning with the bodies of military personnel killed during the war. In later years the policy was sometimes ignored, but in 2003 the George W. Bush administration decreed that there would be "no arrival ceremony for, or media coverage of, deceased military personnel returning [from Iraq or Afghanistan]...to the Dover (Delaware) base." The government enforced the policy strictly.

The Washington Post/Getty Images

Members of the news media strongly protested, as did many others, chiefly on the basis of these arguments:

- The administration was trying to sanitize the war; that is, the government was depriving the public of important information—images—that showed the war's real cost.

- Grief for the deaths of military personnel is not a matter only for the families of the deceased. The sacrifices were made on behalf of the nation, and the nation should be allowed to grieve. Canada and Britain have no such ban; when military coffins are transported there, the public lines the streets to honor the fallen warriors. In fact, in Canada a portion of the highway near the Canadian base has been renamed "Highway of Heroes."

- The coffins at Dover Air Force base are not identified by name, so there is no issue about intruding on the privacy of grieving families.

The chief arguments in defense of the ban were as follows:

- Photographs violate the families' privacy.

- If the arrival of the coffins at Dover is publicized, some grieving families will think they should travel to Dover to be present when the bodies arrive. This may cause a financial hardship on the families.

- If the families give their consent, the press is *not* barred from individual graveside ceremonies at hometown burials. The ban extends only to the coffins' arrival at Dover Air Force Base.

In February 2009, President Obama changed the policy and permitted coverage of the transfer of bodily remains. In his Address to the Joint Session of Congress on February 24, 2009, he said, "For seven years we have been a nation at war. No longer will we hide its price." On February 27, Defense Secretary Robert M. Gates announced that the government ban was lifted and that families will decide whether to allow photographs and videos of the "dignified transfer process at Dover."

Inside Work: Exercise

In an argumentative essay of about 250 words—perhaps two or three paragraphs—give your view of the issue of permitting photos of military coffins. In an opening paragraph, you may want to both explain the issue and summarize the arguments that you reject. The second paragraph of a two-paragraph essay may present your reasons for rejecting those arguments. Additionally, you might devote a third paragraph to a more general reflection.

Discussion Questions: Topics for Critical Thinking and Writing

1. Marvin Kalb, a distinguished journalist, was quoted as saying that the public has a right to see the tape of Daniel Pearl's murder but that "common sense, decency, [and] humanity would encourage editors… to say 'no, it is not necessary to put this out.' There is no urgent demand on the part of the American people to see Daniel Pearl's death." What is your view?

2. In June 2006, two American soldiers were captured in Iraq. Later their bodies were found, dismembered and beheaded. Should newspapers have shown photographs of the mutilated bodies? Why, or why not? (In July 2006, insurgents in Iraq posted images on the Internet showing a soldier's severed head beside his body.)

Another issue concerning the appropriateness of showing certain images arose early in 2006. In September 2005, a Danish newspaper, accused of being afraid to show political cartoons that were hostile to Muslim terrorists, responded by publishing twelve cartoons. One cartoon showed the prophet Muhammad wearing a turban that looked like a bomb. The images at first didn't arouse much attention, but when they were reprinted in Norway in January 2006, they attracted worldwide attention and outraged Muslims, most of whom regard any depiction of Muhammad as blasphemous. Some Muslims in various Islamic nations burned Danish embassies and engaged in other acts of violence. Most non-Muslims agreed that the images were in bad taste; and apparently in deference to Islamic sensibilities (but possibly also out of fear of reprisals), very few Western newspapers reprinted the cartoons when they covered the news events. Most newspapers (including the *New York Times*) merely described the images. The editors of these papers believed that readers should be told the news, but that because the drawings were so offensive to some persons, they should be described rather than reprinted. A controversy then arose: Do readers of a newspaper deserve to *see* the evidence for themselves, or can a newspaper adequately fulfill its mission by offering only a verbal description? These questions arose again after the 2007 bombing of the French satirical newspaper *Charlie Hebdo*, and then after another mass shooting at the same newspaper in 2015 that claimed the lives of twelve editors and staff members.

Persons who argued that the images should be reproduced in the media generally made these points:

- Newspapers should yield neither to the delicate sensibilities of some readers nor to threats of violence.

- Jews for the most part do not believe that God should be depicted (the prohibition against "graven images" appears in Exodus 20.3), but they raise no objections to such Christian images as Michelangelo's painting of God awakening Adam, depicted on the ceiling of the Sistine Chapel. Further, when Andres Serrano (a Christian) in 1989 exhibited a photograph of a small plastic crucifix submerged in urine, it outraged a wider public (several U.S. senators condemned it because the artist had received federal funds), but virtually all newspapers showed the image, and many even printed its title, *Piss Christ*. The subject was judged to be newsworthy, and the fact that some viewers would regard the image as blasphemous was not considered highly relevant.

- Our society values freedom of speech, and newspapers should not be intimidated. When certain pictures are a matter of news, readers should be able to see them.

In contrast, opposing voices made these points:

- Newspapers must recognize deep-seated religious beliefs. They should indeed report the news, but there is no reason to *show* images that some people regard as blasphemous. The images can be adequately *described* in words.

- The Jewish response to Christian images of God, and even the tolerant Christians' response to Serrano's image of the crucifix immersed in urine, are irrelevant to the issue of whether a Western newspaper should represent images of the prophet Muhammad. Virtually all Muslims regard depictions of Muhammad as blasphemous, and that's what counts.

- Despite all the Western talk about freedom of the press, the press does *not* reproduce all images that become matters of news. For instance, news items about the sale of child pornography do not include images of the pornographic photos.

Inside Work: Exercises—Thinking about Images

1. Does the display of the Muhammad cartoons constitute an argument? If so, what is the conclusion, and what are the premises? If not, then what sort of statement, if any, does publishing these cartoons constitute?

2. Hugh Hewitt, an Evangelical Christian, offered a comparison to the cartoon of Muhammad wearing a bomblike turban. Suppose, he asked, an abortion clinic were bombed by someone claiming to be an Evangelical Christian. Would newspapers publish "a cartoon of Christ's crown of thorns transformed into sticks of TNT"? Do you think they would? If you were the editor of a newspaper, would you? Why, or why not?

3. One American newspaper, the *Boston Phoenix,* didn't publish any of the cartoons "out of fear of retaliation from the international brotherhood of radical and bloodthirsty Islamists who seek to impose their will on those who do not believe as they do....We could not in good conscience place the men and women who work at the *Phoenix* and its related companies in physical jeopardy." Evaluate this position.

4. A week after the 2015 attack on *Charlie Hebdo*, and in response to media hesitancy to re-publish the offending images of Muhammad, the Index on Censorship and several other journalistic organizations called for all newspapers to publish them simultaneously and globally on January 8, 2015. "This unspeakable act of violence has challenged and assailed the entire press," said Lucie Morillon of Reporters Without Borders. "Journalism as a whole is in mourning. In the name of all those who have fallen in the defence of these fundamental values, we must continue *Charlie Hebdo*'s fight for the right to freedom of information." Evaluate this position.

Writing about a Political Cartoon

Most editorial pages print political cartoons as well as editorials. Like the writers of editorials, cartoonists seek to persuade, but they rarely use words to *argue* a point. True, they may use a few words in speech balloons or in captions, but generally the drawing does most of the work. Because their aim usually is to convince the viewer that some person's action or proposal is ridiculous, cartoonists almost always **caricature** their subjects:

- They exaggerate the subject's distinctive features to the point at which...

- ...the subject becomes grotesque and ridiculous—absurd, laughable, contemptible.

We agree that it's unfair to suggest that because, say, the politician who proposes such-and-such is short, fat, and bald, his proposal is ridiculous; but that's the way cartoonists work. Further, cartoonists are concerned with producing a striking image, not with exploring an issue, so they almost always oversimplify, implying that there really is no other sane view.

In the course of saying that (1) the figures in a cartoon are ridiculous and *therefore* their ideas are contemptible, and (2) there is only one side to the issue, cartoonists often use **symbolism**. Here's a list of common symbols:

- symbolic figures (e.g., the U.S. government as Uncle Sam)

- animals (e.g., the Democratic Party as donkey and the Republican Party as elephant)

- buildings (e.g., the White House as representing the nation's president)

- things (e.g., a bag with a dollar sign on it as representing a bribe)

For anyone brought up in U.S. culture, these symbols (like the human figures they represent) are obvious, and cartoonists assume that viewers will instantly recognize the symbols and figures, will get the joke, and will see the absurdity of whatever issue the cartoonist is seeking to demolish.

In writing about the argument presented in a cartoon, normally you will discuss the ways in which the cartoon makes its point. Caricature usually implies, "This is ridiculous, as you can plainly see by the absurdity of the figures depicted" or "What *X*'s proposal adds up to, despite its apparent complexity, is nothing more than...." As we have said, this sort of persuasion, chiefly by ridicule, probably is unfair: An unattractive person certainly can offer a thoughtful political proposal, and almost always the issue is more complicated than the cartoonist indicates. But cartoons work largely by ridicule and the omission of counterarguments, and we shouldn't reject the possibility that the cartoonist has indeed highlighted the absurdity of the issue.

Walt Handelsman

✓   A Checklist for Evaluating an Analysis of Political Cartoons

☐ Is there a lead-in?

☐ Is there a brief but accurate description of the drawing?

☐ Is the source of the cartoon cited (perhaps with a comment by the cartoonist)?

☐ Is there a brief report of the event or issue that the cartoon is targeting, as well as an explanation of all the symbols?

☐ Is there a statement of the cartoonist's claim (thesis)?

☐ Is there an analysis of the evidence, if any, that the image offers in support of the claim?

☐ Is there an analysis of the ways in which the drawing's content and style help to convey the message?

☐ Is there adequate evaluation of the drawing's effectiveness?

☐ Is there adequate evaluation of the effectiveness of the text (caption or speech balloons) and of the fairness of the cartoon?

Your essay will likely include an *evaluation* of the cartoon. Indeed, the *thesis* underlying your analytic/argumentative essay may be that the cartoon is effective (persuasive) for such-and-such reasons but unfair for such-and-such other reasons.

In analyzing the cartoon—in determining the cartoonist's attitude—consider the following elements:

- the relative size of the figures in the image
- the quality of the lines (e.g., thin and spidery, or thick and seemingly aggressive)
- the amount of empty space in comparison with the amount of heavily inked space (a drawing with lots of inky areas conveys a more oppressive tone than a drawing that's largely open)
- the degree to which text is important, as well as its content and tone (is it witty, heavy-handed, or something else?)

Caution: If your instructor lets you choose a cartoon, be sure to select one with sufficient complexity to make the exercise worthwhile. (See also Thinking Critically: Analysis of a Political Cartoon.)

Let's look at an example.

Jackson Smith—Student Essay

Jackson Smith wrote this essay in a composition course at Tufts University.

Pledging Nothing?

Gary Markstein's cartoon about the Pledge of Allegiance is one of dozens that can be retrieved by a search engine. It happens that every one of the cartoons that I retrieved mocked the courts for ruling that schools cannot require students to recite the Pledge of Allegiance in its present form, which includes the words "under God." I personally object to these words, so the cartoons certainly do not speak for me, but I'll try as impartially as possible to analyze the strength of Markstein's cartoon.

Markstein shows us, in the cartoon, four schoolchildren reciting the Pledge. Coming out of all four mouths is a speech balloon with the words, "One nation under nothing in particular." The children are facing a furled American flag, and to the right of the flag is a middle-aged female teacher, whose speech balloon is in the form of a cloud, indicating that she is *thinking* rather than saying the words, "God help us."

Certainly the image grabs us: little kids lined up reciting the Pledge of Allegiance, an American flag, a maternal-looking teacher, and, in fact, if one examines the cartoon closely, one sees an apple on the teacher's desk. It's almost a Norman Rockwell scene, except, of course, it is a cartoon, so the figures are all a bit grotesque—but, still, they are nice folks. What is *not* nice, Markstein says, is what these kids must recite, "One nation under nothing in particular." In fact, the cartoon is far from telling the truth. Children who recite the Pledge without the words "under God" will still be saying that they are pledging allegiance to something quite specific—the United States:

I pledge allegiance to the flag of the United States of America, and to the Republic for which it stands: one nation indivisible, with Liberty and Justice for all.

That's really quite a lot, very far from Markstein's "under nothing in particular." But no one, I suppose, expects fairness in a political cartoon—and of course this cartoon *is* political, because the issue of the Pledge has become a political football, with liberals on the whole wanting the words "under God" removed and conservatives on the whole wanting the words retained.

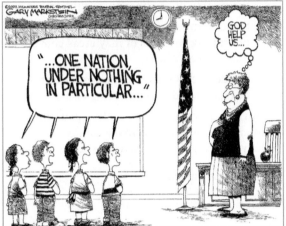

Gary Markstein

Let's now look at some of the subtleties of the cartoon. First, although, as I have said, cartoons present grotesque caricatures, the figures here are all affectionately presented. None of these figures is menacing. The teacher, with her spectacles and her rather dumpy figure, is clearly a benevolent figure, someone who in the eyes of the cartoonist rightly is disturbed about the fate of these little kids who are not allowed to say the words "under God." (Nothing, of course, prevents the children from speaking about God when they are not in the classroom. Those who believe in God can say grace at mealtime, can go to Sunday School, can go to church regularly, can pray before they go to bed, etc.) Markstein suggests that the absence of these words makes the entire Pledge meaningless ("under nothing in particular"), and in a master stroke he has conveyed this idea of impoverishment by showing a tightly furled flag, a flag that is presented as minimally as possible. After all, the flag could have been shown more fully, perhaps hanging from a pole that extended from a wall into the classroom, or the flag could have been displayed extended against a wall. Instead we get the narrowest of flags, something that is not much more than a furled umbrella, identifiable as the American flag by its stripes and a few stars in the upper third. Markstein thus cleverly suggests that with the loss of the words "under God," the flag itself is reduced to almost nothing.

Fair? No. Effective? Yes, and that's the job of a cartoonist. Readers probably give cartoons no more than three or four seconds, and Markstein has made the most of those few seconds. The reader gets his point, and if the reader already holds this view, he or she probably says, "Hey, here's a great cartoon." I don't hold that view, but I am willing to grant that it is a pretty good cartoon, effectively making a point that I think is wrong-headed.

5

Thinking Critically: Analysis of a Political Cartoon

Look at the cartoon on page 142. For each Type of Analysis section in the chart below, provide your own answer based on the cartoon. (Sample answers appear in the third column.)

Type of Analysis	Questions to Ask	Sample Answer	Your Answer
Context	*Who is the artist? Where and when was the cartoon published?*	"This cartoon by Walt Handelsman was originally published in *Newsday* on September 12, 2009. Handelsman, a Pulitzer Prize–winning cartoonist, drew this cartoon in response to recent breaches of political decorum."	
Description	*What does the cartoon look like?*	"It depicts a group of Washington, D.C., tourists being driven past what the guide calls 'The Museum of Modern American Political Discourse,' a building in the shape of a giant toilet."	
Analysis	*How does the cartoon make its point? Is it effective?*	"The toilet as a symbol of the level of political discussion dominates the cartoon, effectively driving home the point that Americans are watching our leaders sink to new lows as they debate the future of our nation. By drawing the toilet on a scale similar to that of familiar monuments in Washington, Handelsman may be pointing out that today's politicians, rather than being remembered for great achievements like those of George Washington or Abraham Lincoln, will instead be remembered for their rudeness and aggression."	

Visuals as Aids to Clarity: Maps, Graphs, and Pie Charts

Maps were part of the argument in the debate over drilling in the Arctic National Wildlife Refuge.

- Advocates of drilling argued that it would take place only in a tiny area. Their map showed Alaska, with an indication (in gray) of the much smaller part of Alaska that was the Refuge, and a further indication (cross-hatched) of what the advocates emphasized was a minuscule part of the Refuge.

- Opponents showed maps indicating the path of migrating caribou and the roads that would have to be constructed across the Refuge to get to the area where the drilling would take place.

Graphs, tables, and pie charts usually present quantitative data in visual form, helping writers to clarify dry statistical assertions. For instance, a line graph may illustrate how many immigrants came to the United States in each decade of the last century.

A bar graph (with bars running either horizontally or vertically) offers similar information. In the Coming to America graph, we can see at a glance that, say, the second bar on the lower left is almost double the length of the first, indicating that the number of immigrants almost doubled between 1850 and 1860.

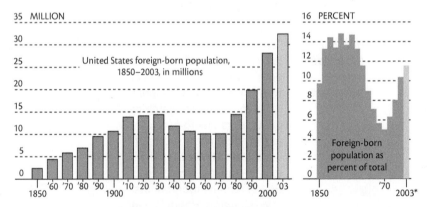

COMING TO AMERICA...

Both the percentage and number of foreign-born people in the United States dropped during much of the twentieth century, but after 1970, the tide was turning again.

A pie chart is a circle divided into wedges so that we can see, literally, how a whole comprises its parts. We can see, for instance, on page 147, that of an entire pie representing the regions of foreign-born U.S. immigrants, 36 percent were born in Central America and Mexico, 26 percent in Asia, 14 percent in Europe, and so on.

Because maps, charts, and graphs offer empirical data to support arguments, they communicate a high degree of reliability and tend to be convincing. "Numbers don't lie," it is sometimes said, and to some extent this is true. It's difficult to spin a fact like 1 + 1 = 2. However, as Charles Seife notes in his book, *Proofiness*, numbers are cold facts, but the measurements that numbers actually chart aren't always so clear or free from bias and manipulation. Consider two examples of advertising claims that Seife cites—one for a L'Oréal mascara offering "twelve times more impact," and another for a new and improved Vaseline product that "delivers 70% more moisture in every drop." Such measurements *sound* good but remain relatively meaningless. (How was eyelash "impact" measured? What is a percentage value of moisture?)

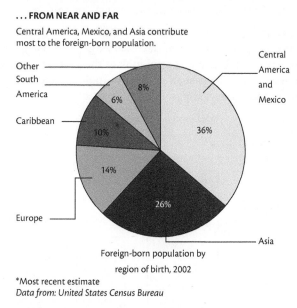

... FROM NEAR AND FAR

Central America, Mexico, and Asia contribute most to the foreign-born population.

Foreign-born population by region of birth, 2002

*Most recent estimate
Data from: United States Census Bureau*

Another way in which data can be relatively meaningless is by addressing only part of the question at stake. In 2013, a Mayo Clinic study found that drinking coffee regularly lowered participants' risk of the liver disease known as primary sclerosing cholangitis (PSC). But PSC is already listed as a "rare disease" by the Centers for Disease Control and Prevention, affecting fewer than 1 in 2,000 people. So even if drinking coffee lowered the risk of PSC by 25 percent, a person's chances would improve only slightly from .0005 percent chance to .0004 percent chance—hardly a change at all, and hardly a rationale for drinking more coffee. Yet, statistical information showing a 25 percent reduction in PSC sounds significant, even more so when provided under a headline proclaiming "Drinking coffee helps prevent liver disease."

Consider other uses of numbers that Seife shows in his book to constitute "proofiness" (his title and word to describe the misuse of numbers as evidence):

- In 2006, George W. Bush declared No Child Left Behind a success in his State of the Union Address: "[B]ecause we acted," he said, "students are performing better in reading and math." (True, fourth to eighth graders showed improved scores, but other grade levels declined. In addition, fourth- to eighth-grade reading and math scores had been improving at an unchanged rate both before and after the NCLB legislation.)

• In 2000, the *New York Times* reported "Researchers Link Bad Debt to Bad Health" (the "dark side of the economic boom"). The researchers claimed that debt causes more illness, but in doing so they committed the correlation-causation fallacy: Just because two phenomena are correlated does not mean they are causally related. (Example: More people wear shorts in the summer and more people eat ice cream in the summer than during other seasons, but wearing shorts does not *cause* higher ice cream consumption.)

Finally, consider the following graph showing that eating Quaker Oats decreases cholesterol levels after just four weeks of daily servings. The bar graph suggests that cholesterol levels will plummet. But a careful look at the graph reveals that the vertical axis doesn't begin at zero. In this case, a relatively small change has been (mis)represented as much bigger than it actually is.

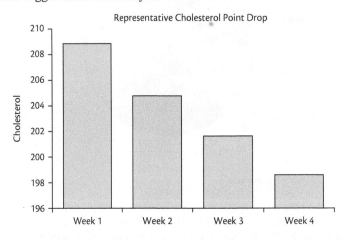

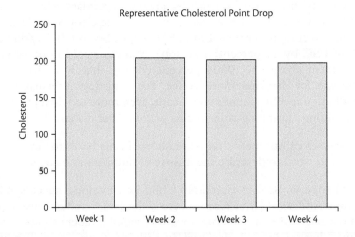

A more accurate representation of cholesterol levels after four weeks of eating Quaker Oats, using a graph that starts at zero, would look more like the second graph—showing essentially unchanged levels.

✓ A Checklist for Charts and Graphs

- ☐ Is the source authoritative?

- ☐ Is the source cited?

- ☐ Will the chart or graph be intelligible to the intended audience?

- ☐ Is the caption, if any, clear and helpful?

Following is another example showing unemployment rates during the Obama presidency. Note that here, too, the vertical axis doesn't start at zero, making the "rise" appear more dramatic than it actually was in reality.

Using Visuals in Your Own Paper

Every paper uses some degree of visual persuasion, merely in its appearance. Consider these elements of a paper's "look": title page; margins (ample, but not so wide that they indicate the writer's inability to produce a paper of the assigned length); double-spacing for the reader's convenience; headings and subheadings that indicate the progression of the argument; paragraphing; and so on. But you may also want to use visuals such as pictures, graphs, or pie charts. Keep a few guidelines in mind as you work with visuals, "writing" them into your own argument with as much care as you would read them in others' arguments:

- Consider your audience's needs and attitudes, and select the type of visuals—graphs, drawings, photographs—likely to be most persuasive to that audience.

- Consider the effect of color, composition, and placement within your document. Because images are most effective when they appear near the text that they supplement, do not group all images at the end of the paper.

In this graph, McDonald's $41 billion in sales are shown to be about 3.5 times higher than the revenues of its next closest competitor, Burger King (at $11.3 billion), but the McDonald's logo graphic is about 13 times larger than Burger King's.

Remember especially that images are almost never self-supporting or self-explanatory. They may be evidence for your argument (e.g., Ut's photograph of napalm victims is *very* compelling evidence of suffering), but they aren't arguments themselves.

- Be sure to explain each visual that you use, integrating it into the verbal text that provides the logic and principal support behind your thesis.

- Be sure to cite the source of any visual that you paste into your argument.

Be alert to common ways in which graphs can be misleading:

- Vertical axis doesn't start at zero or skips numbers.

- Scale is given in very small units to make changes look big.

- Pie charts don't accurately divide on scale with percentages shown.

- Oversized graphics don't match the numbers they represent.

Chapter 5

Writing an Analysis of an Argument

This is what we can all do to nourish and strengthen one another: listen to one another very hard, ask questions, too, send one another away to work again, and laugh in all the right places.

—Nancy Mairs

I don't wait for moods. You accomplish nothing if you do that. Your mind must know it has got to get down to work.

—Pearl S. Buck

Fear not those who argue but those who dodge.

—Marie von Ebner-Eschenbach

Analyzing an Argument

Examining the Author's Thesis

Most of your writing in other courses will require you to write an analysis of someone else's writing. In a course in political science you may have to analyze, say, an essay first published in *Foreign Affairs,* perhaps reprinted in your textbook, that argues against raising tariff barriers to foreign trade. Or a course in sociology may require you to analyze a report on the correlation between fatal accidents and drunk drivers under the age of twenty-one. Much of your writing, in short, will set forth reasoned responses to your reading as preparation for making an argument of your own.

Obviously, you must understand an essay before you can analyze it thoughtfully. You must read it several times—not just skim it—and (the hard part) you must think critically about it. Again, you'll find that your thinking is stimulated if you take notes and if you ask yourself questions about the material. Are there any Web sites or organizations dedicated to the material you are analyzing? If there are, visit some to see what others are saying about the material you are reviewing. Notes will help you to keep

Chapter 5, "Writing an Analysis of an Argument," from *From Critical Thinking to Argument: A Portable Guide,* by Sylvan Barnet, Hugo Bedau, and John O'Hara, pp. 173–192 (Chapter 5). Copyright © 2017 by Bedford/St. Martin's.

track of the writer's thoughts and also of your own responses to the writer's thesis. The writer probably *does* have a thesis, a claim, a point, and if so, you must try to locate it. Perhaps the thesis is explicitly stated in the title or in a sentence or two near the beginning of the essay or in a concluding paragraph, but perhaps you will have to infer it from the essay as a whole.

Notice that we said the writer *probably* has a thesis. Much of what you read will indeed be primarily an argument; the writer explicitly or implicitly is trying to support some thesis and to convince readers to agree with it. But some of what you read will be relatively neutral, with the argument just faintly discernible—or even with no argument at all. A work may, for instance, chiefly be a report: Here are the data, or here is what *X*, *Y*, and *Z* said; make of it what you will. A report might simply state how various ethnic groups voted in an election. In a report of this sort, of course, the writer hopes to persuade readers that the facts are correct, but no thesis is advanced—at least not explicitly or perhaps even consciously; the writer is not evidently arguing a point and trying to change readers' minds. Such a document differs greatly from an essay by a political analyst who presents similar findings to persuade a candidate to sacrifice the votes of one particular ethnic bloc and thereby get more votes from other blocs.

Examining the Author's Purpose

While reading an argument, try to form a clear idea of the author's **purpose**. Judging from the essay or the book, was the purpose to persuade, or was it to report? An analysis of a pure report (a work apparently without a thesis or argumentative angle) on ethnic voting will deal chiefly with the accuracy of the report. It will, for example, consider whether the sample poll was representative.

Much material that poses as a report really has a thesis built into it, consciously or unconsciously. The best evidence that the prose you are reading is argumentative is the presence of two kinds of key terms: transitions that imply the drawing of a conclusion (such as *therefore, because, for the reason that,* and *consequently*) and verbs that imply proof (such as *confirms, verifies, accounts for, implies, proves, disproves, is [in]consistent with, refutes,* and *it follows that*). Keep your eye out for such terms, and scrutinize their precise role whenever they appear. If the essay does not advance a thesis, think of one that it might support or some conventional belief that it might undermine. (See also Thinking Critically: Drawing Conclusions and Implying Proof on page 161.)

Examining the Author's Methods

If the essay advances a thesis, you will want to analyze the strategies or methods of argument that allegedly support the thesis.

- Does the writer quote authorities? Are these authorities competent in this field? Does the writer consider equally competent authorities who take a different view?

- Does the writer use statistics? If so, who compiled them, and are they appropriate to the point being argued? Can they be interpreted differently?

- Does the writer build the argument by using examples or analogies? Are they satisfactory?

- Are the writer's assumptions acceptable?

- Does the writer consider all relevant factors? Has he or she omitted some points that you think should be discussed? For instance, should the author recognize certain opposing positions and perhaps concede something to them?

- Does the writer seek to persuade by means of ridicule? If so, is the ridicule fair? Is it supported also by rational argument?

- Is the argument aimed at a particular audience?

In writing your analysis, you will want to tell readers something about the author's purpose and something about the author's methods. It is usually a good idea at the start of your analysis—if not in the first paragraph, then in the second or third—to let the reader know the purpose (and thesis, if there is one) of the work you are analyzing and then to summarize the work briefly.

Next, you will probably find it useful (readers will certainly find it helpful) to write out *your* thesis (your evaluation or judgment). You might say, for instance, that the essay is impressive but not conclusive, or is undermined by convincing contrary evidence, or relies too much on unsupported generalizations, or is wholly admirable. Remember, because your paper is itself an argument, it needs its own thesis.

And then, of course, comes the job of setting forth your analysis and the support for your thesis. There is no one way of going about this work. If, say, the author whose work you're analyzing gives four arguments (e.g., an appeal to common sense, the testimony of authorities, the evidence of comparisons, and an appeal to self-interest), you might want to do one of the following:

- Take up these four arguments in sequence.

- Discuss the simplest of the four, and then go on to the more difficult ones.

- Discuss the author's two arguments that you think are sound, and then turn to the two that you think are not sound (or perhaps the reverse).

- Apply one of these approaches, and then clinch your case by constructing a fifth argument that is absent from the work under scrutiny but is, in your view, highly important.

In short, the organization of your analysis may or may not follow the organization of the work you are analyzing.

Examining the Author's Persona

You will probably also want to analyze something a bit more elusive than the author's explicit arguments: the author's self-presentation. Does the author seek to persuade readers partly by presenting himself or herself as conscientious, friendly, self-effacing, authoritative, tentative, or in some other light? Most writers do two things:

- They present evidence.

- They present themselves (or, more precisely, they present the image of themselves that they wish us to behold).

In some persuasive writing this **persona** or **voice** or presentation of the self may be no less important than the presentation of evidence. In other cases, the persona may not much matter, but our point is that you should spend a little time looking at the author's self-presentation to consider if it's significant.

In establishing a persona, writers adopt various rhetorical strategies, ranging from the use of characteristic words to the use of a particular form of organization. For instance:

- The writer who speaks of an opponent's "gimmicks" instead of "strategy" probably is trying to downgrade the opponent and also to convey the self-image of a streetwise person.

- On a larger scale, consider the way in which evidence is presented and the kind of evidence that's offered. One writer may first bombard the reader with facts and then spend relatively little time drawing conclusions. Another may rely chiefly on generalizations, waiting until the end of the essay to bring the thesis home with a few details. Another may begin with a few facts and spend most of the space reflecting on these. One writer may seem professorial or pedantic, offering examples of an academic sort; another, whose examples are drawn from ordinary life, may seem like a regular guy.

All such devices deserve comment in your analysis.

The writer's persona, then, may color the thesis and help it develop in a distinctive way. If we accept the thesis, it is partly because the writer has won our goodwill by persuading us of his or her good character (*ethos*, in Aristotle's terms). Later we talk more about the appeal to the speaker's character—the so-called *ethical appeal*, but here we may say that good writers present themselves not as wise-guys, bullies, or pompous asses but as decent people whom the reader would like to invite to dinner.

The author of an essay may, for example, seem fair-minded and open-minded, treating the opposition with great courtesy and expressing interest in hearing other views. Such a tactic is itself a persuasive device. Another author may appear to rely on hard evidence such as statistics. This reliance on seemingly objective truths is itself a way of seeking to persuade—a rational way, to be sure, but a mode of persuasion nonetheless.

Especially in analyzing a work in which the author's persona and ideas are blended, you will want to spend some time commenting on the persona. Whether you discuss it near the beginning of your analysis or near the end will depend on how you want to construct your essay, and this decision will partly depend on the work you are analyzing. For example, if the author's persona is kept in the background and is thus relatively invisible, you may want to make that point fairly early to get it out of the way and then concentrate on more interesting matters. If, however, the persona is interesting—and perhaps seductive, whether because it seems so scrupulously objective or so engagingly subjective—you may want to hint at this quality early in your essay and then develop the point while you consider the arguments.

In short, the author's self-presentation usually matters. Recognize its effect, whether positive or negative.

Examining Persona and Intended Audience

A key element in understanding an argument lies in thinking about the intended audience—how the author perceives the audience and what strategies the author uses to connect to it. We have already said something about the creation of the author's persona. An author with a loyal following is, almost by definition, someone who in earlier writings has presented an engaging persona, a persona with a trustworthy *ethos*. A trusted author can sometimes cut corners and can perhaps adopt a colloquial tone that would be unacceptable in the writing of an unknown author.

Authors who want to win the assent of their audiences need to think about how they present information and how they present *themselves*. Consider how you prefer people to talk to you. What sorts of language do you find engaging? Much of course depends on the circumstances, notably the topic, the audience, and the place. A joke may be useful in an argument about whether the government should regulate junk food, but almost surely a joke will be inappropriate—will backfire, will alienate the audience—

in an argument about abortion. The *way* an author addresses the reader (through an invented persona) can have a significant impact on the reader's perception of the author, which is to say perception of the author's *views*, the author's *argument*. A slip in tone or an error of fact, however small, may be enough for the audience to dismiss the author's argument. Understanding audience means thinking about all of the possible audiences who may come into contact with your writing or your message, and thinking about the consequences of what you write and where it is published.

You may recall a tweet by LeBron James, who formerly played basketball for the Cleveland Cavaliers but left to play for the Miami Heat. After James left the Cavaliers (and his home state of Ohio), the Los Angeles Lakers beat the Cavaliers by fifty-five points, and James tweeted: "Crazy. Karma is a b****. Gets you every time. It's not good to wish bad on anybody. God sees everything!" Cleveland fans not surprisingly

LeBron James, considering his audience while he was with the Miami Heat.

Layne Murdoch/Getty Images

perceived his tweet as a slap in the face. The broader audience, too, outside of Cleveland, perceived it as inappropriate. Though he has since returned to Cleveland and been largely forgiven by fans, LeBron James clearly did not think about his audience(s). To put it in rhetorical terms, LeBron James vastly diminished his *ethos*. Doubtless he wishes he could retract the tweet, but as the ancient Roman poet Horace said, *"Nescit vox missa reverti"* ("The word once spoken can never be recalled"), or, in plain proverbial English, "Think twice before you speak."

Consider Facebook status updates. Have you ever posted a status update and wished you could take it back only to find out it was too late? People you did not want to see it saw it before you could remove it. Have you ever tweeted or even texted something you wished you hadn't? When reading and writing more formal essays, it is equally important to think about who wrote what you are reading, and who will read what you are writing.

✓   A Checklist for Analyzing an Author's Intended Audience

☐   Where did the piece appear? Who published it? Why, in your view, might someone have found it worth publishing?

☐   In what technological format does this piece appear? Print journal? Online magazine? Blog? What does the technological format say about the piece or the author?

☐   Is the writing relatively informal—for instance, a tweet or a Facebook status update? Who is the intended audience? Are there other audiences who may also have an interest but whom the author has failed to consider? Why is this medium good or bad for the message?

☐   If *you* are the intended audience, what shared values do you have with the author?

☐   What strategies does the writer use to create a connection with the audience?

Summary

In the last few pages we have tried to persuade you that, in writing an analysis of a reading, you must do the following:

• Read and reread thoughtfully. Composing and keeping notes will help you to think about what you are reading.

• Be aware of the purpose of the material to which you are responding.

We have also tried to point out these facts:

- Most of the nonliterary material that you will read is designed to argue, to report, or to do both.

- Most of this material also presents the writer's personality, or voice, and this voice usually merits attention in an analysis. An essay on, say, nuclear war, in a journal devoted to political science, may include a voice that moves from an objective tone to a mildly ironic tone to a hortatory tone, and this voice is worth commenting on.

Possibly all this explanation is obvious. There is yet another point, equally obvious but often neglected by students who begin by writing an analysis and end up by writing only a summary, a shortened version of the work they have read: Although your essay is an analysis of someone else's writing, and you may have to include a summary of the work you are writing about, your essay is *your* essay, your analysis, not a mere summary. The thesis, the organization, and the tone are yours.

- Your thesis, for example, may be that although the author is convinced she has presented a strong case, her case is far from proved because...

- Your organization may be deeply indebted to the work you are analyzing, but it need not be. The author may have begun with specific examples and then gone on to make generalizations and to draw conclusions, but you may begin with the conclusions.

- Your tone, similarly, may resemble your subject's (let's say the voice is courteous academic), but it will nevertheless have its own ring, its own tone of, say, urgency, caution, or coolness.

Most of the essays that we have included thus far are more or less in an academic style, and indeed several are by students and by professors. But argumentative writing is not limited to academicians—if it were, your college would not be requiring you to take a course in the subject. The following essay, in a breezy style, comes from a columnist who writes for the *New York Times*.

An Argument, Its Elements, and a Student's Analysis of the Argument

Nicholas D. Kristof

Nicholas D. Kristof (b. 1959), a two-time Pulitzer Prize winner, grew up on a farm in Oregon. After graduating from Harvard, he was awarded a Rhodes scholarship to Oxford, where he studied law. In 1984 he joined the *New York Times* as a correspondent, and since 2001 he has written as a columnist. The editorial that follows first appeared in the *New York Times* in 2005.

For Environmental Balance, Pick Up a Rifle

Here's a quick quiz: Which large American mammal kills the most humans each year?

It's not the bear, which kills about two people a year in North America. Nor is it the wolf, which in modern times hasn't killed anyone in this country. It's not the cougar, which kills one person every year or two.

Rather, it's the deer. Unchecked by predators, deer populations are exploding in a way that is profoundly unnatural and that is destroying the ecosystem in many parts of the country. In a wilderness, there might be ten deer per square mile; in parts of New Jersey, there are up to 200 per square mile.

One result is ticks and Lyme disease, but deer also kill people more directly. A study for the insurance industry estimated that deer kill about 150 people a year in car crashes nationwide and cause $1 billion in damage. Granted, deer aren't stalking us, and they come out worse in these collisions—but it's still true that in a typical year, an American is less likely to be killed by Osama bin Laden than by Bambi.

If the symbol of the environment's being out of whack in the 1960s was the Cuyahoga River in Cleveland catching fire, one such symbol today is deer congregating around what they think of as salad bars and what we think of as suburbs.   5

So what do we do? Let's bring back hunting.

Now, you've probably just spilled your coffee. These days, among the university-educated crowd in the cities, hunting is viewed as barbaric.

The upshot is that towns in New York and New Jersey are talking about using birth control to keep deer populations down. (Liberals presumably support free condoms, while conservatives back abstinence education.) Deer contraception hasn't been very successful, though.

Meanwhile, the same population bomb has spread to bears. A bear hunt has been scheduled for this week in New Jersey—prompting outrage from some animal rights groups (there's also talk of bear contraception: make love, not cubs).

As for deer, partly because hunting is perceived as brutal and vaguely psychopathic, towns are taking out contracts on deer through discreet private companies. Greenwich, Connecticut, budgeted $47,000 this year to pay a company to shoot eighty deer from raised platforms over four nights—as well as $8,000 for deer birth control.   10

Look, this is ridiculous.

We have an environmental imbalance caused in part by the decline of hunting. Humans first wiped out certain predators—like wolves and cougars—but then expanded their own role as predators to sustain a rough ecological balance. These days, though, hunters are on the decline.

According to "Families Afield: An Initiative for the Future of Hunting," a report by an alliance of shooting organizations, for every hundred hunters who die or stop hunting, only sixty-nine hunters take their place.

I was raised on *Bambi*—but also, as an Oregon farm boy, on venison and elk meat. But deer are not pets, and dead deer are as natural as live deer. To wring one's hands over them, perhaps after polishing off a hamburger, is soggy sentimentality.

What's the alternative to hunting? Is it preferable that deer die of disease and hun-   15
ger? Or, as the editor of *Adirondack Explorer* magazine suggested, do we introduce wolves into the burbs?

To their credit, many environmentalists agree that hunting can be green. The New Jersey Audubon Society this year advocated deer hunting as an ecological necessity.

There's another reason to encourage hunting: it connects people with the outdoors and creates a broader constituency for wilderness preservation. At a time when America's wilderness is being gobbled away for logging, mining, or oil drilling, that's a huge boon.

Granted, hunting isn't advisable in suburban backyards, and I don't expect many soccer moms to install gun racks in their minivans. But it's an abdication of environmental responsibility to eliminate other predators and then refuse to assume the job ourselves. In that case, the collisions with humans will simply get worse.

In October, for example, Wayne Goldsberry was sitting in a home in northwestern Arkansas when he heard glass breaking in the next room. It was a home invasion—by a buck.

Mr. Goldsberry, who is six feet one inch and weighs two hundred pounds, wrestled   20
with the intruder for forty minutes. Blood spattered the walls before he managed to break the buck's neck.

So it's time to reestablish a balance in the natural world—by accepting the idea that hunting is as natural as bird-watching.

✓ A Checklist for Analyzing a Text

Have I considered all of the following matters?

- ☐ Who is the author? What stake might he or she have in writing this piece?

- ☐ Is the piece aimed at a particular audience? A neutral audience? Persons who are already sympathetic to the author's point of view? A hostile audience? What evidence enables me to identify the target audience?

- ☐ What is the author's thesis (argument, main point, claim)?

☐   What assumptions does the author make? Do I share them? If not, why not?

☐   Does the author ever confuse facts with beliefs or opinions?

☐   What appeals does the author make? To reason (*logos*), for instance, with statistics, the testimony of authorities, and personal experience? To the emotions (*pathos*), for instance, by an appeal to "our better nature" or to widely shared values? To our sense that the speaker is trustworthy (*ethos*)?

☐   How convincing is the evidence? Why do I think so?

☐   Are significant objections and counterevidence adequately discussed?

☐   How is the text organized, and is the organization effective? Are the title, the opening paragraphs, and the concluding paragraphs effective? In what ways?

☐   If visual materials such as graphs, pie charts, or pictures are used, how persuasive are they? Do they make a logical appeal? (Charts and graphs presumably make a logical appeal.) Do they make an emotional appeal? An ethical appeal?

☐   What is the author's tone? Is it appropriate?

☐   To what extent has the author convinced me? Why?

Discussion Questions: Topics for Critical Thinking and Writing

1. What is Nicholas Kristof's chief thesis? (State it in one sentence.)

2. Does Kristof make any assumptions—tacit or explicit—with which you disagree? With which you agree? Write them down.

3. Is the slightly humorous tone of Kristof's essay inappropriate for a discussion of deliberately killing wild animals? Why, or why not?

4. If you are familiar with *Bambi,* does the story make any *argument* against killing deer, or does the story appeal only to our emotions?

5. Do you agree that "hunting is as natural as bird-watching" (para. 21)? In any case, do you think that an appeal to what is "natural" is a good argument for expanding the use of hunting?

6. To whom is Kristof talking? How do you know?

Thinking Critically: Drawing Conclusions and Implying Proof

Look at Nicholas D. Kristof's essay on page 157. Provide two examples of sentences from Kristof's essay that use each type of conclusion or proof.

Indicator of Conclusion or Proof	Examples	Two Examples from Kristof's Essay
Transitions that imply the drawing of a conclusion	*therefore, because, for the reason that, consequently*	
Verbs that imply proof	*confirms, verifies, accounts for, implies, proves, disproves, is (in)consistent with, refutes, it follows that*	

The Essay Analyzed

OK, time's up. Let's examine Kristof's essay with an eye to identifying those elements we mentioned earlier in this chapter (pp. 151–56) that deserve notice when examining *any* argument: the author's *thesis, purpose, methods, persona,* and *audience.* And while we're at it, let's also notice some other features of Kristof's essay that will help us appreciate its effects and evaluate it. We will thus be in a good position to write an evaluation or an argument that confirms, extends, or even rebuts Kristof's argument.

But first, a caution: Kristof's essay appeared in a newspaper where paragraphs are customarily very short, partly to allow for easy reading and partly because the columns are narrow and even short paragraphs may extend for an inch or two. If his essay were to appear in a book, doubtless the author would run many of the paragraphs together, making longer units. In analyzing a work, think about where it originally appeared. A blog, a print journal, an online magazine? Does the format in some measure influence the piece?

Title   By combining "Environmental Balance" with "Rifle"—terms that don't seem to go together—Kristof starts off with a bang. He gives a hint of his *topic* (something about the environment) and of his thesis (some sort of way of introducing ecological balance). He also conveys something of his persona by introducing a rifle into the environment. He is, the title suggests, a no-nonsense, hard-hitting guy.

Opening Paragraphs   Kristof immediately grabs hold of us ("Here's a quick quiz") and asks a simple question, but one that we probably have not thought much about: "Which large American mammal kills the most humans each year?" In paragraph 2 he tells us it is *not* the bear—the answer most readers probably come up with—nor is it the cougar. Not until paragraph 3 does Kristof give us the answer, the deer. But remember, Kristof is writing in a newspaper, where paragraphs customarily are very short. It takes us only a few seconds to get to the third paragraph and the answer.

Thesis   What is the basic thesis Kristof is arguing? Somewhat unusually, Kristof does *not* announce it in its full form until paragraph 6 ("Let's bring back hunting"), but, again, his paragraphs are very short, and if the essay were published in a book, Kristof's first two paragraphs probably would be combined, as would the third and fourth.

Purpose   Kristof's purpose is clear: He wants to *persuade* readers to adopt his view. This amounts to trying to persuade us that his thesis (stated above) is *true*. Kristof, however, does not show that his essay is argumentative or persuasive by using many of the key terms that normally mark argumentative prose. He doesn't call anything his *conclusion*, none of his statements is labeled *my premises*, and he doesn't connect clauses or sentences with *therefore* or *because*. Almost the only traces of the language of argument are "Granted" (para. 18) and "So" (i.e., *therefore*) in his final paragraph.

Despite the lack of argumentative language, the argumentative nature of his essay is clear. He has a thesis—one that will strike many readers as highly unusual—and he wants readers to accept it, so he must go on to *support* it; accordingly, after his introductory paragraphs, in which he calls attention to a problem and offers a solution (his thesis), he must offer evidence. And that is what much of the rest of the essay seeks to do.

Methods   Although Kristof will have to offer evidence, he begins by recognizing the folks on the other side, "the university-educated crowd in the cities, [for whom] hunting is viewed as barbaric" (para. 7). He goes on to spoof this "crowd" when, speaking of methods of keeping the deer population down, he says in paragraph 8, "Liberals presumably support free condoms, while conservatives back abstinence education." Ordinarily, it is a bad idea to make fun of persons who hold views other than your own—after all, they just may be on to something, they just might know something you don't know, and, in any case, impartial readers rarely want to align themselves with someone who mocks others. In the essay we are looking at, however, Kristof gets away with this smart-guy tone because he not only has loyal readers but also has written the entire essay in a highly informal or playful manner. Think again about paragraph 1, which begins "Here's a quick quiz." The informality is not only in the contraction (*Here's* versus *Here is*), but in the very idea of beginning by grabbing the readers and thrusting a quiz at them. The playfulness is evident throughout: For instance, immediately after Kristof announces his thesis, "Let's bring back hunting," he begins a new paragraph (7) with "Now, you've probably just spilled your coffee."

Kristof's methods of presenting evidence include providing *statistics* (paras. 3, 4, 10, and 13), giving *examples* (paras. 10, 19–20), and citing *authorities* (paras. 13 and 16).

Persona   Kristof presents himself as a confident, no-nonsense fellow, a persona that not many writers can get away with, but that probably is acceptable in a journalist who regularly writes a newspaper column. His readers know what to expect, and they read him with pleasure. But it would be inadvisable for an unknown writer to adopt this persona, unless perhaps he or she were writing for an audience that could be counted on to be friendly (in this instance, an audience of hunters). If this essay appeared in a hunting magazine, doubtless it would please and entertain its audience. It would not convert anybody, but conversion would not be its point if it appeared in a magazine read by hunters. In the *New York Times*, where the essay originally appeared, Kristof could count on a moderately sympathetic audience because he has a large number of faithful readers, but one can guess that many of these readers—chiefly city dwellers—read him for entertainment rather than for information about how they should actually behave.

By the way, when we speak of "faithful readers" we are in effect saying that the author has established good *ethos*, has convinced those readers that he or she is *worth* reading.

Closing Paragraphs   The first two of the last three paragraphs report an episode (the home invasion by a buck) that Kristof presumably thinks is pretty conclusive evidence. The final paragraph begins with "So," strongly implying a logical conclusion to the essay.

Let's now turn to a student's analysis of Kristof's essay and then to our own analysis of the student's analysis. (We should say that the analysis of Kristof's essay that you have just read is partly indebted to the student's essay that you are about to read.)

Swinton 1

Betsy Swinton

Professor Knowles

English 101B

March 12, 2016

Tracking Kristof

Nicholas D. Kristof's "For Environmental Balance, Pick Up a Rifle" is an engaging piece of writing, but whether it is convincing is something I am not sure about. And I am not sure about it for two reasons: (1) I don't know much about the deer problem, and that's my fault; (2) I don't know much about the deer problem, and that's Kristof's fault. The first point needs no explanation, but let me explain the second.

Kristof is making an argument, offering a thesis: Deer are causing destruction, and the best way to reduce the destruction is to hunt deer. For all that I know, he may be correct both in his comment about what deer are doing and also in his comment about what must be done about deer. My ignorance of the situation is regrettable, but I don't think that I am the only reader from Chicago who doesn't know much about the deer problems in New Jersey, Connecticut, and Arkansas, the states that Kristof specifically mentions in connection with the deer problem. He announces his thesis early enough, in his sixth paragraph, and he is entertaining throughout his essay, but does he make a convincing case? To ask "Does he make a convincing case?" is to ask "Does he offer adequate evidence?" and "Does he show that his solution is better than other possible solutions?"

To take the first question: In a short essay Kristof can hardly give overwhelming evidence, but he does convince me that there is a problem. The most convincing evidence he gives appears in paragraph 16, where he says that the New Jersey Audubon Society "advocated deer hunting as an ecological necessity." I don't really know anything about the New Jersey Audubon Society, but I suppose that they are people with a deep interest in nature and in conservation, and if even such a group advocates deer hunting, there must be something to this solution.

I am even willing to accept his argument that, in this nation of meat-eaters, "to wring one's hands over them [dead deer], perhaps after polishing off a hamburger, is soggy sentimentality" (para. 14). According to Kristof, the present alternative to hunting deer is that we leave the deer to "die of disease and hunger" (para. 15). But what I am not convinced of is that there is no way to reduce the deer population other than by hunting. I don't think Kristof adequately explains why some sort of birth control is inadequate. In his eighth paragraph he makes a joke about controlling the birth of deer ("Liberals presumably support free condoms, while conservatives back abstinence education"), and the joke is funny, but it isn't an argument, it's just a joke. Why can't food containing some sort of sterilizing medicine be put out for the starving deer, food that will nourish them and yet make them unreproductive? In short, I don't think he has fairly informed his readers of alternatives to his own positions, and because he fails to look at counterproposals, he weakens his own proposal.

Although Kristof occasionally uses a word or phrase that suggests argument, such as "Granted" (para. 18), "So" (final paragraph), and "There's another reason" (para. 17), he relies chiefly on forceful writing rather than on reasoning. And the second of his two reasons for hunting seems utterly unconvincing to me. His first, as we have seen, is that the deer population (and apparently the bear population) is out of control. His second (para. 17) is that hunting "connects people with the outdoors and creates a broader constituency for wilderness preservation." I am not a hunter and I have never been one. Perhaps that's my misfortune, but I don't think I am missing anything. And when I hear Kristof say, in his final sentence—the climactic place in his essay—that "hunting is as natural as bird-watching," I rub my eyes in

Swinton 3

disbelief. If he had me at least half-convinced by his statistics and his citation of the Audubon Society, he now loses me when he argues that hunting is "natural." One might as well say that war is natural, rape is natural, bribery is natural—all these terrible things occur, but we ought to deplore them and we ought to make every effort to see that they disappear.

In short, I think that Kristof has written an engaging essay, and he may well have an important idea, but I think that in his glib final paragraph, where he tells us that "hunting is as natural as bird-watching," he utterly loses the reader's confidence.

An Analysis of the Student's Analysis

Swinton's essay seems to us to be excellent, doubtless the product of a good deal of thoughtful revision. She does not cover every possible aspect of Kristof's essay—she concentrates on his reasoning and says very little about his style—but we think that given the limits of space (about 500 words), she does a good job. What makes this student's essay effective?

- The essay has a title ("Tracking Kristof") that is of at least a little interest; it picks up Kristof's point about hunting, and it gives a hint of what is to come.

- The author promptly identifies her subject (she names the writer and the title of his essay) early.

- Early in the essay she gives us a hint of where she will be going (in her first paragraph she tells us that Kristof's essay is "engaging... *but...*").

- She recognizes Kristof's audience at the start, and she suggests that he may not have given thought to this matter of the audience.

- She uses a few brief quotations, to give us a feel for Kristof's essay and to let us hear the evidence for itself, but she does not pad her essay with long quotations.

- She takes up all of Kristof's main points.

- She gives her essay a reasonable organization, letting us hear Kristof's thesis, letting us know the degree to which she accepts it, and finally letting us know her specific reservations about the essay.

- She concludes without the formality of "in conclusion"; "in short" nicely does the trick.

- Notice, finally, that she sticks closely to Kristof's essay. She does not go off on a tangent about the virtues of vegetarianism or the dreadful politics of the *New York Times*, the newspaper that published Kristof's essay. She was asked to analyze the essay, and she has done so.

✓   A Checklist for Writing an Analysis of an Argument

Have I asked myself the following questions?

☐   Early in my essay have I accurately stated the writer's thesis (claim) and summarized his or her supporting reasons? Have I explained to my reader any disagreement about definitions of important terms?

☐   Have I, again fairly early in my essay, indicated where I will be taking my reader (i.e., have I indicated my general response to the essay I am analyzing)?

☐   Have I called attention to the strengths, if any, and the weaknesses, if any, of the essay?

☐   Have I commented not only on the *logos* (logic, reasoning) but also on the *ethos* (character of the writer, as presented in the essay)? For instance, has the author convinced me that he or she is well informed and is a person of goodwill? Or, in contrast, does the writer seem to be chiefly concerned with ridiculing those who hold a different view?

☐   If there is an appeal to *pathos* (emotion, originally meaning "pity for suffering," but now interpreted more broadly to include appeals to patriotism, humor, or loyalty to family, for example), is it acceptable? If not, why not?

☐   Have I used occasional brief quotations to let my reader hear the author's tone and to ensure fairness and accuracy?

☐   Is my analysis effectively organized?

☐   Have I taken account of the author's audience(s)?

☐   Does my essay, perhaps in the concluding paragraphs, indicate my agreement or disagreement with the writer but also my view of the essay as a piece of argumentative writing?

☐   Is my tone appropriate?

Inside Work: Exercise

Take one of the essays not yet discussed in class or an essay assigned now by your instructor, and in an essay of 500 words analyze and evaluate it, guided by the checklists and examples we have provided.

Chapter 6

Developing an Argument of Your Own

The difficult part in an argument is not to defend one's opinion but to know what it is.

—André Maurois

Imagine that you enter a parlor. You come late. When you arrive, others have long preceded you, and they are engaged in a heated discussion, a discussion too heated for them to pause and tell you exactly what it is about. In fact, the discussion had already begun long before any of them got there, so that no one present is qualified to retrace for you all the steps that had gone before. You listen for a while, until you decide that you have caught the tenor of the argument; then you put in your oar. Someone answers; you answer him; another comes to your defense; another aligns himself against you, to either the embarrassment or gratification of your opponent, depending upon the quality of your ally's assistance. However, the discussion is interminable. The hour grows late, you must depart. And you do depart, with the discussion still vigorously in progress.

—Kenneth Burke

No greater misfortune could happen to anyone than that of developing a dislike for argument.

—Plato

Planning, Drafting, and Revising an Argument

First, hear the wisdom of Mark Twain: "When the Lord finished the world, He pronounced it good. That is what I said about my first work, too. But Time, I tell you, Time takes the confidence out of these incautious early opinions."

All of us, teachers and students, have our moments of confidence, but for the most part we know that it takes considerable effort to write clear, thoughtful, seemingly effortless prose. In a conversation we can cover ourselves with such expressions as

"Well, I don't know, but I sort of think…" and we can always revise our position ("Oh, well, I didn't mean it that way"), but once we have handed in the final version of our writing, we are helpless. We are (putting it strongly) naked to our enemies.

Getting Ideas: Argument as an Instrument of Inquiry

In Chapter 1 we quoted Robert Frost, "To learn to write is to learn to have ideas," and we offered suggestions about generating ideas, a process traditionally called **invention**. A moment ago we said that we often improve our ideas when explaining them to someone else. Partly, of course, we're responding to questions or objections raised by our companion in the conversation. But partly we're responding to ourselves: Almost as soon as we hear what we have to say, we may find that it won't do, and if we're lucky, we may find a better idea surfacing. One of the best ways of getting ideas is to talk things over.

The process of talking things over usually begins with the text that you're reading: Your notes, your summary, and your annotations are a kind of dialogue between you and the author. You are also having a dialogue when you talk with friends about your topic. You are trying out and developing ideas. You're arguing, but not chiefly to persuade; rather, you're using argument in order to find the truth. Finally, after reading, taking notes, and talking, you may feel that you have some clear ideas and need only put them into writing. So you take up a sheet of blank paper, but then a paralyzing thought suddenly strikes: "I have ideas but just can't put them into words." The blank white page (or screen) stares back at you and you just can't seem to begin.

All writers, even professional ones, are familiar with this experience. Good writers know that waiting for inspiration is usually not the best strategy. You may be waiting a long time. The best thing to do is begin. Recall some of what we said in Chapter 1: *Writing is a way of thinking.* It's a way of *getting and developing ideas. Argument* is an instrument of inquiry as well as persuasion. It is an important part of *critical thinking.* It helps us clarify what we think. One reason we have trouble writing is our fear of putting ourselves on record, but another reason is our fear that we have no ideas worth putting down. However, by writing notes—or even free associations—and by writing a draft, no matter how weak, we can begin to think our way toward good ideas.

Three Brainstorming Strategies: Freewriting, Listing, and Diagramming

If you are facing an issue, debate, or topic and don't know what to write, this is likely because you don't yet know what you think. If, after talking about the topic with yourself (via your reading notes) and others, you are still unclear on what you think, try one of these three strategies:

Freewriting

Write for five or six minutes, nonstop, without censoring what you produce. You may use what you write to improve your thinking. You may even dim your computer screen so you won't be tempted to look up and fiddle too soon with what you've just written.

Once you have spent the time writing out your ideas, you can use what you've written to look further into the subject at hand.

Freewriting should be totally free. If you have some initial ideas, a good freewrite might look like this. (As a topic, let's imagine the writer below is thinking about how children's toys are constructed for different genders. The student is reflecting on the release of the Nerf Rebelle, a type of toy gun made specifically for girls.)

> FREEWRITING: This year Nerf released a new toy made for girls, the Nerf Rebelle gun, an attempt the company made to offer toys for girls traditionally made for boys. This seems good—showing an effort toward equality between the sexes. Or is Nerf just trying to broaden its market and sell more toys (after all, boys are only half the population)? Or is it both? That could be my central question. But it is not like the gun makes no distinction between boys and girls. It is pink and purple and has feminine-looking designs on it. And with its "elle" ending the gun sounds small, cute, and girly. Does this toy represent true equality between the sexes, or does it just offer more in the way of feminine stereotypes? It shoots foam arrows, unlike the boys' version of the gun, which shoots bullets. This suggests Cupid, maybe—that is, the figure whose arrows inspire love—a stereotype that girls aren't saving the world but seeking love and marriage. Maybe it's also related to Katniss Everdeen from the *Hunger Games* movie. She carries a bow and arrow, too. Like a lot of female superheroes, Katniss is presented as both strong and sexy, powerful and vulnerable, masculine and feminine at the same time. What kind of messages does this send to young girls? Is it the same message suggested by the gun? Why do powerful women have to project traditional or stereotypical femininity at the same time? How does this work in other areas of life, like business and politics?

Notice that the writer here is jumping around, generating and exploring ideas while writing. Later she can return to the freewriting and begin organizing her ideas and observations. Notice that right in the middle of the freewriting she made a connection between the toy and the *Hunger Games* movie, and by extension to the larger culture in which forms of contemporary femininity can be found. This connection seems significant, and it may help the student to broaden her argument from a critique of the company's motives early on, to a more evidence-based piece about assumptions underlying certain trends in consumer and media culture. The point is that freewriting in this case led to new paths of inquiry and may have inspired further research into different kinds of toys and media.

Listing

Writing down keywords, just as you do when making a shopping list, is another way of generating ideas. When you make a shopping list, you write *ketchup,* and the act of writing it reminds you that you also need hamburger rolls—and *that* in turn reminds you that you also need tuna fish. Similarly, when preparing a list of ideas for a paper, just writing down one item will often generate another. Of course, when you look over the list, you'll probably drop some of these ideas—the dinner menu will change—but you'll be making progress. If you have a smartphone or tablet, use it to write down your thoughts. You can even e-mail these notes to yourself so you can access them later.

Here's an example of a student listing questions and making associations that could help him focus on a specific argument within a larger debate. The subject here is whether prostitution should be legalized.

LIST: Prostitutes—Law—How has the law traditionally policed sex?—What types of prostitutes exist?—What is prostitution?—Where is it already legal?—How does it work in places where it is legal?—Individual rights vs. public good?—Why shouldn't people be allowed to sell sex?—What are the "bad" effects of prostitution socially?—How many prostitutes are arrested every year?—Could prostitution be taxed?—Who suffers most from enforcement?—Who would suffer most if it were legal?—If it were legal, could its negative effects be better controlled?—Aren't "escort services" really prostitution rings for people with more money?—How is that dealt with?—Who goes into the "oldest business" and why?

Notice that the student doesn't really know the answers yet but is asking questions by free-associating and seeing what turns up as a productive line of analysis. The questions range from the definition of prostitution to its effects, and they might inspire the student to do some basic Internet research or even deeper research. Once you make a list, see if you can observe patterns or similarities among the items you listed, or if you invented a question worthy of its own thesis statement (e.g., "The enforcement of prostitution laws hurts *X* group unequally, and it uses a lot of public money that could better be used in other areas or toward regulating the trade rather than jailing people").

Diagramming

Sketching a visual representation of an essay is a kind of listing. Three methods of diagramming are especially common.

- *Clustering*   As we discuss on page 5, you can make an effective cluster by writing, in the middle of a sheet of paper, a word or phrase summarizing your topic (e.g., *fracking;* see diagram below), circling it, and then writing down and circling a related word (e.g., *energy independence*). Perhaps this leads you to write *lower gas prices* and *clean energy.* You then circle these phrases and continue making connections. The next thing you think of is *environmental impact,* so you draw a line to *clean energy.* Then you think of *water pollution,* write it down and circle it, and draw another line to *environmental impact.* The next thing that occurs to you is *job creation,* so you write this down and circle it. You won't connect this to *clean energy,* but you might connect it to *lower gas prices* because both are generally positive economic effects. (If you can think of negative economic impacts on other industries or workers, write them down and circle them.) Keep going, jotting down ideas and making connections where possible, indicating relationships. Notice that you appear to be detailing and weighing the economic and environmental impacts of fracking. Whether you realized it or not, an argument is taking shape.

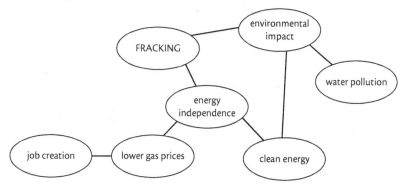

- *Branching*   Some writers find it useful to draw a tree, moving from the central topic to the main branches (chief ideas) and then to the twigs (aspects of the chief ideas).

- *Comparing in columns*   Draw a line down the middle of the page, and then set up two columns showing oppositions. For instance, if you are concerned with the environmental and economic impacts of fracking, you might head one column ENVIRONMENTAL and the other ECONOMIC. In the first column, you might write *water pollution, chemicals used,* and *other hazards?* In the second column, you might write *clean air, employment,* and *independence from unstable oil-producing countries.* You might go on to write, in the first column, *gas leaks* and *toxic waste,* and in the second, *cheaper fuel* and *cheaper electricity*—or whatever else relevant comes to mind.

All these methods can, of course, be executed with pen and paper, but you may also be able to use them on your computer depending on the capabilities of your software.

Whether you're using a computer or a pen, you put down some words and almost immediately see that they need improvement, not simply a little polishing but a substantial overhaul. You write, "Race should be counted in college admissions for two reasons," and as soon as you write those words, a third reason comes to mind. Or perhaps one of those "two reasons" no longer seems very good. As E. M. Forster said, "How can I know what I think till I see what I say?" We have to see what we say—we have to get something down on paper—before we realize that we need to make it better.

Writing, then, is really **rewriting**—that is, **revising**—and a revision is a *re-vision,* a second look. The essay that you submit—whether as hard copy or as a .doc file—should be clear and may appear to be effortlessly composed, but in all likelihood the clarity and apparent ease are the result of a struggle with yourself during which you refined your first thoughts. You begin by putting down ideas, perhaps in random order, but sooner or later comes the job of looking at them critically,

developing what's useful in them and removing what isn't. If you follow this procedure you will be in the company of Picasso, who said that he "advanced by means
of destruction." Any passages that you cut or destroy can be kept in another file
in case you want to revisit those deletions later. Sometimes, you end up restoring
them and developing what you discarded into a new essay with a new direction.

Whether you advance bit by bit (writing a sentence, revising it, writing the next, etc.)
or whether you write an entire first draft and then revise it and revise it again and again
is chiefly a matter of temperament. Probably most people combine both approaches,
backing up occasionally but trying to get to the end fairly soon so that they can see
rather quickly what they know, or think they know, and can then start the real work of
thinking, of converting their initial ideas into something substantial.

Further Invention Strategies: Asking Good Questions

Asking Questions

Generating ideas, we said when talking about **topics** and **invention** strategies in
Chapter 1 (p. 20) is mostly a matter of asking (and then thinking about) questions.
In this part of the book we include questions at the end of each argumentative essay,
not to torment you but to help you think about the arguments—for instance, to turn
your attention to especially important matters. If your instructor asks you to write an
answer to one of these questions, you are lucky: Examining the question will stimulate
your mind to work in a specific direction.

If your instructor doesn't assign a topic for an argumentative essay, you'll find that
some ideas (possibly poor ones initially, but that doesn't matter because you'll soon
revise) come to mind if you ask yourself questions. Begin determining where you
stand on an issue (**stasis**) by asking the following five basic questions:

1. What is X?

2. What is the value of X?

3. What are the causes (or the consequences) of X?

4. What should (or ought or must) we do about X?

5. What is the evidence for my claims about X?

Let's spend a moment looking at each of these questions.

1. *What is X?* We can hardly argue about the number of people sentenced to death
   in the United States in 2000—a glance at the appropriate government report
   will give the answer—but we can argue about whether capital punishment as
   administered in the United States is discriminatory. Does the evidence support
   the view that in the United States the death penalty is unfair? Similarly, we can
   ask whether a human fetus is a human being (in saying what something is, must
   we take account of its potentiality?), and even if we agree that a fetus is a human

being, we can further ask whether it is a person. In *Roe v. Wade* the U.S. Supreme Court ruled that even the "viable" unborn human fetus is not a "person" as that term is used in the Fifth and Fourteenth Amendments. Here the question is this: Is the essential fact about the fetus that it is a person?

An argument of this sort makes a claim—that is, it takes a stand; but notice that it does not also have to argue for an action. Thus, it may argue that the death penalty is administered unfairly—that's a big enough issue—but it need not go on to argue that the death penalty should be abolished. After all, another possibility is that the death penalty should be administered fairly. The writer of the essay may be doing enough if he or she establishes the truth of the claim and leaves to others the possible responses.

2. *What is the value of X?*   College courses often call for literary judgments. No one can argue if you say you prefer the plays of Tennessee Williams to those of Arthur Miller. But academic papers are not mere declarations of preferences. As soon as you say that Williams is a better playwright than Miller, you have based your preference on implicit standards, and you must support your preference by giving evidence about the relative skill, insight, and accomplishments of both Williams and Miller. Your argument is an evaluation. The question now at issue is the merits of the two authors and the standards appropriate for making such an appraisal.

In short, an essay offering an evaluation normally has two purposes:

- to set forth an assessment
- to convince the reader that the assessment is reasonable

In writing an evaluation, you have to rely on criteria, and these will vary depending on your topic. For instance, in comparing the artistic merit of plays by Williams and by Miller, you may want to talk about the quality of the characterization, the importance of the theme, and so on. But if the topic is "Which playwright is more suitable to be taught in high school?" other criteria may be appropriate, such as these:

- the difficulty of the author's language
- the sexual content of some scenes
- the presence of obscene words

Alternatively, consider a nonliterary issue: On balance, are college fraternities and sororities good or bad? If good, how good? If bad, how bad? What criteria serve best in making our evaluation? Probably some or all of the following:

- testimony of authorities (e.g., persons who can offer firsthand testimony about the good or bad effects)
- inductive evidence (examples of good or bad effects)
- appeals to logic ("it follows, therefore, that...")
- appeals to emotion (e.g., an appeal to our sense of fairness)

3. *What are the causes (or the consequences) of X?*   Why did the rate of auto theft increase during a specific period? If the death penalty is abolished, will that cause the rate of murder to increase? Problems such as these may be complex. The phenomena that people usually argue about—such as inflation, war, suicide, crime—have many causes, and it can be a mistake to speak of *the* cause of *X*. A writer in *Time* mentioned that the life expectancy of an average American male is about sixty-seven years, a figure that compares unfavorably with the life expectancy of males in Japan and Israel. The *Time* writer suggested that an important cause of the American male's relatively short life span is "the pressure to perform well in business." Perhaps. But the life expectancy of plumbers is no greater than that of managers and executives. Nutrition authority Jean Mayer, in an article in *Life*, attributed the relatively poor longevity of American males to a diet that is "rich in fat and poor in nutrients." Doubtless other authorities propose other causes, and in all likelihood no one cause entirely accounts for the phenomenon.

Consider a second example of discussions of causality, this one concerning the academic performance of girls in single-sex elementary schools, middle schools, and high schools. It is pretty much agreed (based on statistical evidence) that the graduates of these schools do better, as a group, than girls who graduate from coeducational schools. *Why* do girls in single-sex schools tend, as a group, to do better? What is the *cause*? The administrators of girls' schools usually attribute the success to the fact (we're putting the matter bluntly here) that young women flourish better in an atmosphere free from male intimidation: They allegedly gain confidence and become more expressive when they aren't threatened by the presence of males. This may be the answer, but skeptics have attributed the graduates' success to two other causes:

•   Most single-sex schools require parents to pay tuition, and it is a documented fact that the children of well-to-do parents do better, academically, than the children of poor parents.

•   Most single-sex schools are private schools, and they select students from a pool of candidates. Admissions officers select those candidates who seem to be academically promising—that is, students who have *already done well academically*.

In short, the girls who graduate from single-sex schools may owe their later academic success not to the schools' single-sex environment but to the fact that even at admission the students were academically stronger (again, we're speaking of a cohort, not of individuals) than the girls who attend coeducational schools.

The lesson? Be cautious in attributing a cause. There may be several causes.

The kinds of support that usually accompany claims of cause include the following:

•   factual data, especially statistics

•   analogies ("The Roman Empire declined because of *X* and *Y*"; "Our society exhibits *X* and *Y*; therefore…")

•   inductive evidence

4. *What should (or ought or must) we do about X?*   Must we always obey the law? Should the law allow eighteen-year-olds to drink alcohol? Should eighteen-year-olds be drafted to do one year of social service? Should pornography be censored? Should steroid use by athletes be banned? Ought there to be Good Samaritan laws, making it a legal duty for a stranger to intervene to save a person from death or great bodily harm, when one might do so with little or no risk to oneself? These questions involve conduct and policy; how we answer them will reveal our values and principles.

An essay answering questions of this sort usually has the following characteristics:

- It begins by explaining what the issue (the problem) is.

- Then it states why the reader should care about the issue.

- Next, it offers the proposed solution.

- Then it considers alternative solutions.

- Finally, it reaffirms the merit of the proposed solution, especially in light of the audience's interests and needs.

You'll recall that throughout this book we have spoken about devices that help a writer to generate ideas. If in drafting an essay concerned with policy you begin by writing down your thoughts on the five bulleted items listed above, you'll almost surely uncover ideas that you didn't know you had.

Support for claims of policy usually include the following:

- statistics

- appeals to common sense and to the reader's moral sense

- testimony of authorities

5. *What is the evidence for my claims about X?*   In commenting on the four previous topics, we have talked about the kinds of support that writers commonly offer. However, a few additional points are important.

Critical reading, writing, and thinking depend on identifying and evaluating the evidence for and against the claims one makes and encounters in the writings of others. It isn't enough to have an *opinion* or belief one way or the other; you need to be able to support your opinions—the bare fact of your sincere belief in what you say or write is not itself any *evidence* that what you believe is true.

What constitutes good reasons for opinions and adequate evidence for beliefs? The answer depends on the type of belief or opinion, assertion or hypothesis, claim or principle you want to assert. For example, there is good evidence that President John F. Kennedy was assassinated on November 22, 1963, because this is the date for his death reported in standard almanacs. You could further substantiate the date by checking the back issues of the *New York Times*. But a different kind of evidence is needed to support the proposition that the chemical composition of water is H_2O.

And you would need still other kinds of evidence to support your beliefs about the likelihood of rain tomorrow, the probability that the Red Sox will win the pennant this year, the twelfth digit in the decimal expansion of pi, the average cumulative grades of graduating seniors over the past three years in your college, the relative merits of *Hamlet* and *Death of a Salesman*, and the moral dimensions of sexual harassment. None of these issues is merely a matter of opinion; yet about some of them, educated and informed people may disagree over the reasons, the evidence, and what they show. Sometimes, equally qualified experts examine the same evidence and draw different conclusions. Your job as a critical thinker is to be alert to the relevant reasons and evidence, as well as the basis of various conclusions, and to make the most of them as you present your views.

Again, an argument may answer two or more of our five basic questions. Someone who argues that pornography should (or should not) be censored will have to do the following:

- Mark out the territory of the discussion by defining pornography (our first question: What is *X*?).

- Examine the consequences of adopting the preferred policy (our third question).

- Perhaps argue about the value of that policy (our second question). Some people maintain that pornography produces crime, but others maintain that it provides a harmless outlet for impulses that otherwise might vent themselves in criminal behavior.

- Address the possible objection that censorship, however desirable on account of some of its consequences, may be unconstitutional and that even if censorship were constitutional, it would (or might) have undesirable side effects, such as repressing freedom of political opinion.

- Keep in mind our fifth question: What is the evidence for my claims?

Thinking about one or more of these questions may get you going. For instance, thinking about What is *X*? will require you to produce a definition; and as you do this, new ideas might arise. If a question seems relevant, it's a good idea to start writing—even just a fragmentary sentence. You'll probably find that one word leads to another and that ideas begin to appear. Even if these ideas seem weak as you write them, don't be discouraged; you will have put something on paper, and returning to these words, perhaps in five minutes or the next day, you'll probably find that some aren't at all bad and that others will stimulate you to better ones.

It may be useful to record your ideas in a special notebook or in a private digital notebook or document reserved for the purpose. Such a journal can be a valuable resource when it comes time to write your paper. Many students find it easier to focus their thoughts on writing if during the gestation period they've been jotting down relevant ideas on something more substantial than slips of paper or loose sheets. The very act of designating a traditional or digital notebook or document file as your journal for a course can be the first step in focusing your attention on the eventual need to write a paper.

Take advantage of the free tools at your disposal. Use the Internet and free Web tools, including RSS feeds, Google (Drive, sites, and others), Yahoo!, blogs, and wikis to organize your initial ideas and to solicit feedback. Talking with others can help, but sometimes there isn't time to chat. By using an RSS feed on a Web site that you think will provide good information on your topic (or a topic you're considering), you can receive notifications if the site has uploaded new material such as news links or op-eds. Posting a blog entry in a public space about your topic can also foster conversations about the topic and help you discover other opinions. Using the Internet to uncover and refine a topic is common practice, especially early in the research process.

If what we have just said doesn't sound convincing, and if you know from experience that you have trouble getting started with writing, don't despair. First aid is at hand in a sure-fire method that we will explain next.

The Thesis or Main Point

Let's assume that you are writing an argumentative essay—perhaps an evaluation of an argument in this book—and you have what seems to be a pretty good draft or at least a collection of notes that are the result of hard thinking. You really do have ideas now, and you want to present them effectively. How will you organize your essay? No one formula works best for every essayist and for every essay, but it is usually advisable to formulate a basic **thesis** (a claim, a central point, a chief position) and to state it early. Every essay that is any good, even a book-length one, has a thesis (a main point), which can be stated briefly—usually, in a sentence. Remember Coolidge's remark on the preacher's sermon on sin: "He was against it." Don't confuse the **topic** (sin) with the thesis (sin is bad). The thesis is the argumentative theme, the author's primary claim or contention, the proposition that the rest of the essay will explain and defend. Of course, the thesis may sound commonplace, but the book or essay or sermon ought to develop it in an interesting and convincing way.

Raising the Stakes of Your Thesis

Imagine walking across campus and coming upon a person ready to perform on a tightrope suspended between two buildings. He is wearing a glittering leotard and is eyeing up his challenge very seriously. Here's the thing, though: His tightrope is only *one foot off the ground.* Would you stop and watch him walk across it? Maybe, maybe not. Most people are likely to take a look and move on. If you did spend a few minutes watching, you wouldn't be very worried about the performer falling. If he lost his balance momentarily, you wouldn't gasp in horror. And if he walked across the tightrope masterfully, you might be somewhat impressed but not enraptured.

Now imagine the rope being a hundred feet off the ground. You and many others would almost certainly stop and witness the feat. The audience would likely be captivated, nervous about the performer potentially falling, "oohing" if he momentarily lost his balance, and cheering if he crossed the rope successfully.

Consider the tightrope as your thesis statement, the performer as writer, and the act of crossing as the argument. What we call "low-stakes" thesis statements are comparable to low tightropes: A low-stakes thesis statement itself may be interesting, but not much about it is vital to any particular audience. Low-stakes thesis statements lack a sense of importance or relevance. They may restate what is already widely known and accepted, or they may make a good point but not discuss any consequences. Some examples:

> Good nutrition and exercise can lead to a healthy life.

> Our education system focuses too much on standardized tests.

> Children's beauty pageants are exploitative.

Students can write well-organized, clear, and direct papers on these topics, but if the thesis is "low stakes" like these, then the performance would be similar to that of an expert walking across a tightrope *one foot off the ground.* The argument may be well executed, but few in the audience will be inspired by it.

However, if you raise the stakes by "raising the tightrope," you can compel readers to *want* to read and keep reading. There are several ways to raise the tightrope. First, *think about what is socially, culturally, or politically important* about your thesis statement and argument. Some writing instructors tell students to ask themselves "so what?" about the thesis, but this can be a vague directive. Here are some better questions: Why is your thesis important? What is the impact of your thesis on a particular group or demographic? What are the consequences of what you claim? What could happen if your position were *not* recognized? How can your argument benefit readers or compel them to action (by doing something or adopting a new belief)? What will readers *gain* by accepting your argument as convincing?

In formulating your thesis, keep in mind these points:

Different thesis statements may speak to different target audiences. An argument about changes in estate tax laws may not thrill all audiences, but for a defined group—accountants, lawyers, or the elderly, for instance—this may be quite controversial and highly relevant.

Tightropes, like these, can be raised to many different levels.

Not all audiences are equal—or equally interested in your thesis or argument. In this book, we generally select topics of broad importance. However, in a literature course, a film history course, or a political science course, you'll calibrate your thesis statements and arguments to an audience who is invested in those fields. In writing about the steep decline in bee populations, your argument might look quite different if you're speaking to ecologists as opposed to gardeners. (We will discuss audience in greater detail in the following section.)

Be wary of compare-and-contrast arguments. One of the most basic approaches to writing is to compare and contrast, a maneuver that produces a low-tightrope thesis. It normally looks like this: "X *and* Y *are similar in some ways and different in others*." But if you think about it, *anything* can be compared and contrasted in this way, and doing so doesn't necessarily *tell* anything important. So, if you're writing a compare-and-contrast paper, make sure to include the reasons why it is important to compare and contrast these things. What benefit does the comparison yield? What significance does it have to some audience, some area of knowledge, some field of study?

Thinking Critically: "Walking the Tightrope"

Examine the low-stakes thesis statements provided below, and expand each one into a high-stakes thesis by including the importance of asserting it and by proposing a possible response. The first one has been done as an example.

Low-Stakes Thesis	High-Stakes Thesis
Good nutrition and exercise can lead to a healthy life.	One way to help solve the epidemic obesity problem in the United States is to remind consumers of a basic fact accepted by nearly all reputable health experts: Good nutrition and exercise can lead to a healthy life.
Every qualified American should vote.	
Spanking children is good/bad.	
Electric cars will reduce air pollution.	

✓   A Checklist for a Thesis Statement

Consider the following questions:

☐   Does the statement make an arguable assertion rather than (1) merely assert an unarguable fact, (2) merely announce a topic, or (3) declare an unarguable opinion or belief?

☐   Is the statement broad enough to cover the entire argument that I will be presenting, and is it narrow enough for me to cover the topic in the space allotted?

Imagining an Audience

Raising the tightrope of your thesis will also require you to imagine the *audience* you're addressing. The questions that you ask yourself in generating thoughts on a topic will primarily relate to the topic, but additional questions that consider the audience are always relevant:

- Who are my readers?
- What do they believe?
- What common ground do we share?
- What do I want my readers to believe?
- What do they need to know?
- Why should they care?

Let's think about these questions. The literal answer to the first probably is "my teacher," but (unless you receive instructions to the contrary) you should not write specifically for your teacher. Instead, you should write for an audience that is, generally speaking, like your classmates. In short, your imagined audience is literate, intelligent, and moderately well informed, but its members don't know everything that you know, and they don't know your response to the problem being addressed. Your audience needs more information along those lines to make an intelligent decision about the issue.

For example, in writing about how children's toys shape the minds of young boys and girls differently, it may not be enough to simply say, "Toys are part of the gender socialization process." ("Sure they are," the audience might already agree.) However, if you raise the stakes, you have an opportunity to frame the questions that result from this observation: You frame the questions, lay out the issues, identify the problems, and note the complications that arise because of your basic thesis. You could point out that toys have a significant impact on the interests, identities, skills, and capabilities that children develop and carry into adulthood. Because toys are so significant, is it important to ask questions about whether they perpetuate gender-based stereotypes?

Do toys help perpetuate social inequalities between the sexes? Most children think toys are "just fun," but they may be teaching kids to conform unthinkingly to the social expectations of their sex, to accept designated sex-based social roles, and to cultivate talents differently based on sex. Is this a good or a bad thing? Do toys facilitate growth, or do they have any limiting effects?

What audiences should be concerned with your topic? Maybe you're addressing the general public who buys toys for children at least some of the time. Maybe you're addressing parents who are raising young children. Maybe you're addressing consumer advocates, encouraging them to pressure toy manufacturers and retailers to produce more gender-neutral offerings. The point is that your essay should contain (and sustain) an assessment of the impact of your high-stakes thesis, and it should set out a clear course of action for a particular audience.

That said, if you know your audience well, you can argue for different courses of action that are most likely to be persuasive. You may not be very convincing if you argue to parents in general that they should never buy princess toys for their girls and avoid all Disney-themed toys. Perhaps you should argue simply that parents should be conscious of the gender messages that toys convey, offer their kids diverse toys, and talk to their children while playing with them about alternatives to the stereotypical messages that the toys convey. However, if you're writing for a magazine called *Radical Parenting* and your essay is titled "Buying Toys the Gender-Neutral Way," your audience and its expectations—therefore, your thesis and argument—may look far different. The bottom line is not just to know your audience but to define it.

The essays in this book are from many different sources with many different audiences. An essay from the *New York Times* addresses educated general readers; an essay from *Ms.* magazine targets readers sympathetic to feminism. An essay from *Commonweal,* a Roman Catholic publication for nonspecialists, is likely to differ in point of view or tone from one in *Time,* even though both articles may advance approximately the same position. The *Commonweal* article may, for example, effectively cite church fathers and distinguished Roman Catholic writers as authorities, whereas the *Time* article would probably cite few or none of these figures because a non-Catholic audience might be unfamiliar with them or, even if familiar, might be unimpressed by their views.

The tone as well as the gist of the argument is in some degree shaped by the audience. For instance, popular journals, such as *National Review* and *Ms.* magazine, are more likely to use ridicule than are journals chiefly addressed to, say, an academic audience.

The Audience as Collaborator

If you imagine a particular audience and ask yourself what it does and doesn't need to be told, you will find that material comes to mind, just as when a friend asks you what a film you saw was about, who was in it, and how you liked it.

Your readers don't have to be told that Thomas Jefferson was an American statesman in the early years of this country's history, but they do have to be told that Elizabeth Cady

Stanton was a late-nineteenth-century American feminist. Why? Because it's your hunch that your classmates never heard of her, or even if they have heard the name, they can't quite identify it. But what if your class has been assigned an essay by Stanton? In that case your imagined readers know Stanton's name and at least a little about her, so you don't have to identify her as an American of the nineteenth century. But you do still have to remind readers about relevant aspects of her essay, and you have to tell them about your responses to those aspects.

After all, even if the instructor has assigned an essay by Stanton, you cannot assume that your classmates know the essay inside out. You can't say, "Stanton's third reason is also unconvincing," without reminding the reader, by means of a brief summary, of her third reason. Again:

- Think of your classmates—people like you—as your imagined readers.
- Be sure that your essay does not make unreasonable demands.

If you ask yourself,

- "What do my readers need to know?" and
- "What do I want them to believe?"

you will find some answers arising, and you will start writing.

We've said that you should imagine your audience as your classmates. But this isn't the whole truth. In a sense, your argument is addressed not simply to your classmates but to the world interested in ideas. Even if you can reasonably assume that your classmates have read only one work by Stanton, you can't begin your essay by writing, "Stanton's essay is deceptively easy." You have to name the work because it's possible that a reader is familiar with some other work by Stanton. And by precisely identifying your subject, you ease the reader into your essay.

Similarly, you won't open with a statement like this:

> The majority opinion in *Walker v. City of Birmingham* held that...

Rather, you'll write something like this:

> In *Walker v. City of Birmingham*, the U.S. Supreme Court ruled in 1966 that city authorities acted lawfully when they jailed Martin Luther King Jr. and other clergymen in 1963 for marching in Birmingham without a permit. Justice Potter Stewart delivered the majority opinion, which held that...

By the way, if you suffer from a writing block, the mere act of writing out such readily available facts will help you to get started. You'll find that writing a few words, perhaps merely copying the essay's title or an interesting quotation from the essay, will stimulate other thoughts that you didn't know you had.

Here, again, are the questions about audience. If you write on a computer, consider putting these questions into a file. For each assignment, copy the questions into the file you're working on, and then, as a way of generating ideas, *enter your responses, indented, under each question.*

1. Who are my readers?

2. What do they believe?

3. What common ground do we share?

4. What do I want my readers to believe?

5. What do they need to know?

6. Why should they care?

Thinking about your audience can help you get started; even more important, it can help you generate ideas. Our second and third questions about the audience ("What do they believe?" and "How much common ground do we share?") will usually help you get ideas flowing.

- Presumably, your imagined audience does not share your views, or at least does not fully share them. But why?

- How can these readers hold a position that to you seems unreasonable?

By putting yourself into your readers' shoes—and your essay will almost surely summarize the views that you're going to speak against—and by thinking about what your audience knows or thinks it knows, you will generate ideas. Spend time online reviewing Web sites dedicated to your topic. What do they have to say, and why do the authors hold these views?

Let's assume that you don't believe that people should be allowed to smoke in enclosed public places, but you know that some people hold a different view. Why do they hold it? Try to state their view *in a way that would be satisfactory to them.* Having done so, you may perceive that your conclusions and theirs differ because they're based on different premises—perhaps different ideas about human rights. Examine the opposition's premises carefully, and explain, first to yourself and ultimately to your readers, why you find some of those premises to be unacceptable.

Perhaps some facts are in dispute, such as whether exposure to tobacco is harmful to nonsmokers. The thing to do, then, is to check the facts. If you find that harm to nonsmokers has not been proved but you nevertheless believe that smoking should be prohibited in enclosed public places, of course you can't premise your argument on the wrongfulness of harming the innocent (in this case, the nonsmokers). You'll have to develop arguments that take account of the facts.

Among the relevant facts there surely are some that your audience or your opponent will not dispute. The same is true of the values relevant to the discussion; both sides very likely believe in some of the same values (such as the principle mentioned above, that it is wrong to harm the innocent). These areas of shared agreement are crucial to effective persuasion in argument.

A Rule for Writers

If you wish to persuade, you have to begin by finding premises that you can share with your audience.

There are two good reasons for identifying and isolating the areas of agreement:

- There is no point in disputing facts or values on which you and your readers already agree.
- It usually helps to establish goodwill between yourself and your opponent when you can point to shared beliefs, assumptions, facts, and values.

In a few moments we will return to the need to share some of the opposition's ideas.

Recall that in composing college papers it's usually best to write for a general audience, an audience rather like your classmates but without the specific knowledge that they all share as students enrolled in one course. If the topic is smoking in public places, the audience presumably consists of smokers and nonsmokers. Thinking about our fifth question on page 180—"What do [readers] need to know?"—may prompt you to give statistics about the harmful effects of smoking. Or if you're arguing on behalf of smokers, it may prompt you to cite studies claiming that no evidence conclusively demonstrates that cigarette smoking is harmful to nonsmokers. If indeed you are writing for a general audience and you are not advancing a highly unfamiliar view, our second question ("What does the audience believe?") is less important here; but if the audience is specialized, such as an antismoking group, a group of restaurant owners who fear that antismoking regulations will interfere with their business, or a group of civil libertarians, an effective essay will have to address their special beliefs.

In addressing their beliefs (let's assume that you don't share them—at least, not fully), you must try to establish some common ground. If you advocate requiring restaurants to provide nonsmoking areas, you should recognize the possibility that this arrangement will result in inconvenience for the proprietor. But perhaps (the good news) the restaurant will regain some lost customers or attract some new customers. This thought should prompt you to think of other kinds of evidence—perhaps testimony or statistics.

When you formulate a thesis and ask questions about it—such as who the readers are, what they believe, what they know, and what they need to know—you begin to get ideas about how to organize the material (or, at least, you realize that you'll have to work out some sort of organization). The thesis may be clear and simple, but the reasons (the argument) may take many pages. The thesis is the point; the argument sets forth the evidence that supports the thesis.

> ## ✓ A Checklist for Imagining an Audience
>
> Have I asked myself the following questions?
>
> ☐ Who are my readers? How do I know?
>
> ☐ How much about the topic do they already know?
>
> ☐ Have I provided necessary background (including definitions of special terms) if the imagined readers probably are not especially familiar with the topic?
>
> ☐ Are these imagined readers likely to be neutral? Sympathetic? Hostile? Have I done enough online research to offer something useful to a hostile audience?
>
> ☐ If they're neutral, have I offered good reasons to persuade them? If they're sympathetic, have I done more than merely reaffirm their present beliefs? That is, have I perhaps enriched their views or encouraged them to act? If they're hostile, have I taken account of their positions, recognized their strengths but also called attention to their limitations, and offered a position that might persuade these hostile readers to modify their position?

The Title

It's a good idea to announce the thesis in your essay's **title**. Here are a few examples of titles that take a position:

> Forgive Student Loans? Worst Idea Ever
>
> Millennials Are Selfish and Entitled, and Helicopter Parents Are to Blame
>
> The Draft Would Compel Us to Share the Sacrifice

True, these titles are not especially engaging, but the reader welcomes them because they give some information about the writer's thesis.

Some titles don't announce the thesis, but they do announce the topic:

> Are We Slaves to Our Online Selves?
>
> On Racist Speech
>
> Should Governments Tax Unhealthy Foods and Drinks?

Although not clever or witty, the above titles are informative.

Some titles seek to attract attention or to stimulate the imagination:

A First Amendment Junkie

Why I Don't Spare "Spare Change"

Building Baby from the Genes Up

All of these are effective, but a word of caution is appropriate here. In seeking to engage your readers' attention, be careful not to sound like a wise guy. You want to engage the readers, not turn them off.

Finally, be prepared to rethink your title *after* completing the last draft of your paper. A title somewhat different from your working title may be an improvement because the finished paper may emphasize something entirely different from what you expected when you first gave it a title.

The Opening Paragraphs

Opening paragraphs are difficult to write, so don't worry about writing an effective opening when you're drafting. Just get some words down on paper and keep going. But when you revise your first draft, you should begin to think seriously about the effect of your opening.

A good introduction arouses readers' interest and prepares them for the rest of the paper. How? Opening paragraphs usually do at least one (and often all) of the following:

- attract readers' interest (often with a bold thesis statement or an interesting relevant statistic, quotation, or anecdote)
- prepare readers by giving some idea of the topic and often of the thesis
- give readers an idea of how the essay is organized
- define a key term

You may not wish to announce your thesis in the title, but if you don't announce it there, you should set it forth early in the argument, in the introductory paragraph or paragraphs. In an essay titled "Human Rights and Foreign Policy" (1982), U.S. ambassador to the United Nations Jeanne J. Kirkpatrick merely announces her topic (subject) as opposed to her thesis (point), but she hints at the thesis in her first paragraph, by deprecating President Jimmy Carter's policy:

> In this paper I deal with three broad subjects: first, the content and consequences of the Carter administration's human rights policy; second, the prerequisites of a more adequate theory of human rights; and third, some characteristics of a more successful human rights policy.

Alternatively, consider this opening paragraph from Peter Singer's "Animal Liberation":

> We are familiar with Black Liberation, Gay Liberation, and a variety of other movements. With Women's Liberation some thought we had come to the end of the road. Discrimination on the basis of sex, it has been said, is the last form of discrimination that is universally accepted and practiced without pretense, even in those liberal circles which have long prided themselves on their freedom from racial discrimination. But one should always be wary of talking of "the last remaining form of discrimination." If we have learned anything from the liberation movements, we should have learned how difficult it is to be aware of the ways in which we discriminate until they are forcefully pointed out to us. A liberation movement demands an expansion of our moral horizons, so that practices that were previously regarded as natural and inevitable are now seen as intolerable.

Although Singer's introductory paragraph nowhere mentions animal liberation, in conjunction with the essay's title it gives a good idea of what Singer is up to and where he is going. He knows that his audience will be skeptical, so he reminds them that in previous years many people were skeptical of reforms that are now taken for granted. He adopts a strategy used fairly often by writers who advance unconventional theses: Rather than beginning with a bold announcement of a thesis that may turn off some readers because it sounds offensive or absurd, Singer warms up his audience, gaining their interest by cautioning them politely that although they may at first be skeptical of animal liberation, if they stay with his essay they may come to feel that they have expanded their horizons.

Notice, too, that Singer begins by establishing common ground with his readers; he assumes, probably correctly, that they share his view that other forms of discrimination (now seen to be unjust) were once widely practiced and were assumed to be acceptable and natural. In this paragraph, then, Singer is not only showing himself to be fair-minded but is also letting readers know that he will advance a daring idea. His opening wins their attention and goodwill. A writer can hardly hope to do more. (Soon we'll talk a little more about winning the audience.)

Keep in mind the following points when writing introductory paragraphs:

- You may have to give background information that readers should keep in mind if they are to follow your essay.

- You may wish to define some terms that are unfamiliar or that you use in an unusual sense.

- If you're writing for an online publication (where your instructor or audience will encounter your argument on the Web), you might establish a context for your argument by linking to a news video that outlines the topic, or you might offer your thesis and then link to a news story that supports your claim.

(Remember that using any videos, images, or links also requires a citation of some kind.) The beauty of publishing the piece in an online environment is that you can link directly to sources and use them more easily than if you were submitting a hard copy.

After announcing the topic, giving the necessary background, and stating your position (and perhaps the opposition's) in as engaging a manner as possible, you will do well to give the reader an idea of *how* you will proceed—that is, what the organization will be. In other words, use the introduction to set up the organization of your essay. Your instructors may assign four- to six-page mini-research papers or ten- to fifteen-page research papers; if they assign an online venue, ask them about the approximate word count. No matter what the length, every paper needs to have a clear organization. The introduction is where you can accomplish three key things:

- hook your reader
- reveal your thesis and topic
- explain how you will organize your discussion of the topic—what you'll do first, second, third, and so on.

Look at Kirkpatrick's opening paragraph (p. 186) for an illustration. She tells her readers that she will address three subjects, and she names them. Her approach in the paragraph is concise, obvious, and effective.

Similarly, you may want to announce fairly early that there are, say, four common objections to your thesis and that you will take them up one by one, beginning with the weakest (or most widely held) and moving to the strongest (or least familiar), after which you will advance your own view in greater detail. Not every argument begins with refuting the other side, though many arguments do. The point to remember is that you usually ought to tell readers where you will be taking them and by what route. In effect, you give them an outline.

A Rule for Writers

In writing or revising introductory paragraphs, keep in mind this question: What do my readers need to know? Remember, your aim throughout is to write *reader-friendly* prose. Keeping the needs and interests of your audience constantly in mind will help you achieve this goal.

Organizing and Revising the Body of the Essay

We begin with a wise remark by a newspaper columnist, Robert Cromier: "The beautiful part of writing is that you don't have to get it right the first time—unlike, say, a brain surgeon."

In drafting an essay, you will of course begin with an organization that seems appropriate, but you may find, in rereading the draft, that some other organization is better. Here, for a start, is an organization that is common in argumentative essays:

1. Statement of the problem or issue

2. Statement of the structure of the essay (its organization)

3. Statement of alternative (but less adequate) solutions

4. Arguments in support of the proposed solution

5. Arguments answering possible objections

6. A summary, resolution, or conclusion

Let's look at each of these six steps.

1. *Statement of the problem or issue*   Whether the problem is stated briefly or at length depends on the nature of the problem and the writer's audience. If you haven't already defined unfamiliar terms or terms you use in a special way, now is the time to do so. In any case, it is advisable here to state the problem objectively (thereby gaining the reader's trust) and to indicate why the reader should care about the issue.

2. *Statement of the structure of the essay*   After stating the problem at the appropriate length, the writer often briefly indicates the structure of the rest of the essay. The structure used most frequently is suggested below, in points 3 and 4.

3. *Statement of alternative (but less adequate) solutions*   In addition to stating the alternatives fairly (letting readers know that you've done your homework), the writer conveys a willingness to recognize not only the integrity of opposing proposals but also the (partial) merit of at least some of the alternative solutions.

Our point in the previous sentence is important and worth amplifying. Because it is important to convey your goodwill—your sense of fairness—to the reader, it's advisable to show that you're familiar with the opposition and that you recognize the integrity of those who hold that view. You accomplish this by granting its merits as far as you can.

The next stage, which constitutes most of the body of the essay, usually is this:

4. *Arguments in support of the proposed solution*   The evidence offered will depend on the nature of the problem. Relevant statistics, authorities, examples, or analogies may come to mind or be available. This is usually the longest part of the essay.

5. *Arguments answering possible objections*   These arguments may suggest the following:

    a. The proposal won't work (perhaps it is alleged to be too expensive, to make unrealistic demands on human nature, or to fail to reach the heart of the problem).

    b. The proposed solution will create problems greater than the problem under discussion. (A good example of a proposal that produced dreadful unexpected results is the law mandating a prison term for anyone over age eighteen in possession of an illegal drug. Heroin dealers then began to use children as runners, and cocaine importers followed the practice.)

6. *A summary, resolution, or conclusion*   Here the writer may seek to accommodate the opposition's views as far as possible but clearly suggest that the writer's own position makes good sense. A conclusion—the word comes from the Latin *claudere*, "to shut"—ought to provide a sense of closure, but it can be much more than a restatement of the writer's thesis. It can, for instance, make a quiet emotional appeal by suggesting that the issue is important and that the ball is now in the reader's court.

Of course, not every essay will follow this six-step pattern. But let's assume that in the introductory paragraphs you have sketched the topic (and have shown, or implied, that the reader doubtless is interested in it) and have fairly and courteously set forth the opposition's view, recognizing its merits ("I grant that," "admittedly," "it is true that") and indicating the degree to which you can share part of that view. You now want to set forth arguments explaining why you differ on some essentials.

In presenting your own position, you can begin with either your strongest or your weakest reasons. Each method of organization has advantages and disadvantages.

•   If you begin with your strongest reason, the essay may seem to peter out.

•   If you begin with your weakest reason, you build to a climax; but readers may not still be with you because they may have felt at the start that the essay was frivolous.

The solution to the latter possibility is to ensure that even your weakest argument demonstrates strength. You can, moreover, assure your readers that stronger points will soon follow and you offer this point first in order to show that you are aware of it and that, slight though it is, it deserves some attention. The body of the essay, then, is devoted to arguing a position, which means offering not only supporting reasons but also refutations of possible objections to these reasons.

Doubtless you'll sometimes be uncertain, while drafting an essay, whether to present a given point before or after another point. When you write, and certainly when you revise, try to put yourself into the reader's shoes: Which point do you think the reader needs to know first? Which point *leads to* which further point? Your argument should not be a mere list of points; rather, it should clearly integrate one point with another in order to develop an idea. However, in all likelihood you won't have a strong sense of the best organization until you have written a draft and have reread it.

Checking Paragraphs

When you revise a draft, watch out for short paragraphs. Although a paragraph of only two or three sentences (like some in this chapter) may occasionally be helpful as a transition between complicated points, most short paragraphs are undeveloped paragraphs. Newspaper editors favor very short paragraphs because they can be read rapidly when printed in the narrow columns typical of newspapers. Many of the essays reprinted in this book originally were published in newspapers and, thus, consist of very short paragraphs, but they should *not* be regarded as models for your own writing.

A second note about paragraphs: Writers for online venues often "chunk" (i.e., they provide extra space for paragraph breaks) rather than write a continuous flow. These writers chunk their text for several reasons, but chiefly because breaking up paragraphs and adding space between them makes some types of writing "scannable": The screen is easier to navigate because it isn't packed with text in a 12-point font. The breaks in paragraphs also allow the reader to see a complete paragraph without having to scroll.

Checking Transitions

Make sure, in revising, that the reader can move easily from the beginning of a paragraph to the end and from one paragraph to the next. Transitions help to signal the connections between units of the argument. For example ("For example" is a transition, indicating that an illustration will follow), they may illustrate, establish a sequence, connect logically, amplify, compare, contrast, summarize, or concede (see Thinking Critically: Using Transitions in Argument). Transitions serve as guideposts that enable the reader to move easily through your essay.

A Rule for Writers

When you revise, make sure that your organization is clear to your readers.

When writers revise an early draft, they chiefly do these tasks:

- They **unify** the essay by eliminating irrelevancies.
- They **organize** the essay by keeping in mind the imagined audience.
- They **clarify** the essay by fleshing out thin paragraphs, by ensuring that the transitions are adequate, and by making certain that generalizations are adequately supported by concrete details and examples.

We are not talking here about polish or elegance; we are talking about fundamental matters. Be especially careful not to abuse the logical connectives (*thus, as a result,* and so on). If you write several sentences followed by *therefore* or a similar word or phrase, be sure that what you write after the *therefore* really *does follow* from what has gone before. Logical connectives are not mere transitional devices that link disconnected bits of prose. They are supposed to mark a real movement of thought, which is the essence of an argument.

The Ending

What about concluding paragraphs, in which you summarize the main points and reaffirm your position?

If you can look back over your essay and add something that both enriches it and wraps it up, fine; but don't feel compelled to say, "Thus, in conclusion, I have argued *X, Y,* and *Z,* and I have refuted Jones." After all, *conclusion* can have two meanings: (1) ending, or finish, as the ending of a joke or a novel; or (2) judgment or decision reached after deliberation. Your essay should finish effectively (the first sense), but it need not announce a judgment (the second).

If the essay is fairly short, so that a reader can keep its general gist in mind, you may not need to restate your view. Just make sure that you have covered the ground and that your last sentence is a good one. Notice that the student essay printed later in this chapter (p. 208) doesn't end with a formal conclusion, although it ends conclusively, with a note of finality.

By "a note of finality" we do *not* mean a triumphant crowing. It's far better to end with the suggestion that you hope you have by now indicated why those who hold a different view may want to modify it and accept yours.

Thinking Critically: Using Transitions in Argument

Fill in examples of the types of transitions listed below, using topics of your choice. The first one has been done as an example.

Type of Transition	Type of Language Used	Example of Transition
Illustrate	*for example, for instance, consider this case*	"Many television crime dramas contain scenes of graphic violence. For example, in the episode of Law and Order titled…"
Establish a sequence	*a more important objection, a stronger example, the best reason*	
Connect logically	*thus, as a result, therefore, so, it follows*	
Amplify	*further, in addition to, moreover*	
Compare	*similarly, in a like manner, just as, analogously*	
Contrast	*on the one hand… on the other hand, in contrast, however, but*	
Summarize	*in short, briefly*	
Concede	*admittedly, granted, to be sure*	

A Rule for Writers

Emulate John Kenneth Galbraith, a distinguished writer on economics. Galbraith said that in his fifth drafts he regularly introduced the note of spontaneity for which his writing was famous.

If you study the essays in this book or the editorials and op-ed pieces in a newspaper, you will notice that writers often provide a sense of closure by using one of the following devices:

- a return to something stated in the introduction

- a glance at the wider implications of the issue (e.g., if smoking is restricted, other liberties are threatened)

- a hint toward unasked or answered questions that the audience might consider in light of the writer's argument

- a suggestion that the reader can take some specific action or do some further research (i.e., the ball is now in the reader's court)

- an anecdote that illustrates the thesis in an engaging way

- a brief summary (*Note:* This sort of ending may seem unnecessary and tedious if the paper is short and the summary merely repeats what the writer has already said.)

Two Uses of an Outline

The Outline as a Preliminary Guide

Some writers sketch an outline as soon as they think they know what they want to say, even before writing a first draft. This procedure can be helpful in planning a tentative organization, but remember that in revising a draft you'll likely generate some new ideas and have to modify the outline accordingly. A preliminary outline is chiefly useful as a means of getting going, not as a guide to the final essay.

The Outline as a Way of Checking a Draft

Whether or not you use a preliminary outline, we strongly suggest that after writing what you hope is your last draft, you make an outline of it; there is no better way of finding out whether the essay is well organized.

Go through the draft, and write down the chief points in the order in which you make them. That is, prepare a table of contents—perhaps a phrase for each paragraph. Next, examine your notes to see what kind of sequence they reveal in your paper:

- Is the sequence reasonable? Can it be improved?

- Are any passages irrelevant?

- Does something important seem to be missing?

If no coherent structure or reasonable sequence clearly appears in the outline, then the full prose version of your argument probably doesn't have any either. Therefore, produce another draft by moving things around, adding or subtracting paragraphs—cutting and pasting them into a new sequence, with transitions as needed—and then make another outline to see if the sequence now is satisfactory.

You're probably familiar with the structure known as a **formal outline**. Major points are indicated by I, II, III; points within major points are indicated by A, B, C; divisions within A, B, C are indicated by 1, 2, 3; and so on. Thus:

I. Arguments for opening all Olympic sports to professionals

    A. Fairness

        1. Some Olympic sports are already open to professionals.

        2. Some athletes who really are not professionals are classified as professionals.

    B. Quality (achievements would be higher)

You may want to outline your draft according to this principle, or you might simply write a phrase for each paragraph and indent the subdivisions. But keep these points in mind:

- It is not enough for the parts to be ordered reasonably.
- The order must be made clear to the reader, usually by means of transitions such as *for instance, on the one hand... on the other hand, we can now turn to an opposing view,* and so on.

Here is another way of thinking about an outline. For each paragraph, write:

- what the paragraph *says,* and
- what the paragraph *does.*

An opening paragraph might be outlined thus:

- What the paragraph *says* is that the words "under God" in the Pledge of Allegiance should be omitted.
- What the paragraph *does* is, first, inform the reader of the thesis, and second, *provide some necessary background*—for instance, that the words were not in the original wording of the Pledge.

A dual outline of this sort will help you to see whether you have a final draft or a draft that needs refinement.

A Last Word about Outlines

Outlines may seem rigid to many writers, especially to those who compose online, where we're accustomed to cutting, copying, moving, and deleting as we draft. However, as mentioned earlier, an outline—whether you write it before drafting a single word or use it to evaluate the organization of something you've already written—is meant to be a guide rather than a straitjacket. Many writers who compose electronically find that the ability to keep banging out words—typing is so much easier than pushing a pen or pencil—and to cut and paste without actually reaching for scissors makes it easy to produce an essay that readers may find difficult to follow. (There is much truth in the proverb "Easy writing makes hard reading.") If you compose electronically, and especially if you continually add, delete, and move text around without a clear organizational goal in mind, be sure to read and outline your draft, and *then* examine the outline to see if indeed there is a reasonable organization.

Outlines are especially helpful for long essays, but even short ones benefit from a bit of advanced planning, a list of a few topics (drawn from notes already taken) that keep the writer moving in an orderly way. A longer work such as an honors or a master's thesis typically requires careful planning. An outline will be a great help in ensuring that you produce something that a reader can easily follow—but, of course, you may find as you write that the outline needs to be altered.

When readers reach the end of a piece of writing, they should feel that the writer has brought them to a decisive point and is not simply stopping abruptly and unexpectedly.

✓ A Checklist for Organizing an Argument

- ☐ Does the introduction let the readers know where the author is taking them?

- ☐ Does the introduction state the problem or issue?

    - ☐ Does it state the claim (the thesis)?

    - ☐ Does it suggest the organization of the essay, thereby helping the reader to follow the argument?

- ☐ Do subsequent paragraphs support the claim?

    - ☐ Do they offer evidence?

    - ☐ Do they face objections to the claim and offer reasonable responses?

    - ☐ Do they indicate why the author's claim is preferable?

    - ☐ Do transitions (signposts such as *Furthermore*, *In contrast*, and *Consider as an example*) guide the reader through the argument?

- ☐ Does the essay end effectively, with a paragraph (at most, two paragraphs) bringing a note of closure — for instance, by indicating that the proposed solution is relatively simple? By admitting that although the proposed solution will be difficult to implement, it is certainly feasible? By reminding the reader of the urgency of the problem?

Tone and the Writer's Persona

Although this book is chiefly about argument in the sense of rational discourse—the presentation of reasons in support of a thesis or conclusion—the appeal to reason is only one form of persuasion. Another form is the appeal to emotion—to pity, for example. Aristotle saw, in addition to appeals to reason and to emotion, a third form of persuasion—the appeal to the speaker's character. He called it the **ethical appeal** (the Greek word for this kind of appeal is *ethos*, meaning "character"). The idea is that effective speakers convey the suggestion that they are

- informed,
- intelligent,
- fair minded (persons of goodwill), and
- honest.

Because they are perceived as trustworthy, their words inspire confidence in their listeners. It is a fact that when reading an argument we're often aware of the *person* or *voice* behind the words, and our assent to the argument depends partly on the extent to which we can share the speaker's assumptions and see the matter from his or her point of view—in short, the extent to which we can *identify* with the speaker.

How can a writer inspire the confidence that lets readers identify with him or her? First, the writer should possess the virtues Aristotle specified: intelligence or good sense, honesty, and benevolence or goodwill. As a Roman proverb puts it, "No one gives what he does not have." Still, possession of these qualities is not a guarantee that you will convey them in your writing. Like all other writers, you'll have to revise your drafts so that these qualities become apparent; stated more moderately, you'll have to revise so that nothing in the essay causes a reader to doubt your intelligence, honesty, and goodwill. A blunder in logic, a misleading quotation, a snide remark, even an error in spelling—all such slips can cause readers to withdraw their sympathy from the writer.

Of course, all good argumentative essays do not sound exactly alike; they do not all reveal the same speaker. Each writer develops his or her own voice, or (as literary critics and instructors call it) **persona**. In fact, one writer may have several voices or personae, depending on the topic and the audience. The president of the United States delivering an address on the State of the Union has one persona; when chatting with a reporter at his summer home, he has another. This change is not a matter of hypocrisy. Different circumstances call for different language. As a French writer put it, there is a time to speak of "Paris" and a time to speak of "the capital of the nation." When Abraham Lincoln spoke at Gettysburg, he didn't say "Eighty-seven years ago"; instead, he intoned "Four score and seven years ago." We might say that just as some occasions required him to be the folksy Honest Abe, the occasion of the dedication of hallowed ground at Gettysburg, where so many Civil War soldiers lost their lives, required him to be formal and solemn—thus, as president of the United States he appropriately used biblical language. Lincoln's election campaigns called for one persona, and the dedication of a military cemetery (an entirely different rhetorical situation) called for a different persona. For examples on how to vary tone, see Thinking Critically: Varying Tone.

A Rule for Writers

Present yourself so that readers see you as knowledgeable, honest, open-minded, and interested in helping them to think about the significance of an issue.

When we talk about a writer's persona, we mean the way in which the writer presents his or her attitudes

- toward *the self,*
- toward *the audience,* and
- toward *the subject.*

Thus, if a writer says:

> I have thought long and hard about this subject, and I can say with assurance that…

we may feel that he is a self-satisfied egotist who probably is mouthing other people's opinions. Certainly he's mouthing clichés: "long and hard," "say with assurance."

Let's look at a subtler example of an utterance that reveals certain attitudes:

> President Nixon was hounded out of office by journalists.

The statement above conveys a respectful attitude toward Nixon ("President Nixon") and a hostile attitude toward the press (they are beasts, curs who "hounded" our elected leader). If the writer's attitudes were reversed, she might have said something like this:

> The press turned the searchlight on Tricky Dick's criminal shenanigans.

"Tricky Dick" and "criminal" are obvious enough, but notice that "shenanigans" also implies the writer's contempt for Nixon, and "turned the searchlight" suggests that the press is a source of illumination, a source of truth. The original version and the opposite version both say that the press was responsible for Nixon's resignation, but the original version ("President Nixon was hounded") conveys indignation toward journalists, whereas the revision conveys contempt for Nixon.

These two versions suggest two speakers who differ not only in their view of Nixon but also in their manner, including the seriousness with which they take themselves. Although the passage is very short, it seems to us that the first speaker conveys righteous indignation ("hounded"), whereas the second conveys amused contempt ("shenanigans"). To our ears the tone, as well as the point, differs in the two versions.

We are talking now about loaded words, which convey the writer's attitude and, through their connotations, seek to win the reader to the writer's side. Compare the words in the left-hand column with those in the right:

freedom fighter	terrorist
pro-choice	pro-abortion
pro-life	antichoice
economic refugee	illegal alien
terrorist surveillance	domestic spying

The words in the left-hand column sound like good things; speakers who use them seek to establish themselves as virtuous people supporting worthy causes. The connotations (associations, overtones) of these pairs of words differ, even though the denotations (explicit meanings, dictionary definitions) are the same—just as the connotations of *mother* and *female parent* differ, although the denotations are the same. Similarly, although Lincoln's "four score and seven" and "eighty-seven" both denote "thirteen less than one hundred," they differ in connotation.

Thinking Critically: Varying Tone

See the example of Abraham Lincoln's tone below. In the spaces provided, rewrite Lincoln's statement in wording that reflects qualities of other tones as indicated in the middle column.

Tone	Qualities of the Tone	Example
Abraham Lincoln	Invokes biblical rhetoric in an appeal to national unity	*Four score and seven years ago our fathers brought forth on this continent a new nation, conceived in liberty, and dedicated to the proposition that all men are created equal.*
More academic tone	Incorporates specific factual information and connects to overarching ideas	
More informal tone	Is accurate but simplified, forgoing much detail	
Too informal for most academic writing	Mischaracterizes or oversimplifies the thought process	

Tone is not only a matter of connotation (*hounded out of office* versus, let's say, *compelled to resign*, or *pro-choice* versus *pro-abortion*); it is also a matter of such things as the selection and type of examples. A writer who offers many examples, especially ones drawn from ordinary life, conveys a persona different from that of a writer who offers no examples or only an occasional invented instance. The first writer seems friendlier, more honest, more down-to-earth.

Last Words on Tone

On the whole, when writing an argument, it's advisable to be courteous and respectful of your topic, your audience, and people who hold views opposite to yours. It is rarely good for one's own intellectual development to regard as villains or fools persons who hold views different from one's own, especially if some of them are in the audience. Keep in mind the story of two strangers on a train who, striking up a conversation, found that both were clergymen, though of different faiths. Then one said to the other, "Well, why shouldn't we be friends? After all, we both serve God, you in your way and I in His."

Complacency is all right when telling a joke, but not when offering an argument:

- Recognize opposing views.
- Assume they are held in good faith.
- State them fairly. If you don't, you do a disservice not only to the opposition but also to your own position because the perceptive reader won't take you seriously.
- Be temperate in arguing your own position: "If I understand their view correctly..."; "It seems reasonable to conclude that..."; "Perhaps, then, we can agree that...."
- Write calmly. If you become overly emotional, readers may interpret you as biased or unreasonable, and they may lose their confidence in you.

One way to practice thinking about tone and persona is to think about your professional e-mails. As a student, you probably send many e-mails to classmates and to your instructors or other offices on campus (e.g., the financial aid office, your academic advisor). As teachers, we are often surprised at how flippant and inattentive students are when e-mailing. How do you present yourself in your professional e-mails?

We, One, Or I?

The use of *we* in the previous paragraph brings us to another point: Is it correct to use the first-person pronouns *I* and *we*? In this part of the book, because three of us are writing, we often use *we* to mean the three authors. And we sometimes use *we* to mean the authors and the readers. This shifting use of one word can be troublesome, but we hope (clearly, the *we* here refers only to the authors) that we have avoided ambiguity. But can, or should, or must an individual use *we* instead of *I*? The short answer is no.

If you're simply speaking for yourself, use *I*. Attempts to avoid the first-person singular by saying things like "This writer thinks..." and "It is thought that..." and "One thinks that..." are far more irritating (and wordy) than the use of *I*. The so-called editorial *we* sounds as odd in a student's argument as the royal *we* does. (Mark Twain said that the only ones who can appropriately say *we* are kings, editors, and people with a tapeworm.) It's advisable to use *we* only when you are sure you're writing or speaking directly to an audience who holds membership in the same group, as in "We *students of* X *university* should..." or "We *the members of Theta Chi fraternity* need to...." If the *we* you refer to has a referent, simply refer to what it means: Say "Americans are" rather than "We are," or "College students should" rather than "We should," or "Republicans need to" rather than "We need to."

Many students assume that using *one* will solve the problem of pronouns. But because one *one* leads to another, the sentence may end up sounding, as James Thurber once said, "like a trombone solo." It's best to admit that you are the author, and to use *I*. However, there is no need to preface every sentence with "I think." The reader knows that the essay is yours and that the opinions are yours; so use *I* when you must, but not needlessly. Do not write, "I think *X* movie is terrible"; simply say, "*X* movie is terrible." And do not add extra words that say more obvious things, like "*It is my idea that* the company needs a new mission statement." Just write, "*The company needs a new mission statement.*"

Thinking Critically: Eliminating *We*, *One*, and *I*

Rewrite the following sentences to eliminate unnecessary uses of *I*, *we*, *one*, and other gratuitous statements of opinion.

Original Sentence	Rewritten Sentence
I think fracking is the best way to achieve energy independence and to create jobs.	Fracking is the best way to achieve energy independence and to create jobs.
In our country, we believe in equality and freedom.	
One should consider one's manners at formal dinner parties.	
In my opinion, the government should not regulate the sizes of sodas we can order.	
It is clearly the case that the new policy treats employees unfairly.	

Often you'll see *I* in journalistic writing and autobiographical writing—and in some argumentative writing, too—but in most argumentative writing it's best to state the facts and (when drawing reasonable conclusions from them) to keep yourself in the background. Why? The more you use *I* in an essay, the more your readers will attach *you* directly to the argument and may regard your position as personal rather than as relevant to themselves.

✓ A Checklist for Attending to the Needs of the Audience

☐ Do I have a sense of what the audience probably knows about the issue?

☐ Do I have a sense of what the audience probably thinks about the issue?

☐ Have I stated the thesis clearly and sufficiently early in the essay?

☐ How much common ground do I probably share with the audience?

☐ Have I tried to establish common ground and then moved on to advance my position?

☐ Have I supported my arguments with sufficient details?

☐ Have I used appropriate language (e.g., defined terms that are likely to be unfamiliar)?

☐ Have I indicated why readers should care about the issue and should accept my views, or at least give them serious consideration?

☐ Is the organization clear?

☐ Have I used transitions where they are needed?

☐ If visual material (charts, graphs, pictures) will enhance my arguments, have I used them?

☐ Have I presented myself as a person who is fair, informed, and worth listening to? In short, have I conveyed a strong *ethos*?

Avoiding Sexist Language

Courtesy as well as common sense requires that you respect your readers' feelings. Many people today find offensive the implicit sexism in the use of male pronouns to denote not only men but also women ("As the reader follows the argument, he will find…"). And sometimes the use of the male pronoun to denote all people is ridiculous ("An individual, no matter what his sex,…").

In most contexts there is no need to use gender-specific nouns or pronouns. One way to avoid using *he* when you mean any person is to use *he or she* (or *she or he*), but the result is sometimes cumbersome—although superior to the overly conspicuous *he/she* and *s/he*.

Here are two simple ways to solve the problem:

- *Use the plural* ("As readers follow the argument, they will find…").
- *Recast the sentence* so that no pronoun is required ("Readers following the argument will find…").

Because *man* and *mankind* strike many readers as sexist when used in such expressions as "Man is a rational animal" and "Mankind has not yet solved this problem," consider using such words as *human being, person, people, humanity,* and *we*. (*Examples:* "Human beings are rational animals"; "We have not yet solved this problem.")

Peer Review

Your instructor may suggest—or require—that you submit an early draft of your essay to a fellow student or small group of students for comment. Such a procedure benefits both author and readers: You get the responses of a reader, and the student-reader gets experience in thinking about the problems of developing an argument, especially such matters as the degree of detail that a writer needs to offer to a reader and the importance of keeping the organization evident to a reader.

Oral peer reviews allow for the give and take of discussion, but probably most students and most instructors find written peer reviews more helpful because reviewers think more carefully about their responses to the draft, and they help essayists to get beyond a knee-jerk response to criticism. Online reviews on a class Web site, through e-mail, or via another file-sharing service are especially helpful precisely because they are not face to face; the peer reviewer gets practice *writing*, and the essayist is not directly challenged. Sharing documents works well for peer review.

✓   A Checklist for Peer Review of a Draft of an Argument

Read through the draft quickly. Then read it again, with the following questions in mind. Remember: You are reading a draft, a work in progress. You're expected to offer suggestions, and you're expected to offer them courteously.

In a sentence, indicate the degree to which the draft shows promise of fulfilling the assignment.

- ☐ Is the writer's tone appropriate? Who is the audience?

- ☐ Looking at the essay as a whole, what thesis (main idea) is advanced?

- ☐ Are the needs of the audience kept in mind? For instance, do some words need to be defined? Is the evidence (e.g., the examples and the testimony of authorities) clear and effective?

- ☐ Can I accept the assumptions? If not, why not?

- ☐ Is any obvious evidence (or counterevidence) overlooked?

- ☐ Is the writer proposing a solution? If so,

  - ☐ Are other equally attractive solutions adequately examined?

  - ☐ Has the writer overlooked some unattractive effects of the proposed solution?

- ☐ Looking at each paragraph separately,

  - ☐ What is the basic point?

  - ☐ How does each paragraph relate to the essay's main idea or to the previous paragraph?

- ☐ Should some paragraphs be deleted? Be divided into two or more paragraphs? Be combined? Be moved elsewhere? (If you outline the essay by writing down the gist of each paragraph, you'll get help in answering these questions.)

- ☐ Is each sentence clearly related to the sentence that precedes and to the sentence that follows? If not, in a sentence or two indicate examples of good and bad transitions.

- ☐ Is each paragraph adequately developed? Are there sufficient details, perhaps brief supporting quotations from the text?

- ☐ Are the introductory and concluding paragraphs effective?

- ☐ What are the paper's chief strengths?

- ☐ Make at least two specific suggestions that you think will assist the author to improve the paper.

A Student's Essay, from Rough Notes to Final Version

While we were revising this textbook, we asked the students in one of our classes to write a short essay (500–750 words) on some ethical problem that concerned them. Because this assignment was the first writing assignment in the course, we explained that a good way to generate ideas is to ask oneself some questions, write down responses, question those responses, and write freely for ten minutes or so, not worrying about contradictions. We invited our students to hand in their initial notes along with the finished essay, so that we could get a sense of how they proceeded as writers. Not all of them chose to hand in their notes, but we were greatly encouraged by those who did. What encouraged us was the confirmation of an old belief—we call it a fact—that students will hand in a thoughtful essay if before preparing a final version they ask themselves *why* they think this or that, write down their responses, and are not afraid to change their minds as they proceed.

Here are the first notes of a student, Emily Andrews, who elected to write about whether to give money to street beggars. She simply put down ideas, one after the other.

Help the poor? Why do I (sometimes) do it?

I feel guilty, and think I should help them: poor, cold, hungry (but also some of them are thirsty for liquor, and will spend the money on liquor, not on food).

I also feel annoyed by them—most of them.

Where does the expression "the deserving poor" come from?

And "poor but honest"? Actually, that sounds odd. Wouldn't "rich but honest" make more sense?

Why don't they work? Fellow with red beard, always by bus stop in front of florist's shop, always wants a handout. He is a regular, there all day every day, so I guess he is in a way "reliable," so why doesn't he put the same time in on a job?

Or why don't they get help? Don't they know they need it? They *must* know they need it.

Maybe that guy with the beard is just a con artist. Maybe he makes more money by panhandling than he would by working, and it's a lot easier!

Kinds of poor—how to classify??

    drunks, druggies, etc.

    mentally ill (maybe drunks belong here, too)

    decent people who have had terrible luck

Why private charity?

Doesn't it make sense to say we (fortunate individuals) should give something—an occasional handout—to people who have had terrible luck? (I suppose some people might say there's no need for any of us to give anything—the government takes care of the truly needy—but I *do* believe in giving charity. A month ago a friend of the family passed away, and the woman's children suggested that people might want to make a donation in her name to a shelter for battered women. I know my parents made a donation.)

BUT how can I tell who is who, which are which? Which of these people asking for "spare change" really need (deserve???) help, and which are phonies? Impossible to tell.

Possibilities:

> Give to no one.

> Give to no one but make an annual donation, maybe to United Way.

> Give a dollar to each person who asks. This would probably not cost me even a dollar a day.

> Occasionally do without something—maybe a CD or a meal in a restaurant—and give the money I save to people who seem worthy.

WORTHY? What am I saying? How can I, or anyone, tell? The neat-looking guy who says he just lost his job may be a phony, and the dirty bum—probably a drunk—may desperately need food. (OK, so what if he spends the money on liquor instead of food? At least he'll get a little pleasure in life. No! It's not all right if he spends it on drink.)

Other possibilities:

> Do some volunteer work?

> To tell the truth, I don't want to put in the time. I don't feel *that* guilty.

So what's the problem?

Is it, How I can help the very poor (handouts, or through an organization)? or

How I can feel less guilty about being lucky enough to be able to go to college and to have a supportive family?

I can't quite bring myself to believe I should help every beggar who approaches, but I also can't bring myself to believe that I should do nothing, on the grounds that:

a.   it's probably their fault

b.   if they are deserving, they can get gov't help. No, I just can't believe that. Maybe some are too proud to look for government help, or don't know that they're entitled to it.

> What to do?
>
> On balance, it seems best to:
>
> a.   give to United Way
>
> b.   maybe also give to an occasional individual, if I happen to be moved, without worrying about whether he or she is "deserving" (since it's probably impossible to know)

A day after making these notes Emily reviewed them, added a few points, and then made a very brief selection from them to serve as an outline for her first draft:

> Opening para.: "poor but honest"? Deserve "spare change"?
>
> Charity: private or through organizations?
>
>   pros and cons
>
>   guy at bus
>
>   it wouldn't cost me much, but… better to give through organizations
>
> Concluding para.: still feel guilty?
>
>   maybe mention guy at bus again?

After writing and revising a draft, Emily submitted her essay to a fellow student for peer review. She then revised her work in light of the peer's suggestions and her own further thinking.

On the next page we give the final essay. If after reading the final version you reread Emily's early notes, you'll notice that some of her notes never made it into the final version. But without the notes, the essay probably wouldn't have been as interesting as it is. When Emily made the notes, she wasn't so much putting down her ideas as *finding* ideas through the process of writing.

Emily Andrews

Professor Barnet

English 102

January 15, 2016

Why I Don't Spare "Spare Change"

"Poor but honest." "The deserving poor." I don't know the origin of these quotations, but they always come to mind when I think of "the poor." But I also think of people who, perhaps through alcohol or drugs, have ruined not only their own lives but also the lives of others in order to indulge in their own pleasure. Perhaps alcoholism and drug addiction really are "diseases," as many people say, but my own feeling—based, of course, not on any serious study—is that most alcoholics and drug addicts can be classified with the "undeserving poor." And that is largely why I don't distribute spare change to panhandlers.

But surely among the street people there are also some who can rightly be called "deserving." Deserving of what? My spare change? Or simply the government's assistance? It happens that I have been brought up to believe that it is appropriate to make contributions to charity—let's say a shelter for battered women—but if I give some change to a panhandler, am I making a contribution to charity and thereby helping someone, or, on the contrary, am I perhaps simply encouraging someone not to get help? Or maybe even worse, am I supporting a con artist?

If one believes in the value of private charity, one can give either to needy individuals or to charitable organizations. In giving to a panhandler one may indeed be helping a person who badly needs help, but one cannot be certain that one is giving to a needy individual. In giving to an organization such as the United Way, in contrast, one can feel that one's money is likely to be used wisely. True, confronted by a beggar one may feel that *this* particular unfortunate individual needs help at *this* moment—a cup of coffee or a sandwich—and the need will not be met unless I put my hand in my pocket right now. But I have come to think that the beggars whom I encounter can get along without my spare change, and indeed perhaps they are actually better off for not having money to buy liquor or drugs.

It happens that in my neighborhood I encounter few panhandlers. There is one fellow who is always by the bus stop where I catch the bus to the college, and I never give him anything precisely because he is always there. He is such a regular that, I think, he ought to be able to hold a regular job. Putting him aside, I probably don't encounter more than three or four beggars in a week. (I'm not counting street

Andrews 2

musicians. These people seem quite able to work for a living. If they see their "work" as playing or singing, let persons who enjoy their performances pay them. I do not consider myself among their audience.) The truth of the matter is that since I meet so few beggars, I could give each one a dollar and hardly feel the loss. At most, I might go without seeing a movie some week. But I know nothing about these people, and it's my impression—admittedly based on almost no evidence—that they simply prefer begging to working. I am not generalizing about street people, and certainly I am not talking about street people in the big urban centers. I am talking only about the people whom I actually encounter.

That's why I usually do not give "spare change," and I don't think I will in the future. These people will get along without me. Someone else will come up with money for their coffee or their liquor, or, at worst, they will just have to do without. I will continue to contribute occasionally to a charitable organization, not simply (I hope) to salve my conscience but because I believe that these organizations actually do good work. But I will not attempt to be a mini-charitable organization, distributing (probably to the unworthy) spare change.

The Essay Analyzed

Finally, here are a few comments about the essay.

The title is informative, alerting the reader to the topic and the author's position. (By the way, the student told us that in her next-to-last draft, the title was "Is It Right to Spare 'Spare Change'?" This title, unlike the revision, introduces the topic but not the author's position.)

The opening paragraph holds a reader's interest, partly by alluding to the familiar phrase "the deserving poor" and partly by introducing the *un*familiar phrase "the *un*deserving poor." Notice, too, that this opening paragraph ends by clearly asserting the author's thesis. Writers need not always announce their thesis early, but it is usually advisable to do so.

Paragraph 2 begins by voicing what probably is the reader's somewhat uneasy—perhaps even negative—response to the first paragraph. That is, *the writer has a sense of her audience;* she knows how her reader feels, and she takes account of the feeling.

Paragraph 3 clearly sets forth the alternatives. A reader may disagree with the writer's attitude, but the alternatives seem to be stated fairly.

Paragraphs 4 and 5 are more personal than the earlier paragraphs. The writer, more or less having stated what she takes to be the facts, now is entitled to offer a highly personal response to them.

The final paragraph nicely wraps things up by means of the words "spare change," which go back to the title and to the end of the first paragraph. The reader thus experiences a sensation of completeness. The essayist, of course, hasn't solved the problem for all of us for all time, but she presents a thoughtful argument and ends the essay effectively.

Inside Work: Exercise

In a brief essay, state a claim and support it with evidence. Choose an issue in which you are genuinely interested and about which you already know something. You may want to interview a few experts and do some reading, but don't try to write a highly researched paper. Sample topics:

1. Students in laboratory courses should not be required to participate in the dissection of animals.

2. Washington, D.C., should be granted statehood.

3. In wartime, women should be subject to the military draft.

4. The annual Miss America contest is an insult to women.

5. The government should not offer financial support to the arts.

6. The chief fault of the curriculum in high school was...

7. No specific courses should be required in colleges or universities.

A Guide to College and College Writing

Part Two

Andrea Tsurumi

Part Two

A Guide to College and College Writing

Chapter 7 Inside Colleges and Universities

What Is Higher Education?

Andrea Tsurumi

This book introduces the expectations about writing you'll likely encounter in college and gives you a set of tools to complete writing tasks successfully. To understand those expectations, you must first understand how colleges and universities are structured; how your other writing experiences in high school, college, and work might compare; and what expectations about writing you might encounter in your particular college or university classes. These expectations will likely differ according to the type of college or university you attend.

As you read through many of the chapters in this book, certain recurring features will help expand your knowledge of college writing:

- *Insider's View* boxes contain excerpts of comments by scholars and students discussing academic writing. Many of these are gleaned from video interviews that complement the instruction in this book. The videos can be viewed for greater insight into the processes and productions of academic writers. Video content and other great resources are available on the LaunchPad Solo designed to accompany this text.

- *Inside Work* activities prompt you to reflect on what you have learned while trying out new insights and techniques.

- *Writing Projects* offer sequences of activities that will help you develop your own compositions.

- *Tip Sheets* summarize key lessons of the chapters.

Before we turn to college writing, however, we ask you to read about and reflect on some of the wider contexts of higher education—in particular, your place in it.

How Do Colleges and Universities Differ from One Another?

As we discuss the expectations you might encounter related to writing in college, you should consider the specific context of the school you're attending. What kind of school is it? What types of students does it serve? What are the school's mission and focus? It's important to realize that different schools have differing missions and values that influence their faculty members' expectations for students.

LHow did you determine where to attend college? Some prospective students send out applications to multiple schools, while others know exactly where they want to start their college careers. Some students transfer from one school to another, and they do so for a variety of reasons. If you researched potential schools, and especially if you visited different campuses as part of your decision-making process, you likely realized that there are many different kinds of schools in the United States (not to mention the variety of institutions of higher education elsewhere in the world). If we just focus on the range of higher education options in the United States, we find:

- **Community Colleges:** schools that typically offer associate's degrees. Some community colleges prepare students to enter careers directly following graduation; others specialize in helping students transfer to bachelor's-granting institutions after completing most of their general education requirements or an associate's degree.

- **Liberal Arts Colleges/Universities:** schools that introduce students to a broad variety of disciplines as they pursue their bachelor's degrees. Liberal arts schools generally focus on undergraduate education, although some offer graduate degrees as well.

- **Doctoral-Granting/Research-Intensive Universities:** schools with an emphasis on research and a focus on both undergraduate and graduate education. Doctoral-granting universities, especially those that are research-intensive, can often be quite large, and they generally have higher expectations for faculty members' research activities than other types of institutions do. As a result, students may have more opportunities for collaborative research with faculty members, and graduate students might teach some undergraduate classes.

andy dean photography/Shutterstock

- **Master's-Granting Institutions:**   schools that offer bachelor's degrees in addition to a selection of master's degrees. Such schools usually have a dual focus on undergraduate and graduate education, but they might not emphasize research expectations for their faculty as intensely as doctoral-granting institutions do.

- **Schools with a Specific Focus:**   schools that serve specific populations or prepare students for particular careers. Such schools might be single-sex institutions, historically black colleges and universities, Hispanic-serving institutions, religious-affiliated schools, or agricultural, technical, and vocational schools.

- **For-Profit Institutions:**   schools that operate on a business model and are privately held or publicly traded companies. Some are regionally accredited institutions; many focus on meeting the needs of students whose schedules or other commitments require a different approach from what a typical non-profit college or university provides.

What kind of school is the institution that you currently attend? Knowing how your particular college or university is structured, and how it fits into the larger context of higher education, can help you understand its institutional values and the emphasis it places on particular kinds of academic preparation. If you know these important factors, you'll be able to anticipate the expectations for your academic work and understand the reasoning behind the requirements for your degree.

Inside Work: Choosing a College

Write brief responses to the following questions, and be prepared to discuss them with your classmates.

- What kind of institution do you attend? What characteristics of your school seem to match that category?

- What degree program or major are you most interested in? Why?

- Was your interest in a particular degree program or major a factor when you decided to go to college? Did it draw you to your particular college? Why or why not?

- What classes are you taking, and how did you choose them?

- What kinds of factors do you consider when choosing your classes? What guidance, requirements, or other influences help you make those choices?

What Is the Purpose of College?

People's reasons for pursuing an undergraduate degree can differ, depending on the school and the individual student. Some schools and degree programs focus on preparing students for particular vocations that they can pursue directly after graduation. Others focus more broadly on developing well-rounded, informed graduates who will be active in their communities regardless of which careers they pursue. Still others emphasize different, and sometimes quite specific, outcomes for their graduates. If you have never done so, consider taking a look at the mission or values statements for your university, college, or department. What do the faculty members and administrators value? What are their expectations of you as a student?

For example, the mission statement of Texas A&M University begins by stating:

> Texas A&M University is dedicated to the discovery, development, communication, and application of knowledge in a wide range of academic and professional fields.

This statement shows a broad commitment to a range of academic interests and professions; therefore, students at Texas A&M can expect to find a wide range of majors represented at the university. The mission statement also emphasizes that knowledge discovery is important at Texas A&M, highlighting the school's role as a research-intensive university.

As another example, the mission statement of San Juan College in New Mexico reads:

> The mission of San Juan College is to improve the quality of life of the citizens it serves by meeting the educational and human needs of the entire community in concert with community agencies, businesses, industries, and other groups.

This statement illustrates San Juan College's emphasis on connection to the community and the agencies, businesses, and industries surrounding and connected to the college. San Juan's mission is connected intricately to the community it serves.

A third example is the mission statement of Endicott College in Massachusetts, which begins by stating:

> The mission of Endicott College is to instill in students an understanding of and an appreciation for professional and liberal studies. Deeply woven within this philosophy is the concept of applied learning, which has been the hallmark of Endicott. Linking classroom and off-campus work experience through required internships remains the most distinguishing feature of the College.

Andrea Tsurumi

Endicott's mission mentions an emphasis on applied learning, which is evident through its requirement of internships to extend classroom learning. Students who enroll at Endicott College should expect to make practical, hands-on application of their learning throughout their coursework.

Of course, different students have different goals and reasons for pursuing undergraduate degrees. Sometimes those goals match the institution's mission fairly closely, but not always. What is your purpose in attending your college or university? How do your personal and professional goals fit within the school's goals and values? What will you need to do while in college to achieve your goals? What have you already accomplished, and what do you still need to know and do?

Inside Work: Writing about College

Read the following questions, and write a brief response to each.

- What goals do you hope to achieve by attending college?
- What steps should you take to maximize your opportunity to achieve your academic goals?

Next, find your college or university's mission statement (usually available on the school's website), and write a brief description that compares your goals for college to the mission statement. How does the mission of your school fit your goals? How might the strengths and mission of your college or university help you achieve your goals?

What Are Academic Disciplines?

Another structural feature of colleges and universities is the way they are divided into academic disciplines. Depending on the school, this might take the form of departments, divisions, colleges, or other groupings. Academic disciplines are, broadly defined, areas of teaching, research, and inquiry that academics pursue. Sometimes these disciplines are listed in broad categories, such as psychology, English, biology, physics, and engineering.

At other times, disciplines are listed in more specialized categories that demonstrate the diversity of areas encompassed within higher education: for example, adolescent psychology, abnormal psychology, sociolinguistics, second language acquisition, molecular biology, physiology, astrophysics, quantum mechanics, civil engineering, mechanical engineering, computer science, Victorian poetry, and medieval literature.

While the specific divisions may differ according to the institution, most college and university faculties are grouped into departments. Larger schools are often further divided into colleges or divisions, which usually cluster departments together that are related in some way to one another. These divisions often, but not always, fall along common lines that divide departments into broader disciplinary areas of the humanities, social sciences, natural sciences, and applied fields. We describe these broad categories in more detail in the next section.

Andrea Tsurumi

How Many Different Academic Disciplines Are There?

You might find that different faculty members give varying answers to the question, "How many different academic disciplines are there?" And those answers differ for good reason. Sometimes academic disciplines are seen as equivalent to departments. Faculty in the history department study history, right? But the subject of history can be divided into many different categories, too: antebellum U.S. history, Middle Eastern history, and African American history, for example. In addition, people in other departments might study and teach topics that are related to history, such as American religious history, medieval literature and culture, and ancient rhetoric. You can probably imagine how categorizing all these different areas of study and research would be difficult.

For the purposes of this text, we're going to explore writing in different disciplinary areas that are grouped together according to (1) the kinds of questions that scholars ask in those disciplines and (2) the research strategies, or methods of inquiry, that they use to answer those questions. As mentioned earlier, we've divided various academic disciplines into four broad disciplinary categories: humanities, social sciences, natural sciences, and applied fields. As we talk about these four areas of study and the disciplines associated with them, both here and in Part Three of the book, you'll notice some similarities and differences within the categories:

- Scholars in the humanities usually ask questions about the human condition. To answer these questions, they often employ methods of inquiry that are based on analysis, interpretation, and speculation. Examples of academic disciplines that are generally considered part of the humanities are history, literature, philosophy, foreign languages, religious studies, and the visual arts. For examples of the kinds of questions humanists ask, see Chapter 12.

- Scholars in the social sciences usually ask questions about human behavior and society. To answer these questions, they often employ methods of inquiry that are based on theory building or empirical research. Examples of academic disciplines that are generally considered part of the social sciences are communication, psychology, sociology, political science, economics, and anthropology. For examples of the kinds of questions social scientists ask, see Chapter 13.

- Scholars in the natural sciences usually ask questions about the natural world and the universe. To answer these questions, they often employ methods of inquiry that are based on experimentation and quantifiable data. Examples of academic disciplines that are generally considered part of the natural sciences are chemistry, biology, physics, astronomy, and mathematics. For examples of the kinds of questions natural scientists ask, see Chapter 14.

- Scholars in applied fields might have their foundation in any one (or more) of the disciplinary categories, but their work is generally focused on practical application. Some disciplines that could fall under the category of applied fields are criminal justice, medicine, nursing, education, business, agriculture, and engineering. Each of these fields has elements that are closely aligned with the humanities, social sciences, and/or natural sciences, but each also focuses on application of that knowledge in specific contexts. For examples of the kinds of questions scholars in applied fields ask, see Chapter 15.

These categories are not perfectly distinct, though; they sometimes overlap with one another. You'll see examples of overlap in the chapters in Part Three, in the student writing examples there, and when you undertake your own research in academic journals. However, the disciplinary categories of humanities, social sciences, natural sciences, and applied fields are useful for understanding some of the distinctions in the ways academics think and do research.

Inside Work: Understanding Disciplinarity

In your own words, write a brief description of the four academic disciplines mentioned in the previous section.

- humanities
- social sciences
- natural sciences
- applied fields

Next, list your current course schedule. How might you classify the classes you're taking in terms of these four categories? For each class, write for a few minutes about what characteristics of the class cause it to fit into the category you've chosen. Finally, compare your answers with a classmate's.

Why Do Academics Write?

As you think about the writing you will do in college, keep in mind that you are learning how to participate in the kinds of discussions that scholars and faculty members engage in about topics and issues of mutual interest. In other words, you're entering into academic conversations that have been going on for a while. As you are writing, you will need to think about who your audience is (other students? teachers? an audience outside of the academic setting?), who has already been participating in the conversations of interest to you (and perhaps who hasn't), and what expectations for your writing you'll need to follow in order to contribute to those conversations. (We'll have much more to say about the concept of audience in Chapter 8.)

As we explore the kinds of writing done in various disciplinary areas, you'll notice that different disciplines have different expectations for writing. In other words, faculty members in a particular discipline might expect a piece of writing to be structured in a particular way, or they might use specific kinds of language, or they might expect you to be familiar with certain research by others and refer to it in prescribed ways. Each of these expectations is an aspect of the writing *conventions* of a particular discipline. Conventions are the customs that scholars in a particular discipline follow in their writing. Sometimes those conventions take the form of repeated patterns in structure or certain choices in language use, just to name a few. As students learn these conventions, we sometimes say that they are developing *literacy* in the conventions of a discipline. Literacy generally refers to the ability to read and write, but it can also refer to the development of familiarity with the conventions and expectations of different situations. As a student, you will be developing academic literacy—or literacies, since you'll be navigating the expectations of several disciplinary contexts.

Inside Work: Thinking about What Academics Write

Look for a published piece that has been written by one of the professors that you have for another class. Try to find something that you can access in full, either online or through your school's library. Some colleges and universities have lists of recent publications by faculty on their websites. Additionally, some faculty members list their publications on personal websites. You might also seek help from librarians at your institution if you aren't familiar with the library's resources. Then write your responses to the following questions.

- What does the professor write about?
- Where was that work published?
- Who is the audience for your professor's work?
- What surprised you most about your professor's published work?

Insider's View

Undergraduate Students on Academic Writing

Sam Stout, Gena Lambrecht, Alexandria Woods, Students

Left to right: Sam, engineering; Gena, design; Alexandria, biology

QUESTION: How does the writing you did in high school compare to the writing you've done in college so far?

SAM: Well, in high school [teachers] mainly chose what we wrote about. And here in college they allow you to write about what you're going to be focusing on and choose something that's actually going to benefit you in the future instead of writing for an assignment grade.

GENA: Well, I thought I would be doing a lot more writing like in my AP English classes, which was analyzing literature and poems and plays and writing to a prompt that talked a lot about specific conventions for that type of literature.

ALEXANDRIA: I expected my college writing to be science-related—doing lab reports and research proposals—rather than what I did before college, in middle school and high school, which was just doing definition papers, analysis of books, and things like that.

Hear more from students about college writing.

Insider's View

We're Looking for Students to Get Their Own Voices

Karen Keaton Jackson, Writing Studies

"In general, the sense that I get is that in high school, writing is more focused on literature. At the college level, we're more interested in critical thinking. We're looking for students to get their own voices in place. Really getting students to think stylistically about the choices they make, really thinking about purpose and audience and the whole rhetorical context. I think that's really key at the college level. By college we're looking at the purpose, and the audience, and the style, and how all of this is determined based on the different writing situation you're in."

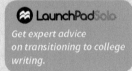

Get expert advice on transitioning to college writing.

To prepare for writing in varied academic contexts, it might be helpful to think about why academics write. Most faculty members at institutions of higher education explain their responsibilities to the institution and their discipline in terms of three categories: their teaching, their research (which generates much of their writing), and their service (what they do outside of their research and teaching that contributes both to the school and to their discipline). Many academics' writing is related to communicating the results of their research, and it might be published or shared with academic audiences or more general audiences. In fact, a scholar might conduct a research project and then find that he or she needs to communicate the results of that project to a variety of audiences.

Imagine that a physiologist who studies diabetes has discovered a new therapy that could potentially benefit diabetic individuals. The researcher might want to publish the results of her study in an academic journal so that other scientists can read about the results, perhaps replicate the study (repeat it to confirm that the results are the same), and maybe expand on the research findings. She might also want to communicate the results of her research to doctors who work with diabetic patients but who don't necessarily read academic journals in physiology. They might read medical journals, though, so in this case the researcher would need to tailor her results to an audience that is primarily interested in the application of research results to patients. In addition, she might want to report the results of her research to the general public, in which case she might write a press release so that newspapers and magazines can develop news stories about her findings. Each of these writing situations involves reporting the same research results, but to different audiences and for different purposes. The physiologist would need to tailor her writing to meet the needs of each writing situation.

How Does Writing in College Compare with Writing in Other Contexts?

Some students find that writing in college focuses less on personal experience and more on academic research than writing they've done in other contexts. Many of your expectations for writing in college might be based on prior experiences, such as the writing you did in high school or in a work setting. Some students are surprised to find that writing instruction in college is not always paired with discussion of literature, as it often is in high school. While some colleges and universities use literature as a starting point for teaching writing, many other schools offer writing instruction that is focused on principles of rhetoric—the study of how language is used to communicate—apart from the study of literature. (Rhetoric will be discussed in detail in subsequent chapters throughout this book.) If you are used to thinking about English courses, and the writing assigned in those courses, as being primarily about literature and literary analysis, you might find that the expectations in your college-level writing courses are somewhat different. Many writing courses at the college level will require you to write about different topics, in different forms, and for different audiences. Depending on your school, writing program, and instructor, the study of literature might be part of that approach, but you might also need to learn about the expectations of instructors in other disciplines.

When we compare the writing expectations in college with what you might have experienced in other contexts, we're making some general assumptions about your experience that may or may not be true. We're also making generalizations about colleges and universities that might differ from the school you're currently attending. One of the most important concepts we'll discuss in this book is the importance of context (see Chapter 8), so you'll need to balance the principles we talk about in this text with your firsthand experience of the context of your particular college or university. You might find that some of our assumptions are true to your particular experience and some are not. When possible, make note of the principles we discuss that are similar to your experience and the ones that are different. As you do so, you'll be learning about and applying these principles in a way that is much more useful than just memorizing information.

Although the approaches toward teaching writing at various colleges and universities differ, we can talk about some common expectations for college-level writing. The Council of Writing Program Administrators (CWPA), a professional organization of hundreds of writing program directors from across the country, published a list of common outcomes for first-year writing courses that has been adapted for use by many schools. The first list of common outcomes was published in 2000, and it has been revised twice since then, most recently in 2014. The purpose of the statement is to provide common expectations for what college students should be able to accomplish in terms of their writing after finishing a first-year course, but the details of those expectations are often revised to fit a specific institution's context. For example, the third outcome deals with "Processes" and states that:

By the end of first-year composition, students should

- Develop a writing project through multiple drafts
- Develop flexible strategies for reading, drafting, reviewing, collaborating, revising, rewriting, rereading, and editing
- Use composing processes and tools as a means to discover and reconsider ideas
- Experience the collaborative and social aspects of writing processes
- Learn to give and act on productive feedback to works in progress
- Adapt composing processes for a variety of technologies and modalities
- Reflect on the development of composing practices and how those practices influence their work

http://wpacouncil.org/positions/outcomes.html

The statement doesn't specify which steps or strategies in a writing process students should practice, or what kinds of writing they should be doing. It is left up to individual schools to determine what will be most helpful for their students.

Some institutions follow the guidelines from the Council of Writing Program Administrators explicitly, while others do not. Even at institutions that use these outcomes as a foundation for the writing curriculum, however, it's often possible to find many different approaches to teaching writing that help students achieve academic literacy. How do your institution's outcomes for writing compare and contrast with your experience in high school English classes? How do the outcomes for writing compare and contrast with your writing experience outside of school (perhaps in work-related or personal settings)?

Inside Work: Understanding the Goals of Your Writing Course

Take a look at the goals, objectives, or outcomes listed for the writing course you are currently taking. You might look for a course description on the school's website or in a course catalog, or you might find goals or learning objectives listed in the course syllabus.

- What surprised you about the goals or objectives for your writing course?
- What is similar to or different from the writing courses you have taken before?
- What is similar to or different from the expectations you had for this course?
- How do the outcomes for the course align with your goals for writing and for college?
- What does the list of goals for your course tell you about what is valued at your institution?

What Do You Already Know about Writing in Different Contexts?

The culminating writing projects in this chapter ask you to explore your own writing and literacy experiences in more detail. Thinking about the experience and skills that you already bring to your college writing will help you to build on them and expand your abilities.

Writing Project: Composing a Literacy Narrative

A *literacy narrative* is an essay that reflects on how someone has developed literacy over time. Literacy is sometimes defined as the ability to read and write, but in this context we'd like you to use a broader definition. Think of literacy not only as the ability to read and write, but also as the ability to successfully function in a specific context or contexts. Your instructor may give you more direction about how to define literacy for the purpose of this assignment, but you could focus on the following questions.

Academic Literacy

- What are your first memories of writing in school?

- How did you learn about the expectations for writing in school?

- Can you think of a time when you struggled to meet the requirements of a school writing assignment? What happened?

Technological Literacy

- What early memories do you have of using technology?

- How do you use technology now to communicate in your daily life? What technologies are most important to you for work, for school, and/or for personal commitments?

Workplace Literacy

- What writing and communication skills are expected in the occupation you aspire to when you graduate? How will you develop those skills?

- Can you think of a time when you encountered a task at work that you didn't know how to accomplish? What did you do? How did you address the challenge?

Social and/or Cultural Literacy

- Have you ever been in a social situation where you didn't know how to act? What did you do?

- What groups do you identify with, and what expectations and shared beliefs make that group cohesive?

A literacy narrative should do three things: (1) make a point about the author's literacy development, (2) read as a story and use narrative strategies to tell the story, and (3) provide specific details that support the point of the narrative.

In a narrative essay, explore the development of your own literacy. You might do this chronologically, at least as you start writing. Be specific in identifying how you define literacy and how you developed your abilities. In your narrative and analysis, provide examples from your experience, and show how they contribute to the development of that literacy. Ultimately, your narrative should be directed to a particular audience for a particular purpose, so think of a context in which you might tell this story. For example, a student who is studying to be a teacher might write about his early literacy experiences and how they led to an interest in teaching other children to read and write. Or an applicant for a job requiring specific technological ability might include a section in an application letter that discusses her development of expertise in technological areas relevant to the job. Be imaginative if you like, but make sure that your narrative provides specific examples and makes a point about your literacy development that you believe is important.

Writing Project: Interviewing a Scholar

Under the guidance of your instructor, find a professor at your college or university who teaches in a discipline that is of interest to you. You might choose a faculty member with whom you already have a connection, either through taking a class, having a mutual acquaintance, or enjoying a shared interest. Ask the scholar if you can interview him or her, either in person or through e-mail. Consider the descriptions of different disciplinary areas in this chapter, and write a profile of the faculty member that addresses questions about his or her writing, such as the following.

- What kinds of writing do scholars in your field do?
- What writing conventions are specific to and important to your field? How did you learn those conventions?
- What was your first experience of writing a scholarly article like? What did you learn through that experience?
- What kinds of writing do you do most often in your work?
- What expectations do you have for students who are learning to write in your field?

Be sure to follow up your questions by asking for specific examples if you need more information to understand the scholar's responses. In addition, you might ask to see an example of his or her academic writing to use as an illustration in your narrative. Above all, be sure to thank the faculty member for taking the time to respond to your questions.

A profile of a faculty member's writing should do two things: (1) make a point about the person being interviewed (in this case, your point should focus on the person's writing), and (2) include details about the person that help develop the point. You might write the questions and answers in an interview format, or you might incorporate the scholar's responses into an essay that uses the interview to make a specific point about his or her development and experience as a writer.

Insider Example

Student Interview with a Faculty Member

Kaitie Gay, a first-year student at North Carolina State University, conducted an interview via e-mail with Marvin Malecha, who is a professor of architecture and dean of the College of Design. Kaitie conducted her interview after reading a selection from one of Malecha's books, *Reconfiguration in the Study and Practice of Design Architecture* (2002). Her interview questions, and Malecha's responses, could lay the foundation for a writing profile.

Courtesy of Kaitie Gay

KAITIE: In your article, you talk about the different ways that individuals learn about the field of architecture. Which do you find more beneficial to students studying architecture, learning by experience or learning in a classroom setting?

MALECHA: I believe both settings are important, as one complements the other. However, it is also true that certain individuals will have their epiphany on a construction site while others will gain insight from theoretical discourse. But in the end, both are important because each gives perspective to the other. For those interested in theory and classroom investigation, the construction site makes real what otherwise would be disconnected ideas. For the individual who is most likely to be inclined to build and ask questions later, the theoretical discussion forces them to be more reflective. It is for this reason that we maintain a close relationship with the architectural profession at NC State. We want students to work in offices as they progress through school. It is also the reason we offer design build experiences during the summer sessions. But the desire to balance a student's experience also justifies our desire to have students study abroad and to participate in scholarship and research. These experiences exercise the mind.

KAITIE: In the article you said, "Technology will reduce the need for a studio-based culture." Is it important that we balance technology and studio, or do you find it a good thing that the field is becoming more technology-driven?

MALECHA: It is easy to forget the rather primitive state of technology in the field of architecture when I wrote this article. The social media and the many tools at our discretion today really amplify my comments. I was speaking to a traditional studio-based culture where students sat at their desks almost solely dependent on the direction and handouts of their instructor. I believed that this sole relationship would be significantly changed by the ability to have incredible amounts of information at hand, including case studies, new materials, programming insights to push along scholarship, and plan development. I believed that it would be possible to check in with a studio instructor from anywhere in the world, blurring the difference between the virtual and the real. It was already true when I wrote this article that joint studios were conducted between schools on different continents utilizing the telephone and fax technology. Given this, I believed that new technologies would enhance such possibilities. I also believed that schools could conduct studios in professional offices, thereby making the bond between practice and education even stronger.

I have never been intimidated by new tools, only concerned that the tools might overwhelm our intentions. The new technologies have brought many wonderful possibilities to the conduct of the design professions. In architecture, ideas such as integrated project delivery would not be possible without the tools. We can build better with fewer errors using new technologies, we can communicate among a diverse set of users and clients using new technologies, and we can archive our work more effectively using new technologies.

It is important, however, that we teach students to control the technology, so as not to be overwhelmed by it.

KAITIE: Later in your piece you talk about the architecture field becoming more competitive, individual, and sometimes arrogant as opposed to cooperative. Throughout your career, have you found that the field is really more individual, or is there a sense of collaboration with other designers when working on a project?

MALECHA: I have found it to be both. There is a very strong culture of the individual within the architecture profession. At times, it will show itself in ugly ways. The prominent celebrity architects are referred to by some as the Black Cape Architects. This reveals the tension between those who take the lead in the concept phase of a project and those who see to the realization of a project through complex phases of design development, construction documents, and construction administration. It is true that great buildings have a personality that is derived most often from the personality of an individual or at least from an office working with a singular mind. It is equally true that the profession is wholly dependent on collaboration to realize even the smallest project.

When I wrote this particular section of the article, I was specifically addressing educators, because in the schools the teaching of collaborative practices was absent for the most part. The school experience had become focused on producing the next great cadre of superstar architects. Of course, this is a flawed strategy, since on a major project such as a hospital or skyscraper there may be a small team of designers led by a strong individual to bring about a design concept and then hundreds within the architectural office and related consultant offices to realize the project. It was my intention to advocate that educators face this dilemma and cause them to teach collaborative methods even as individual design skills were heightened. In addition, it is important to remember that there are many roles architects assume, complementing the obvious role of principal designer. There are those who manage the specification process, those who oversee construction document preparation, those who specialize in construction administration, and those who serve as the primary contact to the clients and users. Each of these roles serves an incredibly important purpose. Again, educators must make students aware of these many roles, give credence to their importance, and encourage students to seek their best place in an interesting and diverse professional culture.

Buildings need the bold ideas of individuals who are strong conceptually. Buildings also need individuals who can put a building together in the most effective way.

KAITIE: What audience were you trying to reach with this article, and what pushed you to write it?

MALECHA: At the time I was writing this article, I was primarily speaking to other educators. However, it is also true that the magazine had a broad audience, and therefore students and practicing architects were very much on my mind. I was trying to get the readers to think differently about the study and practice of architecture.

Discussion Questions

1. Read through Kaitie Gay's questions for Dr. Malecha. What was her purpose in interviewing Dr. Malecha? What did she want to understand?

2. Was there anything that surprised you in Dr. Malecha's responses? If so, what was it?

3. If you were going to add a question to Kaitie's interview, what would it be? Why would you add that question?

4. If Kaitie were to use this interview as the basis for a writing profile of Dr. Malecha, what other information would she need to find? What steps would she need to take?

Tip Sheet Inside Colleges and Universities

- **Colleges and universities are not all the same.** Different kinds of colleges and universities have varying purposes, majors, and degrees, and they appeal to a variety of potential students.

- **The institution you attend has a specific focus.** You may find it helpful to identify this focus and understand how it fits with your academic and career goals.

- **Colleges and universities are divided into disciplinary areas.** You might see these areas at your school as departments, divisions, and/or colleges. In this book, we talk about four broad disciplinary areas: humanities, social sciences, natural sciences, and applied fields.

- **Academic writing follows unique conventions.** When academics write, they often follow conventions specific to their writing situations and to their disciplinary areas.

- **Writing in college is not always the same as writing in other contexts.** In college writing courses, we focus on principles of rhetoric, or how language is used to communicate.

Chapter 8 Reading and Writing Rhetorically

You read and write in many different situations: at school, at home, with your friends, and maybe at work. Perhaps there are other situations in which you read and write, too, likely through a variety of different media. You might read and write in a journal, in a status update on Facebook, in a photo caption on Instagram, in a word processor as you prepare a paper for school, in a text message, or in a note to a friend. You could probably name many other situations in which you read and write on a daily basis.

Have you ever considered how different the processes of reading and writing are in these situations? You're performing the same act (reading or writing a text) in many ways, but several features might change from one situation to another:

- the way the text looks

- the medium or technology you use

- the tone you use

- the words you use (or avoid using)

- the grammar and mechanics that are appropriate

Even within the more specific category of "academic writing" that we address in this book, some of these features might shift depending on the context. In some disciplines, the structure, vocabulary, style, and documentation expectations are different from those in other disciplines. If you've ever written a lab report for a physics class and a literary analysis for a literature class, then you've likely experienced some of those differences. The differences arise because of the specific demands of each of the differing writing situations.

Andrea Tsurumi

Understanding Rhetorical Context

As you read and write, we want you to consider closely the specific situation for which you are writing. In other words, you should always think about the **rhetorical context** in which your writing takes place. In this text, we'll define rhetorical context through four elements:

- who the author is, and what background and experience he or she brings to the text
- who the intended audience is for the text
- what issue or topic the author is addressing
- what the author's purpose is for writing

Each of these elements has an impact on the way a text is written and interpreted. Consider how you might write about your last job in a text message to a friend in comparison with how you might write about it in an application letter for a new job. Even though the author is the same (you) and the topic is the same (your last job), the audience and your purpose for writing are vastly different. These differences thus affect how you characterize your job and your choice in medium for writing the message.

Sometimes writing situations call for more than one audience as well. You might address a **primary audience**, the explicitly addressed audience for the text, but you might also have a **secondary audience**, an implied audience who also might read your text or be interested in it. Imagine you wrote a job application letter as an assignment for a business writing class. Your primary audience would likely be your instructor, but you might also write the letter as a template to use when actually sending out a job application letter in the future. So your future prospective employer might be a secondary audience.

Insider's View

Purpose and Audience Shape Every Decision

Karen Keaton Jackson, Writing Studies

"Purpose and audience essentially shape every decision you will make as a writer. Once you have your topic, and you have the purpose and the audience, then that helps you decide how you're going to structure your sentences, how you're going to organize your essay, the word choices you make, the tone. All those different things are shaped by purpose and audience."

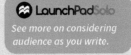

See more on considering audience as you write.

In academic settings, also, these elements of rhetorical context shift depending on the disciplinary context within which you're writing. Consider another example: Imagine a student has decided to research the last presidential election for a school assignment. If the research assignment were given in a history class, then the student might research and write about other political elections that provide a precedent for the outcome of the recent election and the events surrounding it. The student would be approaching the topic from a historical perspective, which would be appropriate for the context of the discipline and audience (a history professor). If the student were writing for an economics class, he or she might focus on the economic impact of elections and how campaign finance laws, voter identification laws, and voters' socioeconomic statuses affected the election. Even though the author, audience, topic, and purpose seem similar at first glance (they're all academic research assignments, right?), the student would focus on different questions and aspects of the topic when examining the election from different disciplinary perspectives and for different audiences. Other elements of the student's writing would likely shift, too, and we'll discuss those differences in Part Three of this book.

Why might it be important to consider the rhetorical context when reading or writing? As you read, noticing the rhetorical context of a text can help you understand choices that the author makes in writing that might at first seem confusing or inconsistent, even in academic writing. For example, writers might use the passive voice in an experimental study report ("the data were collected by...") but not in an essay on the poetry of John Donne. Or the same scholar might write in the first person in one kind of academic text (like this textbook) but not in another (perhaps a scholarly article). In all these writing situations, the author makes choices based on the rhetorical context. In this textbook, the first person ("I" or "We") helps to establish a personal tone that might not be appropriate for an academic journal article. We (first person) made this choice specifically because of our audience for the textbook—students who are learning to navigate academic writing. We wanted the text to have a friendlier and less academically distant tone. Such a conversational tone wouldn't always be appropriate in other rhetorical contexts, though. When you write, understanding the rhetorical context can help you be more effective in achieving your purpose and communicating with your audience because you make choices that are appropriate to the situation.

As you notice the kinds of choices a writer makes, you are analyzing the rhetorical context of the writing: that is, you are taking elements of the writing apart to understand how they work together. Analyzing rhetorical context is a key strategy we'll use throughout this book to understand how different forms of writing work and what the similarities and differences are in writing across various disciplines.

Inside Work: Identifying Rhetorical Context

Think about a specific situation in the past that required you to write something. It could be any kind of text; it doesn't have to be something academic. Then create a map—by drawing a diagram, a chart, or some other visual image—of the rhetorical context of that piece of writing. Consider the following questions as you draw.

- What was your background and role as the author?
- Who was the audience?
- What was the topic?
- What was your purpose for writing?

Understanding Genres

As you learn to analyze the rhetorical context of writing, keep in mind that much writing takes place within communities of people who are interested in similar subjects. They might use similar vocabulary, formats for writing, and grammatical and stylistic rules. In a sense, they speak the same "language." The common practices that they typically employ in their writing are called *conventions*, as we discussed in Chapter 7. As you read and analyze the writing of academic writers, we'll ask you to notice and comment on the conventions that different disciplines use in various rhetorical contexts. When you write, you'll want to keep those conventions in mind, paying attention to the ways you should shape your own writing to meet the expectations of the academic community you are participating in. We'll go into more detail about how to analyze the specific conventions of disciplinary writing in Part Three.

In addition to paying close attention to the conventions that writers employ, we'll ask you to consider the *genre* through which writers communicate their information. **Genres** are approaches to writing situations that share some common features, or conventions. You already write in many genres in your daily life: If you've sent or read e-mail messages, text messages, personal letters, and thank-you notes, then you've written and read examples of four different genres that are all associated with personal writing. If you like to cook, you've probably noticed that recipes in cookbooks follow similar patterns by presenting the ingredients first and then providing step-by-step directions for preparation. The ingredients usually appear in a list, and the instructions generally read as directives (e.g., "Add the eggs one at a time and mix well"), often in more of a prose style. Recipes are a genre. If you've looked for an office job before, you've probably encountered at least three different genres in the job application process: job advertisements, application letters, and résumés. How well you follow the expected conventions of the latter two genres often affects whether or not you get a job.

LaunchPadSolo

See what writing studies instructor Moriah McCracken has to say about genres.

You've also likely had experience producing academic genres. If you've ever written a business letter, an abstract, a mathematical proof, a poem, a book review, a research proposal, or a lab report, then you might have noticed that these kinds of academic writing tasks have certain conventions that make them unique. Lab reports, for example, typically have specific expectations for the organization of information and for the kind of language used to communicate that information. Throughout Part Three of the book, we offer examples of a number of other academic genres—a literature review, an interpretation of an artistic text, as well as a theory response, just to name a few.

Because different writing situations, or rhetorical contexts, call for different approaches, we ask you to think about the genre, as well as associated conventions, that you might be reading or writing in any particular situation. Our goal is not to have you identify a formula to follow for every type of academic writing, but rather to understand the expectations of a writing situation—and how much flexibility you have in meeting those expectations—so that you can make choices appropriate to the genre.

Reading Rhetorically

Since we're talking about paying attention to rhetorical context, we want to explain the difference between the reading you do with an eye toward rhetorical context and the reading you might do in other circumstances. Whenever you read during a typical day, you probably do so for a variety of reasons. You might read:

- **To Communicate:** reading a text message, a letter from a friend, an e-mail, a birthday card, or a post on Instagram
- **To Learn:** reading instructions, a textbook, street signs while you drive, dosage instructions on a medication bottle, or the instructor's comments at the end of a paper that you turned in for a class
- **To Be Entertained:** reading novels, stories, comics, a joke forwarded in e-mail, or a favorite website

The details that you pay attention to, and the level at which you notice those details, vary according to your purpose in reading.

In this text, however, we will ask you to read in a way that is different from reading just to communicate, learn, or be entertained. We want you to *read rhetorically*, paying close attention to the rhetorical context of whatever you are reading. When you read rhetorically, you make note of the different elements of rhetorical context that help to shape the text. You'll notice who the author is (or, if there are multiple authors, who each one is) and what background, experience, knowledge, and potential biases the author brings to the text. In addition, you'll notice who the intended audience is for the text. Is the author writing to a group of peers? To other scholars in the field? How much prior knowledge does that audience have, and how does the intended audience shape the author's approach in the text? Are there multiple audiences (primary and secondary)? You'll also notice what the topic is and how it influences the text. Does the author use a specific approach related to the topic choice? Additionally, you'll notice the author's **purpose** for writing. Sometimes the purpose is stated explicitly, and sometimes it is implied. Why does the author choose to write about this topic at this point? What does the author hope to achieve? Finally, you'll want to notice how these four elements work together to shape the text. How is the choice of audience related to the author's background, topic, and purpose for writing?

Reading Visuals Rhetorically

We should stress that the strategies for understanding rhetorical context and for reading rhetorically are applicable to both verbal and visual texts. In fact, any rhetorical event, or any occasion that requires the production of a text, establishes a writing situation with a specific rhetorical context. Consider the places you might encounter visual advertisements, as one form of visual texts, over the course of a single day: in a magazine, on a website, in stores, on billboards, on television, and so on. Each encounter provides an opportunity to read the visual text rhetorically, or to consider how the four elements of author, audience, topic, and purpose work together to shape the text itself (in this case, an advertisement). This process is called **rhetorical analysis**.

In fact, noticing these elements when you read will help you become a careful and critical reader of all kinds of texts. When we use the term *critical*, we don't use it with any negative connotations. We use it in the way it works in the term *critical thinking*, meaning that you will begin to understand the relationships among author, audience, topic, and purpose by paying close attention to context.

Inside Work: Reading Rhetorically

With the direction of your instructor, choose a text (either verbal or visual) to read and analyze. As you read the text, consider the elements of rhetorical context. Write about who the author is, who the intended audience is, what the topic is, and what the author's purpose is for writing or for creating the text. Finally, consider how these elements work together to influence the way the text is written or designed. In future chapters, we'll ask you to engage in this kind of *rhetorical analysis* to understand the different kinds of texts produced by students and scholars in various academic contexts.

Writing Rhetorically

Writing is about choices. Writing is not a firm set of rules to follow. There are multiple choices available to you anytime you take on a writing task, and the choices you make will help determine how effectively you communicate with your intended audience, about your topic, for your intended purpose. Some choices, of course, are more effective than others, based on the conventions expected for certain situations. And yet, sometimes you might break conventions in order to make a point or draw attention to what you are writing. In both cases, though, it's important to understand the expectations of the rhetorical context for which you are writing so that your choices will have the effect you intend.

When you write rhetorically, you'll analyze the four elements of rhetorical context, examining how those elements shape your text through the choices that you make as a writer. You'll think about the following elements:

- **What You, as the _Author_, Bring to the Writing Situation**   How do your background, experience, and relative position to the audience shape the way you write?

- **Who Your Intended _Audience_ Is**   Is there a specific audience you should address? Has the audience already been determined for you (e.g., by your instructor)? What do you know about your audience? What does your audience value?

- **What Your _Topic_ Is**   What are you writing about? Has the topic been determined for you, or do you have the freedom to focus your topic according to your interests? What is your relationship to the topic? What is your audience's relationship to it?

- **What Your _Purpose_ Is for Writing**   Why are you writing about this topic, at this time? For example, are you writing to inform? To persuade? To entertain?

Outside of school contexts, we often write because we encounter a situation that calls for us to write. Imagine a parent who wants to write a note to thank her son's teacher for inviting her to assist in a class project. The audience is very specific, and the topic is determined by the occasion for writing. Depending on the relationship between the parent and the teacher, the note might be rather informal. But if the parent wants to commend the teacher and copy the school's principal, she might write a longer, more formal note that could be included in the teacher's personnel file. Understanding the rhetorical context would help the parent decide what choices to make in this writing situation.

For school assignments, thinking about the topic is typically the first step because students are often assigned to write about something specific. If your English professor asks you to write a literary interpretation of Toni Morrison's _Song of Solomon_, your topic choice is limited. Even in this situation, though, you have the freedom to determine what aspect of the text you'll focus on. Do you want to look at imagery in the novel? Would you like to examine Morrison's use of language? Would you like to analyze recurring themes, or perhaps interpret the text in the historical and cultural context in which it was written?

In this text, we would like you also to consider the other elements of rhetorical context—author, audience, and purpose—to see how they influence your topic. Considering your purpose in writing can often shape your audience and topic. Are you writing to communicate with a friend? If so, about what? Are you completing an assignment for a class? Are you writing to persuade someone to act on an issue that's important to you? If you are writing to argue for a change in a policy, to whom do you need to write in order to achieve your purpose? How will you reach that audience, and what would the audience's expectations be for your text? What information will you need to provide? Your understanding of the rhetorical context for writing will shape your writing and help you to communicate more effectively with your audience, about your topic, to meet your purpose.

Inside Work: Analyzing Rhetorical Context

Think back to the rhetorical situation you identified in the "Inside Work: Identifying Rhetorical Context" activity on page 234. Consider that situation more analytically now, using the questions from that activity and slightly revised here as a guide. Write your responses to the following questions.

- As the *author*, how did your background, experience, and relative position to the audience shape the way you created your text?

- Were you addressing a specific *audience*? Was the audience already determined for you? What did you know about your audience? What did your audience value or desire?

- What was your text about? Was the *topic* determined for you, or did you have the freedom to focus your topic according to your interests? What was your relationship to the topic? What was your audience's relationship to it?

- What was your *purpose* for creating a text about that topic, at that time? For example, were you writing to inform? To persuade? To entertain?

Rhetorical Writing Processes

In addition to making choices related to the context of a writing situation, writers make choices about their own process of writing. Writers follow different processes, sometimes being influenced by their own writing preferences, their experience with writing, and the specific writing tasks they have to accomplish. Writing can be a messy process that involves lots of drafting, revising, researching, thinking, and sometimes even throwing things out, especially for longer writing tasks. With that said, though, there are several steps in the process that experienced writers often find useful, and each step can be adapted to the specific writing situation in which they find themselves.

You might already be familiar with some of the commonly discussed steps of the writing process from other classes you've taken. Often, writing teachers talk about some variation of the following elements of the writing process:

- **Prewriting/Invention**   The point at which you gather ideas for your writing. There are a number of useful brainstorming strategies that students find helpful to the processes of gathering their thoughts and arranging them for writing. A few of the most widely used strategies are *freewriting*, *listing*, and *idea mapping*.

  - *Freewriting*   As the term implies, **freewriting** involves writing down your thoughts in a free-flow form, typically for a set amount of time. There's no judgment or evaluation of these ideas as they occur to you. You simply write down whatever comes to mind as you consider a topic or idea. Later, of course, you revisit what you've written to see if it contains ideas or information worth examining further.

  - *Listing*   **Listing** is a way of quickly highlighting important information for yourself. The writer starts with a main idea and then just lists whatever comes to mind. These lists are typically done quickly the first time, but you can return to them and rework or refine them at any point in the writing process.

  - *Idea Mapping*   This brainstorming technique is a favorite among students because it allows you to represent your ideas in an easy-to-follow map. **Idea mapping** is sometimes referred to as cluster mapping because as you brainstorm, you use clusters of ideas and lines to keep track of the ideas and the relationships among them.

Insider's View

The Writing Process? It's about Tasks

Jonathan Morris and Jody Baumgartner, Political Science

MORRIS: So often it's not about "I need to write this page." It's that "I have to spend hours and hours and hours doing the analysis. And even once I've done the analysis, taking the statistics and putting them in a way that the reader can understand and is relevant to the story will take days." Now, what I've adjusted to in this *writing* process is "Okay, I don't need to get a page a day. But I've got to have these sets of tasks for today." And it may be doing a series of statistics and then putting them into an Excel to make a nice, pretty chart that'll support the story.

BAUMGARTNER: Well, sure.

MORRIS: So it's about tasks.

LaunchPadSolo

Find additional advice on the writing process.

- **Research**   Sometimes research is considered a separate step in the writing process, and sometimes it is part of prewriting/invention. Of course, depending on the nature of your project, there might be a considerable amount of research or very little research involved. We explore some strategies for conducting research in more detail in Chapter 10.

- **Drafting**   At the drafting stage, you get ideas down on paper or screen. You might already realize that these stages don't happen in isolation in most cases; drafting might occur while you're doing prewriting/invention and research, and you might go back and forth between different stages as you work.

- **Peer Review**   Writers often benefit from seeking the feedback of others before considering a project complete. Peer review is the process of having other students, classmates, or audience members read your work and provide feedback. Later in this text, we'll use the term *peer review* to refer to the specific process that scholars go through when they submit academic writing for publication. It's similar: they submit work for publication, then peers in their discipline read and comment on it (they may or may not recommend it for publication), and then the scholars often revise it again prior to publication.

- **Revising**   At the revision stage, a writer takes another look at his or her writing and makes content-level and organizational changes. This is different from the final step of editing/proofreading.

- **Editing/Proofreading**   Finally, the writer focuses on correcting grammatical, mechanical, stylistic, and referential problems in the text.

Insider's View

The Finished Product Begins with a Hundred or Two Hundred Pages of Just Scribbles

Patrick Bahls, Mathematics

"The more formally recognized genres would be research articles or expository articles or reviews of one another's work. Sometimes you'll see technical reports, depending on what area you're working in. Statisticians will frequently write technical reports for folks for whom they're doing consulting or for government work.

"But I think the day-to-day writing, to me, is much richer and often goes overlooked. When you think about the finished product of a five- or six-page research article—I'll look back over the notes that I would've written to generate the work to end up with that article. And even if you only see five or six pages of polished writing, I look back over my notes and see a hundred or two hundred pages of just scribbles here and scribbles there."

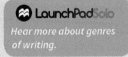

LaunchPadSolo

Hear more about genres of writing.

Depending on the rhetorical context of a writing task, these processes might shift in importance and in the order in which you do them. Imagine you get a last-minute writing assignment at work. You would progress through these stages rather quickly, and you might not have time for more than a cursory peer review. If you're writing a term paper for a class, however, you might be able to do initial prewriting, research, and drafting well before the project's deadline. As we discuss different types of scholarly writing in this text, you might also consider how the writing process for each of these types of writing can vary. When conducting an experimental study, the research stage of the process will take a significant portion of the time allocated to the project.

You might be able to think of examples from your own experience when you wrote in different ways for different projects because the rhetorical context was not the same. We want to encourage you to plan your writing process deliberately and avoid the mistake that many inexperienced writers make—waiting until the last minute and quickly writing a first draft and then turning it in because there is no time left for anything else. The most effective writers carefully plan out their writing and take the time they need to work through different parts of the writing process.

As you consider the influence of rhetorical context on your writing process, also think about the specific preferences you have as a writer. In order to do your best writing, be aware of where and how you write best. Consider these questions: What physical space do you like to write in? Where are you most productive? At what time of day do you write best? If you have a pressing deadline, what environmental factors help you to meet the deadline? Do you need to work someplace quiet? Do you like to have noise in the background? What kind of work space works best for you? Do you usually keep coffee or another favorite drink nearby? An awareness of preferences such as these will help you meet the challenges of different writing situations as you encounter them.

We'll ask you to practice different parts of your writing process throughout this book, both through the exercises you'll participate in and the larger writing assignments that you'll complete. As you work through the exercises, think about what part of the writing process you're addressing.

Writing a Rhetorical Analysis

When you read rhetorically, you analyze a text through a particular lens. Examining a text through the formal framework of author, audience, topic, and purpose can be a way of analyzing a text in a written assignment as well. Such an examination is called a *rhetorical analysis*, a genre of writing that explores elements of a text's rhetorical context. We'll provide several opportunities for you to conduct rhetorical analyses in this book, since it is one of the ways you will begin to discover the features of writing across different academic contexts.

In a rhetorical analysis, the writer uses a rhetorical framework to understand how the context of the text helps to create meaning. One framework you might use involves walking through the different elements of rhetorical context to examine the piece of writing in detail:

Rhetorical Context

Author   What does the author bring to the writing situation?

Audience   Who is the author addressing, and what do they know or think about this topic?

Topic   What is the author writing about, and why did he or she choose it?

Purpose   Why is the author writing about this topic, at this time?

These four components of the rhetorical context function together dynamically. You might analyze the author's background and experience and how he or she develops credibility in the text. Or you could make assertions about the author's primary and secondary audiences based on the author's choices regarding style and language. But in reality, all four of the rhetorical context components function together to shape how someone writes or speaks.

The following text is a letter that George H. W. Bush, the forty-first president of the United States (and father of the forty-third president, George W. Bush), sent to Iraqi president Saddam Hussein on January 9, 1991, shortly before the United States, in cooperation with over thirty other countries, launched an assault to expel Iraqi forces from Kuwait. This action came in response to Iraq's invasion and annexation of Kuwait in 1990, and it became a part of the history that is now referred to as the First Gulf War. While the events that precipitated this letter occurred a long time ago, it is a helpful artifact for understanding the complicated power dynamics at play in the United States' involvement in ongoing events in the Middle East. As you read the letter, pay close attention to the rhetorical moves that President Bush makes. Who are his primary and secondary audiences? Is his audience only Saddam Hussein? If not, then who else is his audience, and what in his letter suggests who the secondary audience is? What is the letter's purpose? Does Bush seem to think Saddam will leave Kuwait? How do you know?

© AP Photo/Dennis Cook

Letter to Saddam Hussein—George H. W. Bush

Mr. President,

We stand today at the brink of war between Iraq and the world. This is a war that began with your invasion of Kuwait; this is a war that can be ended only by Iraq's full and unconditional compliance with UN Security Council resolution 678.

I am writing to you now, directly, because what is at stake demands that no opportunity be lost to avoid what would be a certain calamity for the people of Iraq. I am writing, as well, because it is said by some that you do not understand just how isolated Iraq is and what Iraq faces as a result.

I am not in a position to judge whether this impression is correct; what I can do, though, is try in this letter to reinforce what Secretary of State James A. Baker told your foreign minister and eliminate any uncertainty or ambiguity that might exist in your mind about where we stand and what we are prepared to do.

The international community is united in its call for Iraq to leave all of Kuwait without condition and without further delay. This is not simply the policy of the United States; it is the position of the world community as expressed in no less than twelve Security Council resolutions.

We prefer a peaceful outcome. However, anything less than full compliance with UN Security Council resolution 678 and its predecessors is unacceptable. There can be no reward for aggression.

Nor will there be any negotiation. Principles cannot be compromised. However, by its full compliance, Iraq will gain the opportunity to rejoin the international community. More immediately, the Iraqi military establishment will escape destruction. But unless you withdraw from Kuwait completely and without condition, you will lose more than Kuwait. What is at issue here is not the future of Kuwait—it will be free, its government restored—but rather the future of Iraq. This choice is yours to make.

The United States will not be separated from its coalition partners. Twelve Security Council resolutions, twenty-eight countries providing military units to enforce them, more than one hundred governments complying with sanctions—all highlight the fact that it is not Iraq against the United States, but Iraq against the world. That most Arab and Muslim countries are arrayed against you as well should reinforce what I am saying. Iraq cannot and will not be able to hold on to Kuwait or exact a price for leaving. You may be tempted to find solace in the diversity of opinion that is American democracy. You should resist any such temptation. Diversity ought not to be confused with division. Nor should you underestimate, as others have before you, America's will.

Iraq is already feeling the effects of the sanctions mandated by the United Nations. Should war come, it will be a far greater tragedy for you and your country. Let me state, too, that the United States will not tolerate the use of chemical or biological weapons or the destruction of Kuwait's oil fields and installations. Further, you will be held directly responsible for terrorist actions against any member of the coalition. The American people would demand the strongest possible response. You and your country will pay a terrible price if you order unconscionable acts of this sort.

I write this letter not to threaten, but to inform. I do so with no sense of satisfaction, for the people of the United States have no quarrel with the people of Iraq. Mr. President, UN Security Council resolution 678 establishes the period before January 15 of this year as a "pause of good will" so that this crisis may end without further violence. Whether this pause is used as intended, or merely becomes a prelude to further violence, is in your hands, and yours alone.

I hope you weigh your choice carefully and choose wisely, for much will depend upon it.

Discussion Questions

1. For what purpose(s) does President Bush write this letter?
2. How does Bush establish his credibility, honesty, and resolve in the letter?
3. Who is the primary audience? Who are the secondary audiences?
4. What conventional features for this form of writing (genre) does Bush's letter exhibit?

Insider Example

Student Rhetorical Analysis

The following is a student rhetorical analysis of the letter written from George H. W. Bush to Saddam Hussein. As you read this analysis, consider how the student, Sofia Lopez, uses audience, topic, and purpose to construct meaning from Bush's letter. Additionally, pay attention to how Sofia uses evidence from the letter to support her assertions. These moves will become more important when we discuss using evidence to support claims in Chapter 9 (see pp. 255–57).

Sofia Lopez

Mr. Harris

English 100

January 201–

The Multiple Audiences of George H. W. Bush's Letter to Saddam Hussein

President George H. W. Bush's 1991 letter to Saddam Hussein, then the president of Iraq, is anything but a simple piece of political rhetoric. The topic of the letter is direct and confrontational. On the surface, Bush directly calls upon Hussein to withdraw from Kuwait, and he lays out the potential impact should Hussein choose not to withdraw. But when analyzed according to the rhetorical choices Bush makes in the letter, a complex rhetorical situation emerges. Bush writes to a dual audience in his letter and establishes credibility by developing a complex author position. By the conclusion of the letter, Bush accomplishes multiple purposes by creating a complex rhetorical situation.

While Bush's direct and primary audience is Saddam Hussein, Bush also calls upon a much larger secondary audience in the first sentence of the letter by identifying "the world" as the second party involved in the imminent war that the letter is written to prevent. Bush continues to write the letter directly to Hussein, using second person to address him and describe the choices before him. Bush also continues, however, to engage his secondary audience through-out the letter by referring to resolutions from the UN Security Council in five separate paragraphs (1, 4, 5, 7, and 9). The letter can even be interpreted to have tertiary audiences of the Iraqi and the American people because the letter serves to justify military action should Hussein not comply with the conditions of the letter.

The introduction outlines the writer's approach to analyzing Bush's letter. Based on the introduction, what do you see as the writer's overall purpose for this rhetorical analysis?

In this paragraph, the writer outlines potential audiences for Bush's letter in more detail. Who are those audiences?

In this paragraph, the writer explores the ways Bush is able to align himself with multiple audiences. What evidence does the writer use to demonstrate Bush's associations with his various audiences?

Because Bush is addressing multiple audiences, he establishes a complex author position as well. He is the primary author of the letter, and he uses first person to refer to himself, arguably to emphasize the direct, personal confrontation in the letter. He constructs a more complex author position, however, by speaking for other groups in his letter and, in a sense, writing "for" them. In paragraph 4, he speaks for the international community when he writes, "The international community is united in its call for Iraq to leave all of Kuwait…." He draws on the international community again in paragraph 6 and refers to his coalition partners in paragraph 7, aligning his position with the larger community. Additionally, in paragraph 7, he builds his credibility as an author by emphasizing that he is aligned with other Arab and Muslim countries in their opposition to Hussein's actions. Writing for and aligning himself with such a diverse group of political partners helps him address the multiple audiences of his letter to accomplish his purposes.

The writer frequently refers to Bush's "complex author position." What do you think the writer means by this?

While the primary and literal purpose of the letter is to call upon Iraq to withdraw from Kuwait and to outline the consequences of noncompliance, Bush accomplishes additional purposes directly related to his additional audiences and the complex author position he has established. The primary purpose of his letter, naturally, is addressed to his primary audience, Saddam Hussein. The construction of the letter, however, including the repeated mention of UN Security Council resolutions, the invocation of support from other Arab and Muslim countries, and the reference to other coalition partners and the international community, serves to call upon the world (and specifically the United Nations) to support military action should Hussein not comply with the conditions of the letter. The construction of a letter with a complex audience and author allows Bush to address multiple purposes that support future action.

What other elements of the rhetorical situation might the writer explore to further analyze Bush's letter?

Discussion Questions

1. What does Sofia Lopez identify as Bush's purpose? How does she support that interpretation of Bush's purpose?

2. Whom does Sofia see as Bush's audience? How does she support that reading of the letter?

3. What might you add to the analysis, from a rhetorical perspective?

Writing Project: Analyzing the Rhetorical Features of a Text

In this paper, you will analyze the rhetorical situation of a text of your choosing. You might want to choose something publicly available (already published) that represents a piece of polished writing so that you know that the author(s) has finished making revisions and has had time to think through important rhetorical choices. Alternatively, you might choose something written for an academic, personal, work, or other context. Start by reading the text carefully and rhetorically. Use the elements of rhetorical context to analyze and understand the choices the writer has made in the text.

Rhetorical Context

- author
- audience
- topic
- purpose

In addition to describing the rhetorical features of the article, you will also explore why you believe the author made certain choices. For example, if you're analyzing a blog entry on a political website, you might discuss who the author is and review his or her background. Then you could speculate about the writing choices the author has made and how his or her background might have influenced those choices.

Consider what conclusion you can draw about the text, and highlight that as an assertion you can make in the introduction to your analysis. The body of your paper should be organized around the rhetorical features you are analyzing, demonstrating how you came to your conclusion about the text.

In your conclusion, reflect on what you have found. Are there other issues still to be addressed? What other rhetorical strategies could be explored to analyze the work further? Are there surprises in the choices the writer makes that you should mention?

Keep in mind that your essential aim is to analyze, not to evaluate.

Reading and Writing Rhetorically

- **It is important to consider rhetorical context as you read and write**. Think about how the following four elements have shaped or might shape a text:
  - who the *author* is, and what background and experience he or she brings to the text
  - who the intended *audience* is
  - what issue or *topic* the author is addressing
  - what the author's *purpose* is for writing

- **Genres are approaches to writing situations that share some common features, or conventional expectations**. As you read and write texts, consider the form of writing you're asked to read or produce: Is it a recognizable genre? What kinds of conventional expectations are associated with the genre? How should you shape your text in response to those expectations?

- **Reading rhetorically means reading with an eye toward how the four elements of author, audience, topic, and purpose work together** to influence the way an author shapes a text, verbal or visual or otherwise.

- **Writing rhetorically means crafting your own text based on an understanding of the four elements of your rhetorical context**. Specifically, you consider how your understanding of the rhetorical context should affect the choices you make as a writer, or how your understanding should ultimately shape your text.

- **A rhetorical writing process involves a set of steps that include prewriting, researching, drafting, revising, and editing/proofreading**. The order of the steps and their importance to any writer can be altered or repeated as needed.

- **A rhetorical analysis is a formal piece of writing that examines the different elements of the rhetorical context of a text**. It also often considers how these elements work together to explain the shape of a text targeted for analysis.

Chapter 9 Developing Arguments

Many writing situations, both academic and non-academic, require authors to persuade audiences on a particular topic—in other words, to develop an *argument*. When we refer to arguments, we don't mean heated, emotional sparring matches that are often supported by little else than opinion. Rather, we use **argument** to refer to the process of making a logical case for a particular position, interpretation, or conclusion. You experience and participate in these kinds of arguments around you every day as you decide what to eat for a meal, choose certain classes to take, determine what movie to see with a group of friends, or read (or perhaps choose to ignore) online advertisements about products to purchase.

In academic settings, arguments are frequently research-oriented because the authors are presenting and arguing for a particular interpretation or conclusion from the results of their research. To make such an argument effectively, academics must develop clear, persuasive texts through which to present their research. These arguments make **claims**—arguable assertions—that are supported with evidence from research. The unifying element of any academic argument is its primary or central claim, and although most sustained arguments make a series of claims, there is usually one central claim that makes an argument a coherent whole. Our goal in this chapter is to introduce you to some of the basic principles of argumentation and to help you write clear central claims and develop successful arguments, especially in your academic writing.

Andrea Tsurumi

If arguments are persuasive and effective, they are likely well reasoned and well supported, and they draw on evidence that is chosen for a specific rhetorical context. All writers must pay attention to the audience and purpose of their argument. Often, they do this by developing, either implicitly or explicitly, *proofs* of their arguments and *appeals* that are appropriate to their audience. Proofs and appeals are elements specific to arguments that you'll need to pay attention to in addition to rhetorical context, which is relevant for all writing situations.

Chapter 9, "Developing Arguments" from *An Insider's Guide to Academic Writing* by Susan Miller-Cochran, Roy Stamper, and Stacey Cochran, pp. 59–86 (Chapter 3). Copyright © 2016 by Bedford/St. Martin's.

Understanding Proofs and Appeals

Aristotle, a rhetorician in ancient Greece, developed a method of analyzing arguments that can be useful to us in our own reading and writing today. He explained that arguments are based on a set of proofs that are used as evidence to support a claim. He identified two kinds of proofs: inartistic and artistic. Inartistic proofs are based on factual evidence, such as statistics, raw data, or contracts. Artistic proofs, by contrast, are created by the writer or speaker to support an argument. Many arguments contain a combination of inartistic and artistic proofs, depending on what facts are available for support. Aristotle divided the complex category of artistic proofs into three kinds of rhetorical appeals that speakers and writers can rely on to develop artistic proofs in support of an argument:

• Appeals to *ethos* are based on the author's or speaker's credibility or character. An example might be a brand of motor oil that is endorsed by a celebrity NAS-CAR driver. Another example could be a proposal for grant money to conduct a research study that discusses the grant writer's experience in successfully completing similar research studies in the past. In both examples, the speaker's or writer's experiences (as a NASCAR driver or as an established researcher) are persuasive elements in the argument. We might be more inclined to buy a certain brand of motor oil if our favorite driver says it's the best kind, and a grant-funding agency will likely feel more comfortable giving a large sum of money to a researcher who has demonstrated successful completion of research projects in the past.

• Appeals to *logos* are based on elements of logic and reason. An example might be an argument for change in an attendance policy that outlines the negative effects and potential repercussions of maintaining the current policy. The argument relies on logic and reason because it presents the negative effects and draws a connection to the policy, emphasizing how a change in the policy might reverse those effects.

• Appeals to *pathos* are based on the anticipated emotional response of the audience. Emotion can be a powerful motivator to convince an audience to hear an argument. An example might include telling the story of a particular community affected by current gun control regulation when arguing for a shift in policy. If a politician uses this strategy when arguing for passage of an important bill in Congress, for example, the emotional impact might influence other legislators to vote in favor of the bill.

These types of appeals are present in arguments in both academic and non-academic settings. Many arguments, and often the most effective ones, include elements of more than one kind of appeal, using several strategies to persuade an audience. In the example above of a politician arguing before Congress, the argument would be much stronger and likely more persuasive if other appeals were used in addition to an emotional appeal. The politician might develop an argument that includes raw data and statistics (an inartistic proof), the advice of experts in the field (*ethos*), a cause and effect relationship that points to a particular cause of the problem (*logos*), along with the story of a community affected by current gun control regulation (*pathos*). Understanding the structure of arguments, and knowing the potential ways you can develop your own arguments to persuade an audience, will help you to write more effectively and persuasively.

Inside Work: Writing about Arguments

Choose a text to read that makes either an explicit or an implicit claim. Consider something that interests you—perhaps an advertisement, or even your college's or university's website. Write about the kinds of rhetorical appeals you notice. Do you see evidence of *ethos*? *Logos*? *Pathos*? Is the argument drawing on statistics or raw data, an inartistic proof? Why do you think the author(s) or designer(s) structured the argument in this way? To answer this question, you'll also need to consider the rhetorical context. Who is the author, and who is the intended audience? What is the topic, and what is the purpose of the argument? In other words, what is the ultimate goal of the argument?

Making Claims

As we mentioned earlier, the unifying element of any academic argument is its primary or central claim. In American academic settings, the central claim is often (but not always) presented near the beginning of a piece so that it can tie the elements of the argument together. A form of the central claim that you might be familiar with is the thesis statement. Thesis statements, whether revealed in an argument's introduction or delayed and presented later in an argument (perhaps even in the conclusion), are central claims of arguments that are typical of writing that is centrally focused on civic concerns, as well as writing in some academic fields such as those in the humanities (see Chapter 12).

Imagine for a moment that you've been asked to write an argument taking a position on a current social topic like cell phone usage, and you must decide whether or not to support legislation to limit cell phone use while driving. In this instance, the statement of your position is your claim. It might read something like this: "We should support legislation to limit the use of cell phones while driving," or "We should not support legislation to limit the use of cell phones while driving." There are many types of claims. The statement "We should pass legislation to limit the use of cell phones" is a claim of proposal or policy, indicating that the writer will propose some action or solution to a problem. We could also explore claims of definition ("Cheerleading is a sport") or claims of value ("Supporting a charity is a good thing to do"), just to name a few.

Literary analyses, a genre commonly taught in high school English classes, usually present a thesis statement as part of their introductions. You may be familiar with a thesis statement that reads something like this: "Nathaniel Hawthorne's 'The Birthmark' is a complex tale that cautions us against believing that science is capable of perfecting our natures." This thesis statement makes a claim in support of a specific interpretation of the story. Regardless of the specific type of claim offered, the argument that follows it provides evidence to demonstrate why an audience should find the claim persuasive.

Thesis versus Hypothesis

In an academic setting, thesis statements like those typical of arguments in the humanities are not the only kind of unifying claim you might encounter. In fact, arguments in the natural and social sciences are often organized around a statement of hypothesis, which is different from a thesis statement. Unlike a thesis statement, which serves to convey a final position or conclusion on a topic or issue that a researcher has arrived at based on study, a **hypothesis** is a proposed explanation or conclusion that is usually either confirmed or denied on the basis of rigorous examination or experimentation later in a paper. This means that hypothesis statements are, in a sense, still under consideration by a writer or researcher. A hypothesis is a proposed answer to a research question. Thesis statements, in contrast, represent a writer or researcher's conclusion(s) after much consideration of the issue or topic.

Consider the following examples of a hypothesis and a thesis about the same topic:

Hypothesis	Thesis
Decreased levels of sleep will lead to decreased levels of academic performance for college freshmen.	College freshmen should get at least seven hours of sleep per night because insufficient sleep has been linked to emotional instability and poor academic performance.

The hypothesis example above includes several elements that distinguish it from the thesis statement. First, the hypothesis is written as a prediction, which indicates that the researcher will conduct a study to test the claim. Additionally, it is written in the future tense, indicating that an experiment or study will take place to prove or disprove the hypothesis. The thesis statement, however, makes a claim that indicates it is already supported by evidence gathered by the researcher. A reader would expect to find persuasive evidence from sources later in the essay.

We highlight this distinction in types of claims to underscore that there is no single formula for constructing a good argument in all academic contexts. Instead, expectations for strong arguments are bound up with the expectations of particular writing communities. If you write a lab report with the kind of thesis statement that usually appears in a literary analysis, your work would likely convey the sense that you're a novice to the community of writers and researchers who expect a hypothesis statement instead of a thesis statement. One of the goals of this text is to help you develop awareness of how the expectations for good argumentation change from one academic context to the next.

Developing Reasons

When writing an academic argument that requires a thesis statement, you can choose how detailed to make that thesis statement. When we introduced thesis statements as a type of claim, we asked you to consider two possible statements on the topic of cell phone use while driving: "We should/should not support legislation to limit the use of cell phones while driving." We can also refer to these two possible forms as simple thesis statements because they reveal a writer's central position on a topic but do not include any reasoning as support for that position. When reasons are included as logical support, then we can think about the thesis statement as a complex thesis statement:

Simple Thesis:	We should support legislation to limit the use of cell phones while driving.
Reasons:	They are an unnecessary distraction.
	They increase the incidence of accidents and deaths.

When we combine the simple statement of position or belief with the reasons that support it, then we have a more complex, and fuller, thesis statement:

Complex Thesis:	We should support legislation to limit the use of cell phones because they are an unnecessary distraction for drivers and because they increase needless accidents and deaths on our roadways.

Although constructing complex thesis statements allows you to combine your statement of position with the reasons you'll use to defend that position, you may frequently encounter arguments that do not provide the reasons as part of the thesis. That is, some writers, depending on their rhetorical context, prefer to present a simple thesis and then reveal the reasons for their position throughout their argument. Others choose to write a thesis that both establishes their position and provides the reasoning for it early on. An advantage of providing a complex thesis statement is that it offers a road map to the reader for the argument that you will develop. A disadvantage is that it might provide more information about your argument than you want to or should reveal up front.

Inside Work: Constructing Thesis Statements

Generate a list of six to eight current social issues that require you to take a position. Consider especially issues that are important to your local community. Choose one or two to focus on for the other parts of this activity.

Next, explore multiple positions. Consider competing positions you can take for each of the issues you identified. Write out a simple thesis statement for those positions. Be careful not to limit your positions to pros and cons, especially if you can think of alternative positions that might be reasonable for someone to argue. Often, there are multiple sides to an issue, and we miss the complexity of the issue if we only acknowledge two sides. Then, list as many reasons as you can think of to support each of those positions. It might be helpful to connect your simple statement of thesis to your reasons using the word *because*. This activity can help you to strengthen your argument by anticipating rebuttals or counterarguments. We'll take these issues up later in the chapter.

For example:

Claim: The U.S. Congress should support federal legislation that allows same-sex couples to marry.

Reasons:

because _____.

because _____.

because _____.

Alternate Claim: The U.S. Congress should not support federal legislation that allows same-sex couples to marry.

Reasons:

because _____.

because _____.

because _____.

Alternate Claim: The decision to develop legislation allowing same-sex couples to marry should be made at the state level and not by the federal government.

Reasons:

because _____.

because _____.

because _____.

Finally, combine your simple thesis with your reasoning to construct a complex thesis for each potential position. Write out your thesis statements.

Supporting Reasons with Evidence

Reasons that support a claim are not particularly powerful unless there is evidence to back them up. Evidence that supports an argument can take the form of any of the rhetorical appeals. Let's look again at the complex thesis from the previous section: "We should support legislation to limit the use of cell phones because they are an unnecessary distraction for drivers and because they increase needless accidents and deaths on our roadways." In order to generate the reasons, the writer relied on what he already knew about the dangers of cell phone use. Perhaps the writer had recently read a newspaper article that cited statistics concerning the number of people injured or killed in accidents as a direct result of drivers using their phones instead of paying attention to the roadways. Or perhaps the writer had read an academic study that examined attention rates and variables affecting them in people using cell phones. Maybe the writer even had some personal knowledge or experience to draw upon as evidence for her or his position. Strong, persuasive arguments typically spend a great deal of time unpacking the logic that enables a writer to generate reasons in support of a particular claim, and that evidence can take many forms.

Personal Experience

You may have direct experience with a particular issue or topic that allows you to speak in support of a position on that topic. Your personal experience can be a rich resource for evidence. Additionally, you may know others who can provide evidence based on their experiences with an issue. Stories of personal experience often appeal to either *ethos* (drawing on the credibility of the writer's personal experience) or *pathos* (drawing on readers' emotions for impact). Sometimes these stories appeal to both *ethos* and *pathos* at the same time.

> Imagine the power of telling the story of someone who has been needlessly injured in an accident because another driver was distracted by talking on the phone.

Expert Testimony

Establishing an individual as an expert on a topic and using that person's words or ideas in support of your own position can be an effective way of bolstering your own *ethos* while supporting your central claim. However, the use of expert testimony can be tricky, as you need to carefully establish what makes the person you're relying on for evidence an actual expert on the topic or issue at hand. You must also consider your audience—whom would your audience consider to be an expert? How would you determine the expert's reputation within that community? The use of expert testimony is very common in academic argumentation. Researchers often summarize, paraphrase, or cite experts in their own discipline, as well as from others, to support their reasoning. If you've ever taken a class in which your instructor asked you to use reputable sources to support your argument, then you've probably relied on expert testimony to support a claim or reason already.

Imagine the effectiveness of citing experts who work for the National Transportation and Safety Board about their experiences investigating accidents that resulted from inattentive driving due to cell phone use.

Statistical Data and Research Findings

Statistics frequently serve as support in both popular and academic argumentation. Readers tend to like numbers, partly because they seem so absolute and scientific. However, it is important, as with all evidence, to evaluate statistical data for bias. Consider where statistics come from and how they are produced, if you plan to use them in support of an argument. Additionally, and perhaps most important, consider how those statistics were interpreted in the context of the original research reported. What were the study's conclusions?

Writers also often present the findings, or conclusions, of a research study as support for their reasons and claims. These findings may sometimes appear as qualitative, rather than just statistical, results or outcomes.

Imagine the effectiveness of citing recently produced statistics (rates of accidents) on the highways in your state from materials provided by your state's Department of Transportation.

When selecting the types and amounts of evidence to use in support of your reasons, be sure to study your rhetorical context and pay particular attention to the expectations of your intended audience. Some audiences, especially academic ones, are less likely to be convinced if you only provide evidence that draws on their emotions. Other audiences may be completely turned off by an argument that relies only on statistical data for support.

Insider's View

Figuring Out Who the Experts Are

Moriah McCracken, Writing Studies

"When you jump into a scholarly text, the conversation is so implicit…. For me, the biggest thing that can be kind of disconcerting is that you have to figure out, what are people even talking about? And then you have to figure out, who are the voices that are most popular? Who are the voices that people turn to when they're trying to resolve this issue?"

 LaunchPad Solo

Learn more about entering academic conversations.

So far, we've discussed several types of evidence that are typically used in the construction of arguments—personal experience, expert testimony, statistical data and research findings. Collecting the data you need to make a strong argument can seem like a daunting task at times. It's important to keep in mind, though, that the amount of evidence you provide and the types of data your argument requires will depend entirely on the kind of argument you are constructing, as well as on the potential audience you want to persuade. Therefore, it's essential that you analyze and understand your audience's expectations when selecting support for your argument. Above all, select support that your audience will find credible, reliable, and relevant to your argument.

LaunchPadSolo

Hear criminologist Michelle Richter comment on types of research in her field.

Inside Work: Analyzing Audience Expectations

Choose any one of the complex thesis statements you constructed in the "Inside Work" activity on page 254. Then identify two potential target audiences for your arguments. Freewrite for five to ten minutes in response to the following questions about these audiences' likely expectations for evidence.

- What does each audience already know about your topic? That is, what aspects of it can you assume they already have knowledge about?

- What does each audience need to know? What information do you need to make sure to include?

- What does each audience value in relation to your topic? What kinds of information will motivate them, interest them, or persuade them? How do you know?

- What sources of information about your topic might your audiences find questionably reliable? Why?

Understanding Assumptions

Anytime you stake a claim and provide a reason, or provide evidence to support a reason, you are assuming something about your audience's beliefs and values, and it is important to examine your own assumptions very carefully as you construct arguments. Though assumptions are often unstated, they function to link together the ideas of two claims.

Let's consider a version of the claim and reason we've been looking at throughout this section to examine the role of assumptions: "We should support legislation to limit the use of cell phones while driving because they increase needless accidents and deaths on our roadways." In this instance, the claim and the reason appear logically connected, but let's identify the implied assumptions that the reader must accept in order to be persuaded by the argument:

Claim:	We should support legislation to limit the use of cell phones while driving.
Reason:	They increase needless accidents and deaths on our highways.
Implied Assumptions:	We should do whatever we can to limit accidents and deaths.
	Legislation can reduce accidents and deaths.

Many audiences would agree with these implied assumptions. As a result, it would likely be unnecessary to make the assumptions explicit or provide support for them. However, you can probably imagine an instance when a given audience would argue that legislating peoples' behavior does not affect how people actually behave. To such an audience, passing laws to regulate the use of cell phones while driving might seem ineffective. As a result, the audience might actually challenge the assumption(s) upon which your argument rests, and you may need to provide evidence to support the implied assumption that "legislation can reduce accidents and deaths."

A writer who is concerned that an audience may attack his argument by pointing to problematic assumptions might choose to explicitly state the assumption and provide support for it. In this instance, he might consider whether precedents exist (e.g., the effect of implementing seat belt laws, or statistical data from other states that have passed cell phone use laws) that could support his assumption that "legislation can reduce accidents and deaths."

Inside Work: Considering Assumptions and Audience

In the previous activity, you considered the most appropriate kinds of evidence for supporting thesis statements for differing audiences. This time, we ask you to identify the assumptions in your arguments and to consider whether or not those assumptions would require backing or additional support for varying audiences.

Begin by identifying the assumption(s) for each of your thesis statements. Then consider whether or not those assumptions need backing as the intended audience for your argument changes to the following:

- a friend or relative
- a state legislator
- an opinion news column editor
- a professional academic in a field related to your topic

Anticipating Counterarguments

Initially, it may strike you as odd to think of counterarguments as a strategy to consider when constructing an argument. However, anticipating the objections of those who might disagree with you may actually strengthen your argument by forcing you to consider competing chains of reasoning and evidence. In fact, many writers actually choose to present counterarguments, or rebuttals of their own arguments, as part of the design of their arguments.

Why would anyone do this? Consider for a moment that your argument is like a debate. If you are able to adopt your opponent's position and then explain why that position is wrong, or why her reasoning is flawed, or in what ways her evidence is insufficient to support her own claim, then you support your own position. This is what it means to offer a rebuttal to potential counterarguments. Of course, when you provide rebuttals, you must have appropriate evidence to justify dismissing part or all of the entire counterargument. By anticipating and responding to counterarguments, you also strengthen your own *ethos* as a writer on the topic. Engaging counterarguments demonstrates that you have considered multiple positions and are knowledgeable about your subject.

You can also address possible counterarguments by actually conceding to an opposing position on a particular point or in a limited instance. Now you're probably wondering: Why would anyone do this? Doesn't this mean losing your argument? Not necessarily. Often, such a concession reveals that you're developing a more complex argument and moving past the pro/con positions that can limit productive debate.

Insider's View

Figuring Out the "Right" Side

Mike Brotherton, Astronomy

"In science, we're really worried about which side is right, and you discuss both sides only to the extent of figuring out which one's right. It's not one opinion versus another. It's one set of ideas supported by a certain set of observations against another set of ideas supported, or not supported, by the same set of observations, and trying to figure out which one is a better explanation for how things work."

Hear more about writing to solve problems.

Imagine that you're debating an opponent on a highly controversial issue like fracking (hydraulic fracturing). You're arguing a pro-fracking position, and your opponent makes the point that some people have experienced health issues as a result of the fracking in areas local to their homes. You might choose to concede this point by acknowledging that fracking could be a root cause of some individuals' illnesses. Though you still support fracking, you might now choose to limit the scope of your original position. That is, you could qualify your position by supporting fracking as long as it occurs, say, outside of a five-mile radius of any residence. In this case, your opponents' points are used to adjust or to **qualify** your own position, but this doesn't negate your entire argument. Your position may appear even stronger precisely because you've acknowledged the opponents' points and refined the scope of your claim as a result, or because you've identified instances when your position might not hold true.

Inside Work: Dealing with Counterarguments

Throughout this section, you've been working with a series of claims that you constructed. You've linked those claims to reasons as support, and you've considered the kinds of evidence most appropriate for your theses in light of particular audiences. You've also considered the likely acceptability of your assumptions, according to various potential audiences. This time, consider possible counterarguments for your thesis statements.

- Who might argue against you?
- What will their arguments be based on?
- What might their arguments be?
- How might you use a counterargument to actually support your own claim?

Brainstorm a list of instances in which you might want to concede a point or two as a means of strengthening your own position.

Analyzing Arguments

One way to understand the process of developing a persuasive argument is to study how others structure theirs. If you'll recall, in Chapter 8 we discussed how visual texts, like verbal ones, construct rhetorical situations. In the same way, visual texts may also seek to persuade an audience, and they may use many of the techniques explored throughout this chapter.

The following papers present arguments about visual texts. In the first, Jack Solomon, a professional writer, explores how advertisements reflect what he sees as contradictory impulses in the American character. In the second, Timothy Holtzhauser, a student writer, examines the argument strategies employed in a 1943 American war bonds ad. As you engage with their arguments, keep in mind that each writer is both making an argument and analyzing an argument simultaneously, so you'll want to consider their texts from both perspectives. Also keep in mind that their arguments are supported by evidence found in their own research. We'll explore how to conduct research in more detail in Chapter 10.

Insider Example

Professional Analysis of an Advertisement

In the following passage from "Masters of Desire: The Culture of American Advertising," Jack Solomon uses *semiotics*—a method for studying and interpreting cultural signs and symbols—to analyze the arguments made in two advertisements. As you read Solomon's argument, try to identify which elements of argument discussed in this chapter he uses in his analysis.

Courtesy of Jack Solomon

Jack Solomon

Excerpt from "Masters of Desire: The Culture of American Advertising"

The American dream…has two faces: the one communally egalitarian and the other competitively elitist. This contradiction is no accident; it is fundamental to the structure of American society. Even as America's great myth of equality celebrates the virtues of mom, apple pie, and the girl or boy next door, it also lures us to achieve social distinction, to rise above the crowd and bask alone in the glory. This land is your land and this land is my land, Woody Guthrie's populist anthem tells us, but we keep trying to increase the "my" at the expense of the "your." Rather than fostering contentment, the American dream breeds desire, a longing for a greater share of the pie. It is as if our society were a vast high-school football game, with the bulk of the participants noisily rooting in the stands while, deep down, each of them is wishing he or she could be the star quarterback or head cheerleader.

For the semiotician, the contradictory nature of the American myth of equality is nowhere written so clearly as in the signs that American advertisers use to manipulate us into buying their wares. "Manipulate" is the word here, not "persuade"; for advertising campaigns are not sources of product information, they are exercises in behavior modification. Appealing to our subconscious emotions rather than to our conscious intellects, advertisements are designed to exploit the discontentments fostered by the American dream, the constant desire for social success and the material rewards that accompany it. America's consumer economy runs on desire, and advertising stokes the engines by transforming common objects—from peanut butter to political candidates—into signs of all the things that Americans covet most.

But by semiotically reading the signs that advertising agencies manufacture to stimulate consumption, we can plot the precise state of desire in the audiences to which they are addressed. In this chapter, we'll look at a representative sample of ads and what they say about the emotional climate of the country and the fast-changing trends of American life. Because ours is a highly diverse, pluralistic society, various advertisements may say different things depending on their intended audiences, but in every case they say something about America, about the status of our hopes, fears, desires, and beliefs.

Let's begin with two ad campaigns conducted by the same company that bear out Alexis de Tocqueville's observations about the contradictory nature of American society: General Motors' campaigns for its Cadillac and Chevrolet lines. First, consider an early magazine ad for the Cadillac Allanté. Appearing as a full-color, four-page insert in *Time*, the ad seems to say "I'm special—and so is this car" even before we've begun to read it. Rather than being printed on the ordinary, flimsy pages of the magazine, the Allanté spread appears on glossy coated stock. The unwritten message here is that an extraordinary car deserves an extraordinary advertisement, and that both car and ad are aimed at an extraordinary consumer, or at least one who wishes to appear extraordinary compared to his more ordinary fellow citizens.

Ads of this kind work by creating symbolic associations between their product and what is most coveted by the consumers to whom they are addressed. It is significant, then, that this ad insists that the Allanté is virtually an Italian rather than an American car—an automobile, as its copy runs, "Conceived and Commissioned by America's Luxury Car Leader—Cadillac" but "Designed and Handcrafted by Europe's Renowned Design Leader—Pininfarina, SpA, of Turin, Italy." This is not simply a piece of product information; it's a sign of the prestige that European luxury cars enjoy in today's automotive marketplace. Once the luxury car of choice for America's status drivers, Cadillac has fallen far behind its European competitors in the race for the prestige market. So the Allanté essentially represents Cadillac's decision, after years of resist-ing the trend toward European cars, to introduce its own European import—whose high cost is clearly printed on the last page of the ad. Although $54,700 is a lot of money to pay for a Cadillac, it's about what you'd expect to pay for a top-of-the-line Mercedes-Benz. That's precisely the point the ad is trying to make: the Allanté is no mere car. It's a potent status symbol you can associate with the other major status symbols of the 1980s.

American companies manufacture status symbols because American consumers want them. As Alexis de Tocqueville recognized a century and a half ago, the competitive nature of democratic societies breeds a desire for social distinction, a yearning to rise above the crowd. But given the fact that those who do make it to the top in socially mobile societies have often risen from the lower ranks, they still look like everyone else. In the socially immobile societies of aristocratic Europe, generations of fixed social conditions produced subtle class signals. The accent of one's voice, the shape of one's nose, or even the set of one's chin immediately communicated social status. Aside from the nasal bray and uptilted head of the Boston Brahmin, Americans do not have any native sets of personal status signals. If it weren't for his Mercedes-Benz and Manhattan townhouse, the parvenu Wall Street millionaire often couldn't be distinguished from the man who tailors his suits. Hence, the demand for status symbols, for the objects that mark one off as a social success, is particularly strong in democratic nations—stronger even than in aristocratic societies, where the aristocrat so often looks and sounds different from everyone else.

Status symbols, then, are signs that identify their possessors' place in a social hierarchy, markers of rank and prestige. We can all think of any number of status symbols—Rolls-Royces, Beverly Hills mansions, even Shar Pei puppies (whose rareness has rocketed them beyond Russian wolfhounds as status pets and has inspired whole lines of wrinkle-faced stuffed toys)—but how do we know that something is a status symbol? The explanation is quite simple: when an object (or puppy!) either costs a lot of money or requires influential connections to possess, anyone who possesses it must also possess the necessary means and influence to acquire it. The object itself really doesn't matter, since it ultimately disappears behind the presumed social potency of its owner. Semiotically, what matters is the signal it sends, its value as a sign of power. One traditional sign of social distinction is owning a country estate and enjoying the peace and privacy that attend it. Advertisements for Mercedes-Benz, Jaguar, and Audi automobiles thus frequently feature drivers motoring quietly along a country road, presumably on their way to or from their country houses.

Advertisers have been quick to exploit the status signals that belong to body language as well. As Hegel observed in the early nineteenth century, it is an ancient aristocratic prerogative to be seen by the lower orders without having to look at them in return. Tilting his chin high in the air and gazing down at the world under hooded eyelids, the aristocrat invites observation while refusing to look back. We can find such a pose exploited in an advertisement for Cadillac Seville in which an elegantly dressed woman goes out for a drive with her husband in their new Cadillac. If we look closely at the woman's body language, we see her glance inwardly with a satisfied smile on her face but not outward toward the camera that represents our gaze. She is glad to be seen by us in her Seville, but she isn't interested in looking at us!

Ads that are aimed at a broader market take the opposite approach. If the American dream encourages the desire to arrive, to vault above the mass, it also fosters a desire to be popular, to "belong." Populist commercials accordingly transform products into signs of belonging, utilizing such common icons as country music, small-town life, family picnics, and farmyards. All of these icons are incorporated in GM's "Heartbeat of America" campaign for its Chevrolet line. Unlike the Seville commercial, the faces in the Chevy ads look straight at us and smile. Dress is casual, the mood upbeat. Quick camera cuts take us from rustic to suburban to urban scenes, creating an American montage filmed from sea to shining sea. We all "belong" in a Chevy.

Discussion Questions

1. Jack Solomon sets up an interesting contrast between "manipulate" and "persuade" at the beginning of this excerpt. How does his description of these ads mirror our understanding of arguments? In your own words, how would you describe the differences he establishes between manipulating and persuading?

2. In Solomon's analysis of the Cadillac and Chevrolet ads, where does he address the claims and reasons given by the advertisers to buy their products? Do the ads address assumptions?

3. How does Solomon characterize the appeals made by both advertisements? Where does he describe appeals to *ethos*? *Logos*? *Pathos*?

Insider Example

Student Analysis of an Advertisement

Timothy Holtzhauser, a student in a first-year writing class, wrote the following analysis of an advertisement as a course assignment. He used elements of rhetorical analysis and argument analysis to understand the persuasive effects of the advertisement he chose. Notice, also, that he followed Modern Language Association (MLA) style conventions, especially when citing sources within his paper and documenting them at the end of the paper. (See Chapter 10 for additional information on documentation styles.)

Timothy Holtzhauser

English 101-79

February 13, 201–

Rhetoric of a 1943 War Bonds Ad

From the front covers of magazines at the store, to the ads by Google on sidebars of websites, to the incessant commercials on television, advertisements are visible everywhere. Whether the advertisement announces or insinuates its purpose, all advertisements attempt to change the audience's manner of thinking or acting. In "Masters of Desire: The Culture of American Advertising," Jack Solomon describes the motive behind advertising as pure and simple manipulation: "'Manipulate' is the word here, not 'persuade'; for advertising campaigns are not sources of product information, they are exercises in behavior modification" (60). Even the most innocent advertisement performs this maneuver, and the "Death Warrant…US War Bonds" advertisement drawn by S. J. Woolf is no different. This 1943 ad, printed in the *New York Daily News* for Bloomingdale's department store, not only encourages the purchase of U.S. war bonds by exaggerating Hitler's negative aspects, but also depicts the growing influence and activism of the United States during this era.

The main thesis, or claim.

When this advertisement appeared, the United States was rapidly becoming more involved in the hostilities of World War II. While not yet engaged in the war in Europe, the United States was providing supplies and manpower for the war in the Pacific, and the government was in serious need of funds to keep the war machine rolling. The main method that the government used to obtain these funds was selling war bonds and advertising, to push the sale of these bonds. War bonds were used as a tool to raise money for the government by selling certificates that promised a return on the investment after a period of time in exchange for the investment. In New York City, publishing city of the *New York Daily News* and home of Bloomingdale's main store, there was tremendous outrage at the atrocities being committed as a result of the war. Due to this, the general public showed interest in ending the war, especially the war in the Pacific. For the most part, the city trended toward the progressive democratic mind-set and agreed with the mostly democratic-controlled government of the era (Duranti 666). While factors such as

The next two paragraphs provide the reader with historical context for the ad and its publication. This information clarifies the rhetorical situation for readers and sets the stage for the analyses of the ad's elements that follow.

these propelled the citizens to purchase bonds as the advertisement suggests, there were other factors resisting this push as well. Particularly important was the ever-present aftermath of the Great Depression. The combination of these factors created a mixed feeling about the purchase of war bonds, but the fear of Hitler's reign continuing tended to bias the populace toward purchasing the bonds.

At the time of the release of this ad, the *New York Daily News* was a fairly new newspaper in New York City, as it had been initially released about twenty years beforehand. Even as a new publication, it had an extremely wide reader-ship due to its tabloid format, which focused on images, unlike other New York papers. At the time of the printing of this ad, the *Daily News* was known to be slightly biased toward the democratic mind-set common among the citizens of the city ("New York Daily News"). The publishing of this advertisement at this time could be viewed as an appeal to *ethos* in order to push the patriotic sense of the paper. The advertisement can also be seen as an appeal to *ethos* by Bloomingdale's, as the company

TO BRING CLOSER THE HAPPY DAY SHOWN
ABOVE—BUY MORE AND MORE WAR BONDS
BLOOMINGDALE'S
Lexington Avenue and 59th Street

was seeking to portray itself as a patriotic firm. With that context in mind, several components of the advertisement make more sense and can be more effectively analyzed.

The most prominent feature in the advertisement is Hitler's face, and in particular, his facial expression. Woolf's image here uses two primary components to make the facial expression stand out: the humorously exaggerated bug-eyed stare and the dropped jaw. The effect created by these two factors is compounded by the addition of the buck teeth and the protruding ears. The bug eyes commonly serve in American imagery to express shock, and they perform that role excellently here in this advertisement. The dropped jaw is used very frequently as well, especially in cartoons, and here it strengthens

The analysis now focuses on specific elements of the ad. In this paragraph, the student analyzes features of Hitler's face: the bug eyes, the dropped jaw, the tufts of hair. These, he suggests, express Hitler's fear of American strength, which stems at least partially from the selling and purchasing of war bonds.

the shocked expression. The buck teeth and protruding ears are two images that are used in American culture to convey the idea of a buffoon. In addition to these features, Woolf comically adds in two tufts of hair in imitation of devil horns to further enhance Hitler's evil image. When these two are added to the previous facets, it creates an image of a completely dumbfounded and baffled Hitler. The image was designed in this manner to enhance the feeling that purchasing U.S. war bonds would benefit society by eliminating the severe hindrance known as Hitler.

The next feature that stands out is the death warrant and war bond itself and Hitler's hands clutching it. Woolf draws Hitler's hands in a manner that makes them appear to be tightly gripping the paper as in anger. The paper itself shows only the words "death warrant" and "U.S. War Bonds," but one can infer from the context that the warrant is for Hitler. The fact that the warrant is printed on a war bond suggests that the U.S. government completely backs the killing of Hitler and will take action to see it through. The document appeals to the viewer's *logos* through the suggestion that war bonds will end the war sooner and save countless lives in the process. There is also an inherent appeal to *ethos* in the suggestion of the character of Bloomingdale's as a firm that strongly opposes the horrors committed by Hitler and his followers. In addition, there is an appeal to *pathos*, with the ad attempting to home in on the audience's moral code. This apparent encouragement of killing Hitler, coupled with the text at the bottom of the advertisement, creates a mood of vengeance directed toward Hitler.

The next major feature of the advertisement is the caption at the bottom of the image, which reads, "To bring closer the happy day shown above—buy more and more war bonds." The image shown above the text in most scenarios would not be considered a happy day for most people. The thought of death is normally enough to ruin anyone's day, but this image banks on the public having a burning vengeance that justifies the end of Hitler. The idea of vengeance is generally viewed as having serious negative repercussions, but this article portrays the idea in a positive manner by making an appeal to the audience's *logos*. The appeal here could best be described as sacrificing one to save millions. The caption also makes an appeal to *pathos* in the manner that it tries to connect with the viewer's sense of morals that Hitler has almost definitely broken in numerous ways.

The writer shifts focus to analyze the ad's caption.

The next aspect of the advertisement that stands out is the use of shading. Woolf's decision here may have been influenced by requirements of the *Daily News* at the time, but even viewed in that light it has a rhetorical effect on the advertisement. The usage of shading here creates the appearance of an unfinished image, further enhancing the idea that Hitler has just been served his death warrant hot off the press by the United States and its war bonds. It also creates a worried cast to Hitler's face through the heavy shading in the creases along his jawline. The overall image of Hitler created through the use of shading comes off as dark and sinister, representative of the common American's view on Hitler's character. In contrast, the war bond is virtually untouched by shading, leaving it nearly white. This creates the image of a beacon of hope shining through the darkness that provides a means to eliminate this terror. Additionally, the presence of a heavily shaded advertisement among the more crisp images, popular among tabloids, accents this advertisement and its message.

The final aspect of the advertisement that draws major attention is the overall construction of the image. The layout emphasizes the two key components of the advertisement: Hitler's face and the war bond. Not only does this accentuate the relationship between buying war bonds and bringing the hammer down on Hitler, but it also provides further depth to the image's rhetorical context. Hitler is posed hunched over as if to imply a deformity in his body and represent a deformity of his mind. The statement here runs on the classic American stereotype that a malformed person is either inferior or evil, a stereotype popularly used in comical representations such as this one. In addition, the hunched posture can be interpreted as the weight of the American war machine, fueled by the war bond purchases, dragging Hitler down to end his reign of terror.

With each of these analyzed aspects in mind, the advertisement can serve as an effective description of the period similar to what Jack Solomon suggests is possible in "Masters of Desire." He uses the following statement to show how advertisements are indicative of the culture of their audiences: "But by semiotically reading the signs that advertising agencies manufacture to stimulate consumption, we can plot the precise state of desire in the audiences to which they are addressed" (61). Based upon the patriotic push shown through this advertisement's attack on Hitler and visualization of handing him a death warrant, the advertisement shows the general patriotic mood of America at the time. Given the war footing of the country during this era, this patriotic pride fits well into the time frame. It also shows the growing influence of the United States across the world. Up until this point in time, America was not taken very seriously, and U.S. foreign policy was mostly designed to ignore the rest of the world and preserve America. With the serving of the death warrant to Hitler shown in this advertisement, the change in ideology is starkly apparent. Instead of the wait-and-see mentality common in America before World War II, the highly proactive and aggressive nature of America today begins to show. For a small snippet in a tabloid newspaper, this advertisement packs quite a rhetorical punch.

Taking into account all the elements of this advertisement, rhetorical and otherwise, the advertisement creates an astounding patriotic push for the purchase of war bonds through exaggeration and establishes the United States as a globally significant force through the implications of the death warrant for a foreign citizen. All aspects used in this advertisement work well to cleverly goad readers of the paper to purchase war bonds from Bloomingdale's, holding true to Jack Solomon's statement about advertisements not seeking to provide information, but to manipulate the audience. In the end, however, this advertisement does not convey the negative connotation often associated with manipulative advertising; rather, it uses manipulative elements to try to create a better future for the readers.

Notice how the ending addresses elements of the paper's thesis statement, or how the ad "depicts the growing influence and activism of the United States during this era."

Works Cited

Bloomingdale's. Advertisement. *New York Daily News.* 1943.

Duranti, Marco. "Utopia, Nostalgia, and World War at the 1939–40 New York World's Fair." *Journal of Contemporary History*, vol. 41, no. 4, 2006, pp. 663–83.

"New York Daily News." *Encyclopaedia Britannica Online*, 2016, www .britannica.com/topic/New-York-Daily-News.

Solomon, Jack. "Masters of Desire: The Culture of American Advertising." *The Signs of Our Time: Semiotics: The Hidden Messages of Environments, Objects, and Cultural Images.* Jeremy P. Tarcher, 1988, pp. 59–76.

Discussion Questions

1. Where does Timothy Holtzhauser state his thesis? Why do you think he phrases his thesis in the way that he does?

2. How does Timothy use *logos* in his own argument? Why do you think he relies on *logos* to support his claim?

3. Who is the intended audience for this argument?

4. What scholarly or popular conversation(s) is Timothy joining in?

5. Which claim(s) do you find most convincing and least convincing for Timothy's rhetorical situation? Why?

Writing Project: Composing a Rhetorical Analysis of an Advertisement

For this project, we ask you to consider the ways in which rhetorical context and appeals work together in an advertisement to create an argument.

- To begin, choose a print or online advertisement that you can analyze based on its rhetorical context and the appeals it uses to persuade the intended audience.

- Then, drawing on the principles of rhetorical analysis from Chapter 8 and the discussion of developing arguments in this chapter, compose an analysis examining the ad's use of appeals in light of the rhetorical situation the ad constructs.

Rhetorical Context (see Chapter 8)

Central Question: How do the elements of the rhetorical context affect the way the advertisement is structured?

Author _____

Audience _____

Topic _____

Purpose _____

Rhetorical Appeals (see Chapter 9)

Central Question: What appeals does the advertisement use, and why?

Ethos _____

Logos _____

Pathos _____

Keep in mind that a rhetorical analysis makes an argument, so your analysis should have a central claim that you develop based on what you observed, through the frameworks of rhetorical context and rhetorical appeals, in the advertisement. Make your claim clear, and then support it with reasons and evidence from the advertisement.

Tip Sheet — Developing Arguments

- **Presenting an argument is different from merely stating an opinion.** Presenting and supporting an argument mean establishing a claim that is backed by reasons and evidence.

- **The unifying element of any academic argument is its primary or central claim.** A unifying claim may take the form of a thesis, a hypothesis, or a more general statement of purpose. There are numerous kinds of claims, including claims of value, definition, and policy.

- **Reasons are generated from and supported by evidence.** Evidence may take the form of inartistic proofs (including statistics and raw data) or artistic proofs, including the rhetorical appeals of *ethos* (appeal to credibility), *logos* (appeal to reason and logic), and *pathos* (appeal to emotion).

- **Claims presented as part of a chain of reasoning are linked by (often) unstated assumptions.** Assumptions should be analyzed carefully for their appropriateness (acceptability, believability) in a particular rhetorical context.

- **Considering and/or incorporating counterarguments is an excellent way to strengthen your own arguments.** You may rebut counterarguments, or you may concede (or partially concede) to them and modify your own argument in response.

- **Analyzing others' arguments is a good way to develop your skills at arguing,** particularly in an academic context.

Chapter 10 Academic Research

Conducting Research

Research projects have all kinds of starting points. Sometimes we start them because a course instructor or an employer asks us to. At other times, we embark on research projects because we want to learn about something on our own. In all these cases, though, our research responds to a question or set of questions that we need to answer. These are called **research questions**, and identifying them and narrowing them down is usually the first step of starting a research project, especially in an academic context.

Developing a Research Question

For many students, choosing a subject to research is incredibly difficult. The best way to start is by thinking about issues that matter to you. Writers tend to do their best work when writing about things in which they have a personal investment. Even if you're conducting research in a course with a topic that has been assigned, think about how you might approach the topic from an angle that matters to you or brings in your own unique point of view.

Another challenge that many students face is narrowing down a solid research question once they've selected an issue of interest. If a research question is too broad, then it may not be feasible to respond to it adequately in the scope of your research assignment. If it's too narrow, though, it might not be researchable; in other words, you might not be able to find enough sources to support a solid position on the issue.

Andrea Tsurumi

As you work on drafting a research question, keep these five criteria in mind:

1. **Personal Investment**   Is this an issue you care about?

2. **Debatable Subject**   Might reasonable people looking at evidence about this issue come to different conclusions?

3. **Researchable Issue**   Is there adequate published evidence to support a position on this issue?

4. **Feasibility**   Is the scope of the research question manageable?

5. **Contribution**   Will your response to the question contribute to the ongoing conversation about the issue?

Inside Work: Writing a Research Question

As you begin your research project, you should identify a research question that will guide your research and keep you on track. Start by brainstorming a list of possible research questions for ten minutes, and then use the five criteria below to narrow down your list to a research question that might work for you. If your answer to any of the questions is a definitive "No," then the research question might not be a good choice, or you might need to revise it to make it work for a research project.

1. **Personal Investment**   Is this an issue you care about? If the issue is too broad, is there a way you can narrow down the topic to an aspect of the issue that is of the most importance to you?

2. **Debatable Subject**   Could two reasonable people looking at evidence about this issue come to different conclusions?

3. **Researchable Issue**   Can you find adequate published evidence to support a position on this issue?

4. **Feasibility**   Is the scope of the research question manageable, given the amount of time you have to research the issue and the amount of space in which you will make your argument?

5. **Contribution**   Will your response to your question contribute to the ongoing conversation about the issue?

Choosing Primary and Secondary Sources

To respond to any research question, a writer must collect evidence to prove or disprove a hypothesis or to support a claim. Once you have identified a solid research question, you must decide whether you need to collect *primary* and/or *secondary sources* to support your research aims.

Writers can choose from among several types of sources to support their research. When considering sources to support an argument, writers must study them for information that can serve as specific *evidence* to address aspects of their claims, all the while keeping their target audience in mind. What kind of evidence will likely be convincing to the target audience? If researchers are reviewing the existing literature on a topic or are trying to understand what has already been written about an issue before conducting a study of their own, they must search for sources that provide information about the ongoing conversation concerning that topic or issue. Then the researchers might collect data to answer a clearly defined research question that has grown out of reading those sources.

LaunchPadSolo

A political scientist emphasizes the importance of supporting evidence.

Primary sources include the results of data that researchers might collect on their own. If you're making a claim about how to interpret a work of art and you've studied the piece carefully for images and symbols that you discuss in your argument, then the work of art is your primary source. Or perhaps you've designed and conducted a survey of people's experiences with a particular phenomenon. In this case, the results you've gathered from your survey are a primary source from which you can provide evidence to answer a research question or support an argument. Other forms of primary sources include original historical documents and results from interviews you may have conducted.

Inside Work: Collecting Primary Evidence

Freewrite for five to ten minutes about a time in the past when you had to collect data on your own to answer a research question.

- Why were you collecting the data? What question were you trying to answer?
- What data did you collect, and how did you collect it? Did you observe something? Conduct a survey? Interview someone?
- If you were to try to answer that research question now, what data would you collect? Would you do anything differently? Why or why not?

Based on the scope of your argument and the expectations of your audience, you may also need to engage **secondary sources**, or research collected by and/or commented on by others. Let's say that your literature professor wants you to offer an interpretation of a poem. You study the poem carefully as your primary source and arrive at a conclusion or claim about the work. But imagine that the assignment also requires you to use scholarly opinions to support your own position or interpretation. As a result, you spend time in the library or searching online databases to locate articles or books by scholars who provide their own interpretations or perspectives on the poem. The articles or books you rely on to support your interpretation are secondary sources because the interpretations were developed by others, commenting on the poem. Likewise, if you cite as part of your own argument the results of a survey published in an academic article, then that article serves as a secondary source of information to you. Other secondary sources include newspapers and magazines, textbooks, and encyclopedias. Many of the researched arguments you'll produce in college will require you to use both primary and secondary sources as support.

Inside Work: Using Primary and Secondary Sources

Read Timothy Holtzhauser's ad analysis on pages 265–69 of Chapter 9. After reviewing his analysis, look at the list of works cited at the end of his essay. Then answer the following questions.

- What primary source(s) does Timothy use to support his argument? Why do you think he chooses the primary source(s) he does?

- What would the impact be if Timothy didn't use primary sources in his argument? Would his argument be more or less persuasive to his audience?

- What secondary sources does Timothy use to support his argument?

- Why do you think he chooses these particular secondary sources? What impact do they have on the development of his argument?

- If Timothy had only used primary sources and no secondary sources, what would the impact have been on the persuasiveness of his argument?

Insider's View

Primary Research in Writing Studies

Moriah McCracken, Writing Studies

"I like to try to introduce my students to qualitative research in their first year, when our students have to interview a professor. Sometimes I'll help them develop survey questions and questionnaires so they can have that kind of experience, and I'll teach them about double-entry notebooks so they can do some observations in the classroom. I like to bring in qualitative methods so that students realize there are different kinds of questions to ask, and depending on my question, I'm going to have to try something a little bit different and learn how to do this kind of research in my discipline."

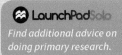

Find additional advice on doing primary research.

Searching for Sources

In Part Three, we discuss collecting primary sources to support claims in specific disciplinary areas or genres in more detail. In the rest of this chapter, though, we provide support for collecting secondary sources, which provide a foundation for research and writing in academic contexts. Even if the main evidence used to support an academic research project comes from primary sources, secondary sources can provide an overview of what other scholars have already argued with regard to a particular issue or topic. Keep in mind that academic writing and research essentially comprise a series of extended conversations about different issues, and secondary sources help you understand what part of the conversation has already happened before you start researching a topic on your own, or before you consider entering an established conversation on a topic or issue.

Identifying Search Terms

The school, college, or university you attend likely offers many avenues to help navigate the processes for conducting library research at your institution. Most of these processes include searching for source materials online. When you search for secondary sources online to support the development of a research study or to support a claim in an argument, it's important to consider your **search terms**, the key words and phrases you'll use while you're searching. Let's say that you're interested in understanding the effects of using cell phones while driving, a topic we explored in Chapter 8. You might begin your research with a question that reads something like this:

What are the effects of using cell phones while driving?

The first step in your research process would likely be to find out what others have already written about this issue. To start, you might rephrase your research question to ask:

What have scholars written about the effects of using cell phones while driving?

To respond, you'll need to identify the key terms of your question that will focus your search for secondary sources about the subject. You might highlight some of the key terms in the question:

What have scholars written about the effects of using cell phones while driving?

If you started your search by typing "cell phones and driving" into Google, your search would return millions of results:

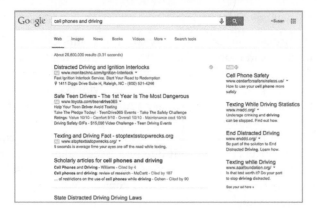

These results include links to images of people on cell phones in their cars, to news articles, and to statistics from insurance companies, to name a few. After careful evaluation, you may decide that some of these sources of data would be useful for your research, but you can also see that the results produce far too many hits to manage. There's simply no way you can comb through the millions of hits to find information that is appropriate for your purposes. As a result, you may choose to narrow your search to something that emerges as a specific issue, like "reaction time." If you narrowed your search to "cell phones and reaction time," you would see results like this:

Focusing your research terms further narrows the scope of your search somewhat, but you still have far too many results to review. One concern to keep in mind, then, is that basic Google searches are not very useful in helping to locate the kinds of sources you might rely on for your research, especially in an academic context. If you want to understand what scholars have written about your topic, then you need to find scholarly or academic sources as support. A basic Google search doesn't filter different kinds of sources, so it's not generally very helpful.

Instead, you might choose to search Google Scholar to understand the ongoing conversation among scholars about your topic. Conducting a search for "cell phones and driving accidents and reaction time" in Google Scholar returns tens of thousands of results:

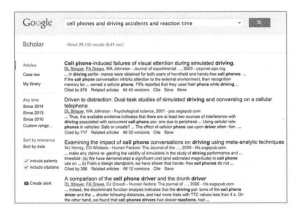

If you take a close look at the left-hand side of the screen, however, you'll notice that you can limit your search in several ways. By limiting the search to sources published since 2014, you can reduce your results significantly:

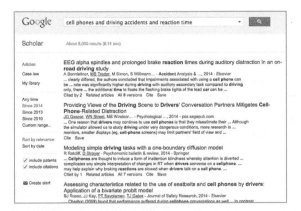

You can continue refining your search until you end up with a more manageable number of hits to comb through. Although the number is still large, thousands of results are more manageable than millions. Of course, you would likely need to continue narrowing your results. As part of this narrowing process, you are simultaneously focusing in on the conversation you originally wanted to understand: what scholars have written about your topic. Consider the criteria that would be most meaningful for your project as you refine your search by revising your search terms.

Inside Work: Generating Search Terms

Think of a controversial social issue that interests you. We chose driving while using a cell phone, but you should choose something you would potentially be interested in learning more about. Then follow these instructions, preferably working with classmates.

- Brainstorm the search terms you would use for that topic. What terms would you enter into a search engine?

- List your search terms in the box for Round 1 below, and then try doing a search using your preferred web search engine.

- How many hits did you get? Write the number in the box for Round 1.

- Switch seats with a classmate so that you can look at someone else's search terms. Should the search be narrowed? If so, revise your classmate's search terms to narrow them slightly. Write those in the box for Round 2. Try the search, and record the number of hits.

- Follow the instructions again for Rounds 3 and 4.

	Search Terms	Number of Hits
Round 1		
Round 2		
Round 3		
Round 4		

After you have finished the exercise, reflect on the following questions.

- How did your classmates narrow your search terms? What changes worked well, and what changes didn't work as well?

- If you were going to write advice for students using search engines for research, what advice would you give about search terms?

Keep in mind that general search engines such as Google are not always the best places to conduct academic research, although they can often be useful starting points. Experienced researchers generally rely on more specialized databases to find the kinds of sources that will support their research most effectively.

Using Journal Databases

If you are conducting academic research, then one of the first types of sources you should look for is peer-reviewed journal articles. You may wonder why we don't recommend beginning your search by scouring your library's catalog for books. The answer is that academic books, which are often an excellent source of information, generally take much longer to make their way through the publishing process before they appear in libraries. Publishing the results of research in academic journal articles, however, is a faster method for academics to share their work with their scholarly communities. Academic journals, therefore, are a valuable resource precisely because they offer insight into the most current research being conducted in a field.

Additionally, like other scholarly work, most academic journals publish research only after it has undergone rigorous scrutiny through a peer-review process by other scholars in the relevant academic field. Work that has gone through the academic peer-review process has been sent out, with the authors' identifying information removed, and reviewed by other scholars who determine whether it makes a sufficiently significant contribution to the field to be published. Work published in a peer-reviewed academic journal has been approved not only by the journal's editor but also by other scholars in the field.

If you've ever browsed through your school's library, you've probably noticed that there are thousands of academic journals, and many are available online and easy to locate via the Internet. If you're associated with a college or university, you likely have access to a wide array of online academic journals that can be explored through databases via the library's website. You can search general library databases by refining search terms, as we discussed in the examples of using Google, but you can also find relevant resources by searching in specific disciplinary databases.

Searching for Journal Articles by Discipline

One way of searching for journal articles through your school's library is to explore the academic databases by subject or discipline. These databases usually break down the major fields of study into the many subfields that make up smaller disciplinary communities. Individual schools, colleges, and universities choose which databases they subscribe to. In the image to the right from the North Carolina State University's library website, you can see that agriculture is divided into various subfields: agricultural economics, animal science, crop science, and so on.

Let's say you need to find information on post-traumatic stress disorder (PTSD) among veterans of the Iraq War that began in March 2003. Consider the

Select databases by subject (see all)

Agriculture	› Agricultural Economics
Design	› Agriculture
Education	› Animal Science
Engineering	› Crop Science
Humanities	› Entomology
Life Sciences	› Family & Consumer Sciences
Management	› Fisheries & Wildlife Sciences
Mathematics	› Food Science
Natural Resources	› Forestry
Physical Sciences	› Genetics & Genomics
Social Sciences	› Horticulture
	› Nutrition

Not sure where to start?
Search General/Multi-Subject databases.

Psychology

Databases

PsycINFO

PsycINFO, from the American Psychological Association (APA), contains more than 2 million citations and summaries of scholarly journal articles, book chapters, books, and dissertations, all in psychology and related disciplines, dating as far back as the 1800s. The database also includes information about the psychological aspects of related fields such as medicine, psychiatry, nursing, sociology, education, pharmacology, physiology, linguistics, anthropology, business, law and others. Journal coverage, which spans 1887 to present, includes international material selected from nearly 2,000 periodicals in more than 25 languages.

subfields of the social sciences where you're most likely to find research on PTSD. You might search databases in history, sociology, political science, and psychology, for instance. If you choose "Psychology," then you see a screen that lists major research databases in psychology, along with some related databases. Choosing the database at the top of the page, "PsycINFO," gains you access to one of the most comprehensive databases in that field of study.

Selecting "PsycINFO" grants access to the PsycINFO database via a search engine—in this case, EbscoHOST. You can now input search terms such as "PTSD and Iraq war veterans" to see your results.

Notice that the search engine allows you to refine your search in a number of ways, very similar to the limitations you can use in Google Scholar: you can limit the years of publication for research articles, you can limit the search to sources that are available full-text online, you can limit the search to peer-reviewed journal articles, and more. The results look like this:

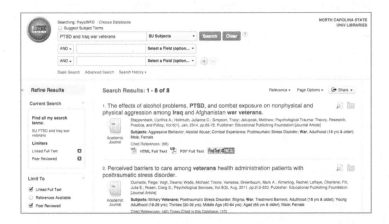

You can now access the texts of journal articles that you find interesting or that might be most relevant to your research purposes. Depending on the number and content of the results, you may choose to revise your search terms and run the search again.

Evaluating Sources

Distinguishing between Scholarly and Popular Sources

As we have said, using search engines makes finding sources easy. The difficult part is deciding which sources are worth your time. If you are working on an academic paper, it is particularly useful to be able to distinguish between popular and scholarly sources.

Depending on your research and writing context, you might be able to use both scholarly and popular sources to support your research. However, in some writing situations it is most appropriate to rely on scholarly sources. For this reason, you should understand the difference between scholarly and popular sources, which comes down to a matter of audience and the publication process. Scholarly sources are produced for an audience of other scholars, and popular sources are produced for a general audience. Scholarly sources have undergone the peer-review process prior to publication, while popular sources typically have been vetted only by an editor. Generally speaking, popular sources are not very useful for supporting academic research. Let's examine a number of publication types in terms of the kind of information, scholarly or popular, they most often provide:

Examples of Scholarly Sources

- Academic Journals   Most journal articles are produced for an audience of other scholars, and the vast majority are peer-reviewed before they are published in academic journals.

- Books Published by Academic Presses   Academic presses publish books that also go through the peer-review process. You can sometimes identify academic presses by their names (e.g., a university press), but sometimes you need to dig deeper to find out whether a press generally publishes scholarly or popular sources. Looking at the press's website can often help answer that question.

Examples of Popular Sources

- Newspapers   Most newspaper articles are reviewed by editors for accuracy and reliability. However, they typically provide only information that would be of interest to a general audience. They are not specifically intended for an academic audience. A newspaper might report the results of a study published in an academic journal, but it will generally not publish original academic research.

- Magazines   Like newspaper articles, magazine articles are typically reviewed by editors and are intended for a general reading audience, not an academic one.

Although it may seem easy to classify sources into one of these two categories, in fact it is often difficult to determine if a source is scholarly or not. Understanding the nature of scholarly and popular sources and recognizing their differences as you do your research will help you develop more effective arguments.

Insider's View

On Distinguishing Scholarly Sources

Jonathan Morris, Political Science

"We have to teach our students what's scholarly literature and what isn't. Peer-review journal articles, books—that's scholarly literature. When you pull things off of Wikipedia, when you go even to newspaper articles from the *New York Times*—that's not scholarly research. They need to know that differentiation.'"

LaunchPadSolo

Get expert advice on finding scholarly sources.

Scholarly works, for instance, are typically built on other sources, so they generally include references to other works that are documented in the text and listed in a complete bibliography at the end. Imagine for a moment, though, that you locate a study published on the Internet that you think would be a really good source for your research. It looks just like an article that might appear in a journal, and it has a bibliography that includes other academic sources. However, as part of your analysis of the source, you discover that the article, published only on a website, has never been published by a journal. Is this a scholarly work? It might be. Could this still be a useful scholarly work for your purposes? Perhaps. Still, as a writer and researcher, you would need to know that the article you're using as part of your own research has never been peer-reviewed or published by a journal or an academic press. This means that the validity of the work has never been assessed by other experts in the field. If you use the source in your own work, you would probably want to indicate that it has never been peer-reviewed or published in an academic journal as part of your discussion of that source.

Answering the following questions about your sources can help you evaluate their credibility and reliability:

1. Who are the authors?

2. Who is the intended audience?

3. Where is the work published?

4. Does the work rely on other reputable sources for information?

5. Does the work seem biased?

As a writer, you must ultimately make the decisions about what is or is not an appropriate source, based on your goals and an analysis of your audience. Answering the questions above can help you assess the appropriateness of sources.

Inside Work: Evaluating Sources

For this exercise, either look at the sample essay from Timothy Holtzhauser on pages 265–69 of Chapter 9 or look at an essay that you wrote for a class in the past. Choose one of the references listed in the essay's bibliography, and write answers to the following questions.

1. Who are the authors? Do they possess any particular credentials that make them experts on the topic? With what institutions or organizations are the authors associated?

2. Who is the intended audience—the general public or a group of scholars? How do you know?

3. Where is the work published? Do works published there undergo a peer-review process?

4. Does the work rely on other reputable sources for information? What are those sources, and how do you know they are reputable?

5. Does the work seem biased? How do you know this? Is the work funded or supported by individuals or parties who might have a vested interest in the results? If so, is there a potential conflict of interest?

Summarizing, Paraphrasing, and Quoting from Sources

Once you've located and studied the sources you want to use in a research paper, then you're ready to begin considering ways to integrate that material into your own work. There are a number of ways to integrate the words and ideas of others into your research, and you've likely already had experience summarizing, paraphrasing, and quoting from sources as part of an academic writing assignment. For many students, though, the specifics of how to summarize, paraphrase, and quote accurately are often unclear, so we'll walk through these processes in some detail.

Summarizing

Summarizing a text is a way of condensing the work to its main ideas. A summary therefore requires you to choose the most important elements of a text and to answer these questions: *What* is this work really trying to say, and *how* does it say it? Composing a summary of a source can be valuable for a number of reasons. Writing a summary can help you carefully analyze the content of a text and understand it better, but a summary can also help you identify and keep track of the sources you want to use in the various parts of your research. You may sometimes be able to summarize a source in only a sentence or two. We suggest a simple method for analyzing a source and composing a summary:

1. Read the source carefully, noting the rhetorical context. Who composed the source? For whom is the source intended? Where was it published? Identify the source and provide answers to these questions at the beginning of your summary, as appropriate.

2. Identify the main points. Pay close attention to topic sentences at the beginning of paragraphs, as they often highlight central ideas in the overall structure of an argument. Organize your summary around the main ideas you identify.

3. Identify examples. You will want to be able to summarize the ways the writer illustrates, exemplifies, or argues the main points. Though you will likely not discuss all of the examples or forms of evidence you identify in detail as part of your summary, you will want to comment on one or two, or offer some indication of how the writer supports his or her main points.

The following excerpt is taken from the fuller text of Jack Solomon's "Masters of Desire: The Culture of American Advertising," which appears on pages 261–64 in Chapter 9:

> Status symbols, then, are signs that identify their possessors' place in a social hierarchy, markers of rank and prestige. We can all think of any number of status symbols—Rolls-Royces, Beverly Hills mansions, even Shar Pei puppies (whose rareness and expense has rocketed them beyond Russian wolfhounds as status pets and has even inspired whole lines of wrinkle-faced stuffed toys)—but how do we know that something is a status symbol? The explanation is quite simple: when an object (or puppy!) either costs a lot of money or requires influential connections to possess, anyone who possesses it must also possess the necessary means and influence to acquire it. The object itself really doesn't matter, since it ultimately disappears behind the presumed social potency of its owner. Semiotically, what matters is the signal it sends, its value as a sign of power. One traditional sign of social distinction is owning a country estate and enjoying the peace and privacy that attend it. Advertisements for Mercedes-Benz, Jaguar, and Audi automobiles thus frequently feature drivers motoring quietly along a country road, presumably on their way to or from their country houses.

A summary of this part of Solomon's text might read something like this:

> In "Masters of Desire: The Culture of American Advertising," Jack Solomon acknowledges that certain material possessions may be understood as representations of an individual's rank or status. He illustrates this point by identifying a number of luxury automobiles that, when observed, cause us to consider the elevated economic status of the vehicles' owners (63).

You'll notice that this summary eliminates discussion of the specific examples Solomon provides. Further, it removes any discussion of the concept of semiotics. Though Solomon's ideas are clearly condensed and the writer of this summary has carefully selected the ideas to be summarized in order to further his or her own aims, the core of Solomon's idea is accurately represented.

Paraphrasing

Sometimes a writer doesn't want to summarize a source because condensing its ideas risks losing part of its importance. In such a case, the writer has to choose whether to paraphrase or quote directly from the source. **Paraphrasing** means translating the author's words and sentence structure into your own for the purpose of making the ideas clear for your audience. A paraphrase may be the same length or even longer than the part of a text being paraphrased, so the purpose of paraphrase is not really to condense a passage, as is the case for summary.

Often, writers prefer to paraphrase sources rather than to quote from them, especially if the exact language from the source isn't important, but the ideas are. Depending on your audience, you might want to rephrase highly technical language from a scientific source, for example, and put it in your own words. Or you might want to emphasize a point the author makes in a way that isn't as clear in the original language. Many social scientists and most scientists routinely paraphrase sources as part of the presentation of their own research because the results they're reporting from secondary sources are more important than the exact language used to explain the results. Quotations should be reserved for instances when the exact language of the original source is important to the point being made. Remember that paraphrasing requires you to restate the passage in your own words and in your own sentence structure. Even if you are putting the source's ideas in your own words, you must acknowledge where the information came from by providing an appropriate citation.

The following paragraph was taken from William Thierfelder's article "Twain's *Huckleberry Finn*," published in *The Explicator*, a journal of literary criticism.

An often-noted biblical allusion in *Huckleberry Finn* is that comparing Huck to the prophet Moses. Like Moses, whom Huck learns about from the Widow Douglas, Huck sets out, an orphan on his raft, down the river. In the biblical story, it is Moses' mother who puts him in his little "raft," hoping he will be found. In the novel, Huck/Moses takes charge of his own travels....

Inappropriate Paraphrase

William Thierfelder suggests that Huckleberry is often compared to the prophet Moses. Huck, an orphan like Moses, travels down a river on a raft (194).

Although some of the language has been changed and the paraphrase includes documentation, this paraphrase of the first two sentences of Thierfelder's passage is inappropriate because it relies on the language of the original text and employs the author's sentence structure. An appropriate paraphrase that uses new language and sentence structure might look like this:

> William Thierfelder notes that numerous readers have linked the character of Huckleberry Finn and the biblical figure of Moses. They are both orphans who take a water journey, Thierfelder argues. However, Moses's journey begins because of the actions of his mother, while Huck's journey is undertaken by himself (194).

Quoting

Depending on your rhetorical context, you may find that **quoting** the exact words of a source as part of your argument is the most effective strategy. The use of quotations is much more common in some academic fields than in others. Writers in the humanities, for example, often quote texts directly because the precise language of the original is important to the argument. You'll find, for instance, that literary scholars often quote a short story or poem (a primary source) for evidence. You may also find that a secondary source contains powerful or interesting language that would lose its impact if you paraphrased it. In such circumstances, it is entirely appropriate to quote the text. Keep in mind that your reader should always be able to understand why the quotation is important to your argument. We recommend three methods for integrating quotations into your writing. (The examples below follow American Psychological Association style conventions; see "Understanding Documentation Systems" on pages 290–92 for more information about documentation styles.)

1. **Attributive Tags**   Introduce the quotation with a tag (with words like *notes*, *argues*, *suggests*, *posits*, *maintains*, etc.) that attributes the language and ideas to its author. Notice that different tags suggest different relationships between the author and the idea being cited. For example:

   > De Niet, Tiemens, Lendemeijer, Lendemei, and Hutschemaekers (2009) argued, "Music-assisted relaxation is an effective aid for improving sleep quality in patients with various conditions" (p. 1362).

2. **Further Grammatical Integration**   You may also fully integrate a quotation into the grammar of your own sentences. For example:

   > Their review of the research revealed "scientific support for the effectiveness of the systematic use of music-assisted relaxation to promote sleep quality" in patients (De Niet et al., 2009, p. 1362).

3. **Introduce with Full Sentence + Punctuation**   You can also introduce a quotation with a full sentence and create a transitional link to the quotation with punctuation, like the colon. For example:

> The study reached a final conclusion about music-assisted relaxation: "It is a safe and cheap intervention which may be used to treat sleep problems in various populations" (De Niet et al., 2009, p. 1362).

Inside Work: Summarizing, Paraphrasing, and Quoting from Sources

Choose a source that you have found on a topic of interest to you, and find a short passage (only one or two sentences) that provides information that might be useful in your own research. Then complete the following steps and write down your responses.

1. Summarize the passage. It might help to look at the larger context in which the passage appears.

2. Paraphrase the passage, using your own words and sentence structure.

3. Quote the passage, using the following three ways to integrate the passage into your own text:

    a.   attributive tags

    b.   grammatical integration

    c.   full sentence + punctuation

For your own research, which approach (summarizing, paraphrasing, quoting) do you think would be most useful? Consider your writing context and how you would use the source.

Avoiding Plagiarism

Any language and ideas used in your own writing that belong to others must be fully acknowledged and carefully documented, including in-text citations and full bibliographic documentation. Failure to include either of these when source materials are employed could lead to a charge of plagiarism, perhaps the most serious of academic integrity offenses. The procedures for documenting cited sources vary from one rhetorical and disciplinary context to another, so always clarify the expectations for documentation with your instructor when responding to an assigned writing task. Regardless, you should always acknowledge your sources when you summarize, paraphrase, or quote, and be sure to include the full information for your sources in the bibliography of your project.

Insider's View

On Accidental Plagiarism

Karen Keaton Jackson, Writing Studies

"Many students come in who are already familiar with using direct quotations. But when it comes to paraphrasing and summarizing, that's when I see a lot of accidental plagiarism. So it's really important for students to understand that if you don't do the research yourself, or if you weren't there in the field or doing the survey, then it's not your own idea and you have to give credit."

Hear more on avoiding plagiarism.

Inside Work: Understanding Plagiarism

Most schools, colleges, and universities have established definitions of plagiarism and penalties or sanctions that may be imposed on students found guilty of plagiarism. You should become familiar with the definitions of plagiarism used by your institution as well as by your individual instructors.

- Locate a resource on campus (e.g., a student handbook or the website of your institution's Office of Student Conduct) that provides a definition of plagiarism from the perspective of your institution. You may discover that in addition to defining plagiarism, your institution provides avenues of support to foster academic integrity and/or presents explanations of the consequences or penalties for violating rules of academic integrity.

- Locate a resource from one of your classes (e.g., a course website, a course syllabus) that provides a definition of plagiarism from the perspective of one of your instructors.

- Consider what is similar about the two definitions. Consider the differences between them. What do these similarities and differences reveal about your instructor's expectations and those of the larger academic community in which you participate?

Understanding Documentation Systems

Documentation systems are often discipline-specific, and their conventions reflect the needs and values of researchers and readers in those particular disciplines. For these reasons, you should carefully analyze any writing situation to determine which documentation style to follow. You'll find examples of specific documentation systems in the disciplinary chapters in Part Three. Here are some of the most common ones:

1. Modern Language Association (MLA)

MLA documentation procedures are generally followed by researchers in the humanities. One of the most important elements of the in-text citation requirements for the MLA documentation system is the inclusion of page numbers in a parenthetical reference. Though page numbers are used in other documentation systems for some in-text citations (as in the APA system when quoting a passage directly), page numbers in MLA are especially important because they serve as a means for readers to assess your use of sources, both primary and secondary, and are used whether you are quoting, paraphrasing, or summarizing a passage. Page numbers enable readers to quickly identify cited passages and evaluate the evidence: readers may verify that you've accurately represented a source's intent when citing the author's words, or that you've fully examined all the elements at play in your analysis of a photograph or poem. Of course, this kind of examination is important in all disciplines, but it is especially the case in the fields of the humanities, where evidence typically takes the form of words and images. Unlike some other documentation systems, the MLA system does not require dates for in-text citations, because scholars in this field often find that past discoveries or arguments are just as useful today as when they were first observed or published. Interpretations don't really expire; their usefulness remains valid across exceptionally long periods of time. Learn more about the style guides published by the Modern Language Association, including the *MLA Handbook*, along with more information about the MLA itself, at www.mla.org.

2. American Psychological Association (APA)

APA documentation procedures are generally followed by researchers in many areas of the social sciences and related fields. Although you will encounter page numbers in the in-text citations for direct quotations in APA documents, you're much less likely to find direct quotations overall. Generally, researchers in the social sciences are less interested in the specific language or words used to report research findings than they are in the results or conclusions. Therefore, social science researchers are more likely to paraphrase information than to quote information. Additionally, in-text documentation in the APA system requires the date of publication for research (see the examples on pp. 288–89). This is a striking distinction from the MLA system. Social science research that was conducted fifty years ago may not be as useful as research conducted two years ago, so it's important to cite the date of the source in the text of the argument. Imagine how different the results would be for a study of the effects of violence in video games on youth twenty years ago versus a study conducted last year. Findings from twenty years ago probably have very little bearing on the contemporary social context and would not reflect the same video game content as today's games. As a result, the APA system requires including the date of research publication as part of the in-text citation. The date enables readers to quickly evaluate the currency, and therefore the appropriateness, of the research being referenced. Learn more about the *Publication Manual of the American Psychological Association* and the APA itself at its website: www.apa.org.

3. The Council of Science Editors (CSE)

As the name suggests, the CSE documentation system is most prevalent among disciplines of the natural sciences, although many of the applied fields of the sciences, like engineering and medicine, rely on their own documentation systems. As in the other systems described here, CSE requires writers to document all materials derived from sources. Unlike MLA or APA, however, CSE allows multiple methods for in-text citations, corresponding to alternative forms of the reference page that appears at the end of research reports. For more detailed information on CSE documentation, consult the latest edition of *Scientific Style and Format: The CSE Manual for Authors, Editors, and Publishers.* You can learn more about the Council of Science Editors at its website: www.councilscienceeditors.org.

Writing Project: Writing an Annotated Bibliography

The annotated bibliography is a common genre in several academic disciplines because it provides a way to compile and take notes on—that is, annotate—resources that are potentially useful in a research project. *Annotated bibliographies* are essentially lists of citations, formatted in a consistent documentation style, that include concise summaries of source material. Some annotated bibliographies include additional commentary about the sources—perhaps evaluations of their usefulness for the research project or comments about how the sources complement one another within the bibliography (perhaps by providing multiple perspectives). Annotated bibliographies are usually organized alphabetically, but longer bibliographies can be organized topically or in sections with subheadings. Each source entry gives the citation first and then a paragraph or two of summary, as in this example using MLA style:

> Carter, Michael. "Ways of Knowing, Doing, and Writing in the Disciplines."
> *College Composition and Communication*, vol. 58, no. 3, 2007, pp.
> 385–418.

In this article, Carter outlines a process for helping faculty across different academic disciplines to understand the conventions of writing in their disciplines by encouraging them to think of disciplines as "ways of doing." He provides examples from his own interactions with faculty members in several disciplines, and he draws on data collected from these interactions to describe four "metagenres" that reflect ways of doing that are shared across multiple disciplines: problem-solving, empirical inquiry, research from sources, and performance. Finally, he concludes that the metagenres revealed by examining shared ways of doing can help to identify "metadisciplines."

For this assignment, you should write an annotated bibliography that seeks to find sources that will help you respond to a specific research question. Your purpose in writing the annotated bibliography is threefold: (1) to organize and keep track of the sources you've found on your own topic, (2) to better understand the relationships among different sources that address your topic, and (3) to demonstrate knowledge of the existing research about it.

To meet this purpose, choose sources that will help answer your research question, and think about a specific audience who might be interested in the research you're presenting. Your annotated bibliography should include the following elements.

- An introduction that clearly states your research question and describes the scope of your annotated bibliography.

- As many as eight to twelve sources (depending on the scope of the sources and the number of perspectives you want to represent), organized alphabetically. If you choose a different organization (e.g., topical), explain how you have organized your annotated bibliography in the introduction.

- An annotation for each source that includes:

  - A summary of the source that gives a concise description of the main findings, focused on what is most important for responding to your research question.

  - Relevant information about the authors or sponsors of the source to indicate credibility, bias, perspective, and the like.

  - An indication of what this source brings to your annotated bibliography that is unique and/or how it connects to the other sources.

  - A citation in a consistent documentation style.

Writing Project: Developing a Supported Argument on a Controversial Issue

For this writing assignment, you will apply your knowledge from Chapter 9 about developing an argument and from this chapter on finding and documenting appropriate sources. The sources you find will be evidence for the argument you develop. We ask you to make a claim about a controversial issue that is of importance to you and support that claim with evidence to persuade a particular audience of your position. As you write, you might follow the steps below to develop your argument.

- Begin by identifying an issue that you care about and likely have some experience with. We all write best about things that matter to us. For many students, choosing an issue that is very specific to their experience or local context makes a narrower, more manageable topic to write about. For example, examining recycling options for students on your college campus would be more manageable than tackling the issue of global waste and recycling.

- Once you have identified an issue, start reading about it to discover what people are saying and what positions they are taking. Use the suggestions in this chapter to find scholarly sources about your issue so that you can "listen in on" the conversations already taking place about your issue. You might find that you want to narrow your topic further based on what you find.

- As you read, begin tracking the sources you find. These sources can serve as evidence later for multiple perspectives on the issue; they will be useful both in supporting your claim and in understanding counterarguments.

- Identify a clear claim you would like to support, an audience you would like to persuade, and a purpose for writing to that audience. Whom should you talk to about your issue, and what can they do about it?

As you work to develop your argument, consider the various elements of an argument you read about in Chapter 9.

- Identify a clear central claim, and determine if it should be a simple or complex thesis statement.

- Develop clear reasons for that claim, drawn from your knowledge of the issue and the sources you have found.

- Choose evidence from your sources to support each reason that will be persuasive to your audience, and consider the potential appeals of *ethos*, *logos*, and *pathos*.

- Identify any assumptions that need to be explained to or supported for your audience.

- Develop responses to any counterarguments you should include in your argument.

Insider Example

Student Argument on a Controversial Issue

The following sample student argument, produced in a first-year writing class, illustrates many of the principles discussed in Chapters 9 and 10. As you read, identify the thesis, reasons, and sources used as support for the argument. Notice also that the student, Ashlyn Sims, followed MLA style conventions throughout her paper.

Ashlyn Sims

ENG 100

November 15, 201–

Project II

Condom Distribution in High School

A day rarely goes by when a teenager does not think about sex. It races back and forth in the teenage mind, sneaking its way into conversations all the time. We live in a society where sex is quickly becoming more and more common at younger ages; however, it is still considered a rather taboo topic, generating more discomfort from one generation to the next when you consider the values and beliefs of varying generations. Many teens learn things about sex through their peers because discussions of sex can be less awkward among friends, and thus a chain of risky, uninformed sex patterns can be created. Most teens will avoid talking to their parents about sex at all costs. Typically, this is because parents do not establish an open line of communication, or they make it clear that consequences will be enacted if their kids are having sex. This only keeps the cycle going, spreading sexually transmitted diseases around campuses and causing hundreds of thousands of unwanted pregnancies. So who is left to pick up the slack when parents become unapproach-able to teens? Schools need to step in for the vast number of parents who do not know how to effectively educate their teens. Accessible contraceptives and sex education are necessary in schools because they can prevent sexually transmitted diseases and unwanted pregnancies while recognizing the reality that teens will inevitably have sex and steps need to be taken to ensure it is safe sex.

Sexually transmitted diseases are spreading quickly throughout high schools because teenagers do not know how to engage in safe sex practices by using condoms. Studies show that approximately one in four sexually active teens will contract an STD ("U.S. Teen Sexual Activity"). Schools need to provide condoms to students in order to slow the spread of STDs and keep their schools safer for sexually active teens. The purpose of schools is to educate students and give them every tool necessary in order to succeed in the world. Sex education should be no exception. By giving students informa-tion about using some form of birth control, they can prevent the

Can you begin to identify a specific audience to whom the author is writing?

Compare the author's claim with the principles for writing a claim discussed on pages 251–53 of Chapter 9.

Why do you think the author uses this statistical data to support this reason? Where did this statistic come from? Think about whom she is writing to and what that audience might find persuasive.

As you see places where the student has cited information from sources, think about whether she has paraphrased, summarized, or quoted. Why do you think she makes the choices she does?

negative effects of having an STD, such as low self-esteem and self-worth, and send the strongest possible students out into the world to prosper. In more extreme cases, students can contract HIV, and it becomes a matter of life and death. Approximately half of the new cases of HIV every year occur in people under the age of twenty-five ("U.S. Teen Sexual Activity"). Although contracting HIV is not an end result for all sexually active teens, it is still a major risk factor, and the spread can be slowed with the help of condoms.

Compared to older adults, adolescents are at a higher risk for acquiring STDs for a number of reasons, including limited access to contraceptives and regular health care ("U.S. Teen Sexual Activity"). When parents won't help their children practice safe sex, it becomes the schools' job to protect students and educate them accordingly. Adolescents face many obstacles to obtaining and using condoms given outside of school. Some of these obstacles include confidentiality, cost, access, transportation, embarrassment, objection by a partner, and the perception that the risks of pregnancy and infection are low (Dodd). School should be a place where students go to obtain condoms, which gives students the means to have safe sex. Because STDs are spreading at an alarming rate, schools should do their best to prevent them by distributing condoms.

Here the student reiterates the central point of the paragraph.

The student offers a reason to support the distribution of condoms in schools.

Pregnancies in teenagers are almost always unplanned, and they are usually the consequences of having sex without birth control. Schools need to supply students with contraceptives because a teenage pregnancy is the number one reason girls drop out of high school, and it sets them up for a life of hardships. Girls who get pregnant at an early age drop out 70% of the time (Mangal). The teenagers may not have known the importance of using contraceptives and practicing safe sex because no one ever talked to them about it. It should be the responsibility of our academic institutions to safeguard these students from pregnancies by educating them when nobody else has done so. Schools have the ability to provide contraceptives and sex education in order to prevent pregnancies and ensure that more girls will graduate and have better odds of getting a higher-paying job. The cost of a condom by the government is nothing compared to the cost it takes to raise the child of a mother who did not graduate from high school and needs welfare in order

The student is embedding reasons together here and developing a logical chain of reasons to support her argument.

to survive. It would be absurd to spend thousands of dollars on a child when a condom costs only a few dollars. Additionally, children of teen mothers are 22% more likely to have children of their own before the age of twenty (Maynard). The early childbearing could then become a cycle.

The student's chain of reasons continues here.

The teen years should be focused on learning everything necessary in order to succeed in life. Students need to complete their education and focus solely on making good grades and learning the skills necessary to get into college, and schools should provide anything students need in order to fulfill their greatest potential. Providing condoms is the more effective way to ensure that students can make smart decisions and focus on school, rather than raising a child.

While many schools try to fight the growing numbers of STDs and pregnancies with abstinence-only classes, they are failing to face the reality that the classes do not prevent students from engaging in sex. By providing condoms for students, schools can acknowledge that students will have sex. Many schools ignore the problem and assume that if students need condoms, they can get them themselves. The reality is that many high school students cannot drive because they are under the age of sixteen or do not have a car. Others cannot afford condoms or choose to take the risk in order to avoid spending money. The difficulty in getting a condom behind parents' backs, combined with the preconceived notion that it is unlikely that one will get pregnant or an STD, creates a risky pattern of unsafe behaviors. In 1997, a study followed two thousand middle-school and elementary-aged students into high school. The study concluded that abstinence-only sex education does not keep teenagers from having sex. Neither does it increase or decrease the likelihood that if they do have sex, they will use a condom (Stepp). Changes need to be made to the programs taught in schools to best persuade students to practice safe sex. To be most effective, schools need to meet students halfway: schools will acknowledge the reality of sex among teens but will also teach them safe sex. A school that acknowledges that teens will have sex and provides condoms shows that it cares about the success and safety of its students.

The author makes a controversial claim here. How does she support it with her sources?

The author acknowledges a potential counterargument here. How does she use her sources to refute that counterargument?

Many parents would argue that by providing access to condoms, a school is promoting the sexual behaviors of teens. Then this leads to the fear that by having more sexually active teens, the STD and pregnancy rate will increase and only produce more affected teens who would otherwise not be affected. However, at least one study has shown that a teen who is not sexually active is no more inclined to get a condom and become sexually active just because of the easy access (Kirby and Brown). Students who need condoms will be able to get them, and those who do not will know that they are available but will not have any reason to use them.

The author identifies another possible counterargument. What evidence is provided to refute the counterargument?

People might also argue that it is not a school's place to make decisions for the parents about whether students should have access to condoms. However, the reality is that teens will have sex, and although it is not the school's place to make these decisions, teens who have no other way to gain access will be able to protect themselves. If no more students are influenced to have sex, then the distribution of condoms is not creating any risk; it is only offering protection to the one in four teens who will contract an STD and the thousands of girls who will get pregnant. It is only giving students access to protect themselves. By providing condoms, a school does not encourage sexual activity among young adults, but rather encourages safe sex and provides options for teens who would otherwise have no options and would engage in high-risk activities anyway.

Overall, providing condoms does not encourage risky behavior; it gives high-risk students options when they cannot afford or obtain condoms. The access to condoms helps prevent sexually transmitted diseases and pregnancies. A school that does not acknowledge the high risk of teens having sex is only hurting its students. Schools need to provide condoms so that students have greater chances of fulfilling their full potential in life and do not have to work against the odds when faced with pregnancy. In order to lower the rates of STDs and pregnancies, all schools should provide condoms in the interest of the safety of sexually active students.

Works Cited

Dodd, Keri J. "School Condom Availability." *Advocates for Youth*, 1998, www.advocatesforyouth.org/publications/449?task=view.

Kirby, Douglas B., and Nancy L. Brown. "Condom Availability Programs in U.S. Schools." *Family Planning Perspectives*, vol. 28, no. 5, 1996, pp. 196-202. JSTOR, www.jstor.org/stable/2135838.

Mangal, Linda. "Teen Pregnancy, Discrimination, and the Dropout Rate." *American Civil Liberties Union of Washington*, ACLU, 25 Oct. 2010, www.aclu-wa.org/blog/teen-pregnancy-discrimination-and-dropout-rate.

Maynard, Rebecca A. "Kids Having Kids." *The Urban Institute | Research of Record*, www.urban.org/pubs/khk/summary.html.

Stepp, Laura Sessions. "Study Casts Doubt on Abstinence-Only Programs." *Washington Post*, 14 Apr. 2007, www.washingtonpost.com/wp-dyn/content/article/2007/04/13/AR2007041301003.html.

"U.S. Teen Sexual Activity." *Kaiser Family Foundation*, Jan. 2005, www.kff.org/youthhivstds/upload/U-S-Teen-Sexual-Activity-Fact-Sheet.pdf.

Notice what kinds of sources the author has cited. If she were to conduct additional research to support her argument, what do you think might strengthen it?

Discussion Questions

1. Whom do you think Ashlyn Sims is targeting as her audience in this assignment? Why do you think that is her audience?

2. What is Ashlyn's thesis, and what does she provide as the reasons and evidence for her claim?

3. What assumptions connect her thesis to her reasons? Additionally, what assumptions would her audience have to accept in order to find her evidence persuasive? Really dig into this question, because this area is often where arguments fall apart.

4. What counterarguments does Ashlyn address in her essay? Why do you think she addresses these particular counterarguments? Can you think of others that she might have addressed?

5. What kinds of sources does she use in her essay? How does she integrate them into her argument, and why do you think she has made those choices?

6. What would make this essay more persuasive and effective?

Tip Sheet   Academic Research

- **Research typically begins with a research question, which establishes the purpose and scope of a project**. As you develop research questions, keep in mind the following evaluative criteria: personal investment, debatable subject, researchable issue, feasibility, and contribution.

- **A researcher who has established a clear focus for her research, or who has generated a claim, must decide on the kinds of sources needed to support the research focus**: primary, secondary, or both.

- **While both scholarly and popular sources may be appropriate sources of evidence in differing contexts, be sure to understand what distinguishes these types of sources** so that you can choose evidence types purposefully.

- **Primary sources are the results of data that researchers might collect on their own**. These results could include data from surveys, interviews, or questionnaires. **Secondary sources include research collected by and/or commented on by others.** These might include information taken from newspaper articles, magazines, scholarly journal articles, and scholarly books, to name a few.

- **Keep in mind that as you do research, you will likely have cause to refine your search terms**. This process involves carefully selecting or narrowing the terms you use to locate information via search engines or databases.

- **Be aware of the challenges of conducting basic searches for sources via Internet search engines** like Google. While Google Scholar may be a better means of searching for sources in the academic context, researchers often rely on more specialized research databases.

- **Peer-reviewed academic journals are an excellent source of information for academic arguments**. The publication process for journal articles is typically much shorter than for books, so using journal articles allows you access to the most current research.

- **Be aware of the strategies you can use to integrate the ideas of others into your own writing**: summarizing, paraphrasing, and/or quoting.

- **When you integrate the words or ideas of others, take care to ensure that you are documenting their words and ideas carefully to avoid instances of plagiarism**, and make sure you understand what constitutes plagiarism at your institution and/or in your individual classes. Follow appropriate rules for documenting your sources and constructing a bibliography. In academic contexts, this often means using MLA, APA, or CSE documentation systems.

Inside Academic Writing

Part Three

Andrea Tsurumi

Part Three

Inside Academic Writing

Chapter 11 Reading and Writing in Academic Disciplines

The four chapters that follow this one introduce four broad disciplinary areas in higher education: humanities, social sciences, natural sciences, and applied fields. While some differences distinguish each of these areas, certain similarities show shared values that provide ways to analyze and understand the conventions of writing and research in those areas.

To help you navigate these chapters, we have organized Chapters 12 through 14 around the same key concerns:

- **Research in the Discipline** Every academic discipline has established conventions of research. One thing that unites them is the importance of **observation**. Whether you're a humanities scholar observing texts, or a social scientist observing human behavior, or a scientist observing the natural world, careful methods of observation are central to developing research questions and writing projects in each disciplinary area. Similarly, all disciplines rely on the concepts of **primary research** and **secondary research**. (If you gather data of your own, you're doing primary research. If you gather data by studying the research of others, you're doing secondary research.) Academic writers in a variety of disciplines engage in both primary and secondary research and find that they inform each other. For example, a social scientist studying human behavior might conduct secondary research

Andrea Tsurumi

Chapter 11, "Reading and Writing in Academic Disciplines" from *An Insider's Guide to Academic Writing* by Susan Miller-Cochran, Roy Stamper, and Stacey Cochran, pp. 108–151 (Chapter 5). Copyright © 2016 by Bedford/St. Martin's.

first to learn what others have done and to develop her research questions. Then she might conduct primary research to test a hypothesis and report results. Similarly, a humanities scholar studying historical documents might conduct secondary research to build a preliminary research question and to develop a review of literature before conducting primary research by analyzing a historical document to develop a thesis about his interpretation of that document.

- **Conventions of Writing in the Discipline**   Each academic discipline has expectations about academic writing in its field. The chapters that follow this one all include sections that describe and help you analyze the *conventions* of writing in the disciplines, using the principles of rhetoric (the strategies of communication and persuasion) introduced in this chapter.

- **Genres in the Discipline**   Each chapter also provides examples of *genres*, or common types of academic writing, that often cross disciplines. These *Insider Examples* of writing, not only by professionals in the disciplines but also by students entering the discipline and composing in particular genres, are annotated to reveal key features that prompt your own analysis of them.

Chapter 15 then explores the kinds of work and genres produced in a number of applied fields, including nursing, education, business, and law.

Additionally, the chapters share other common features to help you broaden your understanding of each disciplinary area: *Insider's View* excerpts of scholars discussing disciplinary writing; *Inside Work* activities that prompt you to reflect on what you've learned; *Writing Projects* that help you develop your own academic compositions; and *Tip Sheets* that summarize key information.

Insider's View

Writing Should Be Different in Various Situations

Karen Keaton Jackson, Writing Studies

"I think students should consider that writing has to be and should be different in various situations. Students need to go through a kind of meta-process of thinking about their own writing, one that allows them to see that the skills they learn in first-year writing can transfer. When students go into their history class or psychology class, for instance, the expectations may be different, but they'll see how they can transfer what they've learned in first-year writing to that situation."

Learn more about rhetorical situations.

Throughout these chapters, we ask you to analyze and practice writing in various academic disciplines. Keep in mind, though, that we *do not* expect you to master the writing of these communities by taking just one class or by reading one book. Instead, we introduce you to the concepts associated with **disciplinary discourse**, or the writing and speaking that is specific to different disciplines. Using these concepts, you can analyze future writing situations and make choices appropriate to the rhetorical contexts. It's worth noting that such rhetorical awareness may help you enter other **discourse communities**, or groups that share common values and similar communication practices, outside of your college classes as well, socially and professionally.

Disciplinary conventions and styles are not just patterns to follow; rather, they represent shared values. In other words, there's a reason why academic texts are communicated in the way that they are: scholars in the same discipline might have similar ways of thinking about an issue, and they follow common ways of researching and investigating that represent their shared values and perspectives. The information we offer you on different academic disciplines in this book is not necessarily something to memorize, but rather something to analyze through the frame of *rhetorical context*. Ultimately, we want you to be able to look at an academic text and determine what the rhetorical context is and what conventions influence that text. As you write for different courses throughout your college career, this ability will help you determine and follow the expectations of writing for the different academic contexts you encounter. It will also help you read the assignments in your other classes because you'll understand some of the reasons that texts are written in the way that they are.

Analyzing Genres and Conventions of Academic Writing

As you know, different writing situations call for different types of writing. Different types of writing—from short items such as tweets, bumper stickers, and recipes to longer and more complex compositions such as Ph.D. dissertations, annual reports, and novels—are called *genres*. Scholars write in many different genres depending on their disciplinary areas, the kinds of work they do, and the situation in which they're writing. You have probably written in several different academic genres in your education already. You might have written a literary analysis in an English class, a lab report in a science class, a bibliography for a research paper, and maybe a personal narrative. Each of these genres has a common set of expectations that you must be familiar with in order to communicate effectively with your intended audience. In this text, you'll find information about writing in many of these genres—such as literary/artistic interpretations, rhetorical analyses, annotated bibliographies, reviews of literature, lab reports, and memos—with the ultimate goal of learning to analyze the rhetorical context so that you can determine the expected conventions of a genre in any writing situation.

Genres are not always bound by discipline, however. You'll find that the conventions of some genres are similar from one disciplinary area to another. As you read Chapters 12 through 15 on humanities, the social sciences, the natural sciences, and applied fields, pay attention to which genres are repeated and how the conventions of those genres shift or remain constant from one disciplinary context to another.

You'll notice that similar writing situations within, and even sometimes across, disciplines call for a similar genre. In other words, academics might approach a piece of writing in the same (or a similar) way even though they come from different academic disciplines.

For example, you'll notice that scholars in all disciplines write reviews of literature for their research. Likewise, when reporting on the results of a research study, many academics follow the **IMRAD (Introduction, Methods, Results, and Discussion) format** or a variation of it to record and publish the results of their research, regardless of their discipline. There might be some subtle differences from one discipline or one situation to another, but common elements are evident. Literature reviews and IMRAD reports are two examples of common genres of academic writing.

As we begin to talk about specific disciplinary contexts, keep in mind these strategies to analyze the conventions of academic writing. When you read and write academic texts, you'll want to:

- understand the overall rhetorical context of the piece of writing: the author, the audience, the topic, and the purpose for writing;

- identify and understand the disciplinary area—humanities, the social sciences, the natural sciences, applied fields—and make connections to what you know about that discipline;

Insider's View

Think about Audience, Purpose, and Form

Moriah McCracken, Writing Studies

"I think the three skills that students need to write in college settings are all tied into the rhetorical situation. If they can think about audience, purpose, and form, I think that will at least get them ready to start asking the kinds of questions they need of their professors to determine, how am I going to shape this for this particular audience, this particular discipline, this particular professor?"

Learn more about analyzing genres.

- consider which elements of structure, language, and reference (explained below) govern the writing situation;

- identify the genre, or category, that the writing fits into, and discover the common conventions and expectations for that genre within the rhetorical context;

- analyze the persuasive strategies used, if the author is developing an argument. (What claims are presented? How are they supported by reasons and evidence? What assumptions are in play?)

These analytical strategies will help you to approach any academic writing situation confidently and effectively.

Adapting to Different Rhetorical Contexts: An Academic Writer at Work

Even though some genres are more common in specific disciplines than others, many scholars write in more than one genre on a regular basis. Scholars write for different rhetorical contexts all the time, and they adapt their writing to the audience, topic, and purpose of the occasion. We'd like to take an in-depth look at one scholar's writing to show you an example of how he shifts the conventions of his writing for different contexts—often academic, but sometimes more general. We've chosen to look at a scholar in a scientific field that is rarely discussed in English classes: astronomy. Mike Brotherton is an astronomer at the University of Wyoming, and we'll look at two types of writing that he does on a regular basis. Brotherton writes scholarly articles in his field to report on his research to an audience of other academics—his peers. He also sometimes writes press releases about his research, and these are intended to help journalists report news to the general public. Each piece of writing represents a different genre intended for a different audience, but together they show us the varying ways that Brotherton shares his work in the field of astronomy. Both of these rhetorical contexts call for an awareness of different conventions.

Inside Work: Reflecting on a Discipline

In his Insider's View, "Scientists Must Write All Sorts of Things," Mike Brotherton makes several generalizations about science, scientists, and scientific writing. Which of these comments, if any, surprised you, and which ones didn't? Explain why.

Insider's View

Scientists Must Write All Sorts of Things

Mike Brotherton, Astronomy

"Aspiring scientists often don't appreciate the importance of communication skills. Science doesn't count until it's communicated to the rest of the scientific community, and eventually the public. Moreover, scientists must write all sorts of things to have a successful career, from journal articles to grant applications to press releases.

"Probably the most important thing to do well when writing as a scientist is simply to get everything right. Science is a methodology for developing reliable information about the world we live in, and getting things wrong is the surest way for scientists to lose their reputation; and for a scientist, reputation is the coin of the realm. While nearly everyone scientifically inclined finds getting things right to be an obvious and principal goal, it is also critically important to identify the audience of any particular piece of writing and address that audience in an effective way. The writing examples included in this text are all targeted for a different readership, and that represents a primary difference between them.

"Scientists write and are asked to write for all sorts of audiences. This isn't an easy task, but success in that adaptation can be the difference between a great career and failure, so it's important to treat it seriously. There isn't magic to this, and while brilliance can be challenging to achieve, competence can certainly be learned. It just takes some practice and thought."

Using Rhetorical Context to Analyze Writing for a Non-Academic Audience

First we'll take a look at a piece of writing that Mike Brotherton composed for a non-academic audience of journalists who might be interested in research he conducted. Brotherton wrote a press release to communicate the results of his research in a genre familiar to journalists. As you read the press release, which we've annotated, keep in mind the elements of rhetorical context that are useful in analyzing all kinds of writing:

- *author* (who is the writer, and what does he or she bring to the text?)
- *audience* (for whom is the text intended?)
- *topic* (what issue is the text addressing?)
- *purpose* (why did the author write the text?)

Specifically, consider the following questions:

- How might Brotherton's position as the *author* of the press release influence the way he wrote it? What might have been different if someone else had written the press release after talking to him about his research?

- Who is the *audience* for this piece? What choices do you think Brotherton made that were specific to his audience for the press release?

- How does the *topic* of the press release affect the choices the author made? Would you have made different choices to approach the topic for a general audience? What would they be?

- What is the *purpose* for writing the press release? How might that influence Brotherton's choices as a writer? Do you think he has met that purpose? Why or why not?

Mike Brotherton

Excerpt from "Hubble Space Telescope Spies Galaxy/Black Hole Evolution in Action"

JUNE 2ND, 2008—A set of 29 Hubble Space Telescope (HST) images of an exotic type of active galaxy known as a "post-starburst quasar" show that interactions and mergers drive both galaxy evolution and the growth of super-massive black holes at their centers. Mike Brotherton, Associate Professor at the University of Wyoming, is presenting his team's findings today at the American Astronomical Society meeting in St. Louis, Missouri. Other team members include Sabrina Cales, Rajib Ganguly, and Zhaohui Shang of the University of Wyoming, Gabriella Canalizo of the University of California at Riverside, Aleks Diamond-Stanic of the University of Arizona, and Dan Vanden Berk of the Penn State University. The result is of special interest because the images provide support for a leading theory of the evolution of massive galaxies, but also show that the situation is more complicated than previously thought.

Over the last decade, astronomers have discovered that essentially every galaxy harbors a super-massive black hole at its center, ranging from 10,000 times the mass of the sun to upwards of 1,000,000,000 times solar, and that there exists a close relationship between the mass of the black hole and properties of its host. When the black holes are fueled and grow, the galaxy becomes active, with the most luminous manifestation being a quasar, which can outshine the galaxy and make it difficult to observe.

Identifies the topic of the research study and its relevant findings.

Identifies members of the research team, who are all authors of the study upon which the press release is based.

Fulfills the purpose of a press release by stating the importance of the research project. Appears in the first paragraph to make it prominent for the audience.

Provides relevant background information about the topic for the audience.

In order to explain the relationships between galaxies and their central black holes, theorists have proposed detailed models in which both grow together as the result of galaxy mergers. This hierarchical picture suggests that large galaxies are built up over time through the assembly of smaller galaxies with corresponding bursts of star formation, and that this process also fuels the growth of the black holes, which eventually ignite to shine as quasars. Supernova explosions and their dusty debris shroud the infant starburst until the activated quasar blows out the obscuration.

Provides a brief overview of the study's methods.

Brotherton and his team turned the sharp-eyed Hubble Space Telescope and its Advanced Camera for Surveys to observe a subset of these post-starburst quasars that had the strongest and most luminous stellar content. Looking at these systems 3.5 billion light-years away, Hubble, operating without the distortions of an atmosphere, can resolve sub-kiloparsec scales necessary to see nuclear structure and host galaxy morphology.

"The images started coming in, and we were blown away," said Brotherton. "We see not only merger remnants as in the prototype of the class, but also post-starburst quasars with interacting companion galaxies, double nuclei, starbursting rings, and all sorts of messy structures."

Astronomers have determined that our own Milky Way galaxy and the great spiral galaxy of Andromeda will collide three billion years from now. This event will create massive bursts of star formation and most likely fuel nuclear activity a few hundred million years later. Hubble has imaged post-starburst quasars three and a half billion light-years away, corresponding to three and a half billion years ago, and three and a half billion years from now our own galaxy is probably going to be one of these systems.

Acknowledges funding support for the research project, giving credit to funding agencies that might also be audiences for the journalists' news articles.

This work is supported by grants from NASA, through the Space Telescope Science Institute and the Long-Term Space Astrophysics program, and the National Science Foundation.

Insider's View

The Audience for a Press Release Is Very General

Mike Brotherton, Astronomy

"It isn't always the case that scientists write their own press releases. Often, there are writers on staff at various institutions who specialize in writing press releases and who work with scientists. I've written press releases solo (e.g., the contribution included here) and in collaboration with staff journalists at the University of Texas, Lawrence Livermore National Laboratory, and the University of Wyoming. Press releases should be able to be run as news stories themselves and contain enough content to be adapted or cut to length. The audience for a press release is very general, and you can't assume that they have any background in your field. You have to tell them why your result is important, clearly and briefly, and little else.

"While I don't think my effort here is bad, it is far from perfect and suffers one flaw. Reporters picking up press releases want to know what single result they should focus upon. They want to keep things simple. I tried to include several points in the release, rather than focusing on a single result. Some reporters became distracted about the notion that the Milky Way and Andromeda would someday merge and might become a post-starburst galaxy, which was not a result of my research project. Even though it gave the work some relevance, in hindsight I should have omitted it to keep the focus on the results of my research."

Inside Work: Reflecting on a Rhetorical Context

In his Insider's View, "The Audience for a Press Release Is Very General," Mike Brotherton explains some of the specifics of writing a press release and what he sees as the strengths and weaknesses of his own press release. Review the press release with Brotherton's comments in mind, and explain whether you agree with his assessment of it. What advice might you give him for revising the press release?

Using Structure, Language, and Reference to Analyze Academic Writing

While rhetorical context provides a useful framework for analyzing a variety of types of writing, the categories of structure, language, and reference (SLR)[1] offer more specific help in analyzing the conventions of academic writing at a deeper level. Although discourse conventions vary from discipline to discipline, once you understand how to analyze academic writing through these categories, you can determine what conventions and choices are appropriate for nearly any academic writing situation.

- **Structure, or Format and Organization**   Written texts are often organized according to specific disciplinary conventions. For example, scholars in the social sciences and natural sciences usually organize experimental study reports with an introduction first, followed by a description of their research methods, then their data/results, then the analysis of that data, and finally a discussion and conclusion (IMRAD format, discussed in more detail in Chapters 13 and 14 on the social sciences and natural sciences). By contrast, scholars in the humanities tend to write and value essays that are driven by a clear thesis (or main claim: what you are trying to prove) near the beginning of the essay that indicates the direction the argument will take. Scholars in the humanities also don't tend, as much, to use headings to divide a text.

- **Language, or Style and Word Choice**   The language used in academic writing follows disciplinary conventions. Consider the use of the active and passive voices. You may recall that in the active voice the subject performs the action, while in the passive voice the subject is acted upon. (Active voice: *Inez performed the experiment*; passive voice: *The experiment was performed by Inez*.) Often, the passive voice is acceptable in specific situations in the natural sciences, but it is usually not favored in the humanities. A scholar in the sciences might write, *It was determined that the two variables have a negative correlation*, a sentence that obscures the subject doing the determining (generally, the researcher or research team). Such uses of the passive voice rarely occur in the humanities, where scholars prefer the active voice. Likewise, qualifiers (words such as *might, could, likely*) are often used in the natural and social sciences to indicate the interpretive power of the data collected and to help persuade an audience to accept the results because they are not generalizing inappropriately (*The positive correlation between the variables likely indicates a strong relationship between the motivation of a student and his or her achievement of learning objectives*). When qualifiers are used in the humanities, however, they often demonstrate uncertainty and weaken an argument (*Hamlet's soliloquies in acts 2 and 4 might provide an interesting comparison because they frame the turning point of the play in act 3*).

---

1 The SLR concept originated in the following essay: Patricia Linton, Robert Madigan, and Susan Johnson, "Introducing Students to Disciplinary Genres: The Role of the General Composition Course," *Language and Learning Across the Disciplines* 1, no. 2 (1994): 63–78.

- **Reference, or Citation and Documentation**   The conventions of how scholars refer to one another's work can also shift by discipline. You might already know, for example, that many scholars in the humanities use the documentation style of the Modern Language Association (MLA), while those in the social sciences generally use the style guide published by the American Psychological Association (APA). Conventions of how often scholars quote, paraphrase, and summarize one another's work can also vary.

LaunchPad Solo

Get astronomer Mike Brotherton's take on qualifying and hedging.

In the next example of Mike Brotherton's work, we'll look at the abstract and introduction to a scholarly journal article that he wrote with several co-authors. If we consider the *structure*, *language*, and *reference conventions* used in the piece, we can gain some insight into the way such writing is structured within the sciences—and specifically in the field of astronomy.

As you read the excerpt from Brotherton's co-authored article, notice the structure, language, and reference conventions. The article contains a lot of specific scientific language, and for the purpose of your analysis right now it's not important to understand the concepts as much as it is to recognize some of the elements that make this writing unique from other writing you may have encountered in English classes in the past. Consider the following questions:

- Even though the entire article is not included, what conclusions can you draw about its **structure**? What comes first in the article, and how is it organized in the beginning?

- How would you describe the **language** that Brotherton and his co-authors choose to use in the article? What does it tell you about the audience for the article?

- What **reference conventions** does the article follow? Does the documentation style used for the parenthetical references look familiar? How often are other scholars cited, and what is the context for citing their work? What purpose do those references serve in the article?

M. S. Brotherton, Wil Van Breugel, S. A. Stanford, R. J. Smith, B. J. Boyle, Lance Miller, T. Shanks, S. M. Croom, and Alexei V. Filippenko

Excerpt from "A Spectacular Poststarburst Quasar"

Abstract

The language is highly specific and technical.

We report the discovery of a spectacular "poststarburst quasar" UN J10252−0040 ($B = 19$; $z = 0.634$). The optical spectrum is a chimera, displaying the broad Mg II λ2800 emission line and strong blue continuum characteristic of quasars, but is dominated in the red by a large Balmer jump and prominent high-order Balmer absorption lines indicative of a substantial young stellar population at similar redshift. Stellar synthesis population models show that the stellar component is consistent with a 400 Myr old instantaneous starburst with a mass of $\leq 10^{11} M_\odot$. A deep, K_s-band image taken in ~0″.5 seeing shows a point source surrounded by asymmetric extended fuzz. Approximately 70% of the light is unresolved, the majority of which is expected to be emitted by the starburst. While starbursts and galaxy interactions have been previously associated with quasars, no quasar ever before has been seen with such an extremely luminous young stellar population.

Headings indicate a particular kind of structure.

1. Introduction

Is there a connection between starbursts and quasar activity? There is circumstantial evidence to suggest so. The quasar 3C 48 is surrounded by nebulosity that shows the high-order Balmer absorption lines characteristic of A-type stars (Boroson & Oke 1984; Stockton & Ridgeway 1991). PG 1700+518 shows a nearby starburst ring (Hines et al. 1999) with the spectrum of a 10^8 yr old starburst (Stockton, Canalizo, & Close 1998). Near-IR and CO mapping reveals a massive (~$10^{10} M_\odot$) circumnuclear starburst ring in I Zw 1 (Schinnerer, Eckart, & Tacconi 1998). The binary quasar member FIRST J164311.3+315618B shows a starburst host galaxy spectrum (Brotherton et al. 1999).

In addition to these individual objects, *samples* of active galactic nuclei (AGNs) show evidence of starbursts. Images of quasars taken with the *Hubble Space Telescope* show "chains of emission nebulae" and "near-nuclear emission knots" (e.g., Bahcall et al. 1997). Seyfert 2 and radio galaxies have significant populations of ~100 Myr old stars (e.g., Schmitt, Storchi-Bergmann, & Cid Fernandes 1999). Half of the ultraluminous infrared galaxies (ULIRGs) contain simultaneously an AGN and recent (10–100 Myr) starburst activity in a 1–2 kpc circumnuclear ring (Genzel et al. 1998).

The advent of *IRAS* provided evidence for an evolutionary link between starbursts and AGNs. The ULIRGs ($L_{IR} > 10^{12} L_\odot$) are strongly interacting merger systems with copious molecular gas [$(0.5–2) \times 10^{10}$ $M_\odot$] and dust heated by both starburst and AGN power sources. The ULIRG space density is sufficient to form the quasar parent population. These facts led Sanders et al. (1988) to hypothesize that ULIRGs represent the initial dust-enshrouded stage of a quasar. Supporting this hypothesis is the similarity in the evolution of the quasar luminosity density and the star formation rate (e.g., Boyle & Terlevich 1998; Percival & Miller 1999). Another clue is that supermassive black holes appear ubiquitously in local massive galaxies, which may be out-of-fuel quasars (e.g., Magorrian et al. 1998). AGN activity may therefore reflect a fundamental stage of galaxy evolution.

Introduction references multiple prior studies by other scholars.

We report here the discovery of a poststarburst quasar. The extreme properties of this system may help shed light on the elusive AGN-starburst connection. We adopt $H_0 = 75$ km s^{-1} Mpc^{-1} and $q_0 = 0$.

Insider's View

Accuracy Trumps Strong Writing

Mike Brotherton, Astronomy

"The audience for a scientific journal should be experts in your field but also beginning graduate students. Articles should be specific, succinct, and correct. For better or worse, in scientific articles it is necessary to use a lot of qualifications, adverbs, and modifying phrases, to say exactly what you mean even though the result is not as strong or effective. Accuracy trumps strong writing here, although there is plenty of room for good writing. Every piece of writing, fiction or non-fiction, should tell an interesting story. The format for a scientific article is rather standard.

Insider Example

"There is also an abstract that gives a summary of all the parts of the paper. In many instances, the entire paper is not read but skimmed, so being able to find things quickly and easily makes the paper more useful. Audiences for scientific papers are often measured only in the dozens, if that. While popular papers can be read and used by thousands, most papers have a small audience and contribute to advancement in some niche or other, which may or may not turn out to be important.

"Some people cite heavily, and some people don't cite as heavily. And, again, you need to keep in mind your audience and what's appropriate. In writing a telescope proposal, for instance, which is not quite the same as a scientific article but has the same conventions, some reviewers want you to cite a lot of things just to prove that you know the field. This is especially true for beginning students writing proposals."

Inside Work: Reflecting on a Disciplinary Writing

In his Insider's View "Accuracy Trumps Strong Writing," Mike Brotherton provides some guidelines for analyzing his scientific article through the lenses of structure, language, and reference. Write down a few points he makes about each lens that will be helpful when you approach reading a scientific article on your own.

- Reread the excerpt from "A Spectacular Poststarburst Quasar" (see pp. 314–15) and reflect on any new things you notice.

- Read the excerpt again, this time with an eye to rhetorical context (author, audience, topic, and purpose for writing). Try to generalize about the usefulness of the two approaches to your reading.

- Annotate a paper you've written for another class, noting the rhetorical and SLR elements as we have in our annotations on the press release and the scholarly article. What practices about your own writing do these approaches suggest?

Writing Project: Writing a Rhetorical Analysis of an Academic Article

For this project, you will analyze a full-length study in a discipline of your choice, published as an article in an academic journal. Your instructor may assign an article or may ask you to seek his or her approval for the article you choose to use for this project.

Using the convention categories of *structure*, *language*, and *reference*, describe the basic rhetorical features of the article you've chosen to study. In addition, try to explain why those conventions are the most appropriate for the writer in light of the goals of his or her article and for his or her intended academic audience.

The introduction to your paper should name the article you will analyze, describe the primary methods you will use to analyze it, and explain the goal of your analysis—to demonstrate and analyze features of discourse in an academic article. The body of your paper might be organized around the three convention categories—structure, language, and reference—or you might focus on one or two of the features that are of specific interest in your article. Of course, you can subdivide these categories to address specific elements of the larger categories. Under the conventions of the language category, for instance, you could address the use of qualifiers, the use of passive and active voice, and so on, providing examples from the article and commenting on their usefulness for the writer. In your conclusion, reflect on what you've found. Are there other issues still to be addressed? What other rhetorical strategies could be explored to analyze the work further? How effective are the strategies the author used, given the intended audience?

Writing Project: Writing a Comparative Rhetorical Analysis

The goal of this writing project is to allow you to consider further the shifts in conventional expectations for writing across two disciplinary areas.

Use what you've learned about structure, language, and reference to compare and contrast the conventional expectations for writing in two different disciplines. To begin, you'll need two comparable studies: locate two articles about the same topic in academic journals representing different disciplines. For example, you might find two articles discussing the issue of increasing taxes on the wealthy to deal with the U.S. national debt. You might find one article written by an economist that addresses the impact of the national debt and projects the feasibility of different solutions, and another article written by a humanist discussing how the media has portrayed the issue.

Once you have your articles, begin by thinking about what kinds of questions the authors ask. Then examine both articles in terms of the structure, language, and reference conventions discussed in this chapter. Formulate a thesis that assesses the degree to which the rhetorical features in each category compare or contrast. Throughout your paper (which should be organized around the three areas of convention—structure, language, and reference), execute your comparisons and contrasts by illustrating your findings with examples from the texts. For example, if you find that one article (perhaps from the humanities) uses the active voice almost exclusively, then provide some examples. If the other article relies heavily on the passive voice, then provide examples of this use. End each section with a consideration of the implications of your findings: What does it say about the humanities that the writing is so characterized by active voice? Do not avoid discussing findings that might contradict your assumptions about writing in these two academic domains. Instead, study them closely and try to rationalize the authors' rhetorical decision-making.

Writing Project: Comparing Scholarly and Popular Articles

Choose a scholarly article and an article written for a more general audience on a common topic. You might reread the discussion of the differences between scholarly and popular articles in Chapter 10 as you're looking for articles to choose. Then use the framework for rhetorical context from Chapter 8 to conduct a rhetorical analysis of each article. In your comparison of the rhetorical contexts and decisions the authors have made, consider the questions below.

- How do the rhetorical contexts for writing compare?

- Which writing conventions are similar, and which ones are different?

- Why do you think the authors made the choices that they did in writing?

Finally, use the framework of structure, language, and reference to analyze the scholarly article. What conclusions can you draw about the conventions of the type of academic writing you're looking at by analyzing these three elements?

Translating Scholarly Writing for Different Rhetorical Contexts

At times, writing for an academic context, like Mike Brotherton's work, must be repurposed for presentation in another, more general context. Sometimes the writer does the translating, and sometimes other writers may help communicate the importance of a piece of scholarly writing to another audience.

Insider Example

Student Translation of a Scholarly Article

Jonathan Nastasi, a first-year writing student, translated a scholarly article about the possible habitability of another planet from the journal *Astronomy & Astrophysics* into a press release for a less specialized audience. He condensed the information into a two-page press release for a potential audience interested in publishing these research results in news venues. Also, he followed his writing instructor's advice to apply MLA style even though the article he summarized is scientific.

Release Date: 18 September 2014

Contact: W. von Bloh

bloh@pik-potsdam.de

Potsdam Institute for Climate Impact Research

Life May Be Possible on Other Planets

New data shows that a new planet found outside of our solar system may be habitable for life.

RALEIGH (SEPTEMBER 18, 2014)—A study from the Potsdam Institute for Climate Impact Research shows that a planet in another solar system is in the perfect position to harbor life. Additionally, the quantity of possibly habitable planets in our galaxy is much greater than expected.

Gliese 581g is one of up to six planets found to be orbiting the low-mass star Gliese 581, hence its name. Gliese 581g and its other planetary siblings are so-called "Super Earths," rocky planets from one to ten times the size of our Earth. This entire system is about twenty light-years away from our Sun. W. Von Bloh, M. Cuntz, S. Franck, and C. Bounama from the Potsdam Institute for Climate Impact Research chose to research Gliese 581g because of its size and distance from its star, which make it a perfect candidate to support life.

An artist's rendition of Gliese 581g orbiting its star.

Lynette Rene Cook for NASA

A planet must be a precise distance away from a star in order to sustain life. This distance is referred to as the habitable zone. According to von Bloh et al., the habitable zones "are defined as regions around the central star where the physical conditions are favourable for liquid water to exist at the planet's surface for a period of time sufficient for biological evolution to occur." This "Goldilocks" zone can be affected by a number of variables, including the temperature of the star and the composition of the planet.

The actual distance of Gliese 581g from its star is known; the goal of this study was to find out if the planet is capable of supporting life at that distance. The researchers began by finding the habitable zone of the star Gliese 581—specifically, the zone that allowed for photosynthesis. Photosynthesis is the production of oxygen from organic life forms and is indicative of life. In order for the planet to harbor this kind of life, a habitable zone that allows for a specific concentration of CO_2 in the atmosphere as well as liquid water would have to be found.

The scientists used mathematical models based on Earth's known attributes and adjusted different variables to find out which scenarios yielded the best results. Some of these variables include surface temperature, mass of the planet, and geological activity. The scientists also considered settings where the surface of the planet was all-land, all-water, or a mix of both.

Considering all of these scenarios, von Bloh et al. determined that the habitable zone for Gliese 581g is between 0.125 and 0.155 astronomical units, where an astronomical unit is the distance between the Earth and the Sun. Other studies conclude that the *actual* orbital distance of Gliese 581g is 0.146 astronomical units. Because Gliese 581g is right in the middle of its determined habitable zone, the error and uncertainty in the variables that remain to be determined are negligible.

However, the ratio of land to ocean on the planet's surface is key in determining the "life span" of the habitable zone. The habitable zone can shift over time due to geological phenomena caused by a planet having more land than ocean. According to von Bloh et al., a planet with a land-to-ocean ratio similar to ours would remain in the habitable zone for about seven billion years, shorter than Gliese 581g's estimated age. In other words, if Gliese 581g has an Earth-like composition, it cannot sustain life. But if the ratio is low (more ocean than land), the planet will remain in its habitable zone for a greater period of time, thus allowing for a greater chance of life to develop.

The researchers conclude that Gliese 581g is a strong candidate for life so long as it is a "water world." According to the authors, water worlds are defined as "planets of non-vanishing continental area mostly covered by oceans."

The discovery of Gliese 581g being a strong candidate for sustaining life is especially important considering the vast quantity of planets just like it. According to NASA's *Kepler Discoveries* Web page, the Kepler telescope alone has found over 4,234 planet candidates in just five years. With the collaboration of other research, 120 planets have been deemed "habitable," according to *The Habitable Exoplanets Catalog*.

"Our results are another step toward identifying the possibility of life beyond the Solar System, especially concerning Super-Earth planets, which appear to be more abundant than previously surmised," say the authors. More and more scientists are agreeing with the idea that extraterrestrial life is probable, given the abundance of Earth-like planets found in our galaxy already. If this is true, humanity will be one step closer to finding its place in the universe.

"[W]e have to await future missions to identify the pertinent geodynamical features of Gl[iese] 581g...to gain insight into whether or not Gl[iese] 581g harbors life," write the researchers. The science community agrees: continued focus in researching the cosmos is necessary to confirm if we have neighbors.

The full journal article can be found at <http://www.aanda.org.prox.lib.ncsu.edu/articles/aa/full_html/2011/04/aa16534-11/aa16534-11.html>.

Astronomy & Astrophysics, published by EDP Sciences since 1963, covers important developments in the research of theoretical, observational, and instrumental astronomy and astrophysics. For more information, visit <http://www.aanda.org/>.

Works Cited

Annual Review of Astronomy and Astrophysics. Annual Reviews, 2014, www.annualreviews.org/journal/astro.

"About Astronomy & Astrophysics." *Astronomy & Astrophysics*, www.aanda.org/about-aa.

Cook, Lynette. "Planets of the Gliese 581 System." *NASA Features*, NASA, 29 Sept. 2010, www.nasa.gov/topics/universe/features/Gliese_581.html.

The Habitable Exoplanets Catalog. Planetary Habitability Laboratory, 2 Sept. 2014, phl.upr.edu/projects/habitable-exoplanets-catalog.

Kepler Discoveries. NASA, 24 July 2014, kepler.nasa.gov/Mission/discoveries/

Kepler Launch. NASA, 2 Apr. 2014, www.nasa.gov/mission_pages/kepler/launch/.

Von Bloh, W., et al. "Habitability of the Goldilocks Planet Gliese 581g: Results from Geodynamic Models." *Astronomy & Astrophysics*, vol. 528, no. A133, 2011. *Summon*, doi:10.1051/0004-6361/201116534.

Discussion Questions

1. Who was Jonathan Nastasi's audience as he wrote his press release? What cues in the writing tell you whom Jonathan views as his audience?

2. How well did he tailor his description of the research to that audience?

3. What is the purpose behind Jonathan's communication of the research findings?

4. What other genre might work for translating this research to a public audience? What would Jonathan need to do differently in that rhetorical situation?

Writing Project: Translating a Scholarly Article for a Public Audience

The goal of this project is to translate a scholarly article for a public audience. To do so, you will first analyze the scholarly article rhetorically and then shift the genre through which the information in your article is reported. You will produce two documents in response to this assignment:

- the translation of your scholarly article
- a written analysis of the choices you made as you wrote your translation

Step One: Identifying Your New Audience and Genre

To get started, you'll need to identify a new audience and rhetorical situation for the information in your selected article. The goal here is to shift the audience from an academic one to a public one. You may, for instance, choose to report the findings of the article in a magazine targeted toward a general audience of people who are interested in science, or you may choose to write a newspaper article that announces the research findings. You might also choose to write a script for a news show that reports research findings to a general television audience. Notice that once you change audiences, then the form in which you report will need to shift as well. The genre you produce will be contingent on the audience you're targeting and the rhetorical situation: magazine article, newspaper article, news show script. There is an array of other possibilities for shifting your audience and genre as well.

Step Two: Analyzing Your Target Audience and Genre Expectations

Closely analyze an example or two of the kind of genre you're attempting to create, and consider how those genre examples fulfill the expectations of the target audience. Your project will be assessed according to its ability to reproduce those genre expectations, so you will need to explain, in detail, the rhetorical changes and other choices you had to make in the construction of your piece. Be sure that you're able to explain the rhetorical choices you make in writing your translation. Consider all four elements of rhetorical context: author, audience, topic, purpose.

Step Three: Constructing the Genre

At this point, you're ready to begin constructing or translating the article into the new genre. The genre you're producing could take any number of forms. As such, the form, structure, and development of your ideas are contingent on the genre of public reporting you're attempting to construct. If you're constructing a magazine article, for example, then the article you produce should really look like one that would appear in a magazine. Try to mirror how the genre would appear in a real situation.

Step Four: Writing the Analysis

Once your translation is complete, compose a reflective analysis. As part of your analysis, consider the rhetorical choices you made as you constructed your translation. Offer a rationale for each of your decisions that connects the features of your translation to your larger rhetorical context. For example, if you had to translate the title of the scholarly article for a public audience, explain why your new title is the most appropriate one for your public audience.

Tip Sheet — Reading and Writing in Academic Disciplines

- **You should not expect to master the writing of every academic discipline by reading one book**, even this one.

- **It's important to become familiar with key concepts of disciplinary writing in academic discourse communities:** *research* expectations; *conventions* (expectations) of writing; *genres* (types) of writing.

- **Genres are not always bound by discipline, although their conventions may vary somewhat from discipline to discipline.** For example, you can expect to write literature reviews in many different courses across the curriculum.

- **Analyzing academic writing is a multistep process.** (1) Understand the rhetorical context (author, audience, topic, purpose for writing); (2) identify the disciplinary area and what you know about it; (3) consider how expectations for features of *structure*, *language*, and *reference* govern the writing situation; (4) identify the genre of writing and the conventions that apply; (5) analyze the persuasive strategies if the writer is developing an argument.

- **Remember SLR.** The acronym for *structure*, *language*, and *reference* offers categories that can help you determine conventions and choices appropriate for most academic writing situations.

  - **Structure** concerns how texts are organized. *Example:* IMRAD—signifying Introduction, Methods, Results, and Discussion—is a common format in both the social and natural sciences.

  - **Language** encompasses conventions of style or word choice. *Example:* Active voice is typically favored in the humanities, and passive voice is more characteristic of writing in the social and natural sciences.

  - **Reference** concerns the ways writers engage source material, including their use of conventions of citation and documentation. *Example:* Many humanities scholars use MLA style; many social science scholars use APA style.

- **Academic research is important beyond the academy.** Therefore, academic writing that conveys such research often must be repurposed—translated—for different venues and audiences.

Chapter 12 Reading and Writing in the Humanities

Introduction to the Humanities

An interest in exploring the meaning, or interpretation, of something and how it reflects on the human experience is one of the defining characteristics of the humanities that sets it apart from the social sciences, the natural sciences, and applied fields. Look at the tree at the bottom of this page, and see if you recognize any fields within the humanities with which you're already familiar.

Scholars in the humanities are interested in, and closely observe, human thought, creativity, and experience. The American Council of Learned Societies explains that humanistic scholars "help us appreciate and understand what distinguishes us as human beings as well as what unites us." Scholars in the humanities ask questions such as these:

- What can we learn about human experience from examining the ways we think and express ourselves?

- How do we make sense of the world through various forms of expression?

- How do we interpret what we experience, or make meaning for ourselves and for others?

Andrea Tsurumi

Professor John McCurdy teaches history at Eastern Michigan University. Dr. McCurdy's research focuses on the history of early America, and he teaches courses on the colonial era and the American Revolution. In his Insider's View comments, he offers thoughts on what humanists do and value, as well as the kind of research questions they ask. These comments come from an interview with him about his writing and about research in the humanities in general.

Insider's View

Humanists Seek to Better Understand the Human Condition

John McCurdy, History

Courtesy of John McCurdy

"Humanists seek to better understand the human condition. We seek knowledge for knowledge's sake, realizing that not everything has an immediate or obvious application. Humanists value truth as well as creativity. Before the process of learning begins, humanists need evidence—documents, plays, sculptures, songs—as these are the physical manifestations of human expression. Without evidence, we have nothing to analyze.

"The most important question for the humanist to ask is *why*. To be sure, we all want to know what, where, how, who, and (especially for historians) when, but all of these questions are but a means to an end: why. *Why* is the most important question because it is the most difficult to answer. Why did the Holocaust happen? Why do I fall in love? Why are we here? Although it is difficult to answer such questions, humanists never stop trying because in the process of formulating questions and attempting to answer them, we learn more about the human condition and ourselves. To answer questions of *why*, humanists turn to sources and each other."

Texts and Meaning

To understand the human condition and respond to these questions, humanists often turn to artifacts of human culture that they observe and interpret. These might be films, historical documents, comic strips, paintings, poems, religious artifacts, video games, essays, photographs, and songs. They might even include graffiti on the side of a building, a Facebook status update, or a YouTube video.

In addition to tangible artifacts, humanist writers might turn their attention to events, experiences, rituals, or other elements of human culture to develop meaning. When Ernest Hemingway wrote *Death in the Afternoon* about the traditions of bullfighting in Spain, he carefully observed and interpreted the meaning of a cultural ritual. And when historians interpret Hemingway's text through the lens of historical context, or when literary scholars compare the book to Hemingway's fiction of a later period, they are extending that understanding of human culture. Through such examination and interpretation of specific objects of study, scholars in the humanities can create artistic texts and develop theories that explain human expression and experience.

In this chapter, we'll often refer to artifacts and events that humanistic scholars study as **texts**. The ability to construct meaning from a text is an essential skill within the scholarship of the humanities. In high school English classes, students are often asked to interpret novels, poetry, or plays. You've likely written such analyses in the past, so you've developed a set of observational and interpretive skills that we'd like to build upon in this chapter. The same skills, such as the observational skills that lead you to find evidence in a literary text to develop and support an interpretation, can help you analyze other kinds of texts.

Inside Work: Thinking about Texts

Write your responses to the following questions.

- What experiences do you already have with interpretation of texts in the humanities? Have you had to write a formal interpretation of a text before? If so, what questions did you ask?

- Imagine a text with which you are familiar. It might be a novel, a song, a painting, a sculpture, a play, a building, or a historical document. Brainstorm a list of *why* questions that you could ask about that text.

Observation and Interpretation

You probably engage every day in observation of the kinds of things studied in the humanities, but you might not be doing it in the systematic way that humanistic scholars do. When you listen to music, how do you make meaning? Perhaps you listen to the words, the chord progressions, or repeated phrases. Or maybe you look to specific matters of context such as who wrote the song, what other music the artist has performed, and when it was recorded. You might consider how it is similar to or different from other songs. In order to understand the song's meaning, you might even think about social and cultural events surrounding the period when the song was recorded. These kinds of observational and interpretive acts are the very things humanists do when they research and write; they just use careful methods of observing, documenting, and interpreting that are generally more systematic than what most of us do when listening to music for enjoyment. Humanists also develop and apply theories of interpretation or build on the theories of others that help still other scholars determine how to observe and interpret texts and find meaningful connections among them. In this chapter, you will learn about some of those methods of observation and interpretation, and you will also have the opportunity to practice some of the kinds of writing and research typically seen in the humanities.

Inside Work: Observing and Asking Questions

For this activity, pick a place to sit and observe, and bring something to write with. You might choose to do the activity in your dorm room or apartment, your workplace, a classroom, outside, in a restaurant or coffee shop, or at a gym, to name a few possibilities. For ten minutes, freewrite about all the things you see around you that could be "texts" that a humanist might interpret. Then think about the kinds of questions that a humanist might ask about those texts. Try to avoid writing about the actual activities people are engaging in; human behavior is more within the realm of the social sciences, not the humanities. Instead, think creatively about the kinds of artifacts that a humanist might analyze to understand and interpret human experience.

For example, if you observe and write in a coffee shop, you might consider the following artifacts, or texts.

- **The Sign or Logo Used for the Store**   Is there a logo? What does it include? How is it designed, and why? Is there a slogan? Whom might it relate to? What does it say about the store?

- **The Clothing of the People Working behind the Counter**   Do they have a dress code? Are they wearing uniforms? If so, what do the colors, materials, and/or style of the uniforms represent? What do they potentially tell you about the values of the business?

- **The Furniture**   Is it comfortable? New? Old? How is it arranged? What might the coffee shop be communicating to customers through that arrangement?

- **The Music Playing in the Background**   Is there music? What is playing? How loud is the music? What mood does it convey? Does it match the arrangement of the rest of the space? What emotions might the music evoke from customers?

- **The Materials Used to Serve Coffee**   Are the cups and napkins recycled? Does the store use glass or ceramic cups that can be washed and reused? Are there slogans or logos on the materials? If so, what do they say? What does the store communicate to customers through the materials used?

- **The Menu**   What kinds of items does the coffee shop serve? What language is used to describe menu items? How are the items written on the menu? Where is it displayed? Is food served? If so, what types of food are available, and what does that communicate to customers?

See how many different texts you can identify and how many questions you can generate. You might do this activity separately in the same place with a partner and then compare notes. What texts did you or your partner find in common? Which ones did you each identify that were unique? Why do you think you noticed the things you did? What was the most interesting text you identified?

Research in the Humanities

The collection of information, or data, is an integral part of the research process for scholars in all academic disciplines. The data that researchers collect form the foundation of evidence they use to answer a question. In the humanities, data are generally gathered from texts. Whether you're reading a novel, analyzing a sculpture, or speculating on the significance of a cultural ritual, your object of analysis is a text and the primary source of data you collect to use as evidence typically originates from that text.

Academic fields within the humanities have at their heart the creation and interpretation of texts. A history scholar may pore through photographs of Civil War soldiers for evidence to support a claim. An actor in a theater class might scour a script in order to develop an interpretation of a character he will perform onstage. And those who are primarily the creators of texts—visual artists, novelists, poets, playwrights, screenwriters, musicians—read widely in the field in order to master elements of style and contribute to their art in original and innovative ways. In the humanities, it's all about the text. Humanists are either creators or interpreters of texts, and often they are both.

LaunchPadSolo

Hear more about the different kinds of texts scholars draw on in their research.

Inside Work: Observing and Interpreting Images

Consider each of the following images—a movie poster (A), graffiti (B), and a painting (C)—as texts that have something to say about human experience. Write your ideas in response to the following questions.

- What does the image mean?
- How do you make meaning from the image? What do you analyze to make meaning?
- What does the image make you think about?
- What emotion does the artist want you to feel? What aspect of the text do you base this on?
- Why do you think someone created this image?

A. Movie Poster as Text   B. Graffiti as Text   C. Painting as Text

© Moviestore Collection Ltd/Alamy

Chris Graythen/Getty Images

Luncheon of the Boating Party, 1880–81 (oil on canvas), Renoir, Pierre-Auguste (1841–1919)/The Phillips Collection, Washington, D.C., USA / Acquired 1923/ Bridgeman Images

To understand the research and writing in a specific disciplinary area, it is important to know not only what the objects of study are but also what methods scholars in that area use to analyze and study the objects of their attention. In the humanities, just as in other disciplines, scholars begin with observation. They closely observe the texts that interest them, looking for patterns, meaning, and connections that will help generate and support an interpretation. Humanists use their observations to pose questions about the human condition, to gather evidence to help answer those questions, and to generate theories about the human experience that can extend beyond one text or set of texts.

The Role of Theory in the Humanities

When scholars in the humanities analyze and interpret a text, they often draw on a specific theory of interpretation to help them make meaning. Theories in the humanities offer a particular perspective through which to understand human experience. Sometimes those perspectives are based on ideas about *how* we make meaning from a text; such theories include Formalism (sometimes called New Criticism, though it is far from new), Reader Response, and Deconstruction. Other theories, such as Feminist Theory and Queer Theory, are based more on ideas about how identity informs meaning-making. Still other theories, such as New Historicism, Postcolonialism, and Marxism, are centrally concerned with how historical, social, cultural, and other contexts inform meaning.

These are only a few of the many prominent theories of humanistic interpretation, barely scratching the surface of the theory-building work that has taken place in the humanities. Our goal is not for you to learn specific names of theories at this point, though. Rather, we want you to understand that when scholars in the humanities draw on a theory in the interpretation of a text, the theory gives them a *lens* through which to view the text and a set of questions they might ask about it. Different theories lead to different sets of questions and varying interpretations of the same text.

Close Reading in the Humanities

To develop clear claims about the texts they're interpreting, scholars in the humanities must closely observe their texts and learn about them. Close observation might involve the kinds of reading strategies we discussed in Chapter 8, especially if the text is alphabetic (i.e., letter based), such as a book, a story, or a poem. One method that humanities scholars use is close reading, or careful observation of a text. It's possible to do a close reading of a story, of course, but one can also do a close reading of non-alphabetic texts such as films, buildings, paintings, events, or songs.

Most college students are highly skilled at reading for content knowledge, or for information, because that's what they're most often asked to do as students. This is what a professor generally expects when assigning a reading from a textbook. As you read such texts, you're primarily trying to figure out what the text is saying rather than thinking about how it functions, why the author makes certain stylistic choices, or how others might interpret the text. As we mentioned in Chapter 8, you might also read to be entertained, to learn, or to communicate.

Close observation or *reading* in the humanities, however, requires our focus to shift from reading for information to reading to understand how a text functions and how we can make meaning of it. Because texts are the primary sources of data used in humanistic research, it's important for those who work in the humanities to examine how a text conveys meaning to its audience. This kind of work—observing a text critically to analyze what it means and how it conveys meaning—is what we call close reading.

Insider Example

Professional Close Reading

In the following example of a close reading of a text, Dr. Dale Jacobs discusses how he constructs meaning from comics. He argues that comics are more complicated to interpret than texts composed only of words (e.g., a novel or short story) because graphic novel readers must also interpret visual, gestural, and spatial language at work in the panels. In doing so, Dr. Jacobs offers his own observation. Furthermore, he concludes his interpretation by calling on instructors to challenge students to think critically about how they construct meaning from texts. As you read his article, you might reflect on this question: When reading a text, how do you make meaning?

Dale Jacobs

More Than Words: Comics as a Means of Teaching Multiple Literacies

Over the last several years, comics have been an ever more visible and well-regarded part of mainstream culture. Comics are now reviewed in major newspapers and featured on the shelves of independent and chain bookstores. Major publishing houses such as Pantheon publish work in the comics medium, including books such as Marjane Satrapi's *Persepolis* and David B.'s *Epileptic*. Educational publishers such as Scholastic are also getting in on the act; in January 2005, Scholastic launched its own graphic novels imprint, Graphix, with the publication of Jeff Smith's highly acclaimed Bone series. At the NCTE Annual Convention, graphic novels and comics are displayed in ever greater numbers. School and public libraries are building graphic novels collections to try to get adolescents into the library. Comics have, indeed, emerged from the margins into the mainstream.

With all this activity and discussion surrounding comics, it is timely to consider how we as literacy teachers might think about the practice of using comics in our class-rooms and how this practice fits into ongoing debates about comics and literacy. In examining these links between theory and practice, I wish to move beyond seeing the reading of comics as a debased or simplified word-based literacy. Instead, I want to advance two ideas: (1) reading comics involves a complex, multimodal literacy; and (2) by using comics in our classrooms, we can help students develop as critical and engaged readers of multimodal texts.

The History of Attitudes toward Comics and Literacy

Prior to their current renaissance, comics were often viewed, at best, as popular entertainment and, at worst, as a dangerous influence on youth. Such attitudes were certainly prevalent in the early 1950s when comics were at their most popular, with critics such as Fredric Wertham voicing the most strenuous arguments against comics in his 1954 book *Seduction of the Innocent* (for an extended discussion of this debate, see Dorrell, Curtis, and Rampal). Wertham baldly asserts that "[c]omic books are death on reading" (121). He goes on, "Reading troubles in children are on the increase. An important cause of this increase is the comic book. A very large proportion of children who cannot read well habitually read comic books. They are not really readers, but gaze mostly at the pictures, picking up a word here and there. Among the worst readers is a very high percentage of comic-book addicts who spend very much time 'reading' comic books. They are book-worms without books" (122). According to this thinking, children who read comic books are not really reading; they are simply looking at the pictures as a way to avoid engaging in the complex processes of learning to read. The problem, according to Wertham, is that in reading comics children focus far too much on the image to make meaning and avoid engaging with the written word, a semiotic system that Wertham clearly sees as both more complex and more important. Though he sees the visuality of comics as dangerous, Wertham shares the notion with current proponents of comics that the visual is more easily ingested and interpreted than the written. Whether the visual acts as a hindrance or a help to the acquisition of word-based literacy, the key idea remains that the visual is subservient to the written.

When I was growing up in the 1970s, I never saw comics in school or in the public library unless they were being read surreptitiously behind the cover of a novel or other officially sanctioned book. Over the last decade, however, there has been a movement to claim a value for comics in the literacy education of children. Comics have made their way into schools mainly as a scaffold for later learning that is perceived to be more difficult, in terms of both the literate practices and content involved. For example, *Comics in Education*, the online version of Gene Yang's final project for his master's degree at California State University, Hayward, embodies thinking that is typical of many educators who advocate the use of comics in the classroom. Yang, a teacher and cartoonist, claims that the educational strength of comics is that they are motivating, visual, permanent, intermediary, and popular. In emphasizing the motivational, visual permanency (in the way it slows down the flow of information), intermediacy, and the popular, such approaches inadvertently and ironically align themselves with Wertham's ideas about the relationship between word and image, even while bringing comics into the mainstream of education. Comics in this formulation are seen simply as a stepping stone to the acquisition of other, higher skills. As a teaching tool, then, comics are seen primarily as a way to motivate through their popularity and to help slow-learning students, especially in the acquisition of reading skills (see Haugaard; Koenke). While I agree with these attempts to argue for the value of comics in education, such an approach has limited value.

Libraries have also been important in the reconsideration of the place of comics as appropriate texts for children in their literacy learning and acquisition. Recently, many librarians have been arguing for the introduction of comics into library collections, usually in the form of graphic novels, as a way to get children into the library and interested in reading. The main thrust of this argument is that the presence of graphic novels will make the library seem cool and interesting, especially among the so-called reluctant readers, mainly adolescent boys, who seem to show little interest in reading or in libraries (see Crawford; Simmons). Graphic novels can compete with video games, television, and movies, giving the library the advantage it needs to get this specifically targeted demographic through the door. Many public libraries and librarians have seen the power of comics and graphic novels as a tool for drawing young people into the library, getting them first to read those comics and then building on that scaffold to turn them into lifelong readers. Again, while I agree with the inclusion of comics and graphic novels in library collections, such an approach places severe limitations on the possibilities of our uses of the medium as literacy educators.

To think through these ideas, let's assume that this strategy has some of its desired effects in drawing reluctant readers into the library and coaxing them to read. What can we then say about the effects of this approach and its conception of comics and their relation to developing literate practices? On the one hand, the use of graphic novels is seen as one strategy in teaching and encouraging literacy and literate practices; on the other hand, graphic novels are still regarded as a way station on the road to "higher" forms of literacy and to more challenging and, by implication, worthwhile texts. I'm not trying to suggest that reading comics or graphic novels exists apart from the world of word-based texts as a whole or the complex matrix of literacy acquisition. Rather, I'm simply pointing out that in the development of children's and adolescents' literacies, reading comics has almost always been seen as a debased form of word-based literacy, albeit an important intermediate step to more advanced forms of textual literacy, rather than as a complex form of multimodal literacy.

Comics as Multimodal Literacy: The Theory

If we think about comics as multimodal texts that involve multiple kinds of meaning making, we do not give up the benefits of word-based literacy instruction but strengthen it through the inclusion of visual and other literacies. This complex view of literacy is touched on but never fully fleshed out in two excellent recent articles on comics and education: Rocco Versaci's "How Comic Books Can Change the Way Our Students See Literature: One Teacher's Perspective" and Bonny Norton's "The Motivating Power of Comic Books: Insights from Archie Comic Readers." By situating our thinking about comics, literacy, and education within a framework that views literacy as occurring in multiple modes, we can use comics to greater effectiveness in our teaching at all levels by helping us to arm students with the critical-literacy skills they need to negotiate diverse systems of meaning making.

I'm going to offer an example of how comics engage multiple literacies by looking at Ted Naifeh's *Polly and the Pirates*, but first let me give a brief outline of these multiple systems of meaning making. As texts, comics provide a complex environment for the negotiation of meaning, beginning with the layout of the page itself. The comics page is separated into multiple panels, divided from each other by gutters, physical or conceptual spaces through which connections are made and meanings are negotiated; readers must fill in the blanks within these gutters and make connections between panels. Images of people, objects, animals, and settings, word balloons, lettering, sound effects, and gutters all come together to form page layouts that work to create meaning in distinctive ways and in multiple realms of meaning making. In these multiple realms of meaning making, comics engage in what the New London Group of literacy scholars calls *multimodality*, a way of thinking that seeks to push literacy educators, broadly defined and at all levels of teaching, to think about literacy in ways that move beyond a focus on strictly word-based literacy. In the introduction to the New London Group's collection, *Multiliteracies: Literacy Learning and the Design of Social Futures*, Bill Cope and Mary Kalantzis write that their approach "relates to the increasing multiplicity and integration of significant modes of meaning-making, where the textual is also related to the visual, the audio, the spatial, the behavioural, and so on. . . . Meaning is made in ways that are increasingly multimodal—in which written-linguistic modes of meaning are part and parcel of visual, audio, and spatial patterns of meaning" (5). By embracing the idea of multimodal literacy in relation to comics, then, we can help students engage critically with ways of making meaning that exist all around them, since multimodal texts include much of the content on the Internet, interactive multimedia, newspapers, television, film, instructional textbooks, and many other texts in our contemporary society.

Such a multimodal approach to reading and writing asserts that in engaging with texts, we interact with up to six design elements, including linguistic, audio, visual, gestural, and spatial modes, as well as multimodal design, "of a different order to the others as it represents the patterns of interconnections among the other modes" (New London Group 25). In the first two pages from *Polly and the Pirates*, all of these design elements are present, including a textual and visual representation of the audio element. Despite the existence of these multiple modes of meaning making, however, the focus in thinking about the relationship between comics and education is almost always on the linguistic element, represented here by the words in the words balloons (or, in the conventions of comics, the dialogue from each of the characters) and the narrative text boxes in the first three panels (which we later find out are also spoken dialogue by a narrator present in the story).

As discussed earlier, comics are seen as a simplified version of word-based texts, with the words supplemented and made easier to understand by the pictures. If we take a multimodal approach to texts such as comics, however, the picture of meaning making becomes much more complex. In word-based texts, our interaction with words forms an environment for meaning making that is extremely complex. In comics and other multimodal texts, there are five other elements added to the mix. Thought about in this way, comics are not just simpler versions of word-based texts but can be viewed as the complex textual environments that they are.

Comics as Multimodal Literacy: *Polly and the Pirates* in the Classroom

In comics, there are elements present besides words, but these elements are just as important in making meaning from the text. In fact, it is impossible to make full sense of the words on the page in isolation from the audio, visual, gestural, and spatial. For example, the first page of *Polly and the Pirates* (the first issue of a six-issue miniseries) opens with three panels of words from what the reader takes to be the story's narrative voice. Why? Partially it is because of *what* the words say—how they introduce a character and begin to set up the story—but also it is because of the text boxes that enclose the words. That is, most people understand from their experiences of reading comics at some point in their history that words in text boxes almost always contain the story's narrative voice and denote a different kind of voice than do words in dialogue balloons. What's more, these text boxes deviate in shape and design from the even rectangles usually seen in comics; instead, they are depicted more like scrolls, a visual element that calls to mind both the time period and genre associated with pirates. Not only does this visual element help to place the reader temporally and generically, but it, along with lettering and punctuation, also aids in indicating tone, voice inflection, cadence, and emotional tenor by giving visual representation to the text's audio element. We are better able to "hear" the narrator's voice because we can see what words are emphasized by the bold lettering, and we associate particular kinds of voices with the narrative voice of a pirate's tale, especially emphasized here by the shape of the text boxes. Both the visual and the audio thus influence the way we read the words in a comic, as can be seen in these three opening panels.

It seems to me, however, that the key lies in going beyond the way we make meaning from the words alone and considering the other visual elements, as well as the gestural and spatial. If I were teaching this text, I would engage students in a discussion about how they understand what is going on in the story and how they make meaning from it. Depending on the level of the class, I would stress different elements at varying levels of complexity. Here I will offer an example of how I make meaning from these pages and of some of the elements I might discuss with students.

In talking about the visual, I would consider such things as the use of line and white space, shading, perspective, distance, depth of field, and composition. The gestural refers to facial expression and body posture, while the spatial refers to the meanings of environmental and architectural space, which, in the case of comics, can be conceived as the layout of panels on the page and the relation between these panels through use of gutter space. The opening panel depicts a ship, mainly in silhouette, sailing on the ocean; we are not given details, but instead see the looming presence of a ship that we are led to believe is a pirate ship by the words in the text boxes. The ship is in the center of an unbordered panel and is the only element in focus, though its details are obscured. The unbordered panel indicates openness, literally and metaphorically, and this opening shot thus acts much in the same way as an establishing shot in a film, orienting us both in terms of place and in terms of genre. The second panel pulls in closer to reveal a silhouetted figure standing on the deck of the ship. She is framed between the sails, and the panel's composition draws our eyes toward her as the central figure in the frame. She is clearly at home, one arm thrust forward while the other points back with sword in hand, her legs anchoring herself securely as she gazes across the ocean. The third panel pulls in even farther to a close-up of her face, the top half in shadow and the bottom half showing a slight smile. She is framed by her sword on the left and the riggings of the ship on the right, perfectly in her element, yet obscured from our view. Here and in the previous panel, gestural and visual design indicate who is the center of the story and the way in which she confidently belongs in this setting. At the same time, the spatial layout of the page and the progression of the panels from establishing shot to close-up and from unbordered panels to bordered and internally framed panels help us to establish the relationship of the woman to the ship and to the story; as we move from one panel to the next, we must make connections between the panels that are implied by the gutter. Linguistic, visual, audio, gestural, and spatial elements combine in these first three panels to set up expectations in the reader for the type of story and its narrative approach. Taken together, these elements form a multimodal system of meaning making.

What happens in the fourth panel serves to undercut these expectations as we find out that the narrative voice actually belongs to one of the characters in the story, as evidenced by the shift from text box to dialogue balloon even though the voice is clearly the same as in the first three panels of the page. Spatially, we are presented with a larger panel that is visually dominated by the presence of a book called *A History of the Pirate Queen.* This book presumably details the story to which we had been introduced in the first three panels. The character holding the book is presenting it to someone and, because of the panel's composition, is also effectively presenting it to us, the readers. The gesture becomes one of offering this story up to us, a story that simultaneously becomes a romance as well as a pirate story as evidenced by the words the character says and the way she says them (with the bold emphasis on *dream* and *marry*). At this point, we do not know who this character is or to whom she is speaking, and the answers to these questions will be deferred until we turn to the second page.

On the first panel of page 2, we see three girls, each taking up about a third of the panel, with them and the background in focused detail. Both the words and facial expression of the first girl indicate her stance toward the story, while the words and facial expression of the second girl indicate her indignation at the attitude of the first girl (whom we learn is named Sarah). The third girl is looking to the right, away from the other two, and has a blank expression on her face. The next panel depicts the second and third girls, pulling in to a tighter close-up that balances one girl and either side of the panel and obscures the background so that we will focus on their faces and dialogue. The unbordered panel again indicates openness and momentary detachment from their surroundings. Polly is at a loss for words and is not paying attention to the other girl, as indicated by the ellipses and

truncated dialogue balloons, as well as her eyes that are pointing to the right, away from the other girl. Spatially, the transition to panel 3 once more encloses them in the world that we now see is a classroom in an overhead shot that places the students in relation to the teacher. The teacher's words restore order to the class and, on a narrative level, name the third of the three girls and the narrative voice of the opening page. The story of the pirates that began on page 1 is now contained within the world of school, and we are left to wonder how the tensions between these two stories/worlds will play out in the remaining pages. As you can see, much more than words alone is used to make meaning in these first two pages of *Polly and the Pirates*.

Conclusion

My process of making meaning from these pages of *Polly and the Pirates* is one of many meanings within the matrix of possibilities inherent in the text. As a reader, I am actively engaging with the "grammars," including discourse and genre conventions, within this multimodal text as I seek to create/negotiate meaning; such a theory of meaning making with multimodal texts acknowledges the social and semiotic structures that surround us and within which we exist, while at the same time it recognizes individual agency and experience in the creation of meaning. Knowledge of linguistic, audio, visual, gestural, and spatial conventions within comics affects the ways in which we read and the meanings we assign to texts, just as knowledge of conventions within word-based literacy affects the ways in which those texts are read. For example, the conventions discussed above in terms of the grammar of comics would have been available to Naifeh as he created *Polly and the Pirates*, just as they are also available to me and to all other readers of his text. These conventions form the underlying structure of the process of making meaning, while familiarity with these conventions, practice in reading comics, interest, prior experience, and attention given to that reading all come into play in the exercise of agency on the part of the reader (and writer). Structure and agency interact so that we are influenced by design conventions and grammars as we read but are not determined by them; though we are subject to the same set of grammars, my reading of the text is not necessarily the same as that of someone else.

Reading and writing multimodal texts, then, is an active process, both for creators and for readers who by necessity engage in the active production of meaning and who use all resources available to them based on their familiarity with the comics medium and its inherent grammars, their histories, life experiences, and interests. In turn, every act of creating meaning from a multimodal text, happening as it does at the intersection of structure and agency, contributes to the ongoing process of becoming a multimodally literate person. By teaching students to become conscious and critical of the ways in which they make meaning from multimodal texts such as comics, we can also teach students to become more literate with a wide range of multimodal texts. By complicating our view of comics so that we do not see them as simply an intermediary step to more complex word-based literacy, we can more effectively help students become active creators, rather than passive consumers, of meaning in their interactions with a wide variety of multimodal texts. In doing so, we harness the real power of comics in the classroom and prepare students for better negotiating their worlds of meaning.

Works Cited

B., David. *Epileptic.* New York: Pantheon, 2005.

Cope, Bill, and Mary Kalantzis. "Introduction: Multiliteracies: The Beginnings of an Idea." *Multiliteracies: Literacy Learning and the Design of Social Futures.* Ed. Bill Cope and Mary Kalantzis. New York: Routledge, 2000. 3–8.

Crawford, Philip. "A Novel Approach: Using Graphic Novels to Attract Reluctant Readers." *Library Media Connection* 22.5 (Feb. 2004): 26–28.

Dorrell, Larry D., Dan B. Curtis, and Kuldip R. Rampal. "Book-Worms without Books? Students Reading Comic Books in the School House." *Journal of Popular Culture* 29 (Fall 1995): 223–34.

Haugaard, Kay. "Comic Books: Conduits to Culture?" *The Reading Teacher* 27.1 (Oct. 1973): 54–55.

Koenke, Karl. "The Careful Use of Comic Books." *The Reading Teacher* 34.5 (Feb. 1981): 592–95.

McCloud, Scott. *Understanding Comics: The Invisible Art.* New York: Harper, 1993.

Naifeh, Ted. *Polly and the Pirates* 1 (Sept. 2005): 1–2.

New London Group, The. "A Pedagogy of Multiliteracies: Designing Social Futures." *Multiliteracies: Literacy Learning and the Design of Social Futures*. Ed. Bill Cope and Mary Kalantzis. New York: Routledge, 2000. 9–37.

Norton, Bonny. "The Motivating Power of Comic Books: Insights from Archie Comic Readers." *The Reading Teacher* 57.2 (Oct. 2003): 140–47.

Satrapi, Marjane. *Persepolis.* New York: Pantheon, 2003.

Simmons, Tabitha. "Comic Books in My Library?" *PNLA Quarterly* 67.3 (Spring 2003): 12, 20.

Versaci, Rocco. "How Comic Books Can Change the Way Our Students See Literature: One Teacher's Perspective." *English Journal* 91.2 (Mar. 2001): 61–67.

Wertham, Fredric. *Seduction of the Innocent.* New York: Rinehart, 1954.

Yang, Gene. *Comics in Education.* 2003. 29 Aug. 2006 <http://www.humblecomics .com/comicsedu/index.html>.

Discussion Questions

1. In your own words, describe how Dr. Jacobs constructs meaning from the comics panels analyzed in this article.

2. What do you think he means by the phrase *multimodal text*?

3. Study one of the comics panels for a minute, and consider how you make meaning from it. Freewrite for five minutes about your own process for making sense of what the comic means.

4. Freewrite for five minutes discussing something you were asked to interpret in the past: perhaps a painting, a novel, a poem, or something else. How did you make meaning of what you were observing and interpreting?

Strategies for Close Reading and Observation

For most of us, when we observe a printed text closely, we highlight, underline, and take notes in the margins. If we're analyzing a visual or aural text, we might take notes on our thoughts, observations, and questions. We might keep a separate notebook or computer file in which we expand on our notes or clarify meaning. As with any skill, the more you practice these steps, the better you'll become at interpretation. We encourage you to take detailed notes, underline passages if applicable, and actively engage with a text when conducting your observation.

We recommend two specific data-collection steps for humanistic inquiry. First, we suggest that you take notes in the margins for a printed text or on a separate sheet of paper as you read, view, or listen to a text to be interpreted. These notes will draw your attention to passages that may serve as direct evidence to support points you'll make later. Additionally, you can elaborate in more detail when something meaningful in the text draws your attention. Jotting down page numbers, audio/video file time markers, and paragraph numbers is often a helpful step for cataloging your notes. The key is to commit fully to engaging with a text by systematically recording your observations.

Second, we recommend developing a **content/form-response grid** to organize the essential stages of your interpretation. The "content" is what happens in the text, and the "form" is how the text's creator structures the piece. In the case of a painting, you might comment on the materials used, the artist's technique, the color palette and imagery choice, or the historical context of the piece. In the case of a religious or political text, you might examine style, language, and literary devices used. The "response" is your interpretation of what the elements you've identified might mean.

Now read the opening paragraphs from "The Story of an Hour," a very brief short story by Kate Chopin published in 1894 that is now recognized as a classic work of

American literature. The excerpt includes a student's notes in the margins followed by a content/form-response grid. Notice the frequency of notes the student takes in the margins and the kinds of questions she asks at this early stage. She offers a fairly equal balance of questions and claims. Pay attention to how she follows the two steps of humanistic inquiry mentioned above:

1. Examine the text and take careful notes. Try keeping marginal notes (if appropriate) and/or separate notebook or sheets of paper to expand on your notes.

2. Complete a content/form-response grid based on the notes you collect.

Kate Chopin

Excerpt from "The Story of an Hour"

Knowing that Mrs. Mallard was afflicted with a heart trouble, great care was taken to break to her as gently as possible the news of her husband's death. It was her sister Josephine who told her, in broken sentences; veiled hints that revealed in half concealing. Her husband's friend Richards was there, too, near her. It was he who had been in the newspaper office when intelligence of the railroad disaster was received, with Brently Mallard's name leading the list of "killed." He had only taken the time to assure himself of its truth by a second telegram, and had hastened to forestall any less careful, less tender friend in bearing the sad message.

Heart trouble? I wonder what kind of trouble.

The news of her husband's death is delivered by her sister.

She did not hear the story as many women have heard the same, with a paralyzed inability to accept its significance. She wept at once, with sudden, wild abandonment, in her sister's arms. When the storm of grief had spent itself she went away to her room alone. She would have no one follow her.

Why would she act differently from other women hearing the same kind of news?

Interesting comparison. The storm-like quality of her grief.

There stood, facing the open window, a comfortable, roomy armchair. Into this she sank, pressed down by a physical exhaustion that haunted her body and seemed to reach into her soul.

Why is she "exhausted"? Interesting word choice.

She could see in the open square before her house the tops of trees that were all aquiver with the new spring life. The delicious breath of rain was in the air. In the street below a peddler was crying his wares. The notes of a distant song which some one was singing reached her faintly, and countless sparrows were twittering in the eaves.

There are lots of images of life here. This really contrasts with the dark news of the story's opening.

This student's annotations can be placed into a content/form-response grid that helps her keep track of the ideas she had as she read and observed closely, both for information (*what*) and for ways the text shaped her experience of it (*how*). Notice that the student uses the Content/Form section to summarize the comments from her annotations, and then she reflects on her annotations in the Response section:

Content/Form Notes (*what* and *how*)	Response (What effect does it have on me?)
Heart trouble? I wonder what kind of trouble.	There's a mystery here. What's wrong with Mrs. Mallard's heart?
The news of her husband's death is delivered by her sister.	Interesting that a female relative is chosen to deliver the news. A man would be too rough?
Why would she act differently from other women hearing the same kind of news?	I wonder what is special about Mrs. Mallard that causes her reaction to be different. Is she putting on a show? Story says her reaction was "sudden" and "wild."
Why is she "exhausted"? Interesting word choice.	Maybe this has to do with her heart condition or with how physically draining her mourning is.
There are lots of images of life here. This really contrasts with the dark news of the story's opening.	This is a sudden change in feeling. Everything is so calm and pleasant now. What happened?

The purpose of this activity is to construct meaning from the text based on the student's close observation of it. This is an interpretation. We can already see that major complexities in the story are beginning to emerge in the student's response notes—such as the importance of the story's setting and the change that occurs in Mrs. Mallard.

Because content/form-response grids like the one above allow you to visualize both your ideas and how you arrived at those ideas, we recommend using this activity anytime you have to observe a text closely in order to interpret its meaning. For a non-alphabetic text, start with the content/form-response grid and use it to log your initial notes as you observe; then reflect later. In the end, such an activity provides a log of details that can help explain how you arrived at a particular conclusion or argument about the text.

Inside Work: Annotating a Text

Use this activity as an opportunity to practice close reading. Read the whole text of Kate Chopin's "The Story of an Hour," which follows, and then annotate the text as you read, paying particular attention to the following elements.

- **Content:** what is being said (the facts, the events, and who the characters are)
- **Form:** how it is being said (the style, language, literary techniques, and narrative perspective)

A follow-up activity at the conclusion of the story asks you to draw a content/form-response grid like the example above. It's important to take extensive marginal notes (perhaps one or two comments per paragraph) and highlight and underline passages as you read the story. These notes will help shape your content/form-response grid and will strengthen your interpretation. We encourage you to expand on your notes on a separate sheet of paper while you read the story.

Kate Chopin

The Story of an Hour

Knowing that Mrs. Mallard was afflicted with a heart trouble, great care was taken to break to her as gently as possible the news of her husband's death. It was her sister Josephine who told her, in broken sentences; veiled hints that revealed in half concealing. Her husband's friend Richards was there, too, near her. It was he who had been in the newspaper office when intelligence of the railroad disaster was received, with Brently Mallard's name leading the list of "killed." He had only taken the time to assure himself of its truth by a second telegram, and had hastened to forestall any less careful, less tender friend in bearing the sad message.

She did not hear the story as many women have heard the same, with a paralyzed inability to accept its significance. She wept at once, with sudden, wild abandonment, in her sister's arms. When the storm of grief had spent itself she went away to her room alone. She would have no one follow her.

There stood, facing the open window, a comfortable, roomy armchair. Into this she sank, pressed down by a physical exhaustion that haunted her body and seemed to reach into her soul.

She could see in the open square before her house the tops of trees that were all aquiver with the new spring life. The delicious breath of rain was in the air. In the street below a peddler was crying his wares. The notes of a distant song which some one was singing reached her faintly, and countless sparrows were twittering in the eaves.

There were patches of blue sky showing here and there through the clouds that had met and piled one above the other in the west facing her window.

She sat with her head thrown back upon the cushion of the chair, quite motionless, except when a sob came up into her throat and shook her, as a child who has cried itself to sleep continues to sob in its dreams.

She was young, with a fair, calm face, whose lines bespoke repression and even a certain strength. But now there was a dull stare in her eyes, whose gaze was fixed away off yonder on one of those patches of blue sky. It was not a glance of reflection, but rather indicated a suspension of intelligent thought.

There was something coming to her and she was waiting for it, fearfully. What was it? She did not know; it was too subtle and elusive to name. But she felt it, creeping out of the sky, reaching toward her through the sounds, the scents, the color that filled the air.

Now her bosom rose and fell tumultuously. She was beginning to recognize this thing that was approaching to possess her, and she was striving to beat it back with her will—as powerless as her two white slender hands would have been.

When she abandoned herself a little whispered word escaped her slightly parted lips. She said it over and over under her breath: "free, free, free!" The vacant stare and the look of terror that had followed it went from her eyes. They stayed keen and bright. Her pulses beat fast, and the coursing blood warmed and relaxed every inch of her body.

She did not stop to ask if it were or were not a monstrous joy that held her. A clear and exalted perception enabled her to dismiss the suggestion as trivial.

She knew that she would weep again when she saw the kind, tender hands folded in death; the face that had never looked save with love upon her, fixed and gray and dead. But she saw beyond that bitter moment a long procession of years to come that would belong to her absolutely. And she opened and spread her arms out to them in welcome.

There would be no one to live for during those coming years; she would live for herself. There would be no powerful will bending hers in that blind persistence with which men and women believe they have a right to impose a private will upon a fellow-creature. A kind intention or a cruel intention made the act seem no less a crime as she looked upon it in that brief moment of illumination.

And yet she had loved him—sometimes. Often she had not. What did it matter! What could love, the unsolved mystery, count for in face of this possession of self-assertion which she suddenly recognized as the strongest impulse of her being!

"Free! Body and soul free!" she kept whispering.

Josephine was kneeling before the closed door with her lips to the keyhole, imploring for admission. "Louise, open the door! I beg, open the door—you will make yourself ill. What are you doing, Louise? For heaven's sake open the door."

"Go away. I am not making myself ill." No; she was drinking in a very elixir of life through that open window.

Her fancy was running riot along those days ahead of her. Spring days, and summer days, and all sorts of days that would be her own. She breathed a quick prayer that life might be long. It was only yesterday she had thought with a shudder that life might be long.

She arose at length and opened the door to her sister's importunities. There was a feverish triumph in her eyes, and she carried herself unwittingly like a goddess of Victory. She clasped her sister's waist, and together they descended the stairs. Richards stood waiting for them at the bottom.

Some one was opening the front door with a latchkey. It was Brently Mallard who entered, a little travel-stained, composedly carrying his grip-sack and umbrella. He had been far from the scene of accident, and did not even know there had been one. He stood amazed at Josephine's piercing cry; at Richards' quick motion to screen him from the view of his wife.

But Richards was too late.

When the doctors came they said she had died of heart disease—of joy that kills.

Inside Work: Preparing a Content/Form-Response Grid

Based on your annotations and notes, construct a content/form-response grid modeled after the example on page 342. Be sure to include your responses to the items you identify in the Content/Form column. Remember that in this case "content" relates to what happens in the story, and "form," in the context of a literary text, relates to how the writer makes the story function through style, narrative perspective, and literary techniques.

Once you've completed your close reading, you might pair up with a classmate or two and share your content/form-response grids. When doing so, consider the following questions as part of your discussion.

1. What facts or events did you note about the story?

2. What did you notice about the ways Chopin shapes your experience of the story? What style or literary techniques did you note?

3. What patterns do you see in the notes you've taken in the Form column? What repeated comments did you make, or what elements strike you in a similar way? How would you explain the meaning of those patterns?

Responding to the Interpretations of Others

Before, during, and after observing a text, humanistic scholars also draw on the work of other scholars to build and support their interpretations. If you were interpreting Chopin's story, for example, you might review the notes you made in your content/form-response grid, search for interesting patterns, and then see if other scholars have noticed the same things. You might look for an element of the story that doesn't make sense to you and see if another scholar has already offered an interpretation. If you agree with the interpretation, you might cite it as support for your own argument. If you disagree, you might look for evidence in the story to show why you disagree and then offer your own interpretation.

As in other disciplines, scholars in the humanities draw on the work of others to make sure they're contributing something new to the ongoing conversation about the artifact, event, or phenomenon they're studying. They also read the work of others to determine if they agree or disagree with an interpretation. Because of the importance of specific language and detail in the humanities, scholars in the humanities quote one another's exact words often, and they also quote directly from their primary sources. We'll discuss some of the reasons for these conventions, and others, in the next section.

LaunchPad Solo

Learn more about incorporating sources into your writing.

Conventions of Writing in the Humanities

Some writing conventions are shared across different fields in the humanities. Because the kinds of texts humanistic scholars examine can vary so much, though, there are also sometimes distinctions in writing conventions among its various fields. One of the challenges of learning the conventions of a disciplinary discourse community is figuring out the specific expectations for communicating with a specific academic audience. In this section, we turn our attention from *research in the humanities* to examine and interpret artifacts themselves, to *strategies of rhetorical analysis* that help us examine how scholars in the humanities write about those artifacts.

Many scholars learn about disciplinary writing conventions through imitation and examination of articles in their fields. Recall that in Chapter 11 we introduced a three-part method for analyzing an academic text by examining the conventions of structure, language, and reference. Applying this analytical framework to professional writing in the various humanities fields can help you further understand conventions appropriate for any given subfield. An awareness of the conventions for writing in any academic context may facilitate your success in writing in those contexts.

Dr. Shelley Garrigan teaches Spanish language and literature at North Carolina State University. As Dr. Garrigan describes in her Insider's View, scholars learn conventions of writing in their field through a variety of means, including learning from peers.

Insider's View

Peer-Mentoring Can Play a Role in Understanding Disciplinary Conventions

Shelley Garrigan, Spanish Language and Literature

Courtesy of Shelley Garrigan

"I learned [about the conventions of writing in my discipline] by trial and error. In graduate school, the papers that we wrote were expected to be publishable according to the academic standards of literary analysis, and yet I can recall no specific guidelines, rubrics, or feedback from professors geared toward teaching me to shape my writerly approach to the material. In fact, I remember that the feedback on a final paper that I received back from one professor in particular contained little more than a congratulations for so actively 'seeking my voice.' This effort was evidently enough to earn me an A– on the project, and yet I had no idea specifically what he meant. Nor was I sure that I should feel happy about being on the right track or bothered that I wasn't quite there yet.

"Peer-mentoring probably played the most significant role in the development of my professional writerly voice during graduate school. With a small group of fellow students, we regularly made informal arrangements with one another to read each other's papers. The praise and constructive criticism that we offered one another was a fundamental factor in my own development as a writer."

Structural Conventions

From your experience in high school, you might already be familiar with common structural features of writing in the humanities. Arguments in the humanities are generally "thesis-driven"; that is, they make an interpretive claim about a text and then support that claim with specific evidence from the text and sometimes with material from other sources that support their interpretation. By contrast, arguments in the social sciences and the natural sciences are usually driven by a hypothesis that must be tested to come to a conclusion, which encourages a different structure (see Chapters 13 and 14). First we'll talk about how humanistic scholars develop research questions and thesis statements. Then we'll turn our attention to a common structure that many students learn in secondary school to support their thesis statements with evidence, which is loosely based on the structure of the thesis-driven argument, and we'll compare it with published scholarship in the humanities.

Developing Research Questions and Thesis Statements

An important part of the interpretation process is using observations to pose questions about a text. From these close observations, humanists develop *research questions* that they answer through their research. A research question in the humanities is the primary question a scholar asks about a text or set of texts. It is the first step in interpretation because questions grow out of our observations and the patterns or threads that we notice. A *thesis statement* is an answer to a research question and is most persuasive when supported by logical evidence. Thesis statements are discussed in more detail in Chapter 9 as the central claim of an argument. It's important to note that developing a research question works best when it is generated prior to writing a thesis statement. Novice writers can sometimes overlook this crucial step in the writing process and attempt to make a thesis statement without formulating a well-realized research question first.

As John McCurdy mentions earlier in this chapter, some of the most important questions for humanists begin by asking, "Why?" Why does George befriend Lenny in *Of Mice and Men*? Why did Pablo Picasso begin experimenting with cubism in his paintings in the early 1900s? Why did President Lincoln frequently use religious imagery and language in public discourse? To answer such questions, humanistic scholars must collect evidence to support their claims, and in the humanities, evidence often originates from texts.

Insider's View

The Research Is Going to Support Your Own Ideas

Karen Keaton Jackson, Writing Studies

"When we talk about what the paper should look like, I let them know that the research part of your paper is not the longest part. I always say the longest part of your paper is this brainchild, your program that you're coming up with. And I say that purposely because I don't want the research running your paper. This is your paper, your voice. The research is going to support your own ideas.

Get expert advice on incorporating research.

"I think this sends the message that there's more to it than this; you can be more creative and not just rely on the research."

Many students confess to struggling with the process of writing a good thesis statement. A key to overcoming this hurdle is to realize that a good thesis statement comes first from asking thoughtful questions about a text and searching for answers to those questions through observation.

Examples of Research Questions and Corresponding Thesis Statements

Research Question:	Why does F. Scott Fitzgerald use the adjective *great* to describe Gatsby in *The Great Gatsby*?
Thesis Statement:	The adjective *great* is used both ironically and derisively throughout F. Scott Fitzgerald's novel *The Great Gatsby*, as evidenced by the use of Nick Carraway as the narrator and the carnival-like depictions of Gatsby's home and parties.

© Tech Gadgets/Alamy

Research Question:	Why did Georges-Pierre Seurat experiment with pointillism in the mid-1800s?
Thesis Statement:	Georges-Pierre Seurat drew upon the scientific research of Ogden Rood and other color theorists to create paintings with minute brushstrokes in a style now called pointillism, which Seurat believed unified optically to make colors more vivid than in traditional painting styles of the time.

Sunday Afternoon on the Island of La Grande Jatte, 1884–86 (oil on canvas), Seurat, Georges-Pierre (1859–91)/The Art Institute of Chicago, IL, USA /Bridgeman Images

Once you have carefully observed a text, gathered thorough notes, and developed a content/form-response grid as discussed earlier in the chapter, you're in a great position to begin brainstorming and drafting research questions. Recall that we encourage open-ended questions (*who, what, when, where, why,* and *how*) as opposed to closed, *yes/no* questions (questions that can be answered with a *yes* or *no*) as a pivotal step before drafting a thesis statement. Scholars in the humanities often start by asking questions that begin with *why*, but you might also consider questions of *what* and *how*.

Inside Work: Developing *Why*, *What*, and *How* Questions

The process of asking questions after conducting a close reading of a text is part of interpretation, and it can help you generate effective research questions to guide the development of a thesis. In this activity, we walk you through developing potential research questions from your notes on "The Story of an Hour." You could easily follow these steps after observing another kind of text as well.

1. Review your notes on "The Story of an Hour," and develop three questions about the story's content and form using *Why* as a starter word.

2. Next, develop three questions using *What* as your starter word. Try to focus your questions on different aspects of the story's characters, language, style, literary techniques, or narrative perspective.

3. Then use *How* as a starter word to develop three more questions. Again, write your questions with a different aspect of the story as the central focus for each. That is, don't just repeat the same questions from your *What* or *Why* list, inserting *How* instead. Think of different questions that can help address the story's meaning.

Try sharing your questions with a fellow student, and discuss which ones might lead to promising thesis statements to ground an extended interpretation. Effective research questions have the following characteristics.

- They can be answered with specific evidence from the text and from your notes: an effective research question can be answered with evidence and not just feelings or opinions.

- They can be answered in more than one way (i.e., they might require you to make a claim as opposed to being questions of fact): an effective research question is debatable.

Developing Effective Thesis Statements

The thesis statement, or the central claim, asserts *what* the author intends to prove, and it may also provide insight into *how* it will be proven. Providing both of these elements in a thesis allows writers to establish a blueprint for the structure of their entire argument—what we describe as a complex thesis statement in Chapter 9. Based on the thesis alone, a reader can determine the central claim and see how the writer intends to go about supporting it.

In the following example, Sarah Ray provides a thesis for her interpretation of Chopin's "The Story of an Hour." Notice that she includes clues as to how she will prove her claim in the thesis statement itself:

Through Mrs. Mallard's emotional development and the concomitant juxtaposition of the vitality of nature to the repressive indoors, Chopin exposes the role of marriage in the oppression of one's true self and desires.

Blueprint for how Sarah will prove her claim.

Sarah's interpretation of the story, provided as a clear claim.

Although it's not uncommon for thesis statements in humanistic scholarship to remain implied, as opposed to being stated explicitly, most interpretations explicitly assert a claim close to the beginning of the argument, often in the introductory paragraph (or, in a longer piece, paragraphs). Thesis statements may appear as single-sentence statements or may span multiple sentences.

Notice, for example, how Zenia Kish, a professor of American studies, states her claim at the end of the introductory section to her article "'My FEMA People': Hip-Hop as Disaster Recovery in the Katrina Diaspora." In the full text of the article, Kish builds up to this statement through several paragraphs of explanation, which all contribute to her thesis statement, shown here:

I will examine how both national and local New Orleans artists identify with and rebel against the forces of marginalization that produced different senses of being a refugee, and also how they exploit marginality and the hustle as strategies to return home, however different or new that home may be. Providing listeners with an affective mapping of the social, economic, and discursive contradictions that produced the Katrina diaspora as refugees, post-Katrina hip-hop is a critical site for interrogating the ongoing tragedy of African American bodies that don't matter. (p. 673)

Blueprint for how Kish will prove her claim.

Reasons provided for Kish's claim.

Clear statement of Kish's claim.

Five-Paragraph Essays and Other Thesis-Driven Templates

Many students learn to write academic arguments following a template taught in primary and secondary school as the **five-paragraph essay**. This template places a thesis, or claim, at the front of the argument (often at the end of an introductory paragraph), devotes the body of the essay to supporting the thesis, and then offers a final paragraph of conclusion that connects all the parts of the argument by summarizing the main points and reminding readers of the argument's overall significance.

Inside Work: Drafting Thesis Statements

Review the questions and responses you drafted in the "Developing *Why, What,* and *How* Questions" Inside Work activity. Some scholars use "I" in thesis statements, like the example from Zenia Kish, while others avoid using "I." Make sure you pay attention to requirements for the particular type of writing you're doing in your discipline. (Don't hesitate to ask your professor if "I" statements are acceptable.) You can always edit the thesis statement later to take out "I" if needed, but sometimes it helps when figuring out what you want to say to include yourself in the statement. So, for now, consider structuring your responses to your two selected questions as separate thesis statements, using an "I" statement in the following form.

By examining _____ (a, b, c, etc.—the evidence you have found), I argue that _____ (your claim).

Example Thesis Statement: **By examining Mrs. Mallard's emotional development and the juxtaposition of the vitality of nature to the repressive indoors in the story, I argue that Chopin exposes the role of marriage in the story to show the oppression of a person's true self and desires.**

Now test the appropriateness of your claim by asking the following questions about it.

- **Is the thesis debatable?**   Claims in the humanities are propositions, not statements of fact. For example, the assertion that "The Story of an Hour" deals with a wife's response to the news of her husband's death is a fact. It is not, therefore, debatable and will not be a very useful thesis. If, however, we assert that the wife's response to her husband's death demonstrates some characteristic of her relationship with her husband and with the institution of marriage, then we're proposing a debatable claim. This is a proposition we can try to prove, instead of a fact that is already obviously true.

- **Is the thesis significant?**   Claims about texts should offer substantial insight into the meaning of the artifacts. They should account for as much of the artifacts as possible and avoid reducing their complexity. Have you paid attention to all of the evidence you collected, and have you looked at it in context? Are you considering all of the possible elements of the text that might contribute to your interpretation?

- **Does the thesis contribute to an ongoing scholarly conversation?**   Effective thesis statements contribute to an ongoing conversation without repeating what others have already said about the text. How does the claim extend, contradict, or affirm other interpretations of the text?

Once you've analyzed Chopin's story and constructed two separate thesis statements, consider sharing them with a classmate, identifying strengths and weaknesses in both. How is your claim both argumentative and significant? How many direct quotes from the story would help support your points? Which of the two thesis statements offers a more significant insight into the story's meaning?

While the premise behind this structure is based on some conventions of the humanities, following the template too closely could get you into trouble. Not every thesis has three points to prove, for example, giving you three body paragraphs in which to present evidence. And sometimes an introduction needs to be longer than one paragraph—as in the case of Zenia Kish's article "'My FEMA People': Hip-Hop as Disaster Recovery in the Katrina Diaspora," which originally appeared in the academic journal *American Quarterly.* The elements of the template that tend to be consistent in scholarship in the humanities, though, are these:

See more on the transition into college writing.

- Thesis statements generally appear toward the beginning of the argument in an introduction that explains the scope and importance of the topic.

- The body of the argument presents evidence gathered from the text to support the thesis.

- The conclusion connects the parts of the argument together to reinforce the thesis, summarizing the argument's important elements and reminding readers of its overall significance.

A template such as this one can provide a useful place to start as you organize your argument, but be careful not to allow a template to restrict your argument by oversimplifying your understanding of how humanistic scholars structure their writing.

Other Structural Conventions in the Humanities

There are other structural features conventional of writing in the humanities that you should consider when you begin a project in the discipline.

Title

Scholars in the humanities value the artistic and creative use of language, and titles of their work often reflect that value. In contrast to articles in the social sciences and the natural sciences, which often have descriptive titles that directly state the topic of study, articles in the humanities tend to have titles that play with language in creative ways, sometimes using quotations from the text in interesting ways. Humanistic scholars are also notorious for their love of subtitles. Here are a few examples:

- *Burlesque West: Showgirls, Sex, and Sin in Postwar Vancouver*

- "'The Fault of Being Purely French': The Practice and Theory of Landscape Painting in Post-Revolutionary France"

- "Reforming Bodies: Self-Governance, Anxiety, and Cape Colonial Architecture in South Africa, 1665–1860"

- "Resident Franchise: Theorizing the Science Fiction Genre, Conglomerations, and the Future of Synergy"

Paragraphs and Transitions

In arguments in the humanities, paragraphs tend to link back to the thesis by developing a reason and providing evidence. The paragraphs are often connected through **transitional words or phrases** (e.g., *similarly, in addition, in contrast, for example*) that guide readers by signaling shifts between and among the parts of an argument. These words and phrases help the reader understand the order in which the reasons are presented and how one paragraph connects to the preceding one.

Language Conventions in the Humanities

Writing in the humanities generally follows several conventions of language use that might sound familiar because they're often taught in English classes. Keep in mind, though, that even though these conventions are common in the humanities, they aren't necessarily conventional in other disciplinary areas.

Descriptive and Rhetorical Language

Writers in the humanities often use language that is creative or playful, not only when producing artistic texts but sometimes also when writing interpretations of texts. For example, you might notice that writing in the humanities uses figurative language and rhetorical devices (similes, metaphors, and alliteration, for example) more often than in other disciplines. Because writers in the humanities are studying texts so closely, they often pay similarly close attention to the text they're creating, and they take great care to choose precise, and sometimes artistic, language. In many cases, the language not only conveys information; it also engages in rhetorical activity of its own.

Active Voice

Writing in the humanities tends to privilege the use of the active voice rather than the passive voice. Sentences written in the **active voice** clearly state the subject of the sentence, the agent, as the person or thing doing the action. By contrast, the **passive voice** inverts the structure of the sentence, obscuring or eliminating mention of the agent. Let's look at three simple examples.

> **Active Voice:**   The girl chased the dog.
>
> **Passive Voice (agent obscured):**   The dog was chased by the girl.
>
> **Passive Voice (agent not mentioned):**   The dog was chased.

In the first example, the girl is the subject of the sentence and the person (the agent) doing the action—chasing. In the second sentence, the girl is still there, but her presence is less prominent because the dog takes the subject's position at the beginning of the sentence. In the final sentence, the girl is not mentioned at all.

Now let's look at an example from a student paper in the humanities to understand why active voice is usually preferred. In Sarah Ray's interpretation of "The Story of an Hour" (printed in full on pp. 361–66), she writes this sentence in the introduction, using active voice:

> **Active Voice:**   Kate Chopin presents a completely different view of marriage in "The Story of an Hour," published in 1894.

If Sarah were to write the sentence in the passive voice, eliminating the agent, it would look like this:

> **Passive Voice:**   A completely different view of marriage is presented in "The Story of an Hour," published in 1894.

In this case, the active voice is preferred because it gives credit to the author, Kate Chopin, who created the story and the character. Scholars in the humanities value giving credit to the person doing the action, conducting the study, or creating a text. Active voice also provides the clearest, most transparent meaning—another aspect of writing that is valued in the humanities. In Chapters 13 and 14, we'll discuss why the passive voice is sometimes preferable in the social sciences and the natural sciences.

Hedging

In the humanities, writers sometimes hedge the claims that they make when interpreting a text, even though they are generally quite fervent about defending their arguments once established. In fact, the sentence that you just read contains not one but three **hedges**, or qualifiers. Take a look:

> In the humanities, writers tend to hedge the claims that they make when interpreting a text.

Each highlighted phrase limits the scope of the claim in a way that is important to improve accuracy and to allow for other possibilities. In contrast, consider the next claim:

> Writers hedge the claims that they make.

If we had stated our claim that way, not only would it not be true, but you would immediately begin to think of exceptions. Even if we had limited the claim to writers in the humanities, you still might find exceptions to it. As the original sentence is written, we've allowed for other possibilities while still identifying a predominant trend in humanities writing.

Humanistic scholars hedge their claims for several reasons. The disciplines of the humanities don't tend to claim objectivity or neutrality in their research (for more detail, see Chapters 13 and 14), so they allow for other interpretations of and perspectives on texts. As an example, take a look at the first sentence of Dale Jacobs's Conclusion from his article printed earlier in the chapter:

> My process of making meaning from these pages of *Polly and the Pirates* is one of many meanings within the matrix of possibilities inherent in the text. (par. 16)

In this example, Jacobs not only hedges the interpretation he has offered, but he explicitly states that there are many possible meanings in the text he has just analyzed.

Reference Conventions in the Humanities

Scholars in the humanities frequently cite the work of others in their scholarship, especially when supporting an interpretation of a text. They often quote the language from their primary sources exactly instead of summarizing or paraphrasing, because the exact words or details included in the primary source might be important to the argument.

Engagement with Other Scholars

When humanistic scholars cite the work of other scholars, they show how their research contributes to ongoing conversations about a subject—whether they're agreeing with a previous interpretation, extending someone else's interpretation, or offering an alternative one. These citations can strengthen their own argument and provide direct support by showing that another scholar had a similar idea or by demonstrating how another scholar's ideas are incorrect, imprecise, or not fully developed.

As we mentioned in Chapter 10, you can integrate the work of others into your writing by paraphrasing, summarizing, or quoting directly. Scholars in the humanities use all these options, but they quote directly more often than scholars in other disciplines because the exact language or details from their primary sources are often important to their argument.

Take a look at this example from Zenia Kish's article "'My FEMA People': Hip-Hop as Disaster Recovery in the Katrina Diaspora." She situates her argument about the message of hip-hop music after Hurricane Katrina within the work of another scholar, Hazel Carby, who had written about the cultural meaning of the blues. Although Carby was writing about a genre that preceded hip-hop, Kish makes a connection between Carby's interpretation of the blues and her own interpretation of the message of hip-hop at a particular point in history:

> Where the early blues served to "sp[ea]k the desires which were released in the dramatic shift in social relations that occurred in a historical moment of crisis and dislocation," as Hazel Carby observes (36), I would argue that the post-Katrina moment is the first time that mainstream American hip-hop has taken up the thematic of contemporary black migration as a mass phenomenon in any significant way. (p. 674)

Establishing Focus/Stance

Most scholars in the humanities include references to the work of others early in their writing to establish what the focus and stance of their own research will be. Because abstracts appear in humanities scholarship less frequently than in social sciences and natural sciences research, the introduction to an article in the humanities provides a snapshot of how the researcher is positioning himself or herself in the ongoing conversation about an object of study.

As you read scholarship in the humanities, notice how frequently the text references or cites secondary sources in the opening paragraphs. Look at this example from the second page of Dale Jacobs's article on teaching literacy through the use of comics, on page 332 of this chapter. Jacobs situates his work historically among work published about comics in the 1950s, and he also references the research of other scholars who had already written about that history in more detail:

> Prior to their current renaissance, comics were often viewed, at best, as popular entertainment and, at worst, as a dangerous influence on youth. Such attitudes were certainly prevalent in the early 1950s when comics were at their most popular, with critics such as Fredric Wertham voicing the most strenuous arguments against comics in his 1954 book *Seduction of the Innocent* (for an extended discussion of this debate, see Dorrell, Curtis, and Rampal). (par. 3)

In these two sentences, Jacobs positions his work within that of other scholars, showing how it's connected to and distinct from it. Also, by citing the work of Dorrell, Curtis, and Rampal, Jacobs doesn't have to write a lengthy history about a period that's tangentially related to his argument but not central to it.

Documentation

A few documentation styles are prevalent in the humanities, and those styles tend to highlight elements of a source that are important in humanistic study. Many scholars in the humanities, especially in literature and languages, follow the documentation style of the Modern Language Association (MLA). Scholars in history and some other disciplines of the humanities follow the *Chicago Manual of Style* (CMS). When using CMS, scholars can choose between two kinds of citations. In the humanities, researchers generally use the footnote style of documentation.

The values of the humanities are most prevalent in the in-text citations of both MLA and CMS. In MLA, in-text citations appear in parenthetical references that include the author's last name and a page number, with no comma in between (Miller-Cochran et al. 139). The page number is included regardless of whether the cited passage was paraphrased, summarized, or quoted from—unlike in other common styles like APA, where page numbers are usually given only for direct quotations. One reason for including the page number in the MLA in-text citation is that humanistic scholars highly value the original phrasing of an argument or passage and might want to look at the original source. The page number makes searching easy for the reader, facilitating the possibility of examining the original context of a quotation or the original language of something that was paraphrased or summarized.

CMS style also supports looking for the information in the original source by giving the citation information in a footnote on the same page as the referenced material. Additionally, CMS allows authors to include descriptive details in a footnote that provides more information about where a citation came from in a source.

Inside Work: Analyzing Scholarly Writing in the Humanities

Answer the following questions about a scholarly article in the humanities. You might choose to focus on Zenia Kish's article, referenced earlier in this chapter, or find another article on a topic that interests you more.

A. Structural Elements

- **Title**   Does the title of the interpretation seek to entertain, to challenge, or to impress the reader somehow? Does the title reveal anything about the writer and his or her relationship to the intended audience?

- **Thesis**   Can you identify a clear statement of thesis? Where is it located? Does the thesis preview the stages of the claim that will be discussed throughout the paper? In other words, does the thesis explicitly or implicitly provide a "blueprint" for guiding the reader through the rest of the paper? If so, what is it?

- **Paragraphs and Transitions**   Look closely at four successive body paragraphs in the paper. Explain how each paragraph relates to the paper's guiding thesis. How does the writer transition between each of the paragraphs such that his or her ideas in each one stay linked together?

B. Language Elements

- **Descriptive and Rhetorical Language**   Is the language of the text meant only to convey information, or does it engage in rhetorical activity? In other words, do similes, metaphors, or other rhetorical devices demonstrate attempts to be creative with language? If so, what are they?

- **Voice**   Is the voice of the text primarily active or passive?

- **Conviction and Hedging**   Is the writer convinced that his or her interpretation is correct? If so, in what way(s) does specific language convey that conviction? Alternatively, if the writer doesn't seem convinced of the certainty of his or her argument, is there evidence of hedging? That is, does the writer qualify statements with words and phrases such as *tend, suggest, may, it is probable that*, or *it is reasonable to conclude that*? What is the significance of hedging?

C. Reference Elements

- **Engagement with Other Scholars**   Choose two or three examples from the article showing the author's use of another scholar's words or ideas, if appropriate. Explain how the writer uses the words and ideas of another to support his or her own argument. Keep in mind that a writer may use another's word or ideas as direct support by showing that another scholar has the same or similar ideas, or by demonstrating how another scholar's ideas are incorrect, imprecise, or not fully developed. Also, does the writer use block quotations? Does he or she fully integrate others' words and ideas in his or her own sentences? Further, notice the writer's attitude toward other scholars: Does he or she treat other scholars' ideas fully and respectfully? Is there praise for others' ideas? Or are their ideas quickly dismissed? Is there any evidence of hostility in the writer's treatment of other voices?

- **Establishing Focus/Stance**   How frequently does the text reference or cite secondary source materials in the opening paragraphs? What function do such citations or references serve in the article's overall organization?

- **Documentation**   Look closely at examples of internal documentation as well as the writer's Works Cited or References page. What form of documentation applies? Why might the chosen documentation system be appropriate for writing about texts in the humanities?

Genres of Writing in the Humanities

The disciplines included under the umbrella of the humanities vary widely, but several genres occur frequently across disciplines. In her Insider's View response to interview questions, Dr. Shelley Garrigan, an associate professor of Spanish at North Carolina State University, describes the kind of academic writing that she does most frequently.

Similar to scholars in the social sciences and the natural sciences, scholars in the humanities often present their research at conferences and publish their work in journal articles and books. In some fields of the humanities, books are highly valued, and scholars here tend to work individually more frequently than scholars in the social sciences and the natural sciences. Also, many scholars in the humanities engage in creative work and might present it at an art installation, reading, or exhibit.

Textual Interpretation

One of the primary genres that humanities researchers write is an interpretation of a text or set of texts. The research methods and activities outlined in this chapter provide support for interpretations of texts in a variety of fields in the humanities. A textual interpretation makes a clear claim about the object of study and then supports that claim with evidence from the text, and often with evidence drawn from the interpretations of other scholars.

Insider's View

Academics Often Write for Other Academics

Shelley Garrigan, Spanish Language and Literature

Courtesy of Shelley Garrigan

"I write academic articles and am currently editing a book-length manuscript. The articles that I have are peer-reviewed and published in academic journals, in which the readership is largely limited to other specialists in my field or in fields that touch upon what I study. Although the book has the possibility of inviting a wider range of readers, it is contracted with an academic press, and so the reading public that it may attract will most likely also be associated with or limited to academia."

Writing Project: Interpreting a Text

In this Writing Project, you'll complete a close reading and offer an interpretation of a text for an audience of your peers. Begin by selecting a text that you find particularly interesting. You may choose from a host of categories, including the ones listed here.

paintings	advertisements
photographs	short stories
sculptures	poems
buildings	music videos or recordings

As a model for reading closely, follow the procedures outlined earlier in this chapter for creating a content/form-response grid. As you read, view, listen to, and/or study the text and make notes, consider the ways you are interacting with the text by creating a form-function diagram: *What* are you learning, and *how* is the text itself shaping your experience of it?

Once your close reading is complete, formulate a thesis (or a claim) about the text. You'll need to provide evidence to support your thesis from the text itself. You might also include evidence from secondary sources as support. (See Chapter 9 for more information on developing a clear thesis and Chapter 10 for gathering secondary sources.) Remember that depending on the scope of your thesis, your interpretation may or may not require you to do additional research beyond your close reading of the text. As you compose your interpretation, also keep in mind the conventions of structure, language, and reference that typically appear in scholarship in the humanities. Integrate them into your interpretation as appropriate.

Insider Example

Student Interpretation of a Text

In the following essay, "Till Death Do Us Part: An Analysis of Kate Chopin's 'The Story of an Hour,'" Sarah Ray offers an interpretation of Chopin's story that relies on close observation of the text for support. Read her essay below, and pay particular attention to her thesis statement and to her use of evidence. Note how her thesis responds to the question, "How does Mrs. Mallard's marriage function in the story?" Sarah didn't use outside scholars to support her interpretation, so you could also consider how secondary sources might have provided additional support for her claim.

Ray 1

Sarah Ray

English 101

10 April 201–

Till Death Do Us Part: An Analysis of Kate Chopin's "The Story of an Hour"

The nineteenth century saw the publication of some of the most renowned romances in literary history, including the novels of Jane Austen and the Brontë sisters, Charlotte, Emily, and Anne. While their stories certainly have lasting appeal, they also inspired an unrealistic and sometimes unattainable ideal of joyful love and marriage. In this romanticized vision, a couple is merely two halves of a whole; one without the other compromises the happiness of both. The couple's lives, and even destinies, are so intertwined that neither individual worries about what personal desires and goals are being forsaken by commitment to the other. By the end of the century, in her "The Story of an Hour" (1894), Kate Chopin presents a completely different view of marriage. Through the perspective of a female protagonist, Louise Mallard, who believes her husband has just died, the author explores the more challenging aspects of marriage in a time when divorce was rare and disapproved of. Through Mrs. Mallard's emotional development and the concomitant juxtaposition of the vitality of nature to the repressive indoors, Chopin explores marriage as the oppression of one's true self and desires.

Form: Ray uses a common line from marriage vows to indirectly indicate that she focuses on the role of marriage in her interpretation.

Content: Ray clearly states her thesis and provides a preview about how she will develop and support her claim.

Ray 2

Content: In this
paragraph, Ray
develops the first
part of her thesis,
the stages of Mrs.
Mallard's emotional
development.

"The Story of an Hour" begins its critique of marriage by ending one, when the news of Brently Mallard's death is gently conveyed to his wife, Louise. Chopin then follows Mrs. Mallard's different emotional stages in response to her husband's death. When the news is initially broken to Louise, "[s]he did not hear the story as many women have heard the same, with a paralyzed inability to accept its significance" (Chopin par. 3). She instead weeps suddenly and briefly, a "storm of grief" that passes as quickly as it had come (par. 3). This wild, emotional outburst and quick acceptance says a great deal about Louise's feelings toward her marriage. "[S]he had loved [her husband]—sometimes" (par. 15), but a reader may infer that Louise's quick acceptance implies that she has considered an early death for her spouse before. That she even envisions such a dark prospect reveals her unhappiness with the marriage. She begins to see, and even desire, a future without her husband. This desire is expressed when Louise is easily able to see past her husband's death to "a long procession of years to come that would belong to her absolutely" (par. 13). Furthermore, it is unclear whether her "storm of grief" is genuine or faked for the benefit of the family members surrounding her. The "sudden, wild abandonment" (par. 3) with which she weeps almost seems like Louise is trying to mask that she does not react to the news as a loving wife would. Moreover, the display of grief passes quickly; Chopin devotes only a single sentence to the action. Her tears are quickly succeeded by consideration of the prospects of a future on her own.

Form: Ray primarily
uses active voice to
clarify who is doing
the action in her
sentences.

Chopin uses the setting to create a symbolic context for Louise's emotional outburst in response to the news of her husband's death. Louise is informed of Brently's death in the downstairs level of her home: "It was her sister Josephine who told her, in broken sentences; veiled hints that revealed in half concealing" (par. 2). No mention is made of windows, and the only portal that connects to the outside world is the door that admits the bearers of bad news. By excluding a link to nature, Chopin creates an almost claustrophobic environment to symbolize the oppression Louise feels from her marriage. It is no mistake that this setting plays host to Mrs. Mallard's initial emotional

Ray 3

breakdown. Her desires have been suppressed throughout her relationship, and symbolically, she is being suffocated by the confines of her house. Therefore, in this toxic atmosphere, Louise is only able to feel and show the emotions that are expected of her, not those that she truly experiences. Her earlier expression of "grief" underscores this disconnect, overcompensating for emotions that should come naturally to a wife who has just lost her husband, but that must be forced in Mrs. Mallard's case.

Chopin continues Mrs. Mallard's emotional journey only after she is alone and able to process her genuine feelings. After her brief display of grief has run its course, she migrates to her upstairs bedroom and sits in front of a window looking upon the beauty of nature. It is then and only then that Louise gives in not only to her emotions about the day's exploits, but also to those feelings she could only experience after the oppression of her husband died with him—dark desires barely explored outside the boundaries of her own mind, if at all. They were at first foreign to her, but as soon as Louise began to "recognize this thing that was approaching to possess her…she [strove] to beat it back with her will" (par. 10). Even then, after the source of her repression is gone, she fights to stifle her desires and physical reactions. The habit is so engrained that Louise is unable to release her emotions for fear of the unknown, of that which has been repressed for so long. However, "her bosom rose and fell tumultuously…. When she abandoned herself a little whispered word escaped her slightly parted lips. She said it over and over under her breath: 'free, free, free!'…. Her pulses beat fast, and the coursing blood warmed and relaxed every inch of her body" (pars. 10, 11). When she's allowed to experience them, Louise's feelings and desires provide a glimpse into a possible joyous future without her husband, a future where "[t]here would be no powerful will bending hers in that blind persistence with which men and women believe they have a right to impose" (par. 14). Her marriage is over, and Louise appears finally to be able to liberate her true identity and look upon the future with not dread but anticipation.

Form: Ray uses transitions between paragraphs that indicate her organization and connect different ideas.

Ray 4

The author's setting for this scene is crucial in the development of not only the plot but also her critique of marriage. Chopin sought to encapsulate the freedom Louise began to feel in her room with this scene's depiction of nature. For example, Chopin describes the view from Louise's bedroom window with language that expresses its vitality: "She could see in the open square before her house the tops of trees that were all aquiver with the new spring life" (par. 5). She goes on to say, "The delicious breath of rain was in the air. In the street below a peddler was crying his wares…and countless sparrows were twittering in the eaves" (par. 5). The very adjectives and phrases used to describe the outdoors seem to speak of bustling activity and life. This is in stark contrast to the complete lack of vivacity in the description of downstairs.

The language used in the portrayal of these contrasting settings is not the only way Chopin strives to emphasize the difference between the two. She also uses the effect these scenes have on Mrs. Mallard to convey their meaning and depth. On the one hand, the the wild, perhaps faked, emotional outburst that takes place in the stifling lower level of the house leaves Louise in a state of "physical exhaustion that haunted her body and seemed to reach into her soul" (par. 4). On the other hand, Louise "[drank] in a very elixir of life through that open window" (par. 18) of her bedroom through which nature bloomed. Because the author strove to symbolize Mrs. Mallard's marriage with the oppressive downstairs and her impending life without her husband with the open, healing depiction of nature, Chopin suggests that spouses are sometimes better off without each other because marriage can take a physical toll on a person's well-being while the freedom of living for no one but one's self breathes life into even the most burdened wife. After all, "[w]hat could love, the unsolved mystery, count for in face of this possession of self-assertion" (par. 15) felt by Mrs. Mallard in the wake of her emancipation from oppression?

Chopin goes on to emphasize the healing capabilities and joy of living only for one's self by showing the consequences of brutally taking it all away, in one quick turn of a latchkey. With thoughts of

Form: When making assumptions about the author's intentions, Ray sometimes uses hedging words — in this case, "seem to."

her freedom of days to come, "she carried herself unwittingly like a goddess of Victory. She clasped her sister's waist, and together they descended the stairs" (par. 20). Already Chopin is preparing the reader for Mrs. Mallard's looming fate. Not only is she no longer alone in her room with the proverbial elixir of life pouring in from the window, but also she is once again sinking into the oppression of the downstairs, an area that embodies all marital duties as well as the suffocation of Louise's true self and desires. When Brently Mallard enters the house slightly confused but unharmed, the loss of her newly found freedom is too much for Louise's weak heart to bear. Chopin ends the story with a hint of irony: "When the doctors came they said she had died of heart disease—of joy that kills" (par. 23). It may be easier for society to accept that Mrs. Mallard died of joy at seeing her husband alive, but in all actuality, it was the violent death of her future prospects and the hope she had allowed to blossom that sent Louise to the grave. Here lies Chopin's ultimate critique of marriage: when there was no other viable escape, only death could provide freedom from an oppressive marriage. By killing Louise, Chopin solidifies this ultimatum and also suggests that even death is kinder when the only other option is the slow and continuous addition of the crushing weight of marital oppression.

In "The Story of an Hour," Kate Chopin challenges the typical, romanticized view of love and marriage in the era in which she lived. She chooses to reveal some of the sacrifices one must make in order to bind oneself to another in matrimony. Chopin develops these critiques of marriage through Louise Mallard's emotional responses to her husband's supposed death, whether it is a quick, if not faked, outburst of grief, her body's highly sexualized awakening to the freedoms to come, or the utter despair at finding that he still survives. These are not typical emotions for a "grieving" wife, and Chopin uses this stark contrast as well as the concomitant juxtaposition of nature to the indoors to further emphasize her critique. Louise Mallard may have died in the quest to gain independence from the oppression of her true self and desires, but now she is at least "[f]ree! Body and soul free!" (par. 16).

Content: Ray provides a broad summary of her argument in the concluding paragraph.

Content: In her last sentence, Ray reveals a portion of the significance of the story to an understanding of marital oppression.

Ray 6

Form: Ray cites her source using MLA format.

Work Cited

Chopin, Kate. "The Story of an Hour." 1894. Ann Woodlief's Web
Study Texts, www.vcu.edu/engweb/webtexts/hour.

Discussion Questions

1. Describe how Sarah Ray's thesis is both debatable and significant.
2. How does the author use evidence from the text to support her interpretation?
3. How has she organized her interpretation?
4. How could it help Sarah's interpretation if she looked at the work of other scholars who have studied Chopin's story?

Artistic Texts

Many scholars in the humanities are creators of artistic texts. It has been said about artistic texts that when you create them, they're the arts, and when you study them, they're the humanities. This formulation oversimplifies somewhat, but it's helpful as shorthand for thinking about the relationship between arts and humanities. Artistic texts can occur in many different forms and media. Some of the more common artistic texts that students create include the following:

paintings	songs	stories
sculptures	pottery	video games
poems	models	short films

The process that you follow to create an artistic text will vary according to the type of text you create. In a writing class, an instructor might ask you to create an artistic text and then reflect on the process of creating it. Additionally, he or she might ask you to interpret your own text or that of another student.

Writing Project: Creating an Artistic Text

In this three-part project, you'll create a text, reflect on the process of creating it, and then develop a preliminary interpretation of the text. Your assessment will be based primarily on your reflection on and close reading of your text. We encourage you to try something new; indeed, you might discover a talent you didn't realize you had, or you might understand something new about the creative process by trying an art form you haven't experimented with before.

Part 1

Choose an art form that you'd like to experiment with for this activity. You might try something that you've done before, or you might want to experiment with something new. Some possibilities are listed below.

- sketching or painting a figure or a landscape
- composing a poem or a song
- using a pottery wheel or sculpting with clay
- writing a short story
- creating an advertisement or Public Service Announcement for an issue important to you
- designing a video game
- directing a (very) short film

Part 2

After completing the creative portion of this project, respond to the following prompts for reflection about the process of creating the text.

- First reflect on the process of creating your text and what you learned from it.
- What was the most challenging part of the project for you?
- What was the most enjoyable part of the project?
- What did you discover about yourself as you participated in this activity?
- Did you find yourself trying to imitate other examples you've seen, heard, or experienced, or were you trying to develop something very different?
- What inspired you as you were working?

Part 3

Once you've reflected on the process of creating your text, examine the text closely and take notes regarding the elements of it that you see as important to its meaning. Once you've developed notes, do the following.

1. Complete a content/form-response grid to highlight the notes you see as most important for constructing meaning from the text. Be sure to articulate responses about why you see each note as important and relevant toward interpreting meaning.

2. Brainstorm a list of *how*, *what*, and *why* questions regarding various aspects of the text related to its meaning(s).

3. Select one or two questions that seem most promising to try and answer. You should be able to draw direct evidence from the text (and your notes) that supports your answer.

4. Select and rewrite the best question that has evidence, and then write a thesis statement.

You should construct the remainder of your interpretation of the text based on the thesis statement. Try to develop an interpretation that's organized with clear reasons and evidence (see Chapter 9). Use examples actually taken from your text as evidence.

Tip Sheet   Reading and Writing in the Humanities

- **In the humanities, scholars seek to understand and interpret human experience**. To do so, they often create, analyze, and interpret texts.

- **Scholars in the humanities often conduct close readings of texts** to interpret and make meaning from them, and they might draw on a particular theoretical perspective to ask questions about those texts.

- **Keeping a content/form-response grid can help you track important elements of a text** and your response to them as you do a close reading.

- **Writing in the humanities also draws on the interpretations of others**, either as support or to position an interpretation within other prior scholarship.

- **Arguments in the humanities generally begin with a thesis statement** that asserts *what* the author intends to prove, and it may also provide insight into *how* the author will prove it. Each section of the argument should provide support for the thesis.

Chapter 13 Reading and Writing in the Social Sciences

Introduction to the Social Sciences

Social scientists study human behavior and interaction along with the systems and social structures we create to organize our world. Professionals in the fields of the **social sciences** help us understand why we do what we do as well as how processes (political, economic, personal, etc.) contribute to our lives. As the image at the bottom of this page shows, the social sciences encompass a broad area of academic inquiry that comprises numerous fields of study. These include sociology, psychology, anthropology, communication studies, and political science, among others.

Maybe you've observed a friend or family member spiral into addictive or self-destructive behavior and struggled to understand how it happened. Maybe you've spent time wondering how cliques were formed and maintained among students in your high school, or how friends are typically chosen. Perhaps larger social issues like war, poverty, or famine concern you the most. If you've ever stopped to consider any of these kinds of issues, then you've already begun to explore the world of the social sciences.

Social scientist Kevin Rathunde, who teaches at the University of Utah, shares his perspective on the work and writing of social scientists in Insider's View features in this chapter. Excerpts from Dr. Rathunde's paper entitled "Middle School Students' Motivation and Quality of Experience: A Comparison of Montessori and Traditional School Environments," which he wrote and published with a colleague, Mihaly Csikszentmihalyi, in the

Andrea Tsurumi

American Journal of Education, also appear throughout this chapter. Rathunde and Csikszentmihalyi's study investigated the types of educational settings that contribute to the best outcomes for students. Specifically, they compared traditional public school environments with those of Montessori schools to assess how students learn, interact, and perceive the quality of their experiences in these differing environments.

As a social scientist, you might study issues like therapy options for autism, the effects of substance abuse on families, peer pressure, the dynamics of dating, social networking websites, stress, or the communication practices of men and women. You might study family counseling techniques or the effects of divorce on teens. Or perhaps you might wonder (as Rathunde and Csikszentmihalyi do) about the effects of differing educational environments on student satisfaction and success.

Whatever the case may be, if you're interested in studying human behavior and understanding why we do what we do, you'll want to consider further how social scientists conduct research and how they present their results in writing. As in all the academic domains, progress in the social sciences rests upon researchers' primary skills at making observations of the world around them.

Insider's View

Social Scientists Care about the Conditions That Allow People to Connect

Kevin Rathunde, Social Sciences

"There are many branches of social science. In general, as the name 'social science' implies, the main focus of scientific action and dialogue is on people and social processes. My training was in an

Courtesy of Kevin Rathunde

interdisciplinary program on human development at the University of Chicago. As a result, my perspective on social science tends to reach across disciplinary boundaries. I also work in an interdisciplinary department at the University of Utah. The professional conversations I have with colleagues—both within and outside of my department—are wide-ranging. If there is a common denominator to them, it might be the well-being of individuals, families, and society. Social scientists care about the conditions that allow people to connect with others, participate in the lives of their communities, and reach their full potential."

Inside Work: Observing Behavior

For this activity, pick a place to sit and observe people. You can choose a place that you enjoy going to regularly, but make sure you can observe and take notes without being interrupted or distracted. For example, you might observe people in your school's library or another space on campus. Try to avoid places where you could feel compelled to engage in conversation with people you know.

For ten minutes, freewrite about the people around you and what they're doing. Look for the kinds of interactions and engagements that characterize their behavior. Then draft some questions that you think a social scientist observing the same people might ask about them. For example, if you wrote about behaviors you observed in a college classroom or lecture hall, you might consider questions like the ones listed here.

- How are students arranged around the room? What does the seating arrangement look like? What effect does the room's arrangement have on classroom interaction, if any?

- What are students doing? Are they taking notes? Writing? Sleeping? Typing? Texting? Listening? Doing something else?

- Are students doing different things in different parts of the room, or are the activities uniform throughout the room? Why?

- What is the instructor doing in the classroom? Where is he or she positioned? How are students responding?

- Are students using technology? If so, what kinds of technology? What are they using the technology to do?

- If people are interacting with one another in the classroom, what are they talking about? How are they interacting? How are they positioned when they interact? Are numerous people contributing to the conversation? Is someone leading the conversation? If so, how?

See how many different behaviors, people, and interactions you can observe and how many questions you can generate. You might do this activity in the same place with a partner and then compare notes. What did you or your partner find in common? What did you each observe that was unique? Why do you think you noticed the things you did? What was the most interesting thing you observed?

Research in the Social Sciences

As we've indicated, the social sciences comprise a diverse group of academic fields that aim to understand human behavior and systems. But it may be difficult to see the commonalities among these disciplines that make it possible to refer to them as social sciences. One of the ways we can link these disciplines and the values they share, beyond their basic concern for why and how people do things, is by considering how social scientists conduct and report their research.

The Role of Theory

Unlike in the natural sciences, where research often takes place in a laboratory setting under controlled conditions, research in the social sciences is necessarily "messier." The reason is fairly simple: human beings and the systems they organize cannot generally be studied in laboratory conditions, where variables are controlled. For this reason, social scientists do not generally establish fixed laws or argue for absolute truths, as natural scientists sometimes do. For instance, while natural scientists are able to argue, with certainty, that a water molecule contains two atoms of hydrogen and one of oxygen, social scientists cannot claim to know the absolute fixed nature of a person's psychology (why a person does what she does in any particular instance) or that of a social system or problem (why homelessness persists, for instance).

Much social science research is therefore based on **theories of human behavior and human systems**, which are propositions that scholars use to explain specific phenomena. Theories can be evaluated on the basis of their ability to explain why or how or when a phenomenon occurs, and they generally result from research that has been replicated time and again to confirm their accuracy, appropriateness, and usefulness. Still, it's important to understand that theories are not laws; they are not absolute, fixed, or perfect explanations. Instead, social science theories are always being refined as research on particular social phenomena develops. The Rathunde and Csikszentmihalyi study we highlight in the Insider's View boxes with Dr. Rathunde, for instance, makes use of goal theory and optimal experience theory as part of the research design to evaluate the type of middle school environment that best contributes to students' education.

Insider Example

Exploring Social Science Theory

Read the following excerpt from Kalervo Oberg's "Cultural Shock: Adjustment to New Cultural Environments," and then reflect on his theory by answering the questions that follow the selection. Oberg (1901–1973) was a pioneer in economic anthropology and applied anthropology, and his foundational work in this study has been cited hundreds of times by sociologists and anthropologists who are interested in the phenomenon. Oberg himself coined the term *culture shock*.

Kalervo Oberg

Excerpt from "Cultural Shock: Adjustment to New Cultural Environments"

Culture shock is precipitated by the anxiety that results from losing all our familiar signs and symbols of social intercourse. These signs or cues include the thousand and one ways in which we orient ourselves to the situations of daily life: when to shake hands and what to say when we meet people, when and how to give tips, how to give orders to servants, how to make purchases, when to accept and when to refuse invitations, when to take statements seriously and when not. Now these cues which may be words, gestures, facial expressions, customs, or norms are acquired by all of us in the course of growing up and are as much a part of our culture as the language we speak or the beliefs we accept. All of us depend for our peace of mind and our efficiency on hundreds of these cues, most of which we do not carry on the level of conscious awareness.

Now when an individual enters a strange culture, all or most of these familiar cues are removed. He or she is like a fish out of water. No matter how broad-minded or full of good will you may be, a series of props have been knocked from under you, followed by a feeling of frustration and anxiety. People react to the frustration in much the same way. First they *reject* the environment which causes the discomfort: "the ways of the host country are bad because they make us feel bad." When Americans or other foreigners in a strange land get together to grouse about the host country and its people—you can be sure they are suffering from culture shock. Another phase of culture shock is *regression.* The home environment suddenly assumes a tremendous importance. To an American everything American becomes irrationally glorified. All the difficulties and problems are forgotten and only the good things back home are remembered. It usually takes a trip home to bring one back to reality.

Symptoms of Culture Shock

Some of the symptoms of culture shock are: excessive washing of the hands; excessive concern over drinking water, food, dishes, and bedding; fear of physical contact with attendants or servants; the absent-minded, far-away stare (sometimes called "the tropical stare"); a feeling of helplessness and a desire for dependence on long-term residents of one's own nationality; fits of anger over delays and other minor frustrations; delay and outright refusal to learn the language of the host country; excessive fear of being cheated, robbed, or injured; great concern over minor pains and irruptions of the skin; and finally, that terrible longing to be back home, to be able to have a good cup of coffee and a piece of apple pie, to walk into that corner drugstore, to visit one's relatives, and, in general, to talk to people who really make sense.

Individuals differ greatly in the degree in which culture shock affects them. Although not common, there are individuals who cannot live in foreign countries. Those who have seen people go through culture shock and on to a satisfactory adjustment can discern steps in the process. During the first few weeks most individuals are fascinated by the new. They stay in hotels and associate with nationals who speak their language and are polite and gracious to foreigners. This honeymoon stage may last from a few days or weeks to six months depending on circumstances. If one is a very important person he or she will be shown the show places, will be pampered and petted, and in a press interview will speak glowingly about progress, good will, and international amity, and if he returns home he may well write a book about his pleasant if superficial experience abroad.

But this Cook's tour type of mentality does not normally last if the foreign visitor remains abroad and has seriously to cope with real conditions of life. It is then that the second stage begins, characterized by a hostile and aggressive attitude towards the host country. This hostility evidently grows out of the genuine difficulty which the visitor experiences in the process of adjustment. There is maid trouble, school trouble, language trouble, house trouble, transportation trouble, shopping trouble, and the fact that people in the host country are largely indifferent to all these troubles. They help but they just don't understand your great concern over these difficulties. Therefore, they must be insensible and unsympathetic to you and your worries. The result, "I just don't like them." You become aggressive, you band together with your fellow countrymen and criticize the host country, its ways, and its people. But this criticism is not an objective appraisal but a derogatory one. Instead of trying to account for conditions as they are through an honest analysis of the actual conditions and the historical circumstances which have created them, you talk as if the difficulties you experienced are more or less created by the people of the host country for your special discomfort. You take refuge in the colony of your countrymen and its cocktail circuit, which often becomes the fountain-head of emotionally charged labels known as stereotypes. This is a peculiar kind of invidious shorthand which caricatures the host country and its people in a negative manner. The "dollar-grasping American" and the "indolent Latin American" are samples of mild forms of stereotypes. The use of stereotypes may salve the ego of someone with a severe case of culture shock but it certainly does not lead to any genuine understanding of the host country and its people. This second stage of culture shock is in a sense a crisis in the disease. If you overcome it, you stay; if not, you leave before you reach the stage of a nervous breakdown.

If the visitor succeeds in getting some knowledge of the language and begins to get around by himself, he is beginning to open the way into the new cultural environment. The visitor still has difficulties but he takes a "this is my cross and I have to bear it" attitude. Usually in this stage the visitor takes a superior attitude to people of the host country. His sense of humor begins to exert itself. Instead of criticizing he jokes about the people and even cracks jokes about his or her own difficulties. He or she is now on the way to recovery. And there is also the poor devil who is worse off than yourself whom you can help, which in turn gives you confidence in your ability to speak and get around.

In the fourth stage your adjustment is about as complete as it can be. The visitor now accepts the customs of the country as just another way of living. You operate within the new milieu without a feeling of anxiety although there are moments of strain. Only with a complete grasp of all the cues of social intercourse will this strain disappear. For a long time the individual will understand what the national is saying but he is not always sure what the national means. With a complete adjustment you not only accept the foods, drinks, habits, and customs, but actually begin to enjoy them. When you go on home leave you may even take things back with you and if you leave for good you generally miss the country and the people to whom you have become accustomed.

Discussion Questions

1. In your own words, define what you think Kalervo Oberg means by *culture shock*.

2. What are the four stages of culture shock, according to Oberg?

3. Oberg's essay was written more than half a century ago. In what ways does it seem dated? In what ways does it strike you as still valid or relevant?

Inside Work: Tracing a Theory's Development

As we indicated, theories in the social sciences exist to be developed and refined over time, based on our developing understandings of a social phenomenon as a result of continued research. Conduct a search (using the web or your academic database access) to determine if you can make a rough estimate as to how often Oberg's theory of culture shock has been cited in published research. You might even make a time-line, or another visual representation, of what you find. As you look at the research, identify any evidence or indicators that the theory has been updated or altered since its first appearance. In what ways has the theory been refined?

Research Questions and Hypotheses

As we've noted throughout this book, research questions are typically formulated on the basis of observations. In the social sciences, such observations focus on human behavior, human systems, and/or the interactions between the two. Observations of a social phenomenon can give rise to questions about how a phenomenon operates or what effects it has on people or, as Rathunde suggests, how it could be changed to improve individuals' well-being. For example, in their social science study, "'Under the Radar': Educators and Cyberbullying in Schools," W. Cassidy, K. Brown, and M. Jackson (2012) offer the following as guiding research questions for their investigation:

> Our study of educators focused on three research questions: Do they [educators] consider cyberbullying a problem at their school and how familiar are they with the extent and impact among their students? What policies and practices are in place to prevent or counter cyberbullying? What solutions do they have for encouraging a kinder online world? (p. 522)

Research that is designed to inform a theory of human behavior or to provide data that contributes to a fuller understanding of some social or political structure (i.e., to answer a social science research question) also often begins with the presentation of a *hypothesis*. As we saw in Chapter 9, a hypothesis is a testable proposition that provides an answer or predicts an outcome in response to the research question(s) at hand. It's important to note that not all social science reports include a statement of hypothesis. Some social science research establishes its focus by presenting the questions that guide researchers' inquiry into a particular phenomenon instead of establishing a hypothesis. C. Kern and K. Ko (2010) present the following hypothesis, or predicted outcome, for their social science study, "Exploring Happiness and Performance at Work." The researchers make a prediction concerning what they believed their research would show before presenting their findings later in their research report:

> The intent of this analysis was to review how happiness and performance related to each other in this workplace. It is the authors' belief that for performance to be sustained in an organization, individuals and groups within that organization need to experience a threshold level of happiness. It is difficult for unhappy individuals and work groups to continue performing at high levels without appropriate leadership intervention. (p. 5)

Hypotheses differ from *thesis statements*, which are more commonly associated with arguments in the humanities. While thesis statements offer researchers' final conclusions on a topic or issue, hypothesis statements offer a predicted outcome. The proposition expressed in a hypothesis may be either accepted or rejected based on the results of the research. For example, an educational researcher might hypothesize that teachers' use of open-ended questioning increases students' level of participation in class. However, the researcher wouldn't be able to confirm or reject such a hypothesis until the end of his or her research report.

Inside Work: Developing Hypotheses

1. For five minutes, brainstorm *social science* topics or issues that have affected your life. One approach is to consider issues that are causing you stress in your life right now. Examples might include peer pressure, academic performance, substance abuse, dating, or a relative's cancer treatment.

2. Once you have a list of topics, focus in on two or three that you believe have had the greatest impact on you personally. Next, generate a list of possible *research questions* concerning the topics that, if answered, would offer you a greater understanding of them. Examples: *What triggers most people to try their first drink of alcohol? What types of therapies are most effective for working with children on the autism spectrum? What kinds of technology actually aid in student learning?*

3. When you've reached the stage of proposing a possible answer to one or more of your questions, then you're ready to state a hypothesis. Try proposing a *hypothesis*, or testable proposition, as an answer to one of the research questions you've posed. For example, if your research question is *What triggers most people to try their first drink of alcohol?* then your hypothesis might be *Peer pressure generally causes most people to try their first drink of alcohol, especially for those who try their first drink before reaching the legal drinking age.*

Methods

Research in the diverse fields of the social sciences is, as you probably suspect, quite varied, and social scientists collect data to answer their research questions or test their hypotheses in several different ways. Their choice of methods is directly influenced by the kinds of questions they ask in any particular instance, as well as by their own disciplinary backgrounds. In his Insider's View on page 378, Kevin Rathunde highlights the connection between the kinds of research questions a social scientist asks and the particular methods the researcher uses to answer those questions.

We can group most of the research you're likely to encounter in the fields of the social sciences into three possible types: quantitative, qualitative, and mixed methods. Researchers make choices about which types of methods they'll employ in any given situation based on the nature of their line of inquiry. A particular research question may very well dictate the methods used to answer that question. If you wanted to determine the number of homeless veterans in a specific city, for instance, then collecting numerical, or quantitative, data would likely suffice to answer that question. However, if you wanted to know what factors affect the rates of homelessness among veterans in your community, then you would need to do more than tally the number of homeless veterans. You'd need to collect a different type of data to help construct an answer—perhaps responses to surveys or interview questions.

Quantitative Methods

Quantitative studies include those that rely on collecting numerical data and performing statistical analyses to reveal findings in research. Basic statistical data, like those provided by *means* (averages), *modes* (most often occurring value), and *medians* (middle values), are fundamental to quantitative social science research. More sophisticated statistical procedures commonly used in professional quantitative studies include correlations, chi-square tests, analysis of variance (ANOVA), and multivariate analysis of variance (MANOVA), as well as regression model testing, just to name a few. Not all statistical procedures are appropriate in all situations, however, so researchers must carefully select procedures based on the nature of their data and the kinds of findings they seek. Researchers who engage in advanced statistical procedures as part of their methods are typically highly skilled in such procedures. At the very least, these researchers consult or work in cooperation with statisticians to design their studies and/or to analyze their data.

Insider's View

A Good Question Is Usually Worth Looking at from Multiple Perspectives

Kevin Rathunde, Social Sciences

Courtesy of Kevin Rathunde

"I have strong interests in how people experience their lives and what helps them stay interested, engaged, and on a path of lifelong learning and development. I tend to ask questions about the quality of life and experience. How are students experiencing their time in class? When are they most engaged? How does being interested affect the learning process? How can parents and teachers create conditions in homes and families that facilitate interest?

"The fields of developmental psychology and educational psychology are especially important to my work. The questions I ask, therefore, are framed the way a developmental or educational psychologist might ask them. Social scientists from other disciplines would probably look at the same topic (i.e., human engagement and interest) in a different way. My daughter is studying anthropology in graduate school. She would probably approach this topic from a cultural perspective. Where I might design a study using questionnaires that are administered in family or school contexts, she might focus on interviews and cultural frameworks that shed light on the meaning and organization of educational institutions. Although my research is primarily quantitative and uses statistical analysis to interpret the results, I have also used a variety of qualitative techniques (i.e., interviews and observations) over the years. A good question is usually worth looking at from multiple perspectives."

You may find, in fact, that a team of researchers collaborating on a social science project often includes individuals who are also experienced statisticians. Obviously, we don't expect you to be familiar with the details of statistical procedures, but it's important that you be able to notice when researchers rely on statistical methods to test their hypotheses and to inform their results.

Also, you should take note of how researchers incorporate discussion of such methods into their writing. In the following example, we've highlighted a few elements in the reporting that you'll want to notice when reading social science studies that make use of statistical procedures:

- **Procedure**   What statistical procedures are used?

- **Variables**   What variables are examined in the procedures?

- **Results**   What do the statistical procedures reveal?

- **Participants**   From whom are the data collected, and how are those individuals chosen?

In their study, "Middle School Students' Motivation and Quality of Experience: A Comparison of Montessori and Traditional School Environments," Rathunde and Csikszentmihalyi report on the statistical procedures they used to examine different types of schools:

The first analysis compared the main motivation and quality-of-experience variables across school type (Montessori vs. traditional) and grade level (sixth vs. eighth) using a two-way MANCOVA with parental education, gender, and ethnic background as covariates. Significant differences were found for school context (Wilks's lambda = .84, $F(5, 275) = 10.84$, $p < .001$), indicating that students in the two school contexts reported differences in motivation and quality of experience. After adjusting for the covariates, the multivariate eta squared indicated that 17 percent of the variance of the dependent variables was associated with the school context factor. The omnibus test for grade level was not significant (Wilks's lambda = .99, $F(5, 275) = .68$, $p = .64$), indicating that students in sixth and eighth grade reported similar motivation and quality of experience. Finally, the omnibus test for the interaction of school context x grade level was not significant (Wilks's lambda = .97, $F(5, 275) = 2.02$, $p = .08$). None of the multivariate tests for the covariates—parental education, gender, and ethnic background—reached the .05 level. (p. 357)

Variables examined, participants or populations involved in the study, and statistical procedure employed—MANCOVA, or a multivariate analysis of covariance—are identified.

Results of the statistical procedure are identified.

Qualitative Methods

Qualitative studies generally rely on language, observation, and reporting of individual human experiences to reveal findings in research. Research reports often communicate these methods through the form of a study's results, which rely on in-depth narrative reporting. Methods for collecting data in qualitative studies include interviews, document analysis, surveys, and observations.

We can see examples of these methods put into practice in Barbara Allen's "Environmental Justice, Local Knowledge, and After-Disaster Planning in New Orleans" (2007), published in the academic social science journal *Technology and Society*. In this example, we've highlighted a few elements in the reporting that you'll want to notice when reading qualitative research methods:

- **Method**   What method of data collection is used?

- **Data**   What data is gathered from that method?

- **Results**   What are the results? What explanation do the researchers provide for the data, or what meaning do they find in the data?

- **Participants**   From whom is the data collected, and how are these individuals chosen?

Participants — Six months after the hurricane I contacted public health officials and researchers, many of whom were reluctant to talk. One who did talk

Data-collection method: interview — asked that I did not use her name, but she made some interesting observations. According to my informant, health officials were in a

Data, followed by explanation or meaning of data — difficult position. Half a year after the devastation, only 25% of the city's residents had returned; a year after the storm, that number rose to about 40%. Negative publicity regarding public health issues would deter such repatriation, particularly families with children who had not returned in any large numbers to the city. The informant also

Data — told me to pursue the state public health websites where the most prominent worries were still smoking and obesity, not Hurricane Katrina. While the information on various public health websites did eventually reflect concerns about mold, mildew, and other contamination, it was never presented as the health threat that independent environmental scientists, such as Wilma Subra, thought it was. (pp. 154–55)

...

Participant — About five months after Hurricane Katrina, I received an e-mail from a high school student living in a rural parish west of New Orleans along the Mississippi River (an area EJ advocates have renamed Cancer Alley). After Hurricane Katrina, an old landfill near her house was opened to receive aste and began emitting noxious odors. She took samples of the "black ooze" from the site and contacted the Louisiana Department of Environmental Quality, only to be told that the landfill was accepting only construction waste, and the smell she described was probably decaying gypsum board. I suspect her story will be repeated many times across south Louisiana as these marginal waste sites receive the debris from homes and businesses ruined by the hurricane. The full environmental impact of Hurricane Katrina's waste and its hastily designated removal sites will not be known for many years. (p. 155)

Explanation or meaning of data.

Mixed Methods

Studies that make use of both qualitative and quantitative data-collection techniques are generally referred to as mixed-methodology studies. Rathunde and Csikszentmihalyi's study, "Middle School Students' Motivation and Quality of Experience: A Comparison of Montessori and Traditional School Environments," used mixed methods: the authors report findings from both qualitative and quantitative data. In this excerpt, they share results from qualitative data they collected as they sought to distinguish among the types of educational settings selected for participation in their study:

After verifying that the demographic profile of the two sets of schools was similar, the next step was to determine if the schools differed with respect to the five selection criteria outlined above. We used a variety of qualitative sources to verify contextual differences, including observations by the research staff; teacher and parent interviews; school newsletters, information packets, mission statements, and parent teacher handbooks; summaries from board of education and school council meetings; and a review of class schedules and textbook choices discussed in strategic plans. These sources also provided information about the level of middle grade reform that may or may not have been implemented by the schools and whether the label "traditional" was appropriate. (p. 64)

However, Rathunde and Csikszentmihalyi's central hypothesis, "that students in Montessori middle schools would report more positive perceptions of their school environment and their teachers, more often perceive their classmates as friends, and spend more time in collaborative and/or individual work rather than didactic educational formats such as listening to a lecture" (p. 68), was tested by using quantitative methods:

> The main analyses used two-way multivariate analysis of covariance (MANCOVA) with school type (Montessori vs. traditional) and grade level (sixth vs. eighth) as the two factors. Gender, ethnicity, and parental education were covariates in all of the analyses. Overall multivariate F tests (Wilks's lambda) were performed first on related sets of dependent variables. If an overall F test was significant, we performed univariate ANOVAs as follow-up tests to the MANCOVAs. If necessary, post hoc analyses were done using Bonferroni corrections to control for Type I errors. Only students with at least 15 ESM signals were included in the multivariate analyses, and follow-up ANOVAs used students who had valid scores on all of the dependent variables. (p. 68)

Addressing Bias

Because social scientists study people and organizations, their research is considered more valuable when conducted within a framework that minimizes the influence of personal or researcher bias on the study's outcome(s). When possible, social scientists strive for **objectivity** (in quantitative research) or **neutrality** (in qualitative research) in their research. This means that researchers undertake all possible measures to reduce the influence of biases on their research. Bias is sometimes inevitable, however, so social science research places a high value on honesty and transparency in the reporting of data. Each of the methods outlined above requires social scientists to engage in rigorous procedures and checks (e.g., ensuring appropriate sample sizes and/or using multiple forms of qualitative data) to ensure that the influence of any biases is as limited as possible.

LaunchPadSolo

A political scientist weighs in on avoiding bias.

Inside Work: Considering Research Methods

In the previous activity, we asked you to consider possible hypotheses, or testable propositions, to the research questions you posed. Now choose one of your hypothesis statements, and consider the types of methods that might be appropriate for testing the hypothesis. Think about the kinds of data you'll generate from the different methods.

- Would quantitative, qualitative, or mixed research methods be the most appropriate for testing your hypothesis? Why?

- What specific methods would you use—statistical procedures, surveys, observations, interviews? Why?

- Who would you want to have participate in your research? From whom would you need to collect your data in order to answer your research question?

The IRB Process and Use of Human Subjects

All research, whether student or faculty initiated and directed, must treat its subjects, or participants, with the greatest of care and consider the ethical implications of all its procedures. Although institutions establish their own systems and procedures for verifying the ethical treatment of subjects, most of these include an **institutional review board (IRB)**, or a committee of individuals whose job is to review research proposals in light of ethical concerns for subjects and applicable laws. Such proposals typically include specific forms of documentation that identify a study's purpose; rigorously detail the research procedures to be followed; evaluate potential risks and rewards of a study, especially for study participants; and ensure (whenever possible) that participants are fully informed about a study and the implications of their participation in it.

We encourage you to learn more about the IRB process at your own institution and, when appropriate, to consider your own research in light of the IRB policies and procedures established for your institution. Many schools maintain informational, educational, and interactive websites. You'll notice similarities in the mission statements of institutional review boards from a number of research-intensive universities:

Duke University: To ensure the protection of human research subjects by conducting scientific and ethical review of research studies while providing leadership and education for the research community.

The George Washington University: To support [the] research community in the conduct of innovative and ethical research by providing guidance, education, and oversight for the protection of human subjects.

University of New Mexico: To promote the safety and protection of individuals involved in human research by providing support, guidance, and education to facilitate ethical and scientifically sound research.

Conventions of Writing in the Social Sciences

In light of the variety of research methods used by social scientists, it's not surprising that there are also a number of ways social scientists report their research findings. In this section, we highlight general conventional expectations of *structure*, *language*, and *reference* that social scientists follow to communicate their research to one another. Understanding these conventions, we believe, can help foster your understanding of this academic domain more broadly.

Aya Matsuda is a linguist and social science researcher at Arizona State University, where she studies the use of English as an international language, the integration of a "World Englishes" perspective into U.S. education, and the ways bilingual writers negotiate identity. In her Insider's View, Dr. Matsuda explains that she learned the conventions of writing as a social scientist, and more particularly as a linguist, "mostly through writing, getting feedback, and revising."

As Dr. Matsuda also suggests, reading can be an important part of understanding the writing of a discipline. Furthermore, reading academic writing with a particular focus on the rhetorical elements used is a powerful way to acquire insight into the academic discipline itself, as well as a way to learn the literacy practices that professional writers commonly follow in whatever academic domain you happen to be studying.

Insider's View

Reading the Kind of Writing I Needed to Do Helped Me Learn about the Conventions

Aya Matsuda, Linguistics

Courtesy of Aya Matsuda

"In undergraduate and graduate courses, I had writing assignments that are similar to the kind of writing I do now. For those, I wrote (often using the published materials as a model) and got feedback from the professors. Sometimes I had a chance to revise according to those comments. Other times I didn't, but used the comments when I had to do a similar writing assignment in later courses. As I became more advanced in my academic career (starting in graduate school), I started submitting my papers for publication. I would draft my manuscript and then share it with my professors or fellow students (when I was in graduate school) or with my colleagues (now) to get their feedback. I also got comments from reviewers and editors. The process of writing, getting feedback, and revising helped me not only learn about but also learn to follow and negotiate the conventions.

"Reading the kind of writing I needed to do (e.g., journal articles) helped me learn about the conventions, but that alone did not help me learn to follow them. I needed to write and use what I learned in order to feel I had actually added it to my writing repertoire."

Structural Conventions and IMRAD Format

Structural conventions within the fields of the social sciences can vary quite dramatically, but the structure of a social science report should follow logically from the type of study conducted or the methodological framework (quantitative, qualitative, or mixed-methods) it employs. The more quantitative a study is, the more likely its reporting will reflect the conventions for scientific research, using IMRAD format. Qualitative studies, though, sometimes appear in other organizational forms that reflect the particular qualitative methods used in the study. But just as numerous fields within the social sciences rely on quantitative research methods, so too do many social scientists report their results according to the conventional form for scientific inquiry: *IMRAD (Introduction, Methods, Results, and Discussion) format.*

Introduction

The introduction of a social science report establishes the context for a study, providing appropriate background on the issue or topic under scrutiny. The introduction is also where you're likely to find evidence of researchers' review of previous scholarship on a topic. As part of these reviews, researchers typically report what's already known about a phenomenon or what's relevant in the current scholarship for their own research. They may also situate their research goals within some gap in the scholarship—that is, they explain how their research contributes to the growing body of scholarship on the phenomenon under investigation. If a theoretical perspective drives a study, as often occurs in more qualitative studies, then the introduction may also contain an explanation of the central tenets or the parameters of the researchers' theoretical lens. Regardless, an introduction in the social sciences generally builds to a statement of specific purpose for the study. This may take the form of a hypothesis or thesis, or it may appear explicitly as a general statement of the researchers' purpose, perhaps including a presentation of research questions. The introduction to Rathunde and Csikszentmihalyi's study provides an example:

The difficulties that many young adolescents encounter in middle school have been well documented (Carnegie Council on Adolescent Development 1989, 1995; Eccles et al. 1993; U.S. Department of Education 1991). During this precarious transition from the elementary school years, young adolescents may begin to doubt the value of their academic work and their abilities to succeed (Simmons and Blyth 1987; Wigfield et al. 1991). A central concern of many studies is motivation (Anderman and Maehr 1994); a disturbingly consistent finding associated with middle school is a drop in students' intrinsic motivation to learn (Anderman et al. 1999; Gottfried 1985; Harter et al. 1992).

Provides an introduction to the topic at hand: the problem of motivation for adolescents in middle school. The problem is situated in the scholarship of others.

Such downward trends in motivation are not inevitable. Over the past decade, several researchers have concluded that the typical learning environment in middle school is often mismatched with adolescents' developmental needs (Eccles et al. 1993). Several large-scale research programs have focused on the qualities of classrooms and school cultures that may enhance student achievement and motivation (Ames 1992; Lipsitz et al. 1997; Maehr and Midgley 1991). School environments that provide a more appropriate developmental fit (e.g., more relevant tasks, student-directed learning, less of an emphasis on grades and competition, more collaboration, etc.) have been shown to enhance students' intrinsic, task motivation (Anderman et al. 1999).

Reviews relevant scholarship: the researchers review previous studies that have bearing on their own aims—addressing the decline in motivation among students.

Identifies
researchers'
particular areas of
interest.

The present study explores the issues of developmental fit and young adolescents' quality of experience and motivation by comparing five Montessori middle schools to six "traditional" public middle schools. Although the Montessori educational philosophy is primarily associated with early childhood education, a number of schools have extended its core principles to early adolescent education. These principles are in general agreement with the reform proposals associated with various motivation theories (Anderman et al. 1999; Maehr and Midgley 1991), developmental fit theories (Eccles et al. 1993), as well as insights from various recommendations for middle school reform (e.g., the Carnegie Foundation's "Turning Points" recommendations; see Lipsitz et al. 1997). In addition, the Montessori philosophy is consistent with the theoretical and practical implications of optimal experience (flow) theory (Csikszentmihalyi and Rathunde 1998). The present study places a special emphasis on students' quality of experience in middle school. More specifically, it uses the Experience Sampling Method (ESM) (Csikszentmihalyi and Larson 1987) to compare the school experiences of Montessori middle school students with a comparable sample of public school students in traditional classrooms. (pp. 341–42)

Although the introductory elements of Rathunde and Csikszentmihalyi's study actually continue for a number of pages, these opening paragraphs reveal common rhetorical moves in social science research reporting: establishing a topic of interest, reviewing the scholarship on that topic, and connecting the current study to the ongoing scholarly conversation on the topic.

Methods

Social science researchers are very particular about the precise reporting of their methods of research. No matter what the type of study (quantitative, qualitative, or mixed-methods), researchers are very careful not only to identify the methods used in their research but also to explain why they chose certain ones, in light of the goals of their study. Because researchers want to reduce the influence of researcher bias and to provide enough context so others might replicate or confirm their findings, social scientists make sure that their reports thoroughly explain the kinds of data they have collected and the precise procedures they used to collect that data (interviews, document analysis, surveys, etc.). Also, there is often much discussion of the ways the data were interpreted or analyzed (using case studies, narrative analysis, statistical procedures, etc.).

An excerpt from W. Cassidy, K. Brown, and M. Jackson's study on educators and cyberbullying provides an example of the level of detail at which scholars typically report their methods:

Each participant chose a pseudonym and was asked a series of 16 in-depth, semi-structured, open-ended questions (Lancy, 2001) and three closed-category questions in a private setting, allowing their views to be voiced in confidence (Cook-Sather, 2002). Each 45- to 60-minute audiotaped interview was conducted by one of the authors, while maintaining a neutral, nonjudgmental stance in regards to the responses (Merriam, 1988).

Provides highly specific details about data-collection methods, and emphasizes researchers' neutral stance.

Once the interviews were transcribed, each participant was given the opportunity to review the transcript and make changes. The transcripts were then reviewed and re-reviewed in a backward and forward motion (Glaser & Strauss, 1967; McMillan & Schumacher, 1997) separately by two of the three researchers to determine commonalities and differences among responses as well as any salient themes that surfaced due to the frequency or the strength of the response (Miles & Huberman, 1994). Each researcher's analysis was then compared with the other's to jointly determine emergent themes and perceptions.

Provides detailed explanation of procedures used to support the reliability of the study's findings.

The dominant themes were then reviewed in relation to the existing literature on educators' perceptions and responses to cyberbullying. The approach taken was "bottom-up," to inductively uncover themes and contribute to theory, rather than apply existing theory as a predetermined frame for analysis (Miles & Huberman, 1994). (p. 523)

Connects the research to the development of theory.

You'll notice that the researchers do not simply indicate that the data were collected via interviews. Rather, they go to some lengths to describe the kinds of interviews they conducted and how they were conducted, as well as how those interviews were analyzed. This level of detail supports the writers' ethos, and it further highlights their commitment to reducing bias in their research. Similar studies might also report the interview questions at the end of the report in an appendix. Seeing the actual questions helps readers interpret the results on their own and also provides enough detail for readers to replicate the study or test the hypothesis with a different population, should they desire to do so. Readers of the study need to understand as precisely as possible the methods for data collection and analysis.

Results

There can be much variety in the ways social science reports present the results, or findings, of a study. You may encounter a section identified by the title "Results," especially if the study follows IMRAD format, but you may not find that heading at all. Instead, researchers often present their results by using headings and subheadings that reflect their actual findings. As examples, we provide here excerpts from two studies: (1) Rathunde and Csikszentmihalyi's 2005 study on middle school student motivation, and (2) Cassidy, Brown, and Jackson's 2012 study on educators and cyberbullying.

In the Results section of their report, Rathunde and Csikszentmihalyi provide findings from their study under the subheading "Motivation and Quality-of-Experience Differences: Nonacademic Activities at School." Those results read in part:

Follow-up ANCOVAs were done on each of the five ESM variables. Table 3 summarizes the means, standard errors, and significance levels for each of the variables.

Table 3

Univariate F-Tests for Quality of Experience in Nonacademic Activities at School by School Context

ESM Measure	School Context		F-test	p
	Montessori (N = 131)	Traditional (N = 150)		
Flow %	11.0 (1.7)	17.3 (1.6)	7.19	.008
Affect	.32 (.05)	.14 (.05)	6.87	.009
Potency	.22 (.05)	.16 (.05)	1.90	NS
Motivation	−.03 (.05)	−.12 (.05)	1.70	NS
Salience	−.38 (.04)	−.19 (.04)	11.14	.001

Means are z-scores (i.e., zero is average experience for the entire week) and are adjusted for the covariates gender, parental education, and ethnicity. Standard errors appear in parentheses. Flow percent indicates the amount of time students indicated above-average challenge and skill while doing nonacademic activities.

Result ——— Consistent with the relaxed nature of the activities, students in both school contexts reported higher levels of affect, potency, and intrinsic motivation in nonacademic activities, as well as lower levels of salience and flow (see table 2). In contrast to the findings for aca-

Result ——— demic work, students in both groups reported similar levels of intrinsic motivation and potency. In addition, students in the traditional group reported significantly more flow in nonacademic activities,

Result ——— although the overall percentage of flow was low. Similar to the findings for academic activities, the Montessori students reported better overall affect, and despite the fact that levels of salience were below

Result ——— average for both student groups, the traditional students reported that their activities were more important. (pp. 360–61)

You'll notice that in this section, the researchers remain focused on reporting their findings. They do not, at this point, go into great detail about what those findings mean or what the implications are.

Cassidy, Brown, and Jackson also report their findings in a Results section, and they subdivide their findings into a number of areas of inquiry (identified in the subheadings) examined as part of their larger study. Only the results are presented at this point in the article; they are not yet interpreted:

RESULTS

Familiarity with technology

Despite the district's emphasis on technology, the educators (except for two younger teachers and one vice-principal) indicated that they were not very familiar with chat rooms and blogs, were moderately familiar with YouTube and Facebook and were most familiar with the older forms of communication—email and cellular phones.

— Results

Cyberbullying policies

We asked respondents about specific cyberbullying policies in place at their school and their perceived effectiveness. Despite the district's priorities around technology, neither the school district nor either school had a specific cyberbullying policy; instead educators were supposed to follow the district's bullying policy. When VP17-A was asked if the district's bullying handbook effectively addressed the problem of cyberbullying, he replied: "It effectively addresses the people that are identified as bullying others [but] it doesn't address the educational side of it…about what is proper use of the Internet as a tool."

— Result

P14-B wanted to see a new policy put in place that was flexible enough to deal with the different situations as they arose. VP19-B thought that a cyberbullying policy should be separate from a face-to-face bullying policy since the impact on students is different. He also felt that there should be a concerted district policy regarding "risk assessment in which you have a team that's trained at determining the level of threat and it should be taken very seriously whether it's a phone threat, a verbal threat, or a cyber threat." Participants indicated that they had not considered the idea of a separate cyberbullying policy before the interview, with several commenting that they now saw it as important. (pp. 524, 526–27)

— Result

Visual Representations of Data   The Results section of a report may also provide data sets in the form of charts and/or figures. Figures may appear as photos, images, charts, or graphs. When you find visual representations of data in texts, it's important that you pause to consider these elements carefully. Researchers typically use *tables* when they want to make data sets, or raw data, available for comparisons. These tables, such as the one Rathunde and Csikszentmihalyi include in "Middle School Students' Motivation and Quality of Experience: A Comparison of Montessori and Traditional School Environments," present variables in columns and rows, as seen here.

Table 1

Comparison of Montessori and Traditional Middle School Samples on Various Background Variables

Background Variable	School Context	
	Montessori	Traditional
Ethnicity (%):		
European American	72.6	74.9
Asian American	10.2	7.8
Latino	1.9	3.4
African American	12.7	12.6
Other	2.6	1.2
Parental education	5.5	5.4
Home resources	29.6	29.5
School-related:		
Parental discussion	2.41	2.49
Parental involvement	2.11	2.10
Parental monitoring	1.69	1.66
Number of siblings	1.8	2.0
Mother employment (%)	71.6	74.1
Father employment (%)	83.7	88.1
Intact (two-parent) family (%)	81.0	84.0
Grade point average	1.97	1.93

Note: None of the differences reported in the table was statistically significant.

In this instance, the "background variable[s]" used to describe the student populations are listed in the column, and the rows identify two "school context[s]," Montessori and Traditional schools, for comparison. The table's title reveals its overall purpose: to compare "Montessori and Traditional Middle School Samples on Various Background Variables." Rathunde and Csikszentmihalyi describe the contents of their table this way:

Table 1 summarizes this comparison. The ethnic diversity of the samples was almost identical. Both shared similar advantages in terms of high parental education (baccalaureate degree or higher), high rates of two-parent families, high family resources, and other indicators of strong parental involvement in their children's education. Although only one-third of the Montessori students received grades, *t*-tests indicated that both samples were comprised of good students (i.e., they received about half As and half Bs). (p. 356)

Researchers use *figures* when they want to highlight the results of research or the derived relationships between data sets or variables. *Graphs*, a type of figure, contain two axes—the horizontal x-axis and the vertical y-axis. The relationship between variables on these axes is indicated by the cells of overlap between the two axes in the body of the figure. Conventionally, the *x-axis* identifies an independent variable, or a variable that can be controlled; by contrast, the *y-axis* identifies the dependent variable, which is dependent on the variable identified in the x-axis. Here's a figure from Rathunde and Csikszentmihalyi's study:

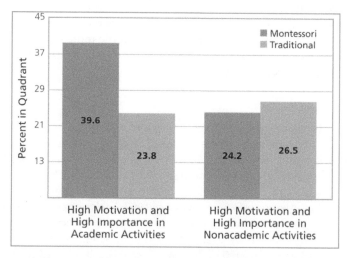

Figure 2. Percentage of undivided interest in academic and nonacademic activities

As with tables, the titles of figures reveal their overall purpose. In this case, the researchers demonstrate the "[p]ercentage of undivided interest in academic and nonacademic activities." Reading the figure, in this instance, comes down to identifying the percentage of "undivided interest" that students in Montessori and traditional middle schools (revealed in different colors, as the legend indicates) expressed in the quadrants "High Motivation and High Importance in Academic Activities" and "High Motivation and

High Importance in Nonacademic Activities." Colored cells in the body of the graph reveal the percentages. Rathunde and Csikszentmihalyi note about this figure: "[O]n the key variable undivided interest, students in the traditional group reported a slightly higher percent of high-motivation and high-importance activities; this noteworthy change from academic activities is illustrated in figure 2" (p. 361).

Whenever you see charts or figures in social science reports, you should take time to do the following:

* study the titles carefully

* look for legends, which provide keys to understanding elements in the chart or figure

* identify the factors or variables represented, and understand how those factors or variables are related, as well as how they are measured

* look closely for possible patterns

Discussion

This section of a social science report explains the significance of the findings in light of the study's aims. This is also where researchers reflect on the study more generally, highlight ways their study could be improved (often called "limitations"), and/ or identify areas of further research that the study has brought to light. Researchers sometimes lay out the groundwork for continued research, based on their contribution, as part of the ongoing scholarly conversation on the topic or issue at hand. A few excerpts from the Discussion section of Rathunde and Csikszentmihalyi's study reveal their adherence to these conventional expectations:

Reveals why their study is important to the ongoing conversation on this topic.

DISCUSSION

Given the well-documented decline in students' motivation and engagement in middle school, and the ongoing emphasis on middle school reform (Cross 1990; Eccles et al. 1993; Lipsitz et al. 1997), an increasing number of studies have explored how to change classroom practices and school cultures in ways that provide a healthier fit for young adolescents (Ames 1992; Eccles et al. 1993; Felner et al. 1997; Maehr and Midgley 1991). The present study adds to this area of research by comparing the motivation and quality of experience of students from five Montessori middle schools and six traditional middle schools. (p. 362)

...

Discusses important findings.

Results from the study showed that while engaged in academic work at school, Montessori students reported higher affect, potency (i.e., feeling alert and energetic), intrinsic motivation (i.e., enjoyment, interest), and flow experience than students from traditional middle schools. (p. 363)

...

The present study did not look at whether such experiential differences translated into positive achievement and behavioral outcomes for the students. This is an important topic for future research. (p. 363)

Identifies limitations in the study and an area for possible future research.

Conclusion

On occasion, researchers separate out coverage of the implications of their findings (as part of a Discussion section) from other elements in the Discussion. When this occurs, these researchers typically construct a separate Conclusion section in which they address conventional content coverage of their study's limitations, as well as their findings' implications for future research.

Following are some additional structural conventions to consider when you are reading or writing in the fields of the social sciences.

Other Structural Conventions

Titles

Research reports in the social sciences, as in the natural sciences, tend to have rather straightforward titles that are concise and that contain key words highlighting important components of the study. Titles in the social sciences tend not to be creative or rhetorical, although there is a greater tendency toward creativity in titles in qualitative studies, which are more typically language driven than numerically driven. The title of Barbara Allen's study reported in the academic journal *Technology in Society*, for instance, identifies the central issues her study examined as well as the study location: "Environmental Justice, Local Knowledge, and After-Disaster Planning in New Orleans." Similarly, the title of Rathunde and Csikszentmihalyi's article is concise in its identification of the study's purpose: "Middle School Students' Motivation and Quality of Experience: A Comparison of Montessori and Traditional School Environments."

Abstracts

Another structural feature of reports in the social sciences is the abstract. **Abstracts** typically follow the title of the report and the identification of the researchers. They provide a brief overview of the study, explaining the topic or issue under study, the specific purpose of the study and its methods, and offering a concise statement of the results. These elements are usually summarized in a few sentences. Abstracts can be useful to other researchers who want to determine if a study might prove useful for their own work or if the methods might inform their own research purposes. Abstracts thus serve to promote collaboration among researchers. Though abstracts appear at the beginning of research reports, they're typically written after both the study and the research report are otherwise completed. Abstracts reduce the most important parts of a study into a compact space.

The following example from Rathunde and Csikszentmihalyi illustrates a number of the conventions of abstracts:

The study's purpose is identified.

Methods are briefly outlined.

Results are provided.

Implications of the research findings are noted.

This study compared the motivation and quality of experience of demographically matched students from Montessori and traditional middle school programs. Approximately 290 students responded to the Experience Sampling Method (ESM) and filled out questionnaires. Multivariate analyses showed that the Montessori students reported greater affect, potency (i.e., feeling energetic), intrinsic motivation, flow experience, and undivided interest (i.e., the combination of high intrinsic motivation and high salience or importance) while engaged in academic activities at school. The traditional middle school students reported higher salience while doing academic work; however, such responses were often accompanied by low intrinsic motivation. When engaged in informal, nonacademic activities, the students in both school contexts reported similar experiences. These results are discussed in terms of current thought on motivation in education and middle school reform.

Acknowledgments

Acknowledgment sections sometimes appear at the end of social science reports. Usually very brief, they offer a quick word of thanks to organizations and/or individuals who have helped to fund a study, collect data, review the study, or provide another form of assistance during the production of the study. This section can be particularly telling if you're interested in the source of a researcher's funding. Barbara Allen's "Environmental Justice, Local Knowledge, and After-Disaster Planning in New Orleans" contains the following Acknowledgments section:

ACKNOWLEDGMENTS

I would like to thank Carl Mitcham, Robert Frodeman, and all the participants of the Cities and Rivers II conference in New Orleans, March 21–25, 2006. The ideas and discussions at this event enabled me to think in a more interdisciplinary manner about the disaster and its impact as well as about my own assumptions regarding environmental justice and citizen participation in science.

In addition, I would like to thank the American Academy in Rome for giving me the time to think and write about this important topic. Conversations with my colleagues at the academy were invaluable in helping me to think in new ways about historic preservation and rebuilding. (p. 159)

References

The documentation system most often used in the social sciences is the style regulated by the American Psychological Association, which is referred to as APA format. (For more details about APA style conventions, see p. 291 of Chapter 10.) Studies in the social sciences end with a References page that follows APA guidelines—or the formatting style used in the study, if not APA.

Appendices

Social science research reports sometimes end with one or more appendices. Items here are often referenced within the body of the report itself, as appropriate. These items may include additional data sets, calculations, interview questions, diagrams, and images. The materials typically offer context or support for discussions that occur in the body of a research report.

Inside Work: Observing Structural Conventions

Although we've discussed a number of structural expectations for reports in the social sciences, we need to stress again that these expectations are conventional. As such, you'll likely encounter numerous studies in the social sciences that rely on only a few of these structural features or that alter the conventional expectations in light of the researchers' particular aims. For this activity, we'd like you to do the following.

- Select a social science topic.

- Locate two articles published in peer-reviewed academic journals that address some aspect of your selected topic.

- Compare and contrast the two articles in terms of their structural features. Note both (1) instances when the articles follow the conventional expectations for social science reporting as explained in this chapter, and (2) instances when the articles alter or diverge from these expectations. Speculate as to the authors' reasoning for following the conventional expectations or diverging from them.

Language Conventions

As with structural conventions, the way social scientists use language can vary widely with respect to differing audiences and/or genres. Nevertheless, we can explore several language-level conventional expectations for writing in the social sciences. In the following sections, we consider the use of both active and passive voice, as well as the use of hedging (or hedge words) to limit the scope and applicability of assertions.

Active and Passive Voice

Many students have had the experience of receiving a graded paper back from an English teacher in high school and discovering that a sentence or two was marked for awkward or inappropriate use of the passive voice. This problem occurs fairly often as students acclimate their writing to differing disciplinary communities. As we discussed in Chapter 12, the passive voice usually appears with less frequency in the fields of the humanities, while writers in the social sciences and natural sciences use it more frequently, and with good purpose. (For a fuller discussion and examples of the differences between active and passive voice constructions, see pp. 354–55 in Chapter 12.)

You may wonder why anyone would want to add words unnecessarily or remove altogether the actor/agent from a sentence. The passive voice is often preferable in writing in the social sciences and natural sciences because, although it may seem wordy or unclear to some readers in some instances, skillful use of the passive voice can actually foster a sense that researchers are acting objectively or with neutrality. This does not mean that natural or social scientists are averse to the active voice. However, in particular instances, the passive voice can go a long way toward supporting an ethos of objectivity, and its use appears most commonly in the Methods sections of social science reports. Consider these two sentences that might appear in the Methods section of a hypothetical social science report:

> **Active Voice:** We asked participants to identify the factors that most influenced their decision.
>
> **Passive Voice:** Participants were asked to identify the factors that most influenced their decision.

With the agent, *we*, removed, the sentence in passive voice deemphasizes the researchers conducting the study. In this way, the researchers maintain more of a sense of objectivity or neutrality in their report.

Hedging

Another language feature common to writing in the social sciences is hedging. Hedging typically occurs when researchers want to make a claim or propose an explanation but also want to be extremely careful not to overstep the scope of their findings based on their actual data set. Consider the following sentences:

> Participants seemed to be anxious about sharing their feelings on the topic.

> Participants were anxious about sharing their feelings on the topic.

When you compare the two, you'll notice that the first sentence "hedges" against making a broad or sweeping claim about the participants. The use of *seemed to be* is a hedge against overstepping, or saying something that may or may not be absolutely true in every case. Other words or phrases that are often used to hedge include the following, just to name a handful:

probably	perhaps
some	possibly
sometimes	might
likely	it appears that
apparently	partially

Considering that social scientists make claims about human behavior, and that participants in a study may or may not agree with the conclusions, it's perhaps not surprising that writers in these fields often make use of hedging.

Inside Work: Observing Language Features

Use the two articles you located for the previous Inside Work exercise, in which you compared and contrasted their structural conventions.

• This time, study the language of the articles for instances of the two language conventions we've discussed in this section. Try to determine in what sections of the reports passive voice and hedging occur most frequently.

• Offer a rationale for your findings. If you find more instances of the use of passive voice in the Methods sections than in the Results sections, for instance, attempt to explain why that would be the case. Or, if you find more instances of verbal hedging in the Results sections than in the Methods sections, what do you think explains those findings?

Reference Conventions

The style guide for writing followed in most (but not all) social science fields is the *Publication Manual of the American Psychological Association* (APA). Many referencing conventions of the social sciences are governed by the APA, and some are worth examining in more detail.

In-Text Documentation

One of the distinguishing features of the APA method for documenting sources that are paraphrased, summarized, or cited as part of a report is the inclusion of a source's year of publication as part of the parenthetical notation in or at the end of a sentence in which a source is used. We can compare this to the MLA documentation system described in Chapter 12 through the following examples:

MLA: The study reports that "in some participants, writing block appears to be tied to exhaustion" (Jacobs 23).

APA: The study reports that "in some participants, writing block appears to be tied to exhaustion" (Jacobs, 2009, p. 23).

Although these examples by no means illustrate all the differences between MLA and APA styles of documentation, they do highlight the elevated importance that social sciences fields place on the year of a source's publication. Why? Imagine that you're reading a sociological study conducted in 2010 that examines the use of tobacco products among teenagers. The study references the finding of a similar study from 1990. By seeing the date of the referenced study in the in-text citation, readers can quickly consider the usefulness of the 1990 study for the one being reported on. Social scientists value recency, or the most current data possible, and their documentation requirements reflect this preference.

Summary and Paraphrase

Another reference distinction among the academic domains concerns how writers reference others' ideas. You've probably had experience writing papers for teachers who required you to cite sources as support for your ideas. You may have done this by copying the language directly from a source. If so, then you noted that these words belonged to another person by putting quotation marks around them and by adding a parenthetical comment identifying the source of the cited language. These practices hold true for writers in the social sciences as well.

However, as you become more familiar with the reference practices of researchers in these fields, you'll discover that social scientists quote researchers in other fields far less frequently than scholars in the humanities do. Why is this so? For humanist scholars, language is of the utmost importance, and how someone conveys an idea can seem almost inseparable from the idea being conveyed. Additionally, for humanists, language is often the "unit of measure"—that is, *how* someone says something (like a novelist or a poet) is actually *what* is being studied. Typically, this is not the case for social science researchers (with the exception of fields such as linguistics and communication, although they primarily address how study participants say something and not how prior research reported its findings). Instead, social scientists tend to be much more interested in other researchers' methodology and findings than they are in the language through which those methods or finding are conveyed. As a result, social scientists are more likely to summarize or paraphrase source materials than to quote them directly.

Inside Work: Observing Reference Features

In this section, we've suggested that two areas of conventional reference features in social science writing are (1) the elevated position of year of publication in the internal documentation of source material, and (2) the preference among social scientists for summarizing and paraphrasing sources.

- Use the same two studies that you examined for the last two Inside Work activities.

- Based on the principle that social scientists are concerned with the recency of research in their areas, examine the References page (the ending bibliography) for each study. How does the form of entries on the References page reflect the social science concern with the recency of sources?

- Look more closely at the introductions of the two articles, and note the number of times in each article another source is referenced. Count the number of times these sources are paraphrased, summarized, or quoted directly. Based on your findings, what can you conclude about the ways social scientists reference source material?

Genres of Writing in the Social Sciences

Scholars in the social sciences share the results of their research in various ways. As Dr. Matsuda reveals in her Insider's View, social scientists write in a variety of forms for differing venues. They might, for instance, present their work at a conference or publish their research results in a journal or a book.

In this section, we offer descriptions of, and steps for producing, two of the most common types of writing, or genres, required of students in introductory-level courses in the social sciences. These are the literature review and the theory-response paper. As genres, literature reviews and responses to social science theories sometimes appear as parts of other, longer works. Sometimes, though, they stand alone as complete works.

The Literature Review

The literature review (also referred to as a review of scholarship) is one of the most common genres you will encounter in academic writing. Though this chapter is dedicated to writing in the social sciences, and the literature review genre occurs quite frequently in the social sciences, you can find evidence of reviews of scholarship in virtually every academic field—including the humanities, the natural sciences, and applied fields. The skills required for this genre are thus important to the kinds of inquiry that occur across all the academic disciplines.

At its core, the literature review is an analysis of published resources related to a specific topic. The purposes of a literature review may vary: students and researchers may conduct a review of scholarship simply to establish what research has already been conducted on a topic, or the review may make a case for how new research can fill in gaps or advance knowledge about a topic. In the former situation, the resulting literature review may appear as a freestanding piece of writing; in the latter, a briefer review of scholarship may be embedded at the start (usually in the introduction) of a research study.

In fact, most published scholarly articles include a review of literature in the first few pages. Besides serving as a means to identify a gap in the scholarship or a place for new scholarship, a literature review helps to establish researchers' credibility by demonstrating their awareness of what has been discovered about a particular topic or issue. It further respectfully acknowledges the hard work of others within the community of scholarship. Equally as important, the literature review illustrates how previous studies interrelate. A good literature review may examine how prior research is similar and different, or it may suggest how a group of researchers' work developed over several years and how scholars have advanced the work of others.

Insider's View

There Are Many Kinds of Writing That Applied Linguists Do

Aya Matsuda, Linguistics

Courtesy of Aya Matsuda

"My writing is mostly in the form of research papers that are published as articles in scholarly journals or chapters in scholarly books. I also review other applied linguists' manuscripts and write evaluation reports on them, usually to help journal editors decide whether or not to publish manuscripts in their journals. I also write book reviews that are published in scholarly journals. But because of the 'real-life' nature of the kinds of questions my field addresses, there are many other kinds of writing that applied linguists do. Textbooks, articles in newspapers and general magazines, policies, consultation reports, and public education materials (e.g., brochures) are some examples of other types of writing that my colleagues do. Grant writing is also an important kind of writing that researchers in my field do."

Insider Example

An Embedded Literature Review

Read the first two paragraphs to "Happiness in Everyday Life: The Uses of Experience Sampling," a social science study reported by Mihaly Csikszentmihalyi and Jeremy Hunter, as an example of a review of scholarship that is embedded within a larger study report. As you read, consider the purposes of a literature review to which it responds, including:

- reviewing what is known on a topic or issue
- identifying a gap in scholarship
- establishing the researchers' ethos

Courtesy of Mihaly Csikszentmihalyi

Courtesy of Jeremy Hunter. Photo by William Vasta

Mihaly Csikszentmihalyi and Jeremy Hunter

Excerpt from "Happiness in Everyday Life: The Uses of Experience Sampling"

INTRODUCTION

Current understanding of human happiness points at five major effects on this emotion. These are, moving from those most impervious to change to those that are most under personal control: genetic determinants, macro-social conditions, chance events, proximal environment, and personality. It is not unlikely that, as behavioral geneticists insist, a "set level" coded in our chromosomes accounts for perhaps as much as half of the variance in self-reported happiness (Lykken & Tellegen, 1996; Tellegen et al., 1988). These effects are probably mediated by temperamental traits like extraversion, which are partly genetically determined and which are in turn linked to happiness (Myers, 1993). Cross-national comparisons suggest that macro-social conditions such as extreme poverty, war, and social injustice are all obstacles to happiness (Inglehart & Klingemann, 2000; Veenhoven, 1995). Chance events like personal tragedies, illness, or sudden strokes of good fortune may drastically affect the level of happiness, but apparently these effects do not last long (Brickman et al., 1978; Diener, 2000). One might include under the

This section of the study's introduction establishes what is known about the topic at hand. It reviews the scholarship of others.

How does this review of previous scholarship affect your view of the writers? What does it say about them?

heading of the proximal environment the social class, community, family, and economic situation—in other words, those factors in the immediate surroundings that may have an impact on a person's well-being. And finally, habits and coping behaviors developed by the individual will have an important effect. Hope, optimism, and the ability to experience flow can be learned and thus moderate one's level of happiness (Csikszentmihalyi, 1997; Seligman, 2002).

Reveals the researchers' purpose in the context of the review of scholarship. Identifies a space, or gap, in the scholarship for investigation.

In this paper, we present a method that allows investigators to study the impact of momentary changes in the environment on people's happiness levels, as well as its more lasting, trait-like correlates. Research on happiness generally considers this emotion to be a personal trait. The overall happiness level of individuals is measured by a survey or questionnaire, and then "happy" people—those who score higher on a one-time response scale—are contrasted with less happy ones. Whatever distinguishes the two groups is then assumed to be a condition affecting happiness. This perspective is a logical outcome of the methods used, namely, one-time measures. If a person's happiness level is measured only once, it is by definition impossible to detect intra-individual variations. Yet, we know quite well that emotional states, including happiness, are quite volatile and responsive to environmental conditions.

Writing a Literature Review

The scope of a freestanding literature review can vary greatly, depending on the knowledge and level of interest of the investigator conducting the review. For instance, you may have very little knowledge about autism, so your review of the scholarship might be aimed at learning about various aspects of the condition and issues related to it. If this is the case, your research would cast a pretty wide net. However, let's say you're quite familiar with certain critical aspects of issues related to autism and are interested in one aspect in particular—for example, the best therapies for addressing autism in young children. If this is the case, then you could conduct a review of scholarship with a more focused purpose, narrowing your net to only the studies that address your specific interest. Regardless of the scope of your research interest, though, literature reviews should begin with a clear sense of your topic. One way to narrow the focus of your topic is by proposing one or more research questions about it. (See Chapter 10 for more support for crafting such research questions.)

Once you've clearly established your topic, the next step is to conduct your research. The research you discover and choose to read, which may be quite substantial for a literature review, is chosen according to the scope of your research interest. (For help in narrowing a search based on key terms in your research question, see Chapter 10.) Here are some tips to conducting research:

- As you search for and review possible sources, pay particular attention to the *abstracts* of studies, as they may help you quickly decide if a study is right for your purposes.

- Unless your review of scholarship targets the tracing of a particular thread of research across a range of years, you should probably focus on the most current research available.

- After you've examined and gathered a range of source materials, determine the best way to keep track of the ideas you discover. Many students find this is a good time to produce an annotated bibliography as a first step in creating a literature review. (See Chapter 10, pp. 292–93, for more help on constructing annotated bibliographies.)

Another useful strategy for organizing your sources is a source synthesis chart. We recommend this as a way to visualize the areas of overlap in your research, whether for a broad focus (*What are researchers studying with regard to autism?*) or a more narrow one (*What are the best therapies for addressing autism in young children?*). Here's an abbreviated example of a source synthesis chart for a broad review of scholarship on autism:

Authors of Study	Topics We Expect to Emerge in Scholarship			
	Issues of Diagnosis	Treatments	Debate over Causes	Wider Familial Effects
Solomon et al. (2012)	pp. 252–55 Notes: emphasizes problems families face with diagnosis	pp. 257–60 Notes: examines and proposes strategies for family therapists	p. 253 Notes: acknowledges a series of possible contributing factors	
Vanderborght et al. (2012)		pp. 359–67 (results) Notes: examines use of robot for storytelling		
Grindle et al. (2012)		pp. 208–313 (results) Notes: school-based behavioral intervention program (ABA)		p. 229 Notes: home-based therapy programs
Lilley (2011)	pp. 135–37 Notes: explores the roles of mothers in diagnosis processes	pp. 143–51 Notes: explores rationales and lived experiences of ABA and non-ABA supporters		

In this case, the studies that we read are named in the column under "Authors of Study." The topics or issues that we anticipated would emerge from our review of the sources are shown in the top row. Based on our reading of a limited number of studies, four at this point, we can already discern a couple of areas of overlap in the scholarship: the diagnosis of autism in children, and intervention programs for children with autism. We can tell which researchers talked about what issues at any given time because we've noted the areas (by page number, along with some detail) where they addressed these issues. The empty cells in the synthesis chart reveal that our review of the sources, thus far at least, suggests there is less concern for those topics. We should note, however, that our review of sources is far from exhaustive. If you're able to create a visual representation of your research such as this one, then you're well on your way to creating a successful literature review. Keep in mind that the more detailed you can make your synthesis chart, the easier your process may be moving forward.

The last step before writing is perhaps the most challenging. You must synthesize the sources. **Synthesizing sources** is the process of identifying and describing the relationships between and among researchers' ideas or approaches: What trends emerge? Does the Grindle et al. study say something similar to the Lilley study about behavioral interventions? Something different? Do they share methods? Do they approach the issue of behavioral interventions similarly or differently? Defining the relationships between the studies and making these relationships explicit is critically important to your success. As you read the sources, you'll likely engage in an internal process of comparing and contrasting the researchers' ideas. You might even recognize similarities and differences in the researchers' approaches to the topic. Many of these ideas will probably be reflected in your synthesis chart, and you might consider color-coding (or highlighting in different colors) various cells to indicate types of relationships among the researchers you note.

A quick review of the abstract to "The Experience of Infertility: A Review of Recent Literature," a freestanding literature review published in the academic journal *Sociology of Health and Illness*, demonstrates the areas of synthesis that emerged from the professionals' examination of recent research on infertility:

Four synthesis points: (1) more recent studies approach the topic of infertility differently; (2) there remains a focus on examining infertility from a clinical viewpoint; (3) there are still questions about research methods, but there have also been "important improvements" in methods; (4) two trends emerged from these scholars' review of the current research.

About 10 years ago Greil published a review and critique of the literature on the socio-psychological impact of infertility. He found at the time that most scholars treated infertility as a medical condition with psychological consequences rather than as a socially constructed reality. This article examines research published since the last review. More studies now place infertility within larger social contexts and social scientific frameworks, although clinical emphases persist. Methodological problems remain, but important improvements are also evident. We identify two vigorous research traditions in the social scientific study of infertility. One tradition uses primarily quantitative techniques to study clinic patients in order to improve service delivery and to assess the need for psychological counseling.

The other tradition uses primarily qualitative research to capture the experiences of infertile people in a sociocultural context. We conclude that more attention is now being paid to the ways in which the experience of infertility is shaped by social context. We call for continued progress in the development of a distinctly sociological approach to infertility and for the continued integration of the two research traditions identified here.

Presents conclusions reached as a result of the literature review project.

Another example, this one a brief excerpt from the introduction to Csikszentmihalyi and Hunter's "Happiness in Everyday Life: The Uses of Experience Sampling," demonstrates the kind of synthesis that typically appears in reviews of scholarship when they're embedded as part of a larger study:

Cross-national comparisons suggest that macro-social conditions such as extreme poverty, war, and social injustice are all obstacles to happiness (Inglehart & Klingemann, 2000; Veenhoven, 1995). Chance events like personal tragedies, illness, or sudden strokes of good fortune may drastically affect the level of happiness, but apparently these effects do not last long (Brickman et al., 1978; Diener, 2000).

The writers indicate that there is agreement between researchers: both Inglehart & Klingemann (2000) and Veenhoven (1995) have confirmed the finding in "cross-national comparisons."

Again, the writers indicate there is agreement between researchers: both Brickman et al. (1978) and Diener (2000) have confirmed this finding.

Writing Project: Writing a Literature Review

Your goal in this writing project, a freestanding literature review, is to provide an overview of the research that has been conducted on a topic of interest to you.

The Introduction

The opening of your literature review should introduce the topic you're exploring and assess the state of the available scholarship on it: What are the current areas of interest? What are the issues or elements related to a particular topic being discussed? Is there general agreement? Are there other clear trends in the scholarship? Are there areas of convergence and divergence?

The Body

Paragraphs within the body of your literature review should be organized according to the issues or synthesized areas you're exploring. For example, based on the synthesis chart shown earlier, we might suggest that one of the body sections of a broadly focused review of scholarship on autism concern issues of diagnosis. We might further reveal, in our topic sentence to that section of the literature review, that we've synthesized the available research in this area and that it seems uniformly to suggest that although many factors have been studied, no credible studies establish a direct link between any contributing factor and the occurrence of autism in children. The rest of that section of our paper would explore the factors that have been examined in the research to reiterate the claim in our topic sentence.

Keep in mind that the body paragraphs should be organized according to a claim about the topic or ideas being explored. They should not be organized merely as successive summaries of the sources. Such an organization does not promote effective synthesis.

The Conclusion

Your conclusion should reiterate your overall assessment of the scholarship. Notify your readers of any gaps you've determined in the scholarship, and consider suggesting areas where future scholarship can make more contributions.

Technical Considerations

Keep in mind the conventions of writing in the social sciences that you've learned about throughout this chapter. Use APA documentation procedures for in-text documentation of summarized, paraphrased, and cited materials, as well as for the References page at the end of your literature review.

Insider Example

Student Literature Review

William O'Brien, a first-year writing student who had a particular interest in understanding the effects of sleep deprivation, composed the following literature review. As you read, notice how William's text indicates evidence of synthesis both between and among the sources he used to build his project. Notice also that he followed APA style conventions in his review.

Running head: SLEEP DEPRIVATION   1

Effects of Sleep Deprivation: A Literature Review

William O'Brien

North Carolina State University

Effects of Sleep Deprivation: A Literature Review

Introduction

Everybody knows the feeling of having to struggle through a long day after a night of poor sleep, or sometimes even none at all. You may feel groggy, cloudy, clumsy, or unable to think of simple things. Sometimes you may even feel completely fine but then get angry or frustrated at things that normally would not affect you. No matter how you deal with it on that particular day, the reality is that even slight sleep deprivation can have extremely negative effects on mental ability. These effects are amplified when poor sleep continues for a long period of time. In a society with an ever-increasing number of distractions, it is becoming harder for many people to get the recommended amount of sleep. Sleep issues plague the majority of the U.S. population in one way or another. The Centers for Disease Control recognizes insufficient sleep as a public health epidemic.

A lot of research is being conducted relating to sleep and sleep deprivation, and for good reason. Most researchers seem to agree that short-term sleep deprivation has purely negative effects on mental functioning in general. However, the particular types of effects caused by poor sleep are still being debated, as are the long-term implications of sleep deprivation. The questions for researchers, then, are under what circumstances do these negative effects begin to show, to what extent do they show, and most significant, what exactly are these negative effects?

Short-Term Effects of Sleep Deprivation

In order to examine the direct and immediate effects of sleep deprivation, numerous researchers rely on experimentation, to control for other variables, for results. Research by Minkel et al. (2012) identified a gap in the research relating to how sleep deprivation affects the stress response (p. 1015). In order to test how inadequate sleep affects the stress response, the researchers divided healthy adults into two groups. Participants in the first group acted as the control and were allowed a 9-hour sleeping opportunity during the night. The second group was not allowed to sleep at all during that night. The next day, the participants completed stressful mental tasks (primarily math) and were asked to report their stress levels and mood via visual scales (Minkel et al., 2012, pp. 1016-1017). The

The writer establishes the general topic, sleep deprivation, in the opening paragraph.

Synthesis point: scholars agree on the negative effects of short-term sleep deprivation.

Synthesis point: questions remain about the effects of long-term sleep deprivation.

Focuses on scholarship that uses experimental studies to examine the effects of short-term sleep deprivation.

SLEEP DEPRIVATION   3

researchers hypothesized that insufficient sleep would increase the
stress response to each stressor as compared to the rested group,
and that sleep loss would increase the stress response in proportion
to the severity of the stressor (p. 1016). Their findings, however,
showed that while the negative response to stressors was more profound for the sleep-deprived group, the differences in stress response
between groups were not significant for the high-stressor condition. Still, the research clearly showed that sleep-deprived people
have "significantly greater subjective stress, anger, and anxiety" in
response to low-level stressors (p. 1019).

Research by Jugovac and Cavallero (2012) also focused on the
immediate effects of sleep deprivation on attention. This study's
purpose was to research the effects of sleep deprivation on attention
through three attentional networks: phasic alerting, covert orienting,
and executive control (Jugovac & Cavallero, 2012, p. 115). The study
tested 30 young adults using the Attention Network Test (ANT), the
Stanford Sleepiness Scale (SSS), and the Global Vigor-Affect Scale
(GVA) before and after a 24-hour sleep deprivation period (p. 116).
(All participants were subjected to sleep deprivation, because the
tests before the sleep deprivation served as the control.) The findings
built upon the idea that sleep deprivation decreases vigilance and
that it impairs the "executive control" attentional network, while
appearing to leave the other components (alerting and orienting)
relatively unchanged (pp. 121-122). These findings help explain how
one night of missed sleep negatively affects a person's attention, by
distinguishing the effects on each of the three particular attentional
networks.

Research by Giesbrecht, Smeets, Leppink, Jelicic, and
Merckelbach (2013) focused on the effects that short-term sleep
deprivation has on dissociation. This research is interesting and different from the other research in that it connects sleep deprivation to
mental illness rather than just temporarily reduced mental functioning. The researchers used 25 healthy undergraduate students and
kept all participants awake throughout one night. Four different
scales were used to record their feelings and dissociative reactions
while being subjected to two different cognitive tasks (Giesbrecht et
al., 2013, pp. 150-152). The cognitive tasks completed before the

Links the two studies reviewed according to their similar focus on short-term effects of sleep deprivation.

The writer links this study to the continuing discussion of short-term effects of sleep deprivation but also notes a difference.

night of sleep deprivation were used to compare the results of the cognitive tasks completed after the night of sleep deprivation. Although the study was small and the implications are still some- what unclear, the study showed a clear link between sleep depriva- tion and dissociative symptoms (pp. 156-158).

This paragraph provides a summative synthesis, or an overview of the findings among the sources reviewed.

It is clear that sleep deprivation negatively affects people in many different ways. These researchers each considered a different type of specific effect, and together they form a wide knowledge base supporting the idea that even a very short-term (24-hour) loss of sleep for a healthy adult may have multiple negative impacts on mental and emotional well-being. These effects include increased anxiety, anger, and stress in response to small stressors (Minkel et al., 2012), inhibited attention—the executive control attentional network more specifically (Jugovac & Cavallero, 2012)—and increased dis- sociative symptoms (Giesbrecht et al., 2013).

Long-Term Effects of Sleep Deprivation

The writer shifts to an examination of the long-term effects of sleep deprivation and acknowledges a shift in the methods for these studies.

Although the research on short-term effects of sleep depriva- tion reveals numerous negative consequences, there may be other, less obvious, implications that studies on short-term effect cannot illuminate. In order to better understand these other implications, we must examine research relating to the possible long-term effects of limited sleep. Unfortunately, long-term sleep deprivation experi- ments do not seem to have been done and are probably not possible (due to ethical reasons and safety reasons, among other factors). A study by Duggan, Reynolds, Kern, and Friedman (2014) pointed out the general lack of previous research into the long-term effects of sleep deprivation, but it examined whether there was a link between average sleep duration during childhood and life-long mortality risk (p. 1195). The researchers analyzed data from 1,145 participants in the Terman Life Cycle Study from the early 1900s, which measured bedtime and wake time along with year of death. The amount of sleep was adjusted by age in order to find the deviations from aver- age sleep time for each age group. The data were also separated by sex (Duggan et al., 2014, pp. 1196-1197). The results showed that, for males, sleeping either more or less than the regular amount of time

SLEEP DEPRIVATION   5

for each age group correlated with an increased life-long mortality
risk (p. 1199). Strangely, this connection was not present for females.
For males, however, this is a very important finding. Since we can
surmise that the childhood sleep patterns are independent of and
unrelated to any underlying health issues that ultimately cause the
deaths later on in life, it is more reasonable to assume causation
rather than simply correlation. Thus, the pattern that emerged may
demonstrate that too little, or too much, sleep during childhood can
cause physiological issues, leading to death earlier in life, which also
reaffirms the idea that sleep is extremely important for maintaining
good health.

Establishes one of the study's central findings related to long-term effects of sleep deprivation.

    While this study examined the relationship between sleep dura-
tion and death, a study by Kelly and El-Sheikh (2014) examined the
relationship between sleep and a slightly less serious, but still very
important, subject: the adjustment and development of children
in school over a period of time. The study followed 176 third grade
children (this number dropped to 113 by the end of the study) as they
progressed through school for five years, recording sleep patterns
and characteristics of adjustment (Kelly & El-Sheikh, 2014, pp. 1137-
1139). Sleep was recorded both subjectively through self-reporting
and objectively though "actigraphy" in order to assess a large variety
of sleep parameters (p. 1137). The study results indicated that
reduced sleep time and poorer-quality sleep are risk factors for problems adjusting over time to new situations. The results also indicate
that the opposite effect is true, but to a lesser extent (p. 1146).

    From this research, we gain the understanding that sleep depri-
vation and poor sleep quality are related to problems adjusting over
time. This effect is likely due to the generally accepted idea that sleep
deprivation negatively affects cognitive performance and emotional
regulation, as described in the Kelly and El-Sheikh article (2014, pp.
1144-1145). If cognitive performance and emotional regulation are
negatively affected by a lack of sleep, then it makes sense that the
sleep-deprived child would struggle to adjust over time as compared
to a well-rested child. This hypothesis has important implications. It
once again affirms the idea that receiving the appropriate amount of
quality sleep is very important for developing children. This basic

SLEEP DEPRIVATION   6

Provides a summative synthesis that examines relationships between the sources and considers implications of findings.

idea does not go against the research by Duggan et al. (2014) in any way; rather, it complements it. The main difference between each study is that the research by Duggan et al. shows that too much sleep can also be related to a greater risk of death earlier in life. Together, both articles provide evidence that deviation from the appropriate amount of sleep causes very negative long-term effects, including, but certainly not limited to, worse adjustment over time (Kelly & El-Sheikh, 2014) and increased mortality rates (Duggan et al., 2014).

Conclusion

Conclusion acknowledges what appears as a gap in the scholarship reviewed.

This research provides great insight into the short-term and long-term effects of sleep deprivation. Duggan et al. (2014) showed increased mortality rates among people who slept too much as well as too little. This result could use some additional research. Through the analysis of each article, we see just how damaging sleep deprivation can be, even after a short period of time, and thus it is important to seriously consider preventative measures. While sleep issues can manifest themselves in many different ways, especially in legitimate sleep disorders such as insomnia, just the simple act of not allowing oneself to get enough sleep every night can have significant negative effects. Building on this, there seems to be a general lack of discussion on *why* people (who do not have sleep disorders) do not get enough time to sleep. One possible reason is the ever-increasing number of distractions, especially in the form of electronics, that may lead to overstimulation. Another answer may be that high demands placed on students and adults through school and work, respectively, do not give them time to sleep enough. The most probable, yet most generalized, answer, however, is that people simply do not appropriately manage their time in order to get enough sleep. People seem to prioritize everything else ahead of sleeping, thus causing the damaging effects of sleep deprivation to emerge. Regardless, this research is valuable for anyone who wants to live a healthy lifestyle and function at full mental capacity. Sleep deprivation seems to have solely negative consequences; thus, it is in every person's best interests to get a full night of quality sleep as often as possible.

References

Duggan, K., Reynolds, C., Kern, M., & Friedman, H. (2014). Childhood sleep duration and lifelong mortality risk. *Health Psychology, 33*(10), 1195-1203. doi:10.1037/hea0000078

Giesbrecht, T., Smeets, T., Leppink, J., Jelicic, M., & Merckelbach, H. (2013). Acute dissociation after one night of sleep loss. *Psychology of Consciousness: Theory, Research, and Practice, 1*(S), 150-159. doi:10.1037/2326-5523.1.S.150

Jugovac, D., & Cavallero, C. (2012). Twenty-four hours of total sleep deprivation selectively impairs attentional networks. *Experimental Psychology, 59*(3), 115-123. doi:10.1027/1618-3169/a000133

Kelly, R., & El-Sheikh, M. (2014). Reciprocal relations between children's sleep and their adjustment over time. *Developmental Psychology, 50*(4), 1137-1147. doi:10.1037/a0034501

Minkel, J., Banks, S., Htaik, O., Moreta, M., Jones, C., McGlinchey, E., Simpson, N., & Dinges, D. (2012). Sleep deprivation and stressors: Evidence for elevated negative affect in response to mild stressors when sleep deprived. *Emotion, 12*(5), 1015-1020. doi:10.1037/a0026871

Theory Response Essay

Faculty in the fields of the social sciences often ask students to apply a social science theory to their own experiences. Psychology, sociology, and communication professors may ask students to use a psychological, sociological, or communication theory as a lens through which to explain their own or others' behaviors. Assignments like these involve writing a **theory response essay**. These assignments are popular for a number of reasons: (1) they allow students to engage with the fundamental elements of social sciences (theories); (2) they allow students to attend to the basic processes of data collection that are common in the social sciences; and (3) they are often quite engaging for faculty to read and are among the most interesting for students to write.

Whether you're using elements of Freud's dream theories to help understand your own dreams or you're using an interpersonal communication theory to understand why people so easily engage with you, the theory you're working with provides the frame for your analysis of some event or action. The theory is the core of any theory response.

Precisely because the theory is the core of such a writing project, it's crucial that in the beginning stage of such a project, you work with a theory that is actually applicable to the event, action, or phenomenon you want to understand better. You also want to choose a theory that genuinely interests you. Luckily, theories of human behavior and human system interactions abound. If you aren't assigned a theory for the project, then consider the places where you might go about locating a workable theory. Textbooks in the social sciences frequently make reference to theories, and numerous academic websites maintain lists and explanations of social science theories. Here are a few categories of theories that students often find interesting:

birth order theories	friendship theories
parenting style theories	stage theories of grieving
addiction theories	

If you're unable to locate a workable theory that's "ready-made" for application to some experience(s), then consider building a theory based on your reading of a social science study. Though this certainly makes completing the assignment challenging, it is not without rewards.

Personal Experience

Regardless of whether you're working with a particular theory or constructing a theory of behavior based on one or more studies, consider making a list of the "moments" or events in your life that the theory might help you understand further. Your next step might be to write out detailed descriptions of those events as you see or remember them. Capture as much detail as you can, especially if you're writing from memory. Then apply the theory (all of its component parts) to your event or moment to see what it can illuminate for you: Where does it really help you understand something?

Where does it fail to help? How might the theory need to change to account for your experiences?

Others' Experiences

Some instructors might ask you to collect and analyze the experiences of others. If you're assigned to do this, then you'll need to consider a data-collection method very carefully and ask your instructor if there are specific procedures at your institution that you should follow when collecting data from other people. We recommend, for now, that you think about the methods most commonly associated with qualitative research: observations, interviews, and open-ended surveys. These rich data-producing methods are most likely to provide the level of detail about others' experiences needed to evaluate the elements of your theory. Trying to understand others' experiences in light of the theory you're working with means considering the same analytical questions that you applied to your own experiences: Where does the theory really help you understand something? Where does it fail to help? How might the theory need to change to account for the experiences of those in your study?

Writing Project: Writing a Theory Response

The goal of this writing project is to apply a theoretical framework from an area of the social sciences to your own experiences. The first step is to choose a theoretical framework that has some relevance to you, providing ample opportunity to reflect on and write about your own experiences in relation to the theory.

The Introduction

The introduction to your study should introduce readers to the theory and explain all of its essential elements. You should also be clear about whether you're applying the theory to your own experiences or the experiences of others, or to both. In light of the work you did applying the theory, formulate a thesis that assesses the value of the theory for helping to understand the "moments," events, or phenomena you studied.

The Body

The body can be organized in a number of ways. If your theory has clear stages or elements, then you can explain each one and apply it to relevant parts of your experiences or those of others. If the theory operates in such a way that it's difficult to break into parts or stages or elements, then consider whether or not it's better to have subheadings that identify either (1) the themes that emerged from your application, or (2) your research subjects (by pseudonym). In this case, your body sections would be more like case studies. Ultimately, the organization strategy you choose will depend on the nature of the theory you're applying and the kinds of events you apply it to. The body of your project should establish connections among the theory's component elements.

The Conclusion

The conclusion of your study should assert your overall assessment of the theory's usefulness. Reiterate how the theory was useful and how it wasn't. Make recommendations for how it might need to be changed in order to account for the experiences you examined in light of the theory.

Technical Considerations

Keep in mind the conventions of writing in the social sciences that you've learned about throughout this chapter. Use APA documentation procedures for in-text documentation of summarized, paraphrased, and cited materials, as well as for the References page at the end of your study.

Insider Example

Student Theory Response Paper

Matt Kapadia, a first-year writing student, was interested in understanding the ways people rationalize their own successes and failures. In the following paper, he analyzes and evaluates a theory about the social science phenomenon of attribution (as described at changingminds.org) through the lenses of both his own and others' experiences. As you read Matt's paper, pay close attention to the moments when he offers evaluation of the theory. Ask yourself if his evaluation in each instance makes sense to you, based on the evidence he provides. Notice also that he followed APA style conventions in his paper.

Running head: THE ATTRIBUTION THEORY 1

Evaluation of the Attribution Theory

Matt Kapadia

North Carolina State University

Evaluation of the Attribution Theory

In an attempt to get a better sense of control, human beings are constantly attributing cause to the events that happen around them (Straker, 2008). Of all the things people attribute causes to, behavior is among the most common. The attribution theory aims to explain how people attribute the causes of their own behaviors compared to the behaviors of those around them. Behaviors can be attributed to both internal and external causes. Internal causes are things that people can control or are part of their personality, whereas external causes are purely circumstantial and people have no control over the resulting events (Straker, 2008). The attribution theory uses these internal and external causes to explain its two major components: the self-serving bias and the fundamental attribution error. The self-serving bias evaluates how we attribute our own behaviors, whereas the fundamental attribution error evaluates how we attribute the behaviors of those around us (Straker, 2008). This paper evaluates how applicable the attribution theory and its components are, using examples from personal experience as well as data collected from others. Based on the findings of this evaluation, I believe the attribution theory holds true on nearly all accounts; however, the category of the self-serving bias might need revision in the specific area dealing with professionals in any field of study or in the case of professional athletes.

Attribution Theory: An Explanation

The foundation of the attribution theory is based in the nature of the causes people attribute behaviors to, whether it be internal or external. A person has no control over an external cause (Straker, 2008). An example would be a student failing a math test because the instructor used the wrong answer key. In this case, the student had no control over the grade he received, and it did not matter how much he had studied. A bad grade was inevitable. A person can also attribute behavioral causes to internal causes. Internal causes are in complete control of the person distributing the behavior and are typically attributed to part of the individual's personality (Straker, 2008). An example would be a student getting a poor grade on his math test because he is generally lazy and does not study. In this case, the student had complete control of his grade and chose not to

The writer establishes a thesis that includes an evaluation of the theory's usefulness in various contexts.

In this paragraph and the next two, the writer reviews and exemplifies the component parts of the theory. That is, the writer offers an explanation of the theory, with examples to illustrate points, as appropriate.

THE ATTRIBUTION THEORY   3

study, which resulted in the poor grade. These two causes build up to the two major categories within the attribution theory.

The first major category of the attribution theory is that of self-serving bias. This category explores how people attribute causes to their own behaviors. It essentially states that people are more likely to give themselves the benefit of the doubt. People tend to attribute their poor behaviors to external causes and their good behaviors to internal causes (Straker, 2008). An example would be a student saying he received a poor grade on a test because his instructor does not like him. In this case, the student is attributing his poor behavior, making a poor grade on the test, to the external cause of his instructor not liking him. However, following the logic of the theory, if the student had made a good grade on the test, then he would attribute that behavior to an internal cause such as his own good study habits.

The second category of the attribution theory, the fundamental attribution error, states the opposite of the self-serving bias. The fundamental attribution error talks about how people attribute cause to the behaviors of those around them. It states that people are more likely to attribute others' poor behaviors to internal causes and their good behaviors to external causes (Straker, 2008). An example would be a student saying his friend got a better grade on the math test than him because the instructor likes his friend more. The student jumps to the conclusion that his friend's good grade was due to the external cause of the instructor liking the friend more. Moreover, if his friend had done poorly on the test, the student would most likely attribute the poor grade to an internal factor, such as his friend not studying for tests.

Personal Experiences

A situation from my personal experiences that exemplifies the ideas of the attribution theory is my high school golfing career. For my first two years of high school, I performed relatively poorly on the golf course. My team consistently placed last in tournaments, and I ranked nowhere near the top golfers from neighboring high schools. I blamed my performance on factors such as the wind and flat-out bad luck. At the same time, I attributed my teammates' poor performances to factors such as not practicing hard enough to compete in tournament play. In doing this, I became no better a golfer because I

The writer details a particular personal experience that he'll later analyze through the lens of the theory.

THE ATTRIBUTION THEORY   4

was denying that the true cause of my poor scores was the fact that I was making bad swings and not putting in the hours of work needed to perform at a higher level. I finally recognized this during my junior year of high school. I started to realize that blaming everything but myself was getting me nowhere and that the only way to improve was to take responsibility for my own play. I started practicing in areas where my game needed improvement and putting in hours at the driving range to improve my swing memory. In doing this, I became a much better player; by the time my senior season came around, I was ranked one of the top golfers in my conference and one of the best amateur players in the state of North Carolina. However, my team still did not perform well due to my teammates' performance, which I continued to attribute to their poor practice habits.

In this section, the writer analyzes his experience through the lens of the theory.

This experience reflects the attribution theory in several ways. I displayed self-serving bias in my early years of high school golf. I attributed all of my poor performances to external causes, such as the wind, that I could not control. At the same time, I was displaying the fundamental attribution error in attributing my teammates' poor performances to internal causes such as not practicing hard enough. Throughout my high school golf career, I displayed the ideas of the attribution theory's category of the fundamental attribution error. However, during my junior and senior seasons my attributions moved away from the attribution theory's category of the self-serving bias. I began to attribute my poor performance to internal causes instead of the external causes I had previously blamed for my mishaps.

I believe that this is generally true for any athlete or professional seeking improvement in his or her prospective field. If a person continues to follow the ideas discussed in the category of the self-serving bias, he is not likely to improve at what he is trying to do. If Tiger Woods had constantly attributed his bad play to external causes and not taken responsibility for his actions as internal causes, he would have never become the best golfer in the world. Without attributing his poor behaviors to internal causes, he would have never gained the motivation to put in the hours of work necessary to make him the best. This observation can be applied to any other professional field, not only athletics. Personal improvement is only likely to take place when a person begins to attribute his or her poor behaviors to internal causes. I believe athletes and professionals represent

THE ATTRIBUTION THEORY   5

problem areas for the theory of self-serving bias. However, the ideas of the fundamental attribution error generally hold true.

Experiences of Others

To evaluate the attribution theory, I conducted an experiment to test both the fundamental attribution error and the self-serving bias. The test subjects were three friends in the same class at North Carolina State University: MEA101, Introduction to Geology. The students were asked to write down if their grades were good or bad on the first test of the semester ("good" meant they received an 80 or higher on the test, and "bad" meant they received below an 80). After the three students had done this for themselves, they were asked to attribute the grades of the others to a cause. This activity provided a clear sample of data that could test the validity of the self-serving bias and the fundamental attribution error. The reason I chose a group of friends versus a group of random strangers was that when people know each other they are more likely to attribute behavioral causes truthfully, without worrying about hurting anyone's feelings.

For the purposes of this experiment, the test subjects will be addressed as Students X, Y, and Z to keep their names confidential. The results of the experiment were as follows. The first student, Student X, received a "bad" grade on the test and attributed this to the instructor not adequately explaining the information in class and not telling the students everything the test would ultimately cover. However, Students Y and Z seemed to conclude that the reason Student X got a "bad" grade was because he did not study enough and is generally lazy when it comes to college test taking. Student Y received a "good" grade on the test and attributed this to studying hard the night before and to the fact that the test was relatively easy if one studied the notes. Students X and Z seemed to conclude that Student Y is a naturally smart student who usually receives good grades on tests regardless of how much he or she studies. Finally, Student Z received a "bad" grade on the test and attributed this to the instructor not covering the material on the test well enough for students to do well, a similar response to Student X. However, Students X and Y attributed Student Z's poor grade to bad study habits and not taking the class seriously.

These results tend to prove the ideas of both of the attribution theory's categories. Student X attributed his poor grade to the

The writer provides some insight into his methods for collecting data on the experiences of others.

In this section, the writer provides the results of his data collection.

THE ATTRIBUTION THEORY   6

In this section, the writer discusses the implications of his findings for his overall evaluation of the theory.

external cause of the instructor not covering the material well enough, demonstrating the self-serving bias. Students Y and Z attributed Student X's poor grade to the internal cause of Student X not studying hard enough and being a generally lazy college student, exemplifying the ideas of the fundamental attribution error. Student Y attributed her good grade to the internal cause of good study habits, also exemplifying the self-serving bias. However, Students X and Z felt that the reason for Student Y's success was the external cause of being a naturally good student who does well with or without study-ing, reflecting the ideas of the fundamental attribution error. Student Z's results also hold true to the theory. Student Z attributed his poor grade to the external cause of the instructor not covering the material adequately, a belief shared by Student X. Also holding true to the fun-damental attribution error, both Students X and Y attributed Student Z's failure to the internal cause of poor study habits. Based on the findings of this experiment, I can say that both the fundamental attribution error and the self-serving bias hold true on all accounts.

Conclusion

The writer concludes his response paper by reviewing his overall evaluation of the theory in light of his own and others' experiences he analyzed.

Overall, I believe the attribution theory's categories of the self-serving bias and the fundamental attribution error are very appli-cable to everyday life. Based on the data gathered through personal experiences and the experiences of others through the experiment described in this analysis, I believe the theory holds true in the vast majority of situations where people attribute causes to behaviors and/or actions. The only area needing revisions is the self-serving bias when applied to the specific situations of professionals in a field of study or in the case of professional athletes. In both situations, improvement must occur in order to become a professional, and the only way this is likely to happen is by accepting internal fault for poor behaviors. By accepting internal fault, a person gains the motivation to put in the hours of work necessary to learn and improve at what he or she is trying to do. Without this improvement and learning, the ability to reach the professional level is slim to none. This displays the exact opposite of the attribution ideas that are described in the self-serving bias. With the exception of this small niche of situations that falsify the self-serving bias, the validity of the attribution theory is confirmed on all accounts.

THE ATTRIBUTION THEORY   7

Reference

Straker, D. (2008). *Attribution theory*. Retrieved from changingminds
.org: http://changingminds.org/explanations/theories/
attribution_theory.htm

Tip Sheet — Reading and Writing in the Social Sciences

- **Observation plays a critical role in the social sciences.** The academic fields of the social sciences, including sociology, psychology, anthropology, communication studies, and political science, among others, make observations about human behavior and interactions, as well as the systems and social structures we create to organize the world around us.

- **Social science research rests on theories of human behavior and human systems.** These are propositions that are used to explain specific phenomena. Social science research contributes to the continual process of refining these theories.

- **Researchers in the social sciences typically establish a hypothesis**, or a testable proposition that provides an answer or predicts an outcome in response to the research question(s) at hand, at the beginning of a research project.

- **Social science researchers must make choices about the types of methods they use** in any research situation, based on the nature of their line of inquiry and the kind of research question(s) they seek to answer. They may use a quantitative, qualitative, or mixed-methods research design to collect data for analysis.

- **Social scientists must guard against bias in their research.** As such, they rely on rigorous procedures and checks (e.g., ensuring appropriate sample sizes and/or using multiple forms of qualitative data) to ensure that the influence of any biases is as limited as possible.

- **IMRAD format—Introduction, Methods, Results, and Discussion—is a common *structure* used for the organization of research reports in the social sciences.** Although research reports in the social sciences may appear in any number of forms, much of the scholarship published in these fields appears in the IMRAD format.

- **The passive voice and hedging are uses of *language*** that characterize, for good reason, social scientific writing.

- **APA style is the most common documentation style used for *reference*** in the fields of the social sciences.

- **The genres of the literature review and the theory response paper are often produced in the fields of the social sciences.**

Introduction to the Natural Sciences

Each of us has likely observed something peculiar in the natural world and asked, "Why does it do that?" or "Why does that happen?" Perhaps you've observed twinkling stars in the night sky and wanted to know why such distant light seems to move and pulse. Or perhaps you've wondered why, as you drive, trees closer to your car appear to rush by much faster than trees in the distance. Maybe you can recall the first time you looked at a living cell under a microscope in a biology course and wondered about the world revealed on the slide.

For most scientists, observation of natural phenomena is the first step in the process of conducting research. Something in the natural world captures their attention and compels them to pose questions. Some moments of scientific observation are iconic—such as Newton's observation of an apple falling from a tree as inspiration for his theory of gravity.

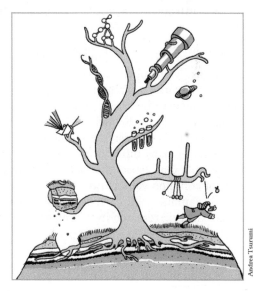

Andrea Tsurumi

We interviewed Sian Proctor, a geologist at South Mountain Community College in Phoenix, Arizona, where she teaches classes in physical, environmental, and historical geology. Dr. Proctor has participated in several unique research team experiences, including the Hawaii Space Exploration Analog and Simulation (HI-SEAS) Mars habitat, the NASA Spaceflight and Life Sciences Training Program (she was a finalist for the 2009 NASA Astronaut Program), and the PolarTREC (Teachers and Researchers Exploring and Collaborating) program in Barrow, Alaska. Her work has taken her out of the college/university setting many times. In her Insider's View, she describes the varied places in which scientists conduct observations and collect data as part of their work to understand the natural world.

Insider's View

Geologists Work out in the Field, in Labs, in Educational Institutions, and in the Corporate World

Sian Proctor, Geology

Courtesy of Sian Proctor

"Geology is an extremely diverse discipline encompassing specialties such as planetary geology, geochemistry, volcanology, paleontology, and more. The goal of a general geologist is to develop understanding of Earth processes such as the formation of mineral or energy resources, the evolution of landscapes, or the cause of natural disasters. Geologists work out in the field, in labs, in educational institutions, and in the corporate world. They collect data, analyze samples, generate maps, and write reports. Geology instructors teach students how to conceptualize all the information and processes mentioned above. It is our job to get students to think like a geologist (if you are teaching majors) or gain an appreciation for the Earth and Earth processes (if you are teaching non-majors)."

As Dr. Proctor's description of her field reveals, those who work in the **natural sciences** study observable phenomena in the natural world and search for answers to the questions that spark researchers' interests about these phenomena. The disciplines of the natural sciences include a wide array of fields of academic research, including those in agricultural and life sciences, as well as physical sciences. As Dr. Proctor's own life experiences suggest, the search for understanding of natural phenomena can take scientists to many different places, and there is much variety in the ways they engage in research. One aspect that holds this diverse group of disciplines together, though, is a set of common values and procedures used in conducting research. You're probably already familiar with or at least have heard about the **scientific method**, a protocol for conducting research in the sciences that includes the following elements, or steps:

1. Observe.

2. Ask a research question.

3. Formulate a hypothesis.

4. Test the hypothesis.

5. Explain the results.

In this chapter, we describe the process of writing activities involved in scientific research. We present this strategy, the scientific writing process, in terms of a four-step process that maps onto the elements of the scientific method. The process begins with careful observation of natural phenomena and leads to the development of research questions. This step is followed by an investigation that culminates in the reporting or publication of the research:

1. Observe and describe.

2. Speculate.

3. Experiment.

4. Report.

The following table illustrates how the elements of the scientific method map onto the scientific writing process:

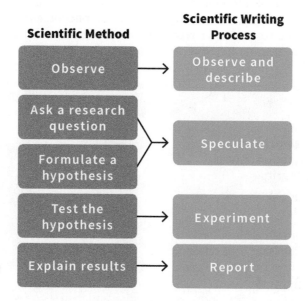

Before we delve too deeply into the research and writing practices of students and scholars of the sciences and how they connect, though, let's consider some of the areas of inquiry that make up the natural sciences.

Astronomy, biology, chemistry, earth science, physics, and mathematics are some of the core disciplinary areas within the natural sciences. Each area of inquiry includes numerous areas of specialty, or fields. For example, quantum physics, acoustics, and thermodynamics are three fields of physics. Conservation biology and marine science are fields of biology. Ecology (the study of organisms and their relationships to their environments) also operates under the umbrella of biology.

Interdisciplinary research is quite common in the natural sciences. An **interdisciplinary field** is an area of study in which different disciplinary perspectives or methods are combined into one. In such instances, methods for data collection often associated with one field may be used within another field of study. Consider biochemistry and biophysics, two interdisciplinary fields. In biochemistry, methods often associated with chemistry research are useful in answering questions about living organisms and biological systems. A biochemist may study aspects of a living organism such as blood alkalinity and its impact on liver function. Likewise, researchers in biophysics may use methods typical of physicists to answer research questions about biological systems. Biophysicists, for instance, might use the methodology of physics to unlock the mysteries of human DNA.

Research in the Natural Sciences

No matter the specific fields in which scientists work, they all collect, analyze, and explain data. Scientists tend to embrace a shared set of values, and as a result they typically share similar desires about how best to conduct research. The importance of any scientific study and its power to explain a natural phenomenon, then, are largely based on how well a researcher or research team designs and carries out a study in light of the shared values and desires of the community's members.

Insider's View

We Value Innovation, Ideas, Accurate Interpretation of Data, and Scientific Integrity

Paige Geiger, Molecular and Integrative Physiology

Courtesy of Paige Geiger

"A biomedical scientist performs basic research on questions that have relevance to human health and disease, biological processes and systems. We design scientific studies to answer a particular research question and then report our results in the form of a manuscript for publication. Good science is only as good as the research study design itself. We value innovation, ideas, accurate interpretation of data, and scientific integrity. There is an honor system to science that the results are accurate and true as reported. Manuscripts are peer-reviewed, and there is inherent trust and belief in this system."

Inside Work: Considering a Natural Science Topic

Generate a list of natural science topics or issues that interest you. Include any you may have read about or heard about recently, perhaps in a magazine or blog or from a television news report. Then select one for further consideration. Try to focus on a topic in which you're genuinely interested or for which you have some concern. If you're currently taking a natural science course or studying in one of the fields of the natural sciences, you might consider a topic that has emerged from your classroom or laboratory experiences. Answer the following questions.

- What is the topic?

- What do you think scientists are currently interested in discovering about this topic? What would you like to know about the topic?

- Could the topic be addressed by researchers in more than one field of the sciences? Is the topic multidisciplinary in nature? What fields of the natural sciences are currently exploring or could potentially explore the topic?

- How do or could scientists observe and collect data on some aspect of the topic?

- In a broader sense, how does the topic connect with you personally?

Completing the steps of a research project in a logical order and reporting the results accurately are keys to mastering research and writing in the natural sciences. You must observe and describe an object of study before you can speculate as to what it is or why it does what it does. Once you've described and speculated about a particular phenomenon, and posed a research question and a hypothesis about it, then you're positioned well to construct an experiment (if appropriate) and collect data to test whether your hypothesis holds true. When you report the results of your research, you must describe these steps and the data collected accurately and clearly. These research and writing steps build on one another, and we explore each step in more detail moving forward.

We interviewed biomedical scientist Paige Geiger, who teaches in the Department of Molecular and Integrative Physiology at the University of Kansas Medical Center, where she conducts experimental research in a laboratory on the effects of exercise and age on muscle metabolism and insulin resistance in Type II diabetes. In her Insider's View, she describes the kind of work that natural scientists do in her field and the importance of conducting careful, thorough data collection in the sciences.

Natural scientists collect evidence through systematic observation and experimentation, and they value methods that are quantifiable and replicable. In some instances, the natural sciences are described as "hard" sciences and the social sciences as "soft." This distinction stems from the tendency for natural scientists to value quantitative methods over qualitative methods, whereas social scientists often engage in both forms of data collection and sometimes combine quantitative and qualitative methods in a single study. (See Chapter 13, pp. 377–82, for more discussion of quantitative and qualitative methods.) Natural scientists value experiments and data collection processes that can be repeated to achieve the same or similar results, often for the purposes of generalizing their findings. Social scientists acknowledge the fluidity and variability of social systems and therefore also highly value qualitative data, which helps them to understand more contextual experiences.

Observation and Description in the Natural Sciences

Observing in the natural world is an important first step in scientific inquiry. Indeed, the first step of the scientific method is observation, as we show in the table on page 427. Beyond simple observation, though, researchers in the natural sciences conduct **systematic observations** of their objects of study. A systematic approach to observation requires a researcher to follow a regular, logical schedule of observation and to conduct focused and *neutral* observations of the object of study. In other words, the researcher tries to minimize or eliminate any bias about the subject matter and simply records everything he or she experiences, using the five senses. These observations, when written up to share with others as part of a research report, form the basis of description of the object of study. In order to move from observation to description, researchers must keep careful notes about their systematic observations. We discuss one method of tracking those observations, an observation logbook, on pages 444–45.

Inside Work: Thinking about Systematic Observation in the Sciences

Read student Kedric Lemon's account of his observations (on pp. 447–54) of various batteries, which he completed between October 11 and October 19, 2013, as part of his observation logbook. Then answer the following questions.

- What do you know about who the author is, based on the language used in this description? Provide at least two specific examples of how the language suggests something about the author's background, knowledge, or frame of reference.

- What can you determine about the observation schedule that the author—the researcher—followed to write this description?

- What kinds of details must the researcher have noted when observing to write this description?

- Did you find any language that seems to reveal bias on the part of the researcher? If so, make a note of this language.

- Based on your answers to the previous questions, what kind of plan for systematic observation would you recommend for the topic you chose in the previous Inside Work activity?

Moving from Description to Speculation

The distinction between description and speculation is a subtle but important one to understand as it relates to scientific inquiry. As we've seen, descriptive writing in the sciences is based on observations. Of course, descriptive writing in the sciences isn't only applicable to a physical space or a stored energy device. A researcher could use similar observational methods to describe, say, the movements of an ant crawling along a sidewalk or tidal erosion along a section of a beach. Descriptive writing, then, is the action outcome associated with the first step of the scientific method—observation.

Speculative writing, in contrast, seeks to explain *how* or *why* something behaves the way that it does, and it is most commonly associated with asking a research question and formulating a hypothesis—the second and third steps of the scientific method. In order to speculate about how or why something exists or behaves as it does, a researcher must first observe and describe. Developing a thorough observational strategy and completing a descriptive writing process will help you to lay a solid foundation for speculating about your object of study so that you can later develop a clear research question and formulate a credible hypothesis worthy of testing through experimentation.

To understand the difference between description and speculation, compare the following two zoo memos written by middle school students.[1] Which one is the better example of descriptive writing? Which one engages more fully in speculative writing?

Middle School Students' Science Memo #1 (12-year-old girls)

On Monday, July 17, DC and I observed the Muntjac. We learned that this animal comes from Asia. And that they eat the bottom part of the grass because it is fresher. We also learned that Muntjacs are very secretive animals. We also observed the difference between a male and female. The male has a [*sic*] earring in his left ear and he has horns. To urinate they stand on three legs. They like to disappear into the bushes. Their habbitat [*sic*] is bushy land.

Another behavior that we observed was the adult Muntjac often moved toward the fence and sniffed. We believe he was sniffing for food. He also rolled back his ears and stuck out his neck. We think he is always alert to protect his family from danger. On one occasion, the male Muntjac came toward the fence. KT [another student] held her shirt toward him. He ran away quickly.

In conclusion, we can say that the Muntjac constantly hunts for food, but is always alert to protect itself and its family.

---

1 From "Revitalizing Instruction in Scientific Genres: Connecting Knowledge Production with Writing to Learn in the Sciences," *Science Education* 83, no. 2 (1999), 115–30.

Middle School Students' Science Memo #2 (13-year-old boys)

Today we went to the Atlanta zoo, where we looked at different animals such as zebras, giraffes, gorilas [*sic*], monkeys, and orangatangs [*sic*]. From my observations of the giraffe I found out that they are rather slow and are always eating. They do many strange things, such as wagging their tails, wiggling their ears, and poking out their tounges [*sic*]. They are very large and I read that they weigh more than a rhinoserous [*sic*], which is close to 2 or 2½ tons, and their necks extend out 7 ft. long. Their tails are 3 ft. long and are sometimes used for swating [*sic*] flies. At times the giraffes will stand completely motionless.

Discussion Questions

1.   What similarities and differences do you notice between the two samples?
2.   Which sample engages in speculative writing more fully, and which one adheres to mostly descriptive writing?

The process of articulating an explanation for an observed phenomenon and speculating about its meaning is an integral part of scientific discovery. By collecting data on your own and then interpreting it, you're engaging in the production of knowledge even before you begin testing a proposed hypothesis. In this respect, scientific discovery is similar to writing in the humanities and the social sciences. Scientists interpret data gained through observation, modeling, or experimentation much in the same way that humanists interpret data collected through observation of texts. The ability to *observe systematically* and *make meaning* is the common thread that runs through all academic research.

Descriptive writing seeks to define an object of study, and it functions like a photograph. Speculative writing engages by asking *how* or *why* something behaves the way that it does, and in this sense it triggers a kind of knowledge production that is essential to scientific discovery. Following a writing process that moves a researcher from describing a phenomenon to considering *how* or *why* something does what it does is a great strategy for supporting scientific inquiry.

To this end, we encourage you to collect original data as modeled in the writing projects presented at the end of this chapter—the observation logbook (p. 446), the research proposal (p. 456), and the lab report (p. 462). Your view on the natural world is your own, and the data you collect and how you interpret that data are yours to decide. The arguments you form based on your data and your interpretation of that data can impact your world in small or very large ways.

Inside Work: Practicing Description and Speculation

For this activity, you should go outdoors and locate any type of animal (a squirrel, bird, butterfly, frog, etc.) as an object of study. Decide beforehand the amount of time you'll spend observing your subject (five minutes may be enough), and write down in a notebook as many observable facts as possible about your subject and its behavior. Consider elements of size, color, weight, distance traveled, and interaction with other animals or physical objects. If you're able to make a video or take a picture (e.g., with a cell phone camera), please do so.

After you've collected your notes and/or video, return to your classroom and write two paragraphs about your subject. Label the first paragraph "Description" and the second paragraph "Speculation," and use the following writing prompt.

Writing Prompt: The director of your local wildlife management agency needs a written report detailing the behaviors that you observed while watching your animal. Be sure to use your notes or video for accuracy. In the first paragraph, write a *description* of the subject and its behavior. Limit your description to observable facts; resist explaining why the subject appears the way it does or behaves the way it does. In the second paragraph, *speculate* about why the animal appears or behaves the way it does. Limit your speculation to the subject's behavior (or appearance) based on the observable data you wrote in your description. Finally, consider writing questions at the end of the second paragraph that might be answered in future research but that cannot be answered on the basis of your observations alone.

Once you've conducted observations and collected data, you can move to speculation, which involves writing research questions and formulating a hypothesis, consistent with the second and third steps of the scientific method. Writing research questions and hypotheses in the natural sciences is a similar process to those activities in the social sciences (see Chapter 13). Devoting time to several days of focused observation, collecting data, and writing and reflecting on your object of study should trigger questions about what you're observing.

As you write research questions, you might consider the difference between open-ended and closed-ended research questions. A closed-ended question can be answered by *yes* or *no*. By contrast, an open-ended question provokes a fuller response. Here are two examples:

Closed-Ended Question: Is acid rain killing off the Fraser fir population near Mount Mitchell in North Carolina?

Open-Ended Question: What factors contribute to killing off the Fraser fir population near Mount Mitchell in North Carolina?

Scientists use both open-ended and closed-ended questions. Open-ended questions usually begin with *What*, *How*, or *Why*. Closed-ended questions can be appropriate in certain instances, but they can also be quite polarizing. They often begin with *Is* or *Does*. Consider the following two questions:

Closed-Ended Question: Is global warming real?

Open-Ended Question: What factors contribute to global warming?

Rhetorically, the closed-ended question divides responses into *yes* or *no* answers, whereas the open-ended question provokes a more thoughtful response. Neither form of question is better per se, but the forms do function differently. If you're engaging in a controversial subject, a closed-ended research question might serve your purpose. If you're looking for a more complete answer to a complex issue, an open-ended question might serve you better.

Once you've established a focused research question, informed by or derived on the basis of your observation and speculation about a natural science phenomenon, then you're ready to formulate a hypothesis. This will be a testable proposition that provides an answer or that predicts an outcome in response to the research question(s) at hand.

Inside Work: Developing Research Questions and a Hypothesis

Review the observation notes and the descriptions and explanations you produced in the Inside Work activity on page 433. What potential research questions emerged? For example, in an observation logbook about house finches and nesting practices written by one of the authors of this textbook, a question that remained unanswered was why two eggs from the initial brood of five were removed from the nest. Potential research questions for a study might include the one shown here.

Research Question: **Do female house finches remove eggs from their own nests?**

From such a question, we can formulate a hypothesis.

Hypothesis: **Our hypothesis is that female house finches do remove eggs from their own nests. Furthermore, our observational data supports other scholars' claims that female house finches cannibalize their brood on occasion.**

Now you try it. Write down at least two research questions that emerged from your observations, and then attempt to answer each question in the form of a hypothesis. Finally, discuss your hypotheses with a classmate or small group, and make the case for which one most warrants further study. Freewrite for five minutes about the evidence you have or additional evidence you could collect that would support your chosen hypothesis.

Designing a Research Study in the Natural Sciences

As we've noted, research in the natural sciences most often relies on quantitative data to answer research questions. While there are many ways to collect and analyze quantitative data, most professional scientists rely on complex statistical procedures to test hypotheses and generate results.

We interviewed Michelle LaRue, a research fellow at the Polar Geospatial Center, a research group based at the University of Minnesota. Her doctorate is in conservation biology, and her research has focused mainly on large-mammal habitat selection and movement—in particular, the phenomenon of potential recolonization of cougars in the American Midwest. In her Insider's View excerpt, Dr. LaRue describes the kinds of questions she asks as a scientist and the kinds of data collection and analysis she typically undertakes as part of her efforts to answer her research questions.

Insider's View

I Typically Form Student Study Questions from Personal Observations or Communication with My Colleagues

Michelle LaRue, Conservation Biology

Courtesy of Michelle LaRue

"I am interested in asking questions that address how populations of animals behave across broad spatial and temporal scales (i.e., large regions such as the Midwest or the Ross Sea, Antarctica, over decades), and which methods are most suitable to answer them. Do suitable habitat or dispersal corridors exist for cougars in midwestern North America? Can we use distance sampling to estimate densities of white-tail deer? How many Weddell seals are there in the Ross Sea? Does glacial retreat impact emigration rates of Adélie penguins?

"I typically form study questions from personal observations or communication with my colleagues. Because my questions come from the perspective of a spatial ecologist, I gather data from myriad sources: field work (e.g., aerial surveys), remote sensing and GIS [Geographic Information Systems] data (land cover, locations of animal occurrence, satellite imagery), population dynamics data (fecundities and survival rates), and climate data (air temperature, wind speed). Compiling data from various disciplines helps me understand the landscape more broadly than focusing on just one aspect. Analysis of these data includes GIS and statistical procedures."

In the previous two sections, we discussed how to conduct systematic observation that leads to description of a phenomenon, and then we explored processes for speculating about what you observed in order to construct a research question and a hypothesis. One way to test a hypothesis is to engage in a systematic observation of the target of your research phenomenon. Imagine that you're interested in discovering factors that affect the migration patterns of bluefin tuna, and you've hypothesized that water temperature has some effect on those patterns. You could then conduct a focused observation to test your hypothesis. You might, for instance, observe bluefin tuna in their migration patterns and measure water temperatures along the routes.

Another way to test a hypothesis, of course, is to design an experiment. Experiments come in all shapes and sizes, and one way to learn about the experimental methods common to your discipline is by reading the Methods sections of peer-reviewed scholarly articles in your field. Every discipline has slightly different approaches to experimental design. Some disciplines, such as astronomy, rely almost exclusively on non-experimental systematic observation, while others rely on highly controlled experiments. Chemistry is a good example of the latter.

One of the most common forms of experimental design is the **comparative experiment**. In a comparative experiment, a researcher tests two or more types of objects and assesses the results. For example, an engineering student may want to test different types of skateboard ball bearings. She may design an experiment that compares a skateboard's distance rolled when using steel versus ceramic bearings. She could measure distances rolled, speed, or the time it takes to cover a preset distance when the skateboard has steel bearings and when it has ceramic bearings.

LaunchPad Solo

Hear more about the prewriting process from a professional mathematician.

In some disciplines of the natural sciences, it's common practice to test different objects against a control group. A **control group** is used in a comparative experimental design to act as a baseline with which to compare other objects. For example, a student researcher might compare how subjects score on a memorization test after having consumed (a) no coffee, (b) two cups of decaf coffee, or (c) two cups of caffeinated coffee. In this example, the group of subjects consuming no coffee would function as a control group.

Regardless of a study's design, it is important to realize that academic institutions have very clear policies regarding experimental designs that involve human subjects, whether that research is being conducted by individuals in the humanities, the social sciences, or the natural sciences. Both professional and student researchers are required to submit proposals through an institutional review board, or IRB. In the United States, *institutional review boards* operate under federal law to ensure that any experiment involving humans is ethical. This is often something entirely new to undergraduate students, and it should be taken seriously. No matter how harmless a test involving human subjects may seem, you should determine if you must submit your research plans through an IRB. This can often be done online. Depending on the nature and scope of your research, though, the processes of outlining the parameters of your research for review may be quite labor-intensive and time-consuming. You should familiarize yourself with the protocol for your particular academic institution. An online search for "institutional review board" and the name of your school should get you started. (For more on the role of institutional review boards, see Chapter 13.)

Inside Work: Freewriting about an Experiment

Start this activity by writing, in one sentence, what your initial research goal was when you began an observation about a phenomenon that interested you. You might draw on your writing from earlier Inside Work activities to start.

> Example: **My goal was to study a bird's nest I discovered on my front porch.**

For many students beginning their inquiry in the sciences, learning about a topic may be the extent of their initial objective. For more advanced students, however, starting an observation from a strong knowledge base may sharpen the objective. The example below draws on prior knowledge of the object of study.

> Example: **My goal was to determine whether a female house finch eats her own eggs.**

Once you've written down what your initial objective was, then freewrite for five minutes about what you now know. What are the most important things you learned about your object of study?

Most important, what hypothesis can you make about your object of study?

> Hypothesis: **My observational data suggest that female house finches often remove eggs from their nest and may occasionally cannibalize their brood.**

After developing a hypothesis, the next step in the scientific method is to test the hypothesis. Keep in mind data in the sciences to support a hypothesis come from either a systematic observation or an experiment.

Freewrite for five minutes about how you could collect data that would test your hypothesis. As you write, consider feasible methods that you could follow soon, as well as methods that might extend beyond the current semester but that you could develop into a larger project for later use in your undergraduate studies. Consider whether an experiment or a systematic observation would be more useful. Most important, use your imagination and have fun.

After observing and describing, speculating and hypothesizing, and conducting an experimental study or systematic observation, scientists move toward publishing the results of their research. This is the final step of the scientific method and the final stage of the scientific writing process that we introduced at the beginning of the chapter: scientists explain their results by reporting their data and discussing its implications. There are multiple forms through which scientists report their findings, and these often depend on the target audience. For instance, a scientist presenting his research results at an academic conference for the consideration of his peers might report results in the form of a poster presentation. Research results can also be presented in the form of an academic journal article. A scientist who wants to present her results to a more general audience, though, might issue a press release. In the next two sections of this chapter, we discuss conventions for reporting results in the natural sciences and provide examples of common genres that researchers in the natural sciences produce as a means of reporting their results.

Conventions of Writing in the Natural Sciences

Although the different fields of study that make up the natural sciences have characteristics that distinguish them from one another, a set of core values and conventions connect these areas of inquiry. The values shared among members of the scientific community have an impact on the communication practices and writing conventions of professionals in natural science fields:

- objectivity
- replicability
- recency
- cooperation and collaboration

In this section, we examine each of these commonly held values in more detail. And we suggest that these values are directly linked to many of the conventions that scientists follow when they write, or to the ways scientists communicate with one another more generally.

Objectivity

In her Insider's View, Michelle LaRue notes the importance of maintaining clarity in the presentation of ideas in science writing. Of course, clarity is a general expectation for all writing, but the desire for clarity in science writing can also be linked to the community's shared value of objectivity. As we noted earlier, objectivity (or neutrality) in observation and experimentation are essential to the research that scientists do. Most researchers in the natural sciences believe that bias undermines the reliability of research results. When scientists report their results, therefore, they often use rhetorical strategies that bolster the appearance of objectivity in their work. (Note that our marginal annotations below indicate which parts of the SLR model apply—structure, language, and reference; see Chapter 11.)

Insider's View

I Also Learned the KISS Principle during My Undergraduate Career

Michelle LaRue, Conservation Biology

Courtesy of Michelle LaRue

"I learned the conventions of science writing through literature review, imitation, and a lot of practice: this often included pages and pages of feedback from advisors and colleagues. Further, reading wildlife and modeling articles helped me focus on the tone, writing style, and format expected for each journal. After that, it was all about practicing my writing skills.

"I also learned the KISS principle during my undergraduate career: Keep It Simple, Stupid. This mantra reminds me to revise my writing so it's clear, concise, and informative. It is my opinion that science writing can be inherently difficult to understand, so it's important to keep the message clear and straightforward.

"I find that as I progress and hone my writing and research skills, sitting down to write gets easier, and I have been able to move up in the caliber of journal in which I publish papers. Writing is a skill that is never perfected; striving for the next best journal keeps me focused on improvement."

Rhetorical Features That Convey Objectivity

- **Titles**   Scientists tend to give their reports very clear titles. Rarely will you find a "creative" or rhetorical title in science writing. Instead, scientists prefer non-rhetorical, descriptive titles, or titles that say exactly what the reports are about.

  Titles may be considered a language and/or a structural feature of a text.

- **IMRAD**   Researchers in the sciences generally expect research reports to appear in the IMRAD format (for more detail, see Chapters 11 and 13):

  The IMRAD format is a common structure used in scientific writing.

  Introduction

  Methods

  Results

  Discussion

Notice how the structure of IMRAD parallels the ordered processes of the scientific writing process (observe and describe, speculate, experiment, and report). This reporting structure underscores the importance of objectivity because it reflects the prescribed steps of the scientific method, which is itself a research process that scientists follow to reduce or eliminate bias.

Jargon is a language feature.

- **Jargon**   Scientists often communicate in highly complex systems of words and symbols that hold specific meaning for other members of the scientific community. These words and symbols enable scientists to communicate their ideas as clearly as possible. For example, a scientific researcher might refer to a rose as *Rosa spinosissima*. By using the Latin name, she communicates that the specific type of rose being referenced is actually the one commonly referred to as the Scotch rose. The use of jargon, in this instance, is actually clarifying for the intended audience. Using jargon is a means of communicating with precision, and precision in language is fundamental to objective expression.

Numbers and other symbol systems function in much the same way as words, so they may be understood as a language feature.

- **Numbers**   Scientific reports are often filled with charts and figures, and these are often filled with numbers. Scientists prefer to communicate in numbers because unlike words, which can inadvertently convey the wrong meaning, numbers are more fixed in terms of their ability to communicate specific meaning. Consider the difference between describing a tree as "tall" and giving a tree's height in feet and inches. This represents the difference between communicating somewhat qualitatively and entirely quantitatively. The preference for communicating in numbers, or quantitatively, enables members of the scientific community to reduce, as much as possible, the use of words. As writers use fewer words and more numbers in scientific reports, the reports appear to be more objective.

Replicability

Like objectivity, the **replicability** of research methods and findings is important to the production and continuation of scientific inquiry. Imagine that a scientific report reveals the discovery that eating an orange every day could help prevent the onset of Alzheimer's disease. This sounds great, right? But how would the larger scientific community go about verifying such a finding? Multiple studies would likely be undertaken in an attempt to replicate the original study's finding. If the finding couldn't be replicated by carefully following the research procedures outlined in the original study, then that discovery wouldn't contribute much, if anything at all, to ongoing research on Alzheimer's disease precisely because the finding's veracity couldn't be confirmed.

Inside Work: Looking for Conventions of Objectivity

Although we've discussed a number of writing expectations related to objectivity in the sciences, we need to stress again that these expectations are conventional. As such, you'll likely encounter numerous studies in the sciences that rely on only a few of these features or that alter the conventional expectations in light of a study's particular aims.

- Choose a scientific topic of interest to you, and locate a research article on some aspect of that topic in a peer-reviewed academic journal article.

- Once you've found an appropriate article, look at the features of the article that reflect the writers' desire for objectivity in science reporting. Note evidence of the following in particular:

  - straightforward, descriptive titles

  - IMRAD

  - jargon

  - numbers

- Take notes on instances where the article follows conventional expectations for science reporting as explained in this chapter, as well as instances where the article alters or diverges from these expectations. Speculate as to the authors' reasoning for their decisions to follow the conventional expectations or to diverge from them.

Several conventional aspects of writing in the natural sciences help ensure the replicability of a study's findings and underscore replicability as an important value shared by members of the scientific community:

- **Detail**   One of the conventional expectations for scientific writing involves the level of detail and specificity, particularly in certain areas of research reporting (e.g., Methods sections). Scientists report their research methods in meticulous detail to ensure that others can replicate their results. This is how scientific knowledge builds. Verification through repeated testing and retesting of results establishes the relative absolute value of particular research findings. It's not surprising, then, that the Methods sections of scientific research reports are typically highly detailed and specific.

  Detail may be considered a language or a structural feature.

- **Hypotheses**   Hypothesis statements predict the outcome of a research study, but the very nature of a prediction leaves open the possibility of other outcomes. By opening this "space" of possibility, scientists acknowledge that other researchers could potentially find results that differ from their own. In this way, scientists confirm the importance of replicability to their inquiry process.

  Hypotheses are a structural feature.

Precision is a language feature of scientific writing.

Precision   Scientific communication must be precise. Just as researchers must choose words and numbers with attention to accuracy and exactness, so too must they present their findings and other elements of scientific communication with absolute precision. As you engage with scientific discourse, you should be able to develop a sense of the precise nature of scientific description and explanation.

Recency

Scientific research is an ongoing process wherein individual studies or research projects contribute bits of information that help fill in a larger picture or research question. As research builds, earlier studies and projects become the bases for additional questioning and research. As in other fields, like the social sciences, it's important that scientific researchers remain current on the developments in research in their respective fields of study. To ensure that their work demonstrates **recency**—that is, it is current and draws on knowledge of other recent work—researchers in the sciences may follow numerous conventions in their writing, including those listed here:

LaunchPadSolo

Learn about putting your research in context.

The purposeful selection of resources is a reference feature.

Reference Selection   Scientific writers typically reference work that has been published recently on their topic. One way to observe the importance of recency is to examine the dates of studies and other materials referenced in a recent scientific publication. If you do this, then you'll likely discover that many studies referenced are relatively recent. By emphasizing recent research in their reports, scientists convey the importance of remaining on top of the current state of research in their areas of expertise. Knowledge production in the natural sciences is highly methodical and builds slowly over time. It's not surprising, then, that the recency of research is important to members of this community.

Scientific documentation systems of reference are often APA or CSE, but they are frequently also specific to the journal in which an article is published.

Documentation   The importance of recency is also evident in the methods of documentation most often employed in the fields of the natural sciences, like APA (American Psychological Association), CSE (Council of Science Editors), and others. Unlike MLA, for instance, where only page numbers appear next to authors' names in parenthetical citations—as in (Jacobs 1109)—the APA system requires a date next to authors' names, both for in-text references to research and, often, in parenthetical remarks when this is not provided in text—as in (Jacobs, 2012, pp. 198–199). The fact that the APA method generally requires a date highlights scientists' concern for the recency of the research they reference and on which they build their own research.

Inside Work: Looking for Conventions of Replicability and Recency

Start with the same article that you used in the previous Inside Work activity to search for writing conventions that demonstrate objectivity. If you don't already have an article selected, search for an academic article published in a peer-reviewed journal on a scientific topic of interest to you.

- Look for at least one example of the researchers' use of the following conventions that might demonstrate how much they value replicability and recency. Note evidence of the following:
  - details
  - precision
  - timely reference selection
  - choice of documentation style
- Take notes on instances where the article follows conventional expectations for science reporting as explained in this chapter and instances where the article alters or diverges from these expectations. Speculate as to the authors' reasoning for their decisions to follow the conventional expectations or to diverge from them.

Cooperation and Collaboration

Unlike the clichéd image of the solitary scientist spending hours alone in a labora-tory, most scientists would probably tell you that research in their fields takes place in a highly cooperative and collaborative manner. In fact, large networks of researchers in any particular area often comprise smaller networks of scholars who are similarly focused on certain aspects of a larger research question. These networks may work together to refine their research goals in light of the work of others in the network, and researchers are constantly sharing—through publication of reports, team researching, and scholarly conferences—the results of their work. Several common elements in scientific writing demonstrate this value:

- **Presentation of Researchers' Names** As you examine published research reports, you'll find that very often they provide a list, prominently, of the names of individuals who contributed to the research and to the reporting of that research. This information usually appears at the top of reports just after the title, and it may also identify the researchers' institutional and/or organizational affiliations. Names typically appear in an order that identifies principal researchers first. Naming all the members of a research team acknowledges the highly cooperative nature of the research-ing processes that many scientists undertake.

The presentation of researchers' names is a structural feature.

Treatment of Other Researchers   Another feature you might notice is the way science professionals treat one another's work. In the humanities, where ideas are a reflection of the individuals who present them, researchers and writers often direct commentary toward individuals for their ideas when there's cause for disagreement or dissatisfaction with other researchers' ideas. Conventionally, however, science researchers treat others in their field more indirectly when objections to their research or findings come up. Instead of linking research problems to individuals, scientists generally direct their dissatisfaction with others' work at problems in the research process or design. This approach highlights the importance of cooperation and collaboration as shared values of members of the scientific community.

Genres of Writing in the Natural Sciences

Once again we interviewed Paige Geiger, whom you met earlier in this chapter. She teaches in the Department of Molecular and Integrative Physiology at the University of Kansas Medical Center. In the following Insider's View, she describes two important genres of writing in her discipline.

In this section, we provide descriptions of, and steps for producing, three of the most common genres that writers in the natural sciences produce: an observation logbook, a research proposal, and a lab report. The observation logbook provides a location for carefully recording systematic observations at the beginning of a research process. The research proposal forms the basis for the important grant proposals that Dr. Geiger describes, and it might draw on information gathered during initial observations. It also incorporates other elements such as a careful review of the literature on a subject. Lab reports are the final results of research, and they reflect the form in which a scientist might ultimately publish a scholarly journal article.

An Observation Logbook

Systematic and carefully recorded observations can lay a solid foundation for further exploration of a subject. These observations might take place as an initial step in the scientific writing process, or they might be part of the data collection that occurs when testing a hypothesis.

One way to focus and record your observations of a phenomenon is to keep an **observation logbook**. The tools that we discuss over the next few pages parallel the kind of systematic observation that's needed to undertake scientific inquiry, and the observation logbook functions as both a data collection tool and a reflective strategy that becomes useful later in research writing and reporting stages. The observation logbook is a foundational part of the research process that precedes the construction of a formal lab report.

Sometimes observation logbooks include speculation in addition to description, but the two types of writing should be clearly separated from each other to ensure that the more objective observations are not confused with any speculation. Speculation, you'll remember, occurs at the stage of formulating research questions and a hypothesis.

Insider's View

Two Different Forms Serve Very Different Purposes

Paige Geiger, Molecular and Integrative Physiology

Courtesy of Paige Geiger

"There are two kinds of writing in my discipline—writing manuscripts for publication and writing grant applications. The two different forms serve very different purposes. We must write grant applications to obtain funding to perform our research. The applications are usually for three to five years of funding and are very broad in scope. These applications describe what you plan to do and the results you expect to see. This requires a comprehensive assessment of the literature, an explanation of what is known and what is unknown regarding the specific research question. You must describe how you will design the studies, how you will collect and analyze data, and how you will handle problems or unexpected results. This kind of writing is considered an art form. It is something that you improve upon throughout your career.

"Writing manuscripts for publication is quite different. A manuscript deals with a very specific research question, and you report the direct results of your investigation. There is some background information to place the study in a greater context, but the focus is on the data and the interpretation of the data from this one study. This form of writing is very direct, and overinterpretation of the data is frowned upon. In addition to these two forms of writing, scientists also write review articles and textbook chapters on their area of expertise."

Writing Project: Keeping an Observation Logbook

For this project, you'll need to decide on a particular object of study and collect at least five days of observations about it. We encourage you to develop a multi-modal data collection process that includes digital photos and videorecorded evidence. For each daily entry, begin with description before moving into speculation. A natural outgrowth of descriptive writing should include brainstormed research questions that could be answered with further experiments, research, or observation.

For each day, you should do the following.

1. Collect and include photographic evidence.
2. Write a description of your object of study and its status.
3. Generate questions for future research.

At the conclusion of five days, answer the following questions.

1. What did I learn about my object of study?
2. What claims can I now make regarding my object of study?
3. What evidence could I use from my observational logbook to support those claims?

Finally, write a one- to two-page paper that includes two sections.

1. Description
2. Speculation

For the **Description** section, write a description of your object of study. Refrain from explaining or speculating about behavior in this section; simply write the observations that are most important to give a clear picture of what you studied and how you studied it. Make use of time measurements and physical measurements such as weight, size, and distance. For the **Speculation** section, assert suggestions as to why certain behaviors emerged in your object of study. You might begin by deciding which behaviors most surprised you or seem most interesting to you.

You might also use the Speculation section as a place to begin thinking about future questions that could be explored as a follow-up to your observations.

Insider Example

Student Observation Logbook

In the following observation logbook, written using APA style conventions, student Kedric Lemon catalogs his observations concerning the efficiency of several types of batteries over a five-day period. His observations form the basis for his experimental study, which appears later on pages 463–70. You'll notice that he carefully separates his observations and description from any speculation about why he observed what he did.

Comparing the Efficiency of Various Batteries

Being Used over Time

Kedric Lemon

North Carolina State University

THE EFFICIENCY OF BATTERIES   2

Comparing the Efficiency of Various Batteries
Being Used over Time

Logbook

Introduction

Establishes the purpose of the study, and outlines an observational protocol.

The purpose of this study is to see if some batteries can hold their charge for longer periods of time than others. Also, this observational study will determine if there is an overwhelming difference between generic brand and the top name-brand batteries, or if people are really just paying for the name. I will perform this study by first recording all of the batteries' initial voltages, and then each day I will allow each of the batteries to go on for an hour and a half and then again check the voltage. It is important that I test the voltage immediately after the batteries come out of the flashlight. Otherwise, results could vary. Before putting in the second set of batteries, I will allow the flashlight to cool down for an hour because after being in use for an hour and a half they are likely hot, and I am unsure if this can affect how fast the other batteries will be consumed. I will look first at how much charge was lost over the duration that they were used in the flashlight. Then I will compare them to one another to determine which one has lost the most over a day, and second, which of the batteries still holds the highest voltage. I hypothesize that the Duracell battery will decrease at the slowest rate and that it will have the highest initial voltage.

Outlines methods

Establishes a hypothesis.

Friday, October 11, 2013

Begins a report on systematic observation of the phenomenon.

Today was the first day that I observed results from my batteries. I believe that the first thing is to state the initial voltages of all three types of batteries. (Also, it is important to note that these are the averages of the batteries, as the flashlight demands two AA batteries.)

THE EFFICIENCY OF BATTERIES   3

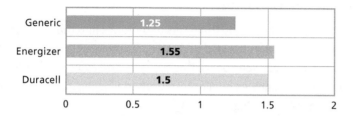

So from these initial observations the Energizer battery has the highest initial voltage.

After allowing all of the batteries to run for an hour and a half, I again took the voltages of the batteries and found this:

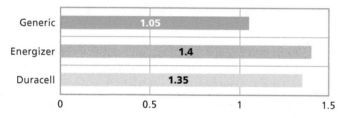

Energizer and Duracell both appear to be decreasing at approximately the same rates thus far in the observation, whereas the generic brand has already dropped much faster than the other two types of batteries. From this observation I have raised the question: What is the composition of the Duracell and Energizer batteries that allows them to hold a better initial charge than the generic brand of batteries?

Observations leading to questions.

THE EFFICIENCY OF BATTERIES   4

Sunday, October 13, 2013

Provides evidence of the researcher's attempt to remain systematic in his observations.

Today I again put the three sets of batteries into the flashlight, in the same order as the trial prior, to allow them all to have close to the same time between usages, again to try and avoid any variables. Today my data showed similar results after allowing all of the batteries to run in the flashlight for an hour and a half:

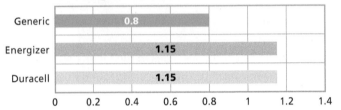

After this day of observing the results I found that the generic brand of batteries did not decrease as significantly as it did after the first trial. This day the generic brand lost close to the same voltage as the other two types of batteries. Another interesting observation I found was that Energizer and Duracell had the same voltages.

Tuesday, October 15, 2013

On this day of observation I again put the batteries into the flashlights for the trial time. The data I found for this day was as follows:

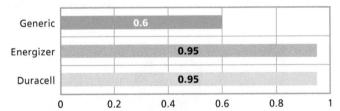

Student's observations continue to raise questions.

On this day I found that again the generic brand decreased by an amount similar to the other two batteries. Also I found that the generic brand's intensity has begun to decrease. However, both the other two batteries still give off a strong light intensity. This observation raises the question: At what voltage does the light intensity begin to waver? Another question is: Will the other two batteries begin to have lower light intensity at approximately the same voltage

THE EFFICIENCY OF BATTERIES   5

as the generic, or will they continue to have a stronger light intensity for longer? The figures below show the change of light intensity of the generic brand of batteries from the beginning until this day's observation.

Figure 1. Before   *Figure 2.* After

Thursday, October 17, 2013

Today is my fourth day of observation. The readings for the voltages for this day were:

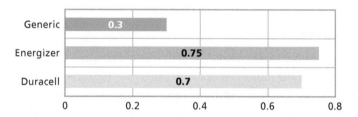

The generic brand is losing even more intensity when it is in the flashlight. It is obvious that it is getting near the end of its battery charge. Today was also the biggest decrease in charge for the generic brand of batteries. This is interesting because it is actually producing less light than before, so why does it lose more voltage toward the end of its life? Also, another thing I observed for this day was that again the Energizer brand holds more voltages than the Duracell, like before. There is still no change in light intensity for the two name brands.

Saturday, October 19, 2013

Today is my final day of observation. This is the data I collected for this day:

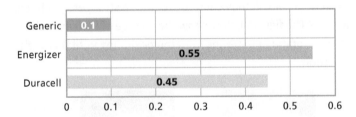

Today the generic battery hardly produced any light out of the flashlight by the end of the time period, although it still didn't drop to 0 voltage, so there are clearly still some electrons flowing in the current throughout the battery. Also, I observed that the Duracell battery has clearly dropped well below the Energizer now. The Duracell has shown a slight decrease in the light intensity compared to when the observational study first started. So what is the composition of the Energizer battery that makes it outlast the Duracell battery?

Narrative

Description

The narrative description provides a summary of the student's systematic observation.

    Five days of observations were conducted over an eight-day period. It did not matter what day of the week I took these observations nor the conditions of the environment around my object of study at the time of the observations. The only thing that I made sure that was constant environmentally for all of the batteries in the study was the temperature because more heat results in higher kinetic energy, which causes electrons to move faster. I had to decide on the types of batteries that I wanted to study for the observational study. The batteries I decided on were: Duracell, Energizer, and a generic brand from Wal-Mart. Before I took my first observation I tested each of the batteries that were to be used with the voltmeter to know the initial charge of the battery. Doing this gave me an idea from the beginning of which battery is typically the most powerful and also how much the batteries would be losing in comparison to their initial charge.

    Each of these battery types was tested for the same amount of time for each day that they were observed. Since the flashlight took

THE EFFICIENCY OF BATTERIES   7

two batteries to run properly I was planning on taking the average of the two batteries, but I found them to be very similar in all of the trials. I believe that this occurrence is a result of the entire circuit acting at the same time, causing equal electron transfer between the two batteries to occur, thus causing them to have equal voltages.

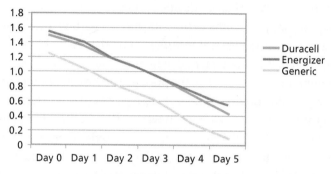

Final Graph from Five Days of Observations

The graph above shows the change in voltage over the five-day period that I took the observations. As you can see, Duracell and Energizer are very similar to one another, with Energizer performing slightly higher than the Duracell brand. The generic has a lower initial voltage than the other two batteries and continues to decrease at a faster rate than the other two batteries. Another thing you can see from this graph is how quickly the generic brand lost its voltage toward the end of its life, whereas the other two batteries seemed to continue to decrease at approximately the same rate throughout.

Speculation

My initial hypothesis that the Duracell battery would decrease at the slowest rate was not supported by this data. I have done a little bit of research on the composition of the cathodes of the Duracell and Energizer batteries. I found that the Duracell battery uses a copper tip on the cathode, whereas the Energizer uses a combination of lithium with the copper tip to allow longer battery life. This would explain why the Energizer battery decreases at a slightly lower rate than the Duracell battery does. Also, the generic brand of batteries

Evaluates initial hypothesis (speculation) in light of the data.

THE EFFICIENCY OF BATTERIES   8

Further speculates about factors that contributed to rejection of the hypothesis.

uses a carbon and copper tip. This would explain why it decreases at a higher rate than the other two name-brand batteries. Also, the cathodes and anodes of the generic batteries may not be as professionally manufactured as the other two types of batteries. All of these reasons could explain why there is a higher voltage density in the Energizer battery than in the other two batteries.

Also, my initial hypothesis that the Duracell battery would have the highest initial voltage was incorrect. From the research that I have gathered, the only explanation for the higher initial voltage in the Energizer battery would be the presence of the alkaline metals that the manufacturer puts into its batteries, whereas the Duracell manufacturer does no such thing. However, there is little information on the Internet about the generic brand of batteries that I used for the experiment, but I was able to find that the reason it has such a lower initial voltage than the other two types of batteries is because it is not packed as well. It takes special equipment to make all the electrons store properly, and the equipment used is not as powerful as the ones that Duracell and Energizer use for their batteries. These ideas all make up my understanding of why there is such a major difference in the rates at which the batteries lose their charge.

Provides suggestions for future research on the subject.

For further research into this topic I would recommend using a larger sample, because I used only two batteries for each type of battery. Also, I would recommend looking into the new rechargeable batteries, as that is what a lot of people are turning to more recently. Another thing that I would try is leaving the batteries on longer because from some of the research that I have done, Duracell does better than Energizer over continuous usage. This means that maybe there is something in the Energizer batteries that causes them to speed up reactions over long periods of use that will cause them to decrease faster over this period. A study like that would be very interesting to compare to my own.

Another interesting topic to follow up on would be the cost of each of the batteries and which battery would be the most cost-effective for users. A lot of people today are buying the generic brand of batteries because they think that this is saving them money. Yes, the generic brand is sold at a lower price, but it is also being used up faster than the other two types of batteries.

Research Proposal

The research proposal is one of the most common genres of academic writing in the natural sciences. Professional scholars use the research proposal to plan out complex studies, to formulate their thoughts, and to submit their research designs to institutional review boards or to grant-funding agencies. The ability to secure grant funding (i.e., to write an effective research proposal and connect it to a realistic, clear budget) is a highly sought-after skill in a job candidate for many academic, government, and private industry positions. In many cases, an effective proposal results from practice with and knowledge of the conventions expected for the genre. No doubt, much of the work of science could not get done without the research proposal, because it is such an important vehicle for securing the funding and materials necessary to conduct research.

Most research proposals include the following sections:

- Title page
- Introduction (and literature review)
- Methods
- References

The *title page* should include (1) the title of your proposal, (2) your name and the names of any co-authors/researchers, and (3) the name of your academic institution. Your instructor may require additional information such as a running header, date, or author's note. Be sure to ask your instructor what documentation and formatting style to use and what information is required in any specific writing context.

The *introduction* of a research proposal explains the topic and purpose of the proposed research. Be sure to include your research question and/or your proposed hypothesis. Additionally, your introduction should contextualize your research by reviewing scholarly articles related to your topic and showing how your proposed research fills a gap in what is already known about the topic. Specifically, the introduction should explain how other researchers have approached your topic (or a closely related one) in the past, with attention to the major overlapping findings in that research. An effective introduction incorporates a literature review that demonstrates your knowledge of other scholars' research. As such, it builds your credibility to conduct your proposed research. (See Chapter 13, pp. 402–05, for more information about writing a literature review.)

The *Methods section* of a research proposal explains exactly what you will do to test your hypothesis (or answer your research question) and how you will do it. It differs from the Methods section of a lab report in several ways: (1) it should be written in future tense, and (2) it should include more detail about your plans. Further, the Methods section should address how long your study will take and should specify how you will collect data (in a step-by-step descriptive manner).

The *references list* for a research proposal is essentially the same as the references list for a lab report or any other academic project. You'll need to include the full citation information for any work you used in your literature review or in planning or researching your topic.

Writing Project: Developing a Research Proposal

Drawing on a topic of interest to you, develop a research proposal that outlines a specific research question and/or hypothesis, and describe how you would go about answering the question or testing the hypothesis. Keep in mind that successful research proposals include the elements listed below.

- Title page
- Introduction (and literature review)
- Methods
- References

You might try drawing on the observations you collected while completing an observation logbook to develop your research question and/or hypothesis.

Insider Example

Research Proposal

In the following example of a professional research proposal by Gary Ritchison, a biologist at Eastern Kentucky University, note how the Introduction section begins with a brief introduction to the topic (par. 1) and then proceeds to review the relevant literature on the topic (pars. 1 and 2). As you read, consider how a potential funding entity would likely view both the content and the form in which that content is presented. Also note that the references list is titled "Literature Cited." Minor variations like this are common from discipline to discipline and in various contexts. Here, Ritchison has followed CSE style conventions in his proposal.

Hunting Behavior, Territory Quality, and Individual Quality
of American Kestrels
(*Falco sparverius*)

Gary Ritchison

Department of Biological Sciences
Eastern Kentucky University

Hunting Behavior 2

Introduction

Establishes the topic and provides background information on American Kestrels.

American Kestrels (*Falco sparverius*) are widely distributed throughout North America. In Kentucky, these falcons are permanent residents and are most abundant in rural farmland, where they hunt over fields and pastures (Palmer-Ball 1996). Although primarily sit-and-wait predators, hunting from elevated perches and scanning the surrounding areas for prey, kestrels also hunt while hovering (Balgooyen 1976). Kellner (1985) reported that nearly 20% of all attacks observed in central Kentucky were made while kestrels were hovering. Habitats used by hunting kestrels in central Kentucky include mowed and unmowed fields, cropland, pastures, and plowed fields (Kellner 1985).

Reveals evidence of a review of previous scholarship.

Several investigators have suggested that male and female American Kestrels may exhibit differences in habitat use during the non-breeding period, with males typically found in areas with greater numbers of trees, such as wooded pastures, and females in open fields and pastures (Stinson et al. 1981; Bohall-Wood and Collopy 1986). However, Smallwood (1988) suggested that, when available, male and female kestrels in south-central Florida established winter territories in the same type of habitat. Differential habitat use occurred only because migratory female kestrels usually arrived on wintering areas before males and, therefore, were more likely to establish territories in the better-quality, more open habitats before males arrived (Smallwood 1988).

Establishes a local context for research.

In central Kentucky, many American Kestrels are residents. As a result, male and female kestrels would likely have equal opportunity to establish winter territories in the higher-quality, open habitats. If so, habitat segregation should be less apparent in central Kentucky than in areas further south, where wintering populations of kestrels are largely migratory. In addition, territory quality should be correlated with individual quality because higher-quality resident kestrels should be able to defend higher-quality territories.

Hunting Behavior 3

The objectives of my proposed study of American Kestrels will be to examine possible relationships among and between hunting behavior, territory quality, and individual quality in male and female American Kestrels. The results of this study will provide important information about habitat and perch selection by American Kestrels in central Kentucky in addition to the possible role of individual quality on hunting behavior and habitat use.

Reveals research purposes and identifies significance of the proposed research.

Methods

Field work will take place from 15 October 2000 through 15 May 2001 at the Blue Grass Army Depot, Madison Co., Kentucky. During the study period, I will search for American Kestrels throughout accessible portions of the depot. Searches will be conducted on foot as well by automobile.

An attempt will be made to capture all kestrels observed using bal-chatri traps baited with mice. Once captured, kestrels will be banded with a numbered aluminum band plus a unique combination of colored plastic bands to permit individual identification. For each captured individual, I will take standard morphological measurements (wing chord, tarsus length, tail length, and mass). In addition, 8 to 10 feathers will be plucked from the head, breast, back, and wing, respectively. Plumage in these areas is either reddish or bluish, and the quality of such colors is known to be correlated with individual quality (Hill 1991, 1992; Keyser 1998). Variation in the color and intensity of plumage will be determined using a reflectance spectrometer (Ocean Optics S2000 fiber optic spectrometer, Dunedin, FL), and these values will be used as a measure of individual quality. To confirm that plumage color and intensity are dependent on condition, we will use tail feather growth rates as a measure of nutritional condition during molt. At the time of capture, the outermost tail feathers will be removed and the mean width of daily growth bars, which is correlated with nutritional condition (Hill and Montgomerie 1994), will be determined.

This section provides a highly detailed description of proposed research procedures, or methods.

References established methods, or those used by other researchers, to support his own method design.

Hunting Behavior 4

Each focal American Kestrel (N = at least 14; 7 males and 7 females) will be observed at least once a week. Observations will be made at various times during the day, with observation periods typically 1 to 3 hours in duration. During focal bird observations, individuals will be monitored using binoculars and spotting scopes. Information will be recorded on a portable tape recorder for later transcription. During each observation, I will record all attacks and whether attacks were initiated from a perch or while hovering. For perches, I will note the time a kestrel lands on a perch and the time until the kestrel either initiates an attack or leaves for another perch (giving up time). If an attack is made, I will note attack distances (the distance from a perch to the point where a prey item was attacked) and outcome (successful or not). If successful, an attempt will be made to identify the prey (to the lowest taxonomic category possible).

The activity budgets of kestrels will also be determined by observing the frequency and duration of kestrel behaviors during randomly selected 20-min observation periods (i.e., a randomly selected period during the 1- to 3-hour observation period). During these 20-minute periods, the frequency of occurrence of each of the following behaviors will be recorded: capturing prey, preening, engaging in nonpreening comfort movements (including scratching, stretching wing or tail, shaking body plumage, cleaning foot with bill, and yawning), vocalizing, and flying. The context in which flight occurs, including pounces on prey, and the duration of flights and of preening bouts will also be recorded.

Territories will be delineated by noting the locations of focal kestrels, and the vegetation in each kestrel's winter territory will be characterized following the methods of Smallwood (1987). Possible relationships among hunting behavior (mode of attack, perch time, attack distance and outcome [successful or unsuccessful], and type of prey attacked), territory vegetation, time budgets, sex, and individual quality will be examined. All analyses will be conducted using the Statistical Analysis System (SAS Institute 1989).

Hunting Behavior 5

Literature Cited

Balgooyen TG. 1976. Behavior and ecology of the American Kestrel in the Sierra Nevada of California. Univ Calif Publ Zool 103:1–83.

Bohall-Wood P, Collopy MW. 1986. Abundance and habitat selection of two American Kestrel subspecies in north-central Florida. Auk 103:557–563.

Craighead JJ, Craighead FC Jr. 1956. Hawks, owls, and wildlife. Harrisburg (PA): Stackpole.

Hill GE. 1991. Plumage coloration is a sexually selected indicator of male quality. Nature 350:337–339.

Hill GE. 1992. Proximate basis of variation in carotenoid pigmentation in male House Finches. Auk 109:1–12.

Hill GE, Montgomerie R. 1994. Plumage colour signals nutritional condition in the House Finch. Proc R Soc Lond B Biol Sci 258:47–52.

Kellner CJ. 1985. A comparative analysis of the foraging behavior of male and female American Kestrels in central Kentucky [master's thesis]. [Richmond (KY)]: Eastern Kentucky University.

Keyser AJ. 1998. Is structural color a reliable signal of quality in Blue Grosbeaks? [master's thesis]. [Auburn (AL)]: Auburn University.

Mengel RM. 1965. The birds of Kentucky. Lawrence (KS): Allen Press. (American Ornithologists' Union monograph; 3).

Palmer-Ball B. 1996. The Kentucky breeding bird atlas. Lexington (KY): Univ. Press of Kentucky.

SAS Institute. 1989. SAS user's guide: statistics. Cary (NC): SAS Institute.

Smallwood JA. 1987. Sexual segregation by habitat in American Kestrels wintering in southcentral Florida: vegetative structure and responses of differential prey availability. Condor 89:842–849.

Smallwood JA. 1988. The relationship of vegetative cover to daily rhythms of prey consumption by American Kestrels wintering in southcentral Florida. J Raptor Res 22:77–80.

Stinson CH, Crawford DL, Lauthner J. 1981. Sex differences in winter habitat of American Kestrels in Georgia. J. Field Ornithol 52:29–35.

Lab Report

Lab reports are the formal reporting mechanism for research in the sciences. When a scientist publishes an article that reports the results of a research study, it is generally in the form of a lab report. Lab reports include information reported in IMRAD format, and the sections of the lab report are often listed exactly in that order:

• Introduction
• Methods
• Results
• Discussion

Be sure to read through the section on pages 385–93 of Chapter 13 that describes the different kinds of information typically presented in each of these sections.

If a group of researchers writes a research proposal before writing a lab report, they've already completed the first two sections of the lab report and only need to revise the report to reflect what they actually accomplished in the study (instead of what they planned to do). The Results and Discussion sections report new information about the data they gathered and what they offer as explanations and interpretations of what those results might mean. The Discussion section might also include suggestions for future research, demonstrating how research in the sciences is always building upon prior research.

Writing Project: Composing a Lab Report

The final writing project for this chapter is a lab report. You might report results from either experimentation or systematic observation. Your research could take place in an actual laboratory setting, or it could just as easily take place in the wider environment around you. Regardless, be sure to check with your instructor about whether your lab report should be based on formal observation or experimentation.

Since lab reports use IMRAD organizational format, your report should include the following sections:

• Introduction
• Methods
• Results
• Discussion

As you report your results and discuss their significance, you might include elements of visual design to help communicate the results to your audience. These might include tables or figures. Also, you might include an abstract, and you'll need to include a reference list that cites all sources used in your report. (See Chapter 13 for more information on writing tables and figures, and more information on abstracts.)

Insider Example

Student Lab Report

In the following sample lab report, Kedric Lemon revisits the question of which battery type is most effective. He draws on the information gathered in his observation logbook (pp. 446–54) to design a research study that allows him to conduct further investigation to answer his research question.

Running head: WHICH BATTERY IS MOST EFFECTIVE?   1

Which Type of Battery Is the Most Effective
When Energy Is Drawn Rapidly?

Kedric Lemon

North Carolina State University

The researcher provides a descriptive, non-rhetorical title.

WHICH BATTERY IS MOST EFFECTIVE?   2

Which Type of Battery Is the Most Effective When Energy Is Drawn Rapidly?

Introduction

The report follows the conventional IMRAD format.

Today batteries are used in many of the products that we use every day, from the TV remote to the car we drive to work. AA batteries are one of the most widely used battery types, but which of these AA batteries is the most effective? Almeida, Xará, Delgado, and Costa (2006) tested five different types of batteries in a study similar to mine. They allowed each of the batteries to run the product for an hour. The product they were powering alternated from open to closed circuit, so the batteries went from not giving off energy to giving off energy very quickly. The researchers then measured the pulse of the battery to determine the charge. The pulse test is a very effective way of reading the battery because it is closed circuit, meaning it doesn't run the battery to find the voltage, and it is highly accurate. They found that the Energizer battery had the largest amount of pulses after the experiment. The energizer had on average 20 more pulses than the Duracell battery, giving the Energizer battery approximately a half hour longer in battery life when being used rapidly. Booth (1999) also performed his experiment using the pulse test. However, this experiment involved allowing the batteries to constantly give off energy for two hours, and then Booth measured the pulse. So his experiment is more comparable to my observational study because it was constantly drawing energy from the battery. In this experiment he found that the Duracell battery was the most effective. The Duracell battery had over 40 more pulses per minute than the Energizer battery, which means that the battery could last for an hour longer than the Energizer battery would.

The researcher establishes a focus for his research by positing a research question.

Reviews previous research, and connects that research to the current research project.

However, in today's market, rechargeable batteries are becoming increasing popular. Zucker (2005) compared 16 different types of rechargeable batteries. Most of these batteries were Nickel Metal Hydride, but a couple of them were the more traditional rechargeable AA battery, the Nickel Cadmium. In his study Zucker was testing how these batteries faired on their second charge after being discharged as closely as they could; rechargeable batteries are not allowed to go to 0 volts because then they cannot be recharged. In the end Zucker found that all but four of the batteries came back

WHICH BATTERY IS MOST EFFECTIVE? 3

up to at least 70% of their initial charge, two of which did not even recharge at all. He found that, not surprisingly, the two most effective rechargeable batteries were Duracell and Energizer, which both came back to 86% of the first charge. However, the Energizer rechargeable battery had the higher initial charge, so Zucker concluded that the Energizer battery was the most effective rechargeable battery. Yu, Lai, Yan, and Wu (1999) looked at the capacity of three different Nickel Metal Hydride (NiMH) rechargeable batteries. They first took three different types of NiMH batteries and found the electrical capacity through a voltmeter. After, they measured the volume of each of the batteries to discover where it fell in the AA battery range of 600 to 660 mAh/cm3. They used this to test the efficiency of the NiMH batteries, as there are slightly different chemical compositions inside the batteries. In the end they concluded that the NiMH battery from the Duracell brand was the most efficient.

Li, Daniel, and Wood (2011) looked at the improvements being made to lithium ion AA batteries. The lithium ion AA batteries are extremely powerful, but in recent years they have become increasingly more popular for studying by many researchers. Li et al. tested the voltage of the lithium ion AA rechargeable battery and found that the starting voltage was on average 3.2 volts. That is more than the average onetime-use AA battery. They further found that what makes modern lithium ion batteries so much more powerful is the cathodes. Research into cathode materials has significantly increased the rate of reactions for lithium ion batteries.

The objective of this study is to determine which brand of batteries is the most efficient and to compare a generic rechargeable battery to these regular AA batteries. My original research question for my logbook was Which brand of AA batteries is the most effective over extended usage? However, for my final study I wanted to look at how batteries reacted when they were being used very quickly, so I formed two research questions for this study: Which type of battery is the most effective for rapid uses? How do regular AA batteries compare to a generic AA rechargeable battery? My hypothesis for this experiment is that the Energizer battery will be the most effective battery when energy is being taken from the battery rapidly.

Prominence of dates points to the researcher's concern for the recency of source materials.

Continues review of previous scholarship on this topic.

Establishes specific research questions on the basis of previous observations.

Hypothesis

WHICH BATTERY IS MOST EFFECTIVE?　　　　　　　4

Method

Observation Logbook

Reports on research previously conducted.

　　In my observation logbook I looked at how different types of batteries compared when they were being tested through a flashlight. The batteries I observed were Duracell, Energizer, and a generic brand. I allowed the flashlight to run for an hour with the set of batteries inside. I did this step for all three types of batteries that I observed in that study. After the hour was up I tested the voltage with a voltmeter. I continued to do this for five consecutive days. For each of the tests I made sure that the temperature was the same for each of the batteries while they were being tested. I also allowed the flashlight to remain off for an hour to let it cool down. These steps were taken to avoid any unknown variables.

　　For my follow-up study, I decided to look at how batteries compare when they are being used in quick bursts, meaning that they quickly change from using no energy to using a lot of energy rapidly. In order to test the battery this way I had to change the flashlight to a strobe light so that it quickly turns on and off automatically. I also decided to add a rechargeable battery to my tests since this is an increasingly popular item today. I found my data by attaching the batteries to a voltmeter immediately after they were taken out of the strobe light. Each of the set of batteries was in the strobe light for 20 minutes.

Provides a detailed account of research procedures.

　　Variables that I made sure remained constant for this experiment were the temperature of the room as well as the temperature of the

WHICH BATTERY IS MOST EFFECTIVE?   5

strobe light. For this reason I allowed the strobe light a 30-minute cooldown before I put the next set of batteries into it.

Limitations

One of the limitations that I faced in this study was an inability to get the thermocouple that I wanted to measure the temperature of the battery. Also I had a small sample size, so if I had taken more samples, then my results would have been more valid. I could improve on these by getting a thermocouple that would measure the temperature. This would allow me to compare the expected voltage of the battery through the thermocouple and the voltmeter. After the battery got out of the strobe light I would hook it up to the thermocouple and then measure the voltage by looking at the voltmeter. I could tell what the voltage of the battery is through the thermocouple using a graph that one of my secondary sources provided. Another limitation that I faced in this experiment was that I lacked better equipment that could have made my results more accurate—like a pulse reader or a better voltmeter, as I was using a fairly inexpensive one.

The researcher uses technical language, or jargon.

The researcher notes limitations he encountered with the methods.

Results

My results from my logbook provided me with primarily quantitative data. For each of the types of batteries I found these results.

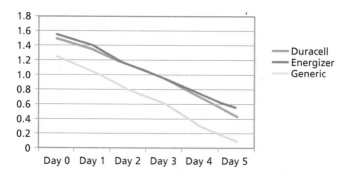

Outlines the major findings of the study. A number of results are also presented visually, in the form of graphs and figures.

The researcher frequently presents results in tables and charts.

For the Energizer battery I found that it started off with the largest initial charge of 1.55 volts. On average the Energizer battery lost .16 volts for every hour. The Duracell battery had an initial charge of 1.5 volts and lost an average of .18 volts per hour. Last, the generic brand of battery had an initial voltage of 1.25 volts and lost on average .23 volts every hour.

WHICH BATTERY IS MOST EFFECTIVE?   6

In this experiment I found that the Energizer battery again had the highest starting charge and highest ending charge. The Duracell AA battery was close behind the Energizer. The generic brand of batteries came next, followed by the rechargeable battery.

This experiment showed similar results to what I had found in my logbook. The Duracell and Energizer batteries were both very similar, while the generic brand lagged behind.

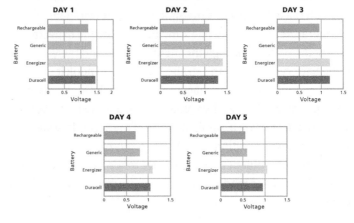

Battery	Initial voltage (volts)	Final voltage (volts)	Average volts lost (volts/20 min)
Energizer	1.60	1.10	0.10
Duracell	1.55	0.95	0.12
Generic	1.40	0.60	0.16
Rechargeable	1.20	0.55	0.13

The table shows that the Energizer battery had the best results in all categories. If I had taken more samples, then I may have found that some of the batteries performed better or worse than they did here, because I could have taken the average of many tests rather than looking at only one. Using a pulse test reader would have been an even more informative way of exploring this experiment because that instrument can estimate the battery life with high precision.

Discussion

Through this experiment I found that the Energizer battery is the most effective battery when used in rapid bursts. Also I found that the rechargeable battery had very bad ratings. Despite the poor

WHICH BATTERY IS MOST EFFECTIVE?   7

ratings, however, it is rechargeable, being a potential reason for its failure. The rechargeable battery is not able to commit as many of its chemicals to solely providing the maximum amount of energy; it has to provide some of the chemicals to the battery's capabilities of recharging. Based on this, the rechargeable battery could be the most effective battery. I found that other studies with similar methods (Booth 1999; Yu, Lai, Yan, & Wu 1999) determined that the Duracell battery was the most effective. However, these studies were conducted years ago.

Provides an overview of the implications of major findings in light of previous scholarship.

If I had had more days to conduct this experiment, I could have more accurately represented the usefulness of the rechargeable battery, because after it exhausted its first charge it came back completely recharged for the next day. Another limitation that I faced in this experiment was that I overestimated how fast the battery voltages would decrease in the strobe light, so I was unable to see how the batteries acted near the end of their charge. An area of study for further research would be to compare different types of rechargeable batteries. For instance, I already know that the lithium ion AA rechargeable batteries carry more volts than regular AA batteries, and they are rechargeable.

Discusses limitations of the study overall.

If I had had more time to perform this experiment or had allowed the batteries to be in the strobe light for a longer time, I think that I would have found that the rechargeable battery would be ahead of the generic battery in terms of the average voltage lost. Also I think that the gap would have been larger between the Duracell battery and the Energizer battery because looking at my results from the observation logbook shows that the Energizer battery does a lot better than the Duracell battery toward the end of its life. This being said, I think that the Duracell battery does not handle the rapid uses as well as the extended uses.

These results show that the Energizer battery is the most effective battery for rapid use and, from my observation logbook, the most effective for extended use. The rechargeable battery used in this experiment is hard to compare to these regular AA batteries because I wasn't able to exploit its sole advantage, recharging. However, this was just a generic brand of rechargeable batteries, so it would be interesting to see how the Duracell and Energizer rechargeable batteries compare to their regular batteries.

WHICH BATTERY IS MOST EFFECTIVE?   8

Provides a list of sources used in the construction of the lab report.

References

Almeida, M. F., Xará, S. M., Delgado, J., & Costa, C. A. (2006). Characterization of spent AA household alkaline batteries. *Waste Management, 26*(5), 466-476. doi:10.1016/j.wasman.2005.04.005

Booth, S. A. (1999). High-drain alkaline AA-batteries. *Popular Electronics, 16*(1), 5.

Li, J., Daniel, C., & Wood, D. (2011). Materials processing for lithium-ion batteries. *Journal of Power Sources, 196*(5), 2452-2460. doi:10.1016/j.jpowsour.2010.11.001

Yu, C. Z., Lai, W. H., Yan, G. J., & Wu, J. Y. (1999). Study of preparation technology for high performance AA size Ni–MH batteries. *Journal of Alloys and Compounds, 293*(1-2), 784-787. doi:10.1016/S0925-8388(99)00463-6

Zucker, P. (2005). AA batteries tested: Rechargeable batteries. *Australian PC User, 17*(6), 51.

Tip Sheet | Reading and Writing in the Natural Sciences

- **Systematic observation plays a critical role in the natural sciences.** The disciplines of the natural sciences rely on methods of observation to generate and answer research questions about how and why natural phenomena act as they do.

- **Many natural scientists work in interdisciplinary fields of study.** These fields, such as biochemistry and biophysics, combine subject matter and methods from more than one field to address research questions.

- **Scientists typically conduct research according to the steps of the scientific method:** observe, ask a research question, formulate a hypothesis, test the hypothesis through experimentation, and explain results.

- **The scientific writing process follows logically from the steps of the scientific method:** observe and describe, speculate, experiment, and report.

- **To test their hypotheses, or their proposed answers to research questions, natural scientists may use multiple methods.** Two common methods are systematic observation and experimentation.

- **Scientific research proposals are typically vetted by institutional review boards (IRB).** Committees that review research proposals are charged with the task of examining all elements of a scientific study to ensure that it treats subjects equitably and ethically.

- **Conventional rhetorical features of the scientific community reflect the shared values of the community's members.** Some of these values are objectivity, replicability, recency, and cooperation and collaboration.

- **Members of the scientific community frequently produce a number of genres.** These include the observation logbook, the research proposal, and the lab report.

Chapter 15 Reading and Writing in the Applied Fields

Introduction to the Applied Fields

In this chapter, we explore some of the applied fields that students often encounter or choose to study as part of their college experience. Throughout the chapter, we also look at some of the genres through which writers in these fields communicate to various audiences.

What Are Applied Fields?

Applied fields are areas of academic study that focus on the production of practical knowledge and that share a core mission of preparing students for specific careers. Often, that preparation includes hands-on training. Examples of applied fields that prepare students for particular careers include nursing, business, law, education, and engineering, but a somewhat more complete list appears below.

Andrea Tsurumi

Some Applied Fields

Sports psychology	Counseling
Business	Statistics
Law	Engineering
Education	Speech pathology
Nursing	Public administration
Applied physics	Architecture
Applied linguistics	Broadcast journalism
Social work	

Research in the applied fields typically attempts to solve problems. An automotive engineering team, for example, might start with a problem like consumers' reluctance to buy an all-electric vehicle. The team must first observe and acknowledge that there is a problem, and then it would need to define the scope of the problem. Why does the problem exist? What are the factors contributing to consumers' reluctance to buy an all-electric vehicle? Once a problem has been identified and defined, the team of researchers can then begin to explore solutions to overcome the problem.

Examples of large-scale problems that require practical applications of research are issues such as: racial inequality in the American criminal justice system, the lack of clean drinking water in some non-industrialized nations, obesity and heart disease, and ways to provide outstanding public education to children with behavioral problems. These are all real-world problems scholars and practitioners in the applied fields are working to solve this very moment.

Inside Work: Defining and Solving Problems

Describe a time when you conducted research to solve a problem. Start by defining the problem and explaining why you needed to solve it. When did you first identify the problem? What caused you to seek solutions to it? How did you research and understand the problem? What methods did you use to solve it?

Professionals in applied fields often work in collaboration with one another, or in teams, to complete research and other projects, and professors who teach in these areas often assign tasks that require interaction and cooperation among a group of students to create a product or to solve a problem. In the field of business management, for example, teams of professionals often must work together to market a new product. Solid communication and interpersonal skills are necessary for a team to manage a budget, design a marketing or advertising campaign, and engage with a client successfully all at the same time. As such, the ability to work cooperatively—to demonstrate effective interpersonal and team communication skills—is highly valued among professionals in the applied fields. You shouldn't be surprised, then, if you're one day applying for a job in an applied field and an interviewer asks you to share a little about your previous experiences working in teams to successfully complete a project. As you learn more about the applied fields examined in this chapter, take care to note those writing tasks completed by teams, or those moments when cooperation among professionals working in a particular field are highlighted by the content of the genres we explore.

Our purpose in this chapter is to offer a basic introduction to a few of the many applied fields of study and to explore some of the kinds of writing that typically occur in these fields. Because the applied fields vary so much, we've chosen to focus on specific disciplines as examples since we cannot generalize conventions across applied fields. The rest of the chapter examines specific applied fields and examples of writing through a rhetorical approach.

Inside Work: Considering Additional Applied Fields

Visit your college or university's website, and locate a listing of the majors or concentrations offered in any academic department. In light of the definition of an *applied field* proposed above, consider whether any of the majors or concentrations identified for that particular discipline could be described as applied fields. Additionally, spend some time considering your own major or potential area of concentration: Are you studying an applied field? Are there areas of study within your major or concentration that could be considered applied fields? If so, what are they, and why would you consider them applied fields?

Rhetoric and the Applied Fields

Because applied fields are centrally focused on preparing professionals who will work in those fields, students are often asked to engage audiences associated with the work they'll do in those fields after graduation. Imagine that you've just graduated from college with a degree in business management and have secured a job as a marketing director for a business. What kinds of writing do you expect to encounter in this new position? What audiences do you expect to be writing for? You may well be asked to prepare business analyses or market reports. You may be asked to involve yourself in new product management or even the advertising campaign for a product. All these activities, which call for different kinds of writing, will require you to manage information and to shape your communication of that information into texts that are designed specifically for other professionals in your field—such as boards of directors, financial officers, or advertising executives. As a student in the applied field of business management, you therefore need to become familiar with the audiences, genres, conventions, and other expectations for writing specific to your career path that extend beyond academic audiences. Being mindful of the rhetorical situation in which you must communicate with other professionals is essential to your potential success as a writer in an applied field.

As with more traditional academic writing, we recommend that you analyze carefully any writing situation you encounter in an applied field. You might begin by responding to the following questions:

LaunchPadSolo

Criminal justice instructor Michelle Richter discusses the role of audience.

1. **Who is my audience?**   Unlike the audience for a lab report for a chemistry class or the audience for an interpretation of a poem in a literature class, your audience for writing in an applied field is just as likely to be non-academic as academic. Certainly, the writing most students will do in their actual careers will be aimed at other professionals in their field, not researchers or professors in a university. In addition to understanding exactly who your audience is, be sure to consider the specific needs of your target audience.

2. **In light of my purpose and the audience's needs, is there an appropriate genre that I should rely on to communicate my information?**   As in the more traditional academic disciplines, there are many genres through which professionals in applied fields communicate. Keeping your purpose for writing in mind, you'll want to consider whether the information you have to share should be reported in a specific genre: Should you write a memorandum, a marketing proposal, or an executive summary, for instance? Answering this question can help you determine if there is an appropriate form, or genre, through which to communicate your information.

3. **Are there additional conventional expectations I should consider for the kind of writing task I need to complete?**   Beyond simply identifying an appropriate genre, answering this question can help you determine how to shape the information you need to communicate to your target audience. If the writing task requires a particular genre, then you're likely to use features that conventionally appear as part of that genre. Of course, there are many good reasons to communicate information in other ways. In these situations, we recommend that you carefully consider the appropriateness of the structural, language, and reference features you employ.

Genres in Selected Applied Fields

In the sections that follow, we offer brief introductions to some applied fields of study and provide examples of genres that students and professionals working in these fields often produce. We explore expectations for these genres by highlighting conventional structure, language, and reference features that writers in these fields frequently rely on.

Nursing

Most of us have had experiences with nurses, who, along with physicians and other medical professionals, serve on the front lines of preventing and treating illness in our society. In addition to their hands-on engagement with individuals in clinical and community settings, nurses spend a good deal of their time writing—whether documenting their observations about patients in medical charts, preparing orders for medical procedures, designing care plans, or communicating with patients. A student of nursing might encounter any number of additional forms of writing tasks, including nursing care plans for individuals, reviews

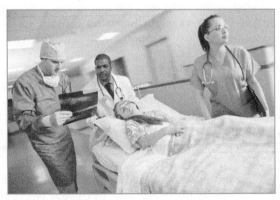
Steve Debenport/Getty Images

of literature, and community or public health assessment papers, just to name a few. Each of these forms of communication requires that nurses be especially attuned to the needs of various audiences. A nurse communicating with a patient, for example, might have to translate medical jargon such that the individual can fully understand his or her treatment. Alternatively, a nurse who is producing a care plan for a patient would likely need to craft the document such that other nurses and medical professionals could follow methodically the assessments and recommendations for care. Some nurses, especially those who undertake advanced study or who prepare others to become nurses, often design, implement, or participate in research studies.

We interviewed Dr. Janna Dieckmann, a registered nurse and clinical associate professor in the School of Nursing at the University of North Carolina at Chapel Hill. In her Insider's View, she offers valuable insights into the writing and researching practices of the nursing community.

As Dr. Dieckmann notes, many nurses, especially those working to prepare other nurses, may also participate in various kinds of scholarly research endeavors. In the section that follows, we provide an excerpted look at a 2005 research study published in *Newborn and Infant Nursing Reviews*, a journal of nursing, along with an example of discharge instructions. The latter is a genre of writing that nurses who work in a clinical setting often produce for patients.

Insider's View

Nurses and Nursing Consider Many Different Areas of Research and Interest

Janna Dieckmann, Nursing

"Research in nursing is varied, including quantitative research into health and illness patterns, as well as intervention to maximize health and reduce illness. Qualitative research varies widely, including research in the history of nursing, which is my focus. There is a wide variety of types of writing demanded in a nursing program. It is so varied that many connections are possible. Cross-discipline collaborations among faculty of various professional schools are valued at many academic institutions today. One of my colleagues conducted research on rats. Another looked at sleep patterns in older adults as a basis for understanding dementia onset. One public health nursing colleague conducts research on out-of-work women, and another examines crosscultural competence. These interests speak to our reasons for becoming nurses—our seeking out of real life, of direct experience, of being right there with people, and of understanding others and their worlds."

Scholarly Research Report

Some nurses are both practitioners and scholars of nursing. As practitioners, they assess and care for patients in cooperation with other medical professionals. As scholars, they may, as Dr. Dieckmann indicates, conduct research on a host of issues, including the history and best practices of nursing. In addition to producing scholarship that advances the field of nursing, these nurses typically work in colleges or universities with programs that prepare individuals for careers in nursing. Such nurses, then, may assume multiple roles as researchers and educators, and as practitioners.

Insider Example

Professional Research Report in Nursing

As you read the following research report, pay particular attention to the structure, language, and reference parallels between the form of the report and those you've encountered already in the fields of the natural sciences and the social sciences. Keep in mind that the text presented here is made up of a series of excerpts from a much lengthier and more substantial research report.

Margaret Shandor Miles, PhD, FAAN;
Diane Holditch-Davis, PhD, FAAN;
Suzanne Thoyre, PhD; Linda Beeber, PhD

Rural African-American Mothers Parenting Prematurely Born Infants: An Ecological Systems Perspective

ABSTRACT

The abstract provides an overview of the report, including a description of the study's purpose, its methods, and its central findings.

This qualitative descriptive study describes the concerns and issues of rural African-American mothers with prematurely born infants. Mothers were part of a larger nurse-parent support intervention. The 18 mothers lived in rural areas in the Southeast, and their infants were younger than 35 weeks gestational age at birth and at high risk for developmental problems because they either weighed less than 1500 grams at birth or required mechanical ventilation. Field notes written by the intervention nurses providing support to the mothers after discharge from the hospital were analyzed using methods of content analysis. Concerns of the mothers related to the infant's health and development, the maternal role in parenting the infant, personal aspects of their lives, and relationship issues particularly with the fathers. Findings support the importance of an ecological systems perspective when designing research and caring for rural African-American mothers with prematurely born children.

REVIEW OF THE LITERATURE

Although mothers are excited about taking the preterm infant home, a number of studies have noted that they are also anxious during this important transition. McHaffie[1] found mothers insecure and lacking in confidence at first, followed by a period of accommodation as they learned about the infant's behavioral cues and needs. During this period, mothers became overwhelmed with responsibilities, and fatigue resulted. As the infants settled into their new surroundings and the mothers felt the rewards of caregiving, they became confident in their maternal role. May[2] also found that mothers went through a process of learning about the added responsibilities of caregiving, and this resulted in strains on their time and energy. Mothers were vigilant about looking for changes in the infant's status and for signs of progress through improved physical health and development. During this process, they looked for signs that their child was normal and sought support from others....

The review of the literature begins with a synthesis point: mothers experience a period of transitioning. Both McHaffie and May confirm this conclusion.

METHOD

This study used a qualitative descriptive design[3] to identify the concerns and issues of the mothers based on field notes written by the intervention nurses providing support to the mothers after discharge from the hospital.[4] The Nursing Support Intervention was an 18-month in-person and telephone intervention provided by master's-prepared nurses starting around the time of discharge of the infant and ending when the infants were around 18 months old corrected for prematurity. The nurses helped the mothers to process the mothering experience and resolve emotional distress that is caused by prematurity, identify and reduce parenting and other life stresses, develop relationships with their infants, and identify and use acceptable resources to meet needs of the infant and the mother....

Qualitative research methods are explained.

RESULTS

The concerns and issues raised by the mothers with the intervention nurses fell into four major categories: infant health and development, parenting, personal concerns, and relationship issues (Table 1).

Results of the study, or categories of concerns identified among mothers, are presented in the form of a summary table. The researchers explore these results in more detail in a number of additional paragraphs.

Table 1

Maternal concerns of rural African-American mothers in parenting prematurely born infants

Infant health and development	Establishing feeding and managing gastrointestinal tract distress
	Managing medical technologies
	Preventing and managing infections
	Establishing sleep patterning
	Learning developmental expectations
Parenting	Learning the infant's needs
	Establishing daily patterns
	Balancing roles
Personal concerns	Coping with financial problems
	Managing stressful jobs while securing appropriate childcare
	Losing and trying to regain educational opportunities toward a better life
	Working toward securing a home of one's own
	Managing depressive symptoms
Relationship issues	Working through relationship with infant's father

> The study's Discussion section connects findings to potential changes in support that could improve outcomes for mothers and their children.

DISCUSSION

Findings from this study provide insight into the needs of mothers of prematurely born infants after discharge from the hospital. In the early months after discharge, support is needed related to caring for the infant. As their infants grow, mothers may need help in identifying and getting resources for developmental problems. Agencies that provide services to mothers need to consider the complex lives of the mothers, especially those who are single and living in poverty. Of utmost importance is helping the mothers to manage issues related to finding a job, managing work, and care of their infant. Finding acceptable day care is a particularly important need. Furthermore, community programs are needed to help the mothers achieve their dreams of furthering their education and finding acceptable homes for themselves and their children.

REFERENCES

1. McHaffie HE. Mothers of very low birthweight babies: how do they adjust? J Adv Nurs. 1990;15:6–11.

2. May KM. Searching for normalcy: mothers' caregiving for low birthweight infants. Pediatr Nurs. 1997;23:17–20.

3. Sandelowski M. Whatever happened to qualitative description? Res Nurs Health. 2000;23:334–340.

4. Holditch-Davis D. A nursing support intervention for mothers of preterm infants. Grant funded by the National Institute of Nursing Research (NR05263). 2001.

Discharge Instructions

If you've ever been hospitalized, then you probably remember the experience quite vividly. It's likely that you interacted with a nurse, who perhaps assessed your health upon arrival. You were also likely cared for by a nurse, or a particular group of nurses, during your stay. Nurses also often play an integral role in a patient's discharge from a hospital. Typically, before a patient is released from a hospital, a nurse provides, in written form, and explains to the patient (and perhaps a family member or two, or another intended primary caregiver) a set of instructions for aftercare. This constitutes the **discharge instructions**.

This document, or series of documents, includes instructions for how to care for oneself at home. The instructions may focus on managing diet and medications, as well as caring for other needs, such as post-operative bandaging procedures. They may also include exercise or diet management plans recommended for long-term recovery and health maintenance. Often presented in bulleted series of items or statements, these lists are usually highly generic; that is, the same instructions frequently apply for patients with the same or similar health conditions. For this reason, discharge instruction forms may include spaces for nurses or other healthcare professionals to write in more specific information relating to a patient's individual circumstances. As well, discharge instructions frequently include information about a patient's follow-up care with his or her doctor or primary caregiver. This could take the form of a future appointment time or directions to call for a follow-up appointment or to consult with another physician. An additional conventional element of discharge instructions is a list of signs of a medical emergency and directions concerning when and how to seek medical attention immediately, should certain signs or symptoms appear in the patient. Finally, discharge instructions are typically signed and dated by a physician or nurse, and they are sometimes signed by the patient as well.

Many patients are in unclear states of mind or are extremely vulnerable at the time of release from a hospital, so nurses who provide and explain discharge instructions to patients are highly skilled at assessing patients' understanding of these instructions.

Insider Example

Discharge Instructions

The following text is an example of a typical set of discharge instructions. As you read the document, consider areas in the instructions that you think a nurse would be more likely to stress to a patient in a discharge meeting: What would a nurse cover quickly? What would he or she want to communicate most clearly to a patient?

Provides identifying information about the patient, as well as name and contact information of healthcare provider.

Much of the information provided in discharge instructions is generic, so nurses can provide "personalized notes" here.

Provides a brief overview of the patient's medical issue treated by the healthcare provider.

Provides specific instructions for the patient to take upon release from the medical facility.

FIRST HOSPITAL
Where Care Comes First

Patient's Name: John Q. Patient
Healthcare Provider's Name: First Hospital
Department: Cardiology
Phone: 617-555-1212
Date: Thursday, May 8, 2014
Notes: **Nurses can write personal notes to the patient here.**

Discharge Instructions for Heart Attack

A heart attack occurs when blood flow to the heart muscle is interrupted. This deprives the heart muscle of oxygen, causing tissue damage or tissue death. Common treatments include lifestyle changes, oxygen, medicines, and surgery.

Steps to Take

Home Care

- Rest until your doctor says it is okay to return to work or other activities.

- Take all medicines as prescribed by your doctor. Beta-blockers, ACE inhibitors, and antiplatelet therapy are often recommended.

- Attend a cardiac rehabilitation program if recommended by your doctor.

Diet

Eat a heart-healthy diet:

- Limit your intake of fat, cholesterol, and sodium. Foods such as ice cream, cheese, baked goods, and red meat are not the best choices.
- Increase your intake of whole grains, fish, fruits, vegetables, and nuts.
- Consume alcohol in moderation: one to two drinks per day for men, one drink per day for women.
- Discuss supplements with your doctor.

Your doctor may refer you to a dietician to advise you on meal planning.

Note that each of these directions begins with a verb, stressing the importance of taking the action indicated.

Physical Activity

The American Heart Association recommends at least 30 minutes of exercise daily, or at least 3–4 times per week, for patients who have had a heart attack. Your doctor will let you know when you are ready to begin regular exercise.

- Ask your doctor when you will be able to return to work.
- Ask your doctor when you may resume sexual activity.
- Do not drive unless your doctor has given you permission to do so.

Medications

The following medicines may be prescribed to prevent you from having another heart attack:

- Aspirin, which has been shown to decrease the risk of heart attacks
  - Certain painkillers, such as ibuprofen, when taken together with aspirin, may put you at high risk for gastrointestinal bleeding and also reduce the effectiveness of aspirin.
- Clopidogrel or prasugrel
  - Avoid omeprazole or esomeprazole if you take clopidogrel. They may make clopidogrel not work. Ask your doctor for other drug choices.
- ACE inhibitors
- Nitroglycerin
- Beta-blockers or calcium channel blockers

Note that specific directions are listed in a series of bulleted sections. Bulleted lists make the information easier to read and follow.

- Cholesterol-lowering medicines
- Blood pressure medicines
- Pain medicines
- Anti-anxiety or antidepressant medicines

If you are taking medicines, follow these general guidelines:

Directions are provided in as few words as possible.

- Take your medicine as directed. Do not change the amount or the schedule.
- Do not stop taking them without talking to your doctor.
- Do not share them.
- Ask what the results and side effects are. Report them to your doctor.
- Some drugs can be dangerous when mixed. Talk to a doctor or pharmacist if you are taking more than one drug. This includes over-the-counter medicine and herbal or dietary supplements.
- Plan ahead for refills so you do not run out.

Lifestyle Changes and Prevention

Together, you and your doctor will plan proper lifestyle changes that will aid in your recovery. Some things to keep in mind to recover and prevent another heart attack include:

- If you smoke, talk to your doctor about ways to help you quit. There are many options to choose from, like using nicotine replacement products, taking prescription medicines to ease cravings and withdrawal symptoms, participating in smoking cessation classes, or doing an online self-help program.
- Have your cholesterol checked regularly.
- Get regular medical check-ups.
- Control your blood pressure.
- Eat a healthful diet, one that is low in saturated fat and rich in whole grains, fruits, and vegetables.
- Have a regular, low-impact exercise program.
- Maintain a healthy weight.
- Manage stress through activities such as yoga, meditation, and counseling.
- If you have diabetes, maintain good control of your condition.

Follow-Up

Since your recovery needs to be monitored, be sure to keep all appointments and have exams done regularly as directed by your doctor. In addition, some people have feelings of depression or anxiety after a heart attack. To get the help you need, be sure to discuss these feelings with your doctor.

Schedule a follow-up appointment as directed by your doctor.

Call for Medical Help Right Away If Any of the Following Occurs

Call for medical help right away if you have symptoms of another heart attack, including:

- Chest pain, which may feel like a crushing weight on your chest
- A sense of fullness, squeezing, or pressure in the chest
- Anxiety, especially feeling a sense of doom or panic without apparent reason
- Rapid, irregular heartbeat
- Pain, tingling, or numbness in the left shoulder and arm, the neck or jaw, or the right arm
- Sweating
- Nausea or vomiting
- Indigestion or heartburn
- Lightheadedness, weakness, or fainting
- Shortness of breath
- Abdominal pain

If you think you have an emergency, call for medical help right away.

Provides directions for how to "follow up" with medical provider(s).

Identifies emergency indicators.

Inside Work: Nurse for a Day

In Table 1 on page 480, the authors of the qualitative research report "Rural African-American Mothers Parenting Prematurely Born Infants: An Ecological Systems Perspective" identify a number of "concerns and issues" among rural mothers with premature infants. Choose one of these "concerns and issues," and develop a discharge plan for a mother and child in response. Using "Discharge Instructions for Heart Attack" as a model for your own set of discharge instructions, complete the following.

- Provide a brief introduction in which you offer a quick overview of the concern or issue.

- Provide supporting instructions for patients in three central areas: Steps to Take, Follow-Up, and Emergency Response. Note that many, or all, of the directives or recommendations that make up your instructions may be non-medical treatments, interventions, or therapies. You may consult additional sources for support, as needed.

- Authorize the discharge orders by signing and dating your document.

Once you've completed the discharge instructions, spend some time reflecting on the challenges you faced in the process of devising your instructions: What were the least and most challenging parts of writing the instructions?

Education

When your teachers tell you that writing is important, they're probably conveying a belief based on their own experiences. Professional educators do a lot of writing. As students, you're aware of many contexts in which teachers write on a daily basis. They have project assignment sheets to design, papers to comment on and grade, websites to design, and e-mails to answer, just to name a few. However, educators also spend a great deal of time planning classes and designing lesson plans. Though students rarely see these written products, they are essential, if challenging and time-consuming, endeavors for teachers. We provide examples and discussion of two forms of writing frequently produced by professionals in the various fields of education: the lesson plan and the Individualized Education Plan (IEP).

© Jaume Gual/agefotostock

Lesson Plan

When designing a **lesson plan**, teachers must consider many factors, including their goals and objectives for student learning, the materials needed to execute a lesson, the activities students will participate in as part of a lesson, and the methods they'll use to assess student learning. Among other considerations, teachers must also make sure their lesson plans help them meet prescribed curricular mandates.

Insider Example

Student Lesson Plan

The following lesson plan for a tenth-grade English class was designed by Dr. Myra Moses, who at the time of writing the plan was a doctoral candidate in education. In this plan, Dr. Moses begins by identifying the state-mandated curricular standards the lesson addresses. She then identifies the broader goals of her lesson plan before establishing the more specific objectives, or exactly what students will do to reach the broader learning goals. As you read, notice that all the plan's statements of objectives begin with a verb, as they identify actions students will take to demonstrate their learning. The plan ends by explaining the classroom activities the teacher will use to facilitate learning and by identifying the methods the instructor will use to assess student learning. These structural moves are conventional for the genre of a lesson plan.

Educational Standard → Goals → Objectives → Materials → Classroom Activities → Assessment

Lesson Plan

Overview and Purpose

This lesson is part of a unit on Homer's *Odyssey*. Prior to this lesson students will have had a lesson on Greek cultural and social values during the time of Homer, and they will have read the *Odyssey*. In the lesson, students will analyze passages from the *Odyssey* to examine author's and characters' point of view. Students will participate in whole class discussion, work in small groups, and work individually to identify and evaluate point of view.

Education Standards Addressed

This lesson addresses the following objectives from the NC Standard Course of Study for Language Arts: English II:

1.02 Respond reflectively (through small group discussion, class discussion, journal entry, essay, letter, dialogue) to written and visual texts by:

Identifies the state-mandated curricular elements, or the educational objectives, the lesson addresses. Notice that these are quite broad in scope.

- relating personal knowledge to textual information or class discussion.

- showing an awareness of one's own culture as well as the cultures of others.

- exhibiting an awareness of culture in which text is set or in which text was written.

1.03 Demonstrate the ability to read, listen to, and view a variety of increasingly complex print and non-print expressive texts appropriate to grade level and course literary focus, by:

- identifying and analyzing text components (such as organizational structures, story elements, organizational features) and evaluating their impact on the text.

- providing textual evidence to support understanding of and reader's response to text.

- making inferences, predicting, and drawing conclusions based on text.

- identifying and analyzing personal, social, historical, or cultural influences, contexts, or biases.

5.01 Read and analyze selected works of world literature by:

- understanding the importance of cultural and historical impact on literary texts.

Goals

Teacher identifies specific goals for the lesson. These goals fit well within the broader state-mandated curricular standards.

1. To teach students how to identify and evaluate an author's point of view and purpose by examining the characters' point of view.

2. To teach students to critically examine alternate points of view.

Objectives

Objectives identify what students will do as part of the lesson. Notice that the statements of objectives begin with verbs.

Students will:

1. Identify point of view in a story by examining the text and evaluating how the main character views his/her world at different points in the story.

2. Demonstrate that they understand point of view by using examples and evidence from the text to support what they state is the character's point of view.

3. Apply their knowledge and understanding of point of view by taking a passage from the text and rewriting it from a supporting character's point of view.

4. Evaluate the rationality of a character's point of view by measuring it against additional information gathered from the text, or their own life experience.

Materials, Resources

In right margin: Identifies materials needed for the lesson.

- Copies of *The Odyssey*
- DVD with video clips from television and/or movies
- Flip chart paper
- Markers
- Directions and rubric for individual assignment

Activities

In right margin: Outlines classroom procedures for the two-day lesson plan.

Session 1

1. Review information from previous lesson about popular cultural and social views held during Homer's time (e.g., Greek law of hospitality). This would be a combination of a quiz and whole class discussion.

2. Teacher-led class discussion defining and examining point of view by viewing clips from popular television shows and movies.

3. Teacher-led discussion of 1 example from *The Odyssey*. E.g., Examine Odysseus's point of view when he violates Greek law of hospitality during his encounter with the Cyclops, Polyphemus. Examine this encounter through the lens of what Homer might be saying about the value Greeks placed on hospitality.

4. In small groups the students will choose 3 places in the epic and evaluate Odysseus's point of view. Students will then determine what Odysseus's point of view might reflect about Homer's point of view and purpose for that part of the epic.

5. Groups will begin to create a visual using flip chart paper and markers to represent their interpretations of Odysseus's point of view to reflect about Homer's point of view and purpose.

Session 2

1. Groups will complete visual.

2. Groups will present their work to the rest of the class.

3. The class will discuss possible alternate interpretations of Homer's point of view and purpose.

4. Class will review aspects of point of view based on information teacher provided at the beginning of the class.

5. Beginning during class and finishing for homework, students will individually take one passage from the epic that was not discussed by their groups and do the following:

- write a brief description of a main character's point of view

- write a response to prompts that guide students in evaluating the rationality of the main character's point of view based on information gathered from the text, or the students' own life experience

- rewrite the passage from a supporting character's point of view

Assessment

Identifies how the teacher will assess students' mastery of the concepts and material covered in the lesson.

- Evaluate students' understanding of Greek cultural/social values from Homer's time through the quiz.

- Evaluate group's understanding of point of view by examining the visual product—this artifact will not be graded, but oral feedback will be provided that should help the students in completing the independent assignment.

- Evaluate the written, individual assignment.

Individualized Education Program (IEP)

Professional educators are often required to design education plans that address the specific needs of individual students who, according to federal definitions, are identified with a disability. These are individualized education programs (IEP). IEP development most often results from cooperation among educational professionals (teachers, school administrators, guidance counselors, etc.) and parents as they plan a student's educational course in light of his or her individual disability and needs. IEPs, like general lesson plans, are guided by the identification of goals and objectives for individual students, taking into account the student's disability or disabilities.

Insider Example

Student IEP

The sample IEP that follows indicates both an academic goal and a functional goal for the student. The academic goal relates to the student's desired academic achievement, while the functional goal specifies a desired behavioral outcome. These goals are followed by statements of objectives that represent steps the student will take to achieve the specified goals. Both sections end with descriptions of how the student's progress toward the desired goals will be measured or assessed.

Student Description for IEP

Joey Smith is a 16-year-old 11th grader. He has a learning disability in reading, and he also has attention deficit hyperactivity disorder.

Joey generally works well with others and has a good sense of humor. He likes to be helpful and is good at encouraging others. He tries hard when assigned tasks, but gets extremely frustrated and gives up quickly when he has difficulty completing a task as easily or quickly as he thinks he should. He responds well to being asked to try again if someone can work with him individually to get him started on the task again. Sometimes he acts up in class, usually in a joking manner. This tends to result in him frequently being off-task, as well as affecting the students around him. He displays the classic characteristics of a student with attention deficit hyperactivity disorder, including losing focus easily, needing to move around frequently, exhibiting difficulty paying attention to details, and continually blurting out inappropriate comments, or talking at inappropriate times.

Check Purpose: ☐ Initial
☒ Annual Review
☐ Reevaluation
☐ Addendum
☐ Transition Part C to B

INDIVIDUALIZED EDUCATION PROGRAM (IEP)

Duration of Special Education and Related Services:
   From: 06/05/2008   To: 06/04/2009

Student: Joey Smith   **DOB: 08/21/1992**

School: ABC High School   **Grade: 10**

Primary Area of Eligibility* Learning Disability

Secondary Area(s) of Eligibility (if applicable): Other Health Impairment

(*Reported on Child Count)

Student Profile

Student's overall strengths:

Joey works hard to complete assignments and accomplish his goals. He interacts well with others, including his peers. He is very helpful and often encourages his peers when they are trying to accomplish their own goals. Joey has a good sense of humor and is good at entertaining others.

Summarize assessment information (e.g., from early intervention providers, child outcome measures, curriculum based measures, state and district assessments results, etc.), and review of progress on current IEP/IFSP goals:

Overall, Joey is making significant progress on his IEP goals. He continues to do well with improving his reading skills. He still struggles with implementing strategies consistently to help him remain focused and committed to completing his tasks; however, he continues to make progress.

INDIVIDUALIZED EDUCATION PROGRAM (IEP)

Duration of Special Education and Related Services:
    From: 06/05/2008   To: 06/04/2009

Student: Joey Smith   **DOB: 08/21/1992**

School: ABC High School   **Grade: 10**

Parent's concerns, if any, for enhancing the student's education:

Parent had no concerns at this time.

Parent's/Student's vision for student's future:

Joey will learn to motivate himself to complete tasks and learn to rely less on external motivation from others. He will complete high school and then attend community college.

Consideration of Transitions

If a transition (e.g., new school, family circumstances, etc.) is anticipated during the life of this IEP/IFSP, what information is known about the student that will assist in facilitating a smooth process?   ☒ N/A

The student is age 14 or older or will be during the duration of the IEP.

                                                              ☒ Yes   ☐ No

Consideration of Special Factors (Note: If you check yes, you must address in the IEP.)

Does the student have behavior(s) that impede his/her learning or that of others?   ☒ Yes   ☐ No

Does the student have Limited English Proficiency?   ☐ Yes   ☒ No

If the student is blind or partially sighted, will the instruction in or use of Braille be needed?   ☐ Yes   ☐ No   ☒ N/A

Does the student have any special communication needs?   ☐ Yes   ☒ No

Is the student deaf or hard of hearing?   ☐ Yes   ☒ No

☐ The child's language and communication needs.

☐ Opportunities for direct communications with peers and professional personnel in the child's language and communication mode.

☐ Academic level.

☐ Full range of needs, including opportunities for direct instruction in the child's language, and

☐ Communication mode.

(Communication Plan Worksheet available at www.ncpublicschools.org/ec/policy/forms.)

Does the student require specially designed physical education?

                                                              ☐ Yes   ☒ No

INDIVIDUALIZED EDUCATION PROGRAM (IEP)

Duration of Special Education and Related Services:
  From: 06/05/2008   To: 06/04/2009

Student: <u>Joey Smith</u>   DOB: **08/21/1992**

School: <u>ABC High School</u>   Grade: **<u>10</u>**

Present Level(s) of Academic and Functional Performance
Include specific descriptions of what the student can and cannot do in relationship to this area. Include current academic and functional performance, behaviors, social/emotional development, other relevant information, and how the student's disability affects his/her involvement and progress in the general curriculum.

> *Joey consistently reads at grade level. He can answer comprehension questions accurately if given additional time. He does well on tests and assignments that require reading if given additional time and if allowed to be in a separate setting with minimized distractions during longer tests.*

Annual Goal
☒ Academic Goal   ☐ Functional Goal

> *Joey will continue to learn and demonstrate functional reading skill at grade level.*

The academic goal for the student is identified here.

Does the student require assistive technology devices and/or services?
                                                         ☐ Yes   ☒ No
If yes, describe needs:

(Address after determination of related services.) Is this goal integrated with related service(s)?   ☐ Yes*   ☒ No
*If yes, list the related service area(s) of integration:

INDIVIDUALIZED EDUCATION PROGRAM (IEP)

Duration of Special Education and Related Services:
  From: 06/05/2008   To: 06/04/2009

Student: Joey Smith   **DOB: 08/21/1992**

School: ABC High School   **Grade: 10**

Competency Goal

> **Required for areas (if any) where student participates in state assessments using modified achievement standards.**
>
> **Select Subject Area:** ☐ Language Arts ☐ Mathematics ☐ Science
>
> **List Competency Goal from the *NC Standard Course of Study*:**
> *(Standard must match the student's assigned grade.)*
>
>
>
> *Note: Selected Grade Standard Competency Goals listed are those identified for specially designed instruction. In addition to those listed, the student has access to grade-level content standards through general education requirements.*

Benchmarks or Short-Term Objectives (if applicable)

(Required for students participating in state alternate assessments aligned to alternate achievement standards)

The IEP identifies specific objectives the student will achieve toward reaching the academic goal.

> 1) Joey will recognize and use vocabulary appropriate for grade level with 90% accuracy.
>
> 2) Joey will recognize the author's point of view and purpose with 85% accuracy.
>
> 3) Joey will apply decoding strategies to comprehend grade-level text with 85% accuracy.

Describe how progress toward the annual goal will be measured

The IEP identifies ways the student's progress will be measured.

> Progress toward this annual goal will be measured by work samples and tests or quizzes.

Present Level(s) of Academic and Functional Performance

Include specific descriptions of what the student can and cannot do in relationship to this area. Include current academic and functional performance, behaviors, social/emotional development, other relevant information, and how the student's disability affects his/her involvement and progress in the general curriculum.

> Joey does well getting back on task with assistance and when he implements attention-focusing strategies. He needs to improve working on his ability to self-monitor and keep himself on task.

INDIVIDUALIZED EDUCATION PROGRAM (IEP)

Duration of Special Education and Related Services:
    From: 06/05/2008   To: 06/04/2009

Student: Joey Smith   **DOB: 08/21/1992**

School: ABC High School   **Grade: 10**

Annual Goal

☐ Academic Goal   ☒ Functional Goal

> *Joey will continue learning to identify situations where he is more likely to lose focus. He will learn to identify and apply appropriate attention-focusing strategies in a variety of situations.*

The functional goal for the student is identified here.

Does the student require assistive technology devices and/or services?

                                                        ☐ Yes   ☒ No

If yes, describe needs:

(Address after determination of related services.) Is this goal integrated with related service(s)?   ☐ Yes*   ☒ No

*If yes, list the related service area(s) of integration:

Competency Goal

Required for areas (if any) where student participates in state assessments using modified achievement standards.

Select Subject Area: ☐ Language Arts   ☐ Mathematics   ☐ Science

List Competency Goal from the *NC Standard Course of Study*:

(Standard must match the student's assigned grade.)

Note: Selected Grade Standard Competency Goals listed are those identified for specially designed instruction. In addition to those listed, the student has access to grade-level content standards through general education requirements.

INDIVIDUALIZED EDUCATION PROGRAM (IEP)

Duration of Special Education and Related Services:
   From: 06/05/2008   To: 06/04/2009

Student: Joey Smith   **DOB: 08/21/1992**

School: ABC High School   **Grade: 10**

Benchmarks or Short-Term Objectives (if applicable)

(Required for students participating in state alternate assessments aligned to alternate achievement standards)

The IEP identifies specific objectives the student will achieve toward reaching the functional goal.

1)   Joey will be able to articulate how he feels when he becomes frustrated when work gets difficult on 4 trials over a 2-week period as evaluated by structured observations every 6 weeks.

2)   By January, Joey will independently request a break from work when he needs it to prevent class disruptions and allow himself to refocus.

Describe how progress toward the annual goal will be measured

The IEP identifies ways that the student's progress will be measured.

Progress will be monitored through documented teacher observation, student self-monitoring checklist, and anecdotal logs.

Inside Work: Teacher for a Day

For this exercise, imagine that you've just taken a job teaching in your major area of study. Identify a specific concept or skill you can see yourself teaching to a group of students. Consider the background and previous knowledge of your target audience. Then, with the concept or skill in mind, design a single-day lesson plan that addresses each of the following elements of a typical lesson plan.

- **Goal(s)**   State the specific goal(s) for the skill you want to teach.

- **Objectives**   Identify what students will do to better understand the concept or learn the target skill.

- **Materials**   Identify the materials needed to carry out the lesson plan successfully.

- **Classroom Activities**   Outline the procedures, in chronological order, for the day's lesson.

- **Assessment**   Explain how you will assess your students' mastery of the concept or skill.

Business

Communication in businesses takes many forms, and professionals writing in business settings may spend substantial amounts of time drafting e-mails and memos, or writing letters and proposals. In some instances, businesses may hire individuals solely for their expertise in business communication practices. Such individuals are highly skilled in the analysis and practice of business communication, and their education and training are often aimed at these purposes. Still, if your experiences lead you to employment in a business setting, you're likely to face the task of communicating in one or more of the genres frequently used in those settings. It's no surprise, then, that schools of business, which prepare students to work in companies and corporations, often require their students to take classes that foster an understanding of the vehicles of communication common to the business setting. In the following section, we provide some introductory context and annotated examples of a couple of the more common forms of communication you're likely to encounter in a business setting: the memorandum and the business plan.

wavebreakmedia/Shutterstock

Memorandum

The **memorandum**, or memo, is a specialized form of communication used within businesses to make announcements and to share information among colleagues and employees. Although memos serve a range of purposes, like sharing information, providing directives, or even arguing a particular position, they are not generally used to communicate with outside parties, like other companies or clients. While they may range in length from a couple of paragraphs to multiple pages, they're typically highly structured according to conventional expectations. In fact, you'd be hard pressed to find an example of a professional memo that didn't follow the conventional format for identifying the writer, the audience, the central subject matter, and the date of production in the header. Also, information in memos typically appears in a block format, and the content is often developed from a clear, centralized purpose that is revealed early on in the memo itself.

Insider Example

Student Memorandum

The following is an example of a memo produced by a student in a professional writing class. His purpose for writing was to share his assessment of the advantages and drawbacks of a particular company he's interested in working for in the future. As you read, notice how the information in the opening paragraphs forecasts the memo's content, along with how the memo summarizes its contents in the concluding passages. We've highlighted a number of the other conventional expectations for the memo that you'll want to notice.

MEMO

To: Jamie Larsen
          Professor, North Carolina State University
From: James Blackwell
          Biological Engineering, North Carolina State University
Date: September 2, 2014
Subject: Investigative Report on Hazen and Sawyer

The writer uses conventional formatting in the To, From, Date, and Subject lines.

I plan on one day using my knowledge gained in biological engineering to help alleviate the growing environmental problems that our society faces. Hazen and Sawyer is a well-known environmental engineering firm. However, I need to research the firm's background in order to decide if it would be a suitable place for me to work. Consequently, I decided to research the following areas of Hazen and Sawyer engineering firm:

Paragraphs are blocked and single-spaced.

- Current and Past Projects
- Opportunities for Employment and Advancement
- Work Environment

Reasons for the student's interest in this company are bulleted and become the developed sections in the remainder of the memo. Important information is often bulleted in memos.

The purpose of this report is to present you with my findings on Hazen and Sawyer, so that you may assist me in writing an application letter that proves my skills and knowledge are worthy of an employment opportunity.

The memo announces its purpose clearly, forecasting the content to follow.

Current and Past Projects

Founded in 1951, Hazen and Sawyer has had a long history of providing clean drinking water and minimizing the effects of water pollution. The company has undertaken many projects in the United States as well as internationally. One of its first projects was improving the infrastructure of Monrovia, Liberia, in 1952. I am interested in using my knowledge of environmental problems to promote sustainability. Designing sustainable solutions for its clients is one of the firm's main goals. Hazen and Sawyer is currently engaged in a project to provide water infrastructure to over one million people in Jordan. Supplying clean drinking water is a problem that is continuously growing, and I hope to work on a similar project someday.

Opportunities for Employment and Advancement

Hazen and Sawyer has over forty offices worldwide, with regional offices in Raleigh, NC, Cincinnati, OH, Dallas, TX, Hollywood, FL, Los Angeles, CA, and its headquarters in New York City. The company currently has over thirty job openings at offices across the United States. I would like to live in the Raleigh area following graduation, so having a regional office here in Raleigh greatly helps my chances of finding a local job with the company. Hazen and Sawyer also has offices in Greensboro and Charlotte, which also helps my chances of finding a job in North Carolina. I am interested in finding a job dealing with stream restoration, and the Raleigh office currently has an opening for a Stream Restoration Designer. The position requires experience with AutoCAD and GIS, and I have used both of these programs in my Biological Engineering courses.

In addition to numerous job openings, Hazen and Sawyer also offers opportunities for professional development within the company. The Pathway Program for Professional Development is designed to keep employees up-to-date on topics in their fields and also stay educated to meet license requirements in different states. Even if I found a job at the Raleigh office, I would most likely have to travel out of state to work on projects, so this program could be very beneficial. I am seeking to work with a company that promotes continuous professional growth, so this program makes me very interested in Hazen and Sawyer.

Work Environment

Hazen and Sawyer supports innovation and creativity, and at the same time tries to limit bureaucracy. I am seeking a company that will allow me to be creative and assist with projects while not being in charge initially. As I gain experience and learn on the job, I hope to move into positions with greater responsibility. The firm offers a mentoring program that places newly hired engineers with someone more experienced. This program would help me adapt to the company and provide guidance as I gain professional experience. I hope to eventually receive my Professional Engineering license, so working under a professional engineer with years of experience would be a great opportunity for me. Hazen and Sawyer supports positive relationships among its employees, by engaging them in social outings such as sporting events, parties, picnics, and other activities.

References

Hazen and Sawyer—Environmental Engineers and Scientists. Web. 2 Sept. 2014. <http://www.hazenandsawyer.com/home/>.

Headers are used to break up the content in memos. In this instance, the student uses headers that correspond to the areas of interest in the company he is exploring for potential employment.

The writer relies on formal language, evidenced here by avoiding contractions.

Double spacing between paragraphs

Notice the organizational pattern employed in the body paragraphs. The writer begins by describing the potential employer and then relates that information to his particular needs, desires, or circumstances.

References are usually indicated in an attachment.

Business Plan

Many people dream of being their own bosses. One avenue for achieving this dream is to create a successful business, or to own and operate a service or company. Anyone undertaking such a task in the economy today will need a solid business background that includes knowledge of the many forms of written communication required to start and continue the operation of a successful business. Two very important genres for these purposes are the business plan and the business proposal. If you're a business owner looking to raise capital, or if you've got a good idea or product that you want to sell to potential investors, then you're going to need a solid business plan, a document that clearly and efficiently describes your business and its essential operations, analyzes your market competition, and assesses the expected expenses and potential for profit. Let's say that you've got a great idea for a new lawn care service, but you need capital to purchase the necessary equipment and to advertise your services to potential customers. To obtain that capital, you're likely going to need a business plan that others can read when deciding whether to invest in your business.

By contrast, the business proposal is a form of communication through which a company proposes a relationship of some sort with another entity—often another company. Companies frequently receive unsolicited business proposals. A photocopying company, for instance, may design a proposal to begin a relationship that involves installing and maintaining all the photocopiers owned by a particular city or municipality. At other times, companies request business proposals. Imagine that you're the president of a landscaping service, for example, and you've decided to outsource all work that involves tree removal. To determine whom you want to hire for those jobs, you call for proposals from those companies or individuals to determine whose services best match your needs. In the world of business, effective communication means making money.

Insider Example

Student Business Plan

The following business plan was produced by a student in a writing class that addressed the communication needs of his major. As you read, notice how the student shaped the plan to satisfy the needs of the target audience, a bank, as a potential source of funding.

The Electricity Monitor Company

Daniel Chase Mills

The Electricity Monitor Company

This document is a request for a start-up business loan for a company that will design, manufacture, and sell an electricity-monitoring product that will answer customers' demands for a solution to high power bills.

To: Ms. Jane Harmon Bausch, President

First National Bank

10 Money Street

Raleigh, North Carolina 27695

Prepared By:

Daniel Chase Mills

The Electricity Monitor Company

100 Satellite Lane

City, North Carolina 20000

Email: dcmills@ncsu.edu

Phone: (919) 555-2233

November 21, 2014

Executive Summary

The Electricity Monitor Company

Prepared by Daniel Chase Mills, November 21, 2014

This document is a start-up business proposal for the Electricity Monitor Company and a request for an investment from First National Bank of Raleigh, North Carolina. The Company will design, manufacture, and sell the Electricity Monitor. Families with a traditional circuit-breaker box often struggle with high power bills, due to their inability to monitor their electricity usage. The Electricity Monitor is a device that will answer this pain point. This device is an adapter that attaches to any existing breaker box with installation simple enough for consumers to perform on their own. The device monitors current electricity usage and determines ways to reduce energy consumption. The device is superior to alternatives in the market in that it is cheaper, easier to install, and more effectively solves the problem of not knowing how much electricity is being used. The overall purpose of the Electricity Monitor Company is to develop a high-quality product that can generate excitement in the electricity monitor market and turn a profit for its business owners and investors. The total loan request from First National Bank is three hundred and fifty-four thousand dollars ($354,000.00).

Table of Contents

List of Tables and Figures

Notice the ordering of elements of the plan. How would you describe the order of these elements?

Introduction to the Electricity Monitor Company

A. Purpose

The purpose of this document is to request funding from First National Bank for a start-up business called the Electricity Monitor Company. This document will contain an overview of the problem that the company will address in the market, how the Electricity Monitor will solve this problem, and a plan for this business.

Briefly identifies the general purpose of the document and offers a preview of the document's contents.

B. Problem: High Power Bills

In twenty-first century America, and in most first world countries, electricity is a necessity. In the home, electricity is used for a variety of devices. Due to the vast number of devices that use electricity, and no good way of knowing how much power they are consuming on a daily basis, families with a traditional circuit-breaker box often struggle with using too much electricity. The problem is high power bills.

Explains a problem that consumers face.

C. Current Alternatives to High Power Bills

There are three currently available solutions to measuring home energy usage in an attempt to lower power bills: Plug-in Meters, Energy Meter Monitors, and Home Energy Monitors. Plug-in Meters are devices that plug in to individual outlets to measure energy usage of a single device. An Energy Meter Monitor attaches to an electricity meter, measures total energy consumption of a home, and estimates what the power bill will be for the month. Neither device is effective in determining energy usage of the entire home across multiple devices. The Home Energy Monitors contain multiple channels to measure energy usage across multiple devices in the home, but these devices are extremely expensive and require detailed installation that increases the cost of the products. Three Home Energy Monitoring Devices are the TED 5000, eGuage, and EnviR, with respective prices of $239, $494, and $129. I have determined that the current solutions in this market are too expensive and do not adequately provide families with an affordable way to monitor their electricity usage. I have developed a better solution to this pain point.

Provides a brief market analysis, and identifies a gap in the market.

How is this section of the report similar to or different from a review of scholarship?

D. The Electricity Monitor

The Electricity Monitor is a device that can solve the pain point of high power bills by measuring the electricity usage of each device in the home. This device can easily attach to any existing breaker box. Installation of the device can be performed by any customer with the instructions provided with the device. At a price of $75, this device will be much cheaper than current solutions to monitoring power usage. A price comparison is shown in Figure 1 below. By measuring

Stresses reasons that support the business's potential for success.

electricity usage of each device in the home, the Electricity Monitor will be able to accurately estimate the power bill for the month (within 1% error) and update daily with changes to electricity usage trends in the home. All data will be transmitted to a monitoring display. This device is also superior to the competition in that it makes suggestions as to how to decrease energy consumption and provides information on which devices in the home are using the most energy. Using the data from the Electricity Monitor, families will finally have the tool they need to save money on their power bill.

Charts and figures appear commonly in business documents for clarification of ideas or to explain relationships between variables.

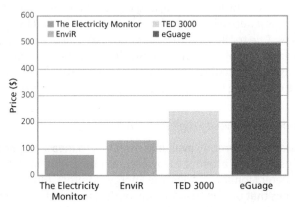

Fig. 1. Price comparison

E. Market for This Product

Performs a more detailed market analysis.

Industry market research from the IBIS World database shows small household appliance manufacturing to have $3.1 billion in annual revenue with $77.9 million in annual profit. This number alone shows the vastness of this market. In addition, IBIS World estimates 38.4% of this market to account for small household devices similar to the Electricity Monitor. Figure 2 below from IBIS World shows the market breakdown. The main demographic for this product will be families of three or more who are unhappy with their current power bill. The United States Census Bureau estimated there to be 4.4 million households with families of three or more people, accounting for 39% of all households in 2011. IBIS World describes the technology change in this market to be "Medium." This leads me to believe that a new product in this market could really shake the market and attract interest from consumers. Assuming that the current trend for revenue and profit in the small household appliance industry performs as predicted, the market for the Electricity Monitor will be large.

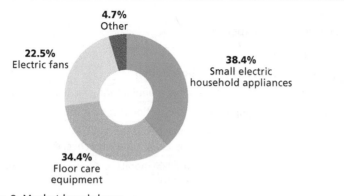

- 4.7% Other
- 22.5% Electric fans
- 38.4% Small electric household appliances
- 34.4% Floor care equipment

Fig. 2. Market breakdown

Plan of Business

A. Overview

I plan to construct the Electricity Monitor Company to hold complete ownership of all business sectors for the Electricity Monitor product. The Company will have an engineering department responsible for the design of the product, a manufacturing facility where the product will be built, and a marketing department responsible for the marketing and selling of the product. The overall cost for the start-up is analyzed below. This breakdown of cost can also be found in the Attachments section of this document.

Explains governance and operating procedures of the proposed company.

B. Cost Analysis

Table 1
Design Expense

Offers a detailed analysis of costs associated with the business start-up.

Design Expense	Description	Total Cost
Building	Rented office space	$ 5,000.00
Software	CAD modeling and FEA software license	$ 4,000.00
Total		**$9,000.00**

Table 1 is an analysis of the cost for designing the product. The requested loan will need to cover the first month of rent for an office and also a license for software that will be used to design the product. The labor is not included in the cost here because I will be designing the product myself.

Table 2
Manufacturing Expense

Manufacturing Expense (First 500 Products)	Description	Total Cost
Building	Small manufacturing facility	$ 100,000.00
Manufacturing equipment	Laser cutting machine, etc.	$ 200,000.00
Tools	Screwdrivers, socket wrenches, Allen wrenches, etc.	$ 5,000.00
Materials	First 500 monitors (avg cost $20/monitor)	$ 10,000.00
Labor	$25/hr with five employees @ 40 hours a week	$ 20,000.00
Total		**$335,000.00**

Table 2 is an analysis of the cost for manufacturing the product. The building and manufacturing equipment are one-time costs for the initial start-up. The materials and labor will be ongoing costs, but the loan request is only enough to cover the first 500 products manufactured. Five hundred products have been estimated as enough to cover the first month of sales and will allow my company to be self-sufficient after selling the first 500 products.

Table 3
Marketing Expense

Marketing Expense	Description	Total Cost
Commercial	Television ad	$ 5,000.00
Web search	Google AdWords	$ 5,000.00
Total		**$ 10,000.00**

Table 3 is an analysis of the total marketing expense. I will additionally market this product to retail stores that could also sell this product, but cost for labor of this marketing is not included here because I will do it myself.

Table 4
Total Cost Analysis

Business Sector	Total Cost
Design	$ 9,000.00
Manufacturing	$ 335,000.00
Marketing	$ 10,000.00
Total	**$354,000.00**

Table 4 is a summary of the total cost analysis for this product. The highlighted cell in Table 4 represents the total start-up cost for the Electricity Monitor Company. This is also the total requested loan amount from First National Bank.

C. Summary

The total cost for this start-up was analyzed in Tables 1 through 4 above. The cost of materials was estimated from current market cost of materials and is subject to change with the market. However, my request for the bottom-line loan amount for this start-up is three hundred and fifty-four thousand dollars ($354,000.00), and this request will not change with cost of materials. A sound business plan has been constructed that will allow the Electricity Monitor Company to become self-sufficient after one month. In order for this business plan to work, the product must be successful in attracting customers quickly as projected by the market research.

Conclusion

The overall purpose of the Electricity Monitor start-up business is to develop a high-quality product that can generate excitement in the electricity monitor market and turn a profit for its business owners and investors. This product will benefit not only its investors, but also its consumers in that it will solve their pain point of not being able to affordably measure their current energy consumption. In comparison to other products in the market that attempt to solve the problem of high power bills, the Electricity Monitor is superior in price, ease of installation, and overall ability to solve the problem. There is nothing quite like this product currently in the market, and this is why it will be successful. The market research has proven that there is a large potential market and that current technology change is not very high. I am excited about starting the Electricity Monitor Company, the potential of this product, and the benefits for all parties involved. Please grant the requested loan amount of three hundred and fifty-four thousand dollars ($354,000.00) and help me make unnecessarily high power bills a thing of the past.

The conclusion reiterates the proposed product's unique characteristics and potential for success in hopes of securing the capital investment.

Bibliography

Documents sources consulted in the preparation of the business document.

Entrepreneur. "TV Ads." Web. <http://www.entrepreneur.com/article/83108>.

IBIS World. "Vacuum, Fan, & Small Household Appliance Manufacturing in the US." Web. <http://clients1.ibisworld.com.prox.lib.ncsu.edu/reports/us/industry/ataglance.aspx?indid=786>.

Kreider, Rose M. "America's Families and Living Arrangements: 2012."
    United States Census Bureau. Web. <https://www.census.gov/
    prod/2013pubs/p20-570.pdf>.

Thornton Oliver Keller Commercial Real Estate. "Rental
    Rate Calculations." Web. <http://tokcommercial.com/
    MarketInformation/LearningCenter/RentalRateCalculations
    .aspx>.

Compiles the costs associated with the business start-up. See the reference to the attachment on page 505.

Attachments

A. Cost Breakdown

Design Expense	Description	Total Cost
Building	Rented office space	$ 5,000.00
Software	CAD modeling and FEA software license	$ 4,000.00
Total		**$ 9,000.00**
Manufacturing Expense (First 500 Products)	**Description**	**Total Cost**
Building	Small manufacturing facility	$ 100,000.00
Manufacturing equipment	Laser cutting machine, etc.	$ 200,000.00
Tools	Screwdrivers, socket wrenches, Allen wrenches, etc.	$ 5,000.00
Materials	First 500 monitors (avg cost $20/monitor)	$ 10,000.00
Labor	$25/hr with five employees @ 40 hours a week	$ 20,000.00
Total		**$ 335,000.00**
Marketing Expense	**Description**	**Total Cost**
Commercial	Television ad	$ 5,000.00
Web search	Google AdWords	$ 5,000.00
Total		**$ 10,000.00**
Business Sector	**Total Cost**	
Design	$ 9,000.00	
Manufacturing	$ 335,000.00	
Marketing	$ 10,000.00	
Total	**$ 354,000.00**	

Inside Work: CFO for a Day

For this exercise, imagine that you're the chief financial officer for a company, Music Studio Emporium. Your company has twenty employees, and you've been charged with the task of notifying ten of them that they'll be receiving a 2 percent annual pay increase, effective immediately, based on their sales records. Unfortunately, you must also notify your other ten employees that they will not be receiving raises. Draft a brief memo to each group of employees—one for those receiving raises and one for those who aren't—in which you explain the company's decisions regarding your employees' compensation. Feel free to provide additional reasoning for those decisions, as you see fit.

Refer to the memo on pages 498–99 as a model of the structural features you'll want to employ in constructing your memo. Once you're done, consider how the nature of the news you had to convey to each audience influenced the way you delivered that news. What did you do the same for each of your audiences? What did you do differently in constructing the two memos?

Law

Most of us probably have clichéd understandings of the law at work. Many of these likely originated from television shows and movies. In these scenarios, there's almost always lots of drama as the lawyers battle in court, parse witnesses' words, and attempt to sway a judge or jury to their side of a case.

In real life, the practice of law may not always be quite as dramatic or enthralling as it appears on the screen. In fact, many lawyers rarely, or maybe never, appear in court. A criminal defense attorney may regularly appear before a judge or jury in a courtroom setting, but a corporate lawyer may spend the majority of her time drafting and analyzing business contracts. This difference is directly related to the field of law an individual specializes in, be it criminal law, family law, tax law, or environmental law, just to name a few.

Regardless of an attorney's chosen specialization, though, the study of law remains fundamentally concerned with debates over the interpretation of language. This is because the various rules that govern our lives—statutes, ordinances, regulations, and laws, for example—are all constructed in language. As you surely recognize, language can be quite slippery, and rules can often be interpreted in

© Rich Legg/Getty Images

many different ways. We need only briefly to consider current debates over free speech issues or the "right to bear arms" or marriage equality to understand how complicated the business of interpreting laws can become. In the United States, the U.S. Supreme Court holds the authority to provide the final interpretation on the meaning of disputed laws. However, there are lots of legal interpretations and arguments that lower courts must make on a daily basis, and only a tiny portion of cases are ever heard by the U.S. Supreme Court.

As in the other applied fields, there are many common forms of communication in the various fields of law, as lawyers must regularly communicate with different kinds of stakeholders, including clients, other lawyers, judges, and law enforcement officials. For this reason, individuals working in the legal professions are generally expert at composing e-mail messages, memos, letters to clients, and legal briefs, among other genres. The following examples provide a glimpse into two types of writing through which lawyers frequently communicate.

Legal Brief

One of the first forms of writing students of law are likely to encounter in their academic study is the legal brief. Briefs can serve any number of functions, but their primary purpose is to outline the critical components of a legal argument to a specified audience. They may be descriptive or argumentative. A typical assignment for a student in law school might include writing a legal brief that describes a particular court's decision and explains how the court reached that decision. Cases that appear before the U.S. Supreme Court are usually accompanied by numerous legal briefs that are written and filed with the Court by parties who are interested in the outcomes of those cases. Many of these briefs are argumentative. Students of law, then, must be familiar with the basic structural components, or the structural conventions, of the legal brief. And law schools regularly instruct their students to produce legal briefs using the generalized form known as IRAC—an acronym for Introduction, Rule, Application, and Conclusion—as a means to describe past court decisions and/or to present written arguments to a court:

- Identify the Legal Issue(s) in the Case

    Introduction   Legal cases can be very complicated. It is a lawyer's task to explore the facts of a case, along with its legal history, to determine which facts are actually relevant and which are irrelevant as they pertain to a legal question or dispute.

- Identify and Explain the Relevant Law(s) to the Case

    Rule   Often, many different statutes, regulations, laws, or other court precedents are applicable and need exploration as part of a legal dispute. A lawyer must identify the applicable rules of law and explain their relevance to the legal question or dispute at hand.

- **Apply the Relevant Rules to the Facts of the Case**

  Application   The facts of the case are explored through the lens of relevant rules. Arguments are presented in these sections of a brief.

- **Argue for a Particular Decision or Outcome**

  Conclusion   Based on the application of relevant rules to the facts of the case, a lawyer makes a recommendation that the judge or court should reach a particular conclusion.

Insider Example

Professional Legal Brief

The following excerpts are from a 55-page legal brief that was filed with the U.S. Supreme Court on behalf of the University of Texas at Austin, et al., which was sued by an applicant after being denied admission to the university. In arguing their case, attorneys writing on behalf of the respondents, or the university, defended its decision to deny admission to the complainant, or the petitioner, Abigail Fisher. As you read the excerpted sections below, try to identify parts of the brief that correspond to the elements of the IRAC structure for presenting legal arguments: Introduction, Rule, Application, and Conclusion.

No. 11-345

In the
Supreme Court of the United States

ABIGAIL NOEL FISHER,
Petitioner,

v.

UNIVERSITY OF TEXAS AT AUSTIN, ET AL.,
Respondents.

ON WRIT OF CERTIORARI TO THE
UNITED STATES COURT OF APPEALS
FOR THE FIFTH CIRCUIT

BRIEF FOR RESPONDENTS

PATRICIA C. OHLENDORF
VICE PRESIDENT FOR
LEGAL AFFAIRS
THE UNIVERSITY OF
TEXAS AT AUSTIN
Flawn Academic Center
2304 Whitis Avenue
Stop G4800
Austin, TX 78712

DOUGLAS LAYCOCK
UNIVERSITY OF VIRGINIA
SCHOOL OF LAW
580 Massie Road
Charlottesville, VA 22903

GREGORY G. GARRE
COUNSEL OF RECORD
MAUREEN E. MAHONEY
J. SCOTT BALLENGER
LORI ALVINO MCGILL
KATYA S. GEORGIEVA
LATHAM & WATKINS LLP
555 11th Street, NW
Suite 1000
Washington, DC 20004
(202) 637-2207
gregory.garre@lw.com

JAMES C. HO
GIBSON, DUNN &
CRUTCHER LLP
2100 McKinney Avenue
Suite 1110
Dallas, TX 75201-6912

Counsel for Respondents

INTRODUCTION

After considering largely the same objections raised by petitioner and her amici here, this Court strongly embraced Justice Powell's controlling opinion in *Regents of the University of California v. Bakke*, 438 U.S. 265 (1978), and refused to prohibit the consideration of race as a factor in admissions at the Nation's universities and graduate schools. *Grutter v. Bollinger*, 539 U.S. 306 (2003); *see id.* at 387 (Kennedy, J., dissenting). And although the Court has made clear that any consideration of race in this context must be limited, it has been understood for decades that "a university admissions program may take account of race as one, non-predominant factor in a system designed to consider each applicant as an individual, provided the program can meet the test of strict scrutiny by the judiciary." *Id.* at 387 (Kennedy, J., dissenting) (citing *Bakke*, 438 U.S. at 289–91, 315–18 (Powell, J.)); *see id.* at 322–23. The University of Texas at Austin (UT)'s highly individualized consideration of race for applicants not admitted under the State's top 10% law satisfies that demand, and meets strict scrutiny under any conception of that test not designed simply to bar the consideration of race altogether.

That conclusion follows *a fortiori* from existing precedent. UT's admissions plan was modeled on the type of plan upheld in *Grutter* and commended by Justice Powell in *Bakke*. Moreover, UT's plan lacks the features criticized in *Grutter* by Justice Kennedy—who agreed with the majority that *Bakke* is the "correct rule." *Id.* at 387 (dissenting). Justice Kennedy concluded that Michigan Law School's admissions plan used race "to achieve numerical goals indistinguishable from quotas." *Id.* at 389. Here, it is undisputed that UT has not set any "target" or "goal" for minority admissions. JA 131a. Justice Kennedy stressed that Michigan's "admissions officers consulted...daily reports which indicated the composition of the incoming class along racial lines." *Grutter*, 539 U.S. at 391 (dissenting). Here, it is undeniable that no such monitoring occurs. JA 398a. And Justice Kennedy believed that race was "a predominant factor" under Michigan's plan. *Grutter*, 539 U.S. at 393 (dissenting). Here, petitioner argues (at 20) that UT's consideration of race is too "minimal" to be constitutional. That paradoxical contention not only overlooks the indisputably meaningful impact that UT's plan has on diversity, *infra* at 36–38, it turns on its head Justice Powell's conception of the appropriately nuanced and modest consideration of race in this special context.

Because petitioner cannot dispute that UT's consideration of race is both highly individualized and modest, she is forced to take positions directly at odds with the record and existing precedent.

Identifies the critical issue at stake, and lays out the respondents' position.

Reviews relevant precedents, or earlier conclusions reached by the Court.

Presents the complainant's central claims, and offers response.

Her headline claim that UT is engaged in "racial balancing" (Pet. Br. 6–7, 19, 27–28, 45–46) is refuted by her own concession that UT has *not* set any "target" for minority admissions. JA 131a. Her argument that the State's top 10% law bars UT from considering race in its holistic review of applicants not eligible under that law is foreclosed by *Grutter*'s holding that percentage plans are not a complete, workable alternative to the individualized consideration of race in full-file review. 539 U.S. at 340. And her argument that, in 2004, UT had already achieved all the diversity that the Constitution allowed is based on "a limited notion of diversity" (*Parents Involved in Cmty. Schs. v. Seattle Sch. Dist. No. 1*, 551 U.S. 701, 723 (2007)) rejected by this Court—one that crudely lumps together distinct racial groups and ignores the importance of diversity among individuals *within* racial groups.

In the end, petitioner really is just asking this Court to move the goal posts on higher education in America—and overrule its precedent going back 35 years to *Bakke*. Pet. Br. 53–57. *Stare decisis* alone counsels decisively against doing so. Petitioner has provided no persuasive justification for the Court to reexamine, much less overrule, its precedent, just nine years after this Court decided *Grutter* and eliminated any doubt about the controlling force of Justice Powell's opinion in *Bakke*. And overruling *Grutter* and *Bakke* (or effectively gutting them by adopting petitioner's conception of strict scrutiny) would jeopardize the Nation's paramount interest in educating its future leaders in an environment that best prepares them for the society and workforce they will encounter. Moreover, the question that petitioner herself asked this Court to decide is the constitutionality of UT's policy under *existing* precedent, including *Grutter*. *See* Pet. i; Pet. Br. i. Because the court of appeals correctly answered that question, the judgment below should be affirmed.

STATEMENT OF THE CASE

. . .

E. Petitioner's Application for Admission

Petitioner, a Texas resident, applied for admission to UT's Fall 2008 freshman class in Business Administration or Liberal Arts, with a combined SAT score of 1180 out of 1600 and a cumulative 3.59 GPA. JA 40a–41a. Because petitioner was not in the top 10% of her high school class, her application was considered pursuant to the holistic review process described above. JA 40a. Petitioner scored an AI of 3.1, JA 415a, and received a PAI score of less than 6 (the actual score is contained in a sealed brief, ECF No. 52). The summary judgment record is uncontradicted that—due to the

Identifies stakes for the outcome of the decision, and reasserts the respondents' position.

Provides background facts about the case concerning the student's application to UT–Austin.

stiff competition in 2008 and petitioner's relatively low AI score—petitioner would not have been admitted to the Fall 2008 freshman class even if she had received "a 'perfect' PAI score of 6." JA 416a.

Petitioner also was denied admission to the summer program, which offered provisional admission to some applicants who were denied admission to the fall class, subject to completing certain academic requirements over the summer. JA 413a–14a. (UT discontinued this program in 2009.) Although one African-American and four Hispanic applicants with lower combined AI/PAI scores than petitioner's were offered admission to the summer program, so were 42 Caucasian applicants with combined AI/PAI scores identical to or lower than petitioner's. In addition, 168 African-American and Hispanic applicants in this pool who had combined AI/PAI scores identical to or *higher* than petitioner's were *denied* admission to the summer program.[1]

[1]These figures are drawn from UT's admissions data and are provided in response to petitioner's unsupported assertion (at 2) that her "academic credentials exceeded those of many admitted minority applicants." Petitioner presented a subset of this data (admitted minority students) to the district court as Plaintiffs' Exhibits 26 and 27 at the preliminary injunction hearing (the court later returned the exhibits). *See* W.D. Tex. Record Transmittal Letter (July 27, 2012), ECF No. 136. UT summarized additional data in a sealed letter brief after the hearing. ECF No. 52; JA 20a (discussing data and explaining that petitioner had not requested data regarding the applicants "who were *not* admitted to UT"). In denying a preliminary injunction, the district court stated (without citation) that 64 minority applicants with lower AI scores than petitioner were *admitted* to Liberal Arts. *Fisher v. Texas*, 556 F. Supp. 2d 603, 607 & n.2 (W.D. Tex. 2008). That statement is not binding at the merits stage. *University of Texas v. Camenisch*, 451 U.S. 390, 395 (1981). Although the district court did not specify whether it was referring to admissions to the fall class or the summer program, that figure can only encompass admits to the summer program. As explained in the unrebutted summary judgment record, with her AI score, petitioner could not "have gained admission through the fall review process," even with a "perfect" PAI score. JA 415a–16a. Petitioner has submitted no contrary evidence (and UT is aware of none). That leaves the now-defunct summer program. The district court's statement that minority applicants with lower AI scores than petitioner were admitted does not establish that race was a factor in petitioner's denial from the summer program, because (as noted above) many more minority applicants (168) with identical or *higher* AI/PAI scores were *denied* admission to the summer program. It is thus hard to see how petitioner could establish any cognizable injury for her § 1983 damages claim—the only claim still alive in this case—or, for that matter, standing to maintain that claim. *See Texas v. Lesage*, 528 U.S. 18, 19, 21 (1999) (per curiam); *Lujan v. Defenders of Wildlife*, 504 U.S. 555, 562 (1992). (Petitioner's claims for injunctive relief dropped out of the case at least once she graduated from a different university in May 2012, making this issue pertinent now.) And that is just one apparent vehicle—if not jurisdictional—defect with this case. *See* Br. in Opp. 6–22; *see also* Adam D. Chandler, *How (Not) to Bring an Affirmative-Action Challenge*, 122 Yale L. J. Online (forthcoming Sept. 2012), *available at* http://ssrn.com/abstract_id=2122956 (discussing vehicle defects stemming from, among other things, the unusual manner in which this case was framed).

UT did offer petitioner admission to the Coordinated Admissions Program, which allows Texas residents to gain admission to UT for their sophomore year by completing 30 credits at a participating UT System campus and maintaining a 3.2 GPA. JA 414a. Petitioner declined that offer and enrolled at Louisiana State University, from which she graduated in May.

F. Procedural History

Provides a brief history of the case in the courts, explaining decisions by lower courts.

Petitioner and another applicant—"no longer involved in this case," Pet. Br. ii—filed suit in the Western District of Texas against UT and various University officials under 42 U.S.C. § 1983, alleging, *inter alia*, that UT's 2008 full-file admissions procedures violate the Equal Protection Clause. JA 38a. They sued only on their own behalf (not on behalf of any class of applicants) and sought a declaratory judgment and injunctive relief barring UT's consideration of race and requiring UT to reconsider their own applications in a race-blind process. JA 39a. They also sought a "refund of [their] application fees and all associated expenses incurred . . . in connection with applying to UT." *Id.*; *see* App. 3a–4a.

The district court denied petitioner's request for a preliminary injunction. The parties filed cross-motions for summary judgment and supporting statements of fact (JA 103a–51a, 363a–403a). Applying strict scrutiny (App. 139a), the court granted judgment to UT, holding that UT has a compelling interest in attaining a diverse student body and the educational benefits flowing from such diversity, and that UT's individualized and holistic review process is narrowly tailored to further that interest. App. 168–69a.

The Fifth Circuit affirmed. Like the district court, the court of appeals found that "it would be difficult for UT to construct an admissions policy that more closely resembles the policy approved by the Supreme Court in *Grutter*." App. 5a. And the court likewise took it as "a given" that UT's policy "is subject to strict scrutiny with its requirement of narrow tailoring." App. 35a. While acknowledging that *Bakke* and *Grutter* call for some deference to a university's "educational judgment," the court emphasized that "the scrutiny triggered by racial classification 'is no less strict for taking into account' the special circumstances of higher education." App. 34a, 36a. Applying strict scrutiny, the court upheld UT's admissions policy. App. 71a.

Judge Garza concurred. He recognized that the court's opinion was "faithful" to *Grutter*, but argued that *Grutter* was wrongly decided. App. 72a–73a.

SUMMARY OF ARGUMENT

UT's individualized consideration of race in holistic admissions did not subject petitioner to unequal treatment in violation of the Fourteenth Amendment.

I. Racial classifications are subject to strict scrutiny, including in the higher education context. But ever since Justice Powell's opinion in *Bakke*, this Court has recognized that universities have a compelling interest in promoting student body diversity, and that a university may consider the race of applicants in an individualized and modest manner—such that race is just one of many characteristics that form the mosaic presented by an applicant's file.

UT's holistic admissions policy exemplifies the type of plan this Court has allowed: race is only one modest factor among many others weighed; it is considered only in an individualized and contextual way that "examine[s] the student in 'their totality,'" JA 129a; and admissions officers do not know an applicant's race when they decide which "cells" to admit in UT's process. At the same time, UT's policy *lacks* the features that Justice Kennedy found disqualifying in *Grutter*: it is undisputed that UT has not established any race-based target; race is not assigned any automatic value; and the racial or ethnic composition of admits is not monitored during the admissions cycle.

II. Petitioner's arguments that she was nevertheless subjected to unequal treatment in violation of the Fourteenth Amendment are refuted by both the record and existing precedent.

...

III. The Court should decline petitioner's far-reaching request to reopen and overrule *Bakke* and *Grutter*. That request is outside the scope of the question presented, which asks the Court to review UT's policy under *existing* precedent, including *Grutter*. In any event, petitioner has failed to identify any special justification for taking the extraordinary step of overruling *Grutter*, just nine years after this Court decided *Grutter* and unequivocally answered any doubt about the validity of Justice Powell's opinion in *Bakke*. Abruptly reversing course here would upset legitimate expectations in the rule of law—not to mention the profoundly important societal interests in ensuring that the future leaders of America are trained in a campus environment in which they are exposed to the full educational benefits of diversity.

...

Presents a summary of arguments in defense of the respondents' position in light of the facts of the case.

Concludes by asserting the decision that respondents believe the Court should reach.

CONCLUSION

The judgment of the court of appeals should be affirmed.

Respectfully submitted,

PATRICIA C. OHLENDORF
*VICE PRESIDENT FOR
LEGAL AFFAIRS*
THE UNIVERSITY OF
TEXAS AT AUSTIN
Flawn Academic Center
2304 Whitis Avenue
Stop G4800
Austin, TX 78712

DOUGLAS LAYCOCK
UNIVERSITY OF VIRGINIA
SCHOOL OF LAW
580 Massie Road
Charlottesville, VA 22903

AUGUST 2012

GREGORY G. GARRE
COUNSEL OF RECORD
MAUREEN E. MAHONEY
J. SCOTT BALLENGER
LORI ALVINO MCGILL
KATYA S. GEORGIEVA
LATHAM & WATKINS LLP
555 11th Street, NW
Suite 1000
Washington, DC 20004
(202) 637-2207
gregory.garre@lw.com

JAMES C. HO
GIBSON, DUNN &
CRUTCHER LLP
2100 McKinney Avenue
Suite 1110
Dallas, TX 75201-6912

Counsel for Respondents

E-Mail Correspondence

As you might expect, technological advances can have a profound impact on the communication practices of professionals. There may always be a place for hard copies of documents, but e-mail communication has no doubt replaced many of the letters that used to pass between parties via the U.S. Postal Service. Like most professionals these days, those employed in the legal fields often spend a lot of time communicating with stakeholders via e-mail. These professionals carefully assess each rhetorical situation for which an e-mail communication is necessary, both (1) to make sure the ideas they share with stakeholders (the explanations of legal procedures, or legal options, or applicable precedents, etc.) are accurate, and (2) to make sure they communicate those ideas in an appropriate fashion (with the appropriate tone, clarity, precision, etc.).

Insider Example

E-Mail Correspondence from Attorney

The following example is an e-mail sent from a practicing lawyer to a client. In this instance, the lawyer offers legal advice concerning a possible donation from a party to a foundation. As you read the lawyer's description of the documents attached to his e-mail correspondence with the client, pay attention to the ways the attorney demonstrates an acute awareness of his audience, both in terms of the actual legal advice he provides and in terms of the structure and language of his message.

Dear _____

As promised, here are two documents related to the proposed gift of the ABC property to the XYZ Foundation (the "Foundation"). The first document summarizes the recommended due diligence steps (including the creation of a limited liability company) that should take place prior to the acceptance of the property, accompanied by estimated costs associated with each such step. The second document contains a draft "pre-acceptance" agreement that the Foundation could use to recover its documented costs in the event that either the donor or the Foundation backs out of a gift agreement following the due diligence process.

You will note that we have limited the Foundation's ability to recover costs in the event that the Foundation is the party that "pulls the plug." In such a scenario, the Foundation could recover costs only if it reasonably determines that either (i) the property would create a risk of material exposure to environmentally related liabilities or (ii) the remediation of environmental issues would impose material costs on the Foundation. We realize that even in light of this limiting language, the agreement represents a fairly aggressive approach with the donor, and we will be glad to work with you if you wish to take a softer stance.

Please don't hesitate to call me with any questions, concerns, or critiques. As always, we appreciate the opportunity to serve you in furthering the Foundation's good work.

Best regards,

Joe

Joseph E. Miller, Jr.
Partner
joe.miller@FaegreBD.com
Direct: +1 317 237 1415
FaegreBD.com Download vCard
FAEGRE BAKER DANIELS LLP
300 N. Meridian Street
Suite 2700
Indianapolis, IN 46204, USA

Marginal annotations:

Establishes the level of familiarity and tone.

Provides transactional advice, explaining what procedure needs to occur between the two parties involved: a donor and a receiving foundation.

Provides additional advice to protect the interests of the parties in the event that either party decides to back out of the transaction.

Explains more specific details included in the attached legal documents to protect the interests of the Foundation.

Communicates a willingness to continue the relationship with the client.

Provides standard identification and contact information for communication between and among professionals.

Inside Work: Lawyer for a Day

Imagine that you're an attorney, and you've just been hired as a consultant by the Board of Governors of a local college that's in the process of designing new guidelines for student admissions. As part of that process, the Board has asked you to review legal briefs presented on behalf of various stakeholders in *Fisher v. University of Texas at Austin, et al*. Additionally, the Board wants you to provide a summary of UT–Austin's response to the charge that its admissions procedures violated the petitioner's rights under the Fourteenth Amendment to the U.S. Constitution.

Read again the section of the legal brief filed with the U.S. Supreme Court entitled "Summary of Argument" (on p. 517), and then draft an e-mail correspondence to your client (the Board of Governors) in which you offer an overview of UT–Austin's response to its possible violation of a prospective student's constitutional rights. As part of your summary, offer your client an assessment of the likely effectiveness of UT–Austin's argument. Be clear and precise in your presentation of UT–Austin's argument in defense of its position. Keep your audience and your relationship to that audience in mind as you compose your e-mail.

Writing Project: Discovering Genres of Writing in an Applied Field

In this chapter, you've read about some of the conventions of writing in the applied fields of nursing, education, business, and law. You might be interested in a field that's not represented in this chapter, though. For this assignment, you will conduct research to discover more about the kinds of writing that are common within a particular applied field—ideally, one you're interested in. You might conduct either primary or secondary research to respond to this assignment. However, you should focus on collecting examples of the kinds of writing done in the field. Consider following the steps below to complete this assignment.

1. Collect examples of the kinds of writing done in the field.

2. Describe the different genres and how they relate to the work of that applied field.

3. Look for comparisons and contrasts across those genres. Do any commonalities point to conventions shared across genres? Are there differences that are important to notice? What do the patterns across the genres tell you about the work and values of that applied field?

Variation: Imagine that your audience is a group of incoming students interested in the same field of study you've researched for this project. Your task is to write a guide for those students about the conventions of writing expected in this applied field. Depending on what you have found, you may need to identify what conventions are appropriate for specific genres of writing.

Tip Sheet

Reading and Writing in the Applied Fields

- **The applied fields focus on the practical application of knowledge and career preparation.** Many applied fields also focus on problem-solving as part of the practical application of knowledge.

- **When beginning a writing task in applied fields, carefully analyze the rhetorical situation.** Consider your purpose and your audience carefully, and assess the appropriateness of responding in a particular genre.

- **Much of the writing in applied fields follows conventional expectations for structure, language, and reference appropriate to the fields.** Regardless of your writing task, you should be aware of these conventional expectations.

- **Students and professionals in applied fields often communicate information through field-specific genres.** Nurses, for example, often construct discharge directions, just as students and professionals in the fields of law often compose legal briefs.

Team Writing:
Before You Start

Part Four

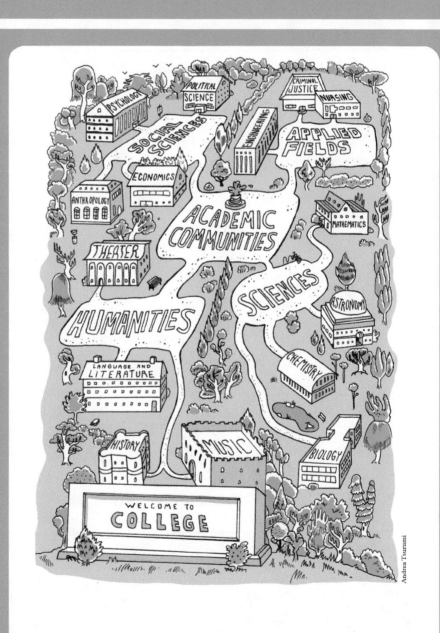

Andrea Tsurumi

Part Four

Team Writing: Before You Start

Chapter 16 Planning Your Collaboration

At the end of a semester-long project on advanced database techniques, Eduardo, a graduate student in computer science, reflected on his team's collaboration:

Interviewer: Did anybody give you any input on the sections of the report that you wrote?

Eduardo: No. No, nobody gave their opinion on anybody's work.

Interviewer: Did you expect them to?

Eduardo: Well, at the beginning, yes...but then everybody submitted at the last minute, so it was rushed. Umm, also we didn't have a chance 'cause we didn't meet after we submitted the draft. At that point, we were in finals, and we weren't going to do anything else.

Interviewer: How do you think your teammates would evaluate your contribution?

Eduardo: Well, I would hope they would say I did the most, but I don't know. I don't think some of them read [the final report].

Thomas, a biology student in a technical writing class, also feels that his collaborative project did not live up to his expectations:

Thomas: Personally, I thought we could have used class time better.

Interviewer: How so?

Thomas: Because I think we could have got more of it done outside of class.... It took us 50 minutes to revise about half a page because of word choice or how we wanted to say it. I think that we thought we were actually more ahead than what we were...and then the final deadline caught up to us. It snuck up on us.

Susan, an undergraduate majoring in math, similarly expresses frustration with a collaborative project she worked on in her technical writing class:

Interviewer: So how did you decide who was going to do what?

Susan: Well, originally we all decided that we were gonna get together and do the Web site, but Rene took the disc and drafted the site herself. And then the rest of the project was just kind of, we volunteered for stuff as it came up, I guess.

Interviewer: And how did you feel about that?

Susan: It kind of destroyed our group working together.... We were going to do it all together because none of us knew how to do a Web site, and then Rene just went and did it all...and then she had to come back and explain it to us.

These three students—and all the other students discussed in this portion of the book—were members of actual student teams observed as they worked on team projects in technical writing and engineering classes. Like the majority of the teams observed, these student groups had problems working together toward a common end. In some cases, students weren't aware of what their teammates had done, other teams failed to budget their time effectively, and still other teams ended up with hurt feelings and resentment. Parts Four and Five of this textbook are intended to teach you to replace such frustrating team situations with ones where you coordinate with your teammates to produce work that is better and much more innovative than what any one of you could have created on your own.

This section of the book focuses on the role of writing in effective teamwork. First, you will learn to produce the types of internal team documents that are *absolutely essential* to a well-run project—documents such as task schedules, meeting minutes, and team agendas as well as e-mails and memos that help head off potential problems. Second, you will learn how to write and revise large documents as a group. This focus on large documents is important because so much collaboration in fields like engineering, business, computer science, medicine, and hard sciences (to name a few) involves major written documents such as design plans, proposals, reports, manuals, and Web sites. This book teaches you specific writing strategies for managing such large documents.

Before you continue reading, take a moment to review the three preceding scenarios and reflect on why these student teams experienced breakdowns. What could these teams have done differently to prevent the problems they experienced?

Why Teamwork?

These three scenarios illustrate the various problems that student teams can encounter. Given the problems with collaboration, why do teachers assign team projects in the first place? Group projects are typically assigned in school for two reasons:

1. To prepare students for the workplace by providing opportunities to learn the social and organizational skills necessary for productive teamwork. Employers in many fields want to hire graduates who already have experience working collaboratively.

2. To improve the educational experience through collaboration with fellow students. Educational research suggests that people learn the most when working with peers toward a common goal. When students discuss problems with an instructor or someone else who is considered an expert, they tend to automatically defer to the expert's viewpoint. However, when students discuss problems with peers, they are freer to debate and think through the problem and all the issues involved.

Let's take each of these reasons separately. First, collaboration has become the norm in most workplaces. On large, complex projects, no one person has all of the expertise and experience (let alone time and energy) to complete the project by himself or herself. Even smaller projects tend to take advantage of teamwork. People working together can often produce better outcomes in less time than any one person could produce independently. Team members benefit from a diversity of approaches and perspectives that lead to innovative insights.

However, teams often fail to work together effectively—and that failure threatens the entire project. For instance, Tom DeMarco and Timothy Lister (1987), experienced software specialists, write:

> The success or failure of a project is seldom due to technical issues.... If the project goes down the tubes it will be non-technical, human interaction problems that do it in. The team will fail to bind, or the developers will fail to gain rapport with the users, or people will fight interminably over meaningless methodological issues. (p. 88)

Because poor team skills waste so much company time, businesses are now putting pressure on educational institutions to provide authentic team experiences that will produce college graduates with strong interpersonal, management, and coauthoring skills. Instructors assign team projects to give students opportunities to develop these skills.

Second, instructors assign team projects so that students have opportunities to learn from their peers. Many students are motivated by collaborative learning. Co-writing and collaborating give students opportunities to share expertise, learn from others' mistakes as well as successes, and—most importantly—solidify what they have learned by teaching it to others.

Unfortunately, teams in school settings do not function just like teams in the workplace. Unlike school-based teams, work-based teams can develop longer histories of working together and are more likely to have clear-cut lines of authority. Thus, school-based teams have some unique challenges that are not present in work-based teams. This textbook attempts to teach you how to navigate some of these challenges using strategies that you can also carry into the workplace.

Understanding Collaboration Methods

The three scenarios that begin this chapter illustrate some of the problems that arise when teams fail to fully plan out a project and agree on a collaboration method. In all three cases, the students being interviewed disagreed with their teammates over the specific steps the team needed to follow. These conflicting views of how the team should go about collaborating hurt the quality of the final projects and led to dissatisfaction with the team.

Understanding different collaboration methods and their respective costs and benefits can help teams identify and negotiate conflicting visions of how the group should proceed. When working on documents, groups can structure their collaboration using one of three basic methods (see Figure 16.1):

1. **Face-to-face**. The entire team sits down and writes the document together. Usually one or two team members sit at the computer and type while others give input.

2. **Divided**. The group breaks the document into sections and assigns each team member a section.

3. **Layered**. Each person on the team is assigned one or more specific roles. Each person works on the document in turn, adding his or her own expertise to the product. The document slowly accumulates in layers as each team member revises and improves upon what already exists.

The type of collaboration method a group uses has significant consequences for how the work proceeds. In the interviews beginning this chapter, Eduardo describes experiences typical of groups that rely on **divided** collaboration. Team members completed their individual sections at the last minute, there was no time for discussion of the final draft, and Eduardo is not sure if his teammates even read the final report. Moreover, one of the team members produced a section that was of particularly low quality—contributing to the disappointing grade this group received.

Whereas Eduardo's group never met to discuss the draft, Thomas's group tried to complete *all* of its work in team meetings. The team members' attempt to draft their entire proposal **face-to-face** not only was inefficient but also lowered project quality because they were rushed for time at the end and ended up dropping sections. In addition, although Thomas was not aware of it at the time, one of the group members was extremely upset with the group dynamics, perceiving the team as not valuing her input. When a team relies too much on face-to-face collaboration, such resentment is common because it is virtually impossible for three or more people sitting around a computer to contribute equally.

Susan's group illustrates how the failure to discuss a collaboration method as a group can produce conflict. Susan felt the group should have created the Web site face-to-face; however, Rene operated using a layered collaboration method in which she completed an initial draft and then tried to hand the project off to others to revise and finish. Although this layered approach seemed more appropriate to this project than Susan's face-to-face method, Rene's failure to discuss her collaboration plans resulted in a major breakdown in group dynamics.

See Table 16.1 for a summary of the advantages and drawbacks of the face-to-face, divided, and layered methods of collaboration.

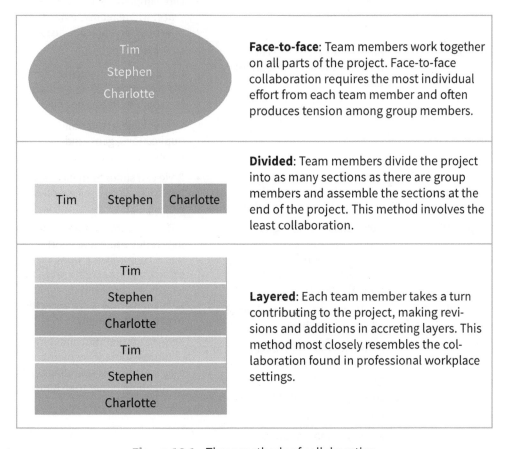

Figure 16.1. Three methods of collaboration.

Table 16.1. Advantages and drawbacks of the three collaboration methods.

Method	Advantages	Drawbacks
Face-to-Face	• Allows team members to quickly share a large number of ideas—particularly useful for brainstorming and debating the pros and cons of different ideas. • Effective for drafting plans, outlines, and task schedules. • Effective for discussing graphic design, such as a company brochure or the layout of a Web page.	• Often difficult to schedule large blocks of time when the team can meet outside of class. • Can be difficult for everyone to have equal input—the person sitting at the keyboard can control what is said. • Ineffective for drafting text and content—wastes individual time and can produce conflict. • Often impossible in the workplace, where team members may be geographically distant.
Divided	• Allows the work to be completed in the least amount of time.	• Minimal collaboration. • Can be difficult to recover if one team member fails to do his or her share or does a poor job. • Content likely to contain duplications, gaps, and inconsistencies. • Style can suffer from inconsistent tone, word choice, and writing quality.
Layered	• Helps ensure a high-quality project because everyone has multiple opportunities to contribute, critique, and improve upon the project. • Maximizes the contributions of all group members. • Motivates the group because everyone feels ownership of the full document. • Particularly effective for drafting and revising. • Mirrors collaboration in the workplace.	• Different team members' roles may require unequal effort—this is common in a work setting but may create problems in a school setting, where all team members are expected to contribute equally. • Requires thoughtful planning up front—some team members may feel anxious spending time on planning rather than jumping into the details.

Despite its substantial advantages, student teams tend to underutilize layered collaboration—probably because it requires the most planning and experience of the three methods. While face-to-face collaboration and divided collaboration seem to come naturally to student teams, layered collaboration requires forethought and some basic training to use it effectively. In part because layered collaboration is unfamiliar to students—and in part because it is the form of collaboration that most frequently leads to higher-quality products—this book stresses layered collaboration in much of the advice and many of the examples provided.

Alternating Collaboration Methods

Often when students are assigned a team project, their first instinct is to schedule a series of face-to-face meetings. Not only does this put a tremendous strain on everyone's personal schedules, but face-to-face collaboration may not even be the most productive form of collaboration for the group at this stage. By figuring out which type of collaboration will be most beneficial at various stages in the project, team members can avoid many problems and ensure that they use their time together productively.

Few experienced teams rely exclusively on a single collaboration method. Most teams alternate collaboration methods throughout the project, depending on what the group is trying to accomplish at each stage. Thus, a team will often begin with face-to-face collaboration in the early stages of a project; switch to layered collaboration to complete the "heavy," detailed work of the project; and then switch back to face-to-face collaboration to discuss revisions or to work out a presentation. Or the team might initially divide up the work so that each team member drafts a section independently and then switch to layered collaboration for the revision process.

Table 16.2 illustrates a group that alternates the face-to-face and layered collaboration methods. In the early stages of the project, the group meets face-to-face to discuss the project's direction and to assign tasks to team members. About a third of the way through the project, the group switches to layered collaboration, with team members successively adding to, elaborating on, critiquing, and revising one another's work. Table 16.3 provides an overview of which types of collaboration are generally most effective at various stages of a project.

Switching collaboration methods might seem complicated at first. However, with a clearly defined **task schedule**, such as the one in Table 16.2, groups can easily stay on task. In fact, if you take away only one lesson from this section of the book, it should be this: a well-planned task schedule is key to the success of any collaborative project. Task schedules will be discussed in more detail in the following chapters.

Table 16.2. **Task schedule from a project that switches from face-to-face to layered collaboration.** Tim is the researcher and client expert; Stephen is the project manager and secondary writer; Charlotte is the primary writer and editor. Note that the task schedule can be color-coded or shaded to highlight each team member's responsibilities.

Deadline	Who	Task
3/02	Everyone	Initial group meeting
3/04	Everyone	Group meeting
3/04	Stephen	E-mail schedule and notes from group meeting
3/13	Tim	Complete client interviews; e-mail interview notes to the group
3/14	Everyone	Group meeting at 3:00 p.m. to discuss interviews
3/14	Stephen	E-mail notes from group meeting
3/21	Charlotte	E-mail rough draft of requirements document minus introduction and conclusion
3/23	Tim	E-mail comments on requirements document
3/29	Stephen	E-mail revised draft of requirements with introduction and conclusion added
3/31	Tim	E-mail draft of cover letter addressed to client
4/03	Charlotte	E-mail revised and polished draft of all materials to group for last-minute comments
4/04 a.m.	Stephen	E-mail editing suggestions to Charlotte
4/04 p.m.	Charlotte	Turn in final draft to professor by 3:00 p.m.

Table 16.3. Most appropriate collaboration method for various stages of a project.

Task or Project Stage	Most Appropriate Collaboration Method
Brainstorming	Face-to-face
Planning a task schedule	Face-to-face
Conducting research	Any, depending on the type of research
Drafting text	Layered or divided
Talking to third parties (instructors, clients, users)	Face-to-face or layered
Discussing a draft	Face-to-face or layered

Task or Project Stage	Most Appropriate Collaboration Method
Resolving disagreements or major changes to project	Face-to-face
Revising text	Layered
Preparing presentations or other visual materials	Layered or face-to-face
Editing text	Layered

Inside Work: Exercises

1. Think of a time when you were involved in a group project at school or at work. Which collaboration method or methods did your group use? How did your choice of collaboration methods contribute to the group's success? How did your choice of collaboration methods lead to conflicts, inefficiencies, or poor project quality? What would you do differently if you were to start this project from scratch?

    The videos in this portion of the textbook are directly based on the interactions of actual student teams. Before you complete any of the video exercises, take a moment to watch the introductory video on the Team Writing *Web site, which describes how the videos were produced and created.*

2. View Team Video 1: Mark, Natalie, and Keith on the *Team Writing* Web site. Answer the following questions about the video:

    Team 1

    a. What method of collaboration does this team seem to be using?

    b. For each team member—Mark (typing at the computer), Natalie, and Keith—provide two or three words or short phrases describing their role on the team.

    c. Based on what you have observed, which team member do you think made the most important contribution, and which one made the least important contribution? Why?

    d. Review Table 16.1. Which drawbacks do you see illustrated in the way the students in this video are collaborating? What problems do you anticipate this team will have in the future if the students continue this style of collaboration?

    e. What changes would you suggest that this group make to improve their collaboration?

3. Once you have completed question 2, read Appendix C, "Responses and Outcomes for Team Video 1." Read about this project's outcome and what the team members themselves said when they viewed a copy of this video after the project was over.

    a. Now that you have more information, how would you modify your original responses to questions 2b–2e?

    b. What actions would you advise the unhappy members of this group to take? How would you have handled the situation if you were Natalie? If you were Mark?

    c. What major lessons can you learn from observing this team?

4. View Team Video 2: Shelly, Will, and Ben on the *Team Writing* Web site. Answer the following questions:

    a. What method of collaboration does this team seem to be using?

    b. For each team member—Shelly, Will, and Ben—provide two or three words or short phrases describing their role on the team.

    c. Review Table 16.1. Which drawbacks do you see illustrated in the way the students in this video are collaborating? What problems do you anticipate this team will have in the future if the students continue this style of collaboration?

    d. What changes would you recommend that this team make to improve their collaboration?

    e. What major lessons can you learn from observing this team?

Team 2

Work Cited

DeMarco, T., & Lister, T. (1987). *Peopleware: Productive products and teams*. New York: Dorset House Publishing.

Chapter 17 Project Management

I n a team evaluation at the end of his project, Ryan commented:

> Audrey was a great project manager. She really kept us on track. There were several times when I wasn't sure what I should do next. Then I just looked at her minutes and saw what it was I needed to finish up.

On another team, Bill similarly attributed team success to good project management:

> Steve did a great job keeping everybody updated. Because of him, everybody knew what their deadlines were and how the group was going. This was the first time I've been on a group project where everybody didn't wait until the last minute to throw everything together.

Project management is one of the least understood aspects of collaboration in student teams. Before we continue discussing how to organize a collaborative project, you should understand what project management involves and why a project manager is necessary—even on small projects.

Why Do You Need a Project Manager?

Students frequently confuse the role of project manager with "boss," "leader," or even "dictator" and quite understandably decide that they do not want a project manager on their team. Instead of viewing the project manager as a kind of supervisor, think of the project manager as someone who plays a specific role on the team by keeping the project on course. The project manager's primary responsibility is to track the status of the project and to ensure that all team members know what they should be doing at any moment.

The larger and more complicated the team project is, the more important the role of project manager becomes. However, even small two-person projects can benefit from someone who acts as project manager by summarizing tasks and deadlines for the group. Often the project manager will do other work for the group; however,

Chapter 17, "Project Management" from *Team Writing: A Guide to Working in Groups* by Joanna Wolfe, pp. 13–26 (Chapter 2). Copyright © 2010 by Bedford/St. Martin's.

according to Charles Stratton, a technical writing consultant, even if he or she does nothing other than coordinate the team, the project manager "has earned his [or her] keep" (Stratton, 1989).

The project manager's specific duties include the following:

- Keeping the project on schedule by publicizing deadlines and responsibilities in the task schedule
- Holding people accountable by documenting action items in the meeting minutes
- Managing disagreements by documenting decisions in the meeting minutes
- Keeping team meetings on task by preparing meeting agendas

In addition, the project manager may, if needed, perform other tasks:

- Sending e-mail reminders of deadlines
- Notifying the instructor of problems, particularly missed deadlines
- Creating the initial straw document of the project
- Producing other documents related to the project, including project plans, team charters, and progress reports

On most projects, the manager will be doing work in addition to coordinating the project. Thus, a project manager might also double up as a co-writer, artist, or some other role on the team. However, on very large projects, it may be sufficient to have a project manager who does nothing other than manage the team.

The remainder of this chapter focuses on the three types of documents that are essential to good project management: task schedules, meeting minutes, and meeting agendas. This chapter also describes additional documents that the project manager should produce.

Task Schedules: Publicizing Deadlines and Responsibilities

Once the team has brainstormed some initial ideas for the project and discussed how to organize the collaboration, the project manager needs to create a written task schedule that documents deadlines, tasks, and responsibilities. Such a document is absolutely essential to effective collaboration.(See Chapter 19, "Getting Started with the Task Schedule," for more details on how to develop and schedule a collaborative process.)

At a minimum, every project (even a two-person project) needs a task schedule that lists the three Ws: *who* is responsible for doing *what* by *when*. This task schedule is continually updated as work is reassigned, new tasks are identified, or deadlines change. Table 17.1 shows a task schedule for a group collaborating on an instruction manual.

Each entry in a task schedule contains three vital pieces of information: a name, a deadline, and a brief description of the task. A good task schedule should also build in padding—additional downtime between major steps that allows the group to recover in case a particular step takes longer than expected. For instance, this group has built in two days of padding between 9/12 (the date that everyone's drafts or tasks are due) and 9/14 (the date that the usability tests are scheduled). Similar padding is built into the schedule between 9/19 (the date that Amy will compile and edit a completed manual) and 9/21 (the date the manual is due). This padding allows the group to stay on schedule even if one or more of the major parts of the project are unexpectedly delayed.

Table 17.1. Task schedule for a three-person group working on an instruction manual.

Deadline	Who	Task	Status
9/04	Amy	Write topic proposal and bring to group meeting	Completed
9/04	Everyone	Review and discuss topic proposal at in-class meeting	Completed
9/06	Amy	Turn in revised topic proposal to instructor	Completed
9/09	Jessica	Bring template with sample layout for manual to meeting	
9/09	Everyone	Discuss and revise template at in-class meeting	
9/12	Bryan	Write instructions for installing motor and arms; e-mail	
9/12	Jessica	Write instructions for assembling base; e-mail	
9/12	Amy	Line up two users for 9/14; prepare all materials for usability tests; e-mail group with status	
9/14	Everyone	Test-drive instructions with users at 3:00 p.m. in the library	
9/14	Amy	E-mail a list of changes to group	
9/17	Bryan and Jessica	Revise instructions; e-mail Amy	
9/19	Amy	Edit manual; prepare overview and table of contents; compile and e-mail completed manual to group	
9/21	Everyone	Group meeting at 3:00 p.m. to review final draft; turn in draft	

To be effective, a task schedule needs to be visible. Thus, the project manager must *distribute the schedule to the entire group* (usually through e-mail) each time it is updated. In addition, it is a good idea to keep a copy of the task schedule in a centralized document server that the entire team can access. The project manager may also want to e-mail a copy of the team's initial task schedule to the instructor so that he or she has a copy in case the group has problems with an individual team member later in the project.

The task schedule in Table 17.1 reflects a layered collaboration model. Each team member has his or her own set of responsibilities but also has opportunities to comment and improve on work created by others. A task schedule is essential for implementing a layered collaboration. Such a carefully structured and planned project has a high potential for success.

Dangers of Operating without a Task Schedule

The need for a task schedule should be obvious; nonetheless, many student teams try to operate without one. Without a task schedule, teams are likely to:

- **Miss deadlines.**
- **Duplicate effort.** Two people may complete the same task because neither one is aware that another teammate has been assigned to do it.
- **Procrastinate.** Without a specific deadline in writing, team members might put off their parts of the project until the last minute, thus ensuring a sloppy, uncoordinated project.
- **Encourage slackers.** Some team members will avoid doing any work on the project at all. They may claim that they didn't know a deliverable was due or that they thought someone else was planning to do it. A clear task schedule eliminates these excuses and holds that person responsible for completing a fair share of the work.

Finally, without a clear task schedule that has been circulated via e-mail and/or stored in a centralized group space, teams have no way to appeal to the instructor if someone on the team fails to do his or her work. Without written documentation, the instructor has to take the word of the complaining student. A written task schedule gives the instructor a resource that he or she can use to implement penalties and reassign work.

Meeting Minutes: Building Accountability and Consensus

The following conversation illustrates a common misconception that students often have about meeting minutes:

> **Interviewer:** Now, I noticed that in team meetings you frequently took notes. What was in those notes?

Jessica: I have them right here…. Here's some, showing what everybody had to do.

Interviewer: Okay. So when you took notes, it was along the lines of what different people had to do?

Jessica: Exactly.

Interviewer: Did you ever e-mail notes out to group members? Or just say this is a reminder of what we did or what we decided on?

Jessica: No, I didn't, but that's a good idea. I think they all saw me write, I think. Maybe I thought they were writing them down too, so they may have them.

Interviewer: Yeah, but different people could have been writing down different things.

Jessica (surprised): That's true. I didn't think of that.

Many teams confuse meeting minutes with individual note taking—or with secretarial work that simply records everything that happened during a meeting. In fact, meeting minutes are managerial documents that direct the project by deciding what information is important enough to include and what needs to happen next. Good meeting minutes help the team come to a consensus on the project's progress, who is responsible for what, and where the team needs to go next.

Good meeting minutes contain the following (see Figure 17.1):

- **Action items.** This is a "to do" list that details who needs to do which tasks. Whenever someone on the team volunteers for a task—or whenever the entire team is given a task—this information needs to be recorded.
- **Decisions.** The minutes should include a brief record of important decisions made during the meeting.
- **Next steps.** The minutes should record the questions or actions that will be taken up at the next meeting.
- **Attendance.** The names of people who attended the meeting should be listed so that the team has a record of who is contributing and who has agreed to team decisions.

In addition, meeting minutes must be distributed to the entire team soon after the meeting, usually within 24 hours. The minutes are useless if team members do not have them in their hands to refer to. If a team does not have time to distribute minutes after a meeting, then it didn't have time for the meeting itself.

Library Project Meeting Minutes
April 8, 2008

Attendance: Alex, Alicia, Sefu (Phil absent because of emergency dental visit)

Action items:

Alex: Double-check room availability and send out confirmation to users

Alicia: E-mail draft of usability script to group by Wednesday night

Sefu: Make changes to artwork and send to Phil by Wednesday night

Phil: Implement changes to home page and insert new artwork by class on Thursday

Discussion:

- Mapped out the details of the usability tests
    - Usability tests will be held in LL15 next Friday from 12:00 to 3:00 p.m. Alex will double-check room availability and send confirmation e-mail to users.
    - Alex will bring his video camera to record the tests.
    - Roles: Alicia will be the moderator for all three tests. Alex will record. Sefu and Phil will take observational notes.
- Discussed changes to the artwork
    - The home page logo/image is taking up too much space. It needs to be cropped or resized.
    - The photo of the computer lab on the "Student Resources" page is too dark. It looks depressing.
- Discussed changes to the home page
    - Main navigation links should be reordered: "Search Catalog" should be first, followed by "Search Journals," "Hours," "Resources," and finally "Contact Information."
    - Link to "Hours" is broken.
    - A copyright logo should be placed in the footer.
- Discussed what we want to get out of the usability tests next Friday
    - What do users think of the artwork? (Maybe have some alternative designs to show them?)
    - Does the order of navigational elements make sense?
    - Are there any broken links?
    - Can users find basic information (such as circulation hours, lab hours, phone numbers) without help?
    - Can users find all journal and book search features without help?

Next steps: Next meeting in class on Thursday, April 10. Need to go over changes to artwork, search for broken links, and take a look at the usability script.

Figure 17.1. Meeting minutes. These minutes contain action items, major decisions, next steps, and attendance. The minutes should be circulated to the team within 24 hours of the meeting.

Randall Walker, an industrial engineer with 15 years of management experience in the military, explains that minutes are essential:

> You can say one thing to five people and they will interpret it five different ways. It's critical to put team decisions in writing because at least it gives them an opportunity to say "No, that's not the context of what I said," or "That's not the way I interpreted what we agreed upon." If you don't have it documented, it's he said/she said three weeks [later].... So I think documentation of those encounters [is] absolutely critical in moving forward; otherwise you take one step forward and four steps back and one step forward and four steps back, and you can only take so many steps back before you drop off the cliff.

Andrew Grove, the CEO of Intel, a major computer chip manufacturer, agrees:

> If a meeting was worth calling in the first place, the effort to produce and distribute the minutes is a small additional investment necessary to realize its full benefits. (Grove, 1995)

The most important information in the minutes is the list of action items detailing who will do what. Ken West, an operations research manager with more than 10 years' experience supervising teams, clarifies:

> Even if you don't produce formal minutes, at the end of the meeting, there should be a page that says you're going to do this, you're going do this, you're going do this, and you're going to do this. The person who is the project manager better make sure that that's written down. It's their responsibility to follow up that things get done.

Dangers of Operating without Meeting Minutes

As the previous quotes from managers testify, meeting minutes are essential to the forward progress of a team. Without a central set of minutes, teams will

- **Waste time.** Without minutes, teams will revisit issues that have already been decided, repeat information that has already been shared, or rehash conversations that have already been completed. Moreover, the minutes allow teams to pick up the next meeting right where they left off.

- **Proceed without consensus.** As Randall Walker stated, you can say something to five people and they will interpret it five different ways. The minutes provide a centralized interpretation of the team's decisions and ensure that everyone is "on the same page."

- **Forget important details.** The minutes serve as a reminder of important material that the team has discussed. Without minutes, teams will almost certainly forget some of this material.

- **Encourage slackers.** The minutes publicize the commitments each person has made and put pressure on everyone to perform up to the team's standards.

Meeting Agenda: Keeping Discussions on Track

A meeting agenda is a *brief* list of topics to be discussed at the meeting. This list of topics does not need to be comprehensive—in other words, the team can discuss items not on the agenda; however, an agenda helps ensure that nothing important gets left out of the discussion. When people who are not part of the team attend a meeting, a brief agenda is particularly important because it lets them know what to expect and allows them to prepare for questions team members might ask.

To allow people time to prepare for the meeting, an agenda should be distributed in advance of the meeting (see Figure 17.2).

TO: Team

FR: Jason

Subject: Agenda for meeting on 3/7, 1:00 p.m., Miller Tech

Hi Team:

We are meeting at 1:00 p.m. on Thursday, 3/7, in the Miller Tech computer lab.

Agenda:

- Confirm meeting time with instructor
- Discuss Karen's revisions (see attachment Karen e-mailed earlier today)
- Report from Susan detailing her research on costs

Let me know if there is anything else that you think should go on the agenda.

Figure 17.2. Meeting agenda sent via e-mail. The agenda contains a short list of items to be discussed, along with a reminder of the meeting time and location. An agenda must be distributed to the team in advance of the meeting.

Dangers of Operating without a Meeting Agenda

A meeting agenda is essential to make sure that the team meeting is really needed and that the team stays on track. Without a clear agenda, teams will

- **Manage their time poorly.** A written agenda allows a team to jump directly to what needs to be accomplished without wasting time figuring out what needs to be discussed. Moreover, without an agenda, the team might overlook important items, thus necessitating another meeting.

- **Show up unprepared.** The agenda gives everyone a chance to think about the items that will be discussed at the meeting, to do any necessary research, and to prepare any information or material that needs to be distributed.

- **Hold unnecessary meetings.** Sometimes, the project manager will begin to prepare a meeting agenda only to realize that there are no issues for the team to discuss. In this case, after checking with the rest of the team, the project manager may cancel the meeting.

E-mail Reminders and Notifications: Stepping In When Problems Occur

The project manager is always focused on the future direction of the group. Even meeting minutes, which at first might seem just to be records of past actions, are produced in order to shape the group's future direction and ensure that everyone follows through on commitments made during the meeting.

In the unfortunate event that some teammates are negligent in performing their duties or a project goes off schedule, the project manager needs to continue this focus on the team's future. Thus, when a project manager steps in to take action on missed deadlines, missed meetings, or unacceptable work, his or her focus needs to be on finding a solution rather than spreading blame.

How forcefully the project manager steps in depends on the situation and the severity of the offense. Usually, small problems can be handled through gentle reminder e-mails. Larger problems that threaten the project's success may require contacting the instructor.

For instance, a project manager should always send a "gentle" reminder to a teammate immediately after a deadline has passed. Figure 17.3 illustrates a gentle reminder sent directly to a teammate who has missed a deadline. This reminder assumes that Susan plans on completing the work but either has encountered unexpected difficulties or has had some personal emergency that has prevented her from completing the work on time. The e-mail focuses on highlighting the effects that this lateness might have on the team's future schedule.

The next step up in severity occurs when a teammate is several days behind schedule, has missed deadlines in the past, or has otherwise shown himself or herself deserving of a more pointed reminder. This reminder should gently point out the consequences that the teammate's actions have on the rest of the team. The project manager may want to copy the entire team in the "cc" section of the e-mail. Figure 17.4 illustrates a pointed reminder.

TO: Susan

FR: Jason

Subject: Draft due date

Dear Susan:

Just a reminder that your draft was due to the team by 5:00 p.m. yesterday. Do you think you can get it out by Wednesday morning? If there is some problem, please let me know ASAP so that I can revise the task schedule.

Thanks,

Jason

Figure 17.3. A gentle reminder that a deadline has passed. Such reminders should be sent (usually directly to the person involved) the first time a team member has missed a deadline.

TO: Susan

FR: Jason

Subject: Draft due date—second notice

Dear Susan:

Your draft was due more than two days ago, and we haven't heard anything from you. Karen needs your materials so that she can compile everything and make revisions by Friday. If you cannot get the materials to us today, please let us know because Karen will have to rearrange her schedule in order to get everything done. I apologize if you are experiencing some crisis. We are starting to get worried about meeting the deadline and will have to contact the instructor if we don't hear from you. Please let us know what to expect.

Thanks,

Jason

Figure 17.4. A more pointed reminder that a deadline has passed. Such reminders should point out the effects that a teammate's delays or poor performance will have on the rest of the team.

If a teammate does not respond appropriately to this pointed reminder, the project manager might want to send an e-mail to the instructor, if for no other reason than to document the team's problems. Figure 17.5 illustrates an e-mail notifying the instructor about a problem.

Chapter 23, "Troubleshooting Team Problems," provides additional advice on handling problematic teammates.

TO: Professor Williams

FR: Jason Carpenter

CC: Carrie S., Matt B.

Subject: Question about a team problem

Dear Professor Williams:

My team would like to notify you and ask your advice about a problem we are having. I have attached a copy of our task schedule. As you can see, a draft of the cost-benefit analysis was due on Monday. I received a brief outline from Susan (the person responsible) on Wednesday night. Not only was this two days late, but it was not what the team needed. It is now Thursday, and the next leg of the project is about to be officially behind schedule.

Since the cost information is key to our proposal, we are unsure how to proceed. Should we give Susan another chance, or should we assign this task to someone else and basically cut her out of the project? Any advice or assistance you can provide would be greatly appreciated.

Thank you very much for your help.

Jason Carpenter

Figure 17.5. **E-mail notifying the instructor about a problem**. Although the e-mail documents the group's past problems, the overall tone and direction of the e-mail focuses on finding a future solution. Jason asks the instructor for advice rather than a solution to the group's problems. Even if the instructor does not take any action, such an e-mail provides documentation of the team's problems and can protect responsible team members if any grading disputes come up in the future.

Other Documents the Project Manager May Produce

Task schedules, meeting minutes, and meeting agendas should be produced for any project, no matter how large or small. These documents are essential to keeping the team on task. Projects that neglect these are destined for trouble and unproductive conflict. However, larger projects may require additional routine maintenance documents with which the project manager keeps the team on track. (See Table 17.2.)

Table 17.2. Additional documents a project manager may need to produce.

Document	Description
Team Charter	An internal document (one that is not shared with others outside of the team) that describes the "big picture" goals and priorities of the project. Teams rely on the team charter to help resolve conceptual conflicts that occur as the project progresses. The team charter is particularly helpful for teams that have not worked together before or for large-scale projects. Chapter 18, "Getting Started with the Team Charter," describes this document in more detail.
Project Plan	A formal document describing the scope of the work for an external audience, which may include instructors, supervisors, or clients. The project plan is used to assure outside stakeholders that the team is headed down the right path. Instructors generally review project plans to make sure that teams have picked projects that meet the assignment guidelines and can be accomplished within the allotted time frame.
	Most project plans contain the following information: (1) what problem the project is addressing; (2) what work is to be done; (3) what major deliverables will be produced; (4) who will be involved and what their responsibilities will be; (5) what major deadlines or milestones will be met.
	Most workplaces have their own unofficial guidelines for project plans. If you are required to complete a project plan, ask your instructor or supervisor for a model you can follow.
Progress Report	Usually an informal document that gives an instructor, supervisor, or client information on the team's progress on a project over a set period of time. This document is used primarily for projects that take at least three months to complete.
	Progress reports contain the following information: (1) how much of the work is complete; (2) what the team is currently working on; (3) what work remains to be done; (4) what problems have arisen; (5) how the project is going in general (whether the project is on schedule).
	There are innumerable variations in the format of a progress report. If you are required to file a progress report, ask your instructor or supervisor for a model you can follow.

Starting the Process with a Straw Document

A "straw" document is an excellent way to start a group writing project that is taking on a complex task for which no clear format exists. A straw document is basically an extremely rough skeleton of the project that the writer expects to be blown down, like a straw house. The purpose of the straw document is to draw the team into a discussion of the pros and cons of various directions the project might take. In this way, the straw document is a tool to facilitate group brainstorming about specific details.

With a straw document, the project manager brings in a very flimsy but relatively complete draft of the entire document or document section. The straw document should contain a comprehensive list of topics or points the document needs to address, but the details do not have to be fully fleshed out. The goal is to have *something* down on paper so that the team can begin to discuss the drawbacks and benefits of various alternatives.

Because of the nature of straw documents, they are used only in the very beginning stages of writing. The writer of the straw document must be ready to stand back and not become upset when others eventually knock down parts of the document. One engineer with extensive experience working on major proposals clarifies this point:

> An important point when you put a straw [document] up is that people mustn't be offended if other people criticize it, tear it apart, offer constructive criticism. You've got to take it in the light that different people have different opinions. It saves a lot of time. If you hadn't written it down [as a straw document,] they wouldn't have thought about it. (Sales, 2006)

Another engineer at the same company states that the great advantage of the straw document is that "it doesn't matter if you get it wrong. In fact, you expect to get it wrong, so you can rush it out any old how. It is safe to do so because you know it will be sorted out later" (Sales, 2006).

Sometimes, groups can benefit from looking at several different straw drafts. This is often the case when there is serious disagreement about how to proceed. In this situation, one or two team members prepare multiple drafts for the group to compare and contrast.

When working with a straw document, everyone in the group needs to understand that it is intended to be a temporary document that will likely be completely rewritten later. It should not be confused with a complete draft of the document (see Chapter 21, "Revising with Others," for information on working with more complete drafts). In other words, the straw document should be used to spark discussions about big, conceptual issues—and not issues such as word choice, formatting, or even the details of much of the content, all of which are more appropriately discussed at the rough-draft stage of the project.

Inside Work: Exercises

1. Review the three scenarios at the beginning of Chapter 16, "Planning Your Collaboration." How might each of these groups' problems have been alleviated with a task schedule?

2. Think of a time when you were involved in a group project. Did this project have a project manager? If so, was this person effective? If you had had the type of project manager described in this chapter, how might any problems that your group experienced have been prevented?

3. Read Appendix B, "Sample Meeting Minutes," which contains three versions of the meeting minutes from one four-person team. All three versions contain the same information. Which version do you think will be the most effective for keeping the team on track? Why?

The videos in this portion of the textbook are directly based on the interactions of actual student teams. Before you complete any of the video exercises, take a moment to watch the introductory video on the Team Writing *Web site, which describes how the videos were produced and created.*

4. View Team Video 3: Jamaal, Jim, Don, and Tonya on the *Team Writing* Web site. This group of students is preparing a proposal to irrigate a third-world country. To the best of your ability based on the information you have, create a brief set of meeting minutes to follow up this group's discussion. What important information has this group failed to discuss? What issues does this team need to take up at its next meeting?

Team 3

5. What collaboration method does the team in this video seem to be using? What problems do you anticipate if the team continues to collaborate using this method?

Works Cited

Grove, A. (1995). *High output management.* New York: Vintage Books.

Sales, H. E. (2006). *Professional communication in engineering.* New York: Palgrave Macmillan.

Stratton, C. R. (1989). Collaborative writing in the workplace. *IEEE Transactions on Professional Communication, 32*(3), 178–182.

Chapter 18
Getting Started with the Team Charter

Kelly and Sean were both members of a four-person team working on a Web site. They made the following observations:

Kelly: Sean has done nothing. We asked him to do the first draft of the project proposal by compiling all of our information into a paper. Instead, he came up with less than one page that didn't meet the requirements of the proposal at all. This is really pitiful since we gave him over four pages of our own work to build on. Also, he was supposed to add what research he had done to the proposal, and there was no mention of it, so I'm assuming that he hasn't done any research. We ended up using the research that Eli got from his interview. Sean has showed up to every meeting; however, he has added nothing during any of the meetings. In fact, during the last meeting, he was chatting on Instant Messenger on his laptop while we were all discussing and working on the project proposal.... In the last week, he has finally shown some interest in helping out, but I'm reluctant in giving him anything important to do as he has so far proven himself unreliable.

Sean: I haven't spent much time at all on the project, sadly. As far as I'm aware, Kelly is the only one who's done much the last two weeks, though I could be wrong—it wouldn't be the first time I've missed something obvious during this project.... The rest of the team seems to work together excellently, but I've felt ignored a few times. I completely missed part of the requirement of the proposal, and instead of saying anything to me, Eli and Angela just completely rewrote it. I've also felt ignored during meetings and thus have been mostly silent during group reviews of papers, which would ordinarily be my strongest moments.... Everything that I've done so far on the project has been incredibly subpar by my own standards. I've done two writing assignments, and both times, I only noticed a fraction of the instructions we were given.... Much of the time I felt confused as to what was going on. This was my own fault—for the first few weeks of the project, I was highly unmotivated. At the time I'm writing this, though, I think I'm about to be given some content to make a page for, so that's not as bad as it could be.

Before you continue reading, take a moment to think about what this team could have done to prevent the problems that it experienced. How would you characterize the problems with this team?

The Team Charter: An Ounce of Prevention Is Worth a Pound of Cure

At the start of a project, the team is usually eager to charge ahead and start productive work right away. However, teams do well to bear in mind the slogan "Failing to plan is planning to fail." A team that spends an hour at the very beginning of the project discussing goals, expectations, and team norms can save substantial time and stress later on in the project.

Many experienced practitioners in a range of fields recommend that teams develop a team charter in the first meetings. A team charter is a brief, informal document that describes the "big picture" goals and priorities of the project. The official purpose of a team charter is to have a written statement of the team's priorities and norms that the team can use to resolve any problems or confusion that may occur later in the project. The unofficial purpose, particularly when team members have not worked together before, is to air any differences that they might have in goals, expectations, and commitment levels *before* the project begins.

For instance, if your project involves a client outside of the classroom, you may find that some team members put a priority on meeting the client's expectations, whereas others prioritize according to the instructor's exact directions. Similarly, you may find that team members have different ideas about the effort they are willing to invest in the project. It is better to know about these differences up front rather than discover them later on.

In general, the bigger the project, the more important the team charter is. Team charters differ greatly in content and format depending on the type of organization and project. For student projects, an effective team charter should contain the following information:

1. Overall, broad team goals for the project

2. Measurable, specific team goals

3. Personal goals

4. Individual level of commitment to the project

5. Other information about team members that may affect the project

6. Statement of how the team will resolve impasses

7. Statement of how the team will handle missed deadlines

8. Statement of what constitutes unacceptable work and how the team will handle this

Team Preparation Worksheet

1. What strengths do you have relative to this project? (Check all that apply.)
    ☐ Above-average writing ability
    ☐ Above-average information-finding/research skills
    ☐ Above-average computing skills
    ☐ Above-average visual design/graphic design skills
    ☐ Above-average leadership or management skills
    ☐ Other (Describe):

2. What would you most like to learn from this project? (Check all that apply.)
    ☐ Improve writing speed
    ☐ Improve writing skills
    ☐ Improve editing skills
    ☐ Improve research skills
    ☐ Improve data analysis skills
    ☐ Improve PowerPoint skills
    ☐ Improve other computer skills
    ☐ Improve visual design skills
    ☐ Improve management skills
    ☐ Other (Describe):

3. What is your level of commitment to the project? (Check the one that best applies.)
    ☐ I plan to get an A on this project and will make whatever sacrifices are necessary.
    ☐ I want an A but am limited in the time/effort I can dedicate to the project.
    ☐ I will be satisfied with a B on this project.
    ☐ My goal is simply to receive a passing grade on this project.

4. What scheduling issues or other commitments do you have that might interfere with this project?

5. What concerns do you have about your skills or abilities that might affect how your team views your performance on this project?

6. Would you like to negotiate an agreement with the team that assigns you less responsibility for the project in exchange for a lower grade?

7. In your opinion, what does this team have to accomplish to make this project a success?

Figure 18.1. Team Preparation Worksheet. You can also download a copy of this worksheet from the *Team Writing* Web site.

Because the team charter is an internal document (something that will be seen only within the team) and because the real point of a team charter lies in discussing it rather than in writing it, this document can be composed in a face-to-face setting. The goal of the team charter is to uncover and discuss potential problems in a low-key setting, before any work has been assigned.

This chapter discusses what goes into a team charter. Before you start working on the charter with your group, take a moment to honestly assess your background, goals, and preparation for this project by completing the team preparation worksheet in Figure 18.1. (You can also download a copy of this worksheet from the *Team Writing* Web site.)

Team Goals: What Constitutes Success?

Your first action as a team should be to agree on what defines a successful project. Spend a few minutes discussing the one or two top broad goals you have for the project. Examples of broad goals include:

- Making an original argument
- Presenting our data accurately and effectively
- Persuading the audience to accept our solution
- Following the format and guidelines of the assignment sheet precisely
- Designing a product that satisfies the client
- Creating instructions that a computer novice can follow without mistakes

Do *not* simply list "getting an A" as one of your priorities. Instead, try to break down what criteria are most important to meet in order to receive an A. It may be that one person believes that getting an A means satisfying the client while another team member believes it means finding an original solution to a problem (whether or not the client wants an original solution). Again, the goal here is to uncover any fundamental differences about what the team is trying to accomplish before you start.

Measurable Goals: How Can You Measure Success?

After your team has set out goals about what defines success, you need to translate your broad goals into measurable goals with objective, specific criteria that are clearly either met or not met. Creating measurable goals is an essential step in workplace teams, which might come up with goals such as *increasing productivity by 20 percent* or *reducing accidents by at least 40 percent*. These goals are specific, objective, and measurable: they can be listed as numbers, so there should be little disagreement over whether or not they are met. Student teams may have more difficulty in generating measurable goals because projects are smaller and fewer external, objective measures are available. Nevertheless, creating measurable goals is an important skill that you should begin to practice now.

Examples of measurable goals include:

- Meeting all 10 of the assignment sheet's guidelines for the report's format
- Meeting or beating all the deadlines set out in the task schedule
- Reducing the word count by 15 percent between the rough draft and the final draft by eliminating wordiness and repetitiveness without deleting any content
- Writing instructions clearly enough that novice users voice no more than two questions or instances of confusion during usability testing
- Creating a Web site that four out of five classmates rank as user-friendly in anonymous surveys
- Citing at least four sources in the works cited page
- Having fewer than one grammatical error or typo per page

Although "getting an A" is a measurable goal, it is not a useful one because the team will not know whether this goal has been achieved until after the project has been completed, at which point it is too late to act on this goal. Instead, try to define measurable goals that can serve as a checklist before turning in the project.

Personal Goals: What Do Team Members Want Out of the Project?

Next, try to uncover what is most important to each member of the team. Examples of personal goals are:

- Improving my writing skills
- Learning how to create a visually compelling PowerPoint presentation
- Creating a document that I can talk about on job interviews
- Having a productive and friendly team experience
- Completing the project with as little effort as possible

This last goal will almost certainly bring you into conflict with other team members, who will understandably wonder if they can trust you. However, there is some benefit to acknowledging this up front in order to avoid becoming a negative contributor (see the section "Negative Contributors").

Understanding what each team member hopes to gain personally from the project will help the group in the next step of defining and assigning roles and tasks. These statements of personal investment in the project should also help the group to determine specific directions for the project.

Individual Commitment: How Much Effort Will Each Person Invest?

In addition to discussing project goals, team members should also discuss their degree of commitment to these goals. Do different team members have different ideas about the amount of time and effort that is needed to succeed? Is everyone truly willing to invest the effort needed to get a good grade on the project? Does everybody feel equally strongly about the importance of getting an A?

Many texts on teamwork assume that everyone on the project will have total commitment to the project—or else can be motivated to contribute 100 percent with just a little prodding. However, in reality, team members have responsibilities outside of the project and different levels of commitment and internal motivation. By frankly discussing what each person is able or willing to contribute up front, teams can anticipate and avoid potential problems.

The team has some concrete options for dealing with team members who have low commitment levels:

1. Team members with low commitment can be **assigned fewer or less critical tasks** on the project so that if they do not follow through, other team members can pick up the slack.

2. The team can consider formalizing an arrangement in which **one team member negotiates to do less work in exchange for a lower grade**. For instance, the team charter might state that John Doe will contribute approximately 25 percent less work than other team members and consequently will receive a one-letter grade reduction on the project. (Check with your instructor to see if this is an option.)

Simply knowing that a particular team member has low motivation can often protect the team against surprises and extreme resentment later on in the project.

Situations in which team members contribute unequal amounts of effort mirror conditions that you might find in the workplace. In workbased teams, one or two team members often may be committed full-time to a project while others have other work priorities and contribute at a much lower level.

Other Information: What Other Factors Might Affect Performance?

Do you have a personal commitment that will make you unavailable during a particular time frame? Do you have a pending personal emergency that may make you less dependable than you are normally? Are you worried that you will have difficulty meeting your team's expectations for the quality of the work? You should express these concerns and potential limitations at the beginning of the project so that you don't become a negative contributor to the group—someone whose presence hurts the team more than it helps.

If the team knows about shortcomings or potential obstacles up front, it can work these constraints into the task schedule. For instance, Cynthia was asked to draft a proposal but had little experience with this type of writing. The team responded by scheduling an extra round of early feedback so that Cynthia could be sure she was going in the right direction. Similarly, Jiang was worried that his poor English skills might hurt the team. The team was able to plan for this by scheduling additional time for Jiang to visit the school's writing center and receive feedback on his grammar before submitting his material to the group.

By understanding your needs and preferences before you start working on a team, you can recognize when your roles and responsibilities on the team are in conflict with your individual needs. Learning to recognize those conflicts and to positively address them represents one of the strongest opportunities for growth that people receive from working in teams.

Negative Contributors

Chris: I think everyone noticed that Stephanie felt like an outsider within the group. This is entirely her fault. If Stephanie would have attended class like she said she would, then we wouldn't have a problem with her feeling left out.... Our presentation is only five days away. Stephanie doesn't have a freakin' clue what is going on.... I don't know what she feels she is contributing, but it isn't that much.

Stephanie is a negative contributor because rather than helping her team finish the project, she has created an additional problem for her teammates to solve. Similarly, Sean (described at the beginning of this chapter) is also a negative contributor. Negative contributors include those who miss deadlines or meetings, turn in substandard work, or engage in unproductive conflict that does not further group goals.

Groups do have options for handling negative contributors: they can be *removed from the team* by the instructor, or they can receive poor evaluations from their teammates at the end of the project that translate into a *lowered project grade*. Of course, these are worst-case scenarios—if possible, it is better to prevent these negative scenarios from occurring.

The best way to avoid becoming a negative contributor is to be honest about your skills and commitments at the beginning of the project. For instance, if you know you will be able to dedicate only a limited number of hours a week or that your skills in a particular area are weak, tell the team about these constraints up front. The team can then factor these constraints into the task schedule. Similarly, if the team knows that you are inexperienced with a particular technology needed for the project, such as FrontPage, someone more experienced can be assigned as your "backup" in case you need to ask for help.

A good, clear task schedule with plenty of overlapping responsibilities and "padding" (extra space in the project for missed deadlines or emergencies) can help prevent any problems that negative contributors might cause. The clear task schedule lets team members know immediately when a task has not been completed, and the padding gives the team a chance to recover in a worst-case scenario.

Irreconcilable Differences: How Will the Team Resolve Impasses?

Chapter 20, "Constructive Conflict," discusses the benefits of constructive conflict and why teams benefit from the healthy debate of ideas. However, there will be times when teams are unable to resolve their disagreements. A team charter that details when and how the team will handle impasses, or stalemates, will help the team progress even in the face of disagreement. The team charter should contain a brief one- or two-sentence statement of how the team will resolve continuing disagreements and at what point (two meetings, 30 minutes of discussion) the team will pursue the resolution method. Table 18.1 describes the four basic methods for resolving impasses and their advantages and disadvantages.

Table 18.1. Four methods for resolving impasses.

Method	Advantages	Disadvantages
Consensus: Discuss the issue until everyone agrees.	• The team will reach the best possible compromise.	• The process is time-consuming. • The consensus may be "fake"—someone on the team may give in just so that the team can move on.
Majority rules: Vote and adopt the majority decision.	• The impasse is resolved quickly. • The solution does not involve anyone outside the team.	• Some team members may feel left out or that others are "ganging up" on them.
Instructor decides: Present both sides anonymously to the instructor and let him or her decide.	• Feelings are unlikely to be hurt. • The team will have more information about what the instructor wants.	• It takes time to contact the instructor and present both sides. • The instructor may not want to intervene.
Third party decides: Present both sides anonymously to a classmate, a client (if applicable), or another party and ask that person to decide.	• Feelings are unlikely to be hurt.	• It may take time to contact a third party and present the information.

Late Work: How Will the Team Handle Missed Deadlines?

Missed deadlines signal a lack of commitment and a breach of trust. Team members rely on one another to make commitments; if a team member fails to honor a commitment, other group members will assume that the person is not trustworthy.

Teams should decide in advance how they will handle missed deadlines. Having procedures in place helps prevent the situation because team members will know there are clear consequences to their actions and also helps defuse the situation if it does occur.

The team charter should spell out how to handle missed deadlines. The following examples show some typical wording:

- The project manager e-mails a reminder to the team member who is late. If the team member does not respond within 24 hours, the project manager contacts the instructor. If the team member does respond with a valid excuse and a reasonable deadline, the project manager informs the rest of the team of the new deadline.
- The project manager e-mails a reminder to the team member who is late. If the team member does not submit acceptable work within 24 hours of this e-mail, the project manager contacts the rest of the team, explaining the situation and asking for input on how to proceed.

See Chapter 23, "Troubleshooting Team Problems," for more information on dealing with tardiness.

Unacceptable Work: How Will the Team Handle Poor-Quality Contributions?

Sometimes, team members meet deadlines but submit work that is clearly unacceptable because it lacks important required information, falls considerably short of the page requirements, is riddled with grammatical errors, or has other shortcomings. Dealing with unacceptable work is often more stressful for the team than coping with missed deadlines because deciding what is unacceptable requires judgment and sometimes awkward discussions.

The team charter should list some general criteria for unacceptable work (for example, rough drafts missing more than 25 percent of the required information; near-final drafts that do not meet all of the assignment criteria), a plan for notifying a team member that the work is unacceptable, and a recommended deadline for revising unacceptable work. Criteria for unacceptable work should distinguish between rough drafts that the team will subsequently revise and more finished work produced closer to the final project deadline. Table 18.2 lists some ways of handling unacceptable work, along with their advantages and disadvantages.

Table 18.2. Methods for responding to a member who has produced unacceptable work.

Method	Advantages	Disadvantages
Project manager says nothing: Project manager asks another team member to rewrite a section (or does it himself or herself) and says nothing to the person directly.	• Avoids an unpleasant conversation. • Resolves the issue quickly. • May be appropriate if the final deadline is approaching and/or this is not the first time this person has produced unacceptable work.	• May be unfair to the person who produced the work, who doesn't have a chance to learn from or correct his or her mistakes. • Places an additional burden on the rest of the team.
Project manager decides: Project manager reviews all work to see if it meets acceptability criteria; contacts anyone who produces unacceptable work; and gives that person suggestions for improvement and a 48-hour deadline to revise.	• Gives the person a chance to correct mistakes. • Enables quick notification that the work was unacceptable.	• Places the entire burden on the project manager.
Team decides: All team members review the work and e-mail the project manager, who then communicates the concerns (without mentioning names) to the person with a 24-hour deadline to revise.	• Avoids burdening the project manager with sole responsibility for deciding whether something is acceptable. • Makes the feedback anonymous (the person does not know who found the work unacceptable).	• May take longer to notify the person of the team's concerns.

Putting It All Together

A team charter not only helps the team plan for negative situations but also prevents these situations from occurring in the first place because team members (1) have a nonthreatening place to **voice concerns** about the project and (2) are aware that there are **clear consequences** for letting the team down. A calm discussion about how the team will handle hypothetical missed deadlines is much less stressful and time-consuming than panicking at the last minute over how to proceed when one or more teammates have not done their work.

Figure 18.2 illustrates a team charter. Note that the tone is informal and that the charter makes good use of formatting (including boldface headings and bulleted and numbered lists) to make information easy to find. The team charter should be stored in a central place (and/or e-mailed to the entire team) so that team members can use it for reference.

Team Charter

Broad Team Goals
1. Clearly communicate the "bottom line" meaning of our results throughout the report.
2. Impress the instructor with the amount of effort we have put into collecting and analyzing our data.

Measurable Team Goals
1. Meet all six of the evaluation criteria listed on the assignment sheet.
2. Meet or beat all deadlines.
3. Obtain data from at least 15 users.
4. Follow all eight guidelines for tables and figures listed in the instructor's PowerPoint presentation.

Personal Goals
- Aaron: Improve management and teamwork skills.
- Bryan: Improve writing skills (be less wordy).
- Yolan: Improve writing skills (improve organization and grammar).
- Mandy: Improve technology skills (especially PowerPoint) and teamwork skills.

Individual Commitment
- Aaron, Yolan, and Mandy are all willing to put in 100 percent effort.
- Bryan would like to put in 100 percent effort but doesn't know whether his job will allow him to commit that much time. He is willing to accept a slightly lower grade if it turns out he cannot keep up.

Other Concerns
- Yolan is worried that her grammar skills may need a lot of work.
- Mandy has done only one PowerPoint presentation before but really wants to improve her tech skills and will work hard to learn.
- Aaron is usually unable to check his e-mail in the evenings and during weekends but will try to check at least twice every school day.
- Bryan is just worried about his job interfering.

Conflict Resolution
If we experience conflict that is not resolved after 30 minutes of respectful discussion of the points, we will present both sides to the instructor and ask him to decide.

Missed Deadlines
If a team member misses a deadline, the project manager will send a "gentle reminder" e-mail. If that team member does not respond within 24 hours, the project manager will contact the instructor, describing the problem. If there is some extenuating circumstance (e.g., personal emergency), the project manager will contact the rest of the team for input on how to proceed.

Unacceptable Work
If a team member turns in work that is clearly unacceptable (e.g., leaves out important information; has major errors; does not meet the assignment criteria; clearly does not meet the team goals of emphasizing the bottom line throughout), other team members should report their concerns to the project manager. The project manager will then contact that team member with a list of concerns and suggest a deadline (usually 48 hours) for when a revised copy of the work is due. If that team member is confused about why the work is unacceptable, that person should seek assistance and e-mail the project manager explaining his or her progress. We want to note that there is no shame in seeking outside assistance!

Figure 18.2. Team Charter.

Inside Work: Exercises

1. Return to the scenario of Kelly and Sean's group at the beginning of this chapter. How might a team charter have helped team members through some of the difficulties they experienced?

2. Have you ever been on a team with a negative contributor? What made this person a negative contributor? How could he or she have avoided this? What are some ways other than failing to follow through on commitments that can make someone a negative contributor?

3. Have you ever been on a team in which different people had different ideas about what the project should be, do, or look like? At what point in the project did you recognize these different perspectives? How might a team charter have helped your group handle these different perspectives?

The videos in this portion of the textbook are directly based on the interactions of actual student teams. Before you complete any of the video exercises, take a moment to watch the introductory video on the Team Writing *Web site, which describes how the videos were produced and created.*

4. View Team Video 5: Jayme, Megan, and Joe on the *Team Writing* Web site. List three problems this group seems to be having and explain how a team charter might have addressed these problems.

Team 5

Chapter 19 Getting Started with the Task Schedule

The **task schedule**, which has been mentioned several times in previous chapters, is the most important document a team produces for managing itself. A task schedule keeps the team on track by documenting who does what by when. Moreover, a task schedule helps the team plan the details of the project so that there are no surprises at the end. This chapter takes you through the steps of producing a task schedule that will help your team implement a layered collaboration. This chapter focuses on four steps:

1. Identifying major tasks

2. Assigning tasks to team members

3. Scheduling the tasks in layers, providing multiple opportunities to comment or revise one another's work

4. Balancing the workload

Identifying Major Tasks

The first step in producing a task schedule is to brainstorm the major tasks that the team will have to perform. Resist assigning tasks to individual team members at this point. Instead, concentrate on making sure that all parts of the project are covered. Listing tasks is a brainstorming activity and is appropriate for face-to-face collaboration.

For example, a team working on a **scientific research report** might identify the following tasks:

- Project management
- Collect data
- Write
  - Introduction
  - Methods
  - Results
  - Discussion
  - Abstract
  - Initial topic proposal
  - Works cited

A team working on a **proposal** might identify the following tasks:

- Project management
- Research
  - Identify audience needs and all relevant stakeholders
  - Identify problems with status quo and collect documentation of problems
  - Investigate potential solutions and costs
- Write
  - Statement of problem and justification for proposal
  - Overview of options
  - Cost-benefit analysis and breakdown
  - Recommendation and rationale
  - Cover letter
  - Executive summary
- Create presentation slides
- Rehearse and deliver final presentation

A team creating a **Web site** might identify the following tasks:

- Project management
- Write initial topic proposal
- Research client
  - Obtain technical information for site from client
  - Find out client's needs and preferences for the site

- Design
  - Site layout (number of links or sections on home page)
  - Home page layout
  - Content page layout
  - Graphics
- Revise content from client for consistency, Web-friendliness
- Assemble the site on test server
- Test and revise the site
  - Create usability script and set up tests
  - Run tests with three users for usability, broken links
  - Make revision tests
- Upload to live site
- Write instructions for maintaining the site
- Write final report for instructor

As the differences in these three task lists demonstrate, your task list needs to be specific to *your* team's project. Some projects will consist primarily of research and writing; other projects will involve additional components, such as preparing presentations, uploading Web sites, or coordinating with other people and teams. Be sure to read your assignment guidelines carefully, and work together with your team to come up with a complete list of tasks. The more complete your list is now, the less you will have to figure out on the spur of the moment later.

Assigning Roles: Motivation versus Experience

Christopher Avery, a consultant on leadership and teamwork, states that when a team assigns roles, matching motivation is far more important than matching skills: "If members don't have the required skills, a high performance team will improvise. The same is not true for motivation, however. Every team performs to the level of its least invested member" (2001). In other words, it is more important to assign team members to tasks that they are motivated to learn or do than to tasks with which they already have experience.

One of the biggest problems with layered collaboration in educational settings is that team members often divide up tasks by expertise (that is, the most experienced writer does most of the writing; the most experienced technical person does most of the computer work) rather than by what will make for the best learning experience. Although this division certainly makes sense and is efficient, it also limits team members' opportunities to develop skills in their weak spots. Team members need to take responsibility for making their time on the project a productive learning experience. Such "on the job" training mirrors the corporate world, where managers will sometimes assign tasks to particular workers in order to make them better-rounded employees.

Not only does dividing tasks up by motivation rather than experience benefit individual team members, but it may also benefit the team. Often, a motivated novice will perform at least as well as a bored expert, especially if the novice can contact an expert as a resource for specific questions. An expert who is bored with a task will put in less effort and be less receptive to the team's feedback than a novice who is eager to show that he or she is able to do the job.

Teams can avoid having to choose between motivation and experience by assigning members a **primary task** that they are motivated to learn and a **secondary, advisory task** that makes use of their existing expertise. The assignment of a secondary task allows each team member to serve as an adviser or primary "go to" person in case another team member completing a given task has questions or runs into difficulties. This structuring is similar to that of workplace teams, in which experienced employees focus on gaining new, more complex skills while at the same time helping newer employees learn more routine skills.

For example, if someone on your team has done numerous PowerPoint presentations or has years of experience writing proposals, this person should serve as an adviser to another team member who is eager to learn this skill. Not only will the novice be able to draw on the expert's advice, but the expert will also have the opportunity to consolidate his or her knowledge on the topic by teaching someone else. Novices often ask interesting questions that challenge more experienced colleagues to reexamine what they think they know and approach the problem from a new perspective. This explains the adage "If you want to truly learn something, then teach it!"

Assigning roles by motivation rather than experience may also help your team avoid a problem that is particularly common in student teams: a **gendered division of labor**, in which women complete writing tasks and men complete technical work. This tendency is at least partly due to a culture that associates tools and equipment with men and language skills with women and is often reinforced on student teams, particularly when team members do not know one another well. Assigning tasks according to what team members want to learn rather than what they already know how to do can help a team break out of traditional, gendered role assignments.

As a team, review the team preparation worksheets that team members completed in Chapter 18, "Getting Started with the Team Charter" (see Figure 18.1), examining what each person perceived as his or her strengths and learning goals for the project. Then discuss how to arrange the project so that motivated teammates can acquire new skills while still having the security of a more experienced adviser who can answer questions or help out if they get "stuck." This information about primary and secondary roles (and any concerns about these roles) should be added to the team charter.

Scheduling the Tasks

Once your team has assigned primary and secondary roles and recorded these in the charter, look over the team preparation worksheets (Figure 18.1) and team charter again to refresh your memory about any scheduling concerns the team needs to keep in mind. Be sure to also review all of the instructor's deadlines in the assignment guidelines.

The project manager should prepare a rough draft of the task schedule, being sure to include plenty of opportunities for team members to revise and comment on one another's work. Although you can find complicated project-management software for maintaining an updated task schedule, a simple table prepared as a word-processing document or a spreadsheet is just as effective for most school projects. Figure 19.1 gives instructions for creating a task schedule in Microsoft Word. You can also download a spreadsheet formatted for a task schedule from the *Team Writing* Web site.

Once the project manager has created a rough draft of the task schedule, he or she should send it to team members for review before their next meeting. This gives them a chance to reflect on the task schedule and think of ways it might be improved. At the next meeting, the team can work together to revise the schedule to everyone's satisfaction and assign contribution values (discussed in the next section).

Balancing the Workload

One of the biggest problems with collaboration in student teams is the **unequal division of labor**. Unequal division of labor is also present in workplace settings, but typically this is not a problem because it is common for employees to dedicate different amounts of time or effort to a project. In the classroom, however, the assumption usually is that everyone will contribute equally to the project. Thus, student teams have a challenge not often found in workplace teams: distributing the workload so that everybody contributes roughly equally to the project.

To help balance the workload fairly, the team can work together to estimate a contribution value for each task. Contribution values can be measured on a five-point scale (where 5 = difficult, time-consuming task critical to group success and 1 = relatively easy, noncritical task). These contribution values can then be totaled for each team member to get an approximation of how much everyone is contributing to the group. The goal should be for each team member to contribute roughly equivalent amounts (unless one team member has negotiated to receive a lower grade in exchange for less work—see Chapter 18, "Getting Started with the Team Charter").

Figure 19.2 shows one team's task schedule worksheet. Each task is clearly assigned to a team member and has a clear-cut deadline. In addition, each task has a contribution value that the team has agreed on. When the contribution values are totaled, it is clear that all three team members are doing roughly equivalent work but that Amy is doing slightly more than the other two team members. Thus, if additional tasks should come up during the project, Steven and Luke should volunteer for those tasks.

Common Mistakes Students Make When Assigning Contribution Values

Your instructor will probably look over your task schedule and the contribution values your team has assigned in order to make sure that the team is crediting work appropriately. Student teams tend to underestimate the amount of effort required to produce good writing (which often requires substantial revision) and to overestimate the amount of effort associated with technology tasks. Be aware of these tendencies when your team assigns values.

To create a task schedule table in Microsoft Word, complete the following steps:

1. Go to the **Insert** tab and click on **Table**. Next, click on **Insert Table**.
2. Type 5 for the number of columns and 20 for the number of rows.

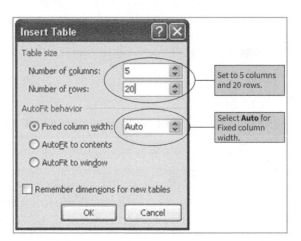

3. Select **Auto** for a fixed column width.
4. Press OK.
5. Enter the words Deadline, Task, Who, Contribution Value, and Status in the first row.
6. Resize the columns:
    a. Hold the cursor over the column boundaries until it changes into the resize pointer .
    b. Click the pointer and wait for a faint vertical line to appear.
    c. Drag the pointer until the column is the width you want.
7. To insert new rows, right-click within the table to bring up a menu. Mouse over **Insert**, and then click **Insert Rows Above** or **Insert Rows Below**.

Figure 19.1. Instructions for creating a task schedule in Microsoft Word.

Technology and Tools for Task Schedules

To maintain the task schedule for short projects, teams should probably use familiar and uncomplicated tools such as tables created with a word-processing program or spreadsheets. However, when projects are long and complex, your team may benefit from using more sophisticated scheduling and project-management tools. Following is a brief overview of common tools for keeping track of projects.

TASK SCHEDULE				

Amy is the group writing expert. Steven is the group technology expert.

Deadline	Task	Assigned to	Contribution Value	Status
9/4	Write topic proposal	Amy	2	
ongoing	Maintain task list and minutes	Amy	3	
9/13	Collect data	Steven	5	
9/14	Enter data and perform initial analysis	Steven	3	
9/20	Write introduction	Luke	3	
9/20	Write methods	Steven	3	
9/20	Write results (with basic graphs)	Luke	5	
9/20	Write discussion	Luke	4	
9/22	Suggest revisions (detailed)	Amy	3	
9/22	Suggest revisions (global issues only)	Steven	2	
9/28	Implement revisions	Luke	5	
ongoing	Help Luke format final graphs in Excel	Steven	1	
10/1	Write abstract for report	Steven	2	
10/1	Make final edits to report	Amy	2	
10/3	Create presentation	Amy	4	
ongoing	Help Amy with presentation	Steven	1	
10/4	Suggest revisions to presentation	Luke	1	
10/4	Suggest revisions to presentation	Steven	1	
10/6	Revise and deliver presentation	Amy	5	

Team member: **Amy**   Total contribution: **19**
Team member: **Steven**   Total contribution: **18**
Team member: **Luke**   Total contribution: **18**

Figure 19.2. Task Schedule. The project manager typically prepares the first draft of the task schedule, assigning names and dates to each task. The team then revises the schedule as needed and collaborates to assign contribution values from 1 to 5 for each task. The task schedule offers several opportunities for team members to comment on and revise one another's work. The Status column is for recording when tasks are completed.

Gantt Charts

A Gantt chart is a type of horizontal bar chart for visualizing the start and end dates of various tasks on a project (see Figure 19.3). Some Gantt charts even show dependencies (when starting one task depends on completing an earlier task). Gantt charts are particularly popular in software development.

One drawback of Gantt charts is that they do not show the complexity of the individual tasks—or the amount of team resources required to complete these tasks—and thus may not provide an accurate representation of the project workload.

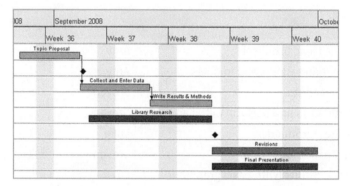

Figure 19.3. Gantt chart for a simple project. Black diamonds indicate milestones, and lines with arrows indicate dependencies.

Project-Management Software

Many companies purchase project-management software to help supervisors keep track of multiple ongoing projects. These tools often have built-in Gantt charts and other scheduling features as well as tools for adjusting employee workloads and allocating company resources. One of the most popular (and most expensive) options is Microsoft Project. Project-management software is rarely free, but many software companies offer free preview trials. Because most project-management software is built with the upper-management company executive in mind, it may be overkill for your school-based project.

Wikis

A wiki is a collection of Web pages that allows those with access to make changes and add new pages. Teams can place a copy of the task schedule on a private wiki that all team members can update to note when items are completed. Most wikis have a revision-history feature that allows the team to track any changes made. The team can also use the wiki to store other documents, such as assignment instructions and PDFs related to the project. (Note: A Web-based editor such as Google Docs has similar functionality but does not allow teams to store external documents. See Chapter 21, "Revising with Others," for more information on tools that help you collaborate.)

Inside Work: Exercises

1. Take a careful look at the task schedule in Figure 19.2. What common team problems might this task schedule help prevent? Why? What could be done to improve this task schedule?

    The videos in this portion of the textbook are directly based on the interactions of actual student teams. Before you complete any of the video exercises, take a moment to watch the introductory video on the Team Writing *Web site, which describes how the videos were produced and created.*

2. Review Day One of Team Video 2: Shelly, Will, and Ben on the *Team Writing* Web site. Write up a task schedule that will take the team through drafting and revising 10 survey questions, administering the survey to 30 students, and writing a two-page document describing the survey results. This section of the project should take two weeks from brainstorming to turning in the survey to the instructor. Be sure to build in opportunities for commenting on and revising one another's work.

    Team 2

Work Cited

Avery, C., with Walker, M. A., & O'Toole, E. (2001). *Teamwork is an individual skill: Getting your work done when sharing responsibility*. San Francisco: Berrett-Koehler Publishers.

Team Writing: Writing Together

Part Five

Andrea Tsurumi

Part Five

Team Writing: Writing Together

Chapter 20 Constructive Conflict

Susan, a member of a team working on a Web site for a small business, expresses her frustration with a teammate:

Susan: I was really upset when Rene just went off and did a draft of the whole Web site. I was really aggravated.

Interviewer: You said before you had problems with the quality of the site. Is that why you were aggravated?

Susan: Yeah. Most of the project time was kind of like me biting my tongue to her because I'm not wanting to say anything to her.

Interviewer: What do you think would have happened if you had said something?

Susan: Well, she didn't seem like a conflict-like person, so I mean it probably could have been talked out. But I think it would have hurt her feelings, like her site wasn't good enough or something.

Interviewer: As it is, do you think you hurt her feelings?

Susan: No. I don't think she knows the rest of us were unhappy.

Interviewer: Now, several times during the project, Rene said stuff like "This is only a draft" and encouraged you all to make changes to the site or start over from scratch. What did you think when she said things like that?

Susan: Like "What's the point?" She already did it. It was supposed to be a group thing.

Susan's comments point to what is the number one problem on some student teams—a lack of substantive conflict. Such teams suffer from a phenomenon called "groupthink," in which creativity and discussion become stifled in favor of a single, group perspective. Such teams suppress any disagreement in the name of group harmony. As a consequence, the team fails to fully consider the merits and drawbacks of competing solutions: the first solution proposed—and not the best solution—dictates how the team proceeds.

In contrast to the conflict avoidance frequently seen on student teams is **constructive conflict**—the healthy, respectful debate of ideas and competing solutions to a problem. Constructive conflict is essential for anticipating problems and working through the pros and cons of different approaches to find the best possible solution. As an operations research manager with more than 20 years of combined military and private-sector experience puts it, "The person who disagrees with you the most is the person whose input you need the most."

The term "constructive conflict" was coined to stress the productive, beneficial role that healthy conflict plays in problem solving. Constructive conflict occurs when two or more people who share the same goal nonetheless hold different ideas about how to accomplish that goal. In carefully debating their different ideas, these people work together to find an optimal solution to a problem.

When team members engage in constructive conflict, they

- **Present evidence and reasons in support of their ideas**. People engaged in constructive conflict do not make emotional arguments or insist that others should listen to them because of their experience or credentials. Constructive conflict involves taking the time to explain the reasoning behind a position.

- **Listen closely to others' viewpoints**. To show that you are a good listener, paraphrase the viewpoint of those you disagree with and ask them to confirm that you have accurately represented their position.

- **Carefully consider the merits and drawbacks of all opinions presented**. Ask the people you disagree with to provide more evidence supporting their position so that you can fully weigh the pros and cons of the issue. Make sure that you have all the information available.

- **Work toward a solution by building and improving on all ideas presented**. Don't just listen to disagreement; try to build on it. Take the time to understand the underlying problems, and use this understanding to think of new alternatives and approaches to the problem.

If your goal is to have the best product possible, you should welcome constructive conflict because it exposes flaws that, when addressed, will lead to an improved product.

One of the biggest differences researchers have found between student and professional teams is that students tend to shut down conflict prematurely. Whereas professionals value conflict and competing ideas as essential to finding the best solution, students often feel that the discussion of competing ideas inhibits group progress. In fact, on a list of problems that student teams experience, business researchers ranked too little conflict and shutting down conflict prematurely as the top problems (Forman &

Katsky, 1986). In other words, a major failure of many student teams is reaching a solution too quickly—before the merits and drawbacks of all the options have been fully weighed and considered.

As evidence of the importance professionals place on constructive conflict, consider the results of a survey taken by 49 experienced scientists and engineers at NASA. These professionals, who worked on projects requiring both complex problem solving and technical expertise, rated the factors shown in Table 20.1 as critical to the working of a successful team (Nowaczyk, 1998).

Of the top nine factors identified as critical to team success, more than half concern constructive conflict (items 3, 4, 5, 7, 8). The NASA scientists and engineers in the survey highly valued open, critical, and healthy debate over various solutions to the problem. During such healthy debates, the discussion focuses on the scientific and technical merits of various solutions; team members take the time to explain their ideas to one another; critical evaluation of ideas is encouraged; and team members don't take disagreements over solutions personally but see them as part of the necessary work of the team.

Table 20.1. Factors NASA professionals rated as important to a successful team.

Factor	Mean Importance Score (1 = no importance; 5 = very important)
1. The team has enough time and resources to complete the task.	4.7
2. There is a sense of "team responsibility" among team members.	4.6
3. The team openly and critically debates various solutions to the problem based on their scientific and technical merits.	4.5
4. The team engages in "healthy" debate over various approaches to the problem or task early on.	4.4
5. During its lifetime, the team experiences a point at which it steps back and critically examines where it is going.	4.4
6. Working on the project is professionally rewarding to individual team members.	4.3
7. Not all team members may agree with the approach or method taken to completing the task but are supportive of the team decision.	4.3
8. Debate and critical evaluation of members' ideas are encouraged.	4.3
9. Team members take the time to explain their ideas and methods so that team members learn from one another.	4.3

Not surprisingly, in a separate questionnaire, these NASA scientists and engineers identified the failure to respond productively to constructive conflict as the number one problematic team behavior. In particular, they were harsh on colleagues who "believe that their technical status insulates their opinions from evaluation by other team members." This behavior was seen as a problem precisely because it shut down a critical and rational discussion of the merits of various ideas and solutions. Team members who insist on their own ideas without listening to the concerns and criticisms of their teammates become an obstacle to group success—no matter what their knowledge or skill level.

Clearly, these NASA scientists and engineers viewed healthy, critical debate as essential to a successful team. This same spirit of healthy debate is needed whether the team is refining a chemical process, writing a proposal to purchase new hardware, developing an online store, or testing the safety features of a new production plant. This chapter helps you distinguish between the constructive conflict necessary for good teamwork and the destructive conflict that occurs when team members react emotionally to criticism or refuse to reconsider ideas. This chapter also provides suggestions for creating a team infrastructure that will lay the groundwork for constructive conflict.

Although this chapter advocates constructive conflict, you should not therefore assume that *all* conflict is good. Constructive conflict is a productive debate of the merits and drawbacks of ideas in pursuit of the best solution to a problem. However, conflict can become destructive when team members refuse to reconsider their positions, mock or ridicule others, treat questions about their ideas as personal attacks, or use emotional appeals rather than evidence and reason to support their positions. Table 20.2 outlines the differences between constructive and destructive conflict.

Table 20.2. Characteristics of constructive versus destructive conflict.

Constructive Conflict	Destructive Conflict
Presenting evidence and reasons in support of ideas	Making emotional arguments; insisting that others should listen to you because of your experience or credentials
Accepting questions and criticisms of your ideas as good for the group	Treating questions and criticisms as personal attacks
Listening closely to others' viewpoints	Rejecting others' viewpoints before you fully understand their position
Asking others to present evidence supporting their positions so that you can make a reasoned decision	Mocking or ridiculing others' positions
Building on others' ideas and suggestions	Ignoring or dismissing others' ideas
Disagreeing in order to find the best solution	Disagreeing for the fun of a fight
Being willing to change your mind	Refusing to reconsider your position

Creating a Constructive Infrastructure for Your Team: Five Key Strategies

Unfortunately, goodwill and responsible behavior alone will not necessarily lead to constructive conflict. The following strategies will help lay the groundwork for constructive conflict in your team.

1.   Clarify Roles and Responsibilities Up Front in a Task Schedule

Many unproductive conflicts occur because team members are unclear and anxious over what is going to happen next. Team members often have different work styles and expectations for the project; if they don't have a clear understanding of their responsibilities and deadlines, their work styles tend to come into conflict just when the team is under the most pressure to finish. As a consequence, one team member will usually back down and let someone else take over. In other words, the team will have maximum destructive conflict and minimum constructive conflict. Taking time at the beginning of the project to prepare a task schedule will eliminate unneeded tension.

2.   Include Revision in the Task Schedule and Allow for Plenty of Time to Implement Revisions

If team members know from the beginning of the project that another team member will revise, edit, or critique their work, they are less likely to take such criticisms personally because they know that such critique is that person's job. Similarly, if team members know that the schedule includes time for revisions—and that they are *expected* to revise one another's work—they will be less anxious about the direction that work takes.

3.   Lay Some Ground Rules for Conversation

Following are some typical guidelines for conversation among team members:

- **Set aside time for brainstorming**. During a brainstorming session, no judgments or criticisms of ideas are allowed. The goal is to hear from everyone and generate as many ideas as possible before weighing the costs and benefits of each approach.

- **Get input from everyone in the group**. Before proceeding to any decision making, the project manager or a group facilitator should make sure that everyone has contributed an idea or opinion. This strategy can work very effectively with e-mail: team members privately e-mail their ideas to the project manager, who compiles them anonymously and distributes them with the next meeting agenda.

- **Restate ideas**. This guideline works particularly well when team members do not seem to be listening to one another. The group can establish a rule that after a person has expressed an opinion, another group member has to summarize and restate that opinion *to the satisfaction of the original speaker*. The group does not move on until that person's opinion has been satisfactorily repeated by the group. This strategy slows down heated debates and ensures that each person's opinion is fully heard *and understood* by the group.

- **Set time limits.** Tired people are more likely to go off on tangents or engage in other unproductive behaviors. Set a time limit on conversations and discuss in advance what will happen if the group still has unresolved issues at the end of that time period.

4.   Decide in Advance How Impasses (Stalemates) Will Be Handled

Methods for resolving a disagreement when the team seems at an impasse include the following:

- **The group finds consensus.** Discuss the issue until consensus is achieved.
- **The majority rules.** Vote and adopt the majority decision.
- **The supervisor decides.** Take the issue to a supervisor, subject-matter expert, instructor, or other authority for a decision.
- **The client (or target audience) decides.** Ask the client or a member of the document's target audience (that is, a potential user or reader) for an opinion. As one workplace manager said, "This is easy for me. I always just ask the client what they prefer." School projects do not always have a clear client or target audience—or it may not be practical to contact that audience for input. In such cases, you might ask one or more classmates to serve as your target audience and to offer their opinions.

5.   Establish Team Priorities in a Team Charter or a Project Plan

This is a particularly useful strategy for large projects. For instance, team members can decide which audience for a document is their priority or whether conciseness is more important than including all of the details. When disagreements occur, they can refer back to the charter to help them weigh the various options.

See also Chapter 21, "Revising with Others," for more specific advice on how to have constructive discussions about revision on your team project.

Inside Work: Exercises

1. Reread the interview with Susan at the beginning of this chapter. Which of the five key strategies listed in the section "Creating a Constructive Infrastructure for Your Team" do you think would have been *most* helpful to this team? Why?

2. Have you ever been on a team—in school or in some other setting—whose members either avoided conflict to the group's detriment or engaged in destructive conflict? What strategies recommended in this chapter might have improved the team's functioning?

The videos in this portion of the textbook are directly based on the interactions of actual student teams. Before you complete any of the video exercises, take a moment to watch the introductory video on the **Team Writing** *Web site, which describes how the videos were produced and created.*

3. View Team Video 4: David, Veronica, and Adam on the *Team Writing* Web site. Answer the following questions about this video:

   a. What model of collaboration does this team seem to be using? (See Chapter 16, "Planning Your Collaboration.")

   Team 4

   b. Review Table 20.2, "Characteristics of Constructive versus Destructive Conflict." Which characteristics of constructive or destructive conflict does this team seem to be demonstrating? Provide specific examples.

   c. What specific behavioral changes did David make between Part I and Part II of the video that improved team collaboration? List as many specific changes in David's speech, body language, attitude, and verbal interactions as possible.

   d. What if David's behavior had not changed so dramatically? Which one or two of the five strategies for creating a constructive infrastructure do you think would be *most* helpful for this team in Part I of the video?

4. Once you have completed question 3, read Appendix F, "Responses and Outcomes for Team Video 4." Considering the outcomes of this project and reactions to the team, what do you think are the major lessons to be learned from this team? Refer to specific concepts from the chapter.

5. View Team Video 5: Jayme, Megan, and Joe on the *Team Writing* Web site. Answer the following questions about this video:

   a. What model of collaboration does this team seem to be using? (See Chapter 16, "Planning Your Collaboration.")

Team 5

   b. Review Table 20.2, "Characteristics of Constructive versus Destructive Conflict." Which characteristics of constructive or destructive conflict does this team seem to be demonstrating? Provide specific examples.

   c. Which one or two of the five strategies for creating a constructive infrastructure do you think would be *most* helpful for this team? Why?

6. Once you have submitted your responses to question 5, turn to Appendix G, "Responses and Outcomes for Team Video 5," and read what professional managers said about this team. Now that you have more information, how would your response to question 5c change?

7. Most people viewing this video immediately identify problems with Joe's behaviors. Do you think that Jayme chose effective strategies for "handling" Joe? What would you have done if you were on a team with Joe?

Works Cited

Forman, J., & Katsky, P. (1986). The group report: A problem in small group or writing processes? *Journal of Business Communication, 23*(4), 23–35.

Nowaczyk, R. H. (1998). *Perceptions of engineers regarding successful engineering team design* (No. NASA/CF-1998-206917 ICASE Report No. 98-9). Hampton, VA: Institute for Computer Applications in Science and Engineering.

Chapter 21 Revising with Others

I n his final interview, Thomas describes his views on suggesting improvements to his teammates' writing:

> **Thomas**: Unless it's really bad, I don't think it's really my place to tell other people what to do. I mean, they're smart people. If it's good enough, I'm not going to criticize it.

Eduardo likewise describes a "hands-off" attitude toward other teammates' writing:

> **Eduardo**: I thought she should have worded that section less strongly. It's not how I would have put it. But she's the one in charge of writing that information, so she can write whatever she wants.

Lily explains how such a "hands-off" attitude eventually caused resentment on her team:

> **Lily**: I remember being so frustrated when Elsa did the whole thing. And she didn't get it. She was like "Well, it's just a rough draft if you want to edit it." And I was like "What's the point? You already did it."

Thomas's, Eduardo's, and Lily's comments illustrate how uncomfortable students can feel when suggesting changes to a teammate's work. Sometimes, the reluctance is due to feelings of ownership—that the person who wrote a section has the right to phrase and organize things the way he or she wants. Sometimes, as Lily suggests, revision seems pointless if the group can simply agree to move forward with what has already been done. At other times, students hesitate to suggest revisions because they fear hurting a teammate's feelings through criticism, or they worry about seeming egotistical, as if they are better than their teammates.

These concerns about revising or critiquing others' work are understandable, but a well-functioning team should be able to overcome this reluctance. Generating a first-rate project involves recognizing that the team owns the work it produces and that every member shares a responsibility to make every part of the project the best it can be. Learning how to revise and critique your teammates' work is an important part of

Chapter 21, "Revising with Others" from *Team Writing: A Guide to Working in Groups* by Joanna Wolfe, pp. 59–79 (Chapter 6). Copyright © 2010 by Bedford/St. Martin's.

this process—as is learning how to take and use the feedback your teammates provide on your own work.

This chapter presents some strategies for building a strong revision process into your team's culture. When team members feel comfortable critiquing and revising one another's work, the team will draw on everyone's strengths and insights and will produce a superior product. Developing a strong revision process and a team culture in which constructive critique is welcomed and encouraged will allow your team to focus on what is best for the project without worrying about hurt feelings or who "owns" a particular section of the project.

Developing a Culture in Which Constructive Feedback Is Encouraged

The quotes that began this chapter were from students who took part in teams whose culture did not promote critique of others' work—and in all three cases, their projects suffered from the lack of feedback and input. These students did not have a team environment that encouraged constructive conflict (see Chapter 20, "Constructive Conflict").

Here are four steps your team can follow to develop a culture in which constructive feedback is encouraged:

- **Build revision and feedback into the task schedule.** Creating a task schedule in which team members are given "credit" for commenting on or revising one another's work not only encourages team members to *give* feedback but also helps them *accept* feedback as part of the necessary work that goes into a successful collaborative document. If writers know that other team members are *required* to provide suggestions for change (or are required to make revisions), they will not take these suggestions or revisions personally. Thus, scheduling revision and feedback into the task schedule creates a team culture in which constructive feedback is simply part of what it takes to get the project done and is not a negative reflection on anybody's work.

- **Decide on a revision process and follow it.** This chapter describes two basic models for revision: feedback and direct revision. Many teams use a combination of these two methods. For instance, a team might use feedback at the beginning of a project to provide global suggestions for a writer and then switch to direct revision at the end. After considering the advantages and disadvantages of these methods (see Table 21.1 on p. 585), your team should decide how revision will be handled at various stages of the project and create a task schedule that reflects this decision.

- **Use writing software that keeps a history of revisions.** This chapter describes three software tools that help with collaborative authoring by tracking all the changes made to a document (see the section "Technology for Collaborative Revising"). These tools allow one team member to revise another member's work while still preserving the original copy. They also make it easy to undo revisions that the team disagrees with and to offer provisional changes that can easily be reversed. The team can use the software to compare different versions of a document and to discuss the pros and cons of individual changes.

*   **Include a statement about the importance of revision and feedback in the team charter.** Once your team decides on a revision process, you can note this in the team charter along with a statement acknowledging that the team agrees that providing honest and constructive feedback is essential to a quality project and that all team members agree to provide thorough feedback on one another's work to the best of their abilities.

Two Types of Revision: Feedback and Direct Revision

Teams can handle revisions in two different ways. In the **feedback** method, one team member drafts some text, submits it to others for feedback, and then implements revisions based on this feedback. This method is sometimes referred to as single-author revision because one person maintains primary responsibility for a section of text. In the **direct-revision** method, one team member drafts some text, and another member implements the revisions, directly changing and revising the text of the previous author. This method is sometimes referred to as multiple-author revision because several people share responsibility for shaping the text.

The Feedback Method

The main benefit of the feedback method is that it is easy to implement. Since one person maintains responsibility for a section of text, there are no opportunities for **version-control problems**, in which two people are simultaneously working from different copies of the text and end up writing over each other's changes. Moreover, the feedback method allows the author to compile comments from several people with different perspectives and can also free up other team members to work on other parts of the project because it usually takes them less time to make comments than to implement direct revisions.

The main drawback of the feedback method is that the quality of the text rests disproportionately on the skills, ability, and efforts of one person. If that person is not a good writer, is defensive about receiving feedback, or does not put sufficient effort or time into drafting and revising, the entire product suffers. For this reason, it is very important to select an author who is highly motivated to improve his or her writing and is therefore eager and willing to listen to others' constructive comments. (Remember: motivation is often more important than experience when selecting people for tasks. See Chapter 19, "Getting Started with the Task Schedule," for more advice on assigning team members to tasks.)

Another drawback of the feedback method is the risk of stylistic inconsistency if the team assigns different sections of text to different authors. Even though these authors may be receiving feedback from one another, the document as a whole can sound disjointed and awkward, especially if the authors have different writing styles or "voices." The following instructor comment on one team's draft illustrates the potential drawbacks of the feedback method:

> Much of the background section is written in the first person plural ("we") while everything else is written in the third person. The "solutions" and "recommendations" sections sound as if they were written for a much more technical audience than the rest of the proposal. Overall, the document sounds like you divided each section up without consulting each other much.

Each section of this document relied on the writing skills of a different team member, and the document lacked a unified "voice" and structure. To avoid this problem, many teams that rely on feedback for revising individual sections of text in the early stages of the project may switch to direct revision toward the end of the project, with one person editing the entire document to make it sound unified and coherent.

The Direct-Revision Method

The main benefit of direct revision is that responsibility for the text is shared by several people who can draw on one another's strengths as they directly change, reorganize, and add to the text. Thus, if one person has strong content knowledge about the topic and another has strong writing and editing skills, the team benefits from combining both of these strengths.

The major drawback of direct revision is that the team can end up with two or more different versions of the same document (known as a version-control problem), a situation that can be frustrating and time-consuming to resolve. Version-control problems can crop up when one team member begins revising a document without knowing that another author is also making revisions to the same text. Moreover, in the direc-revision method, meeting deadlines takes on added importance because the original writer cannot make further changes to the text after handing it off without introducing version-control issues. Some of these problems can be alleviated with a Web-based editor such as Google Docs or a wiki. Nonetheless, "handing off" the text from one writer to the next remains a tricky issue in direct revision.

Choosing a Method

Fortunately, you do not have to choose just one of these methods; teams can and frequently do combine them at different stages of the project. For example, a team may rely on the feedback method for global comments on initial drafts and then switch to direct revision to implement minor changes to the wording and formatting as the document nears completion. Or the team can use the two methods simultaneously: a teammate can hand off a document to another writer for direct revision and at the same time ask the other teammates to provide global feedback. Thus, the person implementing the feedback will be different from the person who wrote the initial draft.

Table 21.1 provides a summary of the benefits and drawbacks of feedback and direct revision.

Table 21.1. Feedback versus direct revision.

Method	Description	Benefits	Drawbacks
Feedback	One person drafts the text, submits it to others for comments, and makes revisions based on these comments.	• Easy to implement: the team does not have to worry about version-control problems. • Particularly useful for obtaining global comments from several people.	• The team "puts all of its eggs in one basket" by depending on a single writer. • Sections of the text written by different authors can sound different. • Writers can ignore or reject feedback from other group members without discussing it.
Direct Revision	One person drafts the text and then hands it off to another team member, who makes revisions directly to the text and then hands it back.	• Draws on the combined strengths of two or more writers. • Particularly useful for making final edits as the document nears completion.	• Easy for one writer to work from the wrong version of the document. • Missed deadlines take on added importance because of the complexity of handing off the text from one author to the next. • Writers can become upset when other authors change their work.

The following questions—while certainly not a complete list of the issues your team should consider—can help you select the method or combination of methods that might be best for your team.

Does your team have...

A writer who really wants to improve his or her writing skills?

A member with both content knowledge and strong writing skills?

Then use...

Feedback so that this writer can have the benefit of receiving and implementing suggestions for improving his or her writing.

Feedback since this writer will be in a good position to see the document as a whole and implement large changes across several sections based on feedback.

| One team member with content knowledge and another with strong writing skills? | Direct revision followed by feedback: the content expert can draft the document, and the writing expert can directly revise it. This direct revision should be followed up with an additional round of feedback from the content expert to ensure that the writer has not accidentally changed the meaning or introduced mistakes into the text. |
| A writer who has trouble accepting feedback? | Direct revision since it may be easier for this person to accept changes once they have already been made than to implement changes suggested through feedback. |

Whether you use feedback or direct revision, you and your teammates should be willing to suggest (or directly implement) both major and minor changes to one another's writing. Moreover, both methods require team members to be open to *receiving* feedback and seeing changes made to their writing. With the feedback method, writers must be willing to implement as many of their teammates' suggestions as possible. With direct revision, writers must be open-minded when someone else changes their text and avoid becoming committed to a particular way of phrasing or organizing the text. To help you handle feedback productively while using either method, the sections that follow offer tips for making and listening to feedback on writing. (See also Chapter 23, "Troubleshooting Team Problems," for additional advice on how to handle problems with giving or receiving feedback.)

Before You Start: Ground Rules for Revision

When writers submit work to teammates for direct revision or comments, they should take a moment to clarify the state of the draft and what they see as the goals for revision.

- **Clarify the state of the draft.** Does the writer see the draft as nearly final, needing only minor editing and polishing? Or as very rough, needing major reorganization and content changes? Has the writer submitted a draft missing major sections, with plans to add those sections later? Whenever writers hand off a draft to others for comment or revision, they should provide a brief statement summarizing the state of the draft and outlining the types of changes they believe the draft needs. This will help teammates gauge their feedback. For instance, if a teammate believes that a draft needs major changes but the writer sees it as close to finished, that teammate should expect some resistance from the writer and therefore should provide detailed justification for the proposed changes.

- **Clarify the goals of the revision or feedback.** If the project is nearing the final deadline, major suggestions or revisions may be inappropriate. If the draft is very rough, sentence-level editing would be a waste of time because entire sections may be deleted or entirely changed during the revision process. Taking a moment to agree up front on the goals of the feedback can help the team use its time more effectively.

Figure 21.1 illustrates how a writer might ask for feedback from teammates, while clarifying what level of feedback she is looking for. In Figure 21.2, one of the writer's teammates requests direct revision on a draft that is nearly at its final stage.

For their part, reviewers and coauthors need to make sure that they understand the goals of the project as a whole before they respond to the writer. Thus, *before responding to or revising a draft, teammates should take time to review the assignment instructions* to ascertain what the final product should look like.

TO: Stephen, Tim

FR: Charlotte

Subject: Feedback

Hey guys!

I'm attaching a rough draft of the results and discussion sections. These are very rough, and right now the discussion section is just a list of topics to cover. I plan to flesh it out in the next draft. In the meantime, could you give me some comments on the results section? Does the organization/order seem right? Do the charts work? Let me know if you find any errors on them (I spent a long time on these!).

As for the discussion section, could you let me know if I left out any topics that I should be sure to cover in the next draft?

We agreed in the task schedule that you'd have these comments to me by Wednesday morning. I've blocked out some time in my schedule Wednesday night to work on this.

Thanks!

Charlotte

Figure 21.1. E-mail requesting feedback. Charlotte explains the state of both sections of her draft and the different levels of feedback she would like on each section.

TO: Charlotte

FR: Stephen

Subject: Moving toward the final draft

Charlotte:

I've attached the transmittal letter, abstract, introduction, and works cited. I think these are ready to go, but if you see something major, IM me right away. Could you be sure to look over the works cited and make sure I did it right? APA always makes me nervous. Also you might double-check to make sure I got the letter format just the way Professor Powell wants it. I think I did, but it won't hurt to double-check. As for the rest, I think you can just look these over for typos/polishing and making sure they are consistent with the rest of the report.

Thanks!

Stephen

Figure 21.2. E-mail handing off a draft to be directly revised. Stephen clarifies that he considers the document close to final, but he directs his teammate to a few places where she might want to double-check the format.

Providing Effective Feedback and Making Good Revisions

If you have been assigned to provide written feedback to a teammate or directly revise a draft a teammate has prepared, you should take time to provide thoughtful suggestions. You don't have to be certain about every suggestion you propose. After all, other people will be commenting as well, and the team can decide which suggestions are good ones. However, you should be constructively critical of the draft. This constructive criticism is key to creating a strong final project and is a major part of teamwork (see Chapter 20, "Constructive Conflict").

Before you provide feedback or make revisions on a draft, make sure you completely understand the project's requirements:

- **Review the assignment instruction sheet.** Make a checklist of the criteria for the assignment. Then read the draft and compare it against this checklist.

- **Check against the grading rubric.** If the instructor has distributed a grading rubric (a sheet that lists the evaluation criteria for the assignment), carefully check your team's document against this rubric to make sure that all the criteria are met.

- **Review the team charter**. Make sure you understand the main goals that the team has set forth in the charter.

Because writers often find it difficult to see shortcomings in their own writing, it is important that someone *other than the original writer(s)* check the assignment for completeness and accuracy. The document will always benefit from having a "fresh set of eyes" take a look at it.

Once you understand the project requirements and have reviewed the draft, you are ready to give feedback or implement revisions. Depending on how far along the project is, you can use one of the following checklists to guide your feedback or direct revisions.

✓ A Checklist for Giving Feedback during the Initial, Rough Stage

- ☐ **Begin with praise**. In your e-mail to the writer, note one or two things that this draft does really well—even if all you can say is that the draft does a good job getting some ideas on the table.

- ☐ **Identify/fix oversights**. Look for parts of the text that do not meet the assignment requirements or do not match what the group decided on.

- ☐ **Suggest/add new material**. What else could be included that would strengthen this draft?

- ☐ **Note/revise misleading or inaccurate information**. Look for places where the information included is presented in a misleading way or is simply wrong.

- ☐ **Suggest/implement alternative organizations**. Do you think the organization could be improved? Would you recommend reordering some of the sections? Or creating new headings to make the material easier to skim? Should the recommendations be in a bulleted list rather than in paragraph form? Should any tables be reorganized to better communicate the data's message?

- ☐ **Identify/resolve inconsistencies in content and argument**. Look for inconsistencies in the information and arguments included. You can address inconsistencies in formatting or vocabulary in later drafts.

✓ A Checklist for Giving Feedback during the Final, Polished Stage

☐ **Begin with praise**. Note one or two things in this draft that are improvements over the previous draft.

☐ **Identify/fix oversights**. Look for parts of the text that do not meet the assignment requirements or do not match what the group decided on.

☐ **Note/revise misleading or inaccurate information**. Look for places where the information included is presented in a misleading way or is simply wrong.

☐ **Identify/resolve inconsistencies in content, organization, vocabulary, and formatting**. Look for inconsistencies not only in the arguments and information included but also in the organization, vocabulary, and format. Does the heading style change from one part of the document to another? Does the document use inconsistent terminology for the same thing? Does the font or formatting suddenly change?

☐ **Suggest/implement alternative formatting**. Do you think a different type of graph or table style should be used? Would you recommend a different heading style or different font throughout?

☐ **Correct grammar and style**. Fix grammatical errors, wordy sentences, or awkward phrases.

Listening to Feedback and Negotiating Revision

Responding to feedback may be one of the most difficult parts of working on a team. When your teammates offer feedback or revisions, do not respond defensively. If someone notes a problem, assume that there *is* some sort of problem—even if that person has mislabeled the problem or presented an incorrect solution. Do not reject any feedback until you have considered it from all angles.

The ability to receive and accept feedback represents a high level of professionalism that, as a student, you may not have had the opportunity to develop yet. If you have difficulty accepting feedback or criticism from others, the strategies in the checklist on page 591 may be helpful.

Sometimes, you will receive feedback that you agree with but don't know how to implement. At other times, you will receive feedback that is confusing or that you don't understand. In these cases, don't simply ignore the feedback. Ignoring your teammates' feedback can make them feel that you don't value their work and input—or it can make them wonder whether you are lazy or closed-minded.

✓ A Checklist for Accepting Feedback

☐ **Count to 10**. Before responding to feedback, give yourself a chance to recover from your initial reaction.

☐ **Ask the person why he or she made this suggestion**. You may find that you and the other person agree more than you originally thought.

☐ **Understand criticism**. Before accepting or rejecting feedback, repeat back the criticism, the rationale, and the proposed solution (if one was supplied), and then ask the person to confirm that you understood him or her correctly.

☐ **Receive comments by e-mail**. If you have trouble accepting feedback in face-to-face situations, ask group members to send you an e-mail with their comments and suggestions. This gives you a chance to react to these suggestions in private and gives you time to tone down your initial reactions.

Instead of ignoring feedback that confuses you, ask for clarification—or for suggestions about how to implement it. Figure 21.3 illustrates an e-mail from a teammate asking for clarification.

TO: Stephen

FR: Charlotte

CC: Tim

Subject: Stephen's feedback

Stephen:

Thanks for your feedback. There were some really good suggestions, and I've implemented almost all of them. But one comment that you made has me stumped. You wrote, "This figure is really hard to read. There is too much information here." I agree that the figure is hard to read, but I'm not sure how to fix it since all the information seems necessary. Do you have any advice on what to cut? Or a better way to organize it? Tim, do you have any ideas or suggestions? (We're talking about Figure 4.)

Thanks!

Charlotte

Figure 21.3. E-mail asking a teammate to clarify a suggestion.

You might also talk to your instructor or a tutor at your university's writing center about how to incorporate confusing feedback. In many cases, your teammates may have correctly identified a problem in your writing but incorrectly identified the solution. A more experienced writer might be able to help you step back and troubleshoot the document from a different perspective.

Sometimes, you will receive feedback that you simply disagree with. If this occurs, try to give yourself 24 hours to cool off and then reconsider the feedback with an open mind. Suggestions that seem impossible at first glance often look much more manageable when you return to them later. Also, if you reread the feedback, you may find that you had initially misunderstood or overreacted to what your teammate was suggesting. A 24-hour cooling-off period allows you to respond to feedback more generously.

If, after cooling off, you still disagree with the feedback or revisions, ask other team members to comment on the issue. You could ask the project manager to put the issue on the agenda for the next team meeting—or the project manager could e-mail the team and ask everyone to comment on the section of text under debate. Sometimes, another team member can provide a suggestion or insight that helps you find a new way to revise that incorporates the best of both your and your teammates' viewpoints. If the disagreement continues, make sure that you abide by the conflict-resolution method you decided on in the team charter—and feel good that your team actually had a substantive discussion about an issue. Most student teams suffer from an avoidance of any kind of substantive disagreement (see Chapter 20, "Constructive Conflict").

If you end up rejecting or disagreeing with the feedback or revisions others have offered, you should provide specific reasons that support your point of view. The best reasons are those that are firmly rooted in the instructor's guidelines, the goals agreed on in the team charter, or the reader's needs. Thus, if you are arguing for or against including particular information or adopting a particular organization—and your instructor has not provided you with clear guidelines on the issue—you will have more success supporting your position if you can make the case that this will meet your audience's needs.

In general, you should try to implement every suggestion your peers provide unless you can clearly articulate a good reason not to. See Chapter 23, "Troubleshooting Team Problems," for more advice on how to handle specific problems that can occur when you are revising with others.

Technology for Collaborative Revising

There are many revision tools available that can help simplify collaborative revising. Some tools are particularly useful for keeping track of direct revisions and reversing controversial changes. Others are particularly useful for providing feedback on text. Some tools help reduce version-control problems by keeping a single, centralized copy of the text on a Web server where it can be edited by everyone. This section discusses some of these tools, starting with the simplest.

E-mail Message

The simplest technology for providing written feedback is to type your constructive criticisms and suggestions for change in an e-mail message. This method is best for providing large, global suggestions for revision. It is not as effective for making minor suggestions to specific sections of text since you cannot easily anchor your comments to a particular paragraph, sentence, or word.

Commenting Features

Many word-processing programs have a commenting feature that allows you to make comments in the "margin" of a document. Figure 21.4 shows Microsoft Word's commenting feature. To make a comment, highlight the section of text you wish to comment on, go up to the Insert toolbar, and select Comment. A box in which you can type your comments will appear in the margin of the text. Once you have commented on the document, you can e-mail it to your teammates. (Hint: If your teammates use a different word-processing program, you can convert the document to Rich Text Format [.rtf] before sending it. RTF is a universal word-processing format.)

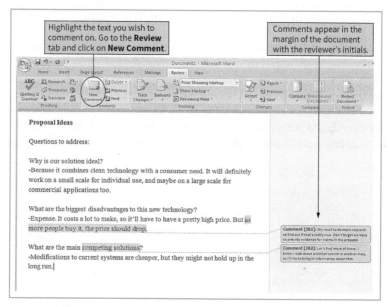

Figure 21.4. Inserting comments. Microsoft Word's commenting feature, which allows you to attach comments to specific sections of text, is a good tool for offering detailed written feedback.

Commenting tools are sometimes combined with Track Changes (see the next section). In this situation, reviewers make large suggestions in the comments and use Track Changes to suggest minor edits and rewordings.

Sometimes, though, when teams use commenting tools, they can end up duplicating their efforts: if several team members are commenting simultaneously, they might spend time pointing out the exact same problems. Moreover, it may be challenging for the writer to collect separate feedback from several people, thereby increasing the chances that some comments get overlooked. To avoid this problem, the team can adopt a "serial commenting" method, in which the document is passed around to teammates one at a time. Each teammate can then respond to the feedback of previous reviewers as well as make additional comments; however, the serial method will lengthen the time it takes to obtain feedback from everyone on the team.

Track Changes

Track Changes is a revision-control feature in Microsoft Word (other word-processing programs have similar tools) that tracks all additions, deletions, and formatting changes to a document. To turn Track Changes on, go to the Review tab and select Track Changes (see Figure 21.5). Using Track Changes, you can make revisions to a document and then give it to other team members, who can then "accept" or "reject" the changes. Figure 21.6 shows a document that has been edited using Track Changes. Figure 21.7 illustrates how other authors can use the reviewing toolbar to implement changes and to switch among different views of the document.

Track Changes is most commonly used for direct revision (although sometimes reviewers also use it to make minor editing suggestions when providing feedback). This feature allows one author to completely revise another author's text without anxiety because coauthors can see exactly what was modified and can easily reverse controversial changes. The main drawback of Track Changes is that coauthors have to carefully coordinate with one another to avoid version-control problems, which can occur when several people are working from different versions of the same text.

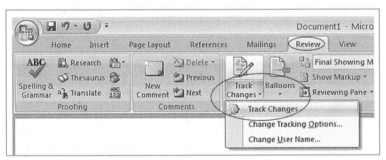

Figure 21.5. Track Changes. To turn Track Changes on, go to the Review tab and select Track Changes. Also in the Review tab is a Changes panel that allows readers to accept or reject changes.

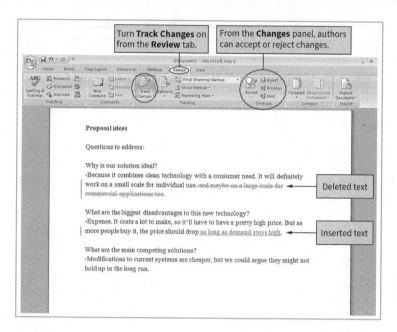

Figure 21.6. Document showing tracked changes. Deleted text is indicated by a strikethrough, while inserted text is underlined. Another author can reverse these changes by going to the Changes panel and "rejecting" them.

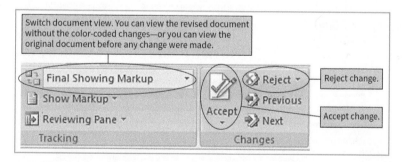

Figure 21.7. Review tab. The Tracking and Changes panels allow authors to accept or reject changes made by a previous author and to switch among various views of the document: Final Showing Markup (with Track Changes shown), Final (with Track Changes turned off), and Original (the document before changes were made).

Google Docs

If several team members are going to be revising a document extensively, the team may want to consider using a Web-based editing environment such as Google Docs (see Figure 21.8) or a wiki-based editor. The main advantage of a Web-based editing environment is that there is only one copy of the document, which stays on the Web site. Multiple authors can edit and revise it without worrying that someone else has a more recently revised version. However, it is usually best to avoid truly simultaneous editing (when two authors are revising at the exact same time) because there are time lags during which one author might move or delete a section of text that another is working on. Thus, truly simultaneous editing can introduce version-control problems into the process—exactly the problem that a Web-based editing environment is intended to prevent.

Most Web-based editing environments keep a revision history that logs who made what changes when. This revision history can help a teammate identify what was changed recently. Revision histories are also good for undoing revisions by reverting back to an earlier version of the document.

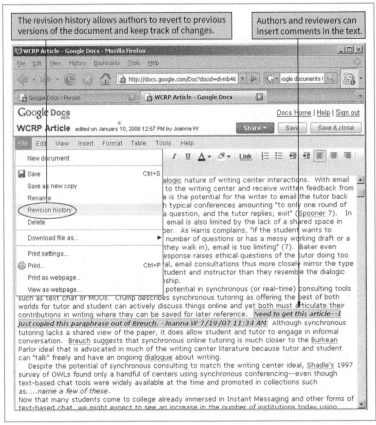

Figure 21.8. Google Docs. Google Docs is a free Web-based editor that allows teams to keep a single version of the document online. Using Google Docs, multiple authors can edit and revise the document simultaneously without having to wonder which version is most current. Commenting features can be used to suggest changes, and the revision history feature allows the team to track changes and reject revisions. However, Google Docs has far fewer formatting features than do desktop-based word-processing programs.

The main drawback of Web-based editors is that they offer far fewer editing features than desktop-based word-processing programs. If your document requires extensive formatting or has lots of tables or figures, you may want to avoid Web-based editors.

Google Docs also allows teams to share and collaboratively edit spreadsheets and presentations. Again, these Web-based tools have far fewer formatting options than the word-processing programs you may be accustomed to.

You can find out more about Google Docs and sign up for a free account for your team at http://docs.google.com. See also www.google.com/google-d-s/tour1.html.

Wikis

Teams can also use another Web-based editing tool for collaborative revision: a wiki, which is a collection of Web pages that allow users to make changes and add new pages. Wikis are particularly useful for putting together complex sets of information. Whereas a Web-based editor such as Google Docs essentially focuses on one document at a time, a wiki allows the team to focus on complex relationships among many separate documents. Wikipedia, an online encyclopedia, is a perfect example of a wiki: it consists of a very large network of small documents that are linked together and collaboratively updated. If your team project involves many small, individual documents that need to coordinate together, you may want to consider using a wiki—especially if your team intends these documents to be open to the public to read, comment on, and possibly even revise.

The main advantage of wikis is that they allow the team to store all the documents associated with a project—including task schedules, external reference documents, discussion boards, instructions, and other materials—in one central place. The main disadvantage of wikis is that they have a much higher learning curve than a tool such as Google Docs, which is specifically designed for drafting written documents. When working with a wiki, team members can easily forget where various documents are placed and can miss important information. For this reason, if you use a wiki for your team project, make sure the team discusses up front a standardized method for notifying everyone of exactly *what* has been changed or added and *where* those changes or additions can be found.

It is impossible to discuss all of the wiki options available, but Table 21.2 lists some common wiki features that are particularly useful for collaborative writing.

The following wikis have many of the features listed in Table 21.2:

- Zoho wiki: http://zoho.com
- PBWiki: http://pbwiki.com/education.wiki
- SocialText: www.socialtext.com

In addition, you might want to consult Wikimatrix (www.wikimatrix.org), which lists hundreds of current wikis. This site also contains a wizard that helps you select a wiki based on your team's needs.

Table 21.2. Wiki features particularly useful for team writing projects.

Feature	Description
Free hosting	With free hosting, the wiki exists on someone else's server and requires no setup before using. Most free wikis place a quota on the amount of content your team is allowed to store. Be sure to check this quota and make sure it will be sufficient for your project's needs. Graphics-intensive projects will need large quotas.
WYSIWYG	WYSIWYG (an acronym for "what you see is what you get") refers to software in which the content displayed during editing appears very similar to the final output. Unless your team has some reason for working with the messy details of markup language, you should make sure the wiki has WYSIWYG capabilities.
E-mail notification	Allows you to e-mail your team when changes have been made. A notification method is extremely important.
Export options	If you are required to print your project, you need to pay careful attention to export and print options. Options include exporting to HTML and PDF.
Page history/ revision history	Allows team members to see what was changed and to undo controversial changes if necessary.
Change summary	Allows a team member who revises a page to include a short summary of the changes made.
Revision diffs	Shows the differences between two pages' revisions, making it easy to spot the differences.
Page permissions	Allows teams to make some pages "public" (available to anyone) or "private" (available only to the team). The team can also "lock" some pages so that they are visible but cannot be edited.
Comments/ discussion pages	Provides a system for discussing individual wiki pages. The most common method is a threaded discussion at the bottom of a page.
Attach files	Allows team members to attach external files to their pages. For instance, team members could upload PDFs of articles or other materials related to the project.
Math formulas	Allows math formulas to be displayed in the wiki page. This feature is needed only for technical projects in which writers are expected to provide examples of the calculations or algorithms used during the project.

More Technology for Revision

Depending on the needs of your specific project, you may want to consider some other, less well-known tools for managing collaborative revision, such as Zoho and Gliffy. Zoho, like Google Docs, is a free Web-based editor.[1] At the time of this writing, it provides a wider range of tools than Google Docs, including an online presentation editor, text chat tools, and project planning tools. It also allows users to import documents directly from Google Docs. However, the sheer number of applications that Zoho supports makes its interface somewhat difficult to navigate. To find out more about Zoho, go to http://zoho.com.

Gliffy is online diagramming software that allows you to create flowcharts, diagrams, floor plans, and technical drawings. You can find out more about this tool at www.gliffy.com.

Selecting a Tool

Table 21.3 summarizes the advantages and drawbacks of the various revision and feedback tools discussed in this chapter. Sometimes, your instructor (or supervisor in the workplace) will require you to use certain tools; however, on most projects you will have some choice, so thinking through the pros and cons of various options up front will save you headaches later.

Table 21.3. Advantages and disadvantages of revision tools.

Tool	Advantages	Disadvantages
E-mail message	• Simple to use. • Allows for quick turnaround. • Good for global feedback. Lack of editing features keeps reviewers focused on "big picture" issues.	• Difficult to comment on specific sections, paragraphs, sentences, and words. • Inappropriate for final editing stages.
Microsoft Word commenting tools	• Reviewers can comment on specific sections of text. Comments are off to the side and easily distinguishable from the main text. • Teammates can respond to one another's comments and discuss the pros and cons of various changes. • Can be combined with Track Changes.	• Reviewers may duplicate efforts by making identical comments. • May be difficult to reconcile feedback from different reviewers unless the team uses "serial" commenting, in which each reviewer comments and then hands the document off to the next reviewer for comments.

---

1 In a detailed review in the online magazine *Computer World*, David DeJean compares Zoho, Google Docs, and ThinkFree (another Web-based editor). The article is available at www.computerworld.com/action/article.do?command=printArticleBasic&articleId=9108799.

Tool	Advantages	Disadvantages
Microsoft Word Track Changes	• Easy to see what was changed and to switch back and forth between original and revised versions. • Easy to accept or reject changes another author has made. • Can be combined with commenting tools to provide justifications of changes or to query coauthors.	• Only one person can work on the document at a time. • Version-control problems can occur when multiple authors work from different versions of the document, writing over each other's changes.
Google Docs	• Writers are always working from the most current version of the document, so the team does not have to worry about version-control problems. • Combines commenting capabilities with direct revision. • Document resides in a common storage space where the team can keep task schedules and other documents associated with the project.	• Lacks a rich set of formatting tools and is inappropriate for documents that have lots of tables or require extensive formatting features. • Comments are inserted directly into the text, sometimes making the text difficult to read.
Wiki	• Pros are similar to those of Google Docs. • Provides maximum flexibility for creating and linking multiple documents. • The team can make project information public and available for comments or edits from outside audiences.	• High learning curve for many users. • Server may not be stable, and technical support may be unavailable. • May be difficult to export or print documents. • Easy to lose, misplace, or miss key information.

Inside Work: Exercises

1. Have you ever been on a team in which you noted a problem with a teammate's work but didn't point it out? What stopped you from providing feedback? Now that you have read this chapter, what are some strategies you could use to politely provide suggestions for revision?

2. Review the assignment materials your instructor has provided. Working together with your team, come up with a checklist of items to look for when commenting on or revising one another's work.

3. Pull up a document that your team has already created (or create a new document of "dummy" text), and try editing it with each of the tools mentioned in this chapter. Which tool do you think will be most effective for your team? Why?

4. Do you ever have problems responding positively to feedback or criticism? Which of the strategies outlined in this chapter for responding productively to feedback do you think would be most helpful in improving how you respond to criticism?

5. Review the team charter and task schedule your team has created, and decide which revision tool you plan to use and which revision method (feedback or direct revision) you plan to implement at various stages in the project. Update the task schedule accordingly. Review the sections of the team charter that state overall team goals and methods for handling impasses. Do you think that any of these sections should be updated?

The videos in this portion of the textbook are directly based on the interactions of actual student teams. Before you complete any of the video exercises, take a moment to watch the introductory video on the Team Writing *Web site, which describes how the videos were produced and created.*

6. View Team Video 3: Jamaal, Jim, Don, and Tonya on the *Team Writing* Web site. Then turn to Appendix E, "Responses and Outcomes for Team Video 3," and read about this project's outcome. What could this team have done differently to avoid the problems it experienced later? What do you think are the major lessons to learn from this team?

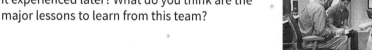

Team 3

Chapter 22

Communication Styles and Team Diversity

When they were asked in their final interviews to comment on how individual team members got along, Veronica and David had this to say about each other:

Veronica: It was a headache because the things that I said weren't being heard. If someone asked a question and I tried to answer it, David especially would interrupt me... . So I just started to sit back and not say anything because I got tired of, you know, having to shout to be heard. It felt like it didn't matter what I said; they're not going to listen.

David: Well, I think Veronica, she might have the worst view of me because she and I just come from different places. With her, I kind of felt like I had to watch what I said because there were some issues there. Do you understand what I'm saying? Whereas with other people, I didn't have to make sure. If I ignored or interrupted them, it wasn't this big issue.

Veronica and David have conflicting communication styles, among other issues. Whereas Veronica perceives interruptions as a sign of disrespect—an indication that others don't care about what she has to say—David sees interruptions as part of the normal ebb and flow of a debate. He feels that he has to curb his normal style of talking in order to accommodate Veronica and wishes that she could be more like the others in his group. As David notes, he and Veronica "just come from different places." He worries about how she perceives him, and vice versa.

Sooner or later, you will find yourself on a team with someone who "comes from a different place" than you do. This chapter teaches you to take the differences between you and your teammate and turn them into something positive. Key to achieving this positive outcome is understanding the differences in communication styles. Many interpersonal problems occur on teams because team members differ in their assumptions about how they should talk to one another, what constitutes productive behavior, and what constitutes rude behavior. Understanding that people can have different assumptions about what is "normal" communication will help you work with others whose communication preferences differ from yours.

The best teams are those that are easy on people but hard on problems. This chapter teaches you about communication styles so that the merit of an idea or a solution—and not how it was communicated—determines whether or not your team adopts it.

The Benefits of Diverse Teams

A diverse team is one composed of people of different genders, ethnicities, or educational backgrounds or from different geographic regions. Although diverse teams sometimes experience social discomfort as people learn to work together, researchers have found that diverse teams outperform homogeneous ones (teams composed of people with similar backgrounds)—particularly on complex tasks without clear solutions (Cordero et al., 1996). These findings should not be surprising if you think back to Chapter 20, "Constructive Conflict," which showed that teams work best when they experience productive conflict by fully considering the merits and drawbacks of a range of ideas. Teams composed of people from diverse perspectives and backgrounds are likely to propose diverse solutions to problems. Such teams will have more opportunities for such constructive conflict than teams in which everybody thinks and acts alike. Thus, diversity often leads to creativity and innovative problem solving.

Moreover, diverse teams are far less likely than homogeneous ones to propose solutions that work only for a single group of people. For instance, when car air bags first became common in the 1980s, designers and auto manufacturers, who were mostly male, tested them on dummies measuring 5 feet 9 inches—the height of the average American man. Only after many women and children were injured and even killed by inappropriately deploying air bags did automakers realize that this safety device could actually harm people with smaller body frames. Today, air bags are now designed and tested for a range of body types, including pregnant women. If more women had been involved in automanufacturing design in the 1980s, this fatal design flaw probably would have been noted and addressed earlier.

However, even if diverse teams didn't have advantages over homogeneous ones, there is at least one practical reason for learning how to work with people different from us: as our culture becomes more global, our workplaces will become increasingly diverse, and therefore homogeneous teams will become less and less common. Learning how to handle diversity successfully is becoming a necessary job skill. Understanding how norms work in interpersonal interactions is the first step in acquiring that skill.

How Differences in Communication Norms Can Cause Interpersonal Conflict

By understanding how norms affect your behavior and your perception of other people's behaviors, you can foster a team environment that reaps the benefits of diversity while minimizing the dissatisfaction that diversity causes. In the realm of communication and other interpersonal issues, a norm is a standard of behavior typical of a particular group. An individual norm is what a particular member of that group considers to be normal behavior. Norms govern how we think, talk, and act. When team members have conflicting norms, they will have different ideas about what is productive or unproductive as well as conflicting ideas about what is polite, mildly offensive, or just plain rude.

An illustration of different communication norms can be seen in how people from different cultures respond to compliments. In the United States, children are usually taught that it is polite to accept compliments, usually by saying "thank you." In Japan and Korea, however, children are taught to deflect or deny compliments by saying "no, no" or "that's not true" (Kim, 2003). A Korean unfamiliar with American cultural norms might think that an American was egotistical for accepting a compliment; conversely, an American might think that a Korean was rude for refusing to accept one. Yet no one way of responding to compliments is inherently better than another—your preference is just a result of what you were brought up to see as normal.

Even within a single culture—especially one as diverse as U.S. culture—there are wide differences in what is considered normal behavior. For instance, some behavior that is considered normal in a crowded area such as New York City may be perceived as rude in other parts of the country. Similarly, what a southerner may view as a polite and necessary conversation-starter might be perceived as an infuriating waste of time by a midwesterner. Even within a particular geographic region, men and women, or people from different social classes, may have different norms. For example, behavior that might be considered normal and appropriate in single-gender settings is often considered inappropriate in mixed company. Similarly, one group of people may find it natural and normal to talk about their accomplishments, whereas another group in the same community may see such talk as egotistical and self-promotional.

Increasing your awareness of social norms can help you reduce unproductive conflict, know how to adjust your behavior to "fit in" to otherwise unfamiliar or uncomfortable social situations, and understand why others might have difficulty fitting in to norms that feel natural to you. This chapter discusses three areas in which different norms often cause conflict in student teams. Before continuing, take the self-assessments in Figures 22.1, 22.2, and 22.3 to see what sort of norms you favor in team interactions. (You can also download a copy of these self-assessments from the *Team Writing* Web site.)

Understanding Norms

Taking these self-assessments will help you identify what feels like a "normal" discussion, self-presentation, or problem-solving style to you. These self-assessments and the discussion in the rest of the chapter offer three basic lessons:

1. What feels "normal" to you may be different from what feels "normal" to others.

2. People whose norms differ from yours are not necessarily egotistical, insecure, or rude—they may just have different ideas and assumptions about what is appropriate behavior.

3. When working in a group setting, you may need to change your norms—in other words, change your normal patterns of talk or behavior—to do what is best for the group as a whole.

> **Note**
>
> You may find that *none* of the communication and interpersonal styles measured in the self-assessments characterize you—or that you have the characteristics of multiple norms. That's perfectly fine, and far more norms exist than this text could possibly cover. The purpose of this chapter is to expose you to some of the norms your *teammates* may exhibit and to provide you with strategies for interacting with people whose norms you may not share.

Table 22.1 provides information about some common norms and their pros and cons. It provides only a small sampling of the norms that sometimes lead to unproductive conflict in teams. You may find that several of these norms describe you—or that none of them describe you. Or, because most of these norms represent extremes, you may find that you fall somewhere in the middle of the spectrum. The goal here is to recognize that people can have some strong differences in their assumptions about what is appropriate and effective communication and teamwork.

Being aware of the norms in Table 22.1 can help you avoid thinking negatively about others. For instance, you might realize that competitive speakers are not deliberately being rude but are acting in ways that feel normal to them. Or you might realize that a self-deprecating speaker is not incompetent but is simply being modest. Understanding norms can also help you change your behavior to better fit in to certain social situations. For example, an American businessperson working in Japan, where a considerate conversational style is often the norm, might want to refrain from interrupting others and to avoid any behavior typically associated with a competitive conversational style.

Each item in the following assessment reflects something that a person might say or think. For each item, indicate how well this statement describes you **when you are interacting with teammates**. Use the following scale:

1 = never (not at all like me)

2 = rarely

3 = sometimes

4 = frequently

5 = always (very much describes me)

Discussion Style

1. When I get a good idea during a team meeting, I say it as soon as possible, even if I have to interrupt to do so.

2. I am careful to wait for my teammates to finish speaking before I jump into a team discussion.

3. My teammates sometimes accuse me of not listening.

4. I nod or agree with teammates while they are talking.

5. I hate feeling as though I have to wait my turn to talk during a team discussion.

6. If I keep getting interrupted during team meetings, I generally give up on trying to talk.

7. I talk over (talk at the same time as) teammates who are trying to speak.

8. I prefer to listen carefully to what my teammates have to say before I form my own opinion.

9. I enjoy challenging my teammates' ideas.

10. If I need to express criticism, I am always careful to avoid hurting my teammates' feelings.

11. When a teammate expresses a new idea, my first instinct is to point out the flaws.

12. When a teammate expresses a new idea, my first instinct is to ask questions.

13. I always say what's on my mind during team meetings.

14. I think it is rude when my teammates never stop to ask me about my opinion.

Add up your responses to the odd-numbered statements. If your score is greater than 25, you exhibit many characteristics of a **competitive discussion style**.

Add up your responses to the even-numbered statements. If your score is greater than 25, you exhibit many characteristics of a **highly considerate discussion style**.

Note: The self-assessments here focus on styles that sometimes come into conflict and are by no means comprehensive. You may find that you score low on both scales or that you exhibit some characteristics of both the competitive and highly considerate discussion styles. In that case, simply choose the description that seems to fit you the best.

Figure 22.1. Self-assessment of discussion style.

SELF-ASSESSMENT

Each item in the following assessment reflects something that a person might say or think. For each item, indicate how well this statement describes you **when you are interacting with teammates**. Use the following scale:

1 = never (not at all like me)

2 = rarely

3 = sometimes

4 = frequently

5 = always (very much describes me)

Presentation Style

1. I frequently express doubts about my skills, knowledge, or preparation to my teammates.

2. I usually assume that I am one of the least skilled people on a team.

3. I almost never let teammates know that I am having difficulty doing something.

4. I hate it when a teammate who knows less than I do questions my ideas.

5. When I make a mistake, I apologize profusely to teammates, even if the mistake is minor.

6. I often say things to my teammates to show that I don't think too highly of myself.

7. I would rather miss a deadline than admit to a teammate that I don't know how to do something.

8. If I think a project isn't challenging enough for me, I might slack off and let some of my teammates take over.

Add up your responses to statements 1, 2, 5, and 6. If your score is greater than 12, you exhibit characteristics of a **self-deprecating presentation style**.

Add up your responses to statements 3, 4, 7, and 8. If your score is greater than 12, you exhibit characteristics of a **self-promotional presentation style**.

Note: The self-assessments here focus on styles that sometimes come into conflict and are by no means comprehensive. You may find that you score low on both scales or that you exhibit some characteristics of both the self-deprecating and self-promotional presentation styles. In that case, simply choose the description that seems to fit you the best.

Figure 22.2. Self-assessment of presentation style.

Each item in the following assessment reflects something that a person might say or think. For each item, indicate how well this statement describes you **when you are interacting with teammates**. Use the following scale:

1 = never (not at all like me)

2 = rarely

3 = sometimes

4 = frequently

5 = always (very much describes me)

Problem-Solving Style

1. I prefer that the team think through an idea completely before we start working on it.

2. I quickly become impatient with long team deliberations.

3. I am always willing to consider new possibilities for solving a problem.

4. When my team is given a technical problem, I prefer that we begin figuring out the technical details as soon as possible.

5. When my team is given a technical problem, I prefer that we make sure we completely understand "the big picture" and end goals before we start thinking about the technical details.

6. I prefer that the team focus on getting things done as quickly as possible.

7. I think it is useful to spend time weighing the pros and cons of different ways to approach a problem before the team begins making any concrete plans.

8. Teams that spend a lot of time talking about ideas up front are just wasting time that could be used actually working on the project.

Add up your responses to the odd-numbered statements. If your score is greater than 13, you exhibit characteristics of a **holistic problem-solving style**.

Add up your responses to the even-numbered statements. If your score is greater than 13, you exhibit characteristics of an **action-oriented problem-solving style**.

Note: The self-assessments here focus on styles that sometimes come into conflict and are by no means comprehensive. You may find that you score low on both scales or that you exhibit some characteristics of both the holistic and action-oriented problem-solving styles. In that case, simply choose the description that seems to fit you the best.

Figure 22.3. Self-assessment of problem-solving style.

Table 22.1. Some communication norms and their pros and cons.

Area	Norm	Definition	Pros and Cons
Discussion Style	Competitive	Conversation is a miniature battle over ideas. Speakers tend to be passionate in supporting their ideas, and interruptions are frequent.	Those who hold this norm like the fast-paced conversation and the challenge of publicly defending ideas in the face of competition. However, those who don't share this norm perceive it as rude and disrespectful. Moreover, this norm works against constructive conflict because speakers are more concerned with defending their own ideas than with carefully listening to their teammates. Often, the most aggressive speaker rather than the best idea wins out.
	Highly considerate	Speakers acknowledge and support one another's contributions, and disagreements are often indirect. Interruptions are rare, and the conversation often pauses to allow new people to speak.	Those who hold this norm like the polite tone, concern for others, and equitable conversations that it fosters. However, those who don't share it find these conversations slow-moving and frustrating and sometimes think that highly considerate speakers have nothing important to say. Moreover, this norm sometimes privileges feelings and emotions over constructive criticism of ideas.
Presentation style	Self-promotional	Speakers aggressively display their own confidence and expertise, often criticizing others to make themselves look better.	This norm sometimes benefits people who may expect special treatment for their expertise but is generally harmful to the group dynamics. Self-promotional speakers tend to see asking for help as a weakness and to see criticism as a direct attack on themselves.
	Self-deprecating	Speakers display their modesty and talk about their own shortcomings.	Even though people (especially men) who engage in humorous self-deprecation may be perceived as likable and easy to get along with, this norm can make group members distrust the speaker's ability to do competent work. Sometimes, self-deprecating speakers are perceived as trying to get out of work.

Area	Norm	Definition	Pros and Cons
Problem-solving style	Action-oriented	People immediately jump into the details of a problem and start working on a solution right away.	This style is very effective for getting things done quickly, but sometimes groups waste time by working on solutions before they fully understand the problem.
	Holistic	People consider the entire problem as a whole and refrain from proposing solutions until the problem is completely understood.	This style generally helps groups propose better solutions because it ensures that they are solving the correct problem. However, the holistic problem-solving style requires more time. Moreover, action-oriented problem solvers sometimes find this style frustrating to work with.

Competitive versus Considerate Conversational Norms

Take a look at the following transcript. It shows the actual discussion of a student team and has not been edited for grammar or completeness. As you read, think about how you would characterize the discussion norms that these speakers seem to hold.

Mark: Okay. Here [are] my thoughts on organization. This is what I call "pre-applying." Stuff you want to have down before you apply.

Natalie: Before you graduate.

Mark: Yeah. And then the next section is applying. Then is the interview process, what to do, how to act. And then I thought maybe the last question would be "after the interview."

Keith: Okay, I'm not sure I buy into a pre-applying section like that. "Pre" implies a time issue, but these [are] done before you go. "Pre" is incorporating everything except the interview.

Mark: Okay, but I'm thinking about the process....

Keith: Yeah, but do you think that should be like the way to organize the paper? You see, pre-applying, that seems to incorporate everything to me. Maybe you could say, um, "Curriculum Requirements," "Deadlines." Something like that, you know....

Mark: No.

Keith: "Pre" is a meaningless title because it would be everything.

Mark: No, what…

Natalie: I think what Mark's saying…

Keith: I understand, but see, having it all under the title of "pre-applying" doesn't make sense.

Mark: When I think about applying, I'm thinking about, July first is when I turn in my materials.

Keith: I understand exactly what you're saying, but I don't understand why you need that under that title of "pre-applying."

Mark: I think it's a natural process.

Keith: I'm suggesting we reword that whole thing.

Natalie: Could we say "Things that should be done prior to…"?

Keith: Find some other way of wording it because the way it's worded right now doesn't make any sense at all.

Natalie: Okay, what I'm saying is we could have "Things that should be done prior to the application process" and then "Things that can be done during the process."

Keith: *(talking over Natalie)* We can stress…

Mark: *(talking at the same time as Keith)* But when I think "during"…

Mark and Keith both demonstrate a **competitive** conversational style in this exchange. They frequently interrupt each other (and Natalie) and often seem more concerned with making their own points than with listening to what the other has to say. Overall, Keith and Mark both tended to enjoy such exchanges, associating them with a high degree of involvement in the project. Many people find the back-and-forth of competitive conversations exciting and enjoy the challenge of scoring a point or winning others over to their side. In many ways, competitive conversations like this one resemble the types of debates you might see on TV programs such as *The O'Reilly Factor* or *Hardball with Chris Matthews*.

Unfortunately, although competitive conversations allow speakers to battle out ideas, speakers are not really involved in coming to a cooperative solution. For instance, in the preceding conversation, both Keith and Mark advocate for their own ideas without ensuring that they have heard the other's counterposition. Keith states that he understands Mark, but he fails to convince Mark of this. The conversation would have been far more productive if Keith had told Mark "I understand your position to be X" and had given Mark a chance to confirm or deny this understanding. This strategy would have given Mark an opportunity to clarify his reasoning; furthermore, it would have assured him that he could stop arguing for his position and would have allowed him to listen more productively to Keith's criticism.

Even worse, though, is that Natalie is having trouble entering the conversation. One of the problems with competitive conversational styles is that they are hierarchical: in other words, speakers who are perceived as having lower status on the team are more likely to be interrupted, ignored, or talked over. On this team, Natalie has consistently been less vocal than her teammates and less assertive when she does speak. As a consequence, her teammates have become accustomed to thinking of her as someone who does not have much to contribute—as someone with less influence than her teammates. Thus, even when she does speak, her teammates have a hard time hearing her: they talk over her and barely consider the suggestion she has made.

Natalie, of course, could be more assertive and speak more competitively, like her teammates. However, this tactic may be difficult for her: as someone out of place in competitive conversations, Natalie has probably been socialized to think of behaviors such as interrupting and talking over others as rude. Unless she has an exceptionally strong investment in the project, Natalie may prefer to stop participating rather than adopt a conversational norm that she finds offensive.

One of the biggest problems with competitive conversations is that they can shut down people who don't share this style and thus can exclude some speakers' ideas. Those who like competitive conversations may think that they are openly debating ideas, but in fact, they are likely hearing and discussing *fewer* ideas than they would if the team had adopted a more cooperative conversational style.

In contrast to competitive conversations, considerate conversations are characterized by a high degree of mutual support through questions and what is known as backchanneling: providing support through brief statements such as "yeah" and "uh-huh" or by nodding your head. As you read the following conversation excerpt of a team planning a Web site, note what specific strategies the speakers are using to create a considerate conversational environment:

> Josh: What we need to do at this point is figure out what resources we need to have ready so that when we sit down with Front Page, we know what we're going to put in the site.

> Rose: Oh, okay. Well, we can do that right now.

> Ming: Yeah.

> Stacy: Yeah, 'cause like whatever paperwork we need I can pick up this weekend, and then, if you want, we can distribute it out so we can all think of different ways to do it.

> Rose: Yeah.

Ming: You know, I was gonna ask…

Stacy: I can pick up all the paperwork Friday. *(to Ming)* Sorry.

Ming: I was gonna ask if she wanted it like the examples in the online book or like a corporate site. It's 30 pages long.

Stacy: I don't think we need to do all 30 pages.

Ming: That's what I was askin'.

Rose: Just do like a miniature version?

Stacy: Yeah.

Josh: Yeah.

Ming: So do we want it like the online one? Because I wasn't sure about that example.

Josh: I thought that's what she wanted.

Rose: Should we ask?

One of the biggest differences between this conversation and the competitive example is that Stacy *repairs her interruption* of Ming halfway through by turning to him and saying "sorry." This simple action gives Ming an opportunity to say what is on his mind. Other effective remarks for inviting silenced speakers to talk include "I'm sorry. What were you trying to say?" or "Ming, you were interrupted just a second ago. Did you have something else to add?"

Moreover, in this conversation, we see speakers *acknowledging ideas* by saying "yeah" and restating ideas rather than immediately tearing them down. We also see team members *asking questions* rather than always arguing for a particular point of view.

A considerate speaking style does not mean that people always have to agree with one another. In the following excerpt, note how Wes and Marissa are able to disagree even while maintaining a considerate communication style:

John: Well, it sounds like we were going to be addressing our proposal to oil companies, but now we're doing something else?

Wes: I was thinking environmental agencies.

Marissa: Do you think we could do both? We could do like, we want to propose this to the environmental place so we can go with them to the oil companies? So we can tell them what we want to say to the companies?

Wes: Yeah, that could work. (*pause*) But one thing that I was thinking, the proposal would be stronger if it was just one thing.

Marissa: I just don't want to lose that focus on the companies themselves.

John: So like make oil companies an indirect audience? A secondary audience?

Marissa: Yeah. (*to Wes*) You think it's too much to do both?

Wes: Yeah, kinda.

This group eventually ends up agreeing with Wes that the proposal would be stronger with a single, clearly defined audience. What is noteworthy here is that even though Wes and Marissa are disagreeing, they still display a considerate conversational style. Before pointing out problems with Marissa's idea, Wes acknowledges that "that could work." This acknowledgment, as well as John's later restatement of Marissa's idea, most likely helps Marissa accept Wes's criticism that she is proposing "too much." Moreover, Marissa "checks in" with Wes by restating his idea and asking if she has understood correctly. This restatement lets Wes know that he was heard and invites him to elaborate on what he thinks.

Competitive speakers often have difficulty providing positive acknowledgment to their teammates and may even feel that all the agreement and "checking in" in the preceding two conversations sound silly. However, to speakers who have more considerate conversational norms, such agreement is necessary to an effective group, and those who fail to provide it appear self-centered or egotistical.

Competitive speakers can adjust their conversational style, although they may find it frustrating to do so. In fact, Wes (in a later interview) explains how he deliberately curbed some of his competitive instincts:

> **Wes:** I wanted to say, "No, we can't do both!" That's not going to work. I mean, oil companies aren't gonna adopt solar energy unless they've gone insane! I wanted to say that. But I had to think of how to say it that didn't make her argument sound absurd because I didn't want to do that.

Later on in the interview, Wes further acknowledged that he was trying to avoid "winning" an argument just based on his conversational style:

> **Wes:** It's a bad habit I have, but when I want people to do something, I usually try to just keep talking until they finally agree with me. I was trying not to do that here, but it was frustrating. It was slow.

Wes's efforts to avoid making his teammates defensive seem to have paid off: at the end of this project, everyone on the team (including Wes) reported being highly satisfied with the way the group had worked together. Moreover, although Wes stated several times that he found the debate over their proposal's audience frustrating, his teammates found the discussion useful:

Interviewer: Do you think this discussion was a productive one?

John: Very.

Interviewer: Why's that?

John: Everybody's just like getting their ideas out and just trying to get a feel for what are we going to do. We figured out what we wanted to talk about in this conversation. So, yeah, it was a very productive day.

Even though considerate conversation styles generally are good support for constructive conflict, in some cases they can interfere with teamwork if team members feel that they always have to wait for an invitation to speak or are so concerned with preserving people's feelings that they hold back on ideas. The goal is to foster a group style that allows everyone to feel that he or she can contribute while still keeping the team focused on finding an effective solution.

How Can Competitive Speakers Adopt a More Considerate Style?

The following strategies—which are good strategies for any team to follow—help mitigate the silencing effects of competitive conversations:

- **Repeat back or restate ideas before disagreeing with them.**

- **Repair interruptions and other competitive behaviors.** Competitive speakers may find themselves unconsciously interrupting, raising their voices, or speaking over someone. When this happens, they (or anyone else on the team) can repair these actions by turning to the silenced person and saying "I'm sorry. You were saying?" or "David, you were interrupted just a second ago. Did you have something else to add?" or just "Sorry, I didn't mean to interrupt."

- **Check in with quiet speakers.** Every so often, the project manager or other team member should check in with anyone who has not spoken recently by saying "Do you have any thoughts?"

- **Pay attention to body language.** Watch the nonverbal behaviors of your teammates. If any of your teammates start to say something but stop, extend their arm or hand toward the center of the group, or lean far forward in their seat, they may be attempting to enter into the conversation. Whenever your teammates display these types of behaviors, invite them to speak by saying something like "Julie, you look like you have something to say."

- **Engage in uncritical brainstorming.** In uncritical brainstorming, teams set aside a limited period (say 10 minutes) during which no criticisms of ideas are allowed. Team members can build on one another's ideas and ask questions but not point out flaws. The goal of this brainstorming period is to get as many ideas as possible on the table and see what is good about these ideas before finding fault with them.

How Can Considerate Speakers Adjust to Competitive Conversations?

If you are a considerate speaker, you may have to deal with situations in which competitive speech is the norm. Rather than giving up on participating or becoming angry at your teammates, you can use the following strategies for getting your ideas across:

- **Learn how to prevent or forestall interruptions.** To stop a competitive speaker from interrupting, you can use gestures while speaking, such as extending your arm forward or holding up your hand like a stop sign. Such gestures tell others that you are not done yet and have more to say. Simple stock phrases, such as "I'm not finished yet" or "One minute please," can also be good ways to stop interruptions.

- **Speak within the first five minutes of a meeting.** Another nonaggressive strategy for dealing with competitive conversations is to get people accustomed to thinking of you as having something important to say. Louisa Ritter, Telecommunications Chief of Staff for a major investment firm, states, "The longer it goes without you saying something, the longer people are going to ignore you, and by the time you do speak up, people are just going to think you're peripheral to the meeting" (Commonwealthclub, 2003).

- **Find gentle ways to interrupt.** Ultimately, you may need to learn how to interrupt if you want to have any hope of getting your say in a competitive conversation. Strategies such as humor can help you. For instance, you might try raising your hand and waving it wildly both to make people laugh and to pause the conversation. You might also learn how to time your interruptions so that they do not seem rude. Cathy G. Lanier, President of Technology Solutions, Inc., states, "I'm an excellent interrupter…. I tend to go with the ebb and flow of meetings and am pretty good at timing my interruptions so they don't seem overly rude or pushy" (Sherman, 2005).

Self-Promoting versus Self-Deprecating Speech

Consider the following comments that students made in final interviews about their team experiences. What do you think about each speaker?

A: I found that [my team] kept looking toward me. Whenever we would get bogged down, when something wasn't right, it seemed to invariably come to me to be fixed.

B: Well, I handled all the, uh, you know, I handled all the Web site. Basically, I built the entire Web site myself…. I'm the type of person, whether I fully know how to understand and know how to do it or not, I'll figure it out. I'll go ahead and take it, take the ball and go with it.

C: To be honest with you, I realized that the scope of this project wasn't large enough for me, so I kind of slacked off on some little things.

D: I can usually go into a class and kind of tell who's, you know, who's gonna do well, who's not gonna do well. Umm, who's a little quicker. Those students, I've had some of them before in other classes, and they're kind of like the lower end of the curve.

E: Probably Stephen made the most valuable contribution 'cause he came up with the main idea, and I know that I would never have been able to come up with that.

F: I did learn quite a bit about computers, and I'm saying that only because I knew so little about that beforehand. But you know, I am learning. I'm having problems publishing, but I feel I have a grasp on them.

G: I kind of know how to do the Web site, but I still have to have people to help me. The directions Charlotte gave me are good, but when there wasn't a direction on how to fix it, when you have something wrong, I would go outside the group.

H: I mean, John and Neal are really, really good at writing reports. I would be at the bottom of that list because I'm, I'm not as good at, you know, putting things together. Umm, I feel, I feel confident in creating a report. I just think that they're better at it.

Comments A through D are examples of **self-promotional** speech, while comments E through H are examples of **self-deprecating** speech. Self-promotional speech is characterized by occasionally aggressive displays of confidence and criticism of others in order to make oneself look better. Self-deprecating speech is characterized by exaggerated displays of modesty and talking about one's own shortcomings. Both types of speech can cause major problems in groups.

Note how self-promotional talk led the speaker in comment C to see certain aspects of the project as beneath him and the speaker in comment D to view certain people as less worthy of respect. Self-promotional talk can also lead speakers to hoard certain parts of the project as their own and to exclude others from any input: this was the case with the speaker in comment B. Thus, self-promotional talk often leads to hierarchical teams in which some work is perceived as more valuable than other work and people at the top of the hierarchy can see themselves as immune to the criticisms and comments of others. This type of mind-set is so counterproductive that NASA engineers who were surveyed about problems with teams rated the statement "Some members believe that their technical status insulates their opinions from evaluation by other team members" as the number one behavior contributing to team problems (Nowaczyk, 1998).

In settings where self-promotional talk is the norm, people can be reluctant to admit weakness or ask one another for help. In student teams, this can lead to projects in which one student takes on too much but never lets the rest of the team know that the project is in danger until the end, when it is too late. In other settings, the consequences can be even higher. For instance, at one major oil company's offshore oil rigs, self-promotional norms that prized heroic accomplishments and disdained any show of weakness encouraged workers to hide mistakes; consequently, many systemic safety issues never came to light because workers did not feel comfortable discussing them. When this company purposefully tried to change the communication norms to develop an atmosphere in which workers felt comfortable productively discussing mistakes and learned to respond to criticism nondefensively, accidents were reduced by 84 percent, while productivity, efficiency, and reliability all increased (Ely & Meyerson, 2007).

Self-deprecating talk may not have such dire consequences, but it can hurt teammates' status on teams and can interfere with team productivity because it takes attention off the problem and puts it on the person and his or her abilities. This is perhaps most evident in comments E and H, in which the speakers talk excessively about how much more inferior their skills are than their teammates'. A teammate listening to this might question whether this person can be trusted with important work—and might even wonder if the speaker is indirectly asking to be given a free ride on the project. Creating this kind of doubt in your teammates' minds does nothing to help the project or yourself.

Even the other two self-deprecating comments (F and G) might make team members wonder whether the speaker is asking for reassurance—in other words, fishing for compliments. Many team members find such comments frustrating because they would rather spend their energy getting to work rather than trying to reassure and bolster the confidence of others.

Both self-promoting talk and self-deprecating talk interfere with team progress, and you should work to avoid both. Be honest about your shortcomings without focusing on them. For instance, if you are assigned a task that you are unfamiliar with, you can state, "I haven't done this before, but I'm looking forward to the challenge" or "I should be able to do that, but I want someone to look over my work just in case." Such statements suggest that you have confidence in yourself without overselling your abilities.

Action-Oriented versus Holistic Problem-Solving Styles

The following comments are by students who exhibit preferences for two different problem-solving styles:

> **Bill:** That whole first day was not productive at all. That was us spinning on our toes until the very end. The whole session was just kind of randomly hashing out what we were going to do and not actually getting anything done. That's the worst thing for me, when we just talk and talk and talk and nothing happens, you know. It's like just do it! I have nothing against going off and talking about stuff. But we didn't have time for that. We needed to start working because it was supposed to be a large-scale project and it was something

that was supposed to take the whole semester and it was something that we needed to start on.

Krista: I just don't like to just rush stuff. I don't like to just throw anything together, and that's what they were wanting to do. Like I said, the rest of the group was so determined to just get it done. I felt like I was the one who kept going "No, we need to go back because if we don't include everything in there he wants, he's gonna send it back. So regardless if you sit here trying to rush it, we're going to have to do it over anyway." I felt like all this was new to me, and I knew we had a time limit, but I wanted to learn too and not just do something.

Bill's comments show that he favors an **action-oriented** problem-solving approach, in which team members jump into the details of the problem and immediately start working on a solution. By contrast, Krista appears to favor a **holistic** problem-solving approach, in which team members begin by considering the entire problem as a whole and refrain from proposing solutions until the problem is completely understood. Action-oriented problem solvers tend to concentrate on solving one piece of the puzzle at a time, whereas holistic problem solvers make sure that the end goal is always in sight.

Those who favor an action-oriented problem-solving style frequently grow impatient with holistic problem solvers and see their slowness in getting started as reflecting insecurity with the details. Being an action-oriented problem solver, Bill expresses his frustration that the group is not getting anything done. Even though the team is at the start of a semester-long project, he wants to see the group take some action.

Those favoring holistic problem solving worry that the action-oriented approach will miss the big picture—for instance, by creating a product that works but that nobody wants to buy. Krista expresses this concern when she claims that her teammates are going to put together a project that the instructor will return and ask them to do over. She wants to ensure that the group understands the requirements and end goals before they begin putting the project together.

Action-oriented problem solvers tend to learn by tinkering and trying out different solutions. This approach works well on small problems but is often less suitable for large, complex problems that require the coordination of several people because the action-oriented approach can lose sight of the big picture. Holistic problem solvers often take longer to arrive at a solution because they spend more time planning up front before they tackle the details of a problem; however, they are more likely to get the correct solution once they get started.

How Can Our Team Balance Different Problem-Solving Styles?

Both the action-oriented and the holistic problem-solving styles are important and necessary on a smoothly functioning team. However, some types of problems are more appropriately addressed by one style than the other. Your team's goal should be to try to balance these styles. The following suggestions will help you use these styles strategically:

- **The best time for holistic problem solving is at the beginning of the project.** When the group is in the early stages of the project, particularly a large project, spend some time making sure that everyone shares the same goals and that the team explores all of its options. Action-oriented problem solvers simply need to be patient at this stage. If you are concerned about deadlines, you might sketch out a brief project schedule and calculate how much time the team can afford to spend on holistic problem solving. Most holistic problem solvers will be able to switch gears and jump into the details when they feel that the time has come.

- **Be patient and strategic.** A particular problem-solving orientation may be better suited to certain tasks than to others. For instance, the group may benefit if the project manager has a more holistic problem-solving style and those working on smaller parts of the project have a more action-oriented style. Remember that differences in problem-solving styles are just that—differences—and do not reflect a person's underlying ability.

- **Refer to the team charter or task schedule to resolve conflicts.** The first two items on your team charter (see Chapter 18, "Getting Started with the Team Charter") should refer to team goals. To remind action-oriented problem solvers of the ultimate goals of the project, holistic problem solvers can refer to the goals that the team agreed on at the outset of the project. Likewise, action-oriented problem solvers can refer to the task schedule to make sure that the project stays on schedule and doesn't get derailed by too many "big picture" conversations (especially when those conversations occur near the end of the project).

Gender and Communication Norms

As you read about the norms in Table 22.1, you may have thought that some of them were more characteristic of men and others more characteristic of women. Such observations may make you uncomfortable since they can lead to stereotyping. However, gender differences are worth discussing because gender influences not only how we act but also how we are perceived—and thinking about gender and communication can help us appreciate how difficult it can be to adapt to certain communication norms.

An easy way to see how gender socialization impacts communication norms is to look at body language. Take a moment to look around a classroom, lab, study area, or other public place. Can you identify differences in how men and women sit? Men typically take up more space when they sit by leaning back in their seats, sitting with legs stretched apart and extending their arms. By contrast, women tend to take up less room when they sit by sitting with knees touching and keeping their arms close to their bodies. Figure 22.4, taken from Team Video 3, illustrates some of these gender-typical differences in body language.

The men in this photograph occupy more physical space and are more likely to lean away from the group than does the one woman. Jamaal, in the foreground, leans back in his chair while extending his arm out to the group; Jim has his arm out to the side and leans slightly forward; Don places one foot across his knee (a position that men use far more frequently than do women, who are more likely to cross their legs at the knee). In contrast to the men, Tonya keeps her body close to her chair; her legs are close to each other, almost touching at the knees; and her arms are close to the center of her body. Even her hands are touching each other.

Of course, there is nothing right or wrong, or good or bad, about these different ways of sitting—but they do illustrate different norms, even different rules, governing men's and women's interpersonal behaviors. For example, if a woman sat like one of the men in the picture, she might be labeled as "unfeminine" for mimicking the body language of a male peer. Have you ever observed a woman behave in a way that you found unfeminine or a man behave in a way that you found unmanly? What specific behavior or action made you draw this conclusion? How would this behavior have appeared if someone of the opposite gender had done the exact same thing?

Figure 22.4. The effect of gender socialization on communication norms. Gender socialization appears to influence the ways in which we communicate with our body language.

Not only do men and women have different norms that govern what they consider acceptable interpersonal behavior, but there are also social rules that affect how others perceive them if they violate these norms. As a consequence, a woman who engages in behaviors typically associated with men may be perceived in much more unflattering ways than a man would be if he did the same thing. In fact, one recent study of negotiation behaviors tested this hypothesis by asking managers to look at videotapes of men and women, all of whom were following the same script, negotiate for a higher salary. The managers perceived the female negotiator as less likable and more difficult to work with than the male negotiator, despite the fact that both had uttered the same words and followed the same nonverbal communication cues (Bowles et al., 2007).

In other words, because of these social rules, women may not be able to figure out the best way to behave by observing men's behavior, and vice versa. Thus, women who find themselves in a competitive discussion (which tends to be a more masculine communication norm) may need to find nonaggressive ways to negotiate this conversational environment without necessarily imitating men's competitive strategies. Likewise, men may need to adapt to considerate conversational styles in ways that do not necessarily mimic "feminine" strategies.

Because the same behavior can be perceived differently depending on *who* is saying it, we can't always expect other people to adjust their communication styles to what we personally perceive as normal. Although all communication styles have pros and cons, some are more *exclusionary* than others in that not everybody is equally free to engage in these behaviors. Some communication styles will produce more negative social consequences for some groups than for others.

A number of researchers have studied the impact of gender and ethnicity on communication norms:

- Men are more likely than women to have competitive speaking norms and to self-promote (Ely & Meyerson, 2007; Fletcher, 1999; McIlwee & Robinson, 1992; Rudman, 1998; Tannen, 1990; West & Zimmerman, 1983; Wolfe & Powell, 2006).

- Women who self-promote are perceived more negatively than are men who self-promote (Bowles et al., 2007; Rudman, 1998).

- Women are more likely than men to use self-deprecating speech, a norm that is thought to hurt women in competitive workplaces (Ingram & Parker, 2002; Kitayama et al., 1997; Rudman, 1998; Tannen, 1990; Wolfe & Powell, 2006).

- African American women are less likely to be silenced by interruptions and other behaviors characteristic of competitive discussions than white women are (hooks, 1989; Kochman, 1981).

- Women are more likely to prefer online discussions (discussions that take place entirely via computer) than men are, although this preference seems to vary by ethnicity (Lind, 1999; Wolfe, 2000). Women in male-dominated teams report more satisfaction with online discussions than with face-to-face discussions (Lind, 1999), possibly because it is not possible to interrupt or talk over someone online.

- People from Asian cultures tend to favor considerate speaking norms; men who have been successful in American and European settings often have difficulty adjusting to professional environments in countries such as Japan (De Mente, 2002; Howden, 1994).

- People from the Northeast self-report more competitive communication behaviors than do people from the Midwest (Sigler, 2005).

- Men are slightly more likely than women to prefer action-oriented problem-solving styles, and women are slightly more likely to prefer holistic styles (Woodfield, 2000).

Inside Work: Exercises

1. Which of the communication or problem-solving styles discussed in this chapter do you tend to favor? Do you prefer the competitive speaking style or the considerate style? Are you a holistic or an action-oriented problem solver? Can you think of a time when your preferences for one style over another interfered with your ability to work productively on a team?

2. Have you ever engaged in either self-promotional or self-deprecating speech on a team? If you think back on it, how might you have spoken differently? How might this have changed the team's interactions?

3. Have you ever been on a team with someone who favored an extreme version of any of the styles discussed in this chapter? How did this person's style interfere with the team's progress? What might the team have done to minimize any negative effects that this style caused?

4. Working with a partner, go through all five *Team Writing* videos and answer the following questions for each video:

   a. Provide examples of both competitive and considerate behaviors in the video. Overall, would you describe this as a competitive or a considerate team? How might this communication style interfere with the team's success?

   b. Do you see any examples of someone being interrupted, silenced, or dismissed? What could team members have done to prevent these behaviors from occurring?

   c. Do you see any examples of self-promotional or self-deprecating behaviors? How do these behaviors seem to interfere with the team's progress?

5. Working with a partner, sit in and observe the meeting of another team in the class. Take notes on any behaviors—positive or negative—that you observe. At the end of the meeting, share notes with your partner and together type up a list of observations. Without naming names, describe the specific behaviors you observed, with quotes if possible. Share your observations with the other team.

Works Cited

Bowles, H. R., Babcock, L., & Lai, L. (2007). Social incentives for gender differences in the propensity to initiate negotiations: Sometimes it does hurt to ask. *Organizational Behavior and Human Decision Processes, 103*, 84–103.

Commonwealthclub. (2003). *Women in business: Lessons learned.* Retrieved August 13, 2008, from http://www.commonwealthclub.org/archive/03/03-08women-speech.html.

Cordero, R., DiTomaso, N., & Ferris, G. F. (1996). Gender and race/ethnic composition of technical work groups: Relationship to creative productivity and morale. *Journal of Engineering and Technology Management, 13*, 205–221.

De Mente, B. L. (2002). Sincerity, Japanese style. Excerpted from *Japanese etiquette & ethics in business.* Retrieved August 13, 2008, from http://www.apmforum.com/columns/boye49.htm.

Ely, R. J., & Meyerson, D. (2007). *Unmasking manly men: The organizational reconstruction of men's identity* (No. 07-054). Boston: Harvard Business School.

Fletcher, J. K. (1999). Disappearing acts: *Gender, power, and relational practice at work.* Cambridge, MA: MIT Press.

hooks, b. (1989). *Talking back: Thinking feminist, thinking black.* Boston: South End Press.

Howden, J. (1994). Competitive and collaborative communicative style: American men and women, American men and Japanese men. *Intercultural Communication Studies, 4*(1), 49–58.

Ingram, S., & Parker, A. (2002). Gender and modes of collaboration in an engineering classroom: A profile of two women on student teams. *Journal of Business and Technical Communication, 16*(1), 33–68.

Kim, H.-J. (2003). *A study of compliments across cultures.* Paper presented at the eighth annual meeting of the Pan-Pacific Association of Applied Linguistics. Retrieved August 1, 2008, from http://www.paaljapan.org/resources/proceedings/PAAL8/pdf/pdf015.pdf.

Kitayama, S., Markus, H. R., Matsumoto, H., & Norasakkunki, V. (1997). Individual and collective processes in the construction of the self: Self-enhancement in the United States and self-criticism in Japan. *Journal of Personality and Social Psychology, 72*(6), 1245–1267.

Kochman, T. (1981). *Black and white styles in conflict.* Chicago: University of Chicago Press.

Lind, M. R. (1999). The gender impact of temporary virtual work groups. *IEEE Transactions on Professional Communication, 42*(4), 276–285.

McIlwee, J. S., & Robinson, J. G. (1992). *Women in engineering: Gender, power, and workplace culture.* Albany: SUNY Press.

Nowaczyk, R. H. (1998). *Perceptions of engineers regarding successful engineering team design* (No. NASA/CF-1998-206917 ICASE Report No. 98-9). Hampton, VA: Institute for Computer Applications in Science and Engineering.

Rudman, L. (1998). Self-promotion as a risk factor for women: The costs and benefits of counterstereotypical impression management. *Journal of Personality and Social Psychology, 74*(3), 629–645.

Sherman, A. (2005). Speak up: Is interrupting a good business tactic or just plain rude? *Entrepreneur.* Retrieved October 7, 2008, from http://findarticles.com/p/articles/mi_m0DTI/is_/ai_n15777261.

Sigler, K. A. (2005). *A regional analysis of assertiveness.* Paper presented at the annual meeting of the International Communication Association. Retrieved June 27, 2008, from http://www.allacademic.com/meta/p14806_index.html.

Tannen, D. (1990). *You just don't understand: Women and men in conversation.* New York: HarperCollins.

West, C., & Zimmerman, D. H. (1983). Small insults: A study of interruptions in cross-sex conversations between unacquainted persons. In B. Throne, C. Kramarae, & N. Henley (Eds.), *Language, gender, and society* (pp. 103–118). Rowley, MA: Newbury House.

Wolfe, J. (2000). Gender, ethnicity, and classroom discourse: Communication patterns of Hispanic and white students in networked classrooms. *Written Communication, 17*(4), 491–519.

Wolfe, J., & Powell, E. (2006). Gender and expressions of dissatisfaction: A study of complaining in mixed-gendered student work groups. *Women and Language, 29*(2), 13–21.

Woodfield, R. (2000). *Women, work, and computing.* Cambridge: Cambridge University Press.

Chapter 23 Troubleshooting Team Problems

n my research on teamwork, more than half of the student teams I observed ran into at least one major breakdown in the course of their project. Although following the advice in this book will help your team avoid many of these breakdowns, problems undoubtedly will still occur. This chapter summarizes some of the problems that your team might encounter and provides advice and strategies for handling these problems at the outset.

Unfortunately, many problems that arise in student teams are never addressed—or are mentioned only at the end of the project, when it may be too late. To help you address problems early, this chapter provides many examples of how you can phrase uncomfortable requests to teammates and some example e-mails you might use.

Problems with Showing Up and Turning in Work

As the final deadline for his project approaches, Chad writes about the problems his group is experiencing:

> Jessica and Dave have not both shown up to class on the same day, much less on time, within the last two weeks. I am beginning to feel like a babysitter. I also feel like the weight of work has shifted onto me. Our presentation is only five days away. Dave is trying to work on a new survey, but this time for professors. Jessica doesn't have a freakin' clue what is going on. This has not been a fun week.

Resa expresses a slightly different problem at the end of her project:

> My biggest complaint is with Gene. All of the reprocessed information that he brought to class was not usable. I think I spent more time making his contributions fit than he spent doing it the first time. I tried to get his input, but it took so long to get responses out of him and then they were worthless.... I really do feel that the project they are taking credit for is about 90 percent mine.

Chapter 23, "Troubleshooting Team Problems" from *Team Writing: A Guide to Working in Groups* by Joanna Wolfe, pp. 104–124 (Chapter 8). Copyright © 2010 by Bedford/St. Martin's.

Teams should never allow problems to go on as long as Chad and Resa did. Creating a clear task schedule and having an effective project manager are the best ways to prevent the problems they experienced; nonetheless, even with these in place, you may still have problems with "slacker" (or just incompetent) teammates. This chapter presents some strategies you can use to handle specific problems with teammates who slack off.

Problem: A Teammate Misses a Meeting

Everybody has emergencies or illnesses (or forgetfulness) that may result in missing a meeting. If any team members miss a meeting, they should contact the project manager as soon as possible to explain their absence and to ask what they missed. If they don't contact the team, the project manager can send a friendly reminder (see Figure 23.1).

If a team member routinely misses meetings, you need to take some action, such as assigning this person some extra work (see Figure 23.2). For instance, you might assign him or her a clerical task that others don't want to do. However, don't use this tactic if the team member has also missed deadlines—assigning additional work to a person who has proved to be untrustworthy may put the group even further behind. The following section outlines how to proceed if a team member misses deadlines.

TO: Jessica

FR: Chad

Subject: Today's meeting

Jessica:

We missed you at today's meeting at noon. I hope everything is okay. I've attached our minutes here. When you get a chance, could you contact me so that I can fill you in on what we did? Be sure to look at the task schedule, too, because we all have deadlines coming up.

Chad

Figure 23.1. Friendly reminder after a missed meeting.

TO: Jessica

FR: Chad

Subject: Today's meeting and revised task schedule

Jessica:

Today was the third team meeting that you missed. To balance out the workload (since everyone is expected to attend meetings), today we decided to update the task schedule and assign you to write the transmittal letter and make photocopies for the final presentation. I've e-mailed Prof. Williams the updated task schedule and task assignment worksheet with a note that your extra workload is due to missed meetings. Please let me know if you have any concerns. I've attached the revised task schedule.

Chad

Figure 23.2. E-mail after a series of missed meetings. The tone is matter-of-fact, and the wording makes it clear that the project manager is implementing the group decision. However, don't use this tactic for a team member who has also missed deadlines—assigning additional work to a person who has proved to be untrustworthy may put the group even further behind.

Problem: A Teammate Misses a Deadline

Failure to meet deadlines—a common problem for teams—is often caused by a team's failure to maintain an up-to-date task schedule. As you learned in Chapter 19, "Getting Started with the Task Schedule," the most important thing you can do to ensure that a team project runs smoothly is to maintain and publicize the task schedule. However, even with a task schedule, team members will sometimes miss deadlines—they might forget about due dates, or run into personal problems, or find that the work took longer than they anticipated. A gentle reminder is appropriate in these cases. In Figure 23.3, note how the presence of a team charter makes Jason's task easier—he simply has to remind his teammate of the consequences that everyone (including Brittany) agreed on at the beginning of the project.

The team charter should specify how long the team should wait before enforcing the consequences of a missed deadline. If at the end of this time period the team member still has not turned in his or her work (or has turned in very incomplete work), you should notify the instructor. When you do so, you don't have to point fingers; instead, just describe the situation as objectively as possible (see Figure 23.4).

TO: Brittany

FR: Jason

Subject: Sketches

Dear Brittany:

Just a reminder that your sketches were due yesterday morning. Please e-mail them as soon as possible. Remember that we agreed in our team charter that the project manager would e-mail the instructor if anything was more than 48 hours late (which would be Wednesday a.m.). If you are having some sort of personal emergency that will prevent you from doing this work, please let me know and I'll consult with the others.

Thanks,

Jason

Figure 23.3. A gentle reminder that a deadline has passed. Without making any accusations, this e-mail matter-of-factly reminds the team member of the consequences for late work.

TO: Professor Williams

FR: Jason

Subject: Problem with team deadlines

Dear Professor Williams:

My team is requesting your advice/help on dealing with a missed deadline. The attached task schedule shows that the initial sketches for our design were due on March 5. I have sent two reminders to Brittany (the person responsible), who said she had a cold but would get them to us by this morning. However, we still have not received the sketches, which are now almost three days late. As you know, the first draft of the project is due on Friday, and we don't quite know how to proceed. Any suggestions you have would be greatly appreciated.

Thanks,

Jason, Project Manager

Figure 23.4. E-mail to an instructor for a missed deadline.

Students often feel that informing the instructor of problems is "tattling" on their teammates. However, you need to think ahead to the workplace, where a team that doesn't report problems to a supervisor will face severe reprimands. Your note to the instructor doesn't need to be accusatory—simply state the facts. Your instructor may respond by sending a strong reminder, removing the offending person from the team and giving the team a new charge or new deadlines, or reducing the offending person's contribution grade.

Some situations may warrant special consideration. For example, a teammate may have a serious medical or personal emergency that prevents him or her from doing the work. In these exceptional cases, the project manager may want to consult with the rest of the team, suggesting a way to revise the task schedule so that another team member takes over this person's deadline—with the understanding that the incapacitated team member will do additional work at the end of the project. Before you do this, however, make sure that the excuse is valid: you don't want to assign an untrustworthy team member too much work at the end of the project, when it can be difficult for the team to recover.

Problem: A Teammate Turns in Incomplete Work

Sometimes, a teammate will meet a deadline but will turn in work that is substantially incomplete. To prevent this problem, the project manager should immediately skim all work that is turned in to ensure that all the required parts are included. If anything is missing, the project manager should immediately e-mail the team member, specifying which parts are missing and giving him or her a deadline for turning in a complete draft. If a complete version is not turned in by the deadline, the project manager should notify the instructor. The next section contains sample e-mails for dealing with this situation.

Problem: A Teammate Turns in Poor-Quality Work

This problem is a little more difficult to handle than the previous two because the difference between an acceptable and an unacceptable draft is often a gray area that requires a judgment call.

When a team member turns in work that the project manager feels is substantially below the group's quality standards, the project manager should contact the other team members privately and ask if anyone else agrees with this assessment. If at least one other person agrees that the team can't use the work, the project manager should e-mail the teammate who turned in the work and ask for a revision. Figure 23.5 illustrates a request for a revised draft. The request for revision should

- briefly explain why the work was considered substandard or unusable
- provide specific suggestions about resources that the teammate can consult for help
- include a specific deadline for turning in the revised work
- ask the teammate to let the project manager know immediately if he or she will not be able to make the deadline or meet the requests

---

TO: Gene

FR: Resa

Subject: Draft of quantitative sections

Dear Gene:

Thanks for turning in your draft on time. I've looked it over and discussed it with some of the other team members, and we think that this is not what Professor Williams is looking for. Specifically:

- The graphs don't meet the guidelines Professor Williams discussed in the "Preparing Effective Charts and Tables" lecture two weeks ago. He put his PowerPoint slides on the course Web site if you need to review them. In particular, be sure to include clear captions since he really emphasized this.

- We were confused on the differences between graphs 2, 3, and 4. Captions would really help, but a different organization might also be useful. I think it makes much more sense to include the overview graph before breaking down the results by product type. This helps the audience see the big picture first before getting into the details and would clarify how the graphs differ.

- The information on comparing costs is missing. Ashley sent this information in an e-mail last week.

- We noticed a lot of grammatical errors and typos. I know this is a draft, but it would really help if you could fix some of this before turning it in.

Thanks for taking these suggestions into consideration. Do you think you can get us a revised draft by Thursday night? Let me know ASAP if you can't make that deadline. I'll update the task schedule with this new information.

Resa, Project Manager

Figure 23.5. Request for revision. Note the detailed suggestions and the specific deadline. Such a request for revision should be made when a team member turns in work that the team finds unacceptable.

Problem: A Teammate Disappears Completely

The sooner you take action when a teammate seems to have disappeared, the less likely it is that this situation will turn into a serious problem. If you believe that someone in your group has dropped out of the picture entirely, you should notify your instructor (see Figure 23.6).

TO: Professor Williams

FR: Audrey

Subject: Missing teammate

Dear Professor Williams:

Mike has missed the last three team meetings and has not responded to any of our e-mails. He hasn't missed any deadlines yet, but we are worried that he will, or that he won't understand what to do because he's missed so many meetings. We are wondering how you would like us to proceed.

If we don't hear from you by Friday (our next meeting), we'll go ahead and update the task schedule assuming that Mike is no longer part of the team. That way we won't get behind on the project. Also, we were wondering if you had any instructions or new guidelines for us now that it looks like we are becoming a three-person team.

Thanks for your help.

Audrey, Project Manager

Figure 23.6. E-mail notifying an instructor that a teammate is missing.

Problems with Personal Interactions

Midway through his project, Brian expresses some concerns about his teammates:

> Things are not going well on our team. I have heard Daniel talk about how he could be writing things so much better than Bethany and about how she is just "getting the job done." Daniel doesn't seem to trust anybody except himself. Bethany is not completely innocent either. If you listen, you'll notice that she basically shoots down most of his ideas or makes fun of them.

Jessica has more pointed things to say about one of her teammates:

> I just didn't, I didn't think that my judgment was respected by Josh at all. He never listened to anything I had to say. I didn't think that he saw me as a person in the group. He saw me as a, a female or something.... And I just cannot cope with somebody like that.

Teams often have problems with interpersonal conflict because teammates just don't seem to get along. This section provides advice for handling situations in which low trust or high resentment is interfering with group progress.

Problem: My Team Doesn't Trust Me to Do Good Work

Teammates may have a number of reasons for not trusting one another to do good work. Sometimes, team members may behave in ways that make others question their competence. At other times, team members may have prejudices against certain groups or particular people. Before you assume that your team is prejudiced against you, make sure that you are not engaging in some behavior that makes them question whether you are capable of doing good work.

The following list describes behaviors that can make your team lose trust in you and provides some ways to regain respect within your team:

Are you failing to submit quality work on time? If you miss a deadline or turn in poor-quality work, your teammates may distrust your ability to do good work: you have already let them down once, and they have reason to worry that you may do it again. If your team has lost trust in you, you need to work extra hard to regain that trust. Some ways to regain trust are:

- **Turn work in early.**
- **Ask questions.** You may think that asking questions would make teammates worry about your competence, but it can often have the opposite effect. When you ask questions, your teammates know that you are working on the problem; if you are asking relevant questions, they know that you are on the right track and will likely meet deadlines. *You should never turn in work late because you are unsure about what to do.* This will ensure that your work not only is late but also may be of poor quality: the worst of both worlds. Instead, ask questions early so that you can get the help you need. If you are uncomfortable asking your team for help, make an appointment with your instructor for individual help on the task (this is what instructors are for) or seek an on-campus tutoring resource. Many schools have writing centers, where you can meet with a tutor to go over writing problems, and computer resource centers, where you can go for assistance on technical matters. In fact, many writing centers can also provide advice on preparing Web sites, PowerPoint presentations, or multimodal projects—ask when you call for an appointment.

Are you being self-deprecating or talking too much about your shortcomings? If you are always talking about how little you know, your lack of skills, how you struggle with grades, your incompetence with computers, or how smart others are in comparison to you, your teammates may believe this talk and be hesitant to trust you with major work. This is particularly the case in masculine environments in which self-promotion may be part of the culture. (See Chapter 22, "Communication Styles and Team Diversity," for more on the problems of both self-promoting and self-deprecating speech.) You don't have to talk about how great you are, but nor should you advertise your shortcomings. If you realize that your teammates have come to distrust you because you have been self-deprecating, you can:

• **Explain that you often sell yourself short and ask for more work.** Let your teammates know that even though you sometimes belittle your abilities, you still want to be challenged. Ask to be assigned additional or more challenging tasks, and offer to complete the work early so that the team doesn't have to worry about being stuck with low-quality work.

Do you appear confused or disengaged in team meetings? Take a look at Team Video 2: Shelly, Will, and Ben. When Ben viewed this video in his final team meeting, he was shocked to see how disengaged he was from the group. He said that he gave the appearance that he didn't care about the project. Judging from this behavior, Ben's teammates would have been justified in wondering whether they could trust him. If you are worried that you may be giving the wrong impression during team meetings, you can:

• **Review the task schedule and read your e-mail before the meeting.** Make sure that you know what the team is doing before you go to the meeting.

• **Start the meeting by saying something.** Show the team that you have something to say by speaking early. Ask a question or make a comment about the task schedule or about a recent e-mail that was sent. If someone has asked for feedback on a draft, make sure that you have something to say (see Chapter 21, "Revising with Others").

• **Sit forward, look up, and make eye contact.** Use body language to show that you are engaged.

Sometimes, however, your teammates may be prejudiced against you for no reason. If you believe that your teammates are reluctant to assign you challenging work because their prejudice makes them distrust your ability to do high-quality work, you can confront this distrust proactively by saying, "You don't seem to have confidence in me. I would like to take on task X. I can do it before the deadline so that I have plenty of time to redo it if the team is unhappy," or "I would like to take on task X. I promise to check with the teaching assistant [or run it past the instructor, or go to the writing center] before turning it in to the team." Such an approach lets your teammates know that you sense their prejudice but are going to turn in high-quality work anyway.

Problem: My Team Isn't Listening to Me—or Is Taking a Direction I Disagree With

Even if your teammates trust you to do good work, you may occasionally have trouble getting your ideas on the table. When team discussions are competitive, speakers with a considerate speaking norm often have difficulty making themselves heard (see Chapter 22, "Communication Styles and Team Diversity").

If you have difficulty getting your teammates to listen to you, try the following strategies:

Learn how to enter competitive conversations. To increase the likelihood that your team will listen to you in face-to-face meetings, try the following strategies:

- **Speak up early in meetings**. Be one of the first people to speak so that your teammates will get used to thinking of you as someone who has something to contribute.

- **Show that you are prepared**. Before the meeting, read all relevant information, check your e-mail, and become familiar with the task schedule. Begin the meeting by saying that you have reviewed all the materials and have some suggestions.

- **Develop strategies for dealing with interruptions**. If you get cut off when you start to speak, hold up your hand like a stop sign or say "Just a minute, I'm not done yet." (See Chapter 22, "Communication Styles and Team Diversity," for more strategies for dealing with interruptions.)

Move the conversation to writing. If you are not an assertive speaker, you might have greater success making yourself heard in writing than in a face-to-face conversation. You can't get interrupted in an e-mail. Moreover, e-mailing your thoughts gives you a chance to state your ideas without the pressure and competition of a face-to-face meeting. You may want to begin the next meeting by reminding teammates of your e-mail and summarizing your main points. Figure 23.7 illustrates how a team member moves the conversation to writing.

Prepare an alternate draft. Because it can be time-consuming, this strategy is probably a last resort. However, if you strongly disagree with what your team is doing, you can prepare another draft (or partial draft) of the document and ask an objective outsider (such as your instructor) to comment on both versions. Don't tell this person which draft is yours. Also, keep your request neutral: simply ask this person to comment on which draft he or she feels is better. Figure 23.8 illustrates this strategy.

TO: Keith, Mark

FR: Natalie

Subject: Another option for organizing

Hey all:

I've been thinking over the discussion we had in class this morning. If I understand correctly, Mark wanted to make clear that students have to do many things before they apply, but Keith was concerned that a heading for "pre-applying" would be too big and that just about everything we wanted to talk about would end up under this heading. I was thinking that a good compromise might be to try the following organization/headings:

1. Ongoing: What should I do before my senior year?

Under this heading, we could list things like volunteering or developing a relationship with a professor.

2. The application process: What do I need to do to put my application together?

Here would go the nitty-gritty details like asking for recommendations and getting transcripts. This would be the longest section.

3. After the application is in: What can I do to prepare for the interview?

Here we can talk about the interview process.

I think this organization addresses both Keith's and Mark's concerns. Also, I want to make a case for including questions in the headings. This structure makes the document reader-friendly and shows students exactly what to expect in each section. A lot of FAQs are organized this way (and really what we're doing is preparing an FAQ of questions about the application process), so people are already familiar with the question-heading format.

Sorry I didn't bring this up in class today. Sometimes, I have trouble thinking on my feet—but I do have strong ideas about things, even if I have trouble getting them out!

If you guys like this organization, maybe Mark could send me what he wrote in class today, and I could move some things around and fill in some blanks. That way we'll have more to work with when we meet again and can use our time more efficiently. Also, we might want to assign sections to people and then meet to discuss them rather than try to do everything together in class. I think I might be able to contribute more that way, and we'd use our group time more efficiently.

Thanks,

Natalie

Figure 23.7. E-mail that moves the conversation to writing. Natalie uses this e-mail to suggest a specific change to the group document as well as changes in how the group works. In addition, she clarifies that she is engaged in the group, even if she is quiet during meetings. Natalie keeps her tone positive by focusing on what will be best for the group. She provides a rationale for all of her suggestions and avoids any wording that might seem accusatory.

TO: Joe, Megan

FR: Jayme

Subject: Our Web site

Joe, Megan:

We were having some disagreement over the layout of our Web site yesterday. Rather than continue to hash it out in person, I went ahead and took the liberty of preparing a version that I thought might be an improvement on the good work Joe has already done. I was thinking that when we meet tomorrow, we might ask Prof. Williams or some of the students in another group to say which of the versions they like better—or what features they like from each of these. I promise to drop my ideas if they don't like my design. I'd just like to get another opinion before we go any further. And Joe, I really appreciate what you've done for the group, even if I sometimes have suggestions for improvement!

Thanks,

Jayme

Figure 23.8. E-mail suggesting that the team consider an alternate draft. Jayme is careful to acknowledge that sometimes people just disagree, and she promises to drop her objections if the outside opinion doesn't support her. This strategy can be an excellent, neutral way to resolve disagreements.

Problem: Other Team Members Are Not Committed to a High-Quality Product

Sometimes, your teammates may not be committed to producing high-quality work. However, if your group has prepared a team charter, you may be able to persuade your teammates to make changes by appealing to the goals and criteria the team agreed on at the start of the project. Base your request for changes closely on the language used in the team charter.

If the team still seems unmotivated to do high-quality work, you might ask your instructor or another knowledgeable outsider to comment on the work done so far. These comments may motivate team members to increase their efforts on the project. Or you might ask your instructor to share his or her grading rubric (a list of the criteria with which the project will be evaluated). Using this rubric, go over the project and point out specific areas where you think the team is failing to meet expectations.

Problem: My Teammates Do and Say Things I Find Disturbing or Demeaning

Some situations are simply intolerable. If, for instance, a team member makes sexist or racist comments, you should report these to your instructor or (if you feel uncomfortable talking to the instructor) to an adviser or a faculty member of a group such as the Society for Women Engineers. These authority figures can advise you on how to handle the situation. Comments do not need to be directed to anyone in the group (or anyone in particular) to be offensive. Even generalized comments about sex or race can make teamwork uncomfortable—even when they're not meant to be taken personally.

If a teammate makes romantic advances or personal comments, you can tell the project manager privately that you feel uncomfortable with this person; you can also request that the task schedule be changed to limit your contact. It is inappropriate for someone to ask a teammate out on a date while the project is ongoing—such personal issues should wait until the project is finished. If the person making you uncomfortable is the project manager, talk to the instructor or ask another team member to intervene on your behalf. Keep in mind that in the workplace, such behavior can lead to harassment suits or worse; therefore, students need to learn what is inappropriate while they are still in school.

Other problems may be more difficult to resolve, especially when it is hard to determine whether a teammate's comments and behavior are based on prejudice, personal dislike, or some other factor. If no outright sexist or racist behavior or harassment is going on, try to resolve the problem through other strategies. To find strategies that might improve your situation, review the sections on how to deal with lack of trust or failure to listen or some of the following sections on revision.

Problem: My Teammates Criticize My Work Excessively

Sometimes, team members may be excessively harsh on someone else on the team in order to avoid work or to keep their own work out of the spotlight. If this appears to be the case, talk to the project manager about updating the task schedule and rebalancing the workload. If you feel that your teammates are using criticism to try to get you to do what should be their work, you might suggest that they be responsible for making revisions.

However, before you take any action, be sure that you are not responding defensively to justifiable and productive criticism. Allow yourself a cooling-off period (24 hours if possible) before taking any action. Then return to the criticism to see whether it is justified. Perhaps your teammate has pointed out a legitimate problem but has suggested an incorrect solution—or has misidentified the problem. Take a critical look at your writing and see if something needs to be changed, even if it's not exactly what your teammate pointed out. If, ultimately, you feel that a teammate is treating you unfairly, ask someone else on the team whether he or she has also noted this behavior. This person may be able to help you find a solution.

Problems with Revision

Erin describes in her final interview how a teammate resisted any revisions that other team members wanted to implement:

> Well, Jin did the first draft of the Web site, and she said we could revise it, but then anytime we wanted to do something different, it was "No, don't do that, you can't do that," that sort of thing. And I remember it was funny because initially she told a story about how when she was in preschool, a little boy was sitting next to her coloring a picture, and she grabbed the picture from him and said, "I'll do it for you. It will be better this way." She told that story, and it kind of fit into the project.

Ben, meanwhile, had the opposite problem with his team:

> And I was disappointed. I thought we'd get a chance to improve, but everybody was just like "yeah, yeah, that's good." So there was no motivation to revise.

Teams often run into conflict when they get into the nitty-gritty details of making revisions. This section describes strategies for handling those who either don't want to listen to their teammates' suggestions for revisions or don't feel comfortable suggesting revisions to their peers' work.

Problem: Team Members Are Not Open to Revisions to Their Work—or Team Members Ignore the Suggestions I Make for Revision

---

Sometimes, you may suggest revisions to material that a teammate has prepared, only to have these suggestions ignored or dismissed. If a teammate ignores your suggestions or just acts as if your feedback doesn't exist, first you need to find out *why* your suggestions were ignored. A teammate might ignore your suggestions because he or she (1) agrees that the suggestions would improve the work but doesn't feel that they are worth the time or effort to implement, (2) disagrees with the suggestions, or (3) overlooked, missed, or forgot about the suggestions. If you want to find out which of these three reasons applies, send a simple "reminder" e-mail to your teammate (see Figure 23.9), with a copy to other team members if necessary.

TO: Jin

FR: Thomas

CC: Josh, Eli

Subject: Revisions to results section

Dear Jin:

I sent some suggestions for the results section last week, but in the revised draft I saw that none of my suggestions were implemented. In case you didn't receive them, I'm attaching them to this e-mail. If you think they're off-base, please let me know.

Josh, could you add a discussion of these revision suggestions to our next team meeting? In our team charter, we said that we would follow all the guidelines for presenting results that Professor Williams gave us. Although I think Jin's draft is a good start, I don't think it contains everything that Professor Williams wants.

Thanks,

Thomas

Figure 23.9. E-mail reminding a teammate about suggestions for revision. Thomas acknowledges the possibility that his teammate didn't receive his earlier suggestions. By asking the project manager to put his revisions on the agenda, Thomas also puts subtle pressure on the team to at least *consider* his suggestions. In addition, he appeals to the team charter to support his request that the team consider his ideas.

If your teammate agrees with the suggestions but doesn't want to implement them, ask the team to discuss whether the suggestions are worth implementing. To make sure that the ideas are discussed, ask the project manager to put this item on the agenda for a future meeting, or ask team members to comment on your suggestions via e-mail. If the changes will be time-consuming, the team may need to consider updating the task schedule and redistributing the workload.

If your team agrees with your suggested revisions but decides that they are not worth the time to implement, you may need to take on additional work to ensure that the project is done right. However, make sure that the project manager updates the task schedule to show the extra work you have done.

If the team disagrees with your suggestions and you feel they are worth pursuing, refer to the section "My Team Isn't Listening to Me—or Is Taking a Direction I Disagree With." In this situation, you might want to create an alternate draft and ask the instructor or someone else to make a judgment call (see Figure 23.8).

Problem: My Team Is Destroying My Work

Occasionally, you may hand off a document to a teammate, only to have that person make radical revisions that you disagree with. In this situation, using Track Changes or another software tool that keeps a history of revisions can be quite useful because everyone can go back and recover material that may have been lost during another person's revisions (see Chapter 21, "Revising with Others").

If you feel that your teammates' revisions *weaken* rather than improve your work, state the reasons for your position and ask the team to reconsider (see Figure 23.10).

You should always feel free to ask teammates to reconsider revisions they have made to your work, but sometimes you need to accede to the group and follow the team's decision. To be sure that you are not just being defensive about your own work, wait 24 hours before responding to the revisions. Then, before you respond, read the revisions again and see whether they do in fact improve the document.

TO: Rene

FR: Gene

CC: Brittany

Subject: Revisions to proposal

Dear Rene:

I just looked over the revisions you made to my draft—I definitely think there are some good changes in here that improve the proposal. However, I noticed that you changed all of the headings from short sentences to single words or phrases. I'd like to offer two reasons for turning them back into sentences:

1. The sentence headings help readers skim the document. That way, if they just read the headings, they'll get an idea of what our proposal is about without having to read any of the details.

2. One of the examples Professor Powell showed us in class had sentence headings. Of all the examples, I thought that one was the best organized, and she seemed to like it too.

Let me know what you think. Maybe Brittany could also comment on which style she prefers?

Thanks! I'll see you in class.

Gene

Figure 23.10. E-mail asking the team to reconsider some revisions. Gene is careful to praise Rene's revisions before objecting to some of them. He provides clear, reader-based reasons for asking the team to reconsider these revisions.

If the team reaches an impasse and cannot agree on revisions to a document, a good strategy is to ask an outsider (such as an instructor or another member of the class) to look over the different versions and comment on which version he or she prefers. The team should agree in advance to abide by that person's decision.

Problem: Team Members Are Not Giving Adequate Feedback

If a teammate has been assigned to provide suggestions on (or make revisions to) your work and simply corrects a few typos or says that it "looks good," you need to encourage your teammate to give more thorough feedback. In such cases, you can try to obtain feedback by asking some specific questions, as shown in Figure 23.11.

TO: Carlos

FR: Marissa

CC: Josh

Subject: Feedback

Dear Carlos:

I just looked over the suggestions you made to my draft. I'll definitely make the corrections you pointed out, but there are a few "big issues" I was worried about that I was hoping you could comment on.

1. I was wondering if you could double-check the graphs I've provided and make sure that I copied all the numbers correctly. Have I forgotten anything on the axis labels? Do you think that a different graph format might be a better representation? Prof. Williams made a really big deal about graphs in class lectures, so I want to make sure they're okay.

2. Right now I've presented speed first (since it's the biggest difference) and then accuracy, but I was wondering if accuracy should go first because it's more important than speed. What do you think?

3. Could you take another look at the assignment sheet and make sure that we haven't left anything off?

Thanks for taking another look at this. I want to make sure we get the benefits of a team project by having as many "eyes" critique this as possible.

Thanks,

Marissa

Figure 23.11. E-mail requesting more thorough feedback. Marissa asks her teammate to comment on several specific questions. Her e-mail focuses on what she would like to happen in the future rather than on what went wrong in the past.

Even with a reminder and another invitation to provide feedback, some teammates may neglect this duty. If so, you may want to contact the project manager and ask that another teammate (or the project manager) be assigned to read and comment on the draft. Make sure that the task schedule gets updated so that this person receives credit for the additional work he or she has done.

Problem: I'm Not Sure How to Give Good Feedback to Team Members

Giving feedback to others can be unnerving—especially if you are worried that your writing skills may not be as good as theirs. Using Track Changes or another software tool that records a history of revisions can be very useful because your teammates can easily go back and recover the original document if they disagree with your revisions (see Chapter 21, "Revising with Others").

Even if you are unsure of your writing abilities, you can take a few steps to ensure that you give good-quality feedback:

- Read the assignment sheet and note *everything* that needs to appear in your document. Then review the document carefully and make sure that nothing has been left out.

- Try to obtain a copy of the grading rubric (a sheet that lists the evaluation criteria) that your instructor will be using to evaluate the project, and note any areas where you think the project might be lacking. Even if you are not sure how to fix these deficiencies, simply pointing them out might prod other team members to think of ways to improve the document.

- Visit your campus writing center and ask a tutor to help you find things to critique. Bring a copy of the assignment instructions (and grading rubric if you have one) so that the tutor can get a general idea of what your instructor expects. Even if the tutor doesn't know all the specifics of the assignment, he or she should be able to point out some weak aspects of your document and to note general writing issues such as poor grammar, inconsistent logic, or poor organization.

Inside Work: Exercises

1. Review the following comments, which teammates made about one another midway through their project. How would you handle the situation if you were Carlos and Veronica? What can Mike do to regain the trust and respect of his teammates?

Carlos: It seems to me that Mike isn't very involved. Mike joins in the discussion we have during class time about the project, but he seems to put very little work in outside of class. After we were working on the project proposal in lab, he told me he felt his voice was not being heard, but then he did not post any changes to the project proposal at the time we all agreed to post our changes.

Mike: The first time we met to work on a document, I felt ignored by the rest of the group. I spoke my concerns to some of the others, however, and have confidence that it won't happen again…. I feel like I've not been doing anything…. For the most part, the aspect of the project that I've been assigned to work on is on hold until I get more information from the rest of the group.

Veronica: The team is working all right together—mostly everything is getting done. The only noteworthy incident would involve Mike, who seems to never know what is going on. He was in charge of compiling the proposal, and we had to extend the date many times…. He even said he couldn't write it because he was missing some info that Carlos had e-mailed out two weeks ago.

2. Two group members exchanged the following e-mails after spending a class period arguing unsuccessfully about changes to a short proposal. This situation does not fit neatly into the scenarios covered in this chapter; however, much of the advice in this chapter can be modified to fit this situation.

TO: Jayme, Megan

FR: Joe

Subject: Time

I have been monitoring our group meetings to see how much we accomplish. We always start out well, but then we waste everybody's time by bickering over the littlest stuff. So we always end up taking waaaay longer than is needed for the task. We spend so much time on little stuff that it is pathetic. There is no reason that a proposal that is only one and a half pages long should take 25 minutes to revise. As adult college students, we should have revised that in 15 to 20 minutes.

Here is another example: we sat in class yesterday for almost 45 minutes discussing the proposal. So what did we really accomplish? Nothing! Because, here again, we were arguing over "you say lemons, I say oranges." Last time I looked, both of those are fruits!

So let's stop wasting all of our time bickering. I propose that we set a time limit for how long a discussion should take. Then, when we reach that time limit, we should just vote. That's it. No more discussion.

Joe

TO: Joe

FR: Jayme

CC: Megan

Subject: Time

In response to your message, I don't think time is the issue. If it takes two hours to write the proposal, then it takes two hours to write the proposal. It took me at least that amount of time to write the first progress report, but I wanted to make sure it was done right.

If I have a problem with something that has my name on it, I want to feel free to voice my opinion. ALL of our opinions ARE worthy because we are all part of the group. I agree that I don't want to argue. The only way to accomplish this is to be open to one another's ideas and not shut them out because we don't have the time to hear them. That causes tension and in the long run is less time-efficient.

If time is the biggest concern, then perhaps we need to give the jobs to those of us in the group who are willing to take that time to get the job done right, the first time.

Jayme

Figure 23.12. E-mail exchange between teammates.

After reading the e-mails in Figure 23.12, answer the following questions:

a. What do you think about the tone of each of these e-mails? How do you think the recipients responded to them? What do you suspect was the outcome of this exchange?

b. The sample e-mails throughout this book try to phrase problems in nonaccusatory language. Reread these sample e-mails and find some wording that Joe and Jayme might have used to make their exchange less accusatory.

c. Overall, what strategies could these students have used to avoid this problem in the first place? Now that the problem has occurred, what strategies could they use to get their team back on the right track?

Appendices

Andrea Tsurumi

Appendices

Peer Evaluation Questionnaire

At the end of your project, answer the following questions about your teammates and your own contributions to the project.

1. List *everything* that each member of the team (including yourself) contributed to the project. Be as specific as possible.

2. For each member of the team (including yourself), list the single most important contribution that he or she made to the project.

3. What advice would you give to each of your teammates to help them improve their teamwork skills?

4. Would you want to work with these teammates again on a future project? Why or why not? (Your answer is confidential.)

You can also download a copy of this questionnaire from the *Team Writing* Web site.

Following are three versions of the meeting minutes from one four-person team. All three versions contain the same information. Which version—version 1, 2, or 3—do you think will be the most effective for keeping the team on track? Why?

Version 1

From:	**Jason**
To:	**Team**
Subject:	**Team meeting—Monday, 3/2/09**

Present: Susan, Jeff, Karen, Jason

Karen started us off by showing us a Web site about oil-tanker transportation. We looked at that for five minutes, and then Jason suggested we review the draft Jeff prepared. Jason noted some incomplete sentences. Susan also noticed some minor grammatical errors. Karen suggested moving the information on oil transportation closer to the beginning. Jason agreed. Susan and Jeff also thought this was a good idea but felt that jumping right into the details on transportation would be too abrupt. The others agreed that the current introduction should remain, but Karen thought that it should be minimized since our audience would already know this information. Jeff liked the current introduction because it has emotional appeal and would catch our audience's attention. Jason and Susan weren't sure which version would be best. Karen suggested that we prepare two different versions and ask the instructor which one would be best for our audience. Jason volunteered to set up a meeting with the instructor later in the week, but Jeff and Karen didn't have copies of their schedules with them. All team members will e-mail Jason tonight with a copy of their schedules. Karen volunteered to write up a revised draft and e-mail it out to the team by Wednesday night. Everybody will read this draft and show up on Thursday with comments.

Appendix B, "Sample Meeting Minutes" from *Team Writing: A Guide to Working in Groups* by Joanna Wolfe, pp. 128–130 (Appendix B). Copyright © 2010 by Bedford/St. Martin's.

Jeff suggested that the team begin working on the next section of the proposal. Susan, Karen, and Jason thought that we needed to include information on costs. Jeff thought that we should look at SPCC regulations next but agreed that costs were also a high priority. Susan's uncle works for Texaco and can provide us with some information on costs. Jason volunteered to draft a section on costs by next Tuesday. Jeff and Susan both have a calculus test on Wednesday and can't work much on the project until then. We set up our next team meeting for Thursday at 1:00 p.m.

Version 2

From: **Jason**

To: **Team**

Subject: **Team meeting—Monday, 3/2/09**

Present: Susan, Jeff, Karen, Jason

To Do:

Everyone: E-mail Jason tonight with your schedule for Friday and Monday.

Karen: Implement the changes the team made on the research review. E-mail revised draft to team by Wednesday.

Jason: Set up meeting with instructor for Friday or Monday.

Susan: Draft a section on costs by next Tuesday.

Everyone: Read the draft Karen e-mails us and show up on Thursday with comments.

Dates: Next team meeting is on Thursday, 3/5, at 1:00 p.m.

Decisions:

1. **Revisions to research review**

    We spent most of the meeting discussing Jeff's draft. We decided to

    (1) move the information on oil transportation closer to the beginning.

    (2) prepare two different versions of the introductory section—one with the current emotional introduction on the environmental impacts of oil spills and one with the abbreviated introduction that doesn't repeat information our audience already knows. We will ask the instructor to decide which works better for our audience.

    (3) make grammatical corrections, especially fixing incomplete sentences.

Karen will make the changes the team suggested and e-mail out a revised version by Wednesday night. We should all read it and come in on Thursday with comments.

2. Meeting with the instructor

Jason will arrange a meeting with the instructor to discuss the two drafts. We all need to e-mail him tonight with times we are available.

3. Costs

We decided that the next step is to estimate the costs of modifying the oil tankers. Susan will research this information and draft a section on costs by next Tuesday.

4. EPA Web site

Karen found some good information about oil transportation on the EPA Web site. The URL is www.epa.gov/oilspill/.

Next meeting (3/5):

(1) Discuss Karen's revisions to research review.

(2) Verify meeting time with instructor.

(3) Discuss costs section if there's time.

Version 3

From: **Jason**

To: **Team**

Subject: **Team meeting—Monday, 3/2/09**

Present: Susan, Jeff, Karen, Jason

The meeting was called to order by Karen at 1:05 p.m.

1. Karen showed us a Web site with good information. The URL is www.epa.gov/oilspill/.

2. The group discussed Jeff's draft. Jason and Susan noted some grammatical errors. Karen thought the information on the environmental impact of oil spills should be condensed. Jeff objected, stating that the current introduction provided emotional appeal and would grab the reader's attention.

3. Karen moved that we prepare two versions of the introduction section and volunteered to complete this task by Wednesday night. The motion was agreed to by the rest of the group.

4. Jason moved that the group set up a meeting with the instructor and volunteered for this task. This motion was agreed to by the rest of the group. All team members need to e-mail Jason with their schedule tonight.

5. Jeff moved that we work on the costs section next. Susan informed the group that her uncle works for Texaco. Susan moved that she will get information on costs from him and draft a costs section by next Tuesday. This motion carried unanimously.

6. Our next team meeting is on Thursday at 1:00 p.m.

The meeting adjourned at 1:50 p.m.

The following information is based on individual interviews conducted with Mark, Natalie, and Keith at the end of their team project. In addition to commenting on the project in general, each of them viewed this video. This video was also viewed by several managers with at least 10 years of professional experience supervising teams.

What Did the Students Think about Their Team?

Keith was the most positive about the project and the group. He described himself as the group's leader and the "creative impetus" behind the project, Mark as the most hardworking and responsible group member, and Natalie as a "tertiary" group member who was too busy to contribute much to the project. Keith's perceptions contradict those of his teammates, largely because Keith valued in-class contributions more than work done outside the class. In fact, Keith did not produce any material outside of class, and his contributions were limited to the types of in-class exchanges you see in the video. This tendency to inflate the importance of face-to-face discussions over work that is contributed independently is a common problem of student teams.

Mark was also fairly positive about the project. Although he was occasionally frustrated with Keith, he generally enjoyed arguing with him and felt that he and Keith shared a leadership role in the group. Mark described Natalie as a reliable group member who, although she frequently missed class, completed a substantial amount of work outside of class and ultimately contributed more than Keith did to the project. He observed that sometimes Natalie may have felt "run over" by himself and Keith. However, when he watched this video at the end of the project, he expressed surprise at *how much* he and Keith were shutting Natalie out.

Natalie, unlike her teammates, described the group project as a very negative experience. She felt that the group spent too much time focusing on small details and as a consequence ended up rushing through and shortchanging parts of the project that she felt were the most important and most interesting to her personally. Although she enjoyed working with Mark, whom she described as reliable and the clear leader of the group, she found Keith impossible to work with because she felt he did not respect her. She commented:

I try to talk to people like that, but when I sense that I'm not being listened to or it's just being passed over, I'd rather just not waste my breath so I usually just kept to myself a lot of times.... I just didn't, I didn't think that my judgment was respected by Keith at all.... I just didn't think that he saw me as a person in the group.

Because she found working with Keith so difficult, Natalie eventually stopped attending class and instead e-mailed her contributions directly to Mark. When Natalie viewed this video clip at the end of the project, she commented:

That's what they're saying. I mean, you heard the man, that's what they were saying, and that's not what they were saying. Keith was trying to say that, I don't know, I never knew what he was trying to change. I don't, there were things that he would always try to change, and it did not need to be changed.... I was so mad there I stopped even listening to what he was saying.

What Did Managers Have to Say about This Team Interaction?

Ken West, Operations Research Manager: What I saw there is they were all trying to do the same thing together.... It looked like Keith was a "this is how you do it" type, while they had Mark doing it, and they might have been better off to split out and have everybody go off and write things separately, then get back together and review the intermediate sections.... It looked like they were trying to write together, and in the environment that they were in, it was not really conducive to having all three of them participate in the project, and as a result I think Natalie was being left out.

Rene Stone, Computer Systems Manager: Keith and Mark are acting like they're racing to some finish line. They're focusing on editing and writing text and producing it. They don't have time for the big picture.... I would counsel them to slow down, sit at a table, and come up with a strategy—not go over it with one person at the screen, the other two behind them. It's hard to have a civilized conversation like that.

Given How Upset Natalie Was with Her Team, What Would You Advise Her to Do?

Stone: She's going to have to do something to get their attention. I would try to get the computer seat because they both want to be controlling the machine. That would get her inside of their circle for a starter. And then I would try to slow it down so when they say something, I would repeat it back to take the urgency out of it.

Interviewer: If that didn't work, what would you recommend?

Stone: Go to the instructor and say, "I don't see that I have a role in this. There might be something else I should work on." Or, "Is there something else you want me to do on this project because they don't appear to need me?"

Appendix D

Responses and Outcomes for Team Video 2: Shelly, Will, and Ben

The following information is based on individual interviews conducted with Shelly, Will, and Ben at the end of their team project. In addition to commenting on the project in general, each of them viewed this video. This video was also viewed by an instructor with experience in guiding team projects.

What Did the Students Think about Their Team?

Shelly was largely satisfied with the project and the way the team divided the work, which she described as going down the list of information required for the proposal and dividing the tasks at random by assigning them to "Shelly, Will, Ben, Shelly, Will, Ben." She felt that the project ran smoothly, although at times she would have liked to review information before her teammates turned it in.

Will described Shelly as "pretty much taking charge" and doing a good job as leader; he described Ben as doing "exactly what he was asked but not much more than that." Will expressed some dissatisfaction with what the team turned in, saying that "the style is still reasonable but the message kind of gets lost. There's a continuity problem." He felt that by handing out five copies of a 20-page document, Shelly deterred him from critiquing anything. As Will said:

> I reviewed the sections to make sure there weren't any gross errors. But looking at it, there's that section I was talking about and a couple of typos and a couple of weird sentence structure things, but nothing that's a crisis. And to print out another five copies of that at 20 pages apiece, I didn't want to put her through the trouble of it.

However, Will never expressed any of his dissatisfaction to his teammates because he doesn't like confrontation and felt that the final document was "acceptable." Overall, Will described the team as "just three people who happened to turn in one thing."

Ben also noted that the teammates did not critique one another's work. He wished that the project could have been more of a learning experience because he did not really understand the content of the parts of the proposal that his teammates wrote.

When Ben was asked about his body language in the video and his tendency to sit apart from his teammates, he said, "That's a good question. I guess I like, kind of like being on the outside looking in." Still, he worried that he might be giving "an impression that I don't really care 'cause I am not part of the group. But really I am. I was just trying to sit back and, uh, listen to what they were saying."

What Did an Instructor Have to Say about This Team Interaction?

John Wang: Well, they're not fighting, but they're not really collaborating either. They have no plan and are just kind of doing everything by the seat of their pants. Nobody knows what the others are doing.... I don't know, but it seems to me like it's going to be a very disjointed project.... At an absolute minimum, any document should go through one round of review, but they're not even doing that. I would describe this as a very weak team.

Appendix E

Responses and Outcomes for Team Video 3: Jamaal, Jim, Don, and Tonya

The following information is based on observations of this student team and individual interviews conducted with Jamaal, Jim, Don, and Tonya at the end of their team project.

How Did This Project Turn Out?

The short clip you saw of team members dividing up tasks shows an apparently friendly group: there is little visible tension, everyone is volunteering for tasks, and the overall atmosphere seems easygoing and collegial. At the end of the project, most of the team members were still very enthusiastic and positive about how well their team had performed.

However, this group had one major problem: Don completely plagiarized his section of the report from the Internet. Only one group member (Jamaal) was aware of this, but Jamaal did not say anything to his teammates because he assumed that the instructor would not penalize the entire group if he discovered the plagiarism. Both Tonya and Jim knew that early on in the project Don had cut-and-pasted information from the Internet onto a handout that he had given to the group, but both of them assumed that he would consolidate this information on the final draft and put it in his own words. However, neither of them did more than skim the final draft for typos. Tonya volunteered that she did not read her teammates' final contributions carefully because she was "so confident that...they could write and they were very articulate. [She] didn't think [she] would be right in telling them to change things."

What Lesson Should You Learn from This Team's Outcome?

This group illustrates that teamwork is much more than face-to-face communication. The group's face-to-face interactions, while far from flawless, do not hint at the major disaster of this team's final project. Although face-to-face interactions are important, they do not necessarily reflect the quality of a team's written output. A person's ability to communicate orally does not necessarily translate into good writing ability (or, in this case, writing ethics)—many people are good speakers but poor writers. Having oral conversations is not a substitute for critically reading and responding to a written draft.

Another variation on the problem of focusing on oral communication at the expense of written communication is reported by Rebecca Burnett (1996), who observed a 13-student cooperative learning (or co-op) team doing an internship at a major engineering research and development corporation. The students had held many oral conversations with one of the chemists in the lab and, based on these conversations, thought they were proceeding in the right direction—only to have this same chemist respond to their final draft by saying that their work was completely unacceptable and showed that they did not understand critical aspects of the basic technology process. When team members asked the chemist why he hadn't mentioned these problems during previous conversations, he responded that until he had something to read—a coherent text that laid out ideas, explanations, and recommendations—he had no way of knowing about the fundamental gaps in their understanding.

In Burnett's study, the students' manager similarly noted how the process of simply drafting the table of contents revealed problems in the project: "It was in the process of deciding to put something on paper that...these vast differences in concepts started coming out." Reflecting back, one of the students on the team agreed with the manager: "The structure of the report should have been the first thing that we did, even though we didn't have...a lot of knowledge about [what] was going to be in it."

These comments reflect the importance of tackling the written part of a project *early* (perhaps even with a straw document—see Chapter 17, "Project Management") and of continually receiving feedback and making revisions on this document. If the students in Team Video 3 had had a stronger revision process and a commitment to truly revise and give feedback to one another, the plagiarism could have been caught before the project was submitted.

Work Cited

Burnett, R. (1996). "Some people weren't able to contribute anything but their technical knowledge": The anatomy of a dysfunctional team. In A. H. Duin & C. J. Hansen (Eds.), *Nonacademic writing: Social theory and technology* (pp. 123–156). Mahwah, NJ: Lawrence Erlbaum Associates.

Appendix F
Responses and Outcomes for Team Video 4: David, Veronica, and Adam

The following information is based on individual interviews conducted with David, Veronica, and Adam at the end of their team project. In addition to commenting on the project in general, each of them viewed this video. This video was also viewed by a manager with experience in supervising team projects.

What Did the Students Have to Say about This Project?

Veronica was initially frustrated with the group and had considered asking the instructor to place her in a different group. She explained why she appreciated the instructor's intervention: "Actually at first I was thinking that I was wrong. I was thinking that maybe I wasn't understanding her right or maybe I just needed to be quiet.... If she hadn't come over, I think I would have been just isolated." However, by the end of the project, Veronica felt that "the group began to value [her] opinion" and gave her "a fair say in the finalization of the documents."

David was initially upset by the instructor's intervention; he felt that that the instructor, by siding with Veronica, was taking on a "guys against girls" role. However, upon later reflection, he realized that he might have "come on a little too strong." So for the remainder of the project, he "held back" and tried to let others give their input: "I just didn't talk as much, that's the main thing.... I sat back sometimes and let other people sit up.... And I let other people finish their sentences and tried to give them adequate feedback for what's said."

Adam noted that the group was initially pressed for time because teammates' schedules were incompatible and that the group did not really consider having teammates create drafts independently and then revise one another's work. He agreed that Veronica was overlooked initially and said that he spoke to David privately after class about trying to include everyone.

What Did a Professional Manager Have to Say about This Team Interaction?

Rene Stone, Computer Systems Manager: I thought Veronica did a good job trying in that first segment. David was blowing her off, and she said, "Well, wait a minute. I want to do some part of it. This is supposed to be a team effort." So she was giving the message, but he wasn't hearing it from her. He only heard it from the instructor, and even then he kind of rejected it too.

Interviewer: So what would you do if you were a manager of this team?

Stone: I would also counsel them that it was important to me that everybody have skills and everybody contribute in private because I wanted input from all of them and that it was going to make it a better product. And I would try to convince David that it was going to be a better product that way. And another tactic would be to make a blatant suggestion that he let the other two do it and then he revise. And that way he would not be involved until it was his turn, and his turn would be clear.

The second segment is much better. They found a way to get him to share—which is getting him off the keyboard. He's listening, and they're being encouraging and saying good things and not just negative. But the Adam guy was left out. They could have asked him more for his opinions and repeat what he said. That would encourage him to speak louder and to be more engaged. He's sitting physically apart. But they're vastly improved over the first one.

Appendix G

Responses and Outcomes for Team Video 5: Jayme, Megan, and Joe

Several professional managers and instructors viewed Team Video 5 and offered their comments and advice.

What Are Your Thoughts on This Group?

Ken West, Operations Research Manager: (*laughing*) I've seen this so many times. Whether he is or not, Joe has set himself to be the technical expert. I don't know whether it's because "I'm the guy and you two are the girls," or whatnot, but he's making all kinds of blanket statements out there that have no basis whatsoever! (*laughing*) Joe is being obstinate and not listening, and the girls are not being successful at convincing him. They're putting forth their ideas, but he's just not seeing it.

Tim Monroe, Deputy Chief Traffic Engineer: The guy's not listening well. I have the idea that he has things set in his mind already and he's not even trying to understand what their point is. Just because you're technically better at getting a color up on the screen doesn't mean necessarily it's got to be your color.... He needs to realize that other people read this thing and it's not necessarily technical people that you're trying to communicate to.

What Would You Recommend to This Team?

Ken West: At this point in time, the best thing to do is bring in a third party. Bring in somebody else and say, "Just take a look at this and give us an honest opinion of what you think about it." In my world, I just bring in the user, and the user takes a look at it and says that they like it or they don't like it.... They could also try to set some ground rules about how they are going to handle disagreements. They could try majority vote, but in this particular case that could also lead to some stalemates because Joe is likely to say, "Well, you two are just ganging up on me, so I'll refuse to play."

Carla Anderson, Technical Writing Instructor: Well, they seem to have decided that they're going to take a "majority rules" approach, but Joe is really unhappy with that. Based on what I've seen here, I don't think he's ever going to hear what the women are saying.... I would recommend that they prepare two or three versions of the layout and then ask the instructor to comment on which one is best. Or find some other way of bringing the instructor into the process. Joe might hear things from an authority that he won't hear from his teammates. Plus, if he continues to act like this in front of the instructor, they have found a neutral way to alert the instructor to problems in the team.

Sample Documents

Acknowledgments

Mike Brotherton. Excerpt from "Hubble Space Telescope Spies Galaxy/Black Hole Evolution in Action." From press release posted on mikebrotherton.com, June 2, 2008. Reproduced with permission of the author.

Mike Brotherton, Wil Van Breugel, S. A. Stanford, R. J. Smith, B. J. Boyle, Lance Miller, T. Shanks, S. M. Croom, and Alexei V. Filippenko. Excerpt from "A Spectacular Poststarburst Quasar." From *The Astrophysical Journal*, August 1, 1999. Copyright © 1999 The American Astronomical Society. Reproduced with permission of the authors.

Wanda Cassidy, Karen Brown, and Margaret Jackson. "'Under the Radar': Educators and Cyberbullying in Schools." From *School Psychology International*, October 2012, Vol. 33, No. 5, pp. 520–32. Copyright © 2012 Psychology International. Reproduced with permission of SAGE.

EBSCO Health. "Sample Discharge Orders." From www.ebscohost.com. Reproduced with permission from EBSCO Information Services.

Nina Fedoroff. "The Genetically Engineered Salmon Is a Boon for Consumers and Sustainability," from *The New York Times*, December 2, 2015 issue. Copyright © 2015 by Nina Fedoroff. All rights reserved. Used by permission of the author.

Arthur L. Greil, Kathleen Slauson-Blevins, and Julia McQuillan. "The Experience of Infertility: A Review of Recent Literature." From *Sociology of Health & Illness*, Vol. 32, Issue 1. Copyright © 2010 by Blackwell Publishing Ltd. Reproduced with permission of Blackwell Publishing Ltd. in the format Book via Copyright Clearance Center.

Sanjay Gupta. "Why I Changed My Mind on Weed," from *CNN*, August 2013. All rights reserved. Used by permission and protected by the copyright laws of the United States. The printing, copying, redistribution, or retransmission of the material without express written permission is prohibited.

Dale Jacobs. "More Than Words: Comics as a Means of Teaching Multiple Literacies." From *English Journal*, Vol. 96, No. 3, January 2007. Copyright © 2007 National Council of Teachers of English. Reproduced with permission.

Susan Jacoby. "A First Amendment Junkie," by Susan Jacoby. Copyright © 1978 by Susan Jacoby. Originally appeared in *The New York Times* (January 26, 1978). Reprinted by permission of Georges Borchardt, Inc. on behalf of the author.

Charles Kerns and Kenneth Ko. "Exploring Happiness at Work." From *Leadership & Organizational Management Journal*. Copyright © 2009. Reproduced with permission of the authors.

Carolyn W. Keys. "Revitalizing Instruction in Scientific Genres: Connection Knowledge Production with Writing to Learn in Science." From *Science Education*, Vol. 83. Copyright © 1999 John Wiley & Sons. Reproduced with permission.